ISBN 978-0-282-55668-6
PIBN 10855919

English
Français
Deutsche
Italiano
Español
Português

www.forgottenbooks.com

Mythology Photography **Fiction**
Fishing Christianity **Art** Cooking
Essays Buddhism Freemasonry
Medicine **Biology** Music **Ancient**
Egypt Evolution Carpentry Physics
Dance Geology **Mathematics** Fitness
Shakespeare **Folklore** Yoga Marketing
Confidence Immortality Biographies
Poetry **Psychology** Witchcraft
Electronics Chemistry History **Law**
Accounting **Philosophy** Anthropology
Alchemy Drama Quantum Mechanics
Atheism Sexual Health **Ancient History**
Entrepreneurship Languages Sport
Paleontology Needlework Islam
Metaphysics Investment Archaeology
Parenting Statistics Criminology
Motivational

Harper's Stereotype Edition.

POLYNESIAN RESEARCHES,

DURING

A RESIDENCE OF NEARLY EIGHT YEARS

IN THE

SOCIETY AND SANDWICH ISLANDS.

BY WILLIAM ELLIS.

FROM THE LATEST LONDON EDITION.

IN FOUR VOLUMES.

VOL. IV.

NEW-YORK:

PRINTED AND PUBLISHED BY J. & J. HARPER,

NO. 82 CLIFF-STREET.

AND SOLD BY THE PRINCIPAL BOOKSELLERS THROUGHOUT THE
UNITED STATES.

·1833.

CONTENTS

OF

THE FOURTH VOLUME.

CHAPTER I.

CHAPTER II.

CHAPTER III.

CHAPTER IV.

CHAPTER V.

FROM PAGE 81 TO PAGE 109.

CHAPTER VI.

FROM PAGE 109 TO PAGE 123.

CHAPTER VII.

FROM PAGE 123 TO PAGE 137.

CHAPTER VIII.

FROM PAGE 137 TO PAGE 153.

CHAPTER IX.

FROM PAGE 153 TO PAGE 169.

CHAPTER XV.

FROM PAGE 285 TO PAGE 309.

CHAPTER XVI.

FROM PAGE 310 TO PAGE 332.

PLATES IN VOL. IV.

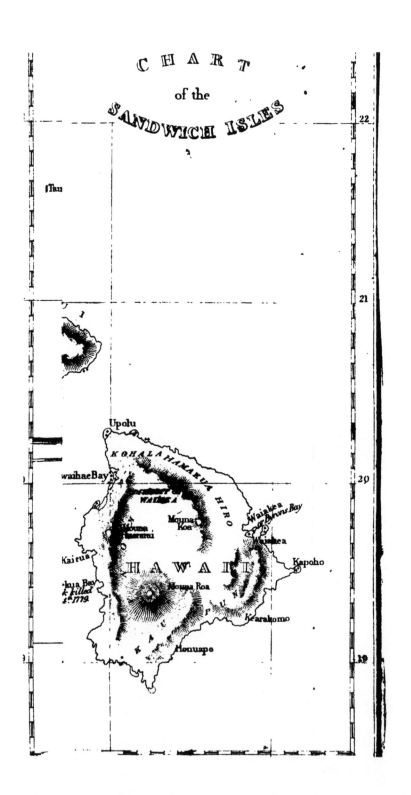

CHART

of the

SANDWICH ISLES

22

Tau

21

Upolu

KOHALA HAMAKUA HIRO

waihaeBay

20

WAIKEA

Mouna
Koa

Waiakea
or Byrons Bay

Mouna
Kaararai

Waakea

Kairua

HAWAII

Kapoho

kua Bay
k killed
1779

Mouna Roa

KAPUNA

Kaarakomo

KAU

Honuapo

19

POLYNESIAN RESEARCHES.

CHAPTER I.

It is now half a century since Captain Cook, in search of a northern passage from the Pacific to the Atlantic, discovered a group of islands, which, in honour of his patron the Earl of Sandwich, first lord of the admiralty, he called the SANDWICH ISLANDS. The importance he attached to this discovery may be gathered from his own words; for, when speaking of the circumstances under which the vessels anchored for the first time in Kearake'kua bay, the appearance of the natives, &c., he remarks, " We could not but be struck with the singularity of this scene; and perhaps there were few on board who now lamented our having failed in our endeavours to find a northern passage homeward last summer. To this disappointment we owed our having it in our power to revisit the Sandwich Islands, and to enrich our voyage with a discovery which, though last, seemed in many respects to be the most important that had hitherto been made by Europeans throughout the extent of the Pacific Ocean." These are the last words recorded in the journal of that enterprising and intelligent navigator; a melancholy event shortly afterward occurred on the shores of this very bay, which arrested his career of discovery, and terminated his existence.

On the return of the survivors, a detailed account of the islands and their inhabitants, which was given to the world, excited no small degree of interest, not only in England, but throughout the continent of Europe.

The descriptions which Captain Cook's Voyages contained of the almost primitive simplicity, natural vivacity, and fascinating manners of a people who had existed for ages isolated and unkhown to the rest of the world, were so entirely new, and the accounts given of the mildness and salubrity of the climate, the spontaneous abundance of delicious fruits, and the varied and delightful appearance of the scenery in the Sandwich and other islands of the Pacific, were so enchanting that many individuals were led to imagine they were a sort of Elysium, where the highly favoured inhabitants, free from the toil and care, the want and disappointment which mar the happiness of civilized communities, dwelt in what they called a state of nature, and spent their lives in unrestrained enjoyment.

These descriptions were, I am convinced, faithful transcripts of the first impressions made on the minds of Captain Cook and his companions, and in every respect correct, so far as their partial observation extended. A residence of eight years in the Society and Sandwich Islands has afforded me an opportunity of becoming familiar with many of the scenes and usages described in their voyages, and I have often been struck with the fidelity with which they are uniformly portrayed. In the inferences they draw, and the reasons they assign, they are sometimes mistaken; but in the description of what they saw and heard, there is throughout a degree of accuracy seldom, if ever, exceeded in accounts equally minute and extended. Still, their acquaintance with the islands and the people was superficial, and the state of society which they witnessed was different from what generally existed.

An event so important and surprising as their arrival, —the ships and the foreigners,—the colour, dress, arms, language, manners, &c. of the latter; whom they regarded at first as superior beings, so powerfully affected the minds of the natives, that the ordinary avocations of life were for a time suspended. The news of such an event spread rapidly through the islands, and multitudes flocked from every quarter to see the return of Orono, or the motus (islands), as they called their ships. The whole island was laid under requisition to supply their wants, or contribute to their satisfaction. Hence the immense quantity of provisions presented by Taraiopu; the dances, &c. with which they were entertained. The effect also produced on the minds of those early visiters, by what they saw during their transient stay among the islands, was heightened by all the attractions of novelty and all the complacency which such discoveries naturally inspire. Far different are the impressions produced on the minds of the missionaries who have resided for some years in the islands. Having acquired their language, observed their domestic economy, and become acquainted with the nature of their government, the sanguinary character of their frequent wars, their absurd and oppressive system of idolatry, and the prevalence of human sacrifices, they are led, from the indubitable facts which have come under their notice, to more just and accurate conclusions—conclusions in awful accordance with the testimony of divine revelation.

Although ten in number, only eight of the Sandwich Islands are inhabited, the other two being barren rocks, principally resorted to by fishermen. They lie within the tropic of Cancer, between 18° 50' and 22° 20' north latitude, and between 154° 53' and 160° 15' west longitude from Greenwich, about one-third of the distance from the western coast of Mexico towards the eastern shores of China. The Sandwich Islands are larger than the Society Islands, or any of the neighbouring clusters.

Ha-wai-i (Owhyhee), the principal island of the group, resembles in shape an equilateral triangle, and is somewhat less than three hundred miles in circumference,—being about ninety-seven miles in length, seventy-eight in breadth, two hundred and eighty miles in circumference, and covering a surface of 4000 square miles. It is the most southern of the whole, and on account of its great elevation, is usually the first land seen from vessels approaching the Sandwich Islands. Its broad base and regular form render its outline different from that of any other island in the Pacific with which we are acquainted. The mountains of Hawaii, unlike the Peak of Teneriffe in the Atlantic, the mountains of Eimeo, and some other islands of the Pacific, do not pierce the clouds like obelisks or spires, but in most parts, and from the southern shore in particular, the ascent is gradual, and comparatively unbroken, from the sea-beach to the lofty summit of Mouna Roa. The whole

appearance of Hawaii is less romantic and picturesque
than that of Tahiti, the principal of the Society Islands,
but more grand and sublime, filling the mind of the beholder with wonder and delight. On approaching the
islands, I have more than once observed the mountains
of the interior long before the coast was visible, or any
of the usual indications of land had been seen. On
these occasions the elevated summit of Mouna Kea, or
Mouna Roa, has appeared above the mass of clouds that
usually skirt the horizon, like a stately pyramid, or the
silvered dome of a magnificent temple, distinguished
from the clouds beneath only by its well-defined outline,
unchanging position, and intensity of brilliancy occasioned by the reflection of the sun's rays from the surface of the snow.

The height of these mountains has been computed by
some navigators who have visited the Sandwich Islands
at 12,000, and by others at 18,000 feet. The estimate
of Captain King,* we think, exceeds their actual elevation; and the peaks of Mouna Kea, in the opinion of those
of our number who have ascended its summit, are not
more than 1000 feet high. But admitting the snow to
remain permanent on the mountains of the torrid zone at
the height of 14,600 feet, the altitude of Mouna Kea
and Mouna Roa is probably not less than 15,000 feet.

The base of these mountains is, at the distance of a
few miles from the seashore, covered with trees;
higher up, their sides are clothed with bushes, ferns, and
alpine plants; but their summits are formed of lava,
partly decomposed, yet destitute of every kind of
verdure.

There are a few inland settlements on the east and
north-west parts of the island; but in general the interior is an uninhabited wilderness. The heart of Hawaii, forming a vast central valley between Mouna Roa,

* In Cook's Voyages, Captain King, speaking of Mouna Kaah (Kea), remarks, that it "may be clearly seen at fourteen leagues' distance." Describing
Mouna Roa, and estimating it according to the tropical line of snow, he ob-
serves, "This mountain must be at least 16,020 feet high, which exceeds the
height of the Pico de Teyde, or Peak of Teneriffe, by 3680 feet, according to
the computation of Chevalier de Borda. The peaks of Mouna Kaah appeared
to be about half a mile high; and as they are entirely covered with snow, the
altitude of their summits cannot be less than 16,400 feet. But it is probable
that both these mountains may be considerably higher; for in insular situations the effects of the warm sea-air must necessarily remove the line of snow
in equal latitudes to a greater height than where the atmosphere is chilled on
all sides by an immense tract of perpetual snow."

Mouna Kea, and Mouna Huararai, is almost unknown; no road leads across it from the eastern to the western shore—but it is reported by the natives who have entered it to be "bristled with forests of ohia," or to exhibit vast tracts of steril and indurated lava. The circumstance of large flocks of wild geese being frequently seen in the mountains would lead to the supposition that there must be large ponds or lakes to which they resort; but if any exist, they have hitherto remained undiscovered.

The greatest part of the land capable of cultivation is found near the seashore, along which the towns and villages of the natives are thickly scattered. The population at present is about 85,000, and this will probably be greatly increased by the establishment of Christianity, whose mild influence, it may reasonably be expected, will effect a cessation of war, an abolition of infanticide, and a diminution of those vices, principally of foreign origin, which have hitherto so materially contributed to the depopulation of the islands.

Hawaii is by far the largest, most populous, and important island of the group; and until within a few years it was the usual residence of the king, and the frequent resort of every chief of importance in the other islands. Foreigners, however, having found the harbours of some of the leeward islands more secure and convenient than those of Hawaii, have been induced more frequently to visit them; and this has led the king and principal chiefs to forsake, in a great degree, the favourite residence of their ancestors—and, excepting the governor and the chiefs of Kaavaroa, to spend the greater part of their time in some of the other islands.

Separated from the northern shore of Hawaii by a strait about twenty-four miles across, the island of Mau-i (Mowee) is situated in lat. 20° N., and long. 157° W. This island is forty-eight miles in length, in the widest part twenty-nine miles across, about one hundred and forty miles in circumference, and covers about six hundred square miles. At a distance it appears like two distinct islands, but on nearer approach, a low isthmus about nine miles across is seen uniting the two peninsulas. The whole island, which is entirely volcanic, was probably produced by the action of two adjacent volcanoes, which have ejected the immense masses of matter of which it is composed. The appearance of Maui resembles Tahiti more than the neighbouring island of Hawaii. The southern peninsula, which is the largest of the two, is lofty; but though its summits are often seen above the clouds, they are never covered with snow. The high land is steep and rugged, and frequently marked with extinct craters, or indurated streams of lava; yet whenever the volcanic matters have undergone any degree of decomposition, the sides of the mountains, as well as the ravines by which they are intersected, are covered with shrubs and trees.

In the northern peninsula there are several extensive tracts of level and well-watered land, in a high state of cultivation; and although this part of the island is evidently of volcanic formation, the marks of recent eruptions, so frequent in the southern peninsula, are seldom seen here. The population of Maui has been estimated at 18,000 or 20,000, and the number of inhabitants does not probably fall short of that amount.

In the month of May, 1823, a Christian mission was commenced at Lahaina, the most important and populous district in the island, and the endeavours of Messrs. Stewart and Richards, and the native teachers by whom they were accompanied, have been attended with the most decisive and extensive success. Public preaching on the Sabbath is regularly attended by numerous audiences, and thousands of the people are daily receiving instruction in useful knowledge and the principles of Christianity, in the various native schools, which are patronised by the young Prince Kauikeouli, younger brother and successor to the late king,—by his sister Nahienaena,—and by all the principal chiefs of Maui. Hence the most lasting benefits may be expected to result, not only to the present race, but to every future generation of the inhabitants.

To the south of Maui, and only a few miles distant from its southern peninsula, is situated the small island of TA-HAU-RA-WE, about eleven miles in length, and eight across. It is low, and almost destitute of every kind of shrub or verdure, excepting a species of coarse grass. The rocks of which it is formed are volcanic, but we are not aware of the existence of any active or extinct craters on the island; and, from its shape and appearance, it is not improbable that it once formed a part of Maui, from which it may have been detached by some violent convulsion connected with the action of the adjacent volcanoes of Maui or Hawaii. There are but few settled residents on the island, and these are considered as under the authority of the governor of Maui.

Mo-ro-ki-ni, a barren rock, which lies between these two islands, would render the navigation of the strait exceedingly dangerous, were it not so much elevated above the sea as to be at all times visible from vessels passing between the islands. Morokini is only visited by fishermen, who on its barren surface spread their nets to dry, and for this purpose it may be considered a convenient appendage to the adjacent islands.

Ra-nai, a compact island, seventeen miles in length, and nine in breadth, lies north-west of Tahaurawe, and west of Lahaina, in Maui; from which it is separated by a channel not more than nine or ten miles across. Though the centre of the island is much more elevated than Tahaurawe, it is neither so high nor broken as any of the other islands: great part of it is barren, and the island in general suffers much from the long droughts which frequently prevail; the ravines and glens, notwithstanding, are filled with thickets of small trees, and to these many of the inhabitants of Maui repair for the purpose of cutting posts and rafters for their small houses. The island is volcanic; the soil shallow, and by no means fertile; the shores, however, abound with shell-fish, and some species of medusæ and cuttle-fish. The inhabitants are but few, probably not exceeding two thousand. Native teachers are endeavouring to instruct them in useful knowledge and religious truth; but no foreign missionary has yet laboured on this or the neighbouring island of Morokai, which is separated from the northern side of Ranai and the eastern end of Maui by a channel, which, though narrow, is sufficiently wide for the purposes of navigation.

Mo-ro-kai is a long irregular island, apparently formed by a chain of volcanic mountains, forty miles in length, and not more than seven miles broad: the mountains are nearly equal in elevation to those of Maui, and are broken by numerous deep ravines and watercourses, the sides of which are frequently clothed with verdure, and ornamented with shrubs and trees. There is but little level land in Morokai, and consequently but few plantations; several spots, however, are fertile, and repay the toils of their cultivators. The population is greater than that of Ranai, though it does not probably exceed three thousand persons. Native teachers are engaged in the instruction of the people; many of the natives also occasionally visit the missionary stations in the adjacent islands of Oahu and Maui, and participate in the advantages connected with these institutions.

O-A-HU, the most romantic and fertile of the Sandwich Islands, resembling, in the varied features of its natural scenery, several of the Society Islands, lies nearly west-north-west of Morokai, from which it is between twenty and thirty miles distant. This beautiful island is about forty-six miles long, and twenty-three wide; its appearance from the roads off Honoruru, or Waititi, is remarkably picturesque: a chain of lofty mountains rises near the centre of the eastern part of the island, and extending perhaps twenty miles, reaches the plain of Eva, which divides it from the distant and elevated mountains that rise in a line parallel with the north-west shore. The plain of Eva is nearly twenty miles in length, from the Pearl river to Waiarua, and in some parts nine or ten miles across: the soil is fertile, and watered by a number of rivulets, which wind their way along the deep watercourses that intersect its surface, and empty themselves into the sea. Though capable of a high state of improvement, only a very small portion of it is enclosed, or under any kind of culture; and in travelling across it, scarce a habitation is to be seen. The whole island is volcanic, and in many parts extinguished craters of large dimensions may be seen; but from the depth of mould with which they are covered, and the trees and shrubs with which they are clothed, it may be presumed that many ages have elapsed since any eruption took place. The plain of Honoruru exhibits in a singular manner the extent and effects of volcanic agency; it is not less than nine or ten miles in length, and, in some parts, two miles from the sea to the foot of the mountains: the whole plain is covered with a rich alluvial soil, frequently two or three feet deep; beneath this, a layer of fine volcanic ashes and cinders extends to the depth of fourteen or sixteen feet; these ashes lie upon a stratum of solid rock, by no means volcanic, but evidently calcareous, and apparently a kind of sediment deposited by the sea, in which branches of white coral, bones of fish and animals, and several varieties of marine shells are often found. A number of wells have been recently dug in different parts of the plain, in which, after penetrating through the calcareous rock, sometimes twelve or thirteen feet, good clear water has been always found; the water in all these wells is perfectly free from any salt or brackish taste, though it invariably rises and falls with the tide, which would lead to the supposition that it is connected with the waters of the adjacent ocean, from which the wells are from 100 yards to three-quarters of a mile distant. The rock is always hard and compact near the surface, but becomes soft and porous as the depth increases; and it is possible that the water in these wells may have percolated through the cells of the rock, and by this process of filtration have lost its saline qualities. The base of the mountains which bound the plain in the interior appears to have formed the original line of coast on this side of the island, but probably in some very remote period an eruption took place from two broad-based truncated mountains, called by foreigners Diamond Hill and Punch-bowl Hill, evidently extinguished craters; the ashes and cinders then thrown out, and wafted by the trade-winds in a westerly direction, filled up the sea, and formed the present extensive plain; the soil of its surface having been subsequently produced either by the decomposition of lava, or the mould and decayed vegetable matter washed down from the mountains during the rainy season of the year.

Across this plain, immediately opposite the harbour of Honoruru, lies the valley of Anuanu, leading to a pass in the mountains, called by the natives *Ka Pari*, the precipice, which is well worth the attention of every intelligent foreigner visiting Oahu. The mouth of the valley, which opens immediately behind the town of Honoruru, is a complete garden, carefully kept by its respective proprietors in a state of high cultivation; and the ground, being irrigated by the water from a river that winds rapidly down the valley, is remarkably productive. The valley rises with a gradual ascent from the shore to the precipice, which is seven or eight miles from the town. After walking about three miles through one unbroken series of plantations, the valley becomes gradually narrower, and the mountains rise more steep on either side. The scenery is romantic and delightful: the bottom of the valley is gently undulated;

a rapid stream takes its serpentine way from one side of the valley to the other, sometimes meandering along with an unruffled surface, at other times rushing down a fall several feet, or dashing and foaming among the rocks that interrupt its progress; the sides of the hills are clothed with verdure; even the barren rocks that project from among the bushes are ornamented with pendulous or creeping plants of various kinds; and in several places beautiful cascades roll their silvery streams down the steep mountain's side into flowing rivulets beneath. The beauty of the scenery around increases, until at length, after walking some time on a rising ground rather more steep than usual, and through a thicket of hibiscus and other trees, the traveller suddenly emerges into an open space, and, turning round a small pile of volcanic rocks, the Pari all at once bursts upon him with an almost overwhelming effect. Immense masses of black and ferruginous volcanic rock, many hundred feet in nearly perpendicular height, present themselves on both sides to his astonished view: while immediately before him, he looks down the fearful steep several hundred feet, and beholds hills and valleys, trees and cottages, meandering streams and winding paths, cultivated plantations and untrodden thickets, and a varied landscape many miles in extent, bounded by lofty mountains on the one side, and the white-crested waves of the ocean on the other—spread out before him as if by the hand of enchantment. I have several times visited this romantic spot, and once climbed the rocky precipice from the district of Kolau, on the northern side: the ascent is at first gradual and easy, but in two places, towards the highest edge, the volcanic rocks appear to rise perpendicularly, presenting an even and apparently projecting front, which it seems impossible to ascend; but though the passage is thus difficult, and the elevation of the upper ridge, over which the path leads, is from four to five hundred feet above the level land below, yet the natives not only pass and repass without much difficulty, but often carry heavy burdens from one side to the other. It is reported that a native female, on one occasion, carried her husband, who was in a state of intoxication, down the precipice in safety; this appears scarcely possible, and the story is probably one of those fabulous wonders with which inquiring foreigners are often entertained during their stay among the islands. On one of my visits, however, I saw a party heavily laden with provisions for the king's household ascend the Pari, and one of them had a pig, of no very small size, fastened on his back, with which he climbed the steep, but not without difficulty.

Within a few yards of the upper edge of the pass, under the shade of surrounding bushes and trees, two rude and shapeless stone idols are fixed, one on each side of the path, which the natives call *Akua no ka Pari*, gods of the precipice; they are usually covered with pieces of white tapa, native cloth; and every native who passes by to the precipice, if he intends to descend, lays a green bough before these idols, encircles them with a garland of flowers, or wraps a piece of tapa round them, to render them propitious to his descent; all who ascend from the opposite side make a similar acknowledgment for the supposed protection of the deities, whom they imagine to preside over the fearful pass. This practice appears universal, for in our travels among the islands we have seldom passed any steep or dangerous paths, at the commencement or termination of which we have not seen these images, with heaps of offerings lying before them. Until very recently, it is evident the influence of superstition was strong in the minds of the great mass of the people; for although the natives who accompanied us in our excursions, either from a conviction of the absurdity of the notions of their countrymen, or from mere wantonness, usually overturned the idols, battered them with stones, or rolled them down the precipice or passage which they were supposed to defend; yet on passing the same path only a very short time afterward, we have invariably found them replaced, or, if broken, their places supplied by fresh ones. This conduct of our native companions was never the consequence of our directions, and seldom received our approbation, for we were not ambitious to become iconoclasts; our object was rather to enlighten the minds of the people, and convince them of the absurdity and evil of idolatry, to present before them the true God as the only legitimate object of rational homage, lead them to the exercise of a better faith, and the adoption of a purer worship; well assured that, if, under the blessing of God, we succeeded in this, they themselves would, with the adoption of the Christian system, not only renounce idolatry, but abolish the observances by which it was upheld.

The Pari of Anuanu was an important position in times of war, and the parties in possession of it were usually masters of the island. In its vicinity many sanguinary battles have been fought, and near it the independence of Oahu was lost in or about the year 1790. Tamehámeha invaded Oahu; the king of the island assembled his forces to defend his country, between Honoruru and the Pearl river; an engagement took place, in which his army was defeated, and his ally, Taeo, king of Tauai and Neehau, was slain. The king of Oahu retreated to the valley of Anuanu, where he was joined by Taiana, an ambitious and warlike chief of Hawaii. Hither Tamehameha and his victorious warriors pursued them, and about two miles from the Pari the last battle in Oahu was fought. Here the king of Oahu was slain; his army then fled towards the precipice, chased by the warriors of Tamehameha: at the edge of the Pari, Taiana made a stand, and defended it till he fell; the troops of the fallen chiefs still continued the conflict, till, being completely routed, a number of them, it is said four hundred, were driven headlong over the precipice, and dashed to pieces among the fragments of rock that lie at its base, leaving Tamehameha master of the field, and sovereign of the island. The natives still point out the spot where the king of the island stood when he hurled his last spear at the advancing foe, and received the fatal wound; and many, as they pass by, turn aside from the path, place their feet on what they describe as the identical spot where he is said to have stood, assume the attitude in which he is said to have received his mortal wound, and poising their staff or their spear, tell their children or companions that there the last king of Oahu died defending his country from its invaders.

Immediately south of the valley of Anuanu is situated the town and harbour of Honoruru: the harbour is the best, and indeed the only secure one at all seasons, in the Sandwich Islands, and is more frequented by foreign vessels than any other; seldom having within it less than three or four, and sometimes upwards of thirty, lying at anchor at the same time. The town has also, since the number of shipping has increased, become populous; it is one of the largest in the islands, usually containing 6000 or 7000 inhabitants; it is the frequent residence of the king and principal chiefs, who are much engaged in traffic with foreigners visiting the islands, or residing on shore, for purposes of trade. There are twelve or fourteen merchants, principally Americans, who have established warehouses on shore for foreign goods, principally piece-goods, hardware, crockery, hats, and shoes, naval stores, &c., which they retail to the natives for Spanish dollars or sandal-wood. On the eastern side of the basin is a strong fort, one hundred yards square, mounting sixty guns. It was begun by the Russians, who were expelled—but finished by the natives, from an apprehension that these foreigners, in connexion with the Russian settlements on the north-west coast of America, were about to take possession of the island. Here, also, in the month of April, 1820, an American mission was commenced, which, under God, has been the means of producing a most happy moral and domestic change in the character of many of the people, whose advancement in the arts of civilized life, as well as Christian knowledge, is truly gratifying. Several thousands are under religious instruction, and numbers regularly attend the preaching of the gospel, which we earnestly hope will result in the conversion of many. Several have forsaken their grass huts, and erected comfortable stone or wooden houses—among which one built by Karaimoku, the prime minister, is highly creditable to his perseverance and his taste.

About six miles to the west of Honoruru, and nearly as far from the village of Eva, on the Pearl river, there is a singular natural curiosity—a small circular lake, situated at a short distance from the seashore, so impregnated with salt that twice in the year the natives take out between two and three hundred barrels of fine, clear, hard, crystallized salt: this lake is an interesting natural curiosity, and is an important appendage to the island. It belongs to the king, and is not only useful in curing large quantities of fish, but furnishes a valuable article of commerce; quantities of it having been sent for sale to Kamtschatka, and used in curing seal-skins at the different islands to which the natives have sent their vessels for that purpose, or sold in the islands to Russian vessels from the settlements on the north-west coast of America. The population of Oahu is estimated at about 20,000.

North-west of Oahu, and distant from it about seventy-five miles, is situated the island of Tauai, which is mountainous and exceedingly romantic in its appearance, but not so fertile as Oahu, or the greater part of Maui. It is forty-six miles in length and twenty-three in breadth, and covers a surface of 520 square miles. The population probably amounts to nearly 10,000. The principal settlements are in the neighbourhood of Waimea river, the roads at the entrance of which are the usual resort of vessels touching at Tauai. Near the mouth of the river is a strong fort, in excellent repair, mounting twenty-two guns. It was erected several years since, and is well adapted for defence. This and the neighbouring island of Nihau were not invaded and conquered by Tamehameha, by whom all the other islands of the group were subdued. Taumuarii, the late king, however, rendered a tacit acknowledgment of dependence on that ambitious prince, and paid annually a nominal tribute, both to him and his son, the late Rihoriho; and shortly before his death, which took place in 1824, he formally ceded the islands which he had governed to Karaimoku, the regent of the Sandwich Islands, for the king, who was then absent on a visit to Great Britain. The son of the late king, and several old warriors, dissatisfied with the conduct of their sovereign, took up arms to rescue the islands from the dominion of the chiefs of the windward islands; but being defeated in a battle fought in a valley near Waimea, the island is now under the authority of the young prince Kauikeouli, the successor to Rihoriho, and the present sovereign of the whole of the Sandwich Islands.

Soon after the commencement of the mission in Oahu, a similar institution was undertaken in Tauai, under the friendly auspices of the late king; this continued to prosper until the civil war, which followed his death, obliged the missionaries to remove from the island, and suspend their endeavours for the instruction of the natives. Since the restoration of peace, however, their labours have been resumed with more extensive and encouraging prospects of success than had been previously enjoyed. The inhabitants are in general a hardy and industrious race. It is remarkable that in their language they employ the t in all those words in which the k would be used by the natives of the other islands.

NI-HAU, a small island, twenty miles in length, and seven miles wide, politically connected with Tauai, lies in a westerly direction, about fifteen miles distant. The inhabitants are not numerous, and in the general features of their character they resemble those of Tauai. These two islands are celebrated throughout the whole group for the manufacture of the fine painted or variegated mats, so much admired by foreigners, and which, for the purpose of sleeping on, the chiefs in all the islands prefer to any others. These mats are sometimes very large, measuring eighteen or twenty yards in length, and three or four yards in breadth; yet they are woven by the hand, without any loom or frame, with surprising regularity and exactness: they are made of a fine kind of rush, part of which they stain of a red colour with vegetable dies, and form their beautiful patterns by weaving them into the mat at its first fabrication, or working them in after it is finished.

The natives of these islands are also distinguished for the cultivation of the yam, which grows very large, both at Tauai and Nihau, and contributes essentially to the support of the inhabitants. As they are not cultivated to any extent in the other islands, many ships are induced to visit these, principally for the purpose of procuring a supply; they are not only an excellent root, but will keep a long time at sea without deterioration.

TAU-RA is another small island belonging to the group, lying in a south-western direction from Tauai; but it is only a barren rock, the resort of vast numbers of aquatic birds, for the purpose of procuring which, it is occasionally visited by the natives of the windward islands.

Adjacent to the shores of most of the islands, small reefs of white coral, common throughout the Pacific, are occasionally found; but they are not so varied in their kind, so frequently met with, nor so extensive, as in all the southern islands.

The climate is not insalubrious, though warm, and debilitating to a European constitution. There is no winter; and the principal variation in the uniformity of the seasons is occasioned by the frequent and heavy rains which usually fall between December and March, and the prevalence of southerly and variable winds during the same season. The following tabular view of a meteorological journal, kept by the American missionaries, will show more fully the state of the weather for a year, from August, 1821, to July, 1822; the thermometer was noted at 8 A. M., 3 P. M., and 8 P. M.

MONTHS.	Greatest heat.	Least heat.	Range.	General range.	Mean temperature.	General course of wind.	GENERAL STATE OF THE WEATHER.
August, 1821,	88°	74°	14°	75° to 85°	79°	N. E.	Clear; rain but once.
September	87	74	13	76—84	78	N. E.	Rained on five days.
October	86	73	13	76—83	78	N. E.	Clear; rain but once.
November	82	71	11	75—80	76	N. E.	Clear; rain but once.
December	80	62	18	70—78	72	N.& N. E.	Clear; rain twice.
January, 1822	80	59	21	68—78	70	Variable.	Rain 1 day; 7 others cloudy.
February	77	61	16	75—75	71	N. E.	Rain 4 days; 10 others cloudy.
March	78	66	12	71—78	72	N. E.	Rain 5 days; 8 others cloudy.
April	81	62	19	72—80	73	Variable.	Rain 5 days; 12 others cloudy.
May	81	72	9	75—81	76	N. E.	Rain 4 days; 3 others cloudy.
June	84	73	13	76—83	78	N. E.	Cloudy six days.
July	84	74	10	76—83	78	N. E.	Rain 5 days; 7 others cloudy.
Result for the year.	88°	61°	27°	70° to 80°	75°	N. E.	Rain on 40 days; generally clear at other times.

Rain falls but seldom on the western shores of any of the islands, excepting in the season above mentioned, though showers are frequent on the eastern or windward side, and in the mountains they occur almost daily.

The soil is rich in those parts which have long been free from volcanic eruptions; but the general appearance of the country is hardly so inviting as when first discovered; many parts then under cultivation are now lying waste.

The natives are in general rather above the middle stature, well formed, with fine muscular limbs, open countenances, and features frequently resembling those of Europeans. Their gait is graceful, and sometimes stately. The chiefs in particular are tall and stout, and their personal appearance is so much superior to that of the common people, that some have imagined them a distinct race. This, however, is not the fact; the great care taken of them in childhood, and their better living, have probably occasioned the difference. Their hair is black or brown, strong, and frequently curly; their complexion is neither yellow like the Malays, nor red like the American Indians, but a kind of olive, and sometimes reddish-brown. Their arms, and other parts of the body, are tattooed; but, except in one of the islands, this is by no means so common as in many parts of the southern sea.

Compared with those of other islands, the inhabitants may be termed numerous. They were estimated by their discoverers at 400,000. There is reason to believe this was somewhat above the actual population at that time, though traces of deserted villages and numerous enclosures, formerly cultivated but now abandoned, are everywhere to be met with. At present it does not exceed 130,000 or 150,000, of which 85,000 inhabit the island of Hawaii. The rapid depopulation which has most certainly taken place within the last fifty years is to be attributed to the frequent and desolating wars which marked the early part of Tamehameha's reign; the ravages of a pestilence brought in the first instance by foreign vessels, which has twice during the above period swept through the islands; the awful prevalence of infanticide; and the melancholy increase of depravity, and destructive consequences of vice.

The natural history of the islands, as it regards the animal kingdom, is exceedingly circumscribed. The only quadrupeds originally found inhabiting them were a small species of hogs, with long heads and small erect ears; dogs, lizards, and an animal larger than a mouse, but smaller than a rat. There were no beasts of prey, nor any ferocious animals except the hogs, which were sometimes found wild in the mountains. There are now large herds of cattle in Hawaii, and some tame ones, in most of the islands, together with flocks of goats and a few horses and sheep, which have been taken thither at different times, principally from the adjacent continent of America. Horses, cattle, and goats thrive well, but the climate appears too warm for sheep, unless they are kept on the mountains, which, in consequence of the keenness of the air, are seldom inhabited by the natives.

Birds, excepting those which are aquatic, and a species of owl that preys upon mice, are seldom seen near the shores. In the mountains they are numerous; and the notes of one kind, whose colour is brown and yellow speckled, are exceedingly sweet, resembling those of the English thrush. Several are remarkably beautiful, among which may be reckoned a small kind of paroquet of a glossy purple, and a species of red, yellow, and green woodpecker, with whose feathers the gods were dressed, and the helmet and handsome cloaks of the chiefs are ornamented. But the feathered tribes of Hawaii are not in general distinguished by variety of plumage, or melody in their notes. There are wild geese in the mountains, and ducks near the lagoons or ponds in the vicinity of the seashore; the domestic fowl was found there by their first discoverer, and, though now seldom used as an article of food, many are raised for the supply of shipping.

In common with the other islands of the Pacific, they are entirely free from every noxious and poisonous reptile, excepting centipedes, which are neither large nor numerous.

Fish are not so abundant on their shores as around many of the other islands; they have, however, several varieties, and the inhabitants procure a tolerable supply.

The vegetable productions, though less valuable and abundant than in some of the islands both to the west and the south, are found in no small variety, and the most serviceable are cultivated with facility. The natives subsist principally on the roots of the *arum esculentum*, which they call *taro*, on the *convolvulus batatas*, of sweet potato, called by them *uära*, and *uhi*, or yam. The principal indigenous fruits are the *wru*, or bread-fruit; the *niu*, or cocoanut; the *maia*, or plantain; the *ohia*, a species of *eugenia*; and the strawberry and rasp-berry. Oranges, limes, citrons, grapes, pine-apples, papaw-apples, cucumbers, and water-melons have been introduced, and, excepting the pine-apples, thrive well. French beans, onions, pumpkins, and cabbages have also been added to their vegetables, and though not esteemed by the natives, are cultivated to some extent, for the purpose of supplying the shipping. Sugar-cane is indigenous, and grows to a large size, though it is not much cultivated. Large tracts of fertile land lie waste in most of the islands; and sugar-cane, together with cotton, coffee, and other valuable intertropical produc-tions, might be easily raised in considerable quantities, which will probably be the case when the natives be-come more industrious and civilized.

The local situation of the Sandwich Islands is im-portant, and highly advantageous for purposes of com-merce, &c. On the north are the Russian settlements in Kamtschatka, and the neighbouring coast; to the north-west, the islands of Japan; due west, the Marian Islands, Manilla in the Philippines, and Canton in China; and on the east, the coast of California and Mexico. Hence they are so frequently resorted to by vessels navigating the Northern Pacific. The establishment of the independent states of South America has greatly in-creased their importance, as they lie in the track of vessels passing from thence to China or Calcutta, and other parts of India, and are not only visited by these, but by those who trade for skins, &c. with the natives of the north-west coast of America.

From the time of their discovery, the Sandwich Islands were unvisited, until 1786, when Captains Dixon and Portlock, in a trading voyage to the north-west coast for furs and sea-otter skins, anchored and procured re-freshments in the island of Oahu. The island of Maui was visited about the same time by the unfortunate La Perouse. After this period the islands were frequently visited by vessels engaged in the fur trade. Capt. Douglas, of the Iphigenia, and Capt. Metcalf, of the Eleanor, an American snow, were nearly cut off by the turbulent chiefs, who were desirous to procure the guns and ammunition belonging to their vessels, to aid them in carrying their purposes of conquest into effect. The son of the latter, a youth of sixteen, who commanded a schooner called the Fair American, which accompanied the Eleanor from Canton, when close in with land off Mouna Huararai, was becalmed; the natives thronged on board, threw young Metcalf overboard, seized and plundered the vessel, and murdered all the crew excepting the mate, whose name was Isaac Davis. He resided many years with Tamehameha, who very severely censured the chief under whose direction this outrage had been committed. A seaman, whose name is Young, belonging to the Eleanor, who was on shore at the time, was prevented from gaining his vessel, but was kindly treated by the king, and is still living at To-waihae.

In the years 1792 and 1793, Captain Vancouver, while engaged in a voyage of discovery in the North Pacific, spent several months at the Sandwich Islands; and, notwithstanding the melancholy catastrophe which had terminated the life of Captain Cook, whom he had accompanied, and the treacherous designs of the warlike and ambitious chiefs towards several of his predecessors, he met with the most friendly treatment from all parties, and received the strongest expressions of confidence from Tamehameha, sovereign of the whole group, who had been wounded in the skirmish that followed the death of their discoverer, but who had ever lamented with deepest regret that melancholy event. He alone had prevented the murderous intentions of his chieftains towards former vessels from being carried into effect; and it was his uniform endeavour to show every mark of friendship to those who visited his dominions. His attachment to the English induced him, during the stay of Capt. Vancouver, to cede the island of Hawaii to the British crown, and to place himself and his dominions under British protection; an act which was repeated by his son, the late king, on his accession to the sovereignty of all the islands.

The natives received many advantages from the visit of Capt. Vancouver; a breed of cattle, and a variety of useful seeds had been given. Generous and disinterested in his whole behaviour, he secured their friendship and attachment, and many still retain grateful recollections of his visit.

After his departure, the islands were seldom resorted

to except by traders from the United States of America, who, having discovered among them the sandal-wood, conveyed large quantities of it to Canton, where it was readily purchased by the Chinese, manufactured into incense, and burnt in their idol temples. Subsequently, when the South Sea whalers began to fish in the North Pacific, the Sandwich Islands afforded a convenient rendezvous for refitting and procuring refreshments during their protracted voyages, particularly since they have found the sperm-whale on the coast of Japan, where of late years the greater part of their cargoes have been procured.

So early as the year 1796, the LONDON MISSIONARY SOCIETY despatched the ship Duff to the South Sea Islands; and early in 1797, missionary settlements were established in the Marquesan, Friendly, and Society Islands. The missionary left at the Marquesas, after spending about a year among the people, returned. The establishment in the Friendly Islands was relinquished, though not till some of the individuals of which it was composed had fallen a sacrifice to the fury of the islanders in their intestine wars. The missionaries in the Society Islands have been enabled to maintain their ground, though exposed to many dangers and privations, and some ill-usage; but their labours were continued with patience and industry for fifteen years from the time of their first establishment, without any apparent effect. After this protracted period of discouragement, God has granted them the most astonishing success; and the happy change in the outward circumstances of the people, and the moral renovation which the reception of the gospel has effected in many, have more than realized the ardent desires of the missionaries themselves, and the most sanguine anticipations of the friends of the mission.

But though the efforts of the London Missionary Society were continued under appearances so inauspicious, with a degree of perseverance which has since been most amply compensated, various causes prevented their making any efforts towards communicating the knowledge of Christ to the Sandwich Islands. While their southern neighbours were enjoying all the advantages of Christianity, they remained under the thick darkness and moral wretchedness of one of the most cruel systems of idolatry that ever enslaved any portion of the human species.

The attention of the American churches was at length directed to the Sandwich Islands; and, their sympathies being awakened, resulted in a generous effort to ameliorate the wretchedness of their inhabitants. A society already existed, under the name of the *American Board of Commissioners for Foreign Missions*, the chief seat of whose operations was in the city of Boston, Massachusetts, though including among its members many distinguished individuals in different states of the Union.

In the autumn of 1819, a select and efficient band of missionaries was appointed by this society to establish a mission in the Sandwich Islands. They landed at Kairua, in Hawaii, on the 4th of February, 1820, and had the satisfaction to find the way in a measure prepared for them, by one of those remarkable events which distinguish the eras in the history of nations, whether barbarous or civilized. This was, the abolition of the national idolatry, which, though it was closely interwoven with all the domestic and civil institutions of every class of the inhabitants, upheld by the combined influence of a numerous body of priests, the arbitrary power of warlike chiefs, and the sanction of venerable antiquity, had been publicly and authoritatively prohibited by the king only a few months before their arrival. The motives which influenced the monarch of Hawaii in this decisive measure, the war it occasioned, and the consequences which ensued, are detailed in the following narrative. The missionaries could not but view it as a remarkable interposition of Divine Providence in their favour, and a happy prelude to the introduction of that gospel which they had conveyed to their shores. They had naturally expected that their landing would be opposed by the institutions of a system which, however degrading and oppressive in its influence, had presented more than human claims to the support of its adherents,—and to be withstood by a numerous and influential class of priests, whose craft would be endangered as soon as they should present the paramount claims of the true God to the homage of the heart and uniform obedience of the life. Instead of this, they found the laws of the *Tabu* entirely abrogated, and priests no longer existing as a distinct body, but merged in the other classes of the community. The whole nation was without any religion—and in this respect, at least, prepared to receive the dispensation of the gospel, recommended as it was by an exemption from all the miseries of their former system, and the animating prospects of life and immortality. Notwithstanding this, the missionaries, in the commencement of their efforts to instruct the natives, met with some opposition from misinformed and jealous individuals, who entertained groundless suspicions as to the ultimate object of their mission. This, however, was overruled by Karaimoku, Keopuolani, and other leading chiefs, and the king willingly allowed them to remain at least for a year.

They were accompanied by several native youths, whom a roving disposition had induced to visit America, where they had been educated in a school for instructing the aborigines of various heathen nations, designated the *Foreign Mission School*, and who, having given pleasing-evidence of piety, and understanding English, were qualified to act as interpreters, and assist the missionaries in the acquisition of the language. The difficult task of settling the orthography of an unwritten language required all their energies; but by diligent application, and the help of the elementary books in the dialects of the Society Islands and New-Zealand, they were enabled, in the beginning of 1822, to put to press the first sheet of a Hawaiian spelling-book, and to present the natives with the elements of the vernacular tongue in a printed form. Schools were established on a scale less extended than the missionaries desired, but not without advantage, as many of their early scholars, who made encouraging proficiency, have since become useful teachers. The more public instructions were generally well received by the people.

CHAPTER II.

Present from the British government to the king of the Sandwich Islands—Voyage to Hawaii—Appearance of the island—Intercourse with the people—Kearakakua bay—Visit to Kuakini, the governor—Voyage to Oahu—Welcome from the American missionaries—Detention in Oahu—Journeys and endeavours to instruct the people—Invitation to reside among them—Labours of Auna and native teachers—Destruction of idols—Observance of the Sabbath by the king and chiefs—Attention to religion—Karaimoku—Religious services in the families of the principal chiefs—Effects of our visit—Departure for the Society Islands—Return to Oahu—Arrival of missionaries—Objects of the projected tour of Hawaii—Remarks on the orthography of native words.

TAMEHAMEHA, who had governed the islands thirty years, and whose decease had taken place less than twelve months before the arrival of the missionaries, had invariably rendered the most prompt and acceptable aid to those English vessels which had touched at the islands. In return for the friendship so uniformly manifested, the British government instructed the governor of New South Wales to order a schooner to be built at Port Jackson, and sent as a present to the king of the Sandwich Islands. In the month of February, 1822, his majesty's colonial cutter Mermaid, having in charge the vessel designed for the king of Hawaii, put into the harbour of Huahine for refreshments. The captain of the Mermaid offered a passage either to the deputation from the London Missionary Society, then at Huahine, or to any of the missionaries who might wish to visit the Sandwich Islands. We had long been anxious to establish a mission among the Marquesas; and as he intended touching at those islands on his return, it appeared a very favourable opportunity for accomplishing it, and at the same time for visiting the American missionaries, the intelligence of whose embarkation for Hawaii had been previously received: Two pious natives, members of the church, and one of them a chief of some rank in the islands, were selected for the Marquesas; and I accompanied the deputation on their visit to Hawaii, for the purpose of aiding in the establishment of the native teachers in the former islands, observing how the people were disposed to receive instructers,

and obtaining such other information as might be serviceable in directing our future endeavours to maintain
permanent missionary stations among them.

An account of the designation of the native teachers
and our embarkation has been given in the preceding
volume. On the 27th of March we came in sight of
Hawaii, and were so near the land during the night as
to perceive the fires on the hills. The next morning,
when the sun appeared, and the mists, which for some
time enveloped the land, had cleared away, the island
spread before us in all its sublimity and romantic beauty.
The summits of the central mountains were concealed
among the clouds. The coast was lofty, and broken
towards the northern extremity. In many parts the
high grounds appeared clothed with verdure, and waterfalls were numerous along the coast. As we sailed
along parallel with the shore, I could sometimes observe
from the ship's deck above twenty beautiful cascades,
of varied elevation and breadth. Passing the straits
between Hawaii and Maui, we reached Towaihai. The
same evening I accompanied the captain towards the
shore, where, near the land, we were met by a little boat
with five persons on board, who were the first Hawaiians that welcomed us to their countrymen. As our
boats approached, one of the natives hailed us with
" Aroha," peace, or attachment. We returned the salutation in Tahitian. Having inquired the name of the
place, we asked where Tamehameha was ; they replied,
" He is dead."—" Who is king now ?" was our next inquiry ; they answered, " His son Rihoriho." We then
asked, " Is it peace ?" They answered, " It is peace ; the
king is at Oahu—he has missionaries there to teach the
people." The chief then asked, " Are you from America ?" We answered, " From Britain." He then said,
" By way of Tahiti !" and, when answered in the affirmative, observed, " There are a number of Tahitians on
shore." This conversation had been carried on as the
boats lay alongside of each other ; but as the chief proposed to visit the ship, we returned on board. There
was a great degree of native dignity about this chief,
who appeared to be about five-and-twenty years of age,
tall, stout, well-made, and remarkably handsome. He
told us his name was Kuakini ; that his sister was the
queen-dowager, his brother governor of the adjacent
island of Maui, and himself governor of Hawaii. He

B 3

entered very freely into conversation with Auna and the other Tahitians on board, and expressed his desire to learn to read and write. From the facility with which we could understand the speech of our guests, and make ourselves understood, we perceived that the Sandwich islanders and Tahitians were members of one great family, and spoke the same language with but slight variations—a fact which we regarded as of great importance in the intercourse we might have with the people. The next morning at sunrise, the chief and his party joined us at our morning devotions, but they did not kneel in prayer. During the day we were astonished and delighted with the appearance of the country; the lofty Mouna Kea, whose summit was covered with snow, impressed very powerfully the minds of our Tahitians. So pleased were they with the sight of the snow, of which we had often endeavoured in vain to give them a correct description, that they proposed, as soon as they should land, to take a journey to the top of the mountain, for the purpose of obtaining some of the white hard water. The signs of recent, vigorous, and extensive volcanic action in the wide and often winding streams of black indurated lava, which covered the greater part of the coast, were not less strange and wonderful to us. During the forenoon of the following day, when we were opposite Kairauea, Kuakini left us, accompanied, agreeably to his urgent request, by Auna, towards whom he manifested much attachment. The next day was the Sabbath: by daylight we found ourselves opposite Kearakekua bay, in which a number of ships appeared lying at anchor. Early in the forenoon we entered the harbour, and were soon boarded by the captains of the ships, and surrounded by natives from the shore. We were scarcely able to hold public worship on deck in the afternoon, on account of the noise and crowds of natives. The striking contrast between the state of the people of the place, their flagrant cheating in barter, &c., and the tranquillity and religious occupations of those we had left at Huahine, deeply affected them; and I endeavoured to excite gratitude to God, and sympathy for the strangers, in the minds of our Tahitian companions, by an address from the words of the apostle, " And such were some of you," &c. The smallness and confinement of the berths below, and the heat of the weather, &c., did not appear to occasion so much unpleasantness to our Tahitian voyagers as the loss of the luxury of bathing, to which they had been accustomed on shore, two or three times every day, in the cool and flowing streams of their native islands; and nothing during the voyage had been more grateful to them than a copious shower. At such seasons they stripped off the greater part of their clothes, and, under the refreshing influence of the rain, could scarcely refrain from dancing about the deck for joy. Early, therefore, on the morning after our arrival in Kearakekua bay, a party of our natives went on shore to bathe. Soon after breakfast we landed on the north side of the bay, surprised at the striking and decisively volcanic aspect of the shore; the whole of that part of the coast seemed one extensive mass of barren lava, with here and there a straggling bush growing between the crevices, or in places where a partial decomposition had taken place. In one of the first houses which we entered, a man and a boy, apparently father and son, entertained us with a *hufa ta raau*, singing to the beating of a stick: we could not comprehend very distinctly the burden of his song; but the name of Rihoriho occurring repeatedly, we presumed that it referred to the new king. Conducted by an old man, whom we induced to be our guide, we visited the spot where Captain Cook was killed—and afterward entered into conversation with the natives, who crowded around us. These all united in confirming the statement of those we first met, that their gods were thrown away, and their temples overturned. In the afternoon, Auna joined our party, and related his proceedings at Kairua, where he had met with Toteta, a native of Eimeo, and where the governor had expressed his desire to embrace the new religion. On the following day a ship arrived, which brought us tidings from England of the coronation of his late majesty George IV., and of the death of his queen.

On the 2d of April, Mr. Tyerman and myself visited the governor at Kairua, his residence. As we approached, we were met by Mr. Young; he conducted us to the governor, who cordially welcomed us, entertained us hospitably, and expressed a wish that I would come and reside at Hawaii. We visited a large temple in ruins, and spent the evening very pleasantly in conversation with the strangers. Mr. Young gave us a full account of the abolition of the tabu, and the overthrow of the former system of idolatry, by the king, on the occasion of a public festival, at which he was present. After we had retired to rest, the governor came with his slate, and sat down by the side of the mat on which we were lying, and requested we would teach him to write; and also made an attempt to read, stating that he had a great desire to learn. It was near two o'clock in the morning before he left us. The next day the governor returned with us to the ship, and we remained nearly a week longer, waiting for the schooner, from which we had parted company soon after leaving Huahine. During this time we had frequent interviews with Kuakini; and though, in consequence of his frequent visits on board the vessels in harbour, we often saw him in a state of inebriation, there was a frankness and apparent sincerity in his expressions of desire after knowledge and improvement, that could not fail to interest us in his behalf.

On the 9th of April we weighed anchor, and sailed for Oahu: through the day we enjoyed the most delightful views of the sublime and magnificent mountains of Hawaii, as we sailed slowly along its shores. We did not enter the harbour in Oahu until the 15th, when we found ourselves at daybreak near the reef, and learned from some fishermen in a canoe that the schooner was at anchor in the bay. We were afterward boarded by Keeaumoku, the governor of Maui and brother of Kuakini, and soon received a pilot, who conducted our little cutter through the intricacies of the channel to the anchorage. We were not long before we proceeded to the shore. On our way we met a canoe, in which the wife of Auna recognised a brother, who had left the Society Islands in the Bounty, when the mutineers took possession of the ship; we were also met by a boat, in which were the American consul and a Frenchman of the name of Rives, who acted as secretary for the king. Messrs. Thurston, Chamberlain, and Loomis, American missionaries, to whom I had written from Hawaii, were also in the boat, and cordially welcomed us.

In a large native house near the shore, we were introduced to the king, his queens, the queen-dowager, and what might be regarded as the Hawaiian court. We were struck with the portly form and gigantic size of the royal party, and many of the chiefs by whom they were attended. The captain delivered the letter from

the governor of New South Wales to the king; and,
after wine had been introduced, Messrs. Bennet, Tyerman, and myself accompanied the American missionaries to their habitation, where we received a pressing
invitation from the whole family to partake of their hospitality and such accommodations as their establishment would afford, so long as we might remain in the
island—a proposal with which we cheerfully complied.
Different lands had given us birth; we had never seen
each other before; but we spoke one language, embraced one faith, had devoted our lives to the accomplishment of one object, which we mutually felt more
important than any other; and found that the influence
of Christian and missionary feeling so united our hearts,
that we were as happy in the society of our friends as
if we had been intimate from childhood. We were
afterward joined by Mr. and Mrs. Bingham, and the
missionaries from Tauai; and the pleasure I derived
from their society, during the four months that we were
detained in Oahu, is still among the most grateful of
my recollections.

The day after our arrival we waited on the chiefs,
and in the evening called on Kaahumanu. Through
the influence of the individual whom we met on our
way from the ship yesterday, Auna and his wife had
been invited to take up their abode in the establishment
of Kaahumanu, who, next to the king and Karaimoku,
was considered the person of greatest influence in the
island. When we called, the greater part of the inmates
of the dwelling were sitting cross-legged on the ground,
playing at cards. Ludicrous spectacles of this kind were
not unfrequently exhibited during our stay: sometimes
we saw a party of large chiefs and chief women sitting
on their mats, or on the grass, under the shade of a tree,
but very partially clothed, playing at cards, with one or
two large pet hogs lying close by them; not small and
cleanly things, that they might take under their arms,
but full-grown, and in a condition, under proper management, to have made good bacon. Auna informed us
that his wife and himself had been treated with kindness; that on the preceding night they read together,
in a retired corner of the house, a portion of the Scriptures, and engaged in prayer; and that this morning,
when Kaahumanu perceived that they were about to do
the same, she requested them to come near, that she

and her people might join. I asked her if she did not
desire to learn to read, to know and serve the true God;
and she answered yes; but said, we cannot, unless the
king does. If he embraces the new religion, we shall
all follow. In the evening of this day we were present
when Anna read the Scripture, and offered family prayers publicly in Kaahumanu's house: we united with no
ordinary feelings, for the first time, in the worship of
the true God with the people around us.

The next day, the 17th of April, being the day on
which our American friends held the weekly religious
service, I had an opportunity of preaching in the Tahitian language. Soon after four in the afternoon, we
went together to the little chapel which stood in the
midst of the plain of Honoruru, not far from the dwelling of the missionaries. It was partly filled with natives. While we were singing a Tahitian hymn, the
king and queen entered, and seated themselves in the
middle of the place. The singing of the natives who
had come with us appeared to surprise and please them,
and they occasionally whispered to each other as it proceeded., I then read the third chapter of the Gospel of
St. John, and offered an extempore prayer, during which
the king and Sandwich islanders remained sitting. I
then delivered a short discourse from the sixteenth
verse of the chapter I had read.. The audience was
attentive, and at the close of the service rose and departed. On being asked, as they went out, whether
they understood what had been said, they answered yes;
though it is probable that they understood but imperfectly, as the whole was in the Tahitian language.

While on board the Mermaid with the king and several of the chiefs, on the day following, the captain informed me that he was going to make a voyage to some
other part of the Pacific, before he returned to Huahine,
and that probably it would be two months before he
could take us back. This was distressing intelligence
—not on our own account, so much as that of Mrs.
Ellis and our friends, who had been distinctly informed
by the captain that before a period so remote our return
might be confidently expected. I communicated the
tidings to the deputation, who were not less surprised
than I had been, and who, while they expressed their
regret on Mrs. Ellis's account, observed, " Perhaps the
Lord has thoughts of mercy towards this people, and

has work for us to do here, that we are deprived for the present of the means of returning."

On the 10th of May, Auna came up to the mission-house, and informed me that Kaahumanu, and Taumuarii, the king of Tauai, had requested him and his wife to take up their abode with them in the Sandwich Islands, and had desired that I would return to Huahine for my family, and then come and dwell with them. As soon as the intelligence was made known to Messrs. Tyerman and Bennet, we unitedly communicated it to our friends the American missionaries, who unanimously expressed their desires that we should comply with the wishes of the chiefs, and expressed their opinion that it would facilitate the introduction of Christianity among the people. Other chiefs afterward expressed a corresponding desire; the king also said it would be well; and as it appeared that our coming would strengthen the hands of our American brethren, facilitate their acquisition of the language, and aid the accomplishment of an object equally desired by us all, we assured the chiefs of our willingness to comply with their wishes. Shortly after this, Auna accompanied Kaahumanu and Taumuarii to Maui, and Messrs. Tyerman, Bennet, Bingham, and myself made a tour of Oahu, which, while it made us acquainted with the number and circumstances of the people, excited our sympathies on their behalf, and enabled us, as opportunity offered, to address them on the subject of religion, favoured us also with the means of observing the extent and varied appearance of the country. In company with Captains Lewis and Brown, and Messrs. Jones, Dix, and Moxley, we sailed as far as the district of Eva, or Pearl river, and travelled on foot the rest of the way. Religious services were continued regularly in the little chapel; but after the effects of their novelty had subsided, few of the natives attended; we had also frequent occasions to lament the inebriation of the king and many of the chiefs, as well as the extensive prevalence and disastrous effects of intoxication among the people; but were encouraged by the diligence and perseverance of Kaahumanu, his favourite queen. In the mean time we were acquiring the language, and were enabled more distinctly to communicate our instructions to the people.

After some weeks' absence, Auna returned, and informed us that they had been to different parts of

Hawaii, that the governor was diligently learning to read and write, and that a young chief, whose name was Lanui, was anxiously desiring to know the Word of the true God; that one Sabbath-day, when there were great crowds of people around, and Auna proposed to retire to a secret place among the bushes for prayer, he said, " No, let us read and pray in my house;" the place was crowded with people, who listened attentively to the reading and prayer. Kaahumanu directed them to fetch the gods that were lying hid in the holes of the rocks and caves, at a distance from the shore. They brought forth great numbers, and in one day burnt no fewer than one hundred and two idols.

Our friends had a small school of fifteen children, whom they were industriously endeavouring to instruct. The king and queen, and several of the principal persons, had become our pupils, and we spent part of every day either in teaching them to read and write, or in conversation on the subject of religion. They were, as might be expected, extremely ignorant; but they were in general willing, and often expressed themselves desirous to be informed. We endeavoured familiarly and with the utmost plainness to exhibit, not the subtleties of theology, or the dogmas of any particular sect, but the great facts and principles of revelation—and were pleased to perceive that they appeared to have obtained an outline of the leading truths of Christianity. On the evening of the 7th of July, which was the Sabbath, when Mr. Bingham and myself went to the king's house, he informed us that he would never again neglect the observance of the Sabbath, but would worship Jehovah; and that he did not intend to drink rum. Our number of hearers now frequently amounted to three hundred persons, to whom we preached twice on the Sabbath, and once during the week: our meetings were enlivened by the introduction of hymns in the native language. A spirit of inquiry was excited among the chiefs and people, and several seemed earnestly desirous to know and serve the living God. Among them Keeaumoku was conspicuous; he not only attended public worship, but collected the people together by ringing a large bell every evening, and invited us to attend and preach to them.

Among the strangers now at Oahu was Mr. Matheson, a gentleman who came as passenger on board an American ship from South America to Canton. In his "Narrative of a Visit to Brazil, Chili, Peru, and the Sandwich Islands, in the years 1821 and 1822," he gives the following account of a visit to the establishment of Keeaumoku, who was also called Cox by the foreigners :—

"August 5.—This morning I went to Cox, intending to purchase some goats. I expected to find him, as usual, either sleeping, or smoking, or drinking, or busy trafficking, like myself. The door of his hut was half-open, and I was about to enter unceremoniously, when a scene too striking ever to be forgotten, and which would require the hand of a master painter to do it justice, suddenly arrested my whole attention.

"About a dozen natives of both sexes were seated in a circle on the matted floor of the apartment, and in the midst of them sat John Honoree, the Hawaiian catechist. All eyes were bent upon him; and the variously expressive features of each individual marked the degree of interest excited by what was passing in his mind. So absorbed, indeed, were they in their reflections, that my abrupt appearance at the door created for some time neither interruption nor remark. The speaker held in his hand the Gospel of St. John, as published at Otaheite, and was endeavouring, by signs and familiar illustrations, to render its contents easy of comprehension. His simple yet energetic manner added weight to his opinions, and proved that he spoke, from personal conviction, the sincere and unpremeditated language of the heart.

"The chief himself stood in the background, a little apart from the rest, leaning upon the shoulder of an attendant. A gleam of light suddenly fell upon his countenance, and disclosed features on which wonder, anxiety, and seriousness were imprinted in the strongest characters. He wore no other dress than the *maro* round the waist; but his tall athletic form and bust, seen bending over the other's shoulders, and dignified demeanour, marked at one glance his rank and superiority over all around. One hand was raised instinctively to his head, in a pensive attitude. His knitted brows bespoke intense thought; and his piercing black eyes were fixed upon the speaker with an inquiring, penetrating look, as much as to say, ' Can what you tell us be really true " I gazed for some minutes with mute astonish-

ment, turning my regards from one to the other, and
dreading to intrude upon the privacy of persons whose
time was so usefully employed. At last the chief turned
round and motioned with his hand, in a dignified manner, for me to withdraw. I did so, but carried away in
my heart the remembrance of a scene, to which the
place, the people, and the occasion united in attaching
a peculiar interest.

"I learned afterward that Cox had promised to build
a school-house, and present it to the missionaries for
their use; a donation which, considering his acknowledged love of money, affords no mean proof that his
inquiries into the truth of the new religion had not been
altogether fruitless."

The chiefs prohibited their people from working on
the Lord's-day; and Keeaumoku, Karaimoku, Kauikeouli, the young prince, Kaahumanu, Taumuarii, Piia,
Naihe, and almost every chief of rank and influence,
were numbered among our pupils, or regular worshippers of the true God. Astonished and gratified by the
wonderful change we had been permitted to witness
during the period of our detention, and having received
every expression of attachment, and desire for our return, from the missionaries and chiefs, we took leave
of them on the 22d of August, and sailed for Huahine in
the Mermaid, which had returned about three weeks
before.

Shortly after our arrival, a public council of the king
and chiefs of Hawaii had been held at Oahu. Auna and
his companion from Huahine were invited to attend,
and had an opportunity of answering the inquiries of the
king and chiefs relative to the events which had transpired in the Society Islands, and of testifying to the
feelings of friendship and esteem entertained by Pomare
and the rulers of those islands, much to the satisfaction
of the latter—who were convinced that the reports
which had been circulated among them respecting the
hostile intentions of the southern islanders, and the dangerous influence of Christian missions there, were totally groundless. The complete removal of those preju-
dices, which had been excited and nurtured by these
means, was one great advantage of our visit. On our
return, we conveyed friendly letters from the king and
chiefs of Hawaii to those of the Society Islands, and

an agreeable correspondence has been ever since maintained.

Early in February, 1823, I returned to Oahu with my family, experienced a kind reception from the king and chiefs, and was privileged to commence my missionary pursuits in harmonious co-operation with my predecessors, the American missionaries, who were diligently employed in their benevolent exertions for the spiritual well-being of the nation; avoiding, as they have uniformly done ever since, all interference with the civil, commercial, and political concerns of the people, and attending solely to their instruction in useful knowledge and religious truth.

The difficulties attending the acquisition of the language and other circumstances had hitherto confined the labours of the missionaries almost entirely to the islands of Oahu and Tauai; but in April, 1823, a reinforcement arriving from America enabled them to extend their efforts, particularly towards Maui and Hawaii. In order that arrangements for the establishment and permanent maintenance of missionary stations in the latter—the largest, most important, and populous island of the group—might be made with all the advantages of local knowledge, it was agreed that three of the American missionaries and myself should visit and explore that interesting island, to investigate the religious and moral condition of the people, communicate to them the knowledge of Christ, unfold the benevolent objects of the mission, inquire whether they were willing to receive Christian teachers, and select the most eligible places for missionary stations. These, though the principal, were not the only objects that occupied our attention during the tour. We availed ourselves of the opportunities it afforded to make observations on the structure of the island, its geographical character, natural scenery, productions, and other objects of curiosity; and to become more fully acquainted with the peculiar features of the system of idolatry, the traditions, manners, and customs of the inhabitants,—a detailed account of which is given in the following narrative.

Before entering upon the tour, a few remarks on the orthography of the Hawaiian names which are occasionally introduced, explaining the reasons for its adoption, and assisting in the pronunciation of native words, will probably be acceptable to most of our readers.

The visits which most foreigners have paid to the Sandwich and other islands of the Pacific have been too transient to allow them, however well qualified they may have been, to obtain any thing beyond an exceedingly superficial acquaintance with the words in most common use among the natives, and certainly insufficient to enable them to discern the nice distinctions of vowel sounds and peculiar structure of the aboriginal languages of the islands; and those individuals whom purposes of commerce have induced to remain a longer period among them, whatever facility they may have acquired in speaking it, have not attended to its orthographical construction, but have adopted those methods of spelling names of persons and places which happen to have been used by those of their predecessors with whose printed accounts they were most familiar.

The want of a standard orthography cannot be better illustrated than by noticing the mistakes, often of a singularly ludicrous, and occasionally of an important kind, which occur even in the present day, or by glancing at the great variety of methods adopted by different voyagers to represent the same word. We have seen the name of Tamehameha, the late king, spelled in various publications twelve or fourteen different ways; and the same variety has also prevailed in other popular names, though perhaps not to an equal extent. The above word is a reduplication of the word *meha* (lonely, or solitary), with the definite article *Ta* prefixed, which is a part of the name; though rejected in Cook's Voyages, where he is called Maihamaiha. Captain Vancouver calls him Tamaahmaah, which is somewhat nearer.

This disagreement in different writers arises, in the first place, from the deficiency in the vowel characters, as used in the English language, for expressing the native vowel sounds. The English language has but one sign, or letter, for the vowel sound in the first syllable of father and fable, or the words tart and tale; but in Hawaiian the sense of these sounds, which frequently occur unconnected with any other, is so different that a distinct character is essential. The first sound is often a distinct word, and frequently marks the past tense of the verb, while the second sound distinguishes the future, and is also a distinct word. These two sounds often occur together, forming two distinct syllables, as

in the interrogation *e-a?* what? and the word *he-a*, to
call. In the English language two letters, called double
vowels, are used to lengthen the same sound, as *ee* in
thee, or to express one totally different, as *oo* in pool:
but in Hawaiian there is often a repetition of the vowel
sound, without any intervening consonant or other vowel
sound, as in *a-a*, a bag or pocket, *e-e*, to embark, *i-i*, a
name of a bird, *o-o*, an agricultural instrument; which
must be sounded as two distinct syllables. Hence, when
the *ee* is employed to express a lengthened sound of *e*,
as in Owhyhee, and *oo* to signify the sound of *u* in rule,
as in Karakakooa, which is generally done by European
visiters, it is not possible to express by any signs those
native words in which the double vowels occur, which
are invariably two distinct syllables.

Another cause of the incorrectness of the orthography of early voyagers to these islands has been a want
of better acquaintance with the structure of the language, which would have prevented their substituting a
compound for a single word. This is the case in the
words Otaheite, Otaha, and Owhyhee, which ought to
be Tahiti, Tahaa, and Hawaii. The O is no part of these
words, but is the preposition *of*, or belonging to; or it
is the sign of the case, denoting it to be the nominative,
answering to the question who or what, which would
be O wai? The sign of the case being prefixed to the
interrogation, the answer uniformly corresponds, as,

Nom.   O wai ia aina?—What that land?
      Ans. O Hawaii—Hawaii.

Pos.   No hea oe?—Of whence you?
      Ans. No Hawaii—Of or belonging to Hawaii.

Obj.   Hoe oe i hea?—Sailing you to where?
      Ans. I Hawaii—To Hawaii.
      Mai hea mai oe?—From whence you?
      Ans. Mai Hawaii mai—From Hawaii.

Any one of these, or other similar combinations, in
which the word Ha-wai-i occurs, might have been given
as the name of the island with as much correctness as
that which commences with the O, which appears sometimes to be a contraction of the pronoun, and is never
used, excepting when the word begins a sentence, and
consequently is, even as a combination, not of frequent
occurrence. The natives are certainly most likely to

know the name of their own island: the designation
they give it we have adopted, and believe that in so doing
we have the approbation of all unprejudiced men, more
than we should have had in perpetuating an error which
their discoverer, had he possessed the means of so doing,
would very cheerfully have corrected.

In pronouncing the word Ha-wai-i, the *Ha* is sounded
short, as in Hah, the *wai* as wye, and the final *i* as e
in me.

Atooi in Cook's Voyages; *Atowai* in Vancouver's, and
Atoui in one of his contemporaries, is also a compound
of two words, a Tauai, literally *and Tauai*. The meaning of the word tauai is, to light upon, or to dry in the
sun; and the name, according to the account of the late
king, was derived from the long droughts which sometimes prevailed, or the large pieces of timber which
have been occasionally washed upon its shores. Being
the most leeward island of importance, it was probably
the last inquired of, or the last name repeated by the
people to the first visiters. For, should the natives be
pointed to the group, and asked the names of the different islands, beginning with that farthest to windward, and proceeding west, they would say, O Hawaii,
Maui, Ranai, Morotai, Oahu, a (and) Tauai: the copu-
lative conjunction preceding the last member of the
sentence would be placed immediately before Tauai;
and hence, in all probability, it has been attached to the
name of that island, which has usually been written,
after Cook's orthography, *Atooi*, or *Atowai*, after Vancouver.

The more intelligent among the natives, particularly
the chiefs, frequently smile at the manner of spelling
the names of places and persons in published accounts
of the islands, which they occasionally see.

The orthography employed in the native names which
occur in the succeeding narrative is in accordance with
the power or sound of the letters composing the Hawaiian alphabet, and the words are represented as nearly
as possible to the manner in which they are pronounced
by the natives. *A* is always as *a* in father, or shorter,
as *a* in the first syllable of aha, *e* as *a* in hate, *i* as *i* in machine, or *ee* in thee, *o* as *o* in note, *u* as *oo* in food, or
short, as in bull, and the diphthong *ai* as *i* in wine or mine.
The consonants are sounded as in English.

The native words may be correctly pronounced by

attending to the above sounds of the vowels. The following list of the principal names will likewise assist in the proper pronunciation of Hawaiian words. The *h* is inserted after the *a* only to secure that vowel's being sounded as in the exclamation *ah!*

PLACES.

Ha-wai-i *pronounced*	Ha-wye-e
O-a-hu	O-ah-hoo
Tau-ai	Tow-i *or* Tow-eye
Mau-i	Mow-e
Kai-ru-a	Ky-roo-ah
Ke-a-ra-ke-ku-a . .	Kay-a-ra-kay-koo-ah
Wai-a-ke-a . . .	Wye-ah-kay-ah
Wai-pi-o	Wye-pe-o
Ki-rau-e-a	Ke-row-ay-ah
Mou-na-hu-a-ra-rai . .	Mow-nah-hoo-ah-ra-rye
Mou-na Ro-a . . .	Mow-nah Ro-ah
Mou-na Ke-a . . .	Mow-nah Kay-ah
Ka-a-va-ro-a . . .	Kah-ah-vah-ro-ah

PERSONS.

Ta-mé-ha-mé-ha . .	Ta-mé-hah-mé-hah
Ri-ho-ri-ho . . .	Ree-ho-ree-ho
Ta-u-mu-a-ri-i . .	Ta-oo-moo-ah-re-e
Ka-a-hu-ma-nu . .	Ka-ah-hoo-ma-noo
Ke-o-pu-o-la-ni . .	Kay-o-poo-o-lah-ne
Ku-a-ki-ni . . .	Koo-ah-ke-ne
Ka-rai-mo-ku . . .	Ka-rye-mo-koo
Bo-ki	Bo-ke
Li-li-ha	Le-le-hah
Mau-ae	Mow-aye
Ma-ko-a	Ma-ko-ah

CHAPTER III.

TAUMUARII, the friendly king of Tauai, having generously offered the missionaries chosen to make the tour
of Hawaii a passage in one of his vessels bound from
Oahu to Kairua, Messrs. Thurston, Bishop, and Goodrich repaired on board in the afternoon of June 24, 1823,
They were accompanied by Mr. Harwood, an ingenious
mechanic, whom curiosity and a desire to assist them
had induced to join their party. The indisposition of
Mrs. Ellis prevented my proceeding in the same vessel,
but I hoped to follow in a few days.

At 4 P. M. the brig was under way, standing to the
S. E. Having cleared the bar and the reefs at the entrance of the harbour, the trade-wind blowing fresh from
the N. E., they were soon out of sight of Honoruru.
They passed the islands of Morokai, Ranai, and the
principal part of Maui during the night, and at daybreak
on the 25th were off Tahaurawe, a small island on the
south side of Maui. The Haaheo Hawaii (Pride of Hawaii), another native vessel, formerly the Cleopatra's
barge, soon after hove in sight; she did not, however,
come up with them, but tacked and stood for Lahaina.
In the evening the wind, usually fresh in the channel
between Maui and Hawaii, blew so strong that they
were obliged to lay-to for about three hours; when it
abated, and allowed them to proceed.

On the 26th, at 4 P. M. the vessel came to anchor
in Kairua bay. The missionaries soon after went on
shore, grateful for the speedy and comfortable passage
with which they had been favoured, having been only
forty-nine hours from Oahu, which is about 150 miles
to the leeward of Kairua. They were heartily welcomed
by the governor, Kuakini, usually called by the foreigners John Adams, from his having adopted the name of a

former president of the United States of America.
They took tea with him; and. after expressing their
gratitude to God in the native language, with the governor and his family, retired to rest in an apartment
kindly furnished for them in his own house.

The next morning their baggage was removed from
the vessel, and deposited in a small comfortable house,
formerly belonging to Tamehameha, but which the governor directed them to occupy so long as they should
remain at Kairua. He also politely invited them to his
table during their stay; in consequence of which, without forgetting their character, they sat down to their
morning repast. Their breakfast-room presented a singular scene. They were seated around a small table
with the governor and one or two of his friends, who,
in addition to the coffee, fish, vegetables, &c. with which
it was furnished, had a large wooden bowl of poë, a sort
of thin paste, made of baked taro, beat up and diluted
with water, placed by the side of their plates, from which
they frequently took very hearty draughts. Two favourite lap-dogs sat on the same sofa with the governor,
one on his right-hand and the other on his left—and
occasionally received a bit from his hand, or the fragments of the plate from which he had eaten. A number of his, *punahele*, favourite chiefs, and some occasional
visiters, sat in circles on the floor, around large dishes
of raw fish, baked hog, or dog, or goat, from which each
helped himself without ceremony, while a huge calabash
of poë passed rapidly round among them. They became exceedingly loquacious and cheerful during their
meal; and several who had been silent before now
laughed aloud, and joined with spirit in the mirth of
their companions. Neat wooden dishes of water were
handed to the governor and his friends, both before and
after eating, in which they washed their hands. Uncivilized nations are seldom distinguished by habits of
cleanliness; but this practice, we believe, is an ancient
custom, generally observed by the chiefs and all the
higher orders of the people throughout the islands.

Kairua, though healthy and populous, is destitute of
fresh water, except what is found in pools or small
streams in the mountains, four or five miles from the
shore. An article so essential to the maintenance of a
missionary station it was desirable to procure, if possible,

nearer at hand.* As soon, therefore, as breakfast was ended, the party walked through the district in a south-east direction, to examine the ground, with a view to discover the most eligible place for digging a well.

The whole face of the country marked decisively its volcanic origin; and in the course of their excursion they entered several hollows in the lava, formed by its having cooled and hardened on the surface, while, in a liquid state underneath, it had continued to flow towards the sea, leaving a crust in the shape of a tunnel, or arched vault, of varied thickness and extent. Before they returned, they also explored a celebrated cavern in the vicinity, called Raniakea. After entering it by a small aperture, they passed on in a direction nearly parallel with the surface—sometimes along a spacious arched way, not less than twenty-five feet high and twenty wide; at other times by a passage so narrow that they could with difficulty press through, till they had proceeded about 1200 feet. Here their progress was arrested by a pool of water, wide, deep, and as salt as that found in the hollows of the lava within a few yards of the sea : this latter circumstance in a great degree damped their hopes of finding fresh water by digging through the lava. More than thirty natives, most of them carrying torches, accompanied them in their descent; and on arriving at the water, simultaneously plunged in, extending their torches with one hand, and swimming about with the other. The partially illuminated heads of the natives, splashing about in this subterranean lake—the reflection of the torch-light on its agitated surface—the frowning sides and lofty arch of the black vault, hung with lava, that had cooled in every imaginable shape—the deep gloom of the cavern beyond the water—the hollow sound of their footsteps —and the varied reverberations of their voices, produced a singular effect; and it would have required but little aid from fancy to have imagined a resemblance between this scene and the fabled Stygian lake of the poets. The mouth of the cave is about half a mile from the sea, and the perpendicular depth to the water probably not

* The late king Tamehameha used frequently to beg a cask of water from the captains of vessels touching at Kairua; and it is one of the most acceptable presents a captain going to this station could make, either to the chiefs or missionaries.

less than fifty or sixty feet. The pool is occasionally
visited by the natives for the purpose of bathing, as its
water is cool and refreshing. From its ebbing and flowing with the tide, it has probably a direct communication
with the sea.

In the afternoon Messrs. Thurston and Bishop explored the northern boundary of the bay, on the eastern
side of which Kairua is situated. It runs three or four
miles into the sea, is composed entirely of lava, and was
formed by an eruption from one of the large craters on
the top of Mouna Huararai (Mount Huararai), which,
about twenty-three years ago, inundated several villages,
destroyed a number of plantations and extensive fish-
ponds, filled up a deep bay twenty miles in length, and
formed the present coast.

An Englishman who has resided thirty-eight years in
the islands, and who witnessed the above eruption, has
frequently told us he was astonished at the irresistible
impetuosity of the torrent. Stone walls, trees, and
houses, all gave way before it; even large masses or
rocks of hard ancient lava, when surrounded by the
fiery stream, soon split into small fragments, and falling
into the burning mass, appeared to melt again, as borne
by it down the mountain's side.

Offerings were presented, and many hogs thrown alive
into the stream, to appease the anger of the gods, by
whom they supposed it was directed, and to stay its devastating course. All seemed unavailing, until one day
the king, Tamehameha, went, attended by a large retinue of chiefs and priests, and, as the most valuable
offering he could make, cut off part of his own hair,
which was always considered sacred, and threw it into
the torrent. A day or two after the lava ceased to flow.
The gods, it was thought, were satisfied; and the king
increased his influence over the minds of the people,
who, from this circumstance, attributed their escape
from threatened destruction, to his supposed interest
with the deities of the volcanoes.

In several places they observed that the sea rushes
with violence twenty or thirty yards along the cavities
beneath the lava, and then, forcing its waters through
the apertures in the surface, forms a number of beautiful jets d'eau, which, falling again on the rocks, roll
rapidly back to the ocean.

They enjoyed a fine view of the town and adjacent

country. The houses, which are neat, are generally erected on the seashore, shaded with cocoanut and kou-trees, which greatly enliven the scene. The environs were cultivated to a considerable extent; small gardens were seen among the barren rocks on which the houses are built, wherever soil could be found sufficient to nourish the sweet-potato, the watermelon, or even a few plants of tobacco, and in many places these seemed to be growing literally in the fragments of lava collected in small heaps around their roots.

The next morning, Messrs. Thurston, Goodrich, and Harwood visited the high and cultivated parts of the district. After travelling over the lava for about a mile, the hollows in the rocks began to be filled with a light brown soil; and, about half a mile farther, the surface was entirely covered with a rich mould, formed by de-cayed vegetable matter and decomposed lava. Here they enjoyed the agreeable shade of bread-fruit and *ohia* trees: the latter is a deciduous plant, a variety of eu-genia, resembling the *eugenia malaccensis*, bearing a beau-tifully red pulpy fruit, of the size and consistence of an apple—juicy, but rather insipid. The trees are elegant in form, and grow to the height of twenty or thirty feet; the leaf is oblong and pointed, and the flowers are at-tached to the branches by a short stem. The fruit, which is abundant, is generally ripe either on different places in the same island, or on different islands, during all the summer months. The path now lay through a beautiful part of the country, quite a garden, compared with that through which they had passed on first leav-ing the shore. It was generally divided into small fields about fifteen rods square, fenced with low stone walls, built with fragments of lava gathered from the surface of the enclosures. These fields were planted with ba-nanas, sweet-potatoes, mountain taro, paper-mulberry plants, melons, and sugar-cane, which flourished luxu-riantly in every direction. Having travelled about three or four miles through this delightful region, and passed several valuable pools of fresh water, they arrived at the thick woods which extend several miles up the sides of the lofty mountain that rises immediately behind Kairua. Among the various plants and trees that now presented themselves, they were much pleased with a species of tree ferns, whose stipes were about five feet long, and the stem about fourteen feet high, and one foot in diameter. A smart shower of rain (a frequent occurrence in the mountains) arrested their farther progress, and obliged them to return to their lodgings, where they arrived about five in the afternoon, gratified, though fatigued, by their excursion.

Mr. Bishop called on Thomas Hopu, the native teacher, who has for some time resided at Kairua, and was pleased to find him patient under the inconveniences to which his situation necessarily subjects him, and anxious to promote the best interests of his countrymen.

29th.—The Sabbath morning dawned upon the missionaries at Kairua under circumstances unusually animating, and they prepared to spend this holy day in extending as widely as possible their labours among the people around them. Mr. Thurston preached in the native language twice at the governor's house, to attentive audiences. Mr. Bishop and Thomas Hopu proceeded early in the morning to Kaavaroa, a village about fourteen miles distant, on the north side of Kearake'kua (Karakakooa), where they arrived at 11 A. M. Kamakau, chief of the place, received them with expressions of gladness, led them to his house, and provided refreshments; after which they walked together to a *ranai* (house of cocoanut-leaves), which he had some time before erected for the public worship of Jehovah. Here they found about a hundred of his people waiting their arrival. Mr. Bishop, with the aid of Thomas, preached to them from John iii. 16, and endeavoured in the most familiar manner to set before them the great love of God in sending his Son to die for sinners, and the necessity of forsaking sin and believing on him, in order to eternal life. Towards the latter part of the discourse, the preacher was interrupted by Kamakau, who, anxious that his people might receive the greatest possible benefit by the word spoken, began earnestly to exhort them to listen and regard, telling them their salvation depended on their attention to what they heard. After the service was concluded, he again addressed them, affectionately recommending them to consider these things.

Kamakau wished them to meet with the people again; but as the day was far spent, they thought it best to return. He then told them, that after their departure, he should assemble his people, and repeat to them what the missionary had said. He asked many questions on

religious subjects, several respecting the heavenly state;
and appeared interested in the answers that were given,
especially when informed that heaven was a holy place,
into which nothing sinful could enter.

As they went from his house to the beach, they passed
by a large idol that Kamakau had formerly worshipped,
lying prostrate and mutilated on the rocks, and washed
by the waves of the sea as they rolled on the shore. It
was a huge log of wood, rudely carved, presenting a
hideous form, well adapted to infuse terror into an ignorant and superstitious mind. On his being asked why
he had worshipped that log of wood, he answered, because he was afraid he would injure his cocoanuts.
" But were you not afraid to destroy it?"—"No; I
found he did me neither good nor harm. I thought he
was no god, and threw him away." Bidding him farewell, they stepped into their canoe, and returned to
Kairua, where they arrived in the evening, encouraged
by the incidents of the day.

Kamakau is a chief of considerable rank and influence
in Hawaii, though not immediately connected with any
of the reigning family. He is cousin to Naihe, the
friend and companion of Tamehameha, and the principal
national orator of the Sandwich Islands. His person,
like that of the chiefs in general, is noble and engaging.
He is about six feet high, stout, well-proportioned, and
more intelligent and enterprising than the people around
him. For some time past he has established family
worship in his house, and the observance of the Sabbath
throughout his district; having erected a place for the
public worship of the true God, in which, every Lord's-
day, he assembles his people for the purpose of exhortation and prayer, which he conducts himself. He is able
to read, writes an easy and legible hand, has a general
knowledge of the first principles of Christianity, and,
what is infinitely better, appears to feel their power on
his heart, and to evince their influence by the purity and
uprightness of his general conduct. His attainments
are surprising, manifesting a degree of industry and perseverance rarely displayed under similar circumstances.
His sources of information have been very limited. An
occasional residence of a few weeks at Honoruru, one
or two visits of the missionaries and of some of the
native teachers to his house, and letters from Naihe,
are the chief advantages he has enjoyed. He appears,

indeed, a modern Cornelius, and is a striking manifestation of the sovereignty of that grace of which we trust he has been made a partaker; and we rejoice in the pleasing` hope that He who has "begun a good work will perform it until the day of Christ."

In the forenoon of the 1st of July, two posts of observation were fixed, and a base line of 200 feet was measured, in order to ascertain the height of Mouna Huararai; but the summit being covered with clouds, the missionaries were obliged to defer their observation. In the afternoon, after an accurate investigation of the places adjacent, in which they thought fresh water might be found by digging, they chose a valley about half a mile from the residence of the governor, and near the entrance of Raniakea, as the spot where they were most likely to meet with success.

The 4th of July, being the anniversary of the American independence, guns were fired at the fort, the colours hoisted, and a hospitable entertainment was given at the governor's table. The missionaries employed the greater part of the day at the well, which early in the morning they had commenced.

In the evening, while at tea, considerable attention was attracted by a slender man, with a downcast look, in conversation with the governor. It afterward appeared that this was a stranger from Maui, who wished to be thought a prophet, affirming that he was inspired by a shark, that enabled him to tell future events. The governor said many of the people believed in him, and from them he obtained a living.

The next day, being the Sabbath, Mr. Bishop preached twice at the governor's house, Thomas Hopu acting as interpreter. The congregation consisted principally of Kuakini's attendants and domestics, the greater part of the population conceiving themselves under no obligation to hear preaching, as they do not know how to read; pretending that ignorance exempts them from all obligation to attend religious exercises.

Leaving Kairua early, in a canoe with four men, provided by the governor, Messrs. Thurston and Goodrich reached Kaavaroa about nine o'clock in the morning. Kamakau was waiting for them, and seemed to rejoice at their arrival. After taking some refreshment, they repaired in company to the ranai for public worship. On reaching it they found about one hundred of the people already there. Before the service commenced, the chief arose, directed them to remain quiet, and pay the greatest attention to the Word of life, which they were about to hear.

Shortly after the conclusion of the service, the missionaries passed over Kearake'kua bay in a canoe, landed on the opposite side, and walked along the shore about a mile, to Karama. Here, in a large house, they collected about three hundred people; to whom Mr. Thurston preached, and was pleased with the interest they manifested. Some who stood near the speaker repeated the whole discourse, sentence by sentence, in a voice too low to create disturbance, yet loud enough to be distinctly heard. There were seven or eight American and English seamen present, who requested that they might be addressed in their own language. Mr. Goodrich accordingly preached to them from Rev. iii. 20.

Returning from Karama to the southern side of Kearake'kua bay, where they had left their canoe, they passed the ruins of an old heiau, the morai mentioned in Captain Cook's voyage, where the observatory was erected. The remaining walls were one hundred feet long and fifteen high, and the space within was strewed with animal and human bones, the relics of the sacrifices once offered there—a scene truly affecting to a Christian mind.

Leaving this melancholy spot, they returned in their canoe to Kaavaroa; and when the people had assembled in the ranai, Mr. Thurston preached to them from Psalm cxviii. 24—*This is the day which the Lord hath made: we will rejoice and be glad in it.*

About sunset Mr. Goodrich ascended a neighbouring height, and visited the spot where the body of the unfortunate Captain Cook was cut to pieces, and the flesh, after being separated from the bones, was burnt. It is a small enclosure, about fifteen feet square, surrounded by a wall five feet high; within is a kind of hearth, raised about eighteen inches from the ground, and encircled by a curb of rude stones. Here the fire was kindled on the above occasion; and the place is still strewed with charcoal. The natives mention the interment of another foreigner on this spot, but could not tell to what country he belonged, or the name of the vessel in which he was brought.

Kamakau and his people had interested the visiters so

much, that they determined to spend the night at his house. After supper, the members of the family, with the domestics and one or two strangers, met for evening worship: a hymn was sung in the native language, and Kamakau himself engaged in prayer with great fervour and propriety. He prayed particularly for the king, chiefs, and people of Hawaii, and the neighbouring islands; and for the missionaries, who had brought the good word of salvation to them. The brethren were surprised to hear him use so much evangelical language in prayer. During the conversation of the evening, he expressed a desire, which has since been gratified, that a missionary might reside in his neighbourhood, that he and his people might be instructed in the Word of God; might learn to read and write, and become acquainted with what the missionaries were teaching at the stations where they dwelt. He is about fifty years of age, and regretted exceedingly, as many others have also done, that he was so far advanced in life before the missionaries arrived at the islands. The Sabbath passed away pleasantly, and it is hoped profitably, both to the interesting inhabitants of the place and their guests; and the latter retired to rest, animated and encouraged by what they had that day witnessed. Early next morning they set out for Kairua, where they arrived about nine o'clock in the forenoon.

Hard and closely imbedded lava rendered the sinking of the well difficult; and, unable to proceed for want of proper instruments with which to drill the rocks, the greater part of this day was spent in ascertaining the population of Kairua. Numbering the houses for one mile along the coast, they found them to be 529; and allowing an average of five persons to each house, the inhabitants in Kairua will amount to 2645 persons. This certainly does not exceed the actual population, as few of the houses are small, and many of them large, containing two or three families each.

The varied and strongly marked volcanic surface of the higher parts of the mountain called *Mouna Huararai*, in the immediate neighbourhood of Kairua—the traditional accounts given by the natives of the eruptions which, from craters on its summit, had in different ages deluged the low land along the coast—the thick woods that skirt its base, and the numerous feathered tribes inhabiting them—rendered it an interesting object,

C 3

and induced the travellers to commence its ascent.
About eight o'clock in the morning of the 9th, they left
Kairua, accompanied by three men, whom they had engaged to conduct them to the summit. Having travelled
about twelve miles in a northerly direction, they arrived
at the last house on the western side of the mountain.
Here their guides wished to remain for the night; and
on being urged to proceed, as it was not more than three
o'clock in the afternoon, declared they did not know
the way, and had never been beyond the spot where
they then were. Notwithstanding this disappointment,
it was determined to proceed. Leaving the path, the
party began to ascend in a south-east direction, and
travelled about six miles over a rough and difficult road,
sometimes across streams of hard lava, full of fissures
and chasms, at other times through thick and closely
interwoven brushwood and fern.

Arriving at a convenient place, and finding themselves
fatigued, drenched also with the showers and the wet
grass through which they had walked, they proposed to
pitch their tent for the night. A temporary hut was
erected with branches of the neighbouring trees, and
covered with the leaves of the tall ferns that grew around
them. At one end of it they lighted a large fire, and,
after the rains had abated, dried their clothes, partook
of the refreshments they had brought with them; and
having commended themselves to the kind protection
of their heavenly Guardian, spread fern-leaves and grass
upon the lava, and lay down to repose. The thermometer, which is usually about 84° on the shore, stood at
60° in the hut where they slept.

The singing of the birds in the surrounding woods
ushering in the early dawn, and the cool temperature of
the pure mountain air excited a variety of pleasing
sensations in the minds of all the party, when they
awoke in the morning, after a comfortable night's rest.
The thermometer, when placed outside of the hut, stood
at 46°. Having united in their morning sacrifice of
thanksgiving to God, and taken a light breakfast, they
resumed their laborious journey. The road, lying
through thick underwood and fern, was wet and fatiguing for about two miles, when they arrived at an
ancient stream of lava, about twenty rods wide, running
in a direction nearly west. Ascending the hardened
surface of this stream of lava, over deep chasms, or

large volcanic stones imbedded in it, for a distance of three or four miles, they reached the top of one of the ridges on the western side of the mountain.

As they travelled along they met with tufts of strawberries, and clusters of raspberry bushes, loaded with fruit, which, as they were both hungry and thirsty, were acceptable. The strawberries had rather an insipid taste; the raspberries were white and large, frequently an inch in diameter, but not so sweet or well-flavoured as those cultivated in Europe and America.

Between nine and ten in the forenoon they arrived at a large extinguished crater, about a mile in circumference, and apparently four hundred feet deep, probably the same that was visited by some of Vancouver's people in 1792. The sides sloped regularly, and at the bottom was a small mound, with an aperture in its centre. By the side of this large crater, divided from it by a narrow ridge of volcanic rocks, was another, fifty-six feet in circumference, from which volumes of sulphureous smoke and vapour continually ascended. No bottom could be seen; and on throwing stones into it, they were heard to strike against its sides for eight seconds, but not to reach the bottom. There were two other apertures near this, nine feet in diameter, and apparently about two hundred feet deep. As the party walked along the giddy verge of the large crater, they could distinguish the course of two principal streams that had issued from it in the great eruption, about the year 1800. One had taken a direction nearly north-east—the other had flowed to the north-west, in a broad irresistible torrent, for a distance of twelve or fifteen miles to the sea—where, driving back the waters, it had extended the boundaries of the island. They attempted to descend this crater, but the steepness of its sides prevented their examining it so fully as they desired.

After spending some time there, they walked along the ridge between three and four miles, and examined sixteen different craters, similar in construction to the first they had met with, though generally of smaller dimensions. The whole ridge along which they walked appeared little else than a continued line of craters—which, in different ages, had deluged the valleys below with floods of lava, or showers of cinders. Some of these craters appeared to have reposed for ages, as trees of considerable size were growing on their sides, and many of them were imbedded in earth, and clothed with verdure. In the vicinity of the craters they found a number of small bushes, bearing red berries in crowded clusters, which in size and shape much resembled whortleberries; though insipid, they were juicy, and supplied the place of fresh water—a comfort they had been destitute of since the preceding evening.

They continued ascending till three P. M., when, having suffered much from thirst, and finding they should not be able to reach the highest peak before dark, the sky also being overcast, and the rain beginning to fall, they judged it best to return to Kairua, without having reached the summit of Mouna Huararai; particularly as they were somewhat scattered, and found a difficulty in pursuing the most direct way, on account of the thick fog which surrounded the mountain.

On their return they found the aid of their pocket-compass necessary to enable them to regain the path by which they had ascended in the morning. After travelling some time, they beheld with gladness the sun breaking through the fog in which they had been so long enveloped—and looking over the clouds that rolled at their feet, saw it gradually sink behind the western wave of the extended ocean. The appearance of the sky at the setting of the sun, in a tropical climate, is usually beautiful and splendid: it was so this evening— and from their great elevation, the party viewed with delight the magnificent yet transient glories of the closing day. They travelled about three miles farther, when, being wet with the fog, and weary with travelling, they erected a hut on the lava, and encamped for the night. They succeeded in making a good fire, dried their clothes, and then partook of their refreshment. It consisted of a small quantity of hard taro paste, called by the natives ai paa. A little water would have been agreeable, but of this they were destitute. Having gathered some fern-leaves, they strewed them on the lava, and laid down to repose.

On the morning of the 11th, the party still felt unwilling to return without reaching the top of the mountain, and hesitated before they began again to descend; but having been a day and two nights without water, and seeing no prospect of procuring any in that elevated region, they directed their steps to Kairua.

Two of the party, in searching for a more direct road

to Kairua, discovered an excellent spring of water.
They soon communicated the agreeable intelligence to
their companions, who hastened to the spot, quenched
their thirst with copious draughts, filled their canteens,
and kept on their way to the town.

Owing to the roughness of the paths, and the circuitous route by which they travelled, they did not arrive
at Kairua until after sunset, much fatigued, and almost
barefoot, their shoes having been destroyed by the sharp
projections in the lava.

After uniting with the governor and his family in
praise to God, they repaired to their lodgings, somewhat disappointed, yet well repaid for the toil of their
journey.

CHAPTER IV.

EIGHT days after the departure of Mr. Thurston and
his companions, I followed in a small schooner belonging
to Keopuolani, bound first to Lahaina, and then to Hawaii, for sandal-wood. Kalakua, one of the queens of
the late Tamehameha, and Kekauruohe, her daughter,
were proceeding in the same vessel to join the king and
other chiefs at Maui. The trade-wind blew fresh from
the north-east, and the sea was unusually rough in the
channel between Oahu and Morokai. The schooner
appeared to be a good sea-boat, but proved a very uncomfortable one: the deck, from stem to stern, being
continually overflowed, all who could not get below
were constantly drenched with the spray. The cabin
was low, and so filled with the chief women and their
companions that, where space could be found sufficient
to stand or sit, it was hardly possible to endure the
heat. The evening, however, was fine, and the night
free from rain.

At daylight next morning, being close in with the west

point of Morokai, we tacked, and stood to the southward
till noon, when we again steered to the northward, and
at four o'clock in the afternoon were within half a mile
of the high bluff rocks which form the southern point
of Ranai.   A light air then came off the land, and carried us slowly along the shore, till about an hour before
sunset, when Kekauruohe said she wished for some fish,
and requested the master to stop the vessel while she
went to procure them among the adjacent rocks.   Her
wishes were gratified, and the boat was hoisted out.
Kekauruohe and three of her female attendants proceeded towards the rocks that lie along the base of the
precipice, about half a mile distant.   The detention thus
occasioned afforded me time to observe more particularly the neighbouring coast.   The face of the high and
perpendicular rocks in this part of the island indicate
that Ranai is either of volcanic origin, or, at some remote period, has undergone the action of fire.   Different strata of lava, of varied colour and thickness, are
distinctly marked from the water's edge to the highest
point.   These strata, lying almost horizontally, are in
some places from twelve to twenty feet thick—in others
not more than a foot or eighteen inches.

After fishing about an hour, Kekauruohe and her companions returned with a quantity of limpets, periwinkles,
&c., of which they made a hearty supper.   The wind
died away with the setting of the sun, until about 9
P. M., when a light breeze came from the land, and
wafted us slowly on our passage.

The southern shore of Ranai is usually avoided by
masters of vessels acquainted with the navigation among
the islands, on account of the light and variable winds
or calms generally experienced there; the course of
the trade-winds being intercepted by the high lands of
Maui and Ranai.

It is not unusual for vessels passing that way to be
becalmed there for six, eight, or even ten days.   The
natives, with the small craft belonging to the islands,
usually keep close in shore, avail themselves of the gentle land-breeze to pass the point in the evening, and run
into Lahaina with the sea-breeze in the morning; but
this is attended with danger, as there is usually a heavy
swell rolling in towards the land.   One or two vessels
have escaped being drifted on the rocks only by the
prompt assistance of their boats.

At daybreak on the 4th we found ourselves within about four miles of Lahaina, which is the principal district in Maui, on account of its being the general residence of the chiefs, and the common resort of ships that touch at the island. A dead calm prevailed; but by means of two large sweeps, or oars, each worked by four men, we reached the roads, and anchored at 6 A. M.

The appearance of Lahaina from the anchorage is singularly romantic and beautiful. A fine sandy beach stretches along the margin of the sea, lined for a considerable distance with houses, and adorned with shady clumps of kou-trees, or waving groves of cocoanuts. The former is a species of cordia—the *sordia sebastina* in Cook's Voyages. The level land of the whole district, for about three miles, is one continued garden, laid out in beds of taro, potatoes, yams, sugar-cane, or cloth-plants. The lowly cottage of the farmer is seen peeping through the leaves of the luxuriant plantain and banana-tree, and in every direction white columns of smoke ascend, curling up among the wide-spreading branches of the bread-fruit tree. The sloping hills immediately behind, and the lofty mountains in the interior, clothed with verdure to their very summits, intersected by deep and dark ravines, frequently enlivened by waterfalls, or divided by winding valleys, terminate the delightful prospect.

Shortly after coming to anchor, a boat came from the barge for the chiefs on board, and I accompanied them to the shore.

On landing, I was kindly greeted by Keóua, governor of the place; and shortly afterward met and welcomed by Mr. Stewart, who was just returned from morning worship with Keopuolani and her husband.

We waited on Rihoriho, the late king, in his tent. He was, as usual, neatly and respectably dressed, having on a suit of superfine blue, made after the European fashion. We were courteously received, and, after spending a few minutes in conversation respecting my journey to Hawaii, and answering his inquiries relative to Oahu, we walked together about half a mile, through groves of plantain and sugar-cane, over a well-cultivated tract of land, to Mr. Butler's establishment, in one of whose houses the missionaries were comfortably accommodated until their own could be erected, and where

I was kindly received by the members of the mission family.

After breakfast I walked to the beach, and there learned that the king had sailed for Morokai, and that Kalakua intended to follow in the schooner in which she had come from Oahu. This obliged me to wait for the *Ainoa*, another native vessel, hourly expected at Lahaina, on her way to Hawaii. The forenoon was spent in conversation with Keopuolani, queen of Maui, and mother of Rihoriho. She, as well as the other chiefs present, appeared gratified with an account of the attention given to the means of instruction at Oahu, and desirous that the people of Lahaina might enjoy all the advantages of Christian education. Taua, the native teacher from Huahine, appeared diligently employed among Keopuolani's people, many of whom were his scholars; and I was happy to learn from Messrs. Stewart and Richards that he was vigilant and faithful in his work.

At sunrise next morning, Mr. Stewart and I walked down to Keopuolani's, to attend the usual morning exercises, in the large house near the sea. About fifty persons were present. In the afternoon I accompanied the missionaries to their schools on the beach. The proficiency of many of the pupils in reading, spelling, and writing on slates was pleasing.

Just as they had finished their afternoon instruction, a party of musicians and dancers arrived before the house of Keopuolani, and commenced a *hura ka raau* (dance to the beating of a stick). Five musicians advanced first, each with a staff in his left hand, five or six feet long, about three or four inches in diameter at one end, and tapering off to a point at the other. In his right hand he held a small stick of hard wood, six or nine inches long, with which he commenced his music, by striking the small stick on the larger one, beating time all the while with his right foot on a stone, placed on the ground beside him for that purpose. Six women, fantastically dressed in yellow tapas, crowned with garlands of flowers, having also wreaths of native manufacture, of the sweet-scented flowers of the *gardenia* on their necks, and branches of the fragrant *mairi* (another native plant) bound round their ankles, now made their way by couples through the crowd—and, arriving at the area, on one side of which the musicians stood, began their dance. Their movements were slow, and, though not always graceful, exhibited nothing offensive to modest propriety. Both musicians and dancers alternately chanted songs in honour of former gods and chiefs of the islands, apparently much to the gratification of the spectators. After they had continued their *hura* (song and dance) for about half an hour, the queen, Keopuolani, requested them to leave off, as the time had arrived for evening worship. The music ceased; the dancers sat down; and after the missionaries and some of the people had sung one of the songs of Zion, I preached to the surrounding multitude with special reference to their former idolatrous dances, and the vicious customs connected therewith, from Acts xvii. 30 —"The times of this ignorance God winked at, but now commandeth all men everywhere to repent." The audience was attentive; and when the service was finished the people dispersed, and the dancers retired to their houses.

On our way home, the voice of lamentation arrested our attention. Listening a few moments, we found it proceeded from a lowly cottage, nearly concealed by close rows of sugar-cane. When we reached the spot, we beheld a middle-aged woman and two elderly men weeping around the mat of a sick man, apparently near his end. Finding him entirely ignorant of God and of a future state, we spoke to him of Jehovah, of the fallen condition of man, of the amazing love of Christ in suffering death for the redemption of the world, and recommended him to pray to the Son of God, who was able to save to the uttermost. He said that, until now, he knew nothing of these things, and was glad he had lived to hear of them. We requested one of his friends to come to our house for some medicine; and having endeavoured to comfort the mourners, bade them farewell.

The Ainoa was seen approaching from the southward on the morning of the 6th. About two P. M. she came to anchor, having been becalmed off Ranai four days.

This day, being the Sabbath, at half-past ten the mission family walked down to the beach to public worship. Most of the chiefs, and about three hundred people, assembled under the pleasant shade of a beautiful clump of kou-trees, in front of Keopuolani's house. After singing and prayer, I preached from Luke x. 23, 24—

"Blessed are the eyes which see the things which ye see: for I tell you, that many prophets and kings have desired to see those things which ye see, and have not seen them; and to hear those things which ye hear, and have not heard them." After service, when we went to present our salutations to Keopuolini, we found her, Kaikioeva, and several chiefs conversing about Tamehameha and others of their ancestors, who had died idolaters, and expressing their regret that the gospel had not been brought to the Sandwich Islands in their day. "But perhaps," said Keopuolani, "they will have less punishment in the other world for worshipping idols than those who, though they do not worship wooden gods, yet see these days, and hear these good things, and still disregard them." As we returned I visited the sick man, found him better than on the preceding evening, and again recommended the Son of God as all-sufficient to save.

I afterward saw a party at *buhénehéne*. This is one of the most popular games in the Sandwich Islands, is the favourite amusement of the king and higher order of chiefs, and frequently occupies them whole days together. It principally consists in hiding a small stone under one of five pieces of native tapa, or cloth, so as to prevent the spectators from discovering under which piece it is hid. The parties at play sit cross-legged on mats spread on the ground, each one holding in his right hand a small elastic rod, about three feet long, and highly polished. At the small end of this stick there is a narrow slit or hole, through which a piece of dog's skin with a tuft of shaggy hair on it, or a piece of *ti* leaf, is usually drawn. Five pieces of tapa of different colours, each loosely folded up like a bundle, are then placed between the two parties, which generally consists of five persons each. One person is then selected on each side to hide the stone. He who is first to hide it takes it in his right hand, lifts up the cloth at one end, puts his arm under as far as his elbow, and passing it along several times underneath the five pieces of cloth, which lie in a line contiguous to each other, he finally leaves it under one of them. The other party sit opposite, watching closely the action in the muscles of the upper part of his arm; and it is said that adepts can discover the place where the stone is deposited, by observing the change that takes place in those muscles when the hand ceases to grasp it. Having deposited the stone, the hider withdraws his arm; and, with many gestures, separates the contiguous pieces of cloth into five distinct heaps, leaving a narrow space between each.

The opposite party, having keenly observed this process, now point with their wands or sticks to the different heaps under which they suppose the stone lies, looking significantly, at the same time, full in the face of the man who hid it. He sits all the while, holding his fingers before his eyes to prevent their noticing any change in his countenance, should one of them point to the heap under which it is hid. Having previously agreed who shall strike first, that individual, looking earnestly at the hider, lifts his rod and strikes a smart blow across the heap he had selected. The cloth is instantly lifted up; and should the stone appear under it, his party have won that hiding with one stroke; if it is not there, the others strike till the stone is found. The same party hide the stone five or ten times successively, according to their agreement at the commencement of the play; and whichever party discovers it the given number of times, with fewest strokes, wins the game. Sometimes they reverse it; and those win who, in a given number of times, strike most heaps without uncovering the stone. Occasionally they play for amusement only, but more frequently for money, or other articles of value, which they stake on the game.

I went to the party whom I found thus engaged, and, after a few minutes' conversation, told them that it was the sacred day of God, and induced them to put aside their play, and promise to attend public worship in the afternoon. Leaving them, I passed through a garden where a man was at work weeding and watering a bed of cloth-plants. I asked him if he did not know it was the sacred day, and improper for him to work! The man answered, yes, he knew it was the la tabu (sacred day), and that Karaimoku had given orders for the people of Lahaina not to work on that day; but said, he was hana maru no (just working secretly); that it was some distance from the beach, and the chiefs would not see him. I then told him he might do it without the chiefs seeing him, but it was prohibited by a higher power than the chiefs, even by the God of heaven and earth, who could see him alike in every place, by night and by day. He said he did not know that before, and would leave off when he had finished the row of cloth-plants he was then weeding!

Mr. Stewart conducted an English service in the afternoon. The sound of the *hura* in a remote part of the district was occasionally heard through the after-part of the day, but whether countenanced by any of the chiefs, or only exhibited for the amusement of the common people, we did not learn.

At four o'clock we again walked down to the beach, and found about two hundred people collected under the kou-trees; many more speedily came, and, after the introductory exercises, I preached to them upon the doctrine of the resurrection and a future state, from John xi. 25. The congregation seemed much interested. Probably it was the first time many had ever heard of the awful hour, when the trumpet shall sound, and the dead shall be raised, and stand before God. At the conclusion of the service, notice was given of the monthly missionary prayer-meeting on the morrow evening, and the people were invited to attend.

Taua, the native teacher of Keopuolani, visited the family in the evening, and gave a very pleasing account of Keopuolani's frequent conversations with him on the love of God in sending his Son, on the death of Christ, and on her great desire to have a new heart and become a true follower of the Redeemer. He informed us, that after most of the attendants had retired, she had several times sent for him, at nine or ten o'clock in the evening, to engage in prayer with her and her husband before they retired to rest. This account was truly gratifying, and tended much to strengthen the pleasing hope which, from her uniform, humble, and Christian conduct, had for some time been indulged, that a saving change had taken place in her heart.

In the afternoon of the seventh I walked to the seaside with Mr. Richards, and waited on the queen Keopuolani, to converse with her respecting the houses and fences which she had kindly engaged to erect for the mission-aries. The interview was satisfactory. Keopuolani seemed anxious to make them comfortable, and assured Mr. Richards that the houses would soon be ready for them. We then visited Maaro, the chief of Waiakea, a large district on the eastern side of Hawaii. He had been on a short visit to the king at Oahu, and was re-turning to his land in the Aino. He received us kindly, and, when informed that I wished to proceed in the vessel to Hawaii, said, "It is good that you should go; we shall sail to-morrow." The eastern part of Lahaina, in which he had his encampment, was highly cultivated and adorned with beautiful groves of kou-trees and cocoanuts. There were also several large ponds well stocked with fish.

On returning from our visit to Maaro, we found the people collecting under the shade of their favourite trees, in front of Keopuolani's house, for the purpose of attending the monthly missionary prayer-meeting. About five o'clock the service commenced. I gave an address from the Saviour's commission to the first missionaries to the heathen, Matt. xxviii. 19,—"Go ye, therefore, and teach all nations." The audience appeared gratified with the brief account given of the missionary operations of the present day, especially those among the southern islands of the Pacific, with whose inhabitants they feel themselves more particularly identified, than with the native tribes of Africa or Asia. It was a circumstance truly animating to see so many of those who, wrapped in the thick darkness of paganism, had till lately worshipped the work of their own hands, and "sacrificed" their fellow-creatures "to devils," now joining with Christians of every nation, in praying for the spread of the gospel of Jesus throughout the world.

After breakfast on the eighth I visited a neat strong brick house which stands on the beach, about the middle of the district. It was erected for Tamehameha; appears well built, is forty feet by twenty, has two stories, and is divided into four rooms by strong boarded partitions. It was the occasional residence of the late king, but by the present is used only as a warehouse. Several persons, who appeared to have the charge of it, were living in one of the apartments; and, having looked over the house, and made some inquiries about the native timber employed for the floor, beams, &c., I sat down on one of the bales of cloth lying in the room where the natives were sitting, and asked them if they knew how to read, or if any of them attended the school, and the religious services on the Sabbath? On their answering in the negative, I advised them not to neglect these advantages, assuring them that it was a good thing to be instructed, and to know the true God, and his Son Jesus Christ, the only Saviour. They said,

"Perhaps it is a good thing for some to attend to the *palapala* and the *pule* (to reading and prayers); but we are the king's servants, and must attend to his concerns. If we (meaning all those that had the care of the king's lands) were to spend our time at our books, there would be nobody to cultivate the ground, to provide food, or cut sandal-wood for the king." I asked them what proportion of their time was taken up in attending to these things? They said they worked in the plantations three or four days in a week, sometimes from daylight till nine or ten o'clock in the forenoon; that preparing an oven of food took an hour; and that when they went for sandal-wood, which was not very often, they were gone three or four days, and sometimes as many weeks. They were the king's servants, and generally work much less than the people who occupy or cultivate lands. I asked them what they did in the remaining part of those days in which they worked at their plantations in the morning, and also on those days when they did not work at all? They said they ate poë, laid down to sleep, or *kamailio no* (just talked for amusement). They were then asked which they thought would be most advantageous to them—to spend that time in learning to read, and seeking the favour of Jehovah and Jesus Christ, that they might live for ever—or wasting it in eating, sleeping, or foolish talking, and remaining ignorant in this world, and liable to wretchedness in that which is to come? They immediately endeavoured to give a different turn to the conversation, by saying, "What a fine country yours must be, compared with this! What large bales of cloth come from thence, while the clothing of Hawaii is small in quantity, and very bad. The soil there must be very prolific, and property easily obtained, or so much of it would not have been brought here." I informed them that the difference was not so great between the countries as between the people; that many ages back the ancestors of the present inhabitants of England and America possessed fewer comforts than the Sandwich islanders now enjoy—wore skins of beasts for clothing—painted their bodies with various colours—and worshipped with inhuman rites their cruel gods; but that since they had become enlightened and industrious, and had embraced Christianity, they had been wise and rich; and many, there was reason to hope, had, after death, gone to a state of happiness in

another world; that they owed all their present wealth
and enjoyment to their intelligence and industry; and
that if the people of either country were to neglect education and religion, and spend as much of their time in
eating, sleeping, and jesting, they would soon become as
poor and as ignorant as the Sandwich islanders. They
said, perhaps it was so; perhaps industry and instruction would make them happier and better, and if the
chiefs wished it, by-and-by they would attend to both.
After again exhorting them to improve the means now
placed within their reach by the residence of the missionaries among them, I took my departure. During the forenoon I went into several other houses, and conversed
with the people on subjects relating to the mission,
récommending their attention to the advantages it was
designed to confer. Some approved, but many seemed
very well satisfied with their present state of ignorance and irreligion, and rather unwilling to be disturbed.

After having united with the family in their evening
devotions, on the 9th I took my leave, grateful for the
hospitable entertainment and kind attention I had experienced during my unexpected stay at their station. I
regretted that the illness of Mr. Stewart, which had
been increasing for several days, prevented his accompanying me on the projected tour. At nine o'clock I
walked down to the beach, but waited till midnight before
an opportunity offered for getting on board. On reaching the brig, I learned that they did not intend to sail till
daylight. There were such multitudes of natives on
board, and every place was so crowded, that it was impossible to pass from the gangway to the companion
without treading on them; and it was difficult anywhere,
either below or upon deck, to find room sufficient to lie
down.

Early in the morning of the 10th the vessel was under
way, but the light winds and strong westerly current
soon rendered it necessary to anchor. Between eight
and nine I went on shore, and, after breakfasting with
the mission family, returned to the beach, that I might
be ready to embark whenever the wind should become
favourable. I sat down in Keopuolani's house, and entered into an interesting conversation with her, Hoapiri,
and several other chiefs, respecting their ancient traditions and mythology.

One of the ancient gods of Maui, prior to its subjugation by Tamehameha, they said, was *Keoroeva*. The body of the image was of wood, and was arrayed in garments of native tapa. The head and neck were formed of a kind of fine basket or wicker-work, covered over with red feathers, so curiously wrought in as to resemble the skin of a beautiful bird.* A native helmet was placed on the idol's head, from the crown of which long tresses of human hair hung over its shoulders. Its mouth, like the greater number of the Hawaiian idols, was large and extended.

In all the temples dedicated to its worship the image was placed within the inner apartment, on the left-hand side of the door, and immediately before it stood the altar, on which the offerings of every kind were usually placed. They did not say whether human victims were ever sacrificed to appease its imagined wrath; but large offerings of every thing valuable were frequent. Sometimes hogs were taken alive, as presents. The large ones were led, and the smaller ones carried in the arms of the priest, into the presence of the idols. The priest then pinched the ears or the tail of the pig till it made a squeaking noise, when he addressed the god, saying, "Here is the offering of such a one of your kaku" (devotees). A hole was then made in the pig's ear, a piece of cinet, formed of the fibres of the cocoanut husk, was fastened in it, and the pig was set at liberty until the priest had occasion for him. In consequence of this mark, which distinguished the sacred hog, he was allowed to range the district at pleasure; and whatever depredations he might commit, driving him away from the enclosures into which he had broken was the only punishment allowed to be inflicted.

Keoroeva's hogs were not the only ones thus privileged. The same lenient conduct was observed towards all the sacred pigs, to whatever idol they had been offered.

Tiha, a female idol, they said was also held in great veneration by the people of Maui, and received nearly the same homage and offerings as Keoroeva.

The people of Ranai, an adjacent island, had a number of idols, but those best known by the chiefs with whom I was conversing were *Raeapua* and *Kaneapua*, two large

* An idol of this kind is deposited in the Missionary Museum, Austin Friars, London.

carved stone images, representing the deities supposed
to preside over the sea, and worshipped chiefly by
fishermen.

Moearii (king of lizards or alligators), a shark, was
also a celebrated marine god, worshipped by the inhabitants of Morokai, another island in the neighbourhood.
The chiefs informed me that on almost every point of
land, projecting any distance into the sea, a temple was
formerly erected for his worship. Several kinds of fish
arrive in shoals on their coast, every year, in their
respective seasons. The first fish of each kind, taken
by the fishermen, were always carried to the heiau, and
offered to their god, whose influence they imagined had
driven them to their shores. In some remote period,
perhaps, they had observed the sharks chasing or devouring these fish, as they passed along among their
islands; and from this circumstance had been led to deify
the monster, supposing themselves indebted to him for
the bountiful supplies thus furnished by a gracious
Providence.

They had a number of sea-gods, besides those, who,
they imagined, directed the shoals of fishes to their
shores. They had also gods who controlled the winds,
and changed the weather. During a storm, or other
season of danger at sea, they offered up their *paro*, or
pule kurana, a particular kind of prayer; but I did not
learn to what idol they addressed it. On these occasions, their dread of perishing at sea frequently led them
to make vows to some favourite deity; and if they ever
reached the land, it was their first business to repair to
the temple and fulfil their vows. These vows were
generally considered most sacred engagements; and it
was expected that, sooner or later, some judgment would
overtake those who failed to perform them. It is not
improbable that the priests of those idols, in order to
maintain their influence over the people, either poisoned
the delinquents, or caused them to sustain some other
injury.

Karaipahoa was also a famous idol, originally belonging to Morokai. It was a middling-sized wooden image,
curiously carved; the arms were extended, the fingers
spread out, the head was ornamented with human hair,
and the widely extended mouth was armed with rows
of shark's teeth.

The wood of which the image was made was so poi-
VOL. IV.—D

sonous, that if a small piece of it was chipped into a dish
of poë, or steeped in water, whoever ate the poë, or
drank the water, the natives reported, would. certainly
die in less than twenty-four hours afterward. We were
never able to procure a sight of this image, though we
have been repeatedly informed that it still exists, not
indeed in one compact figure, as it was divided in several
parts on the death of Tamehameha, and distributed
among the principal chiefs.

It is known that the natives use several kinds of vegetable poison; and probably the wood of which the idol
was made is poisonous. But the report of the virulence
of the poison is most likely one of the many stratagems
so frequently employed by the chiefs and priests, to
maintain their influence over the minds of the people.

A smaller image of the same god was formed of nioi,
a hard yellow wood, of which idols were usually made.
This was left at Morokai, the original being always carried about by Tamehameha, and placed under his pillow
whenever he slept.

The following is the tradition given by the natives of
the original idol.

In the reign of Kamaraua, an ancient king of Moro-
kaai, lived Kanekama, a great gambler. Playing one
day at maita (a Hawaiian game), he lost all that he possessed, except one pig, which, having dedicated to his
god, he durst not stake on any hazard. In the evening
he returned home, lay down on his mat, and fell asleep.
His god appeared to him in a dream, and directed him
to go and play again on the following day, and stake this
pig on his success in a particular part of the play. He
awoke in the morning, did as the god had directed, and
was remarkably successful through the day. Before he
returned home in the evening, he went to the temple
of his idol, and there dedicated the greater part of his
gain.

During his sleep that night the god appeared to him
again, and requested him to go to the king, and tell him
that a clump of trees would be seen growing in a certain
place in the morning; and that if he would have a god
made out of one of them, he would reside in the image,
and impart to it his power; signifying also that Kaneakama should be his priest.

Early the next morning, the man who had received
the communication from his god went and delivered it

to the king, by whom he was directed to take a number of men and cut down one of the trees, and carve it into an image. As they approached Karuakoi, a small valley on the side of one of the mountains in Morokai, they were surprised at beholding a clump of trees where there had been none before, the gods having caused them to grow up in the course of the preceding night. Into these trees Tane and some other gods are reported to have entered. When they arrived at the spot, the gods by some sign directed Kaneakama which tree to cut down. They began to work with their short-handled stone hatchets; but the chips flying on the bodies of one or two of them, they instantly expired. Terrified at the dreadful power of the wood, the others threw down their hatchets, and refused to fell the tree: being urged by Kaneakama, they resumed their work; not, however, till they covered their bodies and faces with native cloth and the leaves of the ti plant, leaving only a small aperture opposite one of their eyes. Instead of their hatchets, they took their long daggers, or pahoas, with which they cut down the tree and carved out the image. From this circumstance, the natives say, the idol derived its name, *Karai-pahoa*, which is literally, dagger cut, or carved; from *karai*, to chip with an adze, or carve, and *pahoa*, a dagger.

Excepting the deities supposed to preside over volcanoes, no god was so much dreaded by the people as Karaipahoa. All who were thought to have died by poison were said to have been slain by him.

Before I left the party, I could not help stating to them the striking identity between some of their traditions and those of the Tahitians, and expressed my conviction that both nations had the same origin. They said tradition informed them that their progenitors were brought into existence on the islands which they now inhabit; that they knew nothing of the origin of the people of the Georgian and Society Islands, yet Tahiti, the name of the largest of the Georgian Islands, was found in many of their ancient songs, though not now applied exclusively to that island. With the people of Borabora (the name they gave to the Society Islands), they said they had no acquaintance before they were visited by Captain Cook, but that since that time, by means of ships passing from one group of islands to the other, several presents and messages of friendship had been interchanged between Tamehameha and Pomare I. ; and that, in order to cement their friendship more firmly, each had agreed to give one of his daughters in marriage to the son of the other. In consequence of this amicable arrangement, a daughter of Pomare was expected from Tahiti, to be the wife of Rihoriho, late king of Hawaii ; and Kekauruohe, one of the daughters of Tamehameha, was selected by her father to be the bride of Pomare, the late king of Tahiti.' Wanting a conveyance from Hawaii to Tahiti, Tamehameha was unable to send Kekauruohe ; which, together with the death of Pomare before he had any opportunity of sending one of his relatives to Hawaii, prevented the intended intermarriages between the reigning families of Hawaii and Tahiti.

About two o'clock in the afternoon the Ainoa hove up her anchor. I went on board in a canoe just as she was leaving the roads. The brig being about ninety tons burden, one of the largest the natives have, was, as has been already observed, much crowded ; and owing to the difference between the motion of the vessel and that experienced in their small canoes, many of the natives soon became sea-sick.

It was calm through the night, but the wind blew fresh in the morning from N. N. E. and continued until noon ; when, being under the lee of the high land of Kohala, one of the large divisions of Hawaii, we were becalmed. At four o'clock P. M. a light air sprang up from the southward, and carried us slowly on towards Towaihae, a district in the division of Kohala, about four miles long, containing a spacious bay and good anchorage. The vessel stood in towards the north side of the bay, leaving a large *heiau* (heathen temple), situated on the brow of a hill, to the southward, and heading directly for a deep gully, or watercourse, called Honokoa, opposite the mouth of which, about seven P. M., she came to anchor in ten fathoms, with a good bottom.

The north side of the bay affords much the best anchorage for shipping, especially for those that wish to lie near the shore. It is the best holding ground, and is also screened by the *kuahive* (high land) of Kohala from those sudden and violent gusts of wind called by the natives mumuku, which come down between the mountains with almost irresistible fury, on the southern part of Towaihae and the adjacent districts.

At six A. M. the next day I went on shore, and walked along the beach about a mile, to the house of Mr. J. Young, an aged Englishman. I had met him before, both at Hawaii and Oahu. He has resided thirty-six years on the island, and rendered the most important services to the late king, not only in his various civil wars, but in all his intercourse with those foreigners who have visited the islands.

I found him recovering from a fit of illness, received from him a cordial welcome, and, as he was just sitting down to his morning repast, joined him with pleasure at his frugal board. After breakfast I visited the large heiau or temple called Bukohola. It stands on an eminence in the southern part of the district, and was built by Tamehameha about thirty years ago, when he was engaged in conquering Hawaii and the rest of the Sandwich Islands. He had subdued Maui, Ranai, and Morokai, and was preparing, from the latter, to invade Oahu; but in consequence of a rebellion in the south and east parts of Hawaii, was obliged to return thither. When he had overcome those who had rebelled he finished the heiau, dedicated it to Tairi, his god of war, and then proceeded to the conquest of Oahu. Its shape is an irregular parallelogram, 224 feet long, and 100 wide. The walls, though built of loose stones, were solid and compact. At both ends, and on the side next the mountains, they were twenty feet high, twelve feet thick at the bottom, but narrowed in gradually towards the top, where a course of smooth stones six feet wide formed a pleasant walk. The walls next the sea were not more than seven or eight feet high, and were proportionably wide. The entrance to the temple is by a narrow passage between two high walls. As I passed along this avenue, an involuntary shuddering seized me, on reflecting how often it had been trodden by the feet of those who relentlessly bore the murdered body of the human victim an offering to their cruel idols. The upper terrace within the area was spacious, and much better finished than the lower ones. It was paved with flat smooth stones, brought from a distance. At the south end was a kind of inner court, which might be called the sanctum sanctorum of the temple, where the principal idol used to stand, surrounded by a number of images of inferior deities.

In the centre of this inner court was the place where
the *anu* was erected, which was a lofty frame of wicker-
work, in shape something like an obelisk, hollow, and
four or five feet square at the bottom. Within this
the priest stood, as the organ of communication from
the god, whenever the king came to inquire his will;
for his principal god was also his oracle, and when it
was to be consulted, the king, accompanied by two or
three attendants, proceeded to the door of the inner
temple, and, standing immediately before the obelisk,
inquired respecting the declaration of war, the conclusion of peace, or any other affair of importance. The
answer was given by the priest in a distinct and audible
voice; though, like that of other oracles, it was frequently very ambiguous. On the return of the king,
the answer he had received was publicly proclaimed, and
generally acted upon. I have frequently asked the people whether on these occasions there was not some
previous agreement between the king and priest. They
generally answered in the negative, or said they did not
know.

On the outside, near the entrance to the inner court,
was the place of the *rere* (altar), on which human and
other sacrices were offered. The remains of one of the
pillars that supported it were pointed out by the natives,
and the pavement around was strewed with bones of
men and animals, the mouldering remains of those numerous offerings once presented there. About the
centre of the terrace was the spot where the king's
sacred house stood, in which he resided during the
season of strict *tabu*—and at the north end, the place
occupied by the houses of priests, who, with the exception of the king, were the only persons permitted to
dwell within the sacred enclosures. Holes were seen
on the walls all around this, as well as the lower ter-
races, where wooden idols of varied size and shape formerly stood, casting their hideous stare in every direction. *Tairi* or *Kukairimoku*, a large wooden image,
crowned with a helmet, and covered with red feathers,
the favourite war-god of Tamehameha, was the principal. To him the heiau was dedicated, and for his occasional residence it was built. On the day in which
he was brought within its precincts vast offerings of
fruit, hogs, and dogs were presented, and no less than

eleven human victims were immolated on his altars. And although the huge pile now resembles a dismantled fortress, whose frown no longer strikes terror through the surrounding country, yet it is impossible to walk over such a golgotha, or contemplate a spot which must often have resembled a pandemonium more than any thing on earth, without a strong feeling of horror at the recollection of the bloody and infernal rites so frequently practised within its walls. Thanks be to God, the idols are destroyed! Thanks to his name, the glorious gospel of his Son, who was manifested to destroy the works of the devil, has reached these heretofore desolate shores! May the Holy Spirit make it the "savour of life unto life" to the remnant of the people!

Leaving Bukohola, accompanied by some natives, I visited *Mairikini*, another heiau, a few hundred yards nearer the shore. It was nearly equal in its dimensions to that on the summit of the hill, but inferior in every other respect. It appeared to have been crowded with idols, but no human sacrifices were offered to any of its gods.

On returning to Mr. Young's house, I was informed that the vessel would sail that evening for Kairua, a circumstance I much regretted, as I hoped to spend the Sabbath at Towaihae. Mr. Young, however, collected his family and neighbours together, to the number of sixty. A short exhortation was given, and followed by prayer; after which I took leave of my kind host, repaired on board, and the vessel soon after got under way.

It was daylight the next morning before we had left Towaihae bay, as the wind during the night had been very light. The sea-breeze had, however, set in early, and carried us along a rugged and barren shore of lava towards Kairua, which is distant from Towaihae about thirty miles. It being the Sabbath, I preached on deck in the afternoon, from Mark iv. 38, 39, to a congregation of about one hundred and fifty natives, including the greater part of the crew. Many of the people were afterward observed sitting together in small groups, and conversing about what they had heard, though some were inclined to make sport of it.

In the evening we were opposite Laemâno (Shark's Point), but strong westerly currents prevented our making much progress.

On the morning of the 14th, we found ourselves becalmed to the southward of Kairua, several leagues from the shore. The snow-covered tops of the mountains were distinctly seen at sunrise—but they soon after became enveloped in clouds, and continued so through the day. A light breeze carried the vessel towards the land, and at nine A. M. the boat was lowered down, and I proceeded to the shore. On my way I met the governor Kuakini, and Messrs. Goodrich and Harwood, who were coming off in the governor's boat. We returned together to the shore, where I was gladly received by Messrs. Thurston and Bishop, whom I found waiting to proceed on the tour of the island.

In the afternoon a party of strolling musicians and dancers arrived at Kairua. About four o'clock they came, followed by crowds of people, and arranged themselves on a fine sandy beach, in front of one of the governor's houses, where they exhibited a native dance, called *hura araapapa*.

The five musicians first seated themselves in a line on the ground, and spread a piece of folded cloth on the sand before them. Their instrument was a large calabash, or rather two—one of an oval shape, about three feet high, the other perfectly round, very neatly fastened to it, having also an aperture about three inches in diameter at the top. Each musician held his instrument before him with both hands, and produced his music by striking it on the ground, where he had laid the piece of cloth, and beating it with his fingers, or the palms of his hands. As soon as they began to sound their calabashes, the dancer, a young man, about the middle stature, advanced through the opening crowd. His jet-black hair hung in loose and flowing ringlets on his naked shoulders; his necklace was made of a vast number of strings of nicely braided human hair, tied together behind, while a *paraoa* (an ornament made of a whale's tooth) hung pendant from it on his breast; his wrists were ornamented with bracelets formed of polished tusks of the hog, and his ankles with loose buskins, thickly set with dog's teeth, the rattle of which, during the dance, kept time with the music of the calabash-drum. A beautiful yellow tapa was tastefully fastened round his loins, reaching to his knees. He began his dance in front of the musicians, and moved forwards and backwards across the area, occasionally chanting tne achievements of former kings of Hawaii. The governor sat at the end of the ring, opposite to the mu. sicians, and appeared gratified with the performance, which continued until the evening.

CHAPTER V.

Proposed route—An ancient fortress—Aid from the governor—Another native dance—Height of Mouna Huararal—Manner of preparing bark for native cloth—Cultivation of the cloth-plant—Method of manufacturing and paint-ing various kinds of cloth—Conversation with the governor—Departure from Kairua—Description of our guide—Several heiaus—Population of the west-ern coast—Tracts of rugged lava—Scene of the battle which took place in consequence of the abolition of idolatry, in 1819—Description of the battle —Tomb of a celebrated priest—Account of Captain Cook's death, and the honours rendered to his remains—Encouraging missionary labours.

July 15th.—Our whole number being now together at the place where we had previously agreed to commence our tour, we no longer delayed to decide on the route we should take, and the manner in which we should endeavour to accomplish the objects of our visit. Anx-ious to gain a thorough acquaintance with the circum-stances of the people, and their disposition relative to missionary operations, we agreed to travel on foot from Kairua, through the villages on the southern shore, to pass round the south point, and continue along the south-east shore, till we should arrive at the path leading to the great volcano, situated at the foot of Mouna Roa, and about twenty-five miles distant from the sea, which we thought it improper to pass unnoticed. We proposed, after visiting the volcano, either to descend to the shore, and travel along the coast through the division of *Puna*, or across the interior to the division of *Hiro*, as circum-stances might then render most expedient. From Wai-akea in Hiro, we agreed to proceed along the eastern shore, till an opportunity should offer for part of our number to cross over the mountains of Kohala, while the rest should travel along the shore round the north point of the island, and meet their companions at To-waihae, whence they could return direct to Oahu, if a means of conveyance should present itself, or to Kairua, and there wait for a vessel. The plan of our tour being

D 3

thus arranged, we were anxious to receive the aid of
the governor in its execution.

I afterward accompanied Mr. Thurston to the well,
where we found the natives boring the hard rocks of
lava, which they intended to blast. We encouraged
them in their laborious work, and then visited the ruins
of an old military fortification, formerly belonging to
the *makaainana* (common people, as distinguished from
the aristocracy, or reigning chiefs). In those periods
of their history during which the island of Hawaii was
divided into a number of independent governments under
different chiefs, which was the case prior to the reign
of Taraiopu, who was king at the time of its discovery
by Captain Cook, this had been a place of considerable
importance. All that at present remains is part of the
wall, about eighteen or twenty feet high, and fourteen
feet thick at the bottom, built of lava, and apparently
entire. In the upper part of the wall were apertures
resembling embrasures; but they could not have been
designed for cannon, that being an engine of war with
which the natives have but recently become acquainted.
The part of the wall now standing is near the mouth
of Raniakea, the spacious cavern already mentioned,
which formed a valuable appendage to the fort. In this
cavern children and aged persons were placed for security during an assault or sally from the fort, and sometimes the wives of the warriors also, when they did not
accompany their husbands to the battle. The fortification was probably extensive, as traces of the ancient
walls are discoverable in several places; but what were
its original dimensions, the natives who were with us
could not tell. They asserted, however, that the cavern,
if not the fort also, was formerly surrounded by a strong
palisade.

In the afternoon, in company with Mr. Thurston, I
waited on the governor, according to appointment—
made him acquainted with our arrangements, and soli-
cited the accommodation of a boat, or canoe, to carry
our baggage, and a man acquainted with the island, to act
as guide, and to procure provisions, offering him at the
same time any remuneration he might require for such
assistance. After inquiring what baggage we intended
to take, and how long we expected to be absent from
Kairua, he generously offered to send a canoe as far as

it could go with safety, and also to furnish a guide for
the whole tour, without any recompense whatever. He
recommended that we should take a few articles for
barter, as occasionally we might perhaps be obliged to
purchase our food, or hire men to carry our baggage.
After thanking him for his kindness, we returned.

About four o'clock in the afternoon, another party of
musicians and dancers, followed by multitudes of people, took their station nearly on the spot occupied yesterday by those from Kaü. The musicians, seven in
number, seated themselves on the sand; a curiously
carved drum, made by hollowing out a solid piece of
wood, and covering the top with sharks-skin, was placed
before each, which they beat with the palm or fingers
of their right hand. A neat little drum, made of the
shell of a large cocoanut, was also fixed on the knee, by
the side of the large drum, and beat with a small stick
held in the left hand. When the musicians had arranged
themselves in a line across the beach, and a bustling
man, who appeared to be master of the ceremonies,
had, with a large branch of a cocoanut-tree, cleared
a circle of considerable extent, two interesting little
children (a boy and a girl), apparently about nine years
of age, came forward, habited in the dancing costume
of the country, with garlands of flowers on their heads,
wreaths around their necks, bracelets on their wrists,
and buskins on their ankles. When they had reached
the centre of the ring, they commenced their dance to
the music of the drums, cantilating alternately with the
musicians a song in honour of some ancient chief of
Hawaii.

The governor of the island was present, accompanied,
as it is customary for every chieftain of distinction to
be on public occasions, by a retinue of favourite chiefs
and attendants. Having almost entirely laid aside the
native costume, and adopted that of the foreigners who
visit the islands, he appeared on this occasion in a light
European dress, and sat on a Canton-made arm-chair,
opposite the dancers, during the whole exhibition. A
servant, with a light *kihei* of painted native cloth thrown
over his shoulder, stood behind his chair, holding a
highly polished spittoon, made of the beautiful brown
wood of the cordia in one hand, and in the other a handsome *kahiri*, an elastic rod, three or four feet long, having the shining feathers of the tropic-bird tastefully fast-

ened round the upper end, with which he fanned away
the flies from the person of his master.

The beach was crowded with spectators, and the exhibition kept up with spirit, till the overspreading shades
of evening put an end to their mirth, and afforded a
respite to the poor children, whose little limbs must
have been very much fatigued by two hours of constant
exercise. We were anxious to address the multitude
on the subject of religion before they should disperse;
but so intent were they on their amusement, that they
could not have been diverted from it. I succeeded,
however, in taking a sketch of the novel assemblage,
in which a youth, who had climbed a high pole (that,
looking over the heads of the throng who surrounded
the dancers, he might witness the scene), formed a conspicuous object.

A messenger now invited us to sup with the governor,
and we soon after joined him and his friends around his
hospitable board. Our repast was not accompanied by
the gladsome sound of " harp in hall" or " aged minstrel's
flowing lay," yet it was enlivened by an interesting
youthful bard, twelve or fourteen years of age, who was
seated on the ground in the large room in which we
were assembled, and who, during the supper, sang, in a
monotonous but pleasing strain, the deeds of former
chiefs, ancestors of our host. His fingers swept no
" classic lyre," but beat, in a manner responsive to his
song, a rustic little drum, formed of a calabash, beautifully stained, and covered at the head with a piece of
shark-skin. The governor and his friends were evidently pleased with his lay, and the youth seemed repaid
by their approbation.

In the morning of the 16th, Messrs. Goodrich and
Harwood endeavoured to ascertain the height of Mouna
Huararai, by means of two observations at the extremity
of a base line of two thousand two hundred and thirty
feet. They made the height of the mountain to be
seven thousand eight hundred and twenty-two feet; but
their quadrant being an inferior one, we thought the
height of the mountain greater than that given above,
though it is never covered with snow.

The accounts the natives gave us of the roads we
were to travel, and the effects the short journeys already
made had produced on our shoes, convinced us that
those we had brought with us would be worn out before

we had proceeded even half-way round the island. We therefore provided a substitute, by procuring a tough bull's hide from the governor's store-house, and making ourselves rude sandals; these we afterward found very serviceable, as they enabled us to travel over large tracts of lava with much more expedition and comfort than we could possibly have done without them.

At four P. M. the musicians from Kaü again collected on the beach, and the dancer commenced a *hura*, similar to that exhibited on Monday evening. We had previously appointed a religious meeting for this time, and about an hour before sunset proposed to the governor to hold it on the beach, where the people were already assembled. He approved, and followed us to the edge of the circle, where we took our station opposite the musicians. At the governor's request the music ceased, and the dancer came and sat down just in front of us. We sang a hymn; I then offered up a short prayer, and afterward addressed the people from Acts xiv. 15— " And preach unto you, that ye should turn from these vanities unto the living God, which made heaven and earth, and the sea, and all things that are therein." The multitude collected was from different and distant parts of the island, and appeared to listen with attention to the word spoken. To many it was doubtless the first time they had heard of the name of Jehovah, or Jesus Christ his Son, and we afterward heard them conversing among themselves about the truths they had heard.

After supper and family worship at the governor's, I spent the evening in conversation with him, partly on traditions respecting some remarkable places in the neighbourhood of Kairua, and partly on the subject of religion. I spoke on the desirableness of his building a place for the public worship of the true God, and the advantages of keeping the Sabbath as a day of holy rest, recommending him to set the common people a good example, and use his influence to induce them to attend public service on the Lord's-day. He said it was his intention to build a church by-and-by, when the *maka-ainana* should become interested in these things, and when they should have a missionary to reside permanently with them; but that at present the people at Kairua were indifferent to all religion.

For several days past we have observed many of the

people bringing home from their plantations bundles of young *wauti* (a variety of the *morus papyrifera*), from which we infer that this is the season for cloth-making in this part of the island.

This morning, the 17th, we perceived Keoua, the governor's wife, and her female attendants, with about forty other women, under the pleasant shade of a beautiful clump of cordia or kou-trees, employed in stripping off the bark from bundles of *wauti*-sticks, for the purpose of making it into cloth. The sticks were generally from six to ten feet long, and about an inch in diameter at the thickest end. They first cut the bark the whole length of the stick, with a sharp serrated shell, and having carefully peeled it off, rolled it into small coils, the inner bark being outside. In this state it is left some time, to make it flat and smooth. Keoua not only worked herself, but appeared to take the superintendence of the whole party. Whenever a fine piece of bark was found it was shown to her, and put aside to be manufactured into *wairiirii*, or some other particular cloth. With lively chat and cheerful song they appeared to béguile the hours of labour until noon, when, having finished their work, they repaired to their dwellings.

The wauti-plant, of which the greater part of the cloth on this side of the island is made, is cultivated with much care in their gardens of sugar-cane, plantain, &c., and whole plantations are sometimes appropriated exclusively to its growth. Slips about a foot long are planted nearly two feet apart, in long rows, four or six feet asunder. Two or three shoots rise from most of the slips, and grow till they are six or twelve feet high, according to the richness of the soil, or the kind of cloth for which they are intended. Any small branches that may sprout out from the side of the long shoot are carefully plucked off, and sometimes the bud at the top of the plant is pulled out, to cause an increase in its size. Occasionally they are two years growing, and seldom reach the size at which they are fit for use in less than twelve, or even eighteen months—when they are cut off near the ground, the old roots being left to produce shoots another year.

The bark, when stripped off and rolled up, as described above, is left several days—when, on being unrolled, it appears flat. The outer bark is then taken off, generally by scraping it with a large shell, and the inner bark, of which the cloth is made, is occasionally laid in water, to extract the resinous substances it may contain. Each piece of bark is then taken singly and laid across a piece of wood twelve or eighteen feet long, six inches square, smooth on the top, but having a groove on the under side, and is beaten with a square mallet of hard heavy wood, about a foot in length, and two inches wide; three sides are carved in grooves or ribs, the other into squares, in order that one mallet may answer for the different kinds of cloth they are accustomed to manufacture.

Various sorts of cloth are made with this plant, some remarkably fine and even; that which has been beaten with a mallet, carved in different patterns, much resembles muslin at first sight, while that made with a grooved mallet appears, until closely examined, something like dimity. There are other kinds very thick and tough, which look like wash-leather; but the most common sort is the paü, worn round the waists of the females. To make this, a piece of bark is beaten till it is four yards long, and more than a yard wide, and of an equal texture throughout. Sometimes two or three pieces of bark are necessary to make one piece of cloth. Five of these pieces, when finished, are spread out one upon the other, and fastened together at one end. These five pieces make one paü. The inside pieces are usually white or yellow; but the outside piece is stained, or painted, with vegetable dies. No gum is used in the manufacture of the paü, except that contained in the bark—yet the fibres adhere firmly together. Those painted red or yellow, &c. are sometimes rubbed over with a vegetable oil, in which chips of sandal-wood or the seeds of the *pandanus odorotissima* have been steeped. This is designed to perfume the cloth, and render it impervious to wet; it is, however, less durable than the common paü.

There is another kind of cloth, called *tapa moe* (sleeping-cloth), made principally for the chiefs, who use it to wrap themselves in at night, while they sleep. It is generally three or four yards square, very thick, being formed of several layers of common tapa, cemented with gum, and beaten with a grooved mallet till they are closely interwoven. The colour is various, either white, yellow, brown, or black, according to the fancy of its owner. Nearly resembling the tapa moe is the kihei,

only it is both thinner and smaller. It is made in the
same manner, and is about the size of a large shawl or
counterpane. Sometimes it is brown, but more frequently white or yellow, intermixed with red and black.
It is generally worn by the men, thrown loosely over
one shoulder, passed under the opposite arm, and tied
in front, or on the other shoulder.

But the best kind of cloth made with the cultivated
plant is the *wauru*, which is made into paüs for the
females, and maros for the men. The paüs are generally four yards long, and about one yard wide, very
thick, beautifully painted with brilliant red, yellow, and
black colours, and covered over with a fine gum and
resinous varnish, which not only preserves the colours,
but renders the cloth impervious and durable. The
maros are about a foot wide, and three or four yards
long.

The colours they employ are procured from the leaves,
bark, berries, or roots of indigenous plants, and require
much skill in their preparation. One or two kinds of
earth are also used in mixing the darker colours. Since
foreigners have visited them, they have found, upon
trial, that our colours are better than theirs, and the
paints they purchase from ships have superseded in a
great degree the native colours, in the painting of the
most valuable kinds of cloth.

Their manner of painting is ingenious. They cut the
pattern they intend to stamp on their cloth, on the
inner side of a narrow piece of bamboo, spread their
cloth before them on a board, and having their colours
properly mixed in a calabash by their side, dip the point
of the bamboo, which they hold in their right hand, into
the paint, strike it against the edge of the calabash, place
it on the right or left side of the cloth, and press it down
with the fingers of the left hand. The pattern is dipped
in the paint after every impression, which is repeated
till the cloth is finished.

The tapa in general lasts but a little while, compared
with any kind of wove cloth—yet if kept free from wet,
which causes it to rend like paper, some kinds may be
worn a considerable time. The fabrication of it shows
both invention and industry: and whether we consider
its different textures, its varied and regular patterns, its
beautiful colours, so admirably preserved by means
of the varnish, we are at once convinced that the people

who manufacture it are neither deficient in taste, nor incapable of receiving the improvements of civilized society.*

During the forenoon, Mr. Harwood made an auger to aid the well-diggers in boring the rocks. I walked with Mr. Thurston to see what progress they had made, and to encourage them to persevere. The rocks, they said, were hard, and their progress slow; yet they were not discouraged, but hoped to find the work easier as they descended.

After dinner the governor entered freely into conversation on religious subjects, particularly respecting the resurrection of the body, the destruction of the heavens and the earth at the last day, and the final judgment. After listening attentively to what was said upon these subjects, he inquired about the locality of heaven and hell. He was told that we did not know where the one or the other was situated, as none had ever returned from either to tell mankind about them; and we only know that there is a place called heaven, where God makes glorious manifestations of his perfections, and where all good men are perfectly happy; and that there is a place where wicked men will endure endless misery. He then said, "How do you know these things?" I asked for his Bible, and translated the passages which inculcate the doctrine of the resurrection, &c., and told him it was from that book we obtained our knowledge of these things; and that it was the contents of that book which we had come to teach the people of Hawaii. He then asked if all the people in our native countries were acquainted with the Bible. I answered, that from the abundant means of instruction enjoyed there, the greater portion of the people had either read the book, or had in some other way become acquainted with its principal contents. He then said, "How is it that such numbers of them swear, get intoxicated, and do so many things prohibited in that book?" He was told that there was a vast difference between knowing the word of God, and obeying it; and that it was most likely those persons knew their conduct was displeasing to God, yet persisted in it, because agreeable to their corrupt inclinations. He asked if God would not be angry with us for troubling him so frequently with our prayers?

* Specimens of the principal kinds of native cloth manufactured in the Sandwich Islands may be seen in the Missionary Museum, Austin Friars.

If he was-like man, he said, he was sure he would.　I
replied that God was always "waiting to be gracious,"
more ready to hear than we were to pray; that indeed
he was not like man, or his patience would have been
exhausted long ago by the wickedness of men; but that
he continued exercising long-suffering and forbearance
towards sinners, that they might turn from their wickedness and live.

ʼ We supped with the governor as usual, and, after
family worship with his household, prepared our baggage for our journey, some of which we left to be forwarded by the Ainoa to Waiakea, a district on the
eastern side of the island.

 About eleven o'clock in the forenoon, on the 18th, we
waited on the governor, to express our grateful sense of
the generous hospitality we had experienced from him
during our stay at Kairua.　We also thanked him for the
advice he had given, and the aid he had so kindly furnished for the prosecution of our journey, and informed
him that we were ready to proceed.　He had before
given instructions to our guide.　He now directed the
man who was going in the canoe to take care of our
things, and told us he would send some men to carry
our baggage by land as far as Kearakekua.　We then
took leave of him, and proceeded on our journey,
Messrs. Bishop and Harwood went in the canoe, the rest
of our number travelled on foot.

 Our guide, *Makoa*, who had been the king's messenger
many years, and was well acquainted with the island,
led the way.　He was rather a singular looking little
man, between forty and fifty years of age.　A thick tuft
of jet-black curling hair shaded his wrinkled forehead,
and a long bunch of the same kind hung down behind
each of his ears.　The rest of his head was cropped as
short as shears could make it.　His small black eyes
were ornamented with tattooed vandyke semicircles.
Two goats, impressed in the same indelible manner,
stood rampant over each of his brows; one, like the
supporter of a coat-of-arms, was fixed on each side of
his nose, and two more guarded the corners of his
mouth.　The upper part of his beard was shaven close;
but that which grew under his chin was drawn together,
braided for an inch or two, and then tied in a knot, while
the extremities below the knot spread out in curls like a
tassel.　A light *kihei* (cloth worn like a shawl) was care-

lessly thrown over one shoulder, and tied in a knot on
the other; and a large fan, made of cocoanut leaf, in his
hand, served to beat away the flies, or the boys, when
either became two numerous or troublesome.

Leaving Kairua, we passed through the villages thickly
scattered along the shore to the southward. The country around looked unusually green and cheerful, owing
to the frequent rains which for some months past have
fallen on this side of the island: Even the barren lava,
over which we travelled, seemed to veil its sterility beneath tufts of tall waving grass, or spreading shrubs and
flowers. The sides of the hills, laid out for a considerable extent in gardens and fields, and generally cultivated with potatoes and other vegetables, were beautiful. The number of heiaus and depositories of the dead
which we passed convinced us that this part of the
island must formerly have been populous. The latter
were built with fragments of lava, laid up evenly on the
outside, generally about eight feet long, from four to six
broad, and about four feet high. Some appeared very ancient, others had evidently been standing but a few years.

At Ruapua we examined an interesting heiau, called
Kauaikahaora, built of immense blocks of lava, and found
its dimensions to be one hundred and fifty feet by
seventy. At the north end was a smaller enclosure,
sixty feet long and ten wide, partitioned off by a high
wall, with but one narrow entrance. The places where
the idols formerly stood were apparent, though the idols
had been removed. The spot where the altar had been
erected could be distinctly traced; it was a mound of
earth, paved with smooth stones, and surrounded by a
firm curb of lava. The adjacent ground was strewed
with bones of the ancient offerings. The natives informed us that four principal idols were formerly worshipped there, one of stone, two of wood, and one
covered with red feathers. One of them, they said,
was brought from a foreign country. Their names
were *Kanenuiakea* (great and wide-spreading Kane), who
was brought from Tauai, *Kaneruruhonua* (earth-shaking
Kane), *Roramakaeha*, and *Kekuaaimanu*.

Leaving the heiau, we passed by a number of smaller
temples, principally on the seashore, dedicated to *Kuura*,
a male, and *Hina*, a female idol, worshipped by fishermen, as they were supposed to preside over the sea, and
to conduct or impel to the shores of Hawaii the various

shoals of fish that visit them at different seasons of the
year. The first of any kind of fish taken in the season
was always presented to them, especially the *operu*, a
kind of herring. This custom exactly accords with the
former practice of the inhabitants of Maui and the adjacent islands, and of the Society islanders.

At two P. M. we reached Horuaroa, a large and populous district. Here we found Keoua the governor's
wife and her attendants, who had come from Kairua
for wauti, with which to make cloth. Shortly after,
we reached a village called Karuaokalani (the second
heaven), where was a fine heiau in good preservation.
It is called Pakiha; its dimensions were two hundred
and seventy feet by two hundred and ten. We could
not learn the idol to which it was dedicated, but were
informed it was built in the time of Keakealani, who,
according to tradition, was queen of Hawaii about eleven
generations back. The walls were solid, thick, and
nearly entire; and the singular manner in which the
stones were piled upon the top, like so many small
spires, gave it an unusually interesting appearance.
Before we left Karuaokalani the inhabitants pointed out
to us a spot called Maukareoreo, the place of a celebrated giant of that name, who was one of the attendants of *Umi*, king of Hawaii, about twelve generations since, and who, they told us, was so tall that he
could pluck the cocoanuts from the trees as he walked
along; and when the king was playing in the surf, where
it was five or six fathoms deep, would walk out to him
without being wet above his loins; and when he was in
a canoe, if he saw any fish lying among the coral at the
same depth, would just put his hand down and take
them. They also told us he was a great warrior, and
that to his prowess principally, Umi was indebted for
many of his victories. The Hawaiians are fond of the
marvellous, as well as many people who are better informed; and probably this passion, together with the
distance of time since Maukareoreo existed, has led
them to magnify one of Umi's followers, of perhaps a
little larger stature than his fellows, into a giant sixty
feet high.

Our road now lay through a pleasant part of the district, thickly inhabited, and ornamented occasionally
with clumps of kou-trees. Several spots were pointed
out to us, where the remains of heiaus, belonging to the

late king Tamehameha, were still visible. After travelling some time we came to Kanekaheilani, a large heiau more than two hundred feet square. In the midst of it was a clear pool of brackish water, which the natives told us was the favourite bathing-place of Tamehameha, and which he allowed no other person to use. A rude figure, carved in stone, standing on one side of the gateway by which we entered, was the only image we saw here. About fifty yards farther on was another heiau, called *Hale o Tairi* (house of Tairi). It was built by Tamehameha soon after he had assumed the government of the island. Only one mutilated image was now standing, though it is evident that, but a few years ago, there had been many. The natives were very desirous to show us the place where the image of Tairi the war-god stood, and told us that frequently in the evening he used to be seen flying about in the neighbourhood in the form of a luminous substance like a flame, or like the tail of a comet. We told them that the luminous appearance which they saw was an occurrence common to other countries, and produced by natural causes · that the natives of the Society Islands formerly, whenever they observed such a phenomenon, supposed it to be *Tane*, one of their gods, taking his flight from one marae to another, or passing through the district seeking whom he might destroy, and were consequently filled with terror; but now, they wondered how they could ever have given way to such fears from so inoffensive a circumstance. We asked them if they did not see the same appearances now, though the god had been destroyed, and his worship discontinued? They said, "No; it has not been seen since the abolition of idolatry." We assured them it did not proceed from the power of the god Tairi, but that it was a luminous vapour under the control of Jehovah, the creator and governor of all things which they beheld.

We walked on to Pahoehoe, where we entered a large house, in which many workmen were employed in making canoes. About fifty people soon after assembled around us. We asked them if they were willing to hear about the true God and the way of salvation? They answered, Yes. I then addressed them for about twenty minutes on the first principles of the gospel. As soon as I began to speak, they all sat down, and observed perfect silence. Shortly after this service we took our leave, and proceeded along the shore to Kahaluu ; where a smart shower of rain obliged us to take shelter in a house by the road-side. While resting there the voice of wailing reached our ears. We inquired whence it came ! and were informed by the people of the house that a sick person in the neighbourhood had just expired. We asked where the soul was gone to ? They answered, they knew not whither, but that it would never return. I spoke to them respecting the condition of departed souls, the resurrection of the body, and the general judgment which will follow.; telling them afterward of the love of Christ, who had brought life and immortality to light, and by his death secured eternal happiness to all that believe in him. They listened attentively, and continued the conversation till the rain abated, when we pursued our journey. We passed another large heiau, and travelled about a mile across a rugged bed of lava, which had evidently been ejected from a volcano more recently than the vast tracts of the same substance by which it was surrounded. It also appeared to have been torn to pieces,·and tossed up in the most confused manner by some violent convulsion of the earth, at the time it was in a semifluid state. There was a kind of path formed across the most level part of it, by large smooth round stones, brought from the seashore, and placed three or four feet apart. By stepping from one to another of these, we passed over the roughest piece of lava we had yet seen; and soon after five P. M. we arrived at Keauhou, a pleasant village, containing one hundred and thirty-five houses, and about eight miles from Kairua. Messrs. Bishop and Harwood reached the same place about an hour earlier, and here we proposed to spend the night. We had not been long in the village, when about one hundred and fifty people collected round the house in which we stopped. After singing and prayer, Mr. Thurston preached to them. They gave good attention ; and though we conversed with them a considerable time after the service was ended, they still thronged our house, and seemed unwilling to disperse. During our walk from Kairua to this place we counted six hundred and ten houses, and allowed one hundred more for those who live among the plantations on the sides of the hills. Reckoning five persons to each house, which we think not far from a correct calculation, the population of the tract through which we have travelled to-day will be about three thousand five hundred and fifty souls. We also passed nineteen heiaus of different dimensions, some of which we carefully examined. Late in the evening we spread our mats on the loose pebbles of which the floor of the house was formed, and, thankful for the mercies we had received, laid ourselves down, and enjoyed a comfortable night's repose. Thermometer at sunset 71°.

Early the next morning, numbers of the natives collected around our lodgings, and, when informed that we intended to perform religious worship, sat down on the ground, and became silent. After singing a hymn in their language, I gave a short exhortation, followed by prayer. They afterward kept us in conversation till about half-past eight, when we left Keauhou, and pursued our journey. Mr. Harwood proceeded in the canoe; the rest of our number travelled on foot. Our way lay across a rough tract of lava, resembling that which we passed over the preceding afternoon. In many places it seemed as if the surface of the lava had become hard, while a few inches underneath it had remained semifluid, and in that state had been broken up, and left in its present confused and irregular form. This rugged appearance of the external lava was probably produced by the expansive force of the heated air beneath the crust, but that could not have caused the deep chasms or fissures which we saw in several places. We also observed many large spherical volcanic stones, the surface of which had been fused, and in some places had peeled off like a crust or shell, an inch or two in thickness. The centre of some of these stones, which we broke, was of a dark blue colour and compact texture, and did not appear to have been affected by the fire which had calcined the surface.

After travelling about two miles over this barren waste, we reached the place where, in the autumn of 1819, the decisive battle was fought between the forces of *Rihoriho*, the present king, and his cousin, *Kekuaokalani*, in which the latter was slain, his followers completely overthrown, and the cruel system of idolatry, which he took up arms to support, effectually destroyed. The natives pointed out to us the place where the king's troops, led on by Karaimoku, were first attacked by the idolatrous party. We saw several small heaps of stones, which our guide informed us were the graves of those who, during the conflict, had fallen there. We were then shown the spot on which the king's troops formed a line from the seashore towards the mountains, and drove the opposing party before them to a rising ground, where a stone fence, about breast high, enabled the enemy to defend themselves for some time, but from which they were at length driven by a party of Karaimoku's warriors. The small *tumuli* increased in number as we passed along, until we came to a place called *Tuamoo*. Here Kekuaokalani made his last stand, rallied his flying forces, and seemed for a moment to turn the scale of victory; but being weak with the loss of blood, from a wound he had received in the early part of the engagement, he fainted and fell. However, he soon revived, and, though unable to stand, sat on a fragment of lava, and twice loaded and fired his musket on the advancing party. He now received a ball in his left breast, and, immediately covering his face with his feather cloak, expired in the midst of his friends. His wife Manona, during the whole of the day, fought by his side with steady and dauntless courage. A few moments after her husband's death, perceiving Karaimoku and his sister advancing, she called out for quarter; but the words had scarcely escaped from her lips, when she received a ball in her left temple, fell upon the lifeless body of her husband, and instantly expired. The idolaters, having lost their chief, made but feeble resistance afterward; yet the combat, which commenced in the forenoon, continued till near sunset, when the king's troops, finding their enemies had all either fled or surrendered, returned to Kairua.

Karaimoku grieved much at the death of Kekuaokalani, who was his own sister's son. He delayed the engagement as long as possible; and the same morning that the battle took place, sent a messenger, addressing the young chief as his son, and requesting him to refrain from hostilities till they could have an interview, and, if possible, effect an accommodation. But the message was rejected, and the messenger obliged to jump into the sea, and swim to save his life. In the moment of victory, also, he acted with humanity; and, contrary to the usual custom, the vanquished were not pursued and murdered in their retreats. A little way south of the spot where the chief fell was a small cave, into which, in the confusion that followed the death of Kekuokalani, a woman attached to his party crept, and, drawing a piece of lava over its mouth, remained until night, beneath whose friendly cover she fled to the mountains, not knowing that the victors had returned without pursuing their foes. The wives of warriors often accompanied their husbands to battle, and were frequently slain. Their practice, in this respect, resembled that of the Society islanders on similar occasions. They generally followed in the rear, carrying calabashes of water, or of poë, a little dried fish, or other portable provision, with which to recruit their husbands' strength when weary, or afford a draught of water when thirsty or faint: but they followed more particularly to be at hand if their husbands should be wounded.

Some women, more courageous than the rest, or urged on by affection, advanced side by side with their husbands to the front of the battle, bearing a small calabash of water in one hand, and a spear, a dart, or a stone in the other; and in the event of the husband's being killed, they seldom survived.

A pile of stones somewhat larger than the rest marked the spot where the rival chief, and his affectionate and heroic wife expired. A few yards nearer the sea, an oblong pile of stones, in the form of a tomb, about ten feet long and six wide, was raised over the grave in which they were both interred. A number of lowly flowering bushes grew around, and a beautiful convolvulus in full bloom almost covered it with foliage and flowers. We could not view this rudely constructed tomb without renewed lamentation over the miseries of war, and a strong feeling of regret for the untimely end of the youthful pair, especially for the affectionate Manona, whom even the horrors of savage fight, in which the demon of war wears his most terrific form, could not prevent from following the fortune, and sharing the dangers, that she might administer to the comfort, of her much-loved husband. This feeling was not a little increased by the recollection of the delusion of which they were the ill-fated victims, and in support of which they were prodigal of their blood. Alas! they knew not, till from the fatal field they entered the eternal world, the value of that life which they had lost, and the true nature of that cause in which they had sacrificed it. The piles of stones rose thick around the spot where they lay; and we were informed that they were the graves of his *kahu* (particular friends and companions), who stood by him to the last, manifesting a steadfastness which even their enemies admired, and a degree of courage worthy of being exercised in a better cause.

Kekuaokalani was first cousin to Rihoriho. He is represented by some as having been an enterprising and restless young man, aspiring to share the government with his cousin, if not to reign in his stead. The late king Tamehameha, a short time before his death, left the government of the islands to his eldest son, Rihoriho, and the care of the gods, their temples, and the support of their worship to the king and Kekuaokalani, together with the rest of the chiefs.

Almost the first public act of the young king Rihoriho, and before the arrival of any missionary, was the abolition of the national idolatry, and all the restrictions of the tabu system by which it was upheld. This system, with all its superstitious cruelty, had existed, and had exerted its degrading yet almost supernatural influence over the people from time immemorial; and it required no small degree of courage by one single act to abrogate its inflexible laws, and destroy its dreaded power. But several acts of Rihoriho's reign show that he possessed a mind well adapted for such undertakings.

His motives for this decisive measure appear to have been, in the first place, a desire to ameliorate the condition of his wives, and the females in general, whom the tabu sank into a state of extreme wretchedness and degradation, obliging them to subsist only on inferior kinds of food, and not allowing them to cook their provisions, such as they were, at the same fire, or even eat in the same place where the men took theirs. And in the second place, he seems to have been influenced by a wish to diminish the power of the priests, and avoid that expenditure of labour and property which the support of idolatry required, and which he was anxious to employ for other purposes. He had also heard what Pomare and the Tahitian chiefs had done in the Society Islands. He consulted some of the principal chiefs, particularly Karaimoku, who declared his intention not to keep or observe any more tabus; and though several of the priests said the gods would recompense any neglect with vengeance, Hevaheva, the high-priest of his father's war-god, said no evil consequences would follow the discontinuance of the worship of the gods. Soon after this, the king made a feast, to' which many chiefs of the different islands were invited. The guests assembled as usual; the men in one place, the women in another. The food was cut up by Mr. Young, from whom, as well as from some of the chiefs, we have received the account, and when all were about to begin their meal, the king ordered his attendants to carry some fowls, and such prohibited food, to the place where his wives and other females were assembled: he then went, and sitting down with them, began to eat, and directed them to do the same. A shout of surprise burst from the multitude around; several other chiefs followed his example. The men and women sat promiscuously, and ate the same food, which they called *ai noa*, general or common eating, in opposition to the former *ai tabu*, restricted or sacred eating. The *ai tabu* was one of the perpetual restrictions imposed by their idolatry on all ranks of the people, from their birth until their death. This public violation of it manifested the king's intention to destroy the whole system, which very shortly after was accomplished by the priest Hevaheva's resigning his office, and the king declaring that there should no longer be any priests, or any worship rendered to the gods.

Kakuaokalani, though he had no share in the government, yet had, in common with the other high chiefs, received a charge concerning the gods. Urged on by the priests, who promised him victory, by a superstitious reverence for the idols of his ancestors, and perhaps also by a hope of defeating Rihoriho, and securing the government to himself, he took up arms.

The abolition of idolatry by Rihoriho was thus the immediate occasion of the war which, terminating in his favour, left him sole monarch of the Sandwich Islands. This was the summit of his ambition, and the consummation of his wishes, though probably the least among the all-wise and benevolent purposes of Him, who ruleth all things after the counsel of his own will, and causeth even the wrath of man to praise him. Little did the pagan chief imagine, when he collected his forces, offered his sacrifices, and, preceded by his war-god, marched to the battle, that he was urging on

E 2

his way to remove the most formidable barrier that
existed to the introduction of a religion which should
finally triumph over every system of idolatry in the
world; and as little did the victorious chiefs, when they
beheld themselves masters of the field, and returned in
triumph to the king, think that success had only prepared
the way for their own subjection to a Prince, whose
heralds (then on their way) should soon proclaim his
laws in their camp, and demand their allegiance to his
crown; whose divine power should erect among them
a kingdom of which they themselves should delight to
become subjects, and commence a reign that should be
everlasting.

Leaving Tuamoo, we passed on to Honuaino, where,
being thirsty and weary, we sat down on the side of a
canoe, under the shade of a fine-spreading *hibiscus*, and
begged a little water of the villagers. We had not remained many minutes before we were surrounded by
about one hundred and fifty people. After explaining
to them in few words our feelings on meeting them,
we asked them if they would like to hear what we had
to say to them. They replied, *Ae* (yes), and sat down
immediately. We sang a hymn and prayed, and I addressed them for about half an hour on the first principles of Christianity. They all appeared gratified, said
they were *naau po* (dark-hearted), and should be glad
to be instructed in all these things, if anybody would
teach them. We now travelled on to Hokukano, where
we passed a *pahu tabu* (sacred enclosure), which the
natives told us was built by Taraiopu,* king of the island
at the time it was discovered by Captain Cook. A little
farther on we examined a *buoa* (tomb) of a celebrated
priest. It was composed of loose stones, neatly laid,
about eight feet square and five high. In the centre
was a small mound of earth, higher than the walls; over
this a house had formerly been erected, but it was now
fallen to decay; around it were long poles, stuck in the
earth, about three or four inches apart, and united together at the top. We asked why the grave was enclosed with those tall sticks? Some said it was a custom so to inter persons of consequence; others said it
was to prevent the spirit from coming out. A mode
of interment corresponding with this, appears to prevail

* Terreeoboo in Cook's Voyages.

among some of the tribes inhabiting the north-west coast of the American continent. On the top of a high mountain, in the neighbourhood, stood the remains of an old heiau, dedicated to Ukanipo, a shark, to which, we were informed, all the people along the coast, for a considerable distance, used to repair, at stated times, with abundant offerings. Passing on along a rugged road, we reached Kaavaroa soon after 2 P. M. Kamakau received us kindly, spread out a mat for us to sit down on, handed us a calabash of good fresh water (a great luxury on this side of the island), and ordered a goat to be prepared for our refreshment. He appeared as zealous in his pursuit of truth, earnest in his desires after his own salvation, and concerned for that of his people, as when formerly visited. One or two inferior chiefs, from a district belonging to him, in the south part of the island, were sitting in the house when he entered. He afterward began to talk with them on matters of religion, with an earnestness and intelligence which surprised us.

In the afternoon Mr. Thurston and I climbed the rocks which rise in a north-east direction from the village, and visited the cave in which the body of Captain Cook was deposited on being first taken from the beach. These rocks, which are entirely composed of lava, are nearly two hundred feet high, and in some parts very steep. A winding path of rather difficult ascent leads to the cave, which is situated on the face of the rocks, about halfway to the top. In front of it is a kind of ledge three or four feet wide, and immediately over it the rocks rise perpendicularly for a yard or two, but afterward the ascent is gradual to the summit.

The cave itself is of volcanic formation, and appears to have been one of those subterranean tunnels so numerous on the island, by which the volcanoes in the interior sometimes discharge their contents upon the shore. It is five feet high, and the entrance about eight or ten feet wide. The roof and sides within are of obsidian or hard vitreous lava; and along the floor, it is evident that in some remote period a stream of the same kind of lava has also flowed.

There are a number of persons at Kaavaroa and other places in the islands, who either were present themselves at the unhappy dispute which in this vicinity terminated the valuable life of the celebrated Captain Cook,

or who, from their connexion with those who were on the
spot, are well acquainted with the particulars of that melancholy event.   With many of them we have frequently
conversed, and though their narratives differ in a few
smaller points, they all agree in the main facts with the
account published by Captain King, his successor.

"The foreigner," they say, "was not to blame; for,
in the first instance, our people stole his boat, and he,
in order to recover it, designed to take our king on board
his ship, and detain him there till it should be restored.
Kapena Kuke* and *Taraiopu* our king were walking together towards the shore, when our people, conscious
of what had been done, thronged round the king, and
objected to his going any farther.   His wife also joined
her entreaties that he would not go on board the ships.
While he was hesitating, a man came running from the
other side of the bay, entered the crowd almost breath-
less, and exclaimed, ' *It is war!*—the foreigners have
commenced hostilities; have fired on a canoe from one
of their boats, and killed a chief.'   This enraged some
of our people, and alarmed the chiefs, as they feared
Captain Cook would kill the king.   The people armed
themselves with stones, clubs, and spears.   Kanona
entreated her husband not to go.   All the chiefs did the
same.   The king sat down.   The captain seemed agitated, and was walking towards his boat, when one of
our men attacked him with a spear: he turned, and
with his double-barrelled gun shot the man who struck
him.   Some of our people then threw stones at him,
which being seen by his men, they fired on us.   Captain
Cook then endeavoured to stop his men from firing, but
could not, on account of the noise.   He was turning again
to speak to us, when he was stabbed in the back with
a *pahoa;* a spear was at the same time driven through
his body; he fell into the water, and spoke no more.†

---

* Captain Cook's name is thus pronounced by the natives.
† We have several times inquired particularly of the natives acquainted with
the circumstances, whether Captain Cook was facing them, or had his back
towards them, when he received the fatal thrust; and their answer in general
has been as here stated, which accords very nearly with Captain King's account, who says, "Our unfortunate commander, the last time he was seen
distinctly, was standing at the water's edge, and calling out to the boats to
cease firing, and pull in.   If it be true, as some of those present have imagined,
that the marines and boatmen fired without his orders, and that he was
desirous of preventing any further bloodshed, it is not improbable that his
humanity on this occasion proved fatal to him; for it was remarked that while
he faced the natives none of them had offered him any violence, but that having

"After he was dead, we all wailed. His bones were separated—the flesh was scraped off and burnt, as was the practice in regard to our own chiefs when they died. We thought he was the god Rono, worshipped him as such, and after his death reverenced his bones."

Not only were his bones so treated, but almost every relic left with them. Among other things, a *sledge*, which, from their description of it, must have come from the north-west coast of America, left at the islands by Captain Cook, or some of his companions, was afterward worshipped by the people. They called it, probably from its singular shape, *Opaitauarii*, a crab or shrimp, for a chief to rest on; from *opai*, a crab or shrimp—*tau*, to rest or sit—and *arii*, a chief.

Many of the chiefs frequently express the sorrow they feel whenever they think of the captain; and even the common people usually speak of these facts with apparent regret. Yet they exonerate the king Taraiopu from all blame, as nothing was done by his orders. I was once in a house in Oahu with Karaimoku and several other chiefs, looking over the plates in the folio edition of Cook's Voyages. They were greatly affected with the print which represented his death, and inquired if I knew the names of those who were slain on that occasion. I perceived Karaimoku more than once wipe the tears from his eyes, while conversing about this melancholy event. He said he recollected Captain Cook's visit, if not also his person, though he was at Maui at the time of his death. More than once, when conversing with us on the length of time the missionaries had been in the Society Islands, they have said, "Why did you not come here sooner? Was it because we killed Captain Cook?"

We have sometimes asked them what inducement they had to steal the boat, when they possessed so many canoes of their own. They have generally answered, that they did not take it to transport themselves from one island to another; for their own canoes were more convenient, and they knew better how to manage them; but because they saw it was not sewed together, but fastened with nails. These they wanted,—therefore

turned about to give his orders to the boats, he was stabbed in the back, and fell with his face into the water."—See Captain King's Continuation of Cook's Voyages, 4to. vol. iii. pages 45 and 46.

they stole the boat, and broke it to pieces the next day, in order to obtain the nails to make fish-hooks with. We have every reason to believe that this was the principal, if not the only, motive by which they were actuated in committing the depredation which ultimately led to such unhappy consequences. They prize nails very highly; and though we do not know that they ever went so far in their endeavours to obtain a more abundant supply as the Society islanders did, who actually planted them in the ground, hoping they would grow like potatoes or any other vegetable, yet such is the value they still set on them, that the fishermen would rather receive a wrought nail, to make of it a fish-hook according to their own taste, than the best English-made fish-hook we could give them.

It has been supposed that the circumstance of Captain Cook's bones being separated, and the flesh taken from them, was evidence of a savage and unrelenting barbarity; but so far from this, it was the result of the highest respect they could show him.

We may also mention here the reason for which the remains of Captain Cook received, as was the case, the worship of a god. Among the kings who governed Hawaii, or an extensive district in the island, during what may in its chronology be called the fabulous age, was *Rono* or *Orono*, who on some account became offended with his wife, and murdered her—but afterward lamented the act so much as to induce a state of mental derangement. In this state he travelled through all the islands, boxing and wrestling with every one he met.

He subsequently set sail in a singularly shaped canoe for Tahiti, or a foreign country. After his departure he was deified by his countrymen, and annual games of boxing and wrestling were instituted to his honour. As soon as Captain Cook arrived, it was supposed and reported that the god Rono was returned; the priests clothed him with the sacred cloth worn only by the god, conducted him to their temples, sacrificed animals to propitiate his favour, and hence the people prostrated themselves before him as he walked through the villages. But when, in the attack made upon him, they saw his blood running, and heard his groans, they said, "No, this is not Rono." Some, however, after his death still supposed him to be Rono, and expected he would appear again. Some of his bones, his ribs, and breast-bone,* were considered sacred, as part of Rono, and deposited in a heiau (temple) dedicated to Rono, on the opposite side of the island. There religious homage was paid to them, and from thence they were annually carried in procession to several other heiaus, or borne by the priests round the island, to collect the offerings of the people for the support of the worship of the god Rono. The bones were preserved in a small basket of wickerwork, completely covered over with red feathers, which in those days were considered to be the most valuable articles the natives possessed.

The missionaries in the Society Islands had, by means of some Sandwich islanders, been long acquainted with the circumstance of some of Capt. Cook's bones being preserved in one of their temples, and receiving religious worship; and since the time of my arrival, in company with the deputation from the London Missionary Society, in 1822, every endeavour has been made to learn, though without success, whether they were still in existence, and where they were kept. All those of whom inquiry has been made have uniformly asserted that they were formerly kept by the priests of Rono, and worshipped, but have never given any satisfactory information as to where they are now. Whenever we have asked the king, or Hevaheva the chief priest, or any of the chiefs, they have either told us they were under the care of those who had themselves said

* Captain King was led to suppose that the bones of the trunk were burnt with the flesh. Part of them probably were so disposed of, but not the whole. It appears that none of them were returned; for, describing those brought to Captain Clarke, which were all they received, he says, "When we arrived at the beach, Eappo came into the pinnace and delivered to the captain the bones, wrapped up in a large quantity of fine new cloth, and covered with a spotted cloak of black and white feathers. We found in it both the hands of Captain Cook entire, which were well known, from a remarkable scar on one of them, that divided the thumb from the forefinger the whole length of the metacarpal bone; the skull, but with the scalp separated from it, and the bones that form the face, wanting; the scalp, with the hair upon it cut short, and the ears adhering to it; the bones of both arms, with the skin of the fore-arms hanging to them; the thigh and leg bones joined together, but without the feet; the ligaments of the joints were entire; and the whole bore evident marks of having been in the fire, except the hands, which had the flesh left upon them, and were cut in several places and crammed with salt, apparently with an intention of preserving them. The lower jaw and feet, which were wanting, Eappo told us had been seized by different chiefs, and that Terreeoboo was using every means to recover them." Speaking of Eappo's first visit after the death of Captain Cook, he says, "We learned from this person that the flesh of all the bodies of our people, together with the bones of the trunks, had been burnt."—Captain King's Continuation of Cook's Voyages, vol. iii. pages 78, 79, and 80.

E 3

they knew nothing about them, or that they were now lost.

The best conclusion we may form is, that part of Captain Cook's bones were preserved by the priests, and were considered sacred by the people, probably till the abolition of idolatry in 1819: that at that period they were committed to the secret care of some chief, or deposited by the priests who had charge of them in a cave, unknown to all besides themselves. The manner in which they were then disposed of will, it is presumed, remain a secret till the knowledge of it is entirely lost. The priests and chiefs always appear unwilling to enter into conversation on the subject, and desirous to avoid the recollection of the unhappy circumstance.

From the above account, as well as every other statement given by the natives, it is evident that the death of Captain Cook was unpremeditated, and resulted from their dread of his anger; a sense of danger, or the momentary impulse of passion, exciting them to revenge the death of the chief who had been shot.

Few intelligent visiters leave Hawaii without making a pilgrimage to the spot where he fell. We have often visited it, and though several natives have been our guides on different occasions, they have invariably conducted us to the same place. A number of cocoanut-trees grow near the shore, and there are perforations through two of them, which the natives say were produced by the balls fired from the boats on the occasion of his death.

We have never walked over these rocks without emotions of melancholy interest. The mind invariably reverts to the circumstances of their discovery, the satisfaction of the visiters, the surprise of the natives, the worship they paid to their discoverer, and the fatal catastrophe which here terminated his days;* and although in every event we acknowledge an overruling Provi-

---

* It will be gratifying to the Christian reader to know that, under the auspices of the governor of the island, and the friendly influence of the present chief of the place, Naihe and his wife Kapiolani, who are steady, intelligent, discreet, and one, if not both, it is hoped, pious persons, a missionary station has since been formed in this village; and that on the shore of the same bay, and not far from the spot where this murderous affray took place, and where Captain Cook was killed, a school has been opened, and a house erected for Christian worship; and that the inhabitants of the neighbourhood are instructed in the elements of learning, and the peaceful principles of the Christian religion; and in their intelligence, cleanliness, order, industry, and good conduct, are exhibiting in a most satisfactory manner its benign effects.

dence, we cannot but lament the untimely end of a man whose discoveries contributed so much to the advancement of science, introduced us to an acquaintance with our antipodes, and led the way for the philosopher in his extended researches, the merchant in his distant commerce, and the missionary in his errand of mercy to the unenlightened heathen at the ends of the earth.

Towards evening we examined another buoa, similar to the one we had passed at Hokukano. On entering it, we found part of a canoe, several calabashes, some mats, tapa, &c., and three small idols about eighteen inches long, carefully wrapped in cloth. The man who accompanied us said, "My father lies here, don't disturb him; I have not yet done weeping for him, though he has been dead some years." We assured him of our sympathy with him in the loss of his father; and having satisfied our curiosity, which he was willing to gratify by allowing us to enter the tomb, we returned to Kamakau's, in conversation with whom we passed the evening. He made many inquiries; such as, if he should bathe on the Sabbath, or eat fish that was caught or brought to him on that day; whether the same body would rise again at the last day; and if the spirit proceeded into the presence of God immediately on quitting the body.

During our journey to-day, we have numbered 443 houses and eight heiaus. In the shade, the thermometer at sunrise stood at 71, at noon 76, at sunset 71.

Much rain fell during the night, but the following morning was bright and serene. It was the Sabbath, and a wide field of usefulness presented its claim to our attention on this holy day, which we felt was to be specially employed in exhibiting to the heathen around the unsearchable riches of Christ.

The village of Kaavaroa, where we lodged, stretched along the north shore of the bay. A number of villages with a considerable population were scattered on the southern shore, and it appeared our duty to go over and preach to them. Mr. Bishop and myself, having procured a canoe from Kamakau, passed over the bay about nine A. M. Messrs. Thurston, Goodrich, and Harwood remained at Kaavaroa, where Mr. Thurston preached to attentive congregations both in the morning and afternoon. The good chief Kamakau was so anxious that his people might profit by the word spoken, that he

could not forbear interrupting the preacher to request
them to be attentive. After the conclusion of the services he also addressed them, and exhorted them to be
in earnest in seeking salvation through Jesus Christ;
and during the day he was frequently engaged in affectionate conversation on religious subjects with his
people.

Landing on the southern shore of Kearake'kua, Mr.
Bishop and I passed through the villages of Kiloa, Wai-
punaula, and Kalama, inviting the people, as we went
along, to attend a religious exercise. At the latter place
we entered a large house, built by Karaimoku's mother,
Kamuaokalani, but at present belonging to Kekauonohi,
his niece. It was the largest in the place; and was
ninety-three feet by thirty in the inside. Here about
three hundred people collected; and I preached to them
from Psalm xxv. 8. After the service, they seemed desirous to enter into conversation on what they had
heard. One man stood up, and called out aloud, " I desire Jehovah, the good Lord, for my God! but we have
no one to tell us about him." In the afternoon we sent
the head man word to collect the people, that they
might hear the word of God again. It rained, but a considerable number soon assembled in the large house, and
I preached to them from 1 Tim. i. 15. Many kept arriving half an hour after the service had commenced, which
induced me to recapitulate the discourse, yet they did
not seem weary. When it was finished, the head man
addressed the people, recommending them to attend to
what they had heard, and proposed that henceforth they
should abstain from all labour on the Sabbath, and pray
to Jehovah and Jesus Christ; assuring them that such
was his own intention. After answering several inquiries, and encouraging them to adopt the proposal that
had been made by the head man, we bade them farewell,
and proceeded to another village.

Two large heaps of ti-root (a variety of dracæna, from
the sweet root of which an intoxicating drink is made),
and one or two vessels of sugar-cane juice in a state of
fermentation, preparatory to its being distilled, were,
during the day, thrown away at this place, in consequence of some public remarks against intoxication.
After leaving Kalama, we walked to Keei, a considerable village on the south point of Kearake'kua bay. As
we approached it, we passed over the ground where,

about forty years ago, Tamehameha encamped with his warriors, previous to his decisive battles with Kivaraao, the son of Taraiopu. On reaching the head man's house, about one hundred people soon collected before the door, and I preached to them from Psalm lxx. 4, concluding, as usual, with prayer. We then went into the house prepared for our lodging, which the good people soon made very comfortable, by spreading some cocoanut leaves on the ground, and covering them with a clean mat. The kind host then proposed to fetch a pig, and have it dressed for supper. We told him we had rather he would not do it on the Sabbath, but that, if agreeable, we should be glad to receive one in the morning. After family worship we laid down on the mats to repose, thankful for the opportunities of doing good which we had enjoyed, and for the encouraging attention manifested by the people.

CHAPTER VI.

Visit to the spot where Capt. Cook was killed—Hawaiian notions of a future state—Account of the battle at Mokuohai—Death of Kaulkeouli—Former prevalence of war in the Sandwich Islands—Warriors—Warlike games—Methods of consulting the gods before determining on war—Human sacrifices—Councils of war—Levying armies—Encampments—Fortifications—Naval fights—Disposition of forces—Weapons—War-dresses—Methods of attack—War-gods carried to battle—Single combats—Sacrificing the slain—Treatment of the vanquished—Manner of concluding peace.

IN the morning of July the 21st, the party at Kamakau's walked through the village of Kaavaroa* to the seaside. The water in some places is deep, and, along the whole extent of the north-west shore, a boat may pull in close to the rocks. The rocks which form the beach, on this and the opposite side of the bay, are not, as was supposed by those who first described them, of black coral, but composed entirely of lava, porous, hard, and of a very dark colour, occasionally tinged with a ferruginous brown, bearing marks of having been in a state of fusion. Part of it has probably flowed through the cavern in which Captain Cook's body was deposited,

* Kowrowa in Cook's Voyages.

as traces of a stream of lava from thence to the plain below are very distinct. The steep rocks at the head of the bay are of the same kind of substance, but apparently more ancient; and judging from appearances, the lava of which they are composed had issued from its volcano before Kearake'kua existed; as part of the coast seems to have been rent from these rocks, and sunk below the level of the sea, which has filled up the indention thus made, and formed the present bay. There are still a number of caves in the face of these rocks, which are seldom resorted to for security in a time of danger, but used as places of sepulture. Several were barricaded, to prevent any but the proprietors entering them, or depositing bodies there. The natives pointed out one in which the remains of Keoua, uncle of Tamehameha, were laid.

Having accomplished the object of their excursion, which was to procure some fragments of the rock on which Captain Cook had been killed, they prepared to return.

On their return, they exchanged a piece of blue cotton, about three yards in length, for four small idols. They were rudely carved imitations of the human figure; one of them between three and four feet in length, the others not more than eighteen inches.

The house in which Mr. Bishop and myself had lodged was early crowded with natives. Morning worship was held in the native language, and a short address given to the people. A very interesting conversation ensued on the resurrection of the dead at the last day, which had been spoken of in the address. The people said they had heard of it by Kapihe, a native priest, who formerly resided in this village, and who, in the time of Tamehameha, told that prince that at his death he would see his ancestors, and that hereafter all the kings, chiefs, and people of Hawaii would live again. I asked them how this would be effected, and with what circumstances it would be attended; whether they would live again on Hawaii, or in Miru, the *Hades* of the Sandwich Islands? They said there were two gods, who conducted the departed spirits of their chiefs to some place in the heavens, where it was supposed the spirits of kings and chiefs sometimes dwelt, and afterward returned with them to the earth, where they accompanied the movements, and watched over the destinies, of their survivors. . The name of one of these gods was *Kaonohio-kala*, the eyeball of the sun ; and of the other, *Kuahairo*. Kapihe was priest to the latter, and, by pretended revelation, informed Tamehameha, that when he should die, Kuahairo would take his spirit to the sky, and accompany it to the earth again, when his body would be re-animated and youthful ; that he would have his wives, and resume his government in Hawaii ; and that, at the same time, the existing generation would see and know their parents and ancestors, and all the people who had died would be restored to life. These, they said, were all the particulars they knew ; but added, that though at Kapihe's suggestion many valuable offerings were made to his god, he proved a false prophet, for Tamehameha died, and did not come to life again.

At breakfast, we were both too ill to partake of the bounty of our host, yet felt grateful for his attention. At nine A. M. we were joined by our companions from Kaavaroa, and shortly after set out on our tour. Mr. Bishop went in the canoe ; the rest of us walked on towards Honaunau, a considerable village about five miles distant.

Leaving Keei, we passed on to Mokuohai, a spot celebrated as the place where, in the year 1780 or 1781, the great battle was fought between *Kauikeouli*,[*] eldest son and successor of Taraiopu, and his cousin *Tamehameha*, by which the latter, though before only possessed of two districts, became sovereign of the whole island. During seven successive days a severe conflict was maintained, with doubtful success. On the morning of the eighth day it was renewed, on both sides, and continued until noon, when the death of Kauikeouli terminated the struggle in favour of his rival. The circumstances attending his death were singular.

Keeaumoku (the father of Kaahumanu, Piia, and Kuakini, present governor of Hawaii), Tamehameha's principal general, with a few of his companions, had advanced a considerable distance beyond the main body of his warriors, and was completely surrounded by Kauikeouli's men. After defending themselves for some time against superior numbers, all the associates of Keeaumoku were slain, he himself was dangerously

[*] Called also Kivarado.

wounded by a number of stabs with the páhoa,* and fell
in the midst of his foes.   His enemies thought him mor-
tally wounded, and were proceeding to despoil him of
his ornaments, &c.   Kauikeouli approached, and called
out to them to take care of the *paraoa*, a finely polished
ornament, made of a whale's tooth, highly valued by the
natives, and worn on the breast, suspended by a necklace of curiously braided human hair, stooping down
himself at the same time to untie it.   Keeaumoku, recovering from a swoon, and seeing Kauikeouli bending
over him, made a sudden spring, and grasped him round
his neck, or (as some of the natives say) by his long
flowing hair, and, being a man of uncommon stature and
strength, held him down.   Kauikeouli endeavoured, but
in vain, to extricate himself from his grasp.   At this instant, Tamehameha and his attendants, having heard that
Keeaumoku had fallen, hastened to the spot, and one
of them, Narimaerua, perceiving the situation of Kauikeouli, rushed forward, and ran a spear through his body;
another stabbed him with a páhoa.   He fell upon the
body of Keeaumoku, and instantly expired.   Keoua, his
uncle, who fought near him, was about the same time
wounded in the thigh by a spear, and obliged to quit the
field.

As soon as the death of Kauikeouli was known, a
panic spread through his men, and they quickly fled.
Many jumped into the sea, and swam to some canoes
lying off the place, and the rest fled to the mountains or
the adjoining puhonua (place of refuge) at Honaunau,
about four miles distant.   Among these was Karaiomoku,
then a youth, now principal chief in the Sandwich
Islands.   Looking one day at the drawing I had made
of the puhonua, he pointed with his finger to the place
by which he entered when fleeing thither for protection.
Tamehameha now remained master of the field, and before evening reached Honaunau, the former residence
of the vanquished chiefs.

The scene of this sanguinary engagement was a large
tract of rugged lava, the whole superficies of which had
been broken up by an earthquake.   Since leaving Keei
we had seen several heaps of stones raised over the
bones of the slain, but they now became much more numerous.   As we passed along, our guide pointed out

* The *páhoa* is a dagger, from eighteen inches to two feet long, made of
wood or iron

the place where Tairi, Tamehameha's war-god, stood, surrounded by the priests, and a little farther on, he showed us the place where Tamehameha himself, his sisters, and friends fought during the early part of the eighth day. A few minutes after we had left it, we reached a large heap of stones overgrown with moss, which marks the spot where Kauikeouli was slain. The numerous piles of stones which we saw in every direction convinced us that the number of those who fell on both sides must have been considerable.

The Sandwich Islands, like many other parts of the world, have frequently felt the cruel scourge of war. Their traditionary history, so far as we have been able to trace it, is distinguished by nothing so much as accounts of the murderous and plundering expeditions of one island against another, or the sanguinary battles between the inhabitants of different parts of the same island. The whole group have seldom, if ever, been united under one authority; but, in general, separate governments and independent kings or chiefs have existed in each of the large islands; and sometimes the six great divisions of Hawaii have been under as many distinct rulers or chieftains. Their inclinations or interests often interfered, and almost every dispute terminated in an appeal to arms. Indeed, a pretext for war was seldom wanting, when one party thought themselves sufficiently powerful to invade with success the territories of their neighbours, and plunder their property. Their modes of warfare must, therefore, necessarily exhibit much of their national character; and having in the course of the narrative already had occasion to describe two of their battles, some account of their system of war will probably be acceptable in this place.

Their armies were composed of individuals from every rank in society. There was no distinct class of men trained exclusively to the use of arms, and warriors by profession, yet there have always been men celebrated for their courage and martial achievements; and there are many now living who distinguished themselves by deeds of valour and strength in the frequent wars which were carried on during the former part of the late Tamehameha's reign; men who left their peaceful home and employment, as agriculturists or fishermen, to follow his fortunes in the field, and resumed their former pursuits on the cessation of hostilities.

Before the introduction of firearms and gunpowder, almost all the men were taught to use the various weapons employed in battle, and frequently engaged in martial exercises or warlike games.

One of the exercises consisted in slinging stones at a mark. They threw their stones with great force and precision, and are supposed to have been able to strike a small stick at fifty yards' distance, four times out of five. They also practised throwing the javelin, and catching and returning those thrown at them, or warding them off, so as to avoid receiving any injury. In this latter exercise, they excelled to an astonishing degree. We know some men who have stood and allowed six men to throw their javelins at them, which they would either catch and return on their assailants, or so dexterously turn aside, that they fell harmless to the ground.

Wrestling was also practised by the more athletic youth, as a preparation to the single combats usual in almost every battle.

Sometimes they had sham-fights, when large numbers engaged, and each party advanced and retreated, attacked and defended, and exercised all the manœuvres employed in actual engagement.

Admirably constituted by nature with finely formed bodies, supple joints, strong and active limbs, accustomed also to a light and cumberless dress, they took great delight in these gymnastic and warlike exercises, and in the practice of them spent no inconsiderable portion of their time.

Whenever war was in contemplation, the *pee kiro* (diviners and priests) were directed to slay the accustomed victims, and consult the gods. Animals only were used on these occasions, generally hogs and fowls. The priests offered their prayers, and the diviners sacrificed the victims, observed the manner in which they expired, the appearance of their entrails, and other signs. Sometimes, when the animal was slain, they embowelled it, took out the spleen, and, holding it in their hands, offered their prayers. If they did not receive an answer, war was deferred. They also slept in the temple where the gods were kept, and after the war-god had revealed his will by a vision or dream, or some other supernatural means, they communicated it to the king and warriors, and war was either determined or relinquished accordingly.

If the expedition in contemplation was of any magnitude or importance, or the danger which threatened imminent, *human* sacrifices were offered, to ensure the co-operation of the war-gods in the destruction of their enemies. They do not appear to have imagined these gods exerted any protecting influence over their devotees, but that their presence and their power destroyed the courage and strength of their enemies, and filled their hearts with terror and dismay. Sometimes the priests proposed that human victims should be slain; sometimes the gods themselves were said to require them, promising victory on condition of their being offered; and at other times they were slain after having consulted the gods as their oracle, and, not having received a favourable answer, they were desirous to consult them again before they abandoned the enterprise. If any of their enemies had been taken captive, the victims were selected from among their number; if not, individuals who had broken tabu, or rendered themselves obnoxious to the chiefs, were fixed upon. A message was sent to the chief under whose authority they were, and at the appointed time he sent his men, who generally despatched them with a stone or club, without any notice, and then carried them away to the temple; sometimes they were bound and taken alive to the heiau, and slain in the outer court, immediately before being placed on the altar. It does not appear that they were slain in the idol's presence, or within the temple, but either on the outside, or at the place where they were first taken; in both cases they appear to have endeavoured to preserve the body entire, or mangled as little as possible. The victims were generally despatched by a blow on the head with a club or stone; sometimes, however, they were stabbed. The number offered at a time varied according to circumstances—two, four, or seven, or ten, or even twenty, we have been informed, have been offered at once. When carried into the temple, every article of clothing they might have on was taken off, and they were laid in a row, with their faces downwards, on the altar immediately before the idol. The priest then, in a kind of prayer, offered them to the gods; and if any offerings of hogs were presented at the same time, they were afterward piled upon them, lying at right angles across the human bodies, where the whole were left to rot and putrefy together.

War was seldom declared without the approbation of the gods, obtained through the medium of the priests, though it is probable the answer of the diviners was given with due regard to the previously known views of the king and chiefs.

Sometimes the question of war or peace was deliberated in a public meeting of chiefs and warriors, and these popular assemblies furnished occasion for the most powerful displays of native eloquence; which, though never present at one of these councils, we should think, from the specimens we have heard repeated, was, like that of their neighbours of the southern isles, at once bold in sentiment, beautiful in imagery, and powerful in effect.

When war was declared, the king and warrior chiefs, together with the priests, fixed the time and place for commencing, and the manner of carrying it on. In the mean time the *Runapai* (messengers of war) were sent to the districts and villages under their authority, to require the services of their tenants, in numbers proportionate to the magnitude of the expedition. These were ordered to come with their weapons, candle-nuts for torches, light calabashes for water, dried fish, or other portable provisions. The summons was in general obeyed with alacrity; and as their spears, clubs, javelins, and slings were usually suspended in some convenient part of every house, they armed with these, and soon joined the forces at the appointed rendezvous.

When the people *en masse* were required, the Tuahaua was sent, whose office it was to bring every individual capable of bearing arms. Sometimes the Uruoki, another officer, was afterward despatched; and if he found any lingering behind who ought to have been with the army, he cut or slit one of their ears, tied a rope round their body, and in this manner led them to the camp. To remain at home when summoned to the field was considered so disgraceful, the circumstances attending detection so humiliating, and the mark of cowardice with which it was punished so indelible, that it was seldom necessary to send round the last-named officer.

These messengers of war were sometimes called Rere, a word which signifies to fly, probably from the rapidity with which they conveyed the orders of the chiefs. They generally travelled at a running pace, and in cases of emergency are reported to have gone round the island of Hawaii in eight or nine days—a distance which, including the circuitous route they would take to call at different villages, exceeds three hundred miles.

When the different parties arrived at the place of rendezvous, the chief of the division or district, with some of inferior rank, waited on the king or commanding chief, and reported the number of warriors they had brought. They then selected a spot for their encampment, and erected their Harepai or Auoro, in which they abode till the army was collected. The former were small huts, built with cocoanut-leaves, or boughs and green ti-leaves, which each party or family erected for their own accommodation around that of their chief, and thus formed a small encampment by themselves. The latter was a large open building, constructed with the same materials, in which the chief and his warriors all dwelt together.

Their camp was near an open space, and they generally selected the most broken and uneven ground, frequently rugged tracts of lava, as their fields of battle. Sometimes they encamped on the banks of a river or deep ravine, which, lying between them and their enemies, secured them from sudden attack. But they do not appear to have thrown up lines or other artificial barriers around their camp; they did not, however, neglect to station pickets at all the passes by which they were likely to be approached. Each party usually had a *pari* or *pakaua*, natural or artificial fortress, where they left their wives and children, and to which they fled if vanquished in the field. These fortresses were either eminences of difficult ascent, and, by walling up the avenues leading to them, sometimes rendered inaccessible; or they were extensive enclosures, including a cave, or spring, or other natural means of sustenance or security. The stone walls around the forts were composed of large blocks of lava, laid up solid, but without cement, sometimes eighteen feet high, and nearly twenty feet thick. On the tops of these walls the warriors fought with slings and stones, or with spears and clubs repelled their assailants. When their pari was an eminence, after they had closed the avenues, they collected large stones and fragments of rock on the edges of the precipices overhanging the path leading to the fortification, which they rolled down on the heads of their enemies.

Sometimes they engaged in fleets amounting to upwards of one hundred canoes on each side. The Sandwich Islands, not being surrounded with coral reefs, there is but little smooth water; and the roughness of the sea, most likely, induced them generally to select terra firma for their theatre of war.

Whenever they expected an action, they proceeded to *hoonoho ka kaua* (fix the war, or set their army in battle array), for which they had a regular system, and adopted various methods for attack and defence, according to the nature of the ground, force of the enemy, &c.

When about to engage in an open plain, their army, drawn up for battle, consisted of a centre and wings, the latter considerably in advance, and the line curved in form of a crescent. The slingers and those who threw the javelin were in general distributed through the whole line. Every chief led his own men to battle, and took his position according to the orders of the commanding chieftain, whose station was always in the centre. The king generally commanded in person, or that authority was exercised by the highest chief among the warriors; occasionally, however, a chief inferior in rank, but distinguished by courage or military talents, has been raised to the supreme command. When they fought in a defile, or narrow pass, in a single column, the first division or advanced guard was called the *verau*, or point, the name they also gave to a bayonet. The other parts of the column were called by different names; the *pohivi*, or shoulder, was generally considered the strongest section. The chief who commanded was in the centre.

Their weapons consisted of the *pololu,* a spear made of hard wood, from sixteen to twenty feet long, and pointed at one end; the *ihe,* or javelin, about six feet in length, made of a species of hard red wood, resembling mahogany, called *kauira,* pointed and barbed; the *raau parau,* a weapon eight or nine feet long, between a club and spear, somewhat resembling a halbert, with which they were accustomed to thrust or strike; and the *pahoa,* or dagger, eighteen inches or two feet in length, made of hard wood, sometimes pointed at both ends, and having a string attached to the handle, which passed round the wrist, to prevent their losing it in action.

Besides these, they employed the sling, and their stones were very destructive. The slings were made of human hair plaited, or the elastic fibres of the cocoanut-husk; the stones they employed were about the size of a hen's egg, generally ponderous pieces of compact lava, from the bed of a stream or the sea-beach, where they had been worn smooth by the action of the water.

They had no shields or weapons of defence, except the javelin, which they used in warding off those that might be thrown at them; they were very expert in avoiding a stone, if they saw it thrown, and the spearmen excelled in parrying the thrusts of their enemies' spears. The warriors seldom went to battle with any other dress than a *maro*, or narrow girdle round their loins. Some, however, wore a quantity of cloth bound round their head, which was called *ahupoonui*, and the chiefs were frequently dressed in their war-cloaks and helmets. The cloaks, though they gave the wearers an imposing appearance, must have proved an encumbrance, without affording much protection. Some of the helmets were made of close wickerwork, exactly fitted the head, and were ornamented along the crown. But those worn by the high chiefs only, and called *mahiori*, though not more useful, were peculiarly beautiful. They were made in the form of the Grecian helmet, with towering crest, and were thickly covered with the glossy red and yellow feathers of a small paroquet found in the mountains (with whose feathers the war-cloaks were also ornamented), and though they did not appear adapted to defend the head, any more than the cloaks were to guard the body, they increased the effect of the towering height and martial air of the chiefs, whose stature was generally above that of the common people. The long cloaks, reaching to the knees, or even to the ankles, were worn only by the king and principal chiefs. The royal colour was yellow, and no one besides the king was allowed to wear a cloak made entirely of yellow feathers. Those of the other chiefs were of red and yellow rhomboidal figures, intermingled or disposed in alternate lines, with sometimes a section of dark purple or glossy black. Tippets were manufactured of the same materials, and worn by the inferior chiefs or some of the principal warriors, whose rank did not entitle them to wear the cloak.

In addition to the helmet and cloak, the high chiefs occasionally wore a *paraoa*, or other ornament, like a breastplate, suspended from the neck by finely braided strings of human hair.

The diviners were consulted immediately before they engaged; they slew their victims, noticed also the face of the heavens, the passage of clouds over the sun, the appearance of the rainbow; and if they augured well, the principal war-god was brought out in the front of the whole army, and placed near the king. The priest then addressed a prayer to the gods, urged them to exercise their power, and prove themselves, in the ensuing engagement, mightier than the gods of their enemies; promising, at the same time, hecatombs of victims in the event of victory. The king, or commander-in-chief, now addressed the assembled warriors; and, if they were to attack, gave the signal for the *hoouta*, or onset, and they rushed to *hui*, or mix in fight.

The national war-god was elevated above the ranks, and carried by the priest near the person of the king, or commander-in-chief. Nor was this the only idol borne to the battle: other chiefs of rank had their war-gods carried near them by their priest; and if the king or chief was killed or taken, the god himself was usually captured also. The presence of their deities inspired the warriors with courage, who supposed their influence essential to victory. A description of Tairi has already been given, and he may be taken as a sample; the image was four or five feet high, the upper part wicker-work, covered with red feathers, the face a hideous form, the mouth armed with triple rows of dog's or shark's teeth, the eyes of mother-of-pearl, the head crowned with a helmet, the crest sometimes formed of long tresses of human hair. We have often conversed with *Hevaheva*, the priest of Tamehameha's war-god, and though there is nothing naturally repulsive in his countenance, we have been told, that, in the battle, he often distorted his face into every frightful form, and uttered most terrific and appalling yells, which were supposed to proceed from the god he bore or attended.

At times the whole army, except the reserve, engaged at once, but their battles were most commonly a succession of skirmishes, or partial engagements. The *hooparau*, single combat, was not unusual. A haughty

and boastful warrior would advance beyond the line
of his companions, and *toho*, or *aa* (insult), in opprobri-
ous terms, his enemies. A warrior from their army
would hasten to meet him, and the encounter was continued till one was disabled or slain. We do not know
whether, like the Grecian heroes, these combatants addressed each other before engaging in the mortal strife,
as did their neighbours in the southern seas,

Their battles were with confused noise, and boastful
shouts. The first that either party slew they called
erehua; frequently the victor jumped upon the expiring
body, or, spurning it contemptuously, dedicated its spirit
to his gods. He then cut or tore off the hair from the
top of the forehead, and elevating it in the air, shouted
aloud, *He oho*, a frontlet; and if it was a chief or warrior of note he had slain, his name was added. *He
oho! He oho!* was reiterated through the ranks of the
victor, while he despoiled the fallen warrior of his ornaments, and then dragged the *heqna*, slain body, to the
king, or the priest, who, in a short address, offered the
victim to his god. The first offering they called *urukoko*,
increasing blood. The second slain was called *maka-
wai*, face of water, and the third *herua-oni*, sand-dug.
They were all likewise brought, and offered to the gods
on the field.

On some occasions, both parties discontinued the
contest, as if by mutual consent, from despair of victory,
or an evil omen revealed by the diviners. Such a battle
was called *rukurua*, both beaten. This, however, was
a rare occurrence; they generally fought till one of the
armies was vanquished. When routed in the field,
some fled to the *pahu tabu*, sacred enclosure, called also
puhonua, or place of refuge; others repaired to their pari
or fortress; and when these were distant, or the way
to them intercepted, they all fled to the mountains,
whither they were pursued by the victors for weeks,
and even months afterward. When discovered, they
were cruelly massacred on the spot, or brought
down to the king and chiefs. When led to the king's
presence, they usually prostrated themselves before
him, and exclaimed, "*E make paha, e ora paha—i runa te
aro? i raro te aro?*" To die perhaps, to live perhaps,—
upwards the face? or downwards the face? If the king
did not speak, or said, "The face down," it was sentence of death, and some one in attendance either

despatched the poor captive in his presence, or led him away to be slaughtered. But if the king said, "Upwards the face," they were spared, though perhaps spared only to be slaves, or to be sacrificed when the priests should require human victims. The persons of the captives were the property of the victors, and their lives entirely at their disposal. A chief taken in the field, or during the retreat, was sometimes spared, and allowed to return to his home.

The victors usually buried their dead; but the bodies of the slain, belonging to the vanquished, were generally left unburied on the field, and were devoured by hogs and dogs, or suffered to rot. Small heaps of stones were afterward piled over their bones, or on the spot where they had fallen, probably as trophies of victory.

When the king or any chief of high rank was known to be humane, or any of the vanquished had formerly been on terms of friendship with him, avoiding carefully the warriors, an individual, risking his life on the conqueror's clemency, would lie in wait for him in his walks, and, prostrating himself in his path, supplicate his compassion, or rush into his house, and throw himself on the ground before him. Though any one might have killed him while on his way thither, none dare touch him within the king's enclosure, without his orders. When the king did not speak, or directed the fugitive to be carried from his presence, which was very unusual, he was taken out and slain. Generally the prince spoke to the individual who had thus thrown himself into his power; and if he did but speak, or only recognise him, he was secure. He might either join the retinue of the sovereign, or return to his own house. No one would molest him, as he was under *maru*, shade, or screening protection, of the king.

When the vanquished were completely routed, or nearly cut off, their country was *hoopahora*, portioned out, by the conqueror, among the chiefs and warriors who had been his companions in the war by whom it was settled. The wives and children of those whom they had defeated were frequently made slaves, and attached to the soil for its cultivation, and, together with the captives, treated with great cruelty. But when there had been a great loss on both sides, or one party wished for peace, an ambassador, with a young plantain-tree, and a green branch of the ti-plant, was sent with

proposals for peace. When these were agreed to, they
all repaired to the temple.... There a pig was slain, its
blood caught in a vessel, and afterward poured on the
ground, probably to signify that thus it should be done
to those who broke the treaty. A wreath of mairi, a
sweet-scented plant, was then woven by the leading
chiefs of both parties, and deposited in the temple.
Peace was ratified, feasting, dances, and public games
followed. The warriors returned to their lands, and the
king's heralds were sent round his districts, to announce
ua pau ka kaua, ended is the war.

The introduction of firearms, which so soon followed
the discovery of the Sandwich Islands, increased the
passion for conquest and plunder in the minds of the
proud and turbulent chiefs, by whom they were governed; and although the recent introduction and partial
reception of Christianity has not induced them to discontinue the practice of war, it has already altered its
ferocious and exterminating character, and the principles of clemency inculcated in the gospel have been
most strikingly exemplified in the humane conduct of
the chiefs by whom it has been embraced.*

There is every reason to hope that Christianity, when
generally received, will subdue their restless and ambitious spirits, and under its influence they may be
expected to delight in the cultivation of the useful arts
of peace.

CHAPTER VII.

Burying-place of the ancient Hawaiian kings—Account of the puhonua, or
city of refuge, at Honaunau—Population of this part of the coast—Advantages of Honaunau for a missionary station—Lodging at Keokea—
Ancient cataract of lava, and irregular vaulted avenue—Journey along the
shore—Mourning ceremonies and customs at the death of the chiefs.

Ever since Saturday last, I had suffered violent pain,
probably induced by the bad water we had been obliged
to drink since leaving Kairua; and shortly after passing
over the battle-ground, I found myself too ill to walk

* After a late civil war in Tauai, when the captives were brought before
Kaahumanu, the chief against whom they had rebelled, he dismissed many of
them with spelling-books, and directed them to go home, and dwell in peace,
cultivate their lands, learn to read and write, and worship the true God.

F 2

any farther. I reclined about an hour on the rocks of
lava, under the shade of a small shrub, and then travelled on slowly to Honaunau, which I reached about
noon. The town contains one hundred and forty-seven
houses; yet we could procure no better accommodation
than what an open house for building canoes afforded.
Here my companions spread a mat on the ground, and
I laid down, grateful for the comfort the shed afforded,
as it screened me from the rays of an almost vertical
sun.

Towards the evening Mr. Thurston preached to the
people of the place, who gave good attention.

After breakfast, Messrs. Thurston and Goodrich examined the inland part of the district, and found, after
proceeding about two miles from the sea, that the
ground was generally cultivated. They passed through
considerable groves of bread-fruit trees, saw many cocoanuts, and numbers of the prickly-pear (*cactus ficus
indicus*) growing very large, and loaded with fruit. They
also found many people residing at the distance of from
two to four miles from the beach, in the midst of their
plantations, who seemed to enjoy an abundance of provisions, seldom possessed by those on the seashore.
They returned about noon.

The night of the 22d was a restless one with us all,
on account of the swarms of vermin that infested our
lodging. We should have been glad to have changed
our quarters, but I was not yet well enough to proceed.

Another day's detention afforded us time for the
more minute examination of whatever was interesting
in the neighbourhood, and the more ample development
of the object of our visit to the people of the village;
and those were the occupations of the day.

Honaunau, we found, was formerly a place of considerable importance, having been the frequent residence of the kings of Hawaii for several successive
generations. The monuments and relics of the ancient
idolatry, with which this place abounds, were, from
some cause unknown to us, spared amid the general destruction of the idols, &c. that followed the abolition
of the ai tabu, in the summer of 1819.

The principal object that attracted our attention was
the *Hare o Keave* (the House of Keave), a sacred deposi-
tory of the bones of departed kings and princes, probably erected for the reception of the bones of the king

whose name it bears, and who reigned in Hawaii about eight generations back. It is a compact building, twenty-four feet by sixteen, constructed with the most durable timber, and thatched with ti-leaves, standing on a bed of lava that runs out a considerable distance into the sea. It is surrounded by a strong fence or paling, leaving an area in the front, and at each end, about twenty-four feet wide. The pavement is of smooth fragments of lava, laid down with considerable skill. Several rudely carved male and female images of wood were placed on the outside of the enclosure; some on low pedestals, under the shade of an adjacent tree; others on high posts, on the jutting rocks that hung over the edge of the water. A number stood on the fence, at unequal distances all around; but the principle assemblage of these frightful representatives of their former deities was at the south-east end of the enclosed space, where, forming a semicircle, twelve of them stood in grim array, as if perpetual guardians of "the mighty dead" reposing in the house adjoining. A pile of stones was neatly laid up in the form of a crescent, about three feet wide, and two feet higher than the pavement, and in this pile the images were fixed. They stood on small pedestals, three or four feet high, though some were placed on pillars, eight or ten feet in height, and curiously carved. The principal idol stood in the centre, the others on either hand; the most powerful being placed nearest to him: he was not so large as some of the others, but distinguished by the variety and superior carvings of his body, and especially of his head. Once they had evidently been clothed, but now they appeared in the most indigent nakedness. A few tattered shreds, round the neck of one that stood on the left-hand side of the door, rotted by the rain, and bleached by the sun, were all that remained of numerous and gaudy garments, with which their votaries had formerly arrayed them. A large pile of broken calabashes and cocoanut-shells lay in the centre, and a considerable heap of dried and partly rotten wreaths of flowers, branches of shrubs and bushes, and fragments of tapa (the accumulated offerings of former days), formed an unsightly mound immediately before each of the images. The horrid stare of these idols, the tattered garments upon some of them, and the heaps of rotting offerings before them, seemed to us no improper emblems of the system they were designed to support; distinguished alike by its cruelty, folly, and wretchedness.

We endeavoured to gain admission to the inside of the house, but were told it was *tabu roa* (strictly prohibited), and that nothing but a direct order from the king, or Karaimoku, could open the door. However, by pushing one of the boards across the doorway a little on one side, we looked in, and saw many large images, some of wood, very much carved, others of red feathers, with distended mouths, large rows of sharks' teeth, and pearl-shell eyes. We also saw several bundles, apparently of human bones, cleaned, carefully tied up with cinet made of cocoanut fibres, and placed in different parts of the house, together with some rich shawls and other valuable articles, probably worn by those to whom the bones belonged, as the wearing apparel and other personal property of the chiefs is generally buried with them.

Adjoining the *Hare o Keave*, to the southward, we found a *pahu tabu* (sacred enclosure) of considerable extent, and were informed by our guide, that it was one of the puhonuas of Hawaii, of which we had so often heard the chiefs and others speak. There are only two on the island; the one which we were then examining, and another at Waipio, on the north-east part of the island, in the district of Kohala.

These *puhonuas* were the Hawaiian cities of refuge, and afforded an inviolable sanctuary to the guilty fugitive who, when flying from the avenging spear, was so favoured as to enter their precincts. This had several wide entrances, some on the side next the sea, the others facing the mountains. Hither the manslayer, the man who had broken a tabu, or failed in the observance of its rigid requirements, the thief, and even the murderer, fled from his incensed pursuers, and was secure. To whomsoever he belonged, and from whatever part he came, he was equally certain of admittance, though liable to be pursued even to the gates of the enclosure. Happily for him, those gates were perpetually open; and as soon as the fugitive had entered, he repaired to the presence of the idol, and made a short ejaculatory address, expressive of his obligations to him in reaching the place with security. Whenever war was proclaimed, and during the period of actual hostilities,

a white flag was unfurled on the top of a tall spear, at
each end of the enclosure, and until the conclusion of
peace, waved the symbol of hope to those who, vanquished in fight, might flee thither for protection. It
was fixed a short distance from the walls on the outside, and to the spot on which this banner was unfurled
the victorious warrior might chase his routed foes; but
here he must himself fall back; beyond it he must not
advance one step, on pain of forfeiting his life. The
priests and their adherents would immediately put to
death any one who should have the temerity to follow
or molest those who were once within the pale of the
pahu tabu; and, as they expressed it, under the shade or
protection of the spirit of Keave, the tutelar deity of
the place.

In one part of the enclosure, houses were formerly
erected for the priests, and others for the refugees, who,
after a certain period, or at the cessation of war, were
dismissed by the priests, and returned unmolested to
their dwellings and families; no one venturing to injure
those who, when they fled to the gods, had been by
them protected. We could not learn the length of time
it was necessary for them to remain in the puahonua;
but it did not appear to be more than two or three days.
After that, they either attached themselves to the service of the priests, or returned to their homes.

The puhonua at Honaunau is capacious, capable of
containing a vast multitude of people. In time of war,
the females, children, and old people of the neighbouring districts were generally left within it, while the
men went to battle. Here they awaited in safety the
issue of the conflict, and were secure against surprise
and destruction, in the event of a defeat.

The form of it was an irregular parallelogram, walled
up on one side and at both ends, the other being formed
by the sea-beach, except on the north-west end, where
there was a low fence. On measuring it, we found it
to be 715 feet in length, and 404 feet wide. The walls
were twelve feet high, and fifteen thick. Holes were
still visible in the top of the wall, where large images
had formerly stood, about four rods apart throughout
its whole extent. Within this enclosure were three
large heiaus, two of which were considerably demolished, while the other was nearly entire. It was a
compact pile of stones, laid up in a solid mass, 126 feet

by 65, and 40 feet high. Many fragments of rock, or pieces of lava, of two or more tons each, were seen in several parts of the wall, raised at least six feet from the ground. The erection of such a place as the puhonua at Honaunau, under the circumstances and with the means by which alone it was reared (as they had no machinery), must have been an Herculean task, and could not have been completed but by the labour of many hands. We could not learn how long it had been standing, but were informed it was built for Keave, who reigned in Hawaii about 250 years ago. The walls and heiaus, indeed, looked as if it might claim such antiquity; but the house of Keave, and the images, must have been renewed since that time.

We had often passed over the ruins of deserted heathen temples, and the vestiges of demolished altars, in the Sandwich Islands, and I had frequently visited those in other groups of the Pacific; but the feelings excited on these occasions had always been those of deep melancholy and horror, at the human immolations and shocking cruelties which they had so often exhibited. Here, however, idolatry appeared at least in the form of clemency, and the sacred enclosure presented a scene unique among the ruins of paganism, which we contemplated with unusual interest.

Whether its establishment was originally projected by the priests, to attach to their interests all who might owe their lives to its institution; or by some mild and humane prince, anxious to diminish the barbarous cruelties of idolatry, and soften the sanguinary character of savage warfare,—or whether derived traditionally from the Israelitish cities of refuge; to which some of its features are strikingly analogous—we do not pretend to determine. However, we could not but rejoice that its abolition was so soon succeeded by the revelation of a refuge more secure,—that the white flag ceased not to wave till another banner was ready to be unfurled, on which was inscribed, "Look unto me, and be ye saved, all the ends of the earth."

Our accommodations at Honaunau were very indifferent. The house where we staid, in addition to other unpleasant circumstances, being entirely open at one end, exposed us by night as well as by day to the unwelcome intrusion of hogs and dogs of every description. As I was able to walk out on the 23d, we resolved to change our lodgings that evening; and about five o'clock in the afternoon we removed nearly half a mile, to a place called Keokea, where we put up in the best house we saw, in hopes of procuring at least a comfortable night's rest. In this, however, we were disappointed, for it rained heavily the greater part of the night, and the roof of the house not being water-proof, we were more than once obliged to shift our mats to different parts of the earthen floor. This was not all: our host, and Makoa our guide, with almost a house-full of natives besides, had been regaling themselves with an immense wooden bowl of fermented juice of the sweet potato, and were very noisy till midnight, when they lay down on their mats, but, to our great annoyance, continued either talking or singing until it was almost day. We frequently spoke to them, and asked them to be still. They answered, "Yes, yes, we will;" but in a few minutes were as boisterous as ever. We were not aware of the intoxicating nature of the simple juice of sweet potatoes, when fermented, till we saw its effects on the party here.

But notwithstanding we were uncomfortable during our short stay at Honaunau, and the people less kind than we usually found them, it appeared to us an eligible place for a missionary station, where one or two devoted men might labour with a prospect of extensive usefulness.

Being sufficiently recovered to proceed on the journey, we left Keokea about eight o'clock on the morning of the 24th. After travelling half a mile, a singular appearance of the lava, at a small distance from the shore, attracted our attention, and on examination presented a curious phenomenon. It consisted of a covered avenue of considerable extent, from fifty to sixty feet in height, formed by the flowing of the lava, in some recent eruption, over the edge of a perpendicular pile of ancient volcanic rocks, from sixty to seventy feet high. It appeared as if, at first, it had flowed over in one vast sheet, but had afterward fallen more slowly, and in detached semifluid masses. These, cooling as they fell, had hardened and formed a pile, which, by continued augmentation from above, had ultimately reached the top, and united with the liquid lava there. It was evident that the lava had still continued to flow, along the outside of the arch thus formed, into the

F 3

plain below, as we observed in several places the
courses of unbroken streams, from the top of the cliff to
the bed of smooth lava, that covered the beach for several miles. The space at the bottom, between the ancient rocks and more recently formed lava, was from
six to twelve feet. On one side, the lava rose perpendicular and smooth, showing distinctly the different and
variously coloured masses of ancient lava of which it
was composed; some of a bright scarlet, others brown
and purple. The whole pile appeared to have undergone, since its formation, the effects of violent heat.
The cracks and hollows, horizontally between the different strata, or obliquely through them, were filled with
lava of a florid red colour, and much less porous than
the general mass. This last kind of lava must have
been brought to a state of most perfect liquefaction, as
it had filled up every crevice that was more than half
an inch wide. It appeared highly glazed, and in some
places we could discover small round pebbles, from the
size of a hazelnut to that of a hen's egg of the same
colour, and having the same vitreous covering, yet
seeming to have remained solid, while the liquid lava
with which they were mixed had been forced by subterranean fire into all the fissures of the ancient rock.

The pile on the other side, formed by the dripping of
the liquid lava from the upper edge of the rocks, presented a striking contrast, but not a less interesting
sight. It was generally of a dark purple or jet black
colour, glittering in the rays of the sun, as if glazed
over with a beautiful vitreous varnish.

On breaking off any fragments, we found them very
porous, and considerably lighter than the ancient lava
on the other side. Its varied forms baffled description,
and were equal to the conceptions of the most fertile
imagination. The archway thus formed continued for
about half a mile, occasionally interrupted by an opening in the pile of recent lava, caused by some projecting rock, or elevation in the precipice above. A spectacle awfully sublime and terrific must have been
presented when this burning stream rolled in one wide
sheet, a fiery cascade, from the lofty steep down upon
the smoking plain.

With what consternation and horror must it have filled
the affrighted inhabitants of the surrounding villages, as
they beheld its irresistible and devastating course, im-

pressed as they were with the belief.that *Pélé*, the goddess whom they had offended, had left her abode in the
volcano, and was in person visiting them with thunder,
lightning, earthquake, and liquid fire, the instruments of
her power and vengeance.

As we passed along this vaulted avenue, called by the
natives Keanaee, we beheld a number of caverns and
tunnels, from some of which streams of lava had flowed.
The mouths of others being walled up with stones, we
supposed they were used as sepulchres.   Mats, spread
upon the slabs of lava, calabashes, &c., indicated some
of them to be the habitations of men; others, near the
openings, were used as workshops, where women were
weaving mats, or beating cloth.   Some we also saw
used as storehouses, or depositories, of sandal-wood.
In many places the water filtered through the lava, and
around the spots where it had dropped on the ground
we observed a quantity of fine white spear-shaped crystals, of a sharp nitrous taste.   Having walked a considerable distance along the covered way, and collected
as many specimens of the lava as we could conveniently
carry, we returned to the seashore.   Mr. Harwood being
indisposed and unable to travel, and being myself but
weak, we proceeded in the canoe to Kalahiti, where we
landed about two P. M., and waited the arrival of our
companions.   The rest of the party travelled along the
shore, by a path often tedious and difficult.   The lava
frequently presented a mural front, from sixty to a hundred feet high, in many places hanging over their heads,
apparently every moment ready to fall; while beneath
them the long rolling billows of the Pacific chafed and
foamed among the huge fragments of volcanic rocks,
along which their road lay.   In many places the lava
had flowed in vast torrents over the top of the precipice
into the sea.   Broad flakes of it, or masses like stalactites, hung from the projecting edge in every direction.
The attention was also attracted by a number of apertures in the face of the rocks, at different distances from
their base, looking like so many glazed tunnels from
which streams of lava had gushed out, and fallen into
the ocean below, probably at the same time that it had
rolled down in a horrid cataract from the lofty rocks
above.

They passed through two villages, containing between
three and four hundred inhabitants, and reached Kala-

hiti about four in the afternoon. Here the people were collected for public worship, and Mr. Thurston preached to them from John vi. 38. They gave good attention, and appeared interested in what they heard. The evening was spent in conversation on religious subjects with those who crowded our lodgings.

At this place we observed many of the people with their hair either cut or shaved close on both sides of their heads, while it was left very long in the middle, from the forehead to the back of the neck. When we inquired the reason of this, they informed us that, according to the custom of their country, they had cut their hair in the manner we perceived on account of their chief, who had been sick, and who they had heard was dead.

The Sandwich islanders observe a number of singular ceremonies on the death of their kings and chiefs, and have been, till very recently, accustomed to make these events occasions for the practice of almost every enormity and vice. The custom we noticed at this place is the most general. The people here had followed only one fashion in cutting their hair, but we have seen it polled in every imaginable form; sometimes a small round place only is made bald, just on the crown, which causes them to look like Romish priests; at other times the whole head is shaved or cropped close, except round the edge, where, for about half an inch in breadth, the hair hangs down its usual length. Some make their heads bald on one side, and leave the hair twelve or eighteen inches long on the other. Occasionally they cut out a patch in the shape of a horse-shoe, either behind or above the forehead; and sometimes we have seen a number of curved furrows cut from ear to ear, or from the forehead to the neck. When a chief, who had lost a relative or friend, had his own hair cut after any particular pattern, his followers and dependants usually imitated it in cutting theirs. Not to cut or shave off the hair indicates want of respect towards the deceased and the surviving friends; but to have it cut close in any form is enough. Each one usually follows his own peculiar taste, which produces the almost endless variety in which this ornamental appendage of the head is worn by the natives during a season of mourning.

Another custom, almost as universal on these occasions, was that of knocking out some of the front teeth,

practised by both sexes, though perhaps most extensively by the men. When a chief died, those most
anxious to show their respect for him or his family
would be the first to knock out with a stone one of
their front teeth. The chiefs related to the deceased,
or on terms of friendship with him, were expected thus
to exhibit their attachment; and when they had done
so, their attendants and tenants felt themselves, by the
influence of custom, obliged to follow their example.
Sometimes a man broke out his own tooth with a stone;
more frequently, however, it was done by another, who
fixed one end of a piece of stick or hard wood against
the tooth, and struck the other end with a stone till it
was broken off. When any of the men deferred this
operation, the women often performed it for them while
they were asleep. More than one tooth was seldom
destroyed at one time; but the mutilation being repeated
on the decease of every chief of rank or authority, there
are few men to be seen, who had arrived at maturity
before the introduction of Christianity to the islands,
with an entire set of teeth; and many by this custom
have lost the front teeth on both the upper and lower
jaw, which, aside from other inconveniences, causes a
great defect in their speech. Some, however, have
dared to be singular; and though they must have seen
many deaths, have parted with but few of their teeth.
Among this number is Karaimoku, a chief next in
authority to the king; not more than one of whose
teeth is deficient.

Cutting one or both ears was formerly practised on
these occasions; but as we never saw more than one or
two old men thus disfigured, the custom appears to have
been discontinued.

Another badge of mourning, assumed principally by
the chiefs, is that of tattooing a black spot or line on the
tongue, in the same manner as other parts of their
bodies are tattooed.

All these usages, though singular, are innocent, compared with others, which, until very recently, were practised on every similar event. As soon as the chief had
expired, the whole neighbourhood exhibited a scene of
confusion, wickedness, and cruelty, seldom witnessed
even in the most barbarous society. The people ran to
and fro without their clothes, appearing and acting more
like demons than human beings; every vice was prac-

tised, and almost every species of crime perpetrated.
Houses were burnt, property plundered, even murder
sometimes committed, and the gratification of every
base and savage feeling sought without restraint. In-
juries or accidents, long forgotten perhaps by the offending party, were now revenged with unrelenting
cruelty. Hence many of the people of Maui, dreading
their recurrence, when Keopuolani was thought to be
near her end, took their effects into the enclosure belonging to the missionaries there, and requested permission to remain there, hoping to find a sanctuary
within their premises amid the general devastation
which they expected would follow her decease.

The inhabitants of several groups in the Pacific have
mourning ceremonies somewhat resembling these. The
Friendly islanders cut off a joint of one of their fingers
at the death of a chief, and, like the Society islanders,
out their temples face, and bosoms with shark's teeth.
The latter also, during their *otohaa*, or mourning, commit almost as many depredations as the Sandwich
islanders. They have, however, one very delicate
method of preserving the recollection of the dead, which
the latter do not appear to employ; that is, of having a
small portion of the hair of the deceased passed through
a perforation in one of their ears, ingeniously braided in
the form of an earring, and worn sometimes for life.

But the Sandwich islanders have another custom,
almost peculiar to themselves, viz. singing at the death
of their chiefs, something in the manner of the ancient
Peruvians. I have been peculiarly affected more than
once on witnessing this ceremony.

A day or two after the decease of Keeaumoku, governor of Maui, and the elder brother of Kuakini, governor
of Hawaii, I was sitting with the surviving relatives,
who were weeping around the couch on which the
corpse was lying, when a middle-aged woman came in
at the other end of the large house, and, having proceeded about half-way towards the spot where the body
lay, began to sing in a plaintive tone, accompanying her
song with affecting gesticulations, such as wringing her
hands, grasping her hair, and beating her breasts. I
wrote down her monody as she repeated it. She described in a feeling manner the benevolence of the deceased, and her own consequent loss. One passage was
as follows —

Ue, ue, ua mate tuu Arü,	Alas, alas, dead is my chief,
Ua mate tuu hatu e tuu hoa,	Dead is my lord and my friend,
Tuu hoa i ta wa o ta wi,	My friend in the season of famine,
Tuu hoa i paa ta aina,	My friend in the time of drought,
Tuu hoa i tuu ilihune,	My friend in my poverty,
Tuu hoa i ta uä e ta matani,	My friend in the rain and the wind,
Tuu hoa i ta vera o ta la,	My friend in the heat and the sun,
Tuu hoa i ta anu o ta mouna,	My friend in the cold from the mountain,
Tuu hoa i ta ino,	My friend in the storm,
Tuu hoa i ta marie,	My friend in the calm,
Tuu hoa i mau tai awaru,	My friend in the eight seas;*
Ue, ue, ua hala tuu hoa,	Alas, alas, gone is my friend,
Aohe e hoi hou mai.	And no more will return.

Other exhibitions of a similar kind I witnessed at Maui. After the death of Keopuolani, we frequently saw the inhabitants of a whole district, that had belonged to her, coming to weep on account of her death. They walked in profound silence, either in single file, or two or three abreast, the old people leading the van, and the children bringing up the rear. They were not covered with ashes, but almost literally clothed in sackcloth. No ornaments, or even decent piece of cloth, was seen on any one. Dressed only in old fishing-nets, dirty and torn pieces of matting, or tattered garments, and these sometimes tied on their bodies with pieces of old canoe-ropes, they appeared the most abject and wretched companies of human beings I ever saw. When they were within a few hundred yards of the house where the corpse was lying, they began to lament and wail. The crowds of mourners around the house opened a passage for them to approach it, and then one or two of their number came forward, and standing a little before the rest, began a song or recitation, showing her birth, rank, honours, and virtues, brandishing a staff or piece of sugar-cane, and accompanying their recitation with attitudes and gestures expressive of the most frantic grief. When they had finished, they sat down, and mingled with the thronging multitudes in their loud and ceaseless wailing.

* A figurative term for the channels between the different islands of the group.

Though these ceremonies were so popular, and almost
universal, on the decease of their chiefs, they do not appear to have been' practised by the common people
among themselves.   The wife did not knock out her
teeth on the death of her husband, nor the son his when
he lost his father or mother; neither did parents thus
express their grief when bereaved of an only child.
Sometimes they cut their hair, but in general only
indulged in lamentations and weeping for several days.

Anxious to make ourselves acquainted with their reasons for these practices, we have frequently conversed
with the natives respecting them.   The former, such as
polling the hair, knocking out the teeth, tattooing the
tongue, &c., they say, is designed to show the loss they
have sustained, and perpetually to remind them of their
departed friends.   Kamehamaru, queen of Rihoriho,
who died on her recent visit to England, gave me a fine
answer to this effect, on the death of Keopuolani, her
husband's mother.   A few days after the interment, I
went into a house where a number of chiefs were assembled for the purpose of having their tongues tattooed;
and the artist was performing this operation on hers
when I entered.   He first immersed the face of the instrument, which was a quarter of an inch wide, and set
with a number of small fish-bones, into the colouring-
matter, placed it on her tongue, and, giving it a quick
and smart stroke with a small rod in his right hand,
punctured the skin and injected the die at the same time.
Her tongue bled much, and a few moments after I entered
she made a sign for him to desist.   She emptied her
mouth of the blood, and then held her hands to it to coun-
teract the pain.   As soon as it appeared to have subsided
a little, I remarked that I was sorry to see her following
so useless a custom : and asked if it was not exceedingly
painful?   She answered, *He eha nui no, he nui roa ra kuu
aroha!*   Pain, great indeed; but greater my affection!
After further remarks, I asked some of the others why
they chose that method of showing their affectionate
remembrance of the dead?   They said, *Aore roa ia e
naro!*   That will never disappear, or be obliterated!

Another method very generally practised by all classes
on these occasions was that of burning on their skin a
large number of semicircles, disposed in different forms.
It was not done by a heated iron, but having stripped
the bark from a small branch of a tree, about an inch in

diameter, they held it in the fire till one end of the bark was perfectly ignited, and in this state applied it to the face or bosom, which instantly raised the skin, and after the blister had subsided, the sears remained a number of days.

We never found any apologists for the enormities practised on these occasions; and the only excuse they have ever given has been, that at the death of a great chief, the paroxysm of grief has been so violent as to deprive the people of their reason; hence they neither knew nor cared what they did, being *hehena*, frantic, or out of their senses, through sorrow.

Since the introduction of the gospel by Christian missionaries, or rather since the death of Keopuolani, in September, 1813, all the wicked practices, and most of the ceremonies, usual on these occasions, have entirely ceased. Knocking out the teeth is discontinued; wailing, cutting the hair, and marking the tongue are still practised; but all the evil customs have been most strictly forbidden by the principal chiefs.

CHAPTER VIII.

Singular pillars of lava—Scarcity of fresh water—Division of Kona—Appearance of the south-west part of the island—Keauaiai—Missionary labours at Patini—Beautiful spouting of water through the lava—Appearance of the southern extremity of Hawaii—Inland route to Kaura—Description of the mountain taro—A congregation of natives at Paapohatu—Valley of Waiohinu—Account of the Pahe, a native game—Conversation respecting the abolition of idolatry, with the people at Kapauku—Superstitions connected with Kaverohea—Reception at Honuapo.

WE took leave of the friendly people of Kalahiti about nine A. M. on the 25th. Messrs. Thurston, Bishop, and Goodrich continued their journey along the shore, and I went in the canoe in company with Mr. Harwood. The coast along which we sailed looked literally ironbound. It was formed of steep rocks of porphyritic lava, whose surface wore the most rugged aspect imaginable. About two P. M. we reached *Tavreonanahoa*, three large pillars of lava, about twenty feet square, and apparently sixty or eighty high, standing in the water, within a few yards of each other, and adjacent to the shore. Two of them were united at the top, but open at their base. The various coloured strata of black, reddish, and brown lava, being distinctly marked, looked like so many courses of masonry. We sailed between them and the mainland; and about five in the afternoon landed at Kapua, a small and desolate-looking village, on the south-west point of Hawaii, and about twenty miles distant from Kalahiti. Here we had the canoe drawn up on the beach until our companions should arrive.

After leaving Kalahiti, Messrs. Thurston, Goodrich, and Bishop proceeded over a rugged tract of lava, broken up in the wildest confusion, apparently by an earth-quake, while it was in a fluid state. About noon they passed a large crater. Its rim, on the side towards the sea, was broken down, and the streams of lava issuing thence, marked the place by which its contents were principally discharged. The lava was not so porous as that at Keanaee, but, like much in the immediate vicin-ity of the craters, was of a dark red, or brown ferru-ginous colour, and but partially glazed. It was exceed-ingly ponderous and compact; many fragments had quite a basaltic shape, and contained quantities of olivine, of a green and brown colour. For about a mile along the coast, they found it impossible to travel without making a considerable circuit inland; they therefore procured a canoe, and passed along the part of the coast where the sea rolled up against the naked rocks; and about one P. M. landed in a very high surf. To a spec-tator on the shore their small canoe would have seemed every moment ready to be buried in the waves; yet by the dexterity of the natives they were safely landed, with no other inconvenience than a slight wetting from the spray of the surf.

Mr. Thurston preached to the people at the place where they landed, after which they took some refresh-ment, and kept on their way over the same broken and rugged tract of lava, till about six P. M., when they reached Honomalino. Here they were so much fatigued with the laborious travelling of the past day, that they were obliged to put up for the night. They procured a little sour poë, and only a small quantity of brackish water. Having conducted family worship with the people of the place, they laid themselves down to rest on their mats, spread on the small fragments of lava of which the floor of the house was composed.

Early the next morning the party at Honomalino proceeded to Kapua, and about eight A. M. joined those who had slept there.

At this place we hired a man to go about seven miles into the mountains for fresh water; but he returned with only one calabash full; a very inadequate supply, as our whole company had suffered much from thirst and the effects of the brackish water we had frequently drunk since leaving Honaunau. Nothing can exceed the barren and solitary appearance of this part of the island, not only from the want of fresh water, but from the rugged and broken tracts of lava of which it appears to be entirely composed.

Unwilling to spend the Sabbath in the desolate and almost forsaken village of Kápua, we prepared for a long day's journey, as we knew of no village before us containing more than five or six houses for nearly thirty miles' distance.

Before we left Kapua, we were so favoured as to procure water enough to fill our canteens, and about ten A. M. resumed our journey. Messrs. Thurston, Bishop, and Goodrich walked on by the seaside. About noon they reached Kaulanamauna, and shortly after left Kona and entered Kaü.

Kona is the most populous of the six great divisions of Hawaii; and being situated on the leeward side, would probably have been the most fertile and beautiful part of the island, had it not been overflowed by floods of lava. It is joined to *Kohala*, a short distance to the southward of Towaihae bay, and extends along the western shore between seventy and eighty miles, including the irregularities of the coast. The northern part, including Kairua, Kearake'kua, and Honaunau, contains a dense population, and the sides of the mountains are cultivated to a considerable extent; but the south part presents a most inhospitable aspect. The population is thin, consisting principally of fishermen, who cultivate but little land, and that at the distance of from five to seven miles from the shore.

The division of Kaü commences at Kaulanamauna, runs down to the south point of the island, and stretches about forty miles along the south-east shore. On enter-

ing it, the same gloomy and cheerless desert of rugged
lava spread itself in every direction from the shore to
the mountains. Here and there, at distant intervals,
they passed a lonely house, or a few wandering fishermen's huts, with a solitary shrub, or species of thistle,
struggling for existence among the crevices in the blocks
of scoriæ and lava. All besides was "one vast desert,
dreary, bleak, and wild."

In many places all traces of a path entirely disap-
peared; for miles together they clambered over huge
pieces of vitreous scoriæ, or rugged piles of lava, which,
like several of the tracts they had passed in Kona, had
been tossed in its present confusion by some violent
convulsion of the earth.

From the state of the lava covering that part of the
country through which we have passed, we should be
induced to think that eruptions and earthquakes had
been, almost without exception, concomitants of each
other; and the shocks must have been exceedingly violent to have torn the lava to pieces, and shaken it up in
such distorted forms as we everywhere beheld.

Slabs of lava, from nine to twelve inches thick, and
from four to twenty or thirty feet in diameter, were frequently piled up edgewise, or stood leaning against several others piled up in a similar manner. Some of them
were six, ten, or twelve feet above the general surface,
fixed in the lava below, which appeared to have flowed
round their base, and filled up the interstices occasioned
by the separation of the different pieces. One side of
these rugged slabs generally presented a compact,
smooth, glazed, and gently undulated surface, while the
other appeared rugged and broken, as if torn with violence from the viscid mass to which it had tenaciously
adhered. Probably these slabs were raised by the expansive force of the heated air beneath the sheet of
lava.

After about eighteen miles of most difficult travelling,
they reached *Keavaiti*, a small opening among the rocks,
where, in case of emergency, a canoe might land in
safety. Here they found Mr. Harwood and myself
waiting; for after leaving Kapua we had sailed along
close to the shore, till the wind, becoming too strong
for us to proceed, we availed ourselves of the opening
which Keavaiti afforded to run the canoe ashore, and
wait till the wind should abate; though, in so doing, we

were completely wet with the surf, and spoiled the provisions we had on board.

The wind was still too strong to allow the canoe to proceed on her voyage, and those who had travelled by land felt too much fatigued to go on without refreshment and rest. Desirous of spending the Sabbath with the people at Tairitii, which was still fourteen or fifteen miles distant, we determined to rest a few hours, and then prosecute our journey by moonlight.

A number of conical hills, from one hundred and fifty to two hundred feet high, rose immediately in our rear, much resembling sandhills in their appearance. On examination, however, we found them composed of volcanic ashes and cinders, but could not discover any mark of their having been craters.

When those of our party who had travelled by land had recovered a little from their fatigue, we partook of such refreshment as remained, and drank the little fresh water we had brought with us in the canoe. Being only about a quart between five persons, it was a very inadequate supply in such a dry and thirsty land; yet we drank it with thankfulness, hoping to procure some at Tairitii early on the following morning.

By the time we had finished our frugal meal, the shades of evening began to close around us. We called our little party together, and after committing ourselves and those who travelled with us to the watchful care of our merciful Father, we spread our mats on the small pieces of lava, and lay down to rest under the canopy of heaven. A pile of blocks of scoriæ and lava, part of which we had built up ourselves, screened our heads from the winds. The thermometer at sunset stood at 73°; yet during the evening the land wind from the snow-covered top of Mouna Roa blew keenly down upon us. We slept, however, tolerably well till midnight, when the wind from the shore being favourable, and the moon having risen, we resumed our voyage.

I went with Mr. Harwood in the canoe to Tairiti, which we reached a short time before daybreak; but the surf rolling high, we were obliged to keep off the shore until daylight enabled us to steer between the rocks to the landing place. Some friendly natives came down to the beach and pointed out the passage; by their aid we landed in safety about half-past five in the morning of the 27th. Our first inquiry was for water; Mauaa, the governor's man, soon procured a calabash full, fresh and cool, of which we drank most copious draughts, then filled the canteens, and preserved them for those who were travelling along the shore.

About half-past eight, Mr. Thurston hastily entered the house; his first expressions were, " Have you got any water ?" A full canteen was handed to him, with which he quenched his thirst, exclaiming, as he returned it, that he had never in his life before suffered so much for want of water. When he first discovered the houses, about two miles distant, he felt his thirst so great, that he left his companions and hastened on, running and walking till he reached the place. After leaving Kea-vaiti, Messrs. Bishop, Goodrich, and Thurston travelled over the rugged lava, till the moon, becoming obscured by dark heavy clouds, they were obliged to halt under a high rock of lava, and wait the dawn of day, for they found it impossible to proceed in the dark, without being every moment in danger of stumbling over the sharp projections of the rocks, or falling into some of the deep and wide fissures that intersected the bed of lava in every direction. After waiting about an hour, they resumed their journey; and Messrs. Bishop and Goodrich reached Tairitii nearly half an hour after Mr. Thurston's arrival.

At 10 A. M. Mr. Thurston preached to the people of Tairitii and the neighbouring village of Patini, all of whom are fishermen. They behaved with propriety, and appeared interested. We had sent out Makoa, our guide, soon after our arrival, to inform the people that there would be a religious meeting, and invite their at. tendance. He had gone much farther than we expected he would; and just as Mr. Thurston had finished his sermon, he returned, followed by a considerable company from an inland settlement, who, to use their own words, had come to hear about Jehovah and Jesus Christ. They seemed disappointed at finding the service over. As they said they could not wait till the evening, they and the people of the village assembled in a large canoe-house, and Mr. Thurston preached again of salvation through Jesus Christ. They sat very quietly, and lis-tened with apparent attention. After they had spent an hour or two in conversation with us, they returned, seemingly interested in what they had heard. In the afternoon Mr. Thurston preached a third time. Between seventy and eighty were present. With most of those who have attended the public worship in this place, this day was probably the first time they ever heard of Jehovah the living God, or Jesus Christ the Saviour. We could not but desire and pray that the Holy Spirit might make the word spoken in this distant and desolate part of the earth the power of God to the salvation of many that heard it.

July 28th.—During the whole of yesterday, a beautiful spouting of the water had attracted our attention, which we found was produced in a manner similar to that we had witnessed at Kairua. The aperture in the lava was about two feet in diameter, and every few seconds a column of water was thrown up with considerable noise, and a pleasing effect, to the height of thirty-five or forty feet. The lava at this place was very ancient, and much heavier than what we had seen in Kona. The vesicles in it were also completely filled with olivine, which appeared in small, green, hard, transparent crystals, in such quantities as to give the rocks quite a green appearance; some of the olivine was brown. In this neighbourhood we also discovered large masses of porphyritic lava, containing crystals of felspar and olivine in great quantities, and apparently black schorls. The trade-winds, blowing along the shore very fresh, and directly against us, obliged us to leave our canoe at this place. Mauae and his companions, having drawn it into an adjacent shed, took off the out-rigger and left it, together with the mast, sails, and paddles, in the care of the man at whose house we had lodged: as he was also desirous to see the volcano, and, after an absence of several years, to revisit Kaimu, in the division of Puna, the place of his birth, he prepared to accompany us by land.

Hitherto we had travelled along the seashore, in order to visit the most populous villages in the districts through which we had passed. But here receiving information that we should find more inhabitants a few miles inland than nearer the sea, we thought it best to direct our course towards the mountains. Makoa, our guide, procured men to carry our baggage, and at nine A. M. we left Tairitii. Our way lay over a bed of ancient lava, smooth, considerably decomposed, and generally covered with a thin layer of soil. We passed along the edge of a more recent stream of lava, rugged, black, and appalling in its aspect, compared with the tract we were walking over, which here and there showed a green tuft of grass, a straggling shrub, or a creeping convolvulus. After travelling about a mile, we reached the foot of a steep precipice. A winding path led to its top, up which we pursued our way, occasionally resting beneath the shade of huge overhanging rocks. This precipice is about three hundred feet high, and the rocks, on fracture, proved a dark gray kind of lava, more compact than that on the adjacent plain. The whole pile appears to have been formed by successive eruptions from some volcano in the interior, as there appeared to be a thin layer of soil between some of the strata, or different inundations, which we supposed had been produced by the decomposition of the lava on the surface of the lower stratum, before it was overflowed by the superincumbent mass. The rocks appeared to have been rent in a line from the seashore towards the mountains, and probably the same convulsion which burst the rocks asunder, sank the plain to its present level. In half an hour we reached its summit.

A beautiful country now appeared before us, and we seemed all at once transported to some happier island, where the devastations attributed to Nahoaarii and Pélé, deities of the volcanoes, had never been known. The rough and desolate tract of lava, with all its distorted forms, was exchanged for the verdant plain, diversified with gently rising hills, and sloping dales, ornamented with shrubs, and gay with blooming flowers. We saw, however, no stream of water during the whole of the day; but, from the luxuriance of the herbage in every direction, the rains must be frequent, or the dews heavy. About noon we reached Kalehu, a small village upwards of four miles from Tairitii. The kind cottagers brought us some fine water-melons, which afforded us a grateful repast, while we rested during the heat of the noonday sun.

Between sixty and seventy persons collected around the house in which we were sitting, and as I was so far recovered as to be able to preach, I addressed them from Matt. i. 21. They seemed interested, and afterward said that they had heard good news. We remained about an hour, conversing on some of the first principles of the religion of Jesus Christ, and then resumed our journey over the same beautiful country, which was partially cultivated, and contained a numerous, though scattered population. The prospect was delightful. On one hand, the Pacific dashed its mighty waves against the rocky shore, and on the other, the *kuahivi* (mountain ridges) of Kaū, and snow-topped Meuna Roa, rose in the interior, with lofty grandeur. Our path led us through several fields of mountain taro (a variety of the arum), extensively cultivated in many parts of Hawaii. It was growing in a dry sandy soil, into which our feet sank two or three inches every step we took. The roots were of an oblong shape, generally from ten inches to a foot in length, and four or six inches in diameter. Seldom more than two or three leaves were attached to a root, and those of a light green colour, frequently blotched and sickly in their appearance. The inside of the root is of a brown or reddish colour, and much inferior to that of the *arum esculentum*, or lowland taro. It is, however, palatable, and forms a prime article of food in those parts of the island where there is a light soil, and but little water.

Between three and four o'clock in the afternoon we reached Kauru, a small village environed with plantations, and pleasantly situated on the side of a wide valley, extending from the mountains to the south point of the island. As the men with our baggage had not come up, we waited about two hours, when Tuite, the head man of the village, arrived, and pressed us to spend the night at his house. We accepted his invitation, and proposed to him to collect the people of the village together, to hear about the true God. He consented, and a little before sunset about a hundred and fifty assembled in front of his house. Mr. Thurston, after the usual devotional exercises, preached to them for about half an hour, and they paid great attention.

At the request of Makoa, Tuite furnished men to carry our baggage to the next district, and soon after daylight on the 29th we left Kauru, and taking an inland direction, travelled over a fertile plain, covered with a thin yet luxuriant soil. Sometimes the surface was strewed with small stones, or fragments of lava, but in general it was covered with brushwood.

The population in this part did not appear concentrated in towns and villages, as it had been along the seashore, but scattered over the whole face of the country, which

appeared divided into farms of varied extent, and upon
these the houses generally stood singly, or in small
clusters, seldom exceeding four or five in number.

After walking six or seven miles, we entered the district of Papapohaku.   When we had nearly passed
through it, we sat down to rest, on a pile of stones by
the way-side.   Between sixty and seventy natives soon
collected around us; presenting a motley group.   Most
of the children were naked, or at best had only a narrow
slip of tapa fastened round their waists.   Several of the
men, on seeing us pass along the road, had left their
work in the fields and gardens, and, although covered
with dust and perspiration, had seated themselves in
the midst, with their o-os* in their hand.   Their only
clothing was the maro, a narrow girdle worn round the
loins, one end of which passes between the legs, and
fastens in front. The old men were most of them
dressed in a *kihei*, as were also some of the women, but
many of the latter wore only a *pau* of native cloth wound
round their bodies.   Their black hair was in several
instances turned up, and painted white all round the
forehead, with a kind of chalk or clay, which is found
in several parts of the island.   Many also wore a small
looking-glass, set in a solid piece of wood, and suspended on the bosom by a handkerchief, or strip of native cloth, fastened round the neck, to which was sometimes added another article, considered equally useful,
and not less ornamental; namely, a small wooden, brass-
tipped tobacco-pipe; the looking-glass and tobacco-
pipe were sometimes combined in one ornament.   Most
of these people had probably never seen so large a
company of foreigners before; and their curiosity, as
might be expected, was unusually excited.   Their countenances, however, indicated no feelings of jealousy,
but manifested a degree of pleasure greater than ordinary.   After conversing with them some time, on the
objects of our tour, and their ideas of the true God, we
proposed to them to listen to his word, and unite with
us in worshipping him.   They seated themselves on
the grass.   We sang a hymn, and I preached, from
Psalm cxxviii. 1.   At the conclusion of our religious

* This o-o is the principal implement of husbandry which a Hawaiian
farmer uses.   Formerly it was a sharp-pointed stick of hard wood; it is now
usually pointed with iron.   The best are made with broad socket chisels, into
which they fix a handle four or six feet long.

service, we resumed our journey, several of the natives following us to the next village.

Our path, running in a northerly direction, seemed leading us towards a ridge of high mountains, but it suddenly turned to the east, and presented to our view a most enchanting valley, clothed with verdure, and ornamented with clumps of kukui and kou trees. On the south-east it was open towards the sea, and on both sides adorned with gardens, and interspersed with cottages, even to the summits of the hills. A fine stream of fresh water, the first we had seen on the island, ran along the centre of the valley, while several smaller ones issued from the rocks on the opposite side, and watered the plantations below. We drank a most grateful draught from the principal stream, and continuing our way along its margin, through Kiolaakaa, travelled towards the sea, till we reached Waiohinu, about ten miles from the place where we slept last night. Here we found a very comfortable house, belonging to Pai, the head man, who invited us in, and kindly entertained us. About noon, a hospitable dinner was prepared, of which, with the additional luxury of fresh water, we made a comfortable meal. At two o'clock in the afternoon, the people of the place were collected outside of the house; and when we had requested them to sit down, we held a religious exercise similar to that in the morning. Much conversation followed, on the subject of religion. They said they had heard of *Iého* (Jehovah) our God, but had never before heard of Jesus Christ; that, until now, they did not know there was a Sabbath-day, on which they ought not to work, but that hereafter they would recollect and observe it. They wished, they said, to become good men, and to be saved by Jesus Christ. Between three and four o'clock we took leave of them, and pursued our journey towards the seashore. Our road, for a considerable distance, lay through the cultivated parts of this beautiful valley: the mountain taro, bordered by sugar-cane and banana, was planted in fields six or eight acres in extent, on the sides of the hills, and seemed to thrive luxuriantly.

In our way, we passed over a *tahua páhe*, or páhe floor, about fifty or sixty yards long, where a number of men were playing at páhe, a favourite amusement with farmers, and common people in general. The

páhe is a blunt kind of dart, varying in length from two
to five feet, and thickest about six inches from the point,
after which it tapers gradually to the other end.   These
darts are made with much ingenuity, of a heavy wood.
They are highly polished, and thrown with great force
or exactness along the level ground, previously prepared
for the game.   Sometimes the excellence of the play
consists in the dexterity with which the páhe is thrown.
On these occasions two darts are laid down at a certain
distance, three or four inches apart, and he who, in a
given number of times, throws his dart most frequently
between these two, without striking either of them, wins
the game.   At other times it is a mere trial of strength;
and those win who, in a certain number of times,
throw their darts farthest.   A mark is made in the
ground, to designate the spot from which they are to
throw it.   The players, balancing the páhe in their
right hand, retreat a few yards from this spot, and then,
springing forward to the mark, dart it along the ground
with great velocity.   The darts remain wherever they
stop, till all are thrown, when the whole party run to
the other end of the floor to see whose have been the
most successful throws.   This latter game is very laborious; yet we have known the men of whole districts
engage in it at once, and have seen them playing several hours together, under the scorching rays of a vertical
sun.

On the same tahua, or floor, they also play at another
game, resembling the páhe, which they call *maita* or *uru
maita*.   Two sticks are stuck in the ground only a few
inches apart, at a distance of thirty or forty yards, and
between these, but without striking either, the parties
at play strive to throw their stone; at other times, the
only contention is, who can bowl it farthest along the
tahua, or floor.   The *uru*, which they use instead of a
dart, is a circular stone, admirably adapted for rolling,
being of compact lava, or a white alluvial rock (found
principally in the island of Oahu), about three or four
inches in diameter, an inch in thickness around the
edge, but thicker in the centre.   These stones are
finely polished, highly valued, and carefully preserved,
being always oiled and wrapped up in native cloth, after
having been used.   The people are, if possible, more
fond of this game than of the páhe; and the inhabitants
of a district not unfrequently challenge the people of

the whole island, or the natives of one island those of all the others, to bring a man who shall try his skill with some favourite player of their own district or island. On such occasions we have seen seven or eight thousand chiefs and people, men and women, assembled to witness the sport, which, as well as the páhe, is often continued for hours together.

Many of these amusements require great bodily exertion; and we have often been struck with the restless avidity and untiring effort with which they pursue even the most toilsome games. Sometimes we have expressed our surprise that they should labour so arduously at their sport, and so leisurely at their plantations or houses, which, in our opinion, would be far more conducive to their advantage and comfort. They have generally answered, that they built houses and cultivated their gardens from necessity, but followed their amusements because their hearts were fond of them. There are some few who play merely for pleasure; but the greater part engage in it in hopes of gain.

Were their games followed only as sources of amusement, they would be comparatively harmless; but the demoralizing influence of the various kinds of gambling existing among them is very extensive. Scarcely an individual resorts to their games but for the purpose of betting; and at these periods all the excitement, anxiety, exultation, and rage which such pursuits invariably produce are not only visible in every countenance, but fully acted out, and all the malignant passions which gambling engenders are indulged without restraint. We have seen females hazarding their beads, scissors, cloth-beating mallets, and every piece of cloth they possessed, except what they wore, on a throw of the *uru* or *páhe*. In the same throng might be frequently seen the farmer, with his *o-o*, and other implements of husbandry; the builder of canoes, with his hatchets and adzes; and some poor man, with a knife, and the mat on which he slept,—all eager to stake every article they possessed on the success of their favourite player; and when they have lost all, we have known them, frantic with rage, tear their hair from their heads on the spot. This is not all; the sport seldom terminates without quarrels, sometimes of a serious nature, ensuing between the adherents of the different parties.

Since schools have been opened in the islands, and

the natives have been induced to direct their attention
to Christian instruction and intellectual improvement,
we have had the satisfaction to observe these games
much less followed than formerly; and we hope the
period is fast approaching when they shall only be the
healthful exercises of children; and when the time and
strength devoted to purposes so useless, and often injurious, shall be employed in cultivating their fertile soil,
augmenting their sources of individual and social happiness, and securing to themselves the enjoyment of the
comforts and privileges of civilized and Christian life.

After travelling about an hour, through a country
which appeared more thickly inhabited than that over
which we had passed in the morning, we came to Kapauku, a pleasant village belonging to Naihe. As we
passed through it, we found tall rows of sugar-cane
lining the path on either side, and beneath their shade we
sat down to rest. A crowd of natives soon gathered
around us; and after a little general conversation, we
asked them who was their god? They said they had
no god; formerly they had many, but now they had
cast them all away. We asked them if they had done
well in abolishing them? They said, Yes, for the tabu
occasioned much labour and inconvenience, and drained
off the best of their property. We asked them if it
was a good thing to have no god, and to know of no
being to whom they ought to render religious homage?
They said, perhaps it was, for they had nothing to provide for the great sacrifices, and were under no fear of
punishment for breaking tabu; that now, one fire cooked
their food, and men and women ate together the same
kind of provisions.

We asked them if they would not like to hear about
the true God, and the only Saviour? They said they
had heard of Jesus Christ, by a boy belonging to Naihe,
who came from Oahu about two months ago; but he had
not told them much, and they should like to hear something more. I then requested them to sit down, and
preached to them on the way of salvation by Jesus
Christ. When the service was ended, many involuntarily exclaimed, "Nui roa maitai! E ake makou i kanaka
makou no Jesu, a i ora roa ia ia:" It is greatly good!
We wish to become the people of Jesus Christ, and to
be saved everlastingly by him.—We recommended them
to think on his love, and to love him in return; to obey

him; to keep the Sabbath-day, by abstaining from
labour; and, meeting together, to talk about what they
had heard; to ask God in prayer to teach them all his
righteous will; and to send to Naihe their chief, or the
missionaries at Oahu, for books, and a person to instruct
them.

Bidding them farewell, we directed our course towards the shore, and in about half an hour came to
Honuapo, an extensive and populous village, standing
on a level bed of lava which runs out a considerable
distance into the sea. As we approached this place,
the natives led us to a steep precipice overhanging the
waves, and pointed out a rock in the water below, called
Kaverohea. They seemed to regard both the place
where we were and the rock below with strong feelings of superstition; at which we were not surprised,
when they informed us that formerly a jealous husband,
who resided a short distance from the place, murdered
his wife in a cruel manner with a stone, and afterward
dragged her down to the spot where we stood, and
threw her into the sea; that she fell on the rock which
we saw, and immediately afterward, while he stood
ruminating on what he had done, called out to him in
the most affectionate and lamentable strains, attesting
her innocence of the crime for which she had been
murdered. From that rock, which is still called by her
name, they said her voice was often heard calling to her
husband, and there her form was sometimes seen.
They also informed us, that her lamentations were considered by them as ominous of some great disaster; as
of war, or famine, or the death of a distinguished chief.
We told them it was in imagination only that she was
seen, and that her supposed lamentations were but the
noise of the surf, or the whistling of the winds.

From the manner in which we were received at Honuapo, we should not think this village had been often
visited by foreigners; for on our descending from the
high land to the lava on which the town stands, the natives came running out to meet us from all quarters, and
soon gathered so thickly around us, that we found it
difficult to proceed. Boys and girls danced and hal-
looed before us; vast numbers walked by our side, or
followed us, occasionally taking us by the hand, or
catching hold of some part of our clothes. They
seemed surprised at our addressing them in their own

tongue, but were much more so when Maaae, who preceded us with a large fan in his hand, told them we were
teachers of religion,—that we had preached and prayed
at every place where we had stopped, and should most
likely do so there before we slept.

We passed through the town to the residence of the
head-man, situated on the farthest point towards the
sea.   He invited us to his house, procured us water to
wash our feet, and immediately sent to an adjacent pond
for some fish for our supper. While that was preparing,
the people assembled in crowds around the house, and
a little before sunset, Mr. Thurston preached to them in
the front yard.   Upwards of two hundred were present,
and during the whole of the service, sat quietly, and
listened attentively, .

A number of the people at this place had one of
their lips tattooed, after the manner of some of the
New-Zealand-tribes.   There was more tattooing here
than we had observed at any other place ; but it was
rudely done, displaying much less taste and elegance
than the figures on the bodies of either the New-Zea-
landers, Tahitians, or Marquesians, which are sometimes
really beautiful.

After the service, some of our number visited the
ruins of a heiau, on a point of lava near our lodging.
During the evening, on making some inquiries respecting it, we found it had been dedicated to Tairi, and was
thrown down in the general destruction of idols, in
1819.   They seemed to think it was well that idolatry
had been prohibited by the king ; said its frequent requisitions kept them very poor, and occasioned them much
labour.   They were, as might be expected, almost entirely ignorant of the religion of Jesus Christ.   And
from what we saw and heard on first arriving among
them, we should fear they were much degraded by im-
morality and vice.

One man only from this place had been at Oahu, since
the king had been favourably disposed towards Christianity : while there, he once attended public worship in
the native language, and heard about Jesus Christ, the
God of the foreigners ; but had given a very imperfect
account of him.   The people seemed inclined to listen
attentively to what was said about salvation through
the Redeemer ; and though fatigued by our journey,
and exercises with the inhabitants of the different places

where we had stopped during the day, we esteemed it
a privilege to spend the evening in conversation on a
topic of so much interest and importance, and experienced no small degree of pleasure, while endeavouring
to convey to their uninformed, but apparently inquiring,
minds a concise and simple view of the leading doctrines and duties of our holy religion. At a late hour,
we asked them to unite with us in our evening worship,
and afterward lay down to rest. Many of the people
in the house, however, continued talking till almost
daylight. The attention given by the people to our instructions is not to be considered as evidencing their
conversion to Christianity, or indicating any decisive
change in their views or feelings, but is merely noticed
as a pleasing manifestation of their willingness to
listen to the truths we are desirous to promulgate
among them.

CHAPTER IX.

Makoa objects to visiting the volcano—Account of the defeat and assassina-
tion of Keoua—Superstitions connected with the pebbly beach at Ninole
—Hospitality of the natives—Methods of dressing the taro—Distant indications of the volcano at Kirauea—Visit to the burning chasm at Ponahohoa
—Journey from Kapapala—Lodging in a cavern—Reflection from the volcano by night.

On the morning of the 30th, we arose much refreshed,
but Makoa not having arrived with our baggage, we did
not leave Honuapo so early as we could have wished.
Great numbers of the people crowded our house at an
early hour, and while breakfast was preparing, they
were addressed from Ps. xcvi. 4. When the service
was ended, the people were anxious to know more
about these things; some time was therefore spent in
conversation with them. We had seldom seen any who
appeared more interested in the truths of the gospel
than the people of Honuapo.

About eight A. M. Makoa arrived, but without our
baggage. The men who were bringing it, he said,
could not be persuaded to come on last night, but had
set out this morning, and would soon overtake us. We
now acquainted him with our intention to visit the vol-
G 3

cano, and requested him to hasten on the men with our
baggage, as we should want more things there than we
could conveniently carry. He objected strongly to our
going thither, as we should most likely he mischievous,
and offend Pélé or Nahoaarii, deities of the volcano, by
plucking the *ohelo* (sacred berries), digging up the sand,
or throwing stones into the crater, and then they would
either rise out of the crater in volumes of smoke, send
up large stones to fall upon us and kill us, or cause
darkness and rain to overtake us, so that we should
never find our way back. We told him we did not
apprehend any danger from the gods; that we knew
there were none; and should certainly visit the volcano.
If we were determined on going, he said, we must go
by ourselves; he would go with us as far as Kapapala,
the last village at which we should stop, and about
twenty miles on this side of it; from thence he would
descend to the seashore, and wait till we overtook
him. The governor, he said, had told him not to go
there, and if he had not, he should not venture near it,
for it was a fearful place.

We waited till after nine o'clock, when, the men not
arriving with our baggage, we proceeded on our way,
leaving Makoa to wait for them, and come after us as
far as Kapapala, where we expected to spend the night.
As we walked through the village, numbers of the
people came out of their houses, and followed us for a
mile or two, after which they gradually fell behind.
When they designed to leave us, they would run on a
little way before us, sit down on a rock, give their parting aroha as we passed, and continue to follow us with
their eyes till we were out of sight.

After travelling some time over a wide tract of lava,
in some places almost as rugged as any we had yet
seen, we reached Hokukaho. Here we found an excellent spring of *fresh* water, the first we had yet seen
on our tour, though we had travelled upwards of a hundred miles. While we were stopping to drink, and rest
ourselves, many natives gathered around us from the
neighbourhood. We requested them to accompany us
to a cluster of houses a little farther on, which they
very cheerfully did; and here I addressed them, and invited all who were athirst, and whosoever would, to
come and take of the water of life freely. They
sat quietly on the lava till the concluding prayer was

finished, when several simultaneously exclaimed, "*He mea maitai ke ora, e maitemake au :*" A good thing is salvation; I desire it. They then proposed several questions, which we answered apparently to their satisfaction, and afterward kept on our way.

We travelled over another rugged tract of lava about two hundred rods wide. It had been most violently torn to pieces, and thrown up in the wildest confusion; in some places it was heaped forty or fifty feet high. The road across it was formed of large smooth round stones, placed in a line two or three feet apart. By stepping along on these stones, we passed over, though not without considerable fatigue. About half-past eleven we reached Hilea, a pleasant village belonging to the governor. As we approached it, we observed a number of artificial fish-ponds, formed by excavating the earth to the depth of two or three feet, and banking up the sides. The sea is let into them occasionally, and they are generally well stocked with excellent fish of the mullet kind. We went into the house of the head man, and asked him to collect the people together, as we wished to speak to them about the true God. He sent out, and most of the people of the village then at home, about two hundred in number, soon collected in his house, which was large; where Mr. Thurston preached to them. They appeared gratified with what they had heard, and pressed us very much to spend the day with them. We could not consent to this, as we had travelled but a short distance since leaving Honuapo. The head man then asked us to stop till he could prepare some refreshment; saying, he had hogs, fish, taro, potatoes, and bananas in abundance. We told him we were not in need of any thing, and would rather go on. He said, probably the governor would be angry with him, banish him, or perhaps take off his head, when he should hear that he had not entertained his friends as they passed through the place. We ate a few ripe plantains which he placed before us, and then took our leave, assuring him that we would speak to the governor on the subject of taking off his head, &c. This in some measure seemed to satisfy him, and after accompanying us a short distance, he gave us his *aroha,* and returned.

As we left Hilea, our guide pointed out a small hill, called Makanau, where *Keoua,* the last rival of Tameha-

meha, surrendered himself up to the warriors under
Taiana, by whom he had been conquered in two successive engagements. He was the younger brother of
Kauikeoule, the eldest son and successor of Taraiopu.
After the battle of Keei, in which his brother was slain,
he fled to *Hiro*, the large eastern division of the island.
The warriors of Hiro, with those of *Puna*, and some
parts of Kaü, on the south-east, together with those of
part of Hamakua, on the north-east, declared themselves in his favour, as the immediate descendant of
Taraiopu. Among them he resided several years, undisturbed by Tamehameha, frequently making attacks
on the northern and western parts of the island, in
which, however, he was generally repulsed with loss.
Notwithstanding the defeats he had experienced, he was
still desirous to obtain the sovereignty of the whole
island, to the throne of which he considered himself the
legitimate heir; and in the year 1789 marched from Hiro
with all his forces to attack Kaü and Kona, on the
western shores. He took the inland road, and on his
way across the island halted for the night in the vicinity
of the volcano. An eruption took place that very night,
and destroyed the warriors of two small villages, in all
about eighty men. This was considered an ill omen.
He however continued his march, and shortly after
reached Taisitii. Here he was met by a body of Tamehameha's warriors under Taiana, a chief of whom frequent mention is made in Meare's and Dixon's voyages.
An engagement took place, in which he was defeated,
and obliged to retreat towards Hiro. The victorious
party pursued, and overtook him at Puakokoki, in the
division of Puna, where another battle was fought, in
which his forces were totally routed, and almost all of
them slain. He saved himself by flying to the mountains attended by a few of his kahu, or faithful companions. Taiana and his warriors returned to Waiohinu,
there to remain till the place of his retreat should be
discovered.
  After some time, Keoua, Kaoreioku his younger
brother, and a few friends that were with them, came
to Makanau. From hence he despatched a messenger
to Taiana, requesting permission to pass to the seashore, in order that he might go and surrender himself
to Tamehameha, who was then at Towaihae. Taiana
and the rest of the warriors agreed to allow him to pass

unmolested through their camp, and Keaveaheuru, the father of Naihe, present chief of Kaavaroa, and Kamahoe, father of Hoapiri, two near relatives of Keoua, though attached to Tamehameha, went back to assure him of his safety, and of the friendly feelings of Tamehameha towards him. He accompanied them to Tairitii, where they embarked in Taiana's canoes, and directed their course along the western shores to Towaihae. On their way he stopped at several places, particularly Honomalino, Honaunau, Kaavaroa, Keauhou, and Kairua. The people at each of the places, at Honaunau in particular, crowded around him, brought him presents of food, hogs, tapa, and fruits, and, by every means in their power, demonstrated their attachment to him. Many of them wept; some on account of the joy they felt at seeing him again, others from a foreboding fear of the result of his surrender to Tamehameha. He stopped two nights at Paraoa, a small village a few miles to the southward of Towaihae, where he received the greatest assurances of Tamehameha's kind intentions; and on the morning of the third day proceeded to Towaihae. Tamehameha, with his chiefs, was standing on the beach as his canoe came in sight, and, with most of the chiefs, intended to protect him; but Keeaumoku, a chief of the most sanguinary disposition, who had grappled with his elder brother in the battle at Keei, had determined on his death; and fearing Tamehameha might frustrate his purpose, if the canoe was allowed to land, he waded above his middle into the sea; and, regardless of the orders of Tamehameha, and the expostulations of the other chiefs, caught hold of the canoe as it approached the shore, and, either with his pahoa or a long knife, stabbed Keoua to the heart as he sat in the stern. He also murdered seven of his companions and friends, who came in the same canoe. In another canoe was Kaoreioku his younger brother, and the father of Panahi, one of the wives of Rihoriho, the late sovereign of the islands. Tamehameha gave strict orders to protect it, and their lives were spared. Tamehameha and many of the chiefs, particularly Keaveaheuru and Kamahoe, are reported to have regretted his death. Keeaumoku, however, justified his horrid act by saying, that if Keoua had been allowed to live, they should never have been secure.

We had not travelled far before we reached Ninole, a

small village on the seashore, celebrated on account of a short pebbly beach called Koroa, the stones of which were reported to possess very singular properties; among others, that of propagating their species. The natives told us it was a *wahi pana* (place famous) for supplying the stones employed in making small adzes and hatchets before they were acquainted with the use of iron; but particularly for furnishing the stones of which the gods were made who presided over most of the games of Hawaii. Some powers of discrimination, they told us, were necessary to discover the stones which would answer to be deified. When selected, they were taken to the heiau, and there several cere- monies were performed over them. Afterward, when dressed, and taken to the place where the games were practised, if the parties to whom they belonged were successful, their fame was established; but, if unsuc- cessful for several times together, they were either broken to pieces, or thrown contemptuously away. When any were removed for the purpose of being trans- formed into gods, one of each sex was generally selected; these were always wrapped very carefully together in a piece of native cloth. Afer a certain time they said a small stone would be found with them, which when grown to the size of its parents, was taken to the heiau, or temple, and afterward made to preside at the games.

We were really surprised at the tenacity with which this last opinion was adhered to, not only by the poor people of the place, but by several others, with whom we have since conversed, and whom we should have supposed better informed. It required all the argument and ridicule that we could employ to make them believe it could not possibly be so. Koroa was also a place of importance in times of war, as the best stones used in their slings were procured here.

This place is also celebrated as furnishing the small black and white stones used by the natives in playing at *konane*, a native game, resembling drafts, and apparently more intricate. The konane-board is generally two feet long, and contains upwards of two hundred squares, usually fourteen in a row. It is a favourite amusement with the old men; and we have known one game, com- menced early in the morning, hardly concluded on the same day.

We examined some of the stones. The black ones

appeared to be pieces of trap, or compact lava. The
white ones were branches of white coral, common to all
the islands of the Pacific. The angles of both were
worn away; and the attrition occasioned by the con-
tinual rolling of the surf on the beach had also given
them a considerable polish.

After travelling about two miles, we came to Punaruu,
where the people of that and the next village, Wailau,
collected together in a large house, and were addressed
on the nature and attributes of the true God and the
way of salvation. In general, speaking to the people
in the open air was preferred, as we then had more
hearers than when we addressed them in a house. But
in the middle of the day we usually found it too hot to
stand so long in the sun. The services which we held
in the morning and evening were always out of doors.

We now left the road by the seaside, and directed our
course towards the mountains. Our path lay over a
rich yellow-looking soil of decomposed lava, or over a
fine black vegetable mould, in which we occasionally
saw a few masses of lava partially decomposed, sufficient to convince us that the whole had once been
overflowed, and that lava was the basis of the whole
tract of country. There was but little cultivation,
though the ground appeared well adapted to the growth
of all the most valuable produce of the islands. After
walking up a gentle ascent about eight miles, we came
to a solitary hamlet called Makaaka, containing four or
five houses, in which three or four families were
residing.

The house which we entered was large, and beneath
one roof included their workshop, kitchen, and sleeping-
room, without any intervening partitions. On one side,
two women were beating native cloth, and the men
were at work on a new canoe. In the same place were
several larger ones, one upwards of sixty feet long, and
between two and three feet deep, hollowed out of a single
tree. The workmen told us they were making a pair
of that size for Kaikioeva, guardian of the young prince
Kauikeouli, whose tenants they were.

Near the south end of the house, which was quite open,
stood their fireplace, where a man was preparing a
quantity of arum or taro for the oven. The roots were
oblong, from six inches to a foot in length, and three or
four inches in diameter. The substance of the root is

somewhat like that of a potato, but more fibrous; and to the taste, before dressed, is exceedingly pungent and acrid. The tender leaves of this plant are sometimes wrapped up in plantain leaves, baked, and eaten by the natives; but in general the root only is used as an article of food. The oven was a hole in the earth, three or four feet in diameter, and nearly a foot deep. A number of small stones were spread over the bottom, a few dried leaves laid on them, and the necessary quantity of sticks and firewood piled up, and covered over with small stones. The dry leaves were then kindled, and while the stones were heating, the man scraped off the skin or rind of the taro with a shell, and split the roots into two or three pieces. When the stones were red-hot, they were spread out with a stick, the remaining fire-brands taken away, and when the dust and ashes on the stones at the bottom had been brushed off with a green bough, the taro, wrapped in leaves, was laid on them till the oven was full, when a few more leaves were spread on the taro; hot stones were then placed on these leaves, and a covering six inches thick, of leaves and earth, spread over the whole. In this state the taro remained to steam or bake about half an hour, when they opened their oven, and took as many roots as were needed. The arum or taro is an excellent vegetable, boiled as we are accustomed to dress potatoes, but is not so farinaceous and pleasant as when baked in a native oven. Sometimes the natives broil their food on heated stones, or roast it before their fire; but these ovens are most generally used for cooking their several kinds of victuals. Potatoes and yams are dressed in the same manner as the taro; but pigs, dogs, fish, and birds are wrapped in green leaves before they are put into the oven.

We saw some Muscovy ducks in the garden, and offered to purchase one; but they said they were rearing them for their landlord, and could not part with any; they furnished us, however, with a fowl, with which, and some buiscuit we had with us, we made a tolerable meal. We remained about two hours, during which we did not omit to speak to the inhabitants respecting the Saviour. We also offered to remunerate them for what we had received, but they refused to take any thing. We therefore made the children a present of a looking-glass and a few strings of beads, and then resumed our journey over the same verdant country, frequently crossing small valleys and watercourses, which, however, were all dry.

The surface of the country was covered with a light yellow soil, and clothed with tall grass, but the sides and bed of every watercourse we passed were composed of volcanic rock, a kind of basaltes, or dark-gray compact lava, with fine grains of olivine, the different strata lying in a direction gently inclined towards the sea.

The land, though very good, was but partially cultivated, till we came to Kaaraara, where we passed through large fields of taro and potatoes, with sugar-cane and plantains growing very luxuriantly. Maruae, the chief of the place, came down to the roadside as we passed by, and asked us to stay for the night at his house; but as Kapapala was only four miles distant, we thought we could reach it before dark, and therefore thanked him, and proposed to walk on. As our boys were tired with their bundles, we asked him to allow a man to carry them to Kapapala. He immediately ordered one to go with us, and we passed on through a continued succession of plantations, in a high state of cultivation.

During the whole of the time we had been travelling on the high land, we had perceived a number of columns of smoke and vapour rising at a considerable distance, and also one large steady column, that seemed little affected by the wind; and this, we were informed, arose from the great crater at Kirauea. The smaller columns were emitted at irregular intervals of several seconds between each. On inquiry we learned that they arose from deep chasms in the earth, and were accompanied by a hot and sulphureous vapour. About seven o'clock in the evening we reached Kapapala, and directed our weary steps to the house of Tapuahi, the head man. He kindly bade us welcome, spread a mat in the front of his house for us to sit down upon, and brought us a most agreeable beverage, a calabash full of good cool fresh water.

The thermometer at sunset stood at 70°, and we sat for some time talking with the people around us. The air from the mountains, however, soon began to be keen. We then went into the house, and although we were in a tropical climate, in the month of July, we found a fire very comfortable. It was kindled in a hollow place in the centre of the earthen floor, surrounded by large square stones, and gave both light and heat. But as there was only one aperture, which, as in the houses of the ancient Britons, answered the triple purpose of a door, a window, and a chimney, the smoke was sometimes rather troublesome.

Few of the Hawaiian females are without some favourite animal. It is usually a dog. Here, however, we observed a species of pet that we had not seen before. It was a curly-tailed pig, about a year and a half old, three or four feet long, and apparently well fed. He belonged to two sisters of our host, who formed part of his family, and joined the social circle around the evening hearth.

In the neighbourhood of Kapapala we noticed a variety of the paper-mulberry, somewhat different from that generally cultivated, which grew spontaneously, and appeared indigenous. Large quantities of the dried bark of this plant, tied up in bundles, like hemp or flax, were piled up in the house where we lodged. It is used in manufacturing a kind of tapa, called mamake, prized throughout the islands on account of its strength and durability.

About eight o'clock a pig was baked, and some taro prepared by our host for supper. At our particular request, he was induced to partake of it, though contrary to the etiquette of his country. When we had finished, Tupuahi and his household assembled for family worship; after which we retired to rest. We had travelled more than twenty miles, and two of our number had, since the morning, spoken four times to the people.

Soon after sunrise on the 31st, the people of the place were collected around our house. I requested them to sit down in front, and, after singing a hymn, preached to them a short and plain discourse. Mr. Thurston concluded the service with prayer. The people remained in the place nearly an hour, and made many inquiries.

After breakfast three of our number went to visit the places where we had seen the columns of smoke rising yesterday; and having travelled about five miles, over a country fertile and generally cultivated, we came to *Ponahohoa*. It was a bed of ancient lava, the surface of which was decomposed; and in many places shrubs and trees had grown to a considerable height.

As we approached the places whence the smoke issued, we passed over a number of fissures and deep chasms, from two inches to six feet in width. The whole mass of rocks had evidently been rent by some violent convulsion of the earth, at no very distant period; and when we came in sight of the ascending columns of smoke and vapour, we beheld immediately before us a valley, or hollow, about half a mile across, formed by the sinking of the whole surface of ancient lava, to a depth of fifty feet below its original level. Its superficies was intersected by fissures in every direction; and along the centre of the hollow, two large chasms, of irregular form and breadth, were seen stretching from the mountain towards the sea, in a south-by-west direction, and extending either way as far as the eye could reach. The principal chasm was in some places so narrow that we could step over it, but in others it was ten or twelve feet across. It was from these wider portions that the smoke and vapours arose.

As we descended into this valley, the ground sounded hollow, and in several places the lava cracked under our feet. Towards the centre it was so hot that we could not stand more than a minute in the same place. As we drew near one of the apertures that emitted smoke and vapour, our guide stopped, and tried to dissuade us from proceeding any farther, assuring us he durst not venture nearer, for fear of Pélé, the deity of the volcanoes. We told him there was no Pélé of which he need be afraid; but that if he did not wish to accompany us, he might go back to the bushes at the edge of the valley, and await our return. He immediately retraced his steps, and we proceeded on, passing as near some of the smoking fissures as the heat and sulphureous vapour rising from them would admit. We looked down into several, but it was only in three or four that we could see any bottom. The depth of these appeared to be about fifty or sixty feet, and the bottoms were composed of loose fragments of rocks and large stones, that had fallen in from the top or sides of the chasm. Most of them appeared to be red-hot, and we thought we saw flames in one; but the smoke was generally so dense, and the heat so great, that we could not look long, nor see very distinctly the bottom of any of them. Our legs, hands, and faces were nearly scorched by the heat. Into one of the small fissures we put our thermometer, which

had stood at 84°; it instantly rose to 118°, and probably
would have risen much higher, could we have held it
longer there.

After walking along the middle of the hollow for
nearly a mile, we came to a place where the chasm was
about three feet across at its upper edge, though apparently much wider below, and about forty feet in
length; and from which a large quantity of lava had
been recently vomited. It had been thrown in detached
semifluid pieces to a considerable distance in every
direction, and from both sides of the opening had flowed
down in a number of smaller streams.

The appearance of the tufts of long grass through
which it had run—the scorched leaves still remaining
on one side of a tree, while the other side was reduced
to charcoal, and the strings of lava hanging from some
of the branches like stalactites—together with the fresh
appearance of the shrubs, partially overflowed and
broken down,—convinced us that the lava had been
thrown out only a few days before. It was highly scoriaceous, of a different kind from the ancient bed of
which the whole valley was composed, being of a jet-
black colour, and bright variegated lustre, brittle, and
porous; while the ancient lava was of a gray or reddish
colour, compact, and broken with difficulty. We found
the heat to vary considerably in different parts of the
surface; and at one of the places, where a quantity of
lava had been thrown out, and from which a volume of
smoke continually issued, we could stand several minutes
together, without inconvenience. We at first attributed
this to the subterranean fires having become extinct beneath; but the greater thickness of the crust of ancient
lava at that place afterward appeared to us the most
probable cause, as the volumes of smoke and vapour
which constantly ascended indicated the vigorous action
of fire below. I took a drawing of this place; and when
we had collected as many specimens of the lava as we
could conveniently carry back to our lodgings, we returned to our guide, whom we found waiting at the spot
where we first entered the hollow.

As he was a resident in Kapapala, and owned a small
garden near, we endeavoured to learn from him something of the history of the phenomenon before us. He
told us that the two large chasms were formed about
eleven moons ago; that nothing else had been visible

till nearly two moons back, when a slight earthquake
was experienced at Kapapala, and the next time he came
by, the ground had fallen in, forming the hollow that
we saw, which also appeared full of fissures. About
three weeks ago, as he was going to his plantation, he
said, he saw a small flame issuing from the apertures,
and a quantity of smoking lava all around; the branches
of the trees that stood near were also broken and
burnt, and several of them still smoking.

Having gratified our curiosity, we prepared to leave
this infant volcano, for such to us it appeared. Although
the surface, at least, of the whole country around had a
volcanic origin, it seems to have remained undisturbed
for a number of years, perhaps ages. The lava is decomposed, frequently a foot in depth, and is mingled
with a prolific soil, fertile in vegetation, and profitable
to its proprietors; and we felt a sort of melancholy interest in witnessing the first exhibitions of returning
action after so long a repose in this mighty agent, whose
irresistible energies will, probably, at no very remote
period, spread desolation over a district now smiling in
verdure, repaying the toils and gladdening the heart of
the industrious cultivator.

Ponahohoa, the place we had visited, is situated in
the district of Kapapala, in the north-east part of the
division of Kaü, and is, as near as we could judge, from
ten to twelve miles from the seashore, and about
twenty miles from the great volcano at the foot of
Mouna Roa.

The road by which we returned lay through a number
of fields of mountain taro, which appears to be cultivated
here more extensively than the sweet potato.

On the edge of one of these fields we sat down in the
grass to rest, beneath a clump of beautiful trees, the
erythrina corollodendrum, a tree we frequently met with
in the mountains, sometimes covered with beautiful
flowers, and always affording an agreeable shade. It
is called by the natives *oviriviri*, or *viriviri*. Its branches
are much used in erecting fences, on account of the
readiness with which they take root when planted in the
ground. The wood is also employed for making the
carved stools placed under their canoes, when drawn
on the beach, or laid up in their houses. The best kind
of surf-boards are also made of this wood, which is
lighter than any other the natives possess.

On our way back we also passed several hills, whose broad base and irregular tops showed them originally to have been craters. They must be very ancient, as they were covered with shrubs and trees. From them must have come the then molten, but now indurated, flood over which we were travelling. Several small columns of smoke were seen rising near them, from fissures recently made.

About two P. M. we reached our lodgings, and dismissed the man who had shown us the way, with a remuneration for his trouble.

Between three and four o'clock in the afternoon of the 31st of July, a party of travellers, consisting of four men and a woman, entered the house in which we were stopping, and sat down to rest. We soon learned that they belonged to Kearakomo, in Puna, whither they were going, by a road that also led to the great volcano; and having before experienced the great inconvenience of travelling without a guide over a country of which we were entirely ignorant, it appeared desirable that some of us, at least, should go with them. We expressed our intention to accompany them. They were pleased, and told us they would wait till we were ready.

No tidings had yet been received of Makoa or our baggage, our biscuit was nearly expended, and being without even a change of linen, we did not think it expedient to leave this place altogether before our baggage should arrive, especially as we knew it would be several days before we should reach any of the villages on the shores of Puna. Messrs. Bishop and Goodrich, therefore, thought best to wait at least another day, while the rest proceeded with the travellers.

Having made this arrangement, we immediately packed up our provisions, which were but a scanty supply, and filled our canteens with water. The natives filled their calabashes; and about five P. M., Messrs. Thurston, Harwood, and myself left Kapapala in company with the people of Puna. We proceeded a short distance to a place called Kapuahi (the hearth of fire), where we stopped at the entrance of a large cave, arched over by a thick crust of ancient lava. Here two or three families, consisting of men, women, and children, were residing. Its interior was rather dark, as the entrance was the only aperture that admitted light; yet the inhabitants of this dreary abode seemed cheerful and con-

tented, and perhaps felt themselves favoured by Péle, in
having a permanent abode furnished free of labour or
expense. The women were employed in making mats
and beating tapa; the children were playing among the
fragments of lava on the outside; and the men were preparing an oven in which to bake some taro. We wished
to purchase a few fowls of them, but they had none to
dispose of. They gave us, however, two or three roots
of taro and a draught of excellent spring-water. Bidding
them farewell, we pursued our way over a beautiful
country, gradually sloping towards the right, and meeting the ocean, at a distance of from ten to fifteen miles,
rising more abruptly on the left, where it was crowned
with the woods, which extended like a vast belt round
the base of the greater part of Mouna Roa. Large slabs
of indurated vesicular lava occasionally appeared amid
the shallow but fertile soil spread over the face of the
country. Although apparently well adapted to the
growth of the sweet potato and the mountain taro, it
was entirely neglected, and every appearance of cultivation ceased on our leaving the immediate vicinity
of Kapapala. We saw no streams or pools of water;
yet from the excellent quality of that furnished by the
natives at Tapuahi, we should suppose it is to be found
in the neighbourhood. In some parts of the islands,
where water is scarce, the natives have recourse to an
ingenious method for procuring a more abundant supply.
They fasten together the leaves of the pandanus, which
are concave on the upper side, from the top of the tree
to the lower branches, and thus form a kind of spout,
along which the rain that falls on the tree descends
into their calabashes or other vessels placed underneath
these vegetable aqueducts for its reception. By this
means, during a shower, they often procure a tolerable
supply.

After travelling between three and four miles, we
reached Keapuana, a large cavern, frequently used as a
lodging-place by travellers. The sun was nearly down,
and the guides proposed to halt for the night in the
cave, rather than proceed any farther, and sleep in the
open air. The proposal was agreed to, and when we
had gathered a quantity of fern leaves and grass for our
bed, and collected some fuel for the evening fire, we
descended about fourteen feet to the mouth of the
cavern, which was probably formed in the same manner

as those we had explored in the vicinity of Kairua.
The entrance, which was eight feet wide and five high,
was formed by an arch of ancient lava, several feet in
thickness. The interior of the cavern was about fifty
feet square, and the arch that covered it ten feet high.
There was an aperture at the northern end, about
three feet in diameter, occasioned by the falling in of
the lava, which admitted a current of keen mountain
air through the whole of the night. While we were
clearing out the small stones between some of the
blocks of lava that lay scattered around, a large fire
was kindled near the entrance, which, throwing its
glimmering light on the dark volcanic sides of the
cavern, and illuminating one side of the huge masses
of lava, exhibited to our view the strange features of
our apartment, which resembled, in no small degre
scenes described in tales of romance. When we had
cleared a sufficient space, we spread our beds of fern-
leaves and grass on the rough floor of the cavern, and
then mingled with the cheerful circle who were sitting
round the fire. We sang a hymn in the native language,
and afterward committed ourselves and fellow-travel-
lers to the kind keeping of Him, whose wakeful eye
and watchful care no dark cavern can exclude.

While the natives were sitting round the fire, Mr.
Thurston and I ascended to the upper region, and walked
to a rising ground at a small distance from the mouth
of the cavern, to try if we could discern the light of the
volcano. The wind blew fresh from the mountains:
the noise of the rolling surf, to which we had been accustomed on the shore, was not heard; and the stillness
of the night was only disturbed by the chirping of the
insects in the grass. The sky was clear, except in the
eastern horizon, where a few light clouds arose, and
slowly floated across the expanse of heaven. On looking towards the north-east, we saw a broad column of
light rising to a considerable elevation in the air, and
immediately above it some bright clouds, or thin vapours,
beautifully tinged with red on the under side. We had
no doubt that the column of light arose from the large
crater, and that its fires illuminated the surrounding atmosphere. The fleecy clouds generally passed over
the luminous column in a south-east direction. As
they approached it, the side towards the place where
we stood became generally bright; afterward the under

edge only reflected the volcanic fire; and in a little time each cloud passed entirely away, and was succeeded by another. We remained some time, to observe the beautiful phenomenon occasioned by the reflection of the volcanic fire, and the more magnificent spectacle presented by the multitude and brilliancy of the heavenly bodies. The season was solemn and delightful, for it was

> " Now the hour
> When Contemplation, from her sunless haunts
> Moves forward, and with radiant finger points
> To yon blue concave, swell'd by breath divine,
> Where one by one the living eyes of heaven
> Awake, quick kindling o'er the face of ether
> One boundless blaze ; ten thousand trembling fires
> And dancing lustres, where the unsteady eye,
> Restless and dazzled, wanders unconfin'd
> O'er all this field of glories—spacious field,
> And worthy of the Maker !
> . . . . From what pure wells
> Of milky light, what soft o'erflowing urn,
> Are all these lamps so fill'd ? These friendly lamps
> For ever streaming o'er the azure deep,
> To point our path, and light us to our home.
> How soft they slide among their lucid spheres !
> How deep the silence, yet how loud the praise !
> But are they silent all ? or is there not
> A tongue in every star, that talks with man,
> And wooes him to be wise ? nor wooes in vain.
> At this still hour, the self-collected soul
> Turns inward, and beholds a stranger there
> Of high descent, and more than mortal rank.
> . . . . A spark of fire divine,
> Which must burn on for ages, when the sun
> (Fair transitory creature of a day)
> Has closed his golden eye, and, wrapp'd in shades,
> Forgets his wonted journey through the east."

VOL. IV.

CHAPTER X.

Departure for the volcano—Volcanic sand—Superstitions of the natives respecting the obele—Description of the great volcano—Pools of water—
Banks of sulphur—Appearance of the volcano at midnight—Traditions and
superstitions of the natives connected with it—Names of the gods by whom
they suppose it inhabited—The little Kirauea—Ancient heiau on the summit
of a precipice—Mouna Roa—Probable structure of the island.

REFRESHED by a comfortable night's sleep, we arose
before daylight on the morning of the 1st of August,
and, after stirring up the embers of our fire, rendered,
with grateful hearts, our morning tribute of praise to
our Almighty Preserver.

As the day began to dawn, we tied on our sandals,
ascended from the subterraneous dormitory, and pursued
our journey, directing our course towards the column
of smoke, which bore E. N. E. from the cavern.

The path for several miles lay through a most fertile
tract of country, covered with bushes, or tall grass and
fern, frequently from three to five feet high, and so
heavily laden with dew, that before we had passed it
we were as completely wet as if we had walked through
a river. The morning air was cool, the singing of birds
enlivened the woods, and we travelled along, in Indian
file, nearly four miles an hour, although most of the
natives carried heavy burdens, which were tied on their
backs with small bands over their shoulders, in the same
manner that a soldier fastens on his knapsack. Having
also ourselves a small leather bag, containing a Bible,
inkstand, note-book, compass, &c. suspended from one
shoulder, a canteen of water from the other, and sometimes a light portfolio, or papers, with specimens of
plants besides, our whole party appeared, in this respect
at least, somewhat *en militaire*.

After travelling a short distance over the open country, we came to a small wood, into which we had not
penetrated far before all traces of a path entirely disap-
peared. We kept on some time, but were soon brought
to a stand by a deep chasm, over which we saw no
means of passing. Here the natives ran about in every
direction, searching for marks of footsteps, as a dog

runs to and fro when he has lost the track of his master.

After searching about half an hour, they discovered a path, which led some distance to the southward, in order to avoid the deep chasm in the lava. Near the place where we crossed over there was an extensive cavern. The natives sat down on the top of the arch by which it was formed, and began eating their sugar-cane, a portable kind of provision, usually carried on their journeys, while we explored the cavern in hopes of finding fresh water. In several places, drops of water, beautifully clear, constantly filtered through the vaulted arch, and fell into calabashes placed underneath to receive it. Unfortunately for us, these were all nearly empty. Probably some thirsty travellers had been there but a short time before.

Leaving the wood, we entered a waste of dry sand, about four miles across. The travelling over it was extremely fatiguing, as we sank in to our ankles at every step. The sand was of a dark olive colour, fine and sparkling, parts of it adhering readily to the magnet, and, being raised up in heaps in every direction, presented a surface resembling, colour excepted, that of drifted snow.

It was undoubtedly volcanic; but whether thrown out of any of the adjacent craters in its present form, or made up of small particles of decomposed lava, and the crystalline olivine we had observed so abundant in the lava of the southern shore, and drifted by the constant trade-wind from the vast tract of lava to the eastward, we could not determine.

When we had nearly passed through it, we sat down on a heap of lava to rest and refresh ourselves, having taken nothing since the preceding noon. About ten o'clock, Messrs. Bishop and Goodrich reached the place where we were sitting. They had heard by some travellers that two or three days would elapse before Makoa would overtake them, and, deeming it inexpedient to wait so long, had procured a guide, and, early this morning, set out from Kapapala to follow the rest of the party.

Having refreshed ourselves, we resumed our journey, taking a northerly direction towards the columns of smoke, which we could now distinctly perceive. Our way lay over a wide waste of ancient lava, of a black colour, compact and heavy, with a shining vitreous sur-

H 2

face, sometimes entirely covered with obsidian, and
frequently thrown up, by the expansive force of vapour
or heated air, into conical mounds, from six to twelve
feet high, which were, probably by the same power,
rent into a number of pieces, from the apex to the base.
The hollows between the mounds and long ridges were
filled with volcanic sand, and fine particles of olivíne, or
decomposed lava.

This vast tract of lava resembled in appearance an inland sea, bounded by distant mountains.   Once it had certainly been in a fluid state, but appeared as if it had become suddenly petrified, or turned into a glassy stone,
while its agitated billows were rolling to and fro.   Not
only were the large swells and hollows distinctly marked,
but in many places the surface of these billows was
covered by a smaller ripple, like that observed on the surface of the sea at the first springing up of a breeze, or
the passing currents of air which produce what the
sailors call a cat's paw.   The billows may have been
raised by the force which elevated the mounds or hills,
but they look as if the whole mass, extending several
miles, had, when in a state of perfect fusion, been agitated with a violent undulating or heaving motion.

The sun had now risen in his strength, and his bright
rays, reflected from the sparkling sand and undulated
surface of the vitreous lava, dazzled our sight, and
caused considerable pain, particularly as the trade-wind
blew fresh in our faces, and continually drove into our
eyes particles of sand.   This part of our journey was
unusually laborious, not only from the heat of the sun
and the reflection from the lava, but also from the unevenness of its surface, which obliged us constantly to
tread on an inclined plane, in some places as smooth
and almost as slippery as glass, where the greatest caution was necessary to avoid a fall.   Frequently we
chose to walk along on the ridge of a billow of lava,
though considerably circuitous, rather than pass up and
down its polished sides.   Taking the trough or hollow
between the waves was found safer, but much more
fatiguing, as we sank every step ankle-deep into the
sand.   The natives ran along the ridges, stepping like
goats from one ridge to another.   They, however, occasionally descended into the hollows, and made several
marks with their feet in the sand, at short distances
for the direction of two or three native boys with our

provisions, and some of their companions, who had fallen behind early in the morning, not being able to keep up with the foremost party.

Between eleven and twelve we passed a number of conical hills on our right, which the natives informed us were craters. A quantity of sand was collected round their base; but whether thrown out by them, or drifted thither by the wind, they could not inform us. In their vicinity we also passed several deep chasms, from which, in a number of places, small columns of vapour arose, at frequent and irregular intervals. They appeared to proceed from Kirauea; the great volcano, and extended towards the sea in a south-east direction. Probably they are connected with Ponahohoa, and may mark the course of a vast subterraneous channel leading from the volcano to the shore. The surface of the lava on both sides was heated, and the vapour had a strong sulphureous smell.

We continued our way beneath the scorching rays of a vertical sun till about noon, when we reached a solitary tree growing in a bed of sand, spreading its roots among the crevices of the rocks, and casting its grateful shade on the barren lava. Here we threw ourselves down on the sand and fragments of lava, stretched out our weary limbs, and drank the little water left in our canteens.

In every direction we observed a number of pieces of spumous lava, of an olive colour, extremely cellular, and as light as sponge. They appeared to have been drifted by the wind into the hollows which they occupied. The high bluff rocks on the north-west side of the volcano were distinctly seen; the smoke and vapours driven past us, and the scent of the fumes of sulphur, which, as we approached from the leeward, we had perceived ever since the wind sprang up, becoming very strong, indicated our proximity to Kirauea.

Impatient to view it, we arose, after resting about half an hour, and pursued our journey. In the way we saw a number of low bushes bearing beautiful red and yellow berries in clusters, each berry being about the size and shape of a large currant. The bushes on which they grew were generally low, seldom reaching two feet in height—the branches small and clear, leaves alternate, obtuse, with a point, and serrated; the flower was monopetalous, and, on being examined, determined

the plant to belong to the class decandria, and order
monogynia. The native name of the plant is ohelo.
The berries looked tempting to persons experiencing
both hunger and thirst, and we eagerly plucked and ate
all that came in our way. They are juicy, but rather
insipid to the taste. As soon as the natives perceived
us eating them, they called out aloud, and begged us to
desist, saying we were now within the precincts of
Pélé's dominions, to whom they belonged, and by whom
they were rahuiia (prohibited) until some had been offered to her, and permission to eat them asked. We
told them we were sorry they should feel uneasy on
this account,—that we acknowledged Jehovah as the
only divine proprietor of the fruits of the earth, and felt
thankful to him for them, especially in our present circumstances. Some of them then said, " We are afraid.
We shall be overtaken by some calamity before we
leave this place." We advised them to dismiss their
fears and eat with us, as we knew they were thirsty
and faint. They shook their heads, and perceiving us
determined to disregard their entreaties, walked along
in silence.

We travelled on, regretting that the natives should
indulge notions so superstitious, but clearing every ohelo
bush that grew near our path, till about two P. M., when
the CRATER OF KIRAUEA suddenly burst upon our view.
We expected to have seen a mountain with a broad
base and rough indented sides, composed of loose slags
or hardened streams of lava, and whose summit would
have presented a rugged wall of scoriæ, forming the rim
of a mighty caldron. But, instead of this, we found
ourselves on the edge of a steep precipice, with a vast
plain before us, fifteen or sixteen miles in circumference,
and sunk from two hundred to four hundred feet below
its original level. The surface of this plain was uneven
and strewed over with large stones and volcanic rocks,
and in the centre of it was the great crater, at the distance of a mile and a half from the precipice on which
we were standing. Our guides led us round towards
the north end of the ridge, in order to find a place by
which we might descend to the plain below. As we
passed along, we observed the natives, who had hitherto
refused to touch any of the ohelo berries, now gather
several bunches, and, after offering a part to Pélé, eat
them very freely. They did not use much ceremony

in their acknowledgment; but when they had plucked a branch, containing several clusters of berries, they turned their faces towards the place whence the greatest quantity of smoke and vapour issued, and, breaking the branch they held in their hand in two, they threw one part down the precipice, saying at the same time, " *E Pélé, eia ka ohelo 'au; e taumaha aku wau ia oe, e`ai hoi au tetahi:*"—Pélé, here are your ohelos: I offer some to you, some I also eat. Several of them told us, as they turned round from the crater, that after such acknowledgments they might eat the fruit with security. We answered, we were sorry to see them offering to an imaginary deity the gifts of the true God; but hoped they would soon know better, and acknowledge Jehovah alone, in all the benefits they received.

We walked on to the north end of the ridge, where, the precipice being less steep, a descent to the plain below seemed practicable. It required, however, the greatest caution, as the stones and fragments of rock frequently gave way under our feet, and rolled down from above; but with all our care, we did not reach the bottom without several falls and slight bruises.

The steep which we had descended was formed of volcanic matter, apparently a light red and gray kind of lava, vesicular, and lying in horizontal strata, varying in thickness from one to forty feet. In a small number of places the different strata of lava were also rent in perpendicular or oblique directions, from the top to the bottom, either by earthquakes or other violent convulsions of the ground, connected with the action of the adjacent volcano. After walking some distance over the sunken plain, which in several places sounded hollow under our feet, we at length came to the edge of the great crater, where a spectacle, sublime and even appalling, presented itself before us—

" We stopped, and trembled."

Astonishment and awe for some moments rendered us mute, and, like statues, we stood fixed to the spot, with our eyes riveted on the abyss below. Immediately before us yawned an immense gulf, in the form of a crescent, about two miles in length, from north-east to south-west, nearly a mile in width, and apparently eight hundred feet deep. The bottom was covered with lava,

and the south-west and northern parts of it were one
vast flood of burning matter, in a state of terrific ebullition, rolling to and fro its "fiery surge" and flaming
billows. Fifty-one conical islands, of varied form and
size, containing as many craters, rose either round
the edge or from the surface of the burning lake.
Twenty-two constantly emitted columns of gray smoke,
or pyramids of brilliant flame; and several of these at
the same time vomited from their ignited mouths
streams of lava, which rolled in blazing torrents down
their black indented sides into the boiling mass below.

The existence of these conical craters led us to conclude that the boiling caldron of lava before us did not
form the focus of the volcano; that this mass of melted
lava was comparatively shallow; and that the basin in
which it was contained was separated, by a stratum of
solid matter, from the great volcanic abyss, which constantly poured out its melted contents through these
numerous craters into this upper reservoir. We were
further inclined to this opinion from the vast columns
of vapour continually ascending from the chasms in the
vicinity of the sulphur banks and pools of water, for
they must have been produced by other fire than that
which caused the ebullition in the lava at the bottom of
the great crater; and also by noticing a number of small
craters in vigorous action, situated high up the sides of
the great gulf, and apparently quite detached from it.
The streams of lava which they emitted rolled down
into the lake and mingled with the melted mass, which,
though thrown up by different apertures, had perhaps
been originally fused in one vast furnace.

The sides of the gulf before us, although composed
of different strata of ancient lava, were perpendicular
for about four hundred feet, and rose from a wide horizontal ledge of solid black lava of irregular breadth, but
extending completely round. Beneath this ledge the
sides sloped gradually towards the burning lake, which
was, as nearly as we could judge, three or four hundred
feet lower. It was evident that the large crater had
been recently filled with liquid lava up to this black
ledge, and had, by some subterranean canal, emptied
itself into the sea, or upon the low land on the shore;
and in all probability this evacuation had caused the inundation of the Kapapala coast, which took place, as
we afterward learned, about three weeks prior to our

visit. The gray, and in some places apparently calcined, sides of the great crater before us—the fissures which intersected the surface of the plain on which we were standing—the long banks of sulphur on the opposite side of the abyss—the vigorous action of the numerous small craters on its borders—the dense columns of vapour and smoke that rose at the north and south end of the plain—together with the ridge of steep rocks by which it was surrounded, rising probably in some places three or four hundred feet in perpendicular height, presented an immense volcanic panorama, the effect of which was greatly augmented by the constant roaring of the vast furnaces below.

After the first feelings of astonishment had subsided, we remained a considerable time contemplating a scene which it is impossible to describe, and which filled us with wonder and admiration at the almost overwhelming manifestation it affords of the power of that dread Being who created the world, and who has declared that by fire he will one day destroy it. We then walked along the west side of the crater, and in half an hour reached the north end.

While walking over the plain, which was covered with a thin layer of what appeared like indurated sand, but which we afterward found to be decomposed lava, the natives requested us not to *kaha a heru ka one*, strike, scratch, or dig the sand, assuring us it would displease Pélé, and be followed by an irruption of lava,* or other expression of vengeance from this goddess of the volcano, of whose power and displeasure they had manifested the greatest apprehensions ever since our approach to Kirauea.

At the north end of the crater we left our provisions and baggage that we had, and went in search of water, which we had been informed was to be found in the neighbourhood of a number of columns of vapour which

* It appears singular that similar ideas respecting the consequences of disturbing the earth in the vicinity of volcanoes should prevail here, as among the natives of the New-Hebrides. Forster, in his account of a visit to a place somewhat resembling this, in the island of Tanna, speaking of their making a hole and burying their thermometer, says, "The natives, who observed that we stirred in the solfaterra" (as he called the places where the smoke and vapour issued), "desired us to leave it, telling us it would take fire and resemble the volcano, which they called Assoor. They seemed to be extremely apprehensive of some mischance, and were very uneasy as often as we made the least attempt to disturb the sulphureous earth."—*Forst. Voy.* vol. ii. p. 308.

we saw rising in a northerly direction. About half a
mile distant, we found two or three small pools of perfectly sweet fresh water—a luxury which, notwithstanding the reports of the natives, we did not expect to meet
with in these regions of fire. It proved a most grateful
refreshment to us after travelling about twenty miles
over a dry barren desert.

These pools appeared great natural curiosities. The
surface of the ground in the vicinity was perceptibly
warm, and rent by several deep irregular chasms, from
which steam and thick vapours continually arose. In
some places these chasms were two feet wide, and from
them a volume of steam ascended, which was immediately condensed by the cool mountain air, and driven,
like drizzling rain, into hollows in the compact lava on
the leeward side of the chasms. The pools, which
were six or eight feet from the chasms, were surrounded
and covered by flags, rushes, and tall grass. Nour-
ished by the moisture of the vapours, these plants flourished luxuriantly, and, in their turn, sheltered the pools
from the heat of the sun, and prevented evaporation.
We expected to find the water warm, but in this we were
also agreeably disappointed. When we had quenched
our thirst with water thus distilled by nature, we directed
the natives to build a hut in which we might pass the
night, in such a situation as to command a view of the
burning lava; and while they were thus employed, we
prepared to examine the many interesting objects around
us. Mr. Bishop returned with a canteen of water, to
meet Mr. Harwood, who had not yet come up.

Mr. Thurston visited the eastern side of the great
crater, and I went with Mr. Goodrich to examine some
extensive beds of sulphur at the north-east end. After
walking about three-quarters of a mile over a tract of
decomposed lava, covered with ohelo bushes and ferns,
we came to a bank about a hundred and fifty yards long,
and in some places upwards of thirty feet high, formed
of sulphur, with a small proportion of red clay or ochre.
The ground was very hot; its surface rent by fissures;
and we were sometimes completely enveloped in the
thick vapours that continually ascended. A number of
apertures were visible along the whole extent of the
bank of sulphur; smoke and vapours arose from these
fissures also; and the heat of the sulphur around them
was more intense than in any other part. Their edges

were fringed with fine crystals, in various combinations, resembling what are called flowers of sulphur. We climbed about half-way up the bank, and endeavoured to break off some parts of the crust, but soon found it too hot to be handled. However, by means of our walking-sticks we detached some curious specimens. Those procured near the surface were crystallized in beautiful acicular prisms of a light-yellow colour; while those found three or four inches deep in the bank were of an orange-yellow, generally in single or double tetra-hedral pyramids, and full an inch in length. A singular hissing and cracking noise was heard among the crystals whenever the outside crust of the sulphur was broken and the atmospheric air admitted. The same noise was produced among the fragments broken off, until they were quite cold. The adjacent stones and pieces of clay were frequently incrusted either with sulphate of ammonia or volcanic sal ammoniac. Considerable quantities were also found in the crevices of some of the neighbouring rocks, which were much more pungent than that exposed to the air. Along the bottom of the sulphur bank we found a number of pieces of tufa, or clay-stone, extremely light and cellular, and which appeared to have been fused. It seemed as if sulphur or some other inflammable substance had formerly occupied the cells in these stones. A thick fog now came on, which, being followed by a shower of rain, obliged us to leave this interesting laboratory of nature, and return to our companions. On the eastern side of the crater we saw banks of sulphur, less pure, yet apparently more extensive, than those we had visited; but their distance from us, and the unfavourable state of the weather, prevented our examining them. On our way to the sulphur banks we saw two flocks of wild geese, which came down from the mountains, and settled among the ohelo bushes, near the pools of water. They were smaller than the common goose, had brown necks, and their wings were tipped with the same colour. The natives informed us there were vast flocks in the interior, although they were never seen near the sea.

Just as the sun was setting we reached the place where we had left our baggage, and found Messrs. Bishop and Harwood sitting near the spot where the natives, with a few green branches of trees, some fern-leaves, and rushes, had erected a hut. We were none of us pleased with the site which they had chosen. It was at the north-east end of the crater, on a pile of rocks overhanging the abyss below, and actually within four feet of the precipice. When we expressed our disapprobation, they said it was the only place where we might expect to pass the night undisturbed by Pélé, and secure from earthquake and other calamity, being the place in which alone Pélé allowed travellers to build a hut. We told them it was unnecessarily near, and, being also very unsafe, we wished to remove. They answered, that as it was within the limits prescribed by Pélé for safe lodging, they should be unwilling to sleep anywhere else, and had not time to build another hut for us.

We then directed them to collect a quantity of fire-wood, as we expected the night would be cold, although the thermometer then stood at 69°. We were the more anxious to have the fuel collected before the shades of night should close upon us, as travelling in some places was extremely dangerous. The ground sounded hollow in every direction, frequently cracked, and in two instances actually gave way while we were passing over it. Mr. Bishop was approaching the hut, when the lava suddenly broke under him. He instantly threw himself forward, and fell flat on his face over a part that was more solid. A boy, who followed me with a basket to the sulphur-banks, and walked about a yard behind Mr. Goodrich and myself, also fell in. There was no crack in the surface of the lava over which he was walking, neither did it bend under his weight, but broke suddenly, when he sank in up to his middle. His legs and thighs were considerably bruised, but providentially he escaped without any other injury. The lava in both places was about two inches in thickness, and broke short, leaving the aperture regular and defined, without even cracking the adjoining parts. On looking into the holes, we could see no bottom; but on both sides, at a short distance from the aperture, the lava was solid, and they appeared to have fallen into a narrow chasm covered over by a thin crust of lava, already in a state of decomposition.

When night came on, we kindled a good fire and prepared our frugal supper. Mr. Thurston, however, had not yet returned, and as the darkness of the night increased we began to feel anxious for his safety. The wind came down from the mountains in violent gusts, dark clouds lowered over us, and a thick fog enveloped every object; even the fires of the volcano were but indistinctly seen: The darkness of the night advanced, but no tidings reached us of Mr. Thurston. About seven o'clock we sent out the natives with torches and firebrands to search for him. They went as far as they durst, hallooing along the border of the crater, till their lights were extinguished, when they returned without having seen or heard any thing of him. We now increased our fire, hoping it might serve as a beacon to direct him to our hut. Eight o'clock came, and he did not appear. We began seriously to fear that he had fallen into the crater itself, or some of the deep and rugged chasms by which it was surrounded.* In this state of painful suspense we remained till nearly half-past eight, when we were happily relieved by his sudden appearance. He had descended, and walked along the dark ledge of lava on the east side of the crater, till a chasm obliged him to ascend. Having with difficulty reached the top, he travelled along the southern and western sides, till the light of our fire directed him to our encampment. The extent of the crater, the unevenness of the path, the numerous fissures and rugged surface of the lava, and the darkness of the night, had prevented his earlier arrival. We now partook with cheerfulness of our evening repast, and afterward, amid the whistling of the winds around, and the roaring of the furnace beneath, rendered our evening sacrifice of praise, and committed ourselves to the secure protection of our God. We then spread our mats on the ground, but as we were all wet through with the rain, against which our hut was but an indifferent shelter, we preferred to sit or stand round the fire, rather than lie down on the ground. Between nine and ten, the dark clouds and heavy fog, that since the setting of the sun had hung over the volcano, gradually cleared away, and the fires of Kirauea, darting their fierce light athwart the midnight gloom, unfolded a sight terrible and sublime beyond all we had yet seen.

The agitated mass of liquid lava, like a flood of melted metal, raged with tumultuous whirl. The lively flame that danced over its undulating surface, tinged with sul-

* A native who accompanied Mr. Goodrich on a subsequent visit to the volcano fell into one of these chasms; he was severely bruised by the fall, and could only be extricated from his perilous situation by a rope lowered from the shore.

phureous blue, or glowing with mineral red, cast a broad
glare of dazzling light on the indented sides of the insulated craters, whose roaring mouths, amid rising flames,
and eddying streams of fire, shot up, at frequent intervals, with very loud detonations, spherical masses of
fusing lava, or bright-ignited stones.

The dark, bold outline of the perpendicular and jutting
rocks around formed a striking contrast with the luminous lake below, whose vivid rays, thrown on the
rugged promontories, and reflected by the overhanging
clouds, combined to complete the awful grandeur of the
imposing scene. We sat gazing at the magnificent phenomena for several hours, when we laid ourselves down
on our mats, in order to observe more leisurely their
varying aspect; for, although we had travelled upwards
of twenty miles since the morning, and were both weary
and cold, we felt but little disposition to sleep. This
disinclination was probably increased by our proximity
to the yawning gulf, and our conviction that the de-
tachment of a fragment from beneath the overhanging
pile on which we were reclining, or the slightest concussion of the earth, which every thing around indicated
to be no unfrequent occurrence, would perhaps precipitate us, amid the horrid crash of falling rocks, into the
burning lake immediately before us.

The natives, who probably viewed the scene with
thoughts and feelings somewhat different from ours,
seemed, however, equally interested. They sat most of
the night talking of the achievements of Pélé, and re-
garding with a superstitious fear, at which we were not
surprised, the brilliant exhibition. They considered it
the primeval abode of their volcanic deities. The conical craters, they said, were their houses, where they
frequently amused themselves by playing at konane;*
the roaring of the furnaces and the crackling of the
flames were the *kani* of their *hura* (*music* of their *dance*),
and the red flaming surge was the surf wherein they
played, sportively swimming on the rolling wave.†

As eight of the natives with us belonged to the adjoining district, we asked them to tell us what they knew
of the history of this volcano, and what their opinions

* The game resembling drafts, described page 158.
† Swimming in the sea, when the weather is tempestuous and the surf
high, is a favourite amusement throughout the Sandwich and other islands in
the Pacific.

were respecting it. From their account, and that of others with whom we conversed, we learned that it had been burning from time immemorial, or, to use their own words, "*mai ka po mai*," from chaos till now,[*] and had overflowed some part of the country during the reign of every king that had governed in Hawaii: that in earlier ages it used to boil up, overflow its banks, and inundate the adjacent country; but that for many kings' reigns past it had kept below the level of the surrounding plain, continually extending its surface and increasing its depth, and occasionally throwing up, with violent explosions, huge rocks, or red-hot stones. These eruptions, they said, were always accompanied by dreadful earthquakes, loud claps of thunder, with vivid and quick-succeeding lightning. No great explosion, they added, had taken place since the days of Keoua; but many places near the sea had since been overflowed, on which occasions they supposed Pélé went by a road under ground from her house in the crater to the shore.

These few facts were gathered from their accounts of its origin and operation; but they were so incorporated with their traditions of its supernatural inhabitants, and fabulous stories of their romantic adventures, that we found no small difficulty in distinguishing fiction from fact. Among other things, we were told that though, according to the traditions preserved in their songs, Kirauea had been burning ever since the island emerged from night, it was not inhabited till after the *Tai-a-kahina'rii*, sea of Kahina'rii, or deluge of the Sandwich Islands. Shortly after that event, they say, the present volcanic family came from Tahiti, a foreign country, to Hawaii.

The names of the principal individuals were: *Komoho-arii*, the king Moho; moho sometimes means a vapour, hence the name might be the king of steam or vapour—*Ta-poha-i-tahi-ora*, the explosion in the place of life—*Te-ua-a-te-po*, the rain of night—*Tane-hetiri*, husband of thunder, or thundering tane[†]—and *'Te-o-ahi-tama-taua*,

---

[*] The Hawaiian traditions, like those of the ancients, refer to night, or a chaotic state, the origin of the world, and almost all things therein, the greater part of their gods not excepted. The present state they call the *Ao marama*, day, or state of light. They speak of creation as a transition from darkness to light: and when they wish to express the existence of any thing from the beginning, they say it has been so *mai ka po mai*, from the night, or state of darkness or confusion, till now.

[†] Tane is the name of one of their gods, as well as the name of the principal god formerly worshipped by the Society islanders; in both languages the word also means a husband.

fire-thrusting child of war, or the child of war with a spear of fire; these were all brothers, and two of them, Vulcan-like, were deformed, having hump-backs—*Pélé*, principal goddess—*Makore-wawahi-waa*, fiery-eyed canoe-breaker—*Hiata-wawahi-lani*, heaven-rending cloud-holder—*Hiata-noholani*, heaven-dwelling cloud-holder—*Hiata-taarewa-mata*, quick-glancing-eyed cloud-holder, or the cloud-holder whose eyes turn quickly, and look frequently over her shoulders—*Hiata-hoi-te-pori-a Pélé*, the cloud-holder embracing or kissing the bosom of Pélé—*Hiata-tabu-enaena*, the red-hot mountain holding or lifting clouds—*Hiata-tareiia*, the wreath or garland-encircled cloud-holder—and *Hiata-opio*, young cloud-holder.

These were all sisters; and with many others in their train, on landing at Hawaii, are said to have taken up their abode in Kirauea. Something of their characters may be inferred from the few names we have given. Whenever the natives speak of them, it is as dreadful beings. This volcano is represented as having been their principal residence ever since their arrival, though they are thought to have many other dwellings in different parts of the island, and not a few on the tops of the snow-covered mountains. To these some of them frequently remove. Sometimes their arrival in a district was foretold by the priests of the heiaus there, and always announced by the convulsive trembling of the earth, the illuminating fire in their houses (craters), the flashes of lightning, and the roar of thunder. They never journeyed on errands of mercy; to receive offerings or execute vengeance were the only objects for which they left their palace. *"Nui wale,"* said the people with whom we were talking, " *ka kanaka i make ia rakou*"*—Great indeed is the number of men slain by them; *ua rau, ua rau, ua rau, ka puaa i horaia na rakou*,† four hundreds, four hundreds, four hundreds of hogs have been thrown to them.‡ The whole island was considered as bound to pay them tribute, or support their heiaus and *kahu* (devotees); and whenever the chiefs or people failed to send the proper offerings, or incurred

---

* Alluding to those destroyed by the inundations.

† This is a figurative expression, signifying a great number, as we are accustomed to hear of thousands, and thousands, and thousands.

‡ Vast numbers of hogs, some alive, others cooked, were thrown into the craters during the time they were in action, or when they threatened an eruption; and also during an inundation, many were thrown into the rolling torrent of lava, to appease the gods and stay its progress.

their displeasure by insulting them or their priests, or breaking the tabu (sacred restrictions) of their domains in the vicinity of the craters, they filled Kirauea with lava, and spouted it out, or, taking a subterranean passage, marched to some of their houses (craters) in the neighbourhood where the offending parties dwelt, and from thence came down upon the delinquents with all their dreadful scourges. If a sufficient number of fish were not taken to them by the inhabitants of the seashore, they would go down and with fire kill the fish, fill up with *pahoehoe* (lava) the shallow places, and destroy all the fishing-grounds.

We were told that several attempts had been made to drive them off the islands, and that once they were nearly overpowered by Tamapuaa, child of a hog, from *tama*, a child, and *puaa*, a hog. He was the *Centaur* of Hawaii, a gigantic animal, half-hog and half-man. He travelled from Oahu to countries beyond the heavens, namely, beyond the visible horizon, the boundary where they supposed the heavens to be, in form of a hollow cone, joined to the sea. He also visited Kirauea, and made proposals to become the guest and suitor of Pélé, the elder sister. When she saw him standing on the edge of the crater, she rejected his proposals with contempt, calling him a hog, the son of a hog. On her ascending from the crater to drive him away, a fierce combat ensued. Pélé was forced to her volcano, and threatened with destruction from waters of the sea, which Tamapuaa poured into the crater till it was almost full, and the fires were nearly extinct. Pélé and her companions drank up the waters, rose again from the craters, and finally succeeded in driving Tamapuaa into the sea, whither she followed him with thunder, lightning, and showers of large stones.

They also related the account of the destruction of part of Keoua's camp by a violent eruption of the volcano, which, from their description, must have been sudden and awful.

Pélé, they said, was propitious to Tamehameha, and availed herself of the opportunity afforded by the contiguous encampment of Keoua to diminish his forces, and aid the cause of his rival. We asked why Keoua was unpopular with Pélé. They said, " We do not exactly know. Some say he had not sent sufficient offerings to the heiaus; others, that he had no right to make

war against Tamehameha, as he had before concluded a
treaty of peace with him; and others, that he had broken
the tabu of the place by eating the oheloes, marking and
disturbing the sand, or pulling up a sacred kind of grass
growing in the neighbourhood." Whatever was the
cause, Pélé, they said, was "*huhu roa*," exceedingly
angry, and soon after sunset repeatedly shook the earth
with the most violent heaving motion, sent up a column
of dense black smoke, followed by the most brilliant
flames. A violent percussion was afterward felt, streams
of bright red lava were spouted up, and immense rocks
in a state of ignition thrown to a great height in the air.
A volley of smaller stones, thrown with much greater
velocity and force, instantly followed the larger ones,
and struck some of them, when the latter frequently
burst with a report like thunder, accompanied by vivid
flashes of lightning. Many of Keoua's people were killed
by the falling fragments of rocks, and a number were actually buried beneath the overwhelming mass of ashes
and lava. Some of the natives say the warriors of two
districts, about eighty men, perished on this occasion.
Not intimidated by this event, which many considered
as a premonition of his fate, Keoua continued his march,
and the volcano continued its action, confining, however, its operation within the boundaries of Kirauea.
We had heard the account several times before, with
some little variation as to the numbers killed, and the
appearance of Pélé to Keoua in the column of smoke as
it rose from the crater, and, with the exception of this
last circumstance, believe it to be true.

Frequently during the night the natives thought they
saw some one or other of the deities, but immediately
afterward they doubted. At these times, if we asked
them where they saw Pélé, they would sometimes point
to the red lava, at others to the variegated flame; and
on our saying we could not perceive any distinct form,
they generally answered by assuring us that during the
night some one or other of them would certainly be
seen. We jocosely requested them to inform us as soon
as any appeared; and even to awake us, should we happen to be asleep. At the same time we told them, that
when we considered their ignorance of the true God,
and of the causes by which the action of volcanoes was
sustained, we were not surprised at their supposing them
to be the habitations of their deities, and their opera-

tions those of supernatural beings. As far as their language and mental capability admitted, we endeavoured to explain some of the causes of volcanic fire; and illustrated them by the force of gunpowder, with the effects of which the natives are familiar; assuring them that the expansive force of steam is much greater than that of gunpowder. Our principal solicitude, however, was to lead their minds to God, who created the world, and whose almighty power controls the elements of nature in all their diversified operations; but of whom, though they beheld the wondrous works of his hand, they were lamentably ignorant.

After two or three hours' sleep, we arose before it was day, and, gathering round our fire, sang our morning hymn of praise, in which we were joined by the natives who were with us. The sun had now risen, and as we had no provisions left, we felt it necessary to prepare for our departure. Mr. Goodrich walked along the north side of the crater, in order to enable us to form as accurate an opinion as possible of its actual dimensions; and from the observations of Mr. Goodrich and Mr. Thurston, as well as those the rest of our party made when we walked along the north and east sides, we think the crater is not less than five, or five and a half, miles in circumference.* We regret that we had not means for ascertaining more accurately its depth. We lowered down a line one hundred feet from the edge of the plain on which our hut was erected, but it did not appear to reach near half-way to the black ledge of lava; and judging the proportion below to be equal to that above, it could not be less than seven or

---

* The following extract of a letter from Mr. Chamberlain is copied from a recent American publication:—

"Mr. Goodrich and myself visited the volcano again, and with a line measured the upper edge of the crater, and found it to be seven miles and a half in circumference. We then descended and measured the side of the ledge, and satisfied ourselves that, at the depth of five or six hundred feet, the circumference is at least five miles and a half. We did not get the exact depth of it, but judge it not less than one thousand feet. We had good opportunities for forming a judgment."—In a letter to Professor Silliman, of New-Haven, Mr. Goodrich corroborates the above, and states also that he walked across the bottom where the lava was hard, the surface of which, though apparently smooth as seen from the top, was raised in hills or sunk in valleys; that dense sulphureous fumes and gases, very suffocating, some of them resembling muriatic gas ascended from almost all parts of the bottom, making in their escape a "tremendous roaring, like the discharge of steam from the boiler of a steam-engine;" at one place the florid lava was boiling like a fountain, and spouting up lava forty or fifty feet into the air.—*Philosophical Magazine for September*, 1826.

eight hundred feet to the liquid lava. We also threw
down some large stones, which after several seconds
struck on the sides, and then bounded down to the bottom, where they were lost in the lava. When they
reached the bottom, they appeared like pebbles, and we
were obliged to watch their course very steadily, to perceive them at all.

In company with Dr. Blatchely, Messrs. Chamberlain
and Ely, American missionaries, and a gentleman resident in Oahu, I have since visited Kirauea, when we
again endeavoured to measure its circumference. Mr.
Chamberlain walked round the northern end from east
to west, as near the edge as it was prudent to go, and,
numbering his paces, made that part of it $3\frac{7}{8}$ miles;
from which, we think, the above estimate does not exceed the actual extent of the crater. We also lowered
down a line-two hundred and thirty feet long, but it did
not reach the horizontal ledge of lava. The fissures in
the vicinity of the sulphur banks and pools of water
were more numerous, and the smoke and vapour that ascended from them greater in quantity than during our
first visit. The volcano was much more quiescent; but
some violent convulsions had taken place in the interim,
for several masses of rock had fallen from the high precipices in the neighbourhood. The fires in the south
and west parts burned but feebly; and though there was
but little fire in the north and east sections of the volcano, it was evident that the whole of the lava in this
part had been in a state of agitation since we had seen
it. Some of the small craters on the southern sides of
the great abyss were extinguished; but several new
craters had been formed on the opposite side, and bore
marks of having been in vigorous action but a very short
period before.

In June, 1825, Mr. Stewart accompanied Lord Byron
and a party from the Blonde frigate to Kirauea; and
the following description of a descent to the bottom of
the crater, and an eruption that took place during the
second night, on their encampment near its borders, is
extracted from his account, which has since been published in England.

"Leaving the sulphur banks on the eastern side behind us, we directed our course along the northern part,
to the western cliffs. As we advanced, these became
more and more perpendicular, till they presented nothing

but the bare and upright face of an immense wall, from eight to ten hundred feet high, on whose surface huge stones and rocks hung, apparently so loosely as to threaten falling at the agitation of a breath. In many places a white curling vapour issued from the sides and summit of the precipice; and in two or three places streams of clay-coloured lava, like small waterfalls, extending almost from the top to the bottom, had cooled, evidently at a very recent period. At almost every step, something new attracted our attention; and by stopping, sometimes to look up, not without a feeling of apprehension at the enormous masses above our heads—at others to gain, by a cautious approach to the brink of the gulf, a nearer glance at the equally frightful depth below —at one time turning aside to ascertain the heat of a column of steam—at another, to secure some unique or beautiful specimen—we occupied more than two hours in proceeding the same number of miles.

"At that distance from our entrance on the ledge, we came to a spot on the western side where it widened many hundred feet, and terminated next the crater— not, as in most other places, perpendicularly, but in an immense heap of broken slabs and blocks of lava, loosely piled together, as they had fallen in some convulsion of the mountain, and jutting off to the bottom in a frightful mass of ruin. Here, we had been informed, the descent into the depth of the crater could be most easily made; but being without a guide, we were entirely at a loss what course to take, till we unexpectedly descried the gentlemen who had preceded us re-ascending. They dissuaded us most strenuously from proceeding farther: knowing that the crater had been crossed at this end, we hastened on, notwithstanding the refusal of the guide to return with us. The descent was as perilous as it had been represented; but by proceeding with great caution, testing well the safety of every step before committing our weight to it, and often stopping to select the course which seemed least hazardous, in the space of about twenty minutes, by a zigzag way, we reached the bottom, without any accident of greater amount than a few scratches on the hands, from the sharpness and roughness of the lava, by which we had occasionally been obliged to support ourselves. When about half-way down, we were encouraged to persevere in our undertaking, by meeting a native who had descended on

the opposite side, and passed over. It was only, however, from the renewed assurance it gave of the prac-
ticability of the attempt; for, besides being greatly
fatigued, he was much cut and bruised from a fall—said
the bottom was " *Ino, ino roa, ka wahi O debelo !*"—Ex-
cessively bad, the place of the devil!—and could be prevailed on to return with us only by the promise of a
large reward.

" It is difficult to say whether sensations of admiration or of terror predominated, on reaching this tremendous spot. As I looked up at the gigantic wall, which
on every side rose to the very clouds, I felt oppressed
to a most unpleasant degree, by a sense of confinement.
Either from the influence of imagination, or from the
actual effect of the intense power of a noonday sun
beating directly on us, in addition to the heated and sulphureous atmosphere of the volcano itself, I for some
moments experienced an agitation of spirits, and difficulty of respiration that made me cast a look of wishful
anxiety towards our little hut, which seemed only like
a bird's nest on the opposite cliff. These emotions,
however, soon passed off, and we began, with great
spirit and activity, the enterprise before us.

" I can compare the general aspect of the bottom of
the crater to nothing that will give a livelier image of it
to your mind, than to the appearance the Otsego Lake
would present if the ice with which it is covered in the
winter were suddenly broken up by a heavy storm, and
as suddenly frozen again, while large slabs and blocks
were still toppling, and dashing, and heaping against
each other with the motion of the waves. Just so rough
and distorted was the black mass under our feet, only a
hundred-fold more terrific, independently of the innumerable cracks, fissures, deep chasms, and holes, from
which sulphureous vapour, steam, and smoke were ex-
haled with a degree of heat that testified to the near
vicinity of fire.

" We had not proceeded far, before our path was intersected by a chasm, at least thirty feet wide, and of a
greater depth than we could ascertain, at the nearest
distance we dare approach. The only alternative was
to return, or to follow its course till it terminated, or
became narrow enough to be crossed. We chose the
latter, but soon met an equally formidable obstacle in a
current of smoke, so highly impregnated with a suffo-

cating gas, as not to allow of respiration. The lava on
which we stood was in many places so hot that we
could not hold for a moment in our hands the pieces
we knocked off for specimens. On one side lay a gulf
of unfathomable depth, on the other an inaccessible pile
of ruins, and immediately in front an oppressive and
deadly vapour. While hesitating what to do, we perceived the smoke to be swept round occasionally by an
eddy of the air, in a direction opposite to that in which
it most of the time ascended ; and watching an opportunity when our way was thus made clear, we held our
breath, and ran as rapidly as the dangerous character of
the path would permit, till we had gained a place beyond its ordinary course. We here unexpectedly found
ourselves also delivered from the other impediment to
our progress ; for the chasm abruptly ran off in a direction far from that we wished to pursue. Our escape
from the vapour, however, was that which we considered the most important ; and so great was our impression of the danger to which we had been exposed
from it, that when we saw our way to the opposite side
open, without any special obstacle before us, we felt disposed formally to return thanks to Almighty God for
our deliverance. But before this was proposed, all our
number, except Lord Byron, Mr. Davis, and myself, had
gone forward so far as to be out of call ; and, for the
time, the external adoration of the Creator, from the
midst of one of the most terrible of his works, was re-
luctantly waived.

"At an inconsiderable distance from us was one of
the largest of the conical craters, whose laborious action
had so greatly impressed our minds during the night,
and we hastened to a nearer examination of it. On
reaching its base, we judged it to be one hundred and
fifty feet high, a huge, irregularly shapen, inverted funnel of lava covered with clefts, orifices, and tunnels,
from which bodies of steam escaped, while pale flames,
ashes, stones, and lava were propelled with equal force
and noise from its rugged mouth. The whole formed
so singularly terrific an object, that in order to secure
a hasty sketch of it, I permitted the other gentlemen
to go a few yards nearer than I did, while I occupied
myself with my pencil. Lord Byron and his servant
ascended the cone several feet, but found the heat too

great to remain longer than to detach, with their sticks, a piece or two of recent lava, burning hot.

"So highly was our admiration excited by the scene, that we forgot the danger to which we might be exposed should any change take place in the currents of destructive gas, which exist in a greater or less degree in every part of the crater; till Mr. Davis, after two or three ineffectual intimations of the propriety of an immediate departure, warned us in a most decided tone of the peril of our situation; assuring us, that three inspirations of the air by which we might be surrounded would prove fatal to every one of us. We felt the truth of the assertion, and notwithstanding the desire we had of visiting a similar cone, covered with a beautiful incrustation of sulphur; at the distance from us of a few hundred yards only, we hastily took the speediest course from so dangerous a spot. The ascent to the ledge was not less difficult and frightful than the descent had been, and, for the last few yards, was almost perpendicular; but we all succeeded in safely gaining its top, not far from the path by which we had in the morning descended the upper cliff.

"We reached the hut about two o'clock, nearly exhausted from fatigue, thirst, and hunger; and had immediate reason to congratulate ourselves on a most narrow escape from extreme danger, if not from death: for, on turning round, we perceived the whole chasm to be filled with thick sulphureous smoke; and within half an hour, it was so completely choked with it, that not an object below us was visible. Even where we were, in the unconfined region above, the air became so oppressive, as to make us think seriously of a precipitate retreat.

"The splendid illuminations of the preceding evening were again lighted up with the closing of the day; and after enjoying their beauties for two or three hours with renewed delight, we early sought a repose, which the fatigue of the morning had rendered most desirable. The chattering of the islanders around our cabins, and the occasional sound of voices in protracted conversation among our own number, had however scarcely ceased long enough to admit of sound sleep, when the volcano again began roaring and labouring with redoubled activity. The confusion of noises was prodigiously great.

These sounds were not fixed or confined to one place, but rolled from one end of the crater to the other; sometimes seeming to be immediately under us, when a sensible tremor of the ground on which we lay took place; and then again rushing to the farthest end with incalculable velocity. The whole air was filled with the tumult; and those most soundly asleep were quickly roused by it to thorough wakefulness. Lord Byron sprang up in his cot, exclaiming, 'We shall certainly have an eruption; such power must burst through every thing!' He had barely ceased speaking, when a dense column of heavy black smoke was seen rising from the crater directly in front of us; the subterranean struggle ceased, and immediately after, flames burst from a large cone, near which we had been in the morning, and which then appeared to have been long inactive. Red-hot stones, cinders, and ashes were also propelled to a great height with immense violence; and shortly after, the molten lava came boiling up, and flowed down the sides of the cone, and over the surrounding scoria, in two beautiful curved streams, glittering with indescribable brilliance.

"At the same time a whole lake of fire opened in a more distant part. This could not have been less than two miles in circumference; and its action was more horribly sublime than any thing I ever imagined to exist, even in the ideal visions of unearthly things. Its surface had all the agitation of an ocean; billow after billow tossed its monstrous bosom in the air, and occasionally those from different directions burst with such violence, as in the concussion to dash the fiery spray forty or fifty feet high. It was at once the most splendidly beautiful and dreadfully fearful of spectacles; and irresistibly turned the thoughts to that lake of fire from whence the smoke of torment ascendeth for ever and ever. No work of him who laid the foundations of the earth, and who by his almighty power still supports them, ever brought to my mind the more awful revelations of his Word with such overwhelming impression. Truly, 'with God is terrible majesty.'—'Let all the nations say unto God—how terrible art thou in thy works!'"

Soon after leaving our encampment on the morning of the 3d of August, we came to the pools of water, where we filled our canteens. Here also our party

separated; Messrs. Goodrich and Harwood proceeding
across the interior through the villages of *Orá* to Waiakea, in the division of Hiro, while the rest passed along
the east side of the crater, towards the seashore. The
path was in many places dangerous, lying along narrow
ridges, with fearful precipices on each side, or across
deep chasms and hollows that required the utmost care
to avoid falling into them, and where a fall would have
been fatal, as several of the chasms seemed narrowest
at the surface.

In one place, we passed along for a considerable distance under a high precipice, where, though the country
was perfectly level at the top, or sloped gradually towards the sea, the impending rocks towered some hundred feet above us on our left, and the appalling flood
of lava rolled almost immediately beneath us on our
right. On this side we descended to some small craters
on the declivity, and also to the black ledge; where
we collected a number of beautiful specimens of highly
scoriaceous lava, the base approaching to volcanic
glass. It was generally of a black or red colour, light,
cellular, brittle, and shining. We also found a quantity
of volcanic glass drawn out into filaments as fine as
human hair, and called by the natives *rauoho o 'Pélé*
(hair of Pélé). It was of a dark olive colour, semi-
transparent, and brittle, though some of the filaments
were several inches long. Probably it had been produced by the bursting of igneous masses of lava, thrown
out from the craters, or separated in fine-spun threads
from the boiling fluid, when in a state of perfect fusion,
and, borne by the smoke or vapour above the edges of
the crater, had been wafted by the winds over the adjacent plain; for we also found quantities of it at least
seven miles distant from the large crater. We entered
several small craters, that had been in vigorous action
but a very short period before, marks of most recent
fusion presenting themselves on every side. Their
size and height were various, and many, which from the
top had appeared insignificant as mole-hills, we now
found twelve or twenty feet high. The outside was
composed of bright shining scoriaceous lava, heaped
up in piles of most singular form. The lava on the inside was of a light or dark red colour, with a glazed
surface, and in several places, where the heat had evidently been intense, we saw a deposite of small and

beautifully white crystals. We also entered several
covered channels, or tunnels, through which the lava
had flowed into the large abyss. They had been formed
by the cooling of the lava on the sides and surface of
the stream, while it had continued to flow on underneath. As the size of the current diminished, it had
left a hard crust of lava of unequal thickness over the
top, supported by walls of the same material on each
side. Their interior was beautiful beyond description.
In many places they were ten or twelve feet high, and
as many wide at the bottom. The roofs formed a regular arch, hung with red and brown stalactitic lava, in
every diversified shape, while the floor appeared like
one continued glassy stream. The winding of its current and the ripple of its surface were so entire, that it
seemed as if, while in rapid motion, the stream of lava
had suddenly stopped, and become indurated, even before the undulations of the surface had subsided.

We traced one of these volcanic chambers to the
edge of the precipice that bounds the great crater, and
looked over the fearful steep down which the fiery cascade had rushed. In the place where it had fallen, the
lava had formed a spacious basin, which, hardening as
it cooled, had retained all those forms which a torrent of
lava, falling several hundred feet, might be expected to
produce on the viscid mass below. In the neighbourhood we saw several large masses of basaltic rock, of
a dark gray colour, weighing probably from one to four
or five tons, which, although they did not bear any
marks of recent fire, must have been ejected from the
great crater during some violent eruption, as the surrounding rocks in every direction presented a very different appearance; or they might have been thrown
out in a liquid state, combined with other matter that
had formed a rock of a less durable kind, which, decom-
posing more rapidly, had been washed away, and left
them in detached masses on the plain. They were
hard, and, when fractured, appeared a lava of basalt,
containing very fine grains of compact felspar and augite;
some of them contained small particles of olivine. We
also saw a number of other rocks in a state of decomposition, which proved to be a species of lava, containing
globules of zeolite. The decomposition of these rocks
appeared to have formed the present surface of much

I 2

of the west, north, and east parts of the plain immediately surrounding the crater.

When we had broken off specimens of these, and of
some red earthy-looking stones, which seemed to have
the same base as the other, but to have lost their compact texture, and to have experienced a change of
colour from a further degree of decomposition,* we
passed along to the east side, where I took a sketch of
the south-west end of the crater.

As we travelled on from this spot, we unexpectedly
came to another deep crater, nearly half as large as the
former. The native name of it is *Kirauea-iti* (little
Kirauea). It is separated from the large crater by an
isthmus nearly a hundred yards wide. Its sides, which
were much less perpendicular than those of the great
crater, were covered with trees and shrubs, but the
bottom was filled with black lava, either fluid or scarcely
cold, and probably supplied by the great crater, as the
trees, shrubs, and grass on its sides showed it had remained many years in a state of quiescence. Though
this was the only small one we saw, our companions
informed us there were many in the neighbourhood.
They also pointed out to us the ruins of Oararano, an
old heiau, which crowned the summit of a lofty precipice on our left. It was formerly a temple of Pélé, of
which *Kamakaakeakua* (the eye of god), a distinguished
soothsayer, who died in the reign of Tamehameha, was
many years priest. Large offerings were frequently
made, of hogs, dogs, fish, and fruits, but we could not
learn that human victims were ever immolated on its
altars. These offerings were always cooked in the
steaming chasms, or the adjoining ground. Had they
been dressed anywhere else, or prepared with other
fire, they would have been considered polluted, and have
been expected to draw down calamities on those who
presented them.

The ground throughout the whole plain is so hot,
that those who come to the mountains to procure wood
for building, or to cut down trees and hollow them out
for canoes, always cook their own food, whether animal or vegetable, by simply wrapping it in fern leaves,

* Specimens of volcanic sulphur, of the several kinds of lava and rocks
found in the immediate neighbourhood of the volcano, and other parts of the
island, with descriptions of their localities, are deposited in the Museum of
the London Missionary Society, Austin Friars.

and burying it in the earth. The east side of the plain was ornamented with several beautiful species of filices; also with several plants much resembling some of the varieties of cycas, and thickly covered with ohelo bushes, the berries of which we ate freely as we walked along, till, coming to a steep precipice, we ascended about 300 feet, and reached the high land on the side towards the sea, which commanded a fine view of Mouna Roa, opposite to which we had been travelling ever since we left Punaruu. The mountain appeared of an oval shape, stretching along in a south-west direction, nearly parallel with the south-east shore, from which its base was generally distant twenty or thirty miles. A ridge of high land appeared to extend from the eastern point to the south-west shore. Between it and the foot of Mouna Roa was a valley, as near as we could judge, from seven to twelve miles wide. The summit of Mouna Roa was never free from snow, the higher parts of the mountain's side were totally destitute of every kind of vegetation; and, by the help of a telescope, we could discover numerous extinguished craters, with brown and black streams of indurated lava over the whole extent of its surface. The foot of the mountain was enriched on this side by trees and shrubs, which extended from its base six or seven miles towards the summit.

The volcano of Kirauea, the largest of which we have any account, and which was, until visited by us, unknown to the civilized parts of the world, is situated in the district of Kapapala, nearly on the boundary line between the divisions of Kaü and Puna, twenty miles from the seashore. We could form no correct estimate of its elevation above the level of the sea; the only means we had of judging being the difference of temperature in the air, as shown by our thermometer, which, on the shore, was usually at sunrise 71°, but which, in the neighbourhood of the volcano, was, at the same hour, no higher than 46°. From the isthmus between *Kiraueanui*, or Great Kirauea, and Little Kirauea, the highest peak of Mouna Kea bore by compass N. N. W., and the centre of Mouna Roa W. S. W. The uneven summits of the steep rocks, that, like a wall many miles in extent, surrounded the crater and all its appendages, showed the original level of the country, or perhaps marked the base, and formed, as it were,

the natural buttresses of some lofty mountain, raised in
the first instance by the accumulation of volcanic matter, whose bowels had been consumed by volcanic fire,
and whose sides had afterward fallen into the vast
furnace, where, reduced a second time to a liquefied
state, they had been again vomited out on the adjacent
plain.

But the magnificent fires of Kirauea, which we had
viewed with such admiration, appeared to dwindle into
insignificance, when we thought of the probable subterranean fires immediately beneath us. The whole island
of Hawaii, covering a space of four thousand square
miles, from the summits of its lofty mountains, perhaps
15,000 or 16,000 feet above the level of the sea, down
to the beach is, according to every observation we
could make, one complete mass of lava, or other volcanic matter, in different stages of decomposition. Perforated with innumerable apertures in the shape of
craters, the island forms a hollow cone over one vast
furnace, situated in the heart of a stupendous submarine
mountain, rising from the bottom of the sea; or possibly the fires may rage with augmented force beneath
the bed of the ocean, rearing, through the superincumbent weight of water, the base of Hawaii, and, at the
same time, forming a pyramidal funnel from the furnace
to the atmosphere.

* In Cook's Voyages, Capt. King, speaking of Mouna Kaah (Kea), remarks,
that it "may be clearly seen at fourteen leagues' distance." Describing
Mouna-Roa, and estimating it according to the tropical line of snow, he ob-
serves, "This mountain must be at least 16,020 feet high, which exceeds the
height of the Pico de Tende, or Peak of Teneriffe, by 724 feet, according to
Dr. Heberden's computation, or 3680 according to that of Chevalier de Borda.
The peaks of Mouna Kaah appeared to be about half a mile high; and, as
they are entirely covered with snow, the altitude of their summits cannot be
less than 18,400 feet. But it is probable that both these mountains may be
considerably higher; for, in insular situations, the effects of the warm sea
air must necessarily remove the line of snow, in equal latitudes, to a greater
height, than where the atmosphere is chilled on all sides by an immense
tract of perpetual snow."

CHAPTER XI.

Journey to Kearakomo—Description of the dracæna, or ti-plant—Account of the application of a priestess of Pélé to the chiefs at Maui, to revenge the insult offered to the goddess—Visit of Kapiolani to the crater—Reported eruption of lava in Kapapala—Sabbath in Kearakomo—Affectionate reception of Makoa—Fragment of a song on his birth—Conversation with the people—Marks of an earthquake—Description of Kaimu—Manner of launching and landing canoes at Kehena—Preaching—Visit to Kinao—Popular superstitions respecting the origin of diseases.

Though we left our encampment at daybreak, it was eleven o'clock in the forenoon before we took our final leave of Kirauea.

The path by which we descended towards the sea was about south-east by east. On the high lands in the vicinity of the crater we found the ground covered with strawberry plants, on some of which were a few berries, but the season for them appeared to be gone by. The plants and vines were small, as was also the fruit, which in its colour and shape resembled the haut-boy-strawberry, though in taste it was much more insipid. Strawberries, as well as raspberries, are indigenous plants, and are found in great abundance over most of the high lands of Hawaii; though we do not know of their existence in any other islands of the group.

The ground over which we walked was composed of ancient lava, of a light brown colour, broken into small pieces, resembling coarse dry gravel, to the depth of two or three inches, below which it appeared one solid mass of lava. The surface was covered with ohelo bushes, and a few straggling ferns and low shrubs, which made travelling more agreeable than when we approached the volcano. Within a few miles of Kirauea, we passed three or four high and extinct craters. One of them, Keanakakoi, the natives told us, sent forth in the days of Riroa king of Hawaii, about fourteen generations back, most of the lava over which we were travelling. The sides of these craters were generally covered with verdure, while the brown irregular-shaped rocks, on their indented summits, frowned like the battlements of a castle in ruins. We occasionally passed through rather extensive shrubberies of bushes and small trees, growing in the decomposed lava and sand, and striking their roots among the cracks which were filled up with the same material. As we approached the sea, the soil became more generally spread over the surface, and vegetation more luxuriant.

We stopped at a solitary cottage, where we procured a draught of fresh water, to us exceedingly grateful, as we had travelled since the morning without any refresh-ment, except a few berries and a piece of sugar-cane. We descended 300 or 400 feet, by a narrow winding path, covered with overhanging trees, and bordered by shrubs and grass. We then walked over a tract of lava, broken and decomposed, and about four or five miles wide, at the end of which another steep appeared. These steep precipices form concentric ridges of vol-canic rock round the greater part of this side of the island. Down this we descended, by following the course of a rugged current of ancient lava, for about 600 feet perpendicular depth, when we arrived at the plain below, which was one extended sheet of lava, without shrub or bush, stretching to the north and south as far as the eye could reach, and from four to six miles across, from the foot of the mountain to the sea. The natives gave us the fabulous story of the combat between Pélé and Támapuaa, as the origin of this flood of lava. This vast tract of lava was black, shining, and cellular, though not very brittle, and was more homogeneous than that which covered the south-ern shores of the island. We crossed it in about two hours, and arrived at Kearakāmo, the second village in the division of Puna. We stopped at the first house we came to, and asked for water. The natives brought us a calabash-full, of which we drank most hearty draughts, though it was little better than the water of the sea, from which it had percolated through the vesicles of the lava into hollows from nine to twelve feet distant from the ocean. It barely quenched our thirst while we were swallowing it, but it was the best we could procure, and we could hardly refrain from drinking at every hollow to which we came. After walking about a mile along the beach, we came to a house, which our guide pointed out as our lodgings. It was a miserable hut, and we asked if we could not find better accommodation; as we intended to spend the Sabbath in the village. Mahae told us it was the only one in the place that was not crowded with people, and he thought the most comfortable one we could procure.

The village is populous, and the natives soon thronged around us. To our great regret, two-thirds of them appeared to be in a state of intoxication, a circumstance we frequently had occasion to lament in the villages through which we passed. Their inebriation was generally the effect of an intoxicating drink made of fermented sugar-cane juice, sweet potatoes, or ti-root.

The ti-plant is common in all the South Sea islands, and is a variety of *dracæna*, resembling the *dracæna terminalis*, except in the colour of its leaves, which are of a lively shining green. It is a slow-growing plant, with a large woody fusiform root, which, when first dug out of the ground, is hard and fibrous, almost tasteless, and of a white or light yellow colour. The natives bake it in large ovens under ground. After baking, it appears like a different substance altogether, being of a yellowish brown colour, soft, though fibrous, and saturated with a highly saccharine juice. It is sweet and pleasant to the taste, and much of it was eaten in this state, but the greater part is employed in making an intoxicating liquor much used by the natives. They bruise the baked roots with a stone, and steep them with water in a barrel or the bottom of an old canoe, till the mass is in a state of fermentation. The liquor is then drawn off, and sometimes distilled, when it produces a strong spirit; but the greater part of it is drunk in its fermented state without any further preparation. The root is certainly capable of being used for many valuable purposes. A good beer may be made from it; and in the Society Islands, though never able to granulate it, we have frequently boiled its juice to a thick syrup, and used it as a substitute for sugar, when destitute of that article.

We should think it an excellent antiscorbutic, and, as such, useful to ships on long voyages. Captains visiting the Society Islands frequently procure large quantities of it, to make beer with during their voyage, as it will keep good six weeks or two months after it is baked.*

* On my return, in the American ship Russell, Captain Coleman, we procured a quantity that had been baked, at Rurutu, near the Society Islands, and brought it round Cape Horn. It lasted five or six weeks, and would

I 3

Other parts of the dracæna are also useful. The natives frequently plant the roots thickly around their enclosures, interweave the stems of the plant, and form a valuable permanent hedge. The branch was always an emblem of peace, and, in times of war, borne, together with a young plantain-tree, as a flag of truce by the messengers who passed between the hostile parties. The leaves, woven together by their stalks, formed a short cloak, which the natives wore in their mountainous journeys; they also make the most durable thatch for the sides and roofs of their best houses.

About sunset we sent to the head man of the village for some refreshment, but he was intoxicated; and though we had walked upwards of twenty miles since morning, and had subsisted on but scanty fare since leaving Kapapala, we could only procure a few cold potatoes, and two or three pieces of raw salt fish. Multitudes crowded around our hut; and with those that were sober we entered into conversation.

The apprehensions uniformly entertained by the natives of the fearful consequences of Pélé's anger prevented their paying very frequent visits to the vicinity of her abode; and when, on their inland journeys, they had occasion to approach Kirauea, they were scrupulously attentive to every injunction of her priests, and regarded with a degree of superstitious veneration and awe the appalling spectacle which the crater and its appendages presented. The violations of her sacred abode, and the insults to her power, of which we had been guilty, appeared to them, and to the natives in general, acts of temerity and sacrilege; and, notwithstanding the fact of our being foreigners, we were subsequently threatened with the vengeance of the volcanic deity, under the following circumstances.

Some months after our visit to Kirauea, a priestess of Pélé came to Lahaina, in Maui, where the principal chiefs of the islands then resided. The object of her visit was noised abroad among the people, and much public interest excited. One or two mornings after her arrival in the district, arrayed in her prophetic robes,

probably have kept longer, as the only change we perceived during that time was a slight degree of acidity in the taste. Cattle, sheep, and goats are fond of the leaves; and, as they contain more nutriment than any other indigenous vegetable, and may be kept on board ships several weeks, they are certainly the best provender that can be procured in the islands for stock taken to sea.

having the edges of her garments burnt with fire, and
holding a short staff or spear in her hand, preceded by
her daughter, who was also a candidate for the office
of priestess, and followed by thousands of the people,
she came into the presence of the chiefs; and, having
told who she was, they asked what communications she
had to make. She replied that, in a trance or vision,
she had been with Pélé, by whom she was charged to
complain to them that a number of foreigners had visited
Kirauea; eaten the sacred berries; broken her houses,
the craters; thrown down large stones, &c.—to request
that the offenders might be sent away,—and to assure
them, that if these foreigners were not banished from
the islands, Pélé would certainly, in a given number of
days, take vengeance, by inundating the country with
lava, and destroying the people.' She also pretended to
have received, in a supernatural manner, Rihoriho's approbation of the request of the goddess. The crowds
of natives who stood waiting the result of her interview
with the chiefs were almost as much astonished as the
priestess herself, when Kaahumanu, and the other
chiefs, ordered all her paraphernalia of office to be
thrown into the fire, told her the message she had delivered was a falsehood, and directed her to return home,
cultivate the ground for her subsistence, and discontinue
her deceiving the people.

This answer was dictated by the chiefs themselves.
The missionaries at the station, although they were
aware of the visit of the priestess, and saw her, followed
by the thronging crowd, pass by their habitation on her
way to the residence of the chiefs, did not think it
necessary to attend or interfere; but relied entirely on
the enlightened judgment and integrity of the chiefs, to
suppress any attempts that might be made to revive the
influence of Pélé over the people; and in the result they
were not disappointed, for the natives returned to their
habitations, and the priestess soon after left the island,
and has not since troubled them with the threatenings
of the goddess.

On another occasion, Kapiolani, a pious chief-woman,
the wife of Naihe chief of Kaavaroa, was passing near
the volcano, and expressed her determination to visit
it. Some of the devotees of the goddess met her, and
attempted to dissuade her from her purpose; assuring
her that though foreigners might go there with security,

yet Pélé would allow no Hawaiian to intrude. Kapiolani, however, was not to be thus diverted, but proposed
that they should all go together; and declaring that if
Pélé appeared, or inflicted any punishment, she would
then worship the goddess, but proposing, that if nothing
of the kind took place, they should renounce their attachment to Pélé, and join with her and her friends in
acknowledging Jehovah as the true God. They all
went together to the volcano; Kapiolani, with her attendants, descended several hundred feet towards the
bottom of the crater, where she spoke to them of the
delusion they had formerly laboured under in supposing
it inhabited by their false gods; they sang a hymn, and
after spending several hours in the vicinity, pursued
their journey. What effect the conduct of Kapiolani,
on this occasion, will have on the natives in general,
remains yet to be discovered.

The people of Kearakomo also told us, that, no longer
than five moons ago, Pélé had issued from a subterranean cavern, and overflowed the low land of Kearaara,
and the southern part of Kapapala. The inundation was
sudden and violent, burnt one canoe, and carried four
more into the sea. At Mahuka, the deep torrent of lava
bore into the sea a large rock, according to their account,
near a hundred feet high, which, a short period before,
had been separated by an earthquake from the main pile
in the neighbourhood. It now stands, they say, in the
sea, nearly a mile from the shore, its bottom surrounded
by lava, its summit rising considerably above the water.
We exceedingly regretted our ignorance of this inundation at the time we passed through the inland parts of
the above-mentioned districts, for, had we known of it
then, we should certainly have descended to the shore,
and examined its extent and appearance. We now felt
convinced that the chasms we had visited at Ponahohoa, and the smoking fissures we afterward saw nearer
Kirauea, marked the course of a stream of lava, and
thought it probable, that though the lava had burst out
five months ago, it was still flowing in a smaller and less
rapid stream. Perhaps the body of lava that had filled
Kirauea up to the black ledge which we saw, between
three and four hundred feet above the liquid lava, at the
time we visited it, had been drawn off by this subterranean channel, though the distance between the great

crater and the land overflowed by it was not less than thirty or thirty-five miles.

When the day began to close, and we wished the natives to retire, we told them that to-morrow was the sacred day of Jehovah, the true God, and directed them to come together early in the morning, to hear his Word, and unite with us in his worship. We then spread our mats upon some poles that lay at one end of the house, and, as we had no lamp, and could procure no candle-nuts, we laid ourselves down as soon as it became dark, and, notwithstanding our uncomfortable lodging-place, slept very soundly till daybreak.

On the morning of the 3d, between six and seven o'clock, about two hundred of the people collected in front of our house. We sang a hymn; one of our number preached to them a discourse, which occupied rather more than half an hour; and another concluded the service with prayer. They were all sober, and appeared attentive. Several proposed questions to us; and when we had answered them, we directed them to return to their houses, to abstain from fishing and other ordinary employments, and when the sun was over their heads (the manner of expressing mid-day), to come together again, and hear more about Jehovah and Jesus Christ. Many, however, continued talking with the natives belonging to our company, and gazing at us through most of the day.

At twelve o'clock, about three hundred of the people again assembled near our dwelling, and we held a religious exercise similar to that which they had attended in the morning. The head man of the village was present during the service. He came into our house after it was over, and told us all his provisions were at his farm, which was some distance inland, and that to-morrow he intended to bring us a pig and some potatoes. We thanked him, but told him probably we should proceed on our way early in the morning. He went away, and in a short time returned with a raw salted albicore and a basket of baked sweet potatoes, which he said was all he could furnish us with to-day. We spent the afternoon in conversation with those who crowded our hut, and wished to inquire more fully about the things of which they had heard. Between five and six in the evening the people again collected for worship in front of our house, when they were addressed from Isaiah lx. 1—" Arise, shine, for thy light is come." They listened with attention to the advantages of Christian light and knowledge, contrasted with pagan ignorance and misery, and several exclaimed at the conclusion of the service, *Oia no. Poereere makou. E ake makou i hoomaramarama ia*—" So it is. We are dark. We desire to be enlightened." In the evening we were so favoured as to procure a calabash full of fresh water from the caves in the mountains, where it had filtered through the strata of lava, and was received into vessels placed there for that purpose. It tasted bitter, from standing long in the calabashes; but yet it was a luxury, for our thirst was great, notwithstanding the quantities of water we had drunk during the day. About sunset we ate some of our raw fish and half-baked potatoes. When it began to grow dark we concluded the day with prayer, imploring the gracious influences of the Holy Spirit to follow our feeble attempts to declare his truth, and make it effectual to the spiritual welfare of the people. We afterward laid down upon our mats, but passed an uncomfortable night, from the swarms of vermin which infested the house, and the indisposition induced by the nature of the food and water we had taken since leaving the volcano.

When, on the morning of the 4th, we had passed Punau, Leapuki, and Kamomoa, the country began to wear a more agreeable aspect. Groves of cocoanuts ornamented the projecting points of land, clumps of koutrees appeared in various directions, and the habitations of the natives were also thickly scattered over the coast.

At noon we passed through Pulana, where we saw a large heiau called *Wahaura*, Red Mouth, or Red-feather Mouth, built by Tamehameha, and dedicated to Tairi, his war-god. Human sacrifices, we were informed, were occasionally offered here. Shortly after, we reached Kupahua, a pleasant village, situated on a rising ground, in the midst of groves of shady trees, and surrounded by a well-cultivated country. Here we stopped, and, having collected the people of the village, I preached to them. They afterward proposed several interesting inquiries connected with what they had heard, and said it was a good thing for us to *aroha*, or have compassion on them. They also asked when we would come again.

Leaving this interesting place, we passed on to Kala-

pana, a small village on the seashore, distinguished as
the residence of *Kapihi*, the priest, who in the days of
Tamehameha told the king that after death he and all
his ancestors would live again on Hawaii. We saw a
large heiau, of which he was priest, but did not see
many people. Kapihi had many disciples, who believed,
or pretended to believe, his predictions. Frequent offerings were made to Kuahairo, his god, at other parts of
the island more frequently visited by the king, and this
probably drew away many of the people from Kalapana.
About three P. M. we approached *Kaimu*. This was the
birth-place of Mauae, and the residence of most of his
relations. He was a young man belonging to the governor, who had been sent with the canoe, and who, since
leaving Honuapo, had acted as our guide. He walked
before us as we entered the village. The old people
from the houses welcomed him as he passed along, and
numbers of the young men and women came out to
meet him, saluted him by touching noses, and wept for
joy at his arrival. Some took off his hat, and crowned
him with a garland of flowers; others hung round his
neck wreaths of a sweet-scented plant resembling ivy,
or necklaces composed of the nut of the fragrant *pandanus odoratissimus*. When we reached the house where
his sister lived, she ran to meet him, threw her arms
around his neck, and having affectionately embraced
him, walked hand in hand with him through the village.
Multitudes of young people and children followed, chanting his name, the names of his parents, the place and
circumstances of his birth, and the most remarkable
events in the history of his family, in a lively song,
which, he afterward informed us, was composed on the
occasion of his birth. The following fragment of the
commencement, which I afterward wrote down from the
mouth of one of his aged relatives who was with us,
will suffice as a specimen—the whole is too long for
insertion:

FRAGMENT OF A SONG ON THE NAME OF MAUAE.

Inoa o Mauae a Para,	Name of Mauae* (son) of Para,
He aha matou auanei?	How shall we declare?
O Mauae, te wahine horua nui,	O *Mauae*, woman famous at *horua*,†
Wahine mahesi pono.	Woman tilling well the ground.
Tuu ra te Ravaia	Give the fisherman,

---

* Mother of the young man.   † Horua, a native game.

I ta wahine maheai,	To the woman (who) tilleth the ground;
I pono wale ai te aina o orua.	Happy will be the land of you two.
Owerawahie i uta i Tapapala.	Burnt were the woods inland of Tapapala.
Tupu mau u ore te pari.	Long parched had been the precipice.
Oneanea te aina o Tuaehu.	Lonely was the land of Tuaehu.
Ua tu ra te manu i te pari Oharahara.	The bird perched on Oharahara rocks.
Ewaru te po, e waru te ao,	Eight the nights, eight the days,
Ua pau te aho o na hoa maheai,	Gone was the breath of those who help the tillage,
I te tanu wale i te rau, a maloa.	With planting herbs (they) were fatigued;
Ua mate i te la,	Fainting under the sun.
Ua tu nevaneva.	(They) looked anxiously around.
I ta matani, ua ino auaurere,	By the wind, the flying, scudding tempest,
Ua tu ta repo i Hiona:	Thrown up was the earth (or dust) at Hiona:
Pura ta onohi i ta u i ta repo.	Red were the eyeballs with the dust.
O Tauai, O Tauai, aroha wale	O Tauai,* O Tauai, loved be
Te aina i roto o te tai,	The land in the midst of the sea,
E noho marie oe i roto o te tai,	Thou dwellest quietly in the midst of the sea,
E fariu ai te aro i rehua.	And turnest thy face to the pleasant wind,
Pura ta onohi i ta matani,	Red were the eyeballs with the wind,
Ta tatau ta iri onionio,	(Of those) whose skin was spotted with tattoo,
Ta repo a tau i Pohaturoa,	The sand of Tau (lay) at Pohaturoa,†
Te ai Ohiaotalani,	The lava at Ohiaotalani.‡
Ma tai te aranui e hiti ai	By the sea was the road to arrive
I te one i Taimu,	At the sandy beach of Taimu,
Ma uta i ta tuohivi,	Inland by the mountain ridges,
Te aranui i hunaia.	The path that was concealed.
Narowale Tirauea i te ino.	Hid was Tirauea§ by the tempest
Noho Pele i Tirauea,	Pele‖ abode in Tirauea,
I tabu mau ana i te rua.	In the pit, ever feeding the fires.

They continued chanting their song, and thus we passed through their plantations and groves of cocoanut-trees, till we reached his father's house, where a general effusion of affection and joy presented itself, which it was impossible to witness without delight. A number of children, who ran on before, had announced his approach; his father, followed by his brothers and several other relations, came out to meet him, and, under the shade of a wide-spreading kou-tree, fell on his neck and wept aloud for some minutes; after which, they took him by the hand, and led him through a neat little garden into the house. He seated himself on a mat on the floor; while his brothers and sisters gathered around him; some unloosed his sandals, and rubbed his limbs and feet; others clasped his hand, frequently saluting

* Atooi.   † Districts: ‡ North peak of the volcano.
§ The great volcano.   ‖ Goddess of volcanoes.

it by touching it with their nose; others brought him a calabash of water, or a lighted tobacco-pipe. One of his sisters, in particular, seemed much affected; she clasped his hand, and sat for some time weeping by his side. At this we should have been surprised, had we not known it to be the usual manner among the South Sea islanders of expressing unusual joy or grief. In the present instance it was the unrestrained expression of joyful feelings. Indeed, every one seemed at a loss how to manifest the sincere pleasure which his unexpected arrival, after several years' absence, had produced. On first reaching the house, we had thrown ourselves down on a mat, and remained silent spectators; not, however, without being considerably affected by the interesting scene.

At six o'clock in the evening, we sent to collect the people of the village to hear preaching. Between three and four hundred assembled under a clump of trees in front of the house, and I preached to them from Psalm xxii. verses 27 and 28. Our singing appeared to interest them, as well as other parts of the service; and, at the conclusion, several exclaimed, "Jehovah is a good God; I desire him for my God."

About this time Makoa arrived with our baggage. We were glad to see him, and inquired where he had been during the past week. He said he remained only one night at Honuapo, and followed on the next morning—observing, at the same time, we must have travelled fast, or he should have been here before us, as he had not gone round by the volcano, but had proceeded in a straight line from Kapapala to Kearakomo.

The evening we spent with the people of the place in conversation on various subjects, but principally respecting he volcano which we had recently visited.

The people recapitulated the contest between Pélé and Tamapaa, and related the adventures of several warriors, who with spear in hand had opposed the volcanic demons when coming down on a torrent of lava. They could not believe that we had descended into the crater, or broken off pieces of Pélé's houses, as they called the small craters, until the specimens of lava, &c. were produced, when some of them looked very significantly, and none of them cared much to handle them.

We tried to convince them of their mistake in sup-

posing Kirauea was inhabited, and unfolded to them in
as simple a manner as possible the nature of volcanoes,
and of their various phenomena, assuring them at the
same time that they were under the sovereign control
of Jehovah; the only true God. Some said, *Ae paha*—
"Yes, perhaps;" others were silent.

Numbers of the people were present at our evening
worship, which was in their language.

After a comfortable night's rest, we arose at daybreak
on the 5th. At sunrise the people assembled more nu-
merously than they had done on the preceding evening,
and I preached to them from these words,—"Herein is
love, not that we love God, but that he loved us, and
sent his Son to be the propitiation for our sins." They
appeared to listen with interest, and numbers sat down
under the kou-trees, talking among themselves on the
subject, for a long time after the services had closed.

After breakfast we examined the effects of an earthquake experienced in this place about two months before.
We were informed that it took place about ten o'clock
in the evening. The ground, after being agitated some
minutes with a violent tremulous motion, suddenly burst
open, for several miles in extent, in a direction from north-
by-east to south-by-west, and emitted, in various places
at the same instant, a considerable quantity of smoke
and luminous vapour, but none of the people were injured
by it. A stone wall four feet thick and six feet high,
enclosing a garden at the north end of the village, was
thrown down. A chasm about a foot wide marked distinctly its course. At the south end of the village it had
passed through a small well, in which originally there
was seldom more than eighteen inches' depth of water,
though since that period there has been upwards of three
feet. The crack was about ten inches wide, running
from north to south across the bottom of the well. The
water has not only increased in quantity, but suffered a
great deterioration in quality, being now very salt; and
its rising and falling with the ebbing and flowing of the
tide indicates its connexion with the waters of the
ocean, from which it appeared distant about three hundred yards.

Convulsions of this kind are common over the whole
island; they are not, however, so frequent in this vicinity as in the northern and western parts, and are seldom
violent, except when they immediately precede the erup-

tion of a volcano. The superstitions of the natives
lead them to believe they are produced by the power
of Pélé, or some of the volcanic deities, and consider
them as requisitions for offerings, or threatenings of still
greater calamities.

Kaimu is pleasantly situated near the seashore, on the
south-east side of the island, standing on a bed of lava
considerably decomposed, and covered over with a light
and fertile soil. It is adorned with plantations, groves
of cocoanuts, and clumps of kou-trees. It has a fine
sandy beach, where canoes may land with safety; and,
according to the houses numbered to-day, contains about
seven hundred and twenty-five inhabitants. Including
the villages in its immediate vicinity along the coast, the
population would probably amount to two thousand; and
if water could be procured near at hand, it would form
an eligible missionary station. There are several wells
in the village, containing brackish water, which has
passed from the sea through the cells of the lava, under-
going a kind of filtration; and is collected in hollows
scooped out to receive it. The natives told us that at the
distance of about a mile there was plenty of fresh water.
The extent of cultivation in the neighbourhood, together
with the decent and orderly appearance of the people,
induced us to think they are more sober and industrious
than those of many villages through which we have
passed.

From the oppression of idolatry the people feel themselves emancipated, and seem also to enjoy, in some
degree, the domestic comfort resulting from their dwelling together in one house, sitting down to the same repast, and eating the same kind of food. But though they
approved of the destruction of the national idols, many
were far from having renounced idolatry, and were in
general destitute of all knowledge of that dispensation
of grace and truth which came by Jesus Christ. They
seemed firm believers in the existence of deities in the
volcanoes.

We endeavoured in the evening to convince those
who crowded our dwelling of their mistake respecting
the objects of their worship, spoke to them of Jehovah,
the only being to whom religious homage should be rendered, and of that life and immortality revealed in the
sacred scriptures.

Before we retired we wrote a letter to the governor,

informing him of our progress, the hospitality of the people in general, and the kind attention we had received from Mauae, who intended to return from this place to Kairua.

Early the next morning, after travelling nearly two hours, we arrived at Keouohana, where we sat down to rest beneath the shade of some cocoanut-trees. Makoa, our guide, spoke to the head man, and he directed the people to assemble near his house. About one hundred soon came; and when we had explained to them, in few words, the object of our visit, we requested them to sit down, and listen to the tidings we had brought. They immediately obeyed. We sang a hymn in their language, after which an address was given, and the service concluded in the usual manner. As soon as it was finished, they began to talk about what we had told them. Some said it was very good: they had never heard before of a God who had sent his Son to save men. Others said it was very well for the *haore* (foreigners) to believe it, but *Tane, Rono, Tanaroa,* and *Tu* were the gods of the Sandwich islanders. Makoa, who was a chief speaker among them on such occasions, said they must all attend to the new word, must forsake thieving and drunkenness, infanticide and murder, and do no work on the *la tabu* (day sacred); adding, at the same time, that the king had received the *palapala,* books, &c., and went to church on the sacred day, as did also Kuakini, the governor. The head man brought us some ripe plantains, of which we ate a few, and then proceeded on our way, leaving them busy in conversation about the news they had heard; which, in all probability, were "strange things" to their ears.

After travelling a mile and a half along the shore, we came to Kehena, a populous village: the people seemed, from the number of their canoes, nets, &c., to be much engaged in fishing. Their contrivance for launching and landing their canoes was curious.

Leaving Kehena, we walked on to Kamaili, a pleasant village, standing in a gently sloping valley, cultivated and shaded by some large cocoanut-trees. Here we stopped to take breakfast, having travelled about four hours and a half. The people who were not employed on their plantations, or in fishing, afterward assembled, and were addressed from Psalm lxvii. 7. Conversation followed, and they detained us some time to answer

their questions, or to explain more fully the things that
had been spoken. It was truly gratifying to notice the
eagerness with which they proposed their inquiries.
After spending about half an hour in endeavouring to
satisfy two or three hundred of them, we took leave, and
pursued our journey. Our path from Kaimu had been
smooth and pleasant, but shortly after leaving Kamaili
we passed a very rugged tract of lava, nearly four miles
across. The lava seemed as if broken to pieces as it
cooled; it had continued to roll on like a stream of large
scoria, or cinders. Our progress across it was slow and
fatiguing. On our way, our guide pointed out Karepa,
an ancient heiau, formerly dedicated to Tu and Rono,
and built in the days of Teavemauhiri, or Tanakini, king
of this part of the island. We could not learn whether
this was the heiau of Rono, in which the bones of Captain Cook were deposited and worshipped. About half-
past one we arrived at Opihikao, another populous village, situated within a short distance of the sea. The
head man, Karaikoa, brought out a mat, spread it under
the umbrageous shade of a kou-tree in front of his door,
and invited us to sit down and rest, as the sun was vertical, and travelling laborious. We seated ourselves
beside him, and so soon as he learned from Makoa the
nature of our errand, he sent of his own accord and collected the people. When they had assembled, we stood
up and sang a hymn, after which one of our number
preached to them from Job xxi. 15. It was undoubtedly
the first time most, if not all, of them had attended a
meeting of the kind; and the preacher was frequently
interrupted by several, who exclaimed, " Owau kahi e
malama ia Jehova,—e ake au i ora ia Jesu Kraist;" I am
one that will serve Jehovah: I desire to be saved by
Jesus Christ.

We invited them to ask us any question respecting
what they had heard; and in answering those they proposed we spent some time after the service was concluded. We then proceeded about two miles, principally through cultivated grounds, to Kauaea. About
three hundred people, excited by curiosity, soon collected around us, to whom Mr. Thurston preached. We
afterward sat down and talked with them, and then resumed our journey through the district of Malama, the
inland part of which was inundated by a volcanic eruption about thirty years since. The part over which we

passed, being nearer the sea than that which the lava had overflowed, was covered with soil, and smiling with verdure. Near five P. M. we reached Keahialaka, the residence of *Kinao*, chief or governor of Puna. We found him lying on a couch of sickness, and felt anxious to administer to his comfort, yet did not like at so early an hour to halt altogether for the night. I therefore remained with the sick chief, while Messrs. Thurston and Bishop went on to a village at the east point, about two miles distant. When they reached Pualaa, the above-mentioned village, they were kindly welcomed by the head man, who soon had the people of the place collected at their request, and to them Mr. Thurston proclaimed the news of salvation through Jesus Christ. The chief entertained the travellers with hospitality, and their lodgings were comfortable.

Just before the setting of the sun, I preached to the people at the village where I was staying, and spent the evening with the chief, who was afflicted with a pulmonary complaint, and almost reduced to a skeleton, earnestly recommending him to apply to Jesus, the great physician of souls. He seemed at first much attached to the superstitions of his ancestors, said he had performed every ceremony that he thought likely to be of any avail, and would do any thing to live; but added, *E make poha auanei*, Perhaps I must soon die. The love of the Saviour, and his suitableness to the situation of the poor chief, were pointed out, and he was requested rather to seek unto Him for the salvation of his soul, than to priests and the incantations of sorcerers for the prolongation of his mortal life, which, although of infinitely less moment than the well-being of his soul, was yet entirely beyond their power. He listened attentively, and at a late hour requested me to pray for him to Jesus Christ. The family collected during the time of prayer, at the close of which the chief reclined on his mat, but said he could not sleep.

We were fatigued with the labours of the day, though we had not travelled so far as usual. The country had been much more populous than any we had passed since leaving Kona, and we felt thankful for the opportunities that we had this day enjoyed of speaking to so many about those things which concern their everlasting peace. May the Holy Spirit water the seed this day sown!

Messrs. Thurston and Bishop conducted the usual worship with the people, who at an early hour the next morning crowded the house where they had lodged. I spent some time in endeavouring to inform the dark mind of the dying chief on points of the last importance; again directed him to that compassionate Saviour who invites all to come unto him, receives even those who apply at the eleventh hour, and is able to save to the uttermost those who trust in his mercy. I afterward prayed with him and his family, and then bade them farewell.

The situation of Kinao was affecting. He appeared in the midst of his days, probably not more than thirty or forty years of age; and though formerly robust and healthy, he was now pale, emaciated, and reduced almost to a skeleton. Enveloped in all the darkness of paganism; and perhaps agitated with fearful uncertainties respecting a future state, he clung eagerly to life, yet seemed to feel a conviction of his approaching end daily increasing. Like his countrymen in general, he supposed his disease inflicted in consequence of the prayers of some malicious enemy, or the vindictive displeasure of the gods of his country; hence he had consulted the sorcerers, expended on them his property, and attended to all their injunctions, if by any means his life might be spared.

The popular superstitions of the islanders lead them to imagine that an individual who possesses the means of employing a sorcerer may afflict with painful disease, and even occasion the death of, any person against whom he may indulge feelings of hatred or revenge. They also believe that the sorcerers, by certain incantations, can discover the author or cause of the disease, and refer it back to the party with whom it originated. So prevalent are these notions, that the people generally believe every individual, who does not meet his death by some act of violence, is destroyed by the immediate power of an unpropitious deity, by poison, or the incantations of the sorcerers employed by some cruel enemy. This belief gives the sorcerers great influence among the middling and lower orders; and in times of protracted sickness, their aid is almost invariably sought by all who can procure a dog and a fowl for the sacrifice, and a piece or two of tapa as a fee for the priest. A dog and a fowl are all that are necessary for the ceremony:

but the offerings to the god and the fees to the priest are regulated according to the wealth or rank of the individual on whose behalf the aid of sorcery is employed.

The ceremonies performed are various; but the most general is the *kuni ahi*, broiling fire, a kind of *anaaná*, or sorcery, used to discover the person whose incantation has induced the illness of the party for whom it is performed. When a chief wishes to resort to it, he sends for a priest, who on his arrival receives a number of hogs, dogs, and fowls, together with several bundles of tapa. Before he commences any of his operations, all persons, except the parties immediately concerned, retire from the house, which the priest tabus, and prohibits strangers from entering. He then kindles a small fire somewhere near the couch of the invalid, and covers it with stones. This being done, he kills one of the dogs by strangling it, and cuts off the head of one of the fowls, muttering all the while his prayers to the god he invokes. The dog, fowl, and pig, if there be one, are then cut open, embowelled, and laid on the heated stones, the priest continuing his incantations, and watching at the same time the offerings broiling on the fire. A small part only of these offerings is eaten by the priest, the rest remain on the fire until consumed, when the priest lies down to sleep; and if his prayers are answered, he informs the poor sufferer, on awaking, who or what is the cause of his sickness. Additional presents are then made to the god, and other prayers offered, that the sickness may seize the person whose incantations, in the first instance, caused it; or, if in consequence of any delinquency towards the god on the part of the sufferer, that he would abate his anger, and remove the disease. But if, during his sleep, the priest has no revelation or dream, he informs his employers, on awaking, that he has not succeeded, and that another kuni ahi must be prepared before he can satisfy them respecting the cause of sickness. On such occasions the unsuccessful priest is often dismissed, and another sent for, to try his influence with the god.

Different priests employ different prayers or incantations, and are careful to keep the knowledge of them confined to their families, as each one supposes, or wishes the people to think, his own form the best; hence we have often heard the natives, when talking on the subject, say, "*He pule mana ko me,*" A powerful-

prayer has such a one : and the priest or sorcerer who
is supposed to have most influence with the god is most
frequently employed by the people, and hence derives
the greatest emoluments from his profession. Though
Uri is the principal god for the sorcerers, each tribe has
its respective deities for these occasions. Thus the
poor deluded people are led to imagine that the beings
they worship are continually exerting their power against
each other.; or that the same god who, when a small
offering only was presented, would allow sickness to
continue till' death should destroy the victim of his
displeasure,. would, for 'a larger offering, restrain his
anger, and withdraw the' disease. The sorcerers were
a distinct class among the priests of the island, and
their art appears to claim equal antiquity with the other
parts of that cruel system of idolatry by which the
people have been so long oppressed; and though it has
survived the destruction of the national idolatry, and is
still practised by many, it is entirely discontinued by the
principal chiefs in every island, and by all who attend
to Christian instruction.

CHAPTER XII.

Conversation with the natives—Appearance of the country in the vicinity of
Pualaa—Extinguished volcano in the valley of Kapoho—Description of
the horua, a native game—Traditionary story of a contest between Pélé
and Kahavari—Incidents on the journey to Hiro—Description of Ora—
Public worship at Waiakea—Conversation with a priestess of Pélé, the
goddess of the volcanoes—Opinion of the natives respecting the permanent
residence of missionaries at Waiakea—Description of native houses.

IT was about eight o'clock in the morning of the
seventh when I joined Messrs. Thurston and Bishop at
Pualaa, where we took breakfast, and afterward spent
the forenoon in conversation with the natives.

Two or three old men, whom we afterward learned
were priests, seemed to dispute what we said about
Jehovah's being the only true God, and the Christian the only true religion. They said they thought
their taö (traditions) respecting Tu, Tanaroa, Rono, or
Orono, and Tairi, were as authentic as the accounts in
our book, though ours, from the circumstance of their

VOL. IV.—K

being written, or, as they expressed it, " *hana paia i ka palapala*" (made fast on the paper), were better preserved, and more *akaaka*, clear, or generally intelligible.

To this we replied at some length, after which the old men ceased to object, but withheld their assent. Numbers sat around, and seemed interested in the discussion. We continued talking to them on the subject of their traditions, one of which we wrote down as they repeated it.

About half-past eleven we took leave of them, and directed our way across the eastern point. A most beautiful and romantic landscape presented itself on our left, as we travelled out of Pualaa.

As we reached Kapoho a cluster apparently of hills three or four miles round, and as many hundred feet high, with deep indented sides, overhung with trees, and clothed with herbage, standing in the midst of the barren plain of lava, attracted our attention. We walked through the gardens that encircled its base, till we reached the south-east side, where it was much lower than on the northern parts. Here we ascended what appeared to us to be one of the hills, and on reaching the summit were agreeably surprised to behold a charming valley opening before us. It was circular, and open towards the sea. The outer boundary of this natural amphitheatre was formed by an uneven ridge of rocks, covered with soil and vegetation. Within these there was a smaller circle of hills, equally verdant, and adorned with trees. The sides of the valley, which gradually sloped from the foot of the hills, were almost entirely laid out in plantations, and enlivened by the cottages of their proprietors. In the centre was an oval hollow, about half a mile across, and probably two hundred feet deep, at the bottom of which was a beautiful lake of brackish water, whose margin was in a high state of cultivation, planted with taro, bananas, and sugar-cane. The steep perpendicular rocks forming the sides of the hollow were adorned with tufts of grass, or blooming pendulous plants; while along the narrow and verdant border of the lake at the bottom, the bread-fruit, the kukui, and the ohia trees appeared, with now and then a lowly native hut standing beneath their shade. We walked to the upper edge of the rocks that form the side of the hollow, where we viewed with pleasure this singularly beautiful scene.

The placid surface of the lake, disturbed only by the boys and girls diving and sporting in its waters, the serpentine walks among the luxuriant gardens along its margin, the tranquil occupations of the inhabitants, some weaving mats, others walking cheerfully up and down the winding paths among the steep rocks, the sound of the cloth-beating mallet from several directions, and the smiling gayety of the whole, contrasted strongly with the panorama we had recently beheld at Kirauea. Yet we felt persuaded that this now cheerful spot had once presented a similar spectacle, less extended, but equally grand and appalling.

The traditions of the people informed us, that the valley itself was originally a crater, the indented rocks along the outer ridge forming its rim, and the opening towards the sea its mouth. But had tradition been silent, the volcanic nature of the rocks, which were basaltic, or of compact lava in some parts and cellular in others, the structure of the large basin in which we were standing, and the deep hollow in the centre which we were viewing, would have carried conviction to the mind of every beholder that it had once been the seat of volcanic fires. We asked several natives of the place if they had any account of the king in whose reign it had burned; or if they knew any songs or traditions in which it was stated how many kings had reigned in Hawaii, or how many chiefs had governed Puna, either since it first broke out or since it became extinct; but they could give us no information on these subjects. They told us the name of the place was *Kapoho* (the sunken in), and of the lake, *Ka Wai a Pélé* (the water of Pélé). The saltness of the water in this extinguished volcano proves the connexion of the lake with the sea, from which it is about a mile distant; but we could not learn that it was at all affected by the rising or falling of the tides. The natives also told us that it was one of the places from which the volcanic goddess threw rocks and lava after *Kahavari*, for refusing his *papa*, or sledge, when playing at *horua*

The *horua* has for many generations been a popular amusement throughout the Sandwich Islands, and is still practised in several places. It consists in sliding down a hill on a narrow sledge; and those who, by strength or skill in balancing themselves, slide farthest, are considered victorious. The *papa*, or sledge, is com-

posed of two narrow runners, from seven to twelve or
eighteen feet long, two or three inches deep, highly
polished, and at the foremost end tapering off from the
under side to a point at the upper edge. These two
runners are fastened together by a number of short
pieces of wood laid horizontally across. To the upper
edge of these short pieces two long tough sticks are
fastened, extending the whole length of the cross-
pieces, and about five or six inches apart. Sometimes a
narrow piece of matting is fastened over the whole
upper surface, except three or four feet at the foremost
end, though in general only a small part for the breast
to rest on is covered. At the foremost end there is a
space of about two inches between the runners, but
they widen gradually towards the hinder part, where
they are distant from each other four or five inches.—
The person about to slide grasps the small side-stick
firmly with his right hand, somewhere about the middle,
runs a few yards to the brow of the hill, or starting-
place, where he grasps it with his left hand, and at the
same time, with all his strength throwing himself forward, falls flat upon it, and slides down the hill, his
hands retaining their hold of the side-sticks, and his
feet being fixed against the hindermost cross-piece of
the sledge. Much practice and address are necessary,
to assume and keep an even balance on so narrow a
vehicle; yet a man accustomed to the sport will throw
himself, with velocity and apparent ease, a hundred and
fifty or two hundred yards down the side of a gradually
sloping hill.

About three o'clock we resumed our journey, and
soon reached Kula, a romantic spot, where Kahavari
took leave of his sister. The hill on which he was
sliding when he incurred the displeasure of the terrible
goddess, the spot where he rested, and first saw her
pursuing him were visible, and the traditionary story of
his encounter with Pélé is so interesting, that we think
we shall be pardoned for inserting it.

In the reign of Keariikukii, an ancient king of Hawaii, Kahavari, chief of Puna, and one of his *punahele*
(favourite companions), went one day to amuse themselves at the horua on the sloping side of a hill, which is
still called *Ka horua-ana o Kahavari* (the sliding place of
Kahavari). Vast numbers of the people collected at
the bottom of the hill, to witness the game; and a

company of musicians and dancers repaired to the spot, to add to the amusement of the spectators. The buskined youths had begun their dance, and, amid the sound of the drums, and the songs of the musicians, the horua commenced between Kahavari and his favourite. Pélé, the goddess of the volcano, came down from Kirauea, to witness the sport. She stood on the top of the hill, in the form of a woman, and challenged Kahavari to slide with her. He accepted the offer, and they set off together down the hill. Pélé, less acquainted with the art of balancing herself on the narrow sledge than her rival, was beaten, and Kahavari was applauded by the spectators as he returned up the side of the hill.

Before they started again, Pélé asked him to give her his papa. He, supposing from her appearance that she was no more than a native woman, said, *Aore*, no! "Are you my wife, that you should obtain my sledge?" and, as if impatient at being delayed, adjusted his papa, ran a few yards to take a spring, and then, with all his strength, threw himself upon it, and shot down the hill. Pélé, incensed at his answer, stamped on the ground, and an earthquake followed, which rent the hill in sunder. She called, and fire and liquid lava arose, and, assuming her supernatural form, with these irresistible ministers of vengeance she followed down the hill. When Kahavari reached the bottom of the hill, he arose, and, on looking behind, saw Pélé, accompanied by thunder and lightning, earthquake, and streams of burning lava, closely pursuing him. He took up his broad spear, which he had stuck in the ground at the beginning of the game, and, accompanied by his friend, fled for his life. The musicians, dancers, and crowds of spectators were instantly buried beneath the fiery torrent, which, bearing on its foremost wave the enraged goddess, continued to pursue Kahavari and his friend. They ran till they came to an eminence, called Buukea. Here Kahavari threw off his tuirai, cloak of netted ti-leaves, and proceeded towards his house, which stood near the shore. He met his favourite hog Aróipuaa, saluted him by touching noses, and ran to the house of his mother, who lived at Kukii, saluted her by touching noses, and said, *Aroha ino oe, eia ihonei paha oe e make aike ai mainei Pélé:* Compassion great to you, close here perhaps is your death; Pélé comes devouring.

Leaving her, he met his wife, Kanakawahine. He saluted her. The burning torrent approached, and she said, "Stay with me here, and let us die together." He said, "No; I go, I go." He then saluted his two children, Paupouru and Kahoe, and said, *Ke ue nei au ia orua*, I grieve for you two. The lava rolled near, and he ran till a deep chasm arrested his progress; he laid down his spear, and on it walked safely over. His friend called out for his help; he held out his spear over the chasm; his friend took hold of it, and he drew him securely over. By this time Pélé was coming down the chasm with accelerated motion. He ran till he reached the place where we were sitting.

Here he met his sister Koae, but had only time to say, *Aroha oe!* "Alas for you!" and then ran on to the seashore. His younger brother had just landed from his fishing-canoe, and had hastened to his house, to provide for the safety of his family, when Kahavari arrived; he and his friend leaped into the canoe, and with his broad spear paddled out to sea. Pélé, perceiving his escape, ran to the shore, and hurled after him, with prodigious force, huge stones and fragments of rock, which fell thickly around, but did not strike his canoe. When they had paddled a short distance from the shore, the *Kumukahi* (east wind) sprang up. He fixed his broad spear upright in the canoe, which, answering the double purpose of mast and sail, he soon reached the island of Maui. Here they rested one night, and proceeded to Ranai. On the day following, he removed to Morokai, and from thence to Oahu, the abode of Koronohairaau his father and Kanewahinekeaho his sister, to whom he related his perils, and with whom he took up his abode.

The above tale is a tolerable specimen of their traditions, though not among the most marvellous we have met with, and the truth may easily be separated from the fiction. A sudden and unexpected eruption of a volcano, when a chief and his people were playing at horua, is probably its only foundation. It exhibits, however, much of the general character of the people, the low estimation in which the females were held, and the wretched state of their domestic society, in which those fond attachments that in civilized and Christian life endear the different members of kindred and family to each other appear scarcely to have existed. The absence of relative affections shown by Kahavari, who, notwithstanding the entreaties of his wife, could leave her, his children, his mother, and his sister to certain destruction, meets with no reprehension; neither is any censure passed on his unjust seizure of the canoe belonging to his brother, who was engaged in saving his own family, while his adroitness in escaping the dreadful calamity of which he had been the sole cause is applauded in terms too indelicate to be recorded. The natives pointed out a number of rocks in the sea, which, they said, were thrown by Pélé, to sink the canoe in which Kahavari escaped.

After travelling a short distance, we saw the *Bu o Kahavari* (Hill of Kahavari), the place where he stopped, after sliding down-hill, and perceived the goddess pursuing him. It was a black frowning crater, about one hundred feet high, with a deep gap in its rim on the eastern side, from which the course of the current of lava could be distinctly traced. Our way now lay over a very rugged tract of country. Sometimes for a mile or two we were obliged to walk along on the top of a wall, four feet high, and about three feet wide, formed of fragments of lava that had been collected from the surface of the enclosures which these walls surrounded. We were, however, cheered with a beautiful prospect; for the land, which rose gradually towards the mountains a few miles to the westward of us, presented an almost enchanting appearance. The plain was covered with verdure; and as we advanced, a woody eminence, probably some ancient crater, frequently arose from the gently undulated surface, while groups of hills, clothed with trees of various foliage, agreeably diversified the scene. The shore, which was about a mile to the eastward of us, was occasionally lined with the spiral pandanus, the waving cocoanut, or the clustering huts of the natives. At half-past four we reached Kahuwai, where we sat down and took some refreshment, while Makoa was engaged in bringing the people of the place together. About one hundred and fifty assembled around the door, and were addressed. After conversing some time, we travelled in an inland direction to Honoruru, a small village situated in the midst of a wood, where we arrived just at the setting of the sun. A discourse was delivered from John xii. 46—"I am come a light into the world," &c.

We arose early on the 8th, and Mr. Thurston held
morning worship with the people of the place. Although
I had been much indisposed through the night, we left
Honoruru soon after six A. M., and, travelling slowly towards the seashore, reached Waiakaheula about eight.
Messrs. Thurston and Bishop walked up to the settlement situated half a mile inland, where the former
preached to the people.

We had seen the eastern division of Hiro yesterday
afternoon; and Mr. Bishop, hoping to reach Waiakea in
a few hours, left Mr. Thurston and the natives with me,
and proceeded thither. About noon we resumed our
journey, and soon after five P. M. we reached Kaau, the
last village in the division of Puna. It was extensive
and populous, abounding with well-cultivated plantations
of taro, sweet potatoes, and sugar-cane; and probably
owes its fertility to a fine rapid stream of water, which,
descending from the mountains, runs through it into the
sea. It was the second stream we had seen on the
island. Having quenched our thirst, we passed over it
by stepping on some large stones, and directed our way
to the house of the head man, where we put up for the
night.

Early on the 9th the house was crowded with natives,
and a little before sun-rise morning worship was performed as usual. Some of the natives observed, in conversation, "We shall never obtain the things of which
you have told us, for we are a wicked and unbelieving
people." Before we left the place, the people offered
for sale some curious deep oval baskets, with covers,
made of the fibrous roots of *ië*. We purchased two,
intending to preserve them as specimens of native
ingenuity.

Leaving the village of Kaau, we resumed our journey, and, after walking between two and three hours,
stopped in the midst of a thicket to rest and prepare
some breakfast. The natives produced fire by rubbing
two dry sticks of the *hibiscus tiliaceus* together; and
having suspended over it a small iron pot, in gipsy style,
upon three sticks, soon prepared our food. At half-past
ten we resumed our walk, and, passing about two miles
through a wood of pretty large timber, came to the open
country in the vicinity of Waiakea. At one P. M. we
reached the house of the chief, where we were wel-

comed by our companions, and Maaro the chief, who, though very ill, was glad to see us.

In company with Messrs. Chamberlain, Ely, and Blatchly, I have since travelled from this place to the volcano, and during that journey had an opportunity of preaching at most of the villages of Ora. The distance is probably between thirty and forty miles, and the ascent gradual from the shore to the volcano. The soil is generally rich and fertile, and the face of the country, though more uniform than some parts which we passed over on leaving the southern shore, is varied by occasional undulations. We travelled through two or three extensive woods, in which were many large trees, and saw also several pools and small currents of excellent fresh water.

The construction of the swineherds' houses at the village of Ka-pu-o-ka-ahi (the hill of the fire) was singular. There were no walls nor upright posts along the sides, but the rafters were fixed in the ground, united at the top, and thatched about half-way down. In the neighbourhood of this village we also saw hedges of raspberry bushes, which the natives informed us bore white berries, and were abundant in the mountains, though they would not grow nearer the shore. Nine or ten miles from the sea we met with ohelo bushes, and after we had travelled about twenty miles we found strawberry plants in abundance, and saw several in blossom, although it was in the month of January. The latter plant, as well as the raspberry, is found in all the higher parts of Hawaii, which induces us to think them both indigenous.

It was six months after our tour along the coast that we passed through the villages of Ora, and we were gratified to find that several of the people, at different places, had received some general ideas of the true God from the reports of those natives who had heard us preach when travelling along the shore, and had subsequently visited these inland districts. At one place where we halted for the night, on our return from the volcano, I preached to the people in the evening, and the natives afterward maintained an interesting conversation on religious subjects till midnight. Among other things, respecting the salvation of the soul through Jesus Christ, they said, " Our fathers, from time immemorial, and we, ever since we can remember any thing,

K 3

have been seeking the *ora roa* (enduring life), or a state in which we should not die; but we have never found it yet: perhaps this is it, of which you are telling us."

During the same journey we overtook *Maaro*, the chief of Waiakea, and three or four hundred people, returning with sandal wood, which they had been cutting in the mountains. The bark and sap had been chipped off with small adzes, and the wood appeared lighter in colour than what is usually sold at Oahu, probably from its having been but recently cut down.

The sandal wood is the same as in the East Indies, and is probably the *santalum album*. It is a tolerably heavy and solid wood, and after the sap, or part next the bark, is taken off, is of a light-yellow or brown colour, containing a quantity of aromatic oil. Although a plant of slow growth, it is found in abundance in all the mountainous parts of the Sandwich Islands, and is cut in great quantities by the natives, as it constitutes their principal article of exportation. It is brought down to the beach in pieces from a foot to eighteen inches in diameter, and six or eight feet long, to small sticks not more than an inch thick and a foot and a half long. It is sold by weight; and the merchants, who exchange for it articles of European or Chinese manufacture, take it to the Canton market, where it is bought by the Chinese for the purpose of preparing incense to burn in their idol temples.

Shortly after ten o'clock on the 10th, the chiefs and people in considerable numbers assembled in a large house adjacent to that in which we resided, agreeably to the invitation given them last evening. The worship commenced as usual, and I preached from the text, " Happy is that people whose God is the Lord." The attention was not so good as that generally given by the congregations we had addressed. Many, however, quietly listened till the service was over. As we arose to depart, an old woman, who during the discourse sat near the speaker, and had listened very attentively, all at once exclaimed, " Powerful are the gods of Hawaii, and great is Pélé, the goddess of Hawaii; she shall save Maaro" (the sick chief who was present). Another began to chant a song in praise of Pélé, to which the people generally listened, though some began to laugh. We supposed they were intoxicated, and therefore took no notice of them; but, on our leaving the house, some of

our people told us they were not *ona i ka ruma* (intoxicated or poisoned with rum), but inspired by the *akua*
(goddess) of the volcano, or that one of them was Pélé
herself in the form of one of her priestesses. On hearing this I turned back into the house, and when the song
was ended, immediately entered into conversation with
the principal one, by asking her if she had attended to
the discourse that had been delivered there? She answered that she had listened, and understood it. I then
asked if she thought Jehovah was good, and those happy
who made him their God? She answered, "He is your
good God (or best God), and it is right that you should
worship him; but Pélé is my deity, and the great goddess of Hawaii. Kirauea is the place of her abode.
Ohiaotelani (the northern peak of the volcano) is one
corner of her house. From the land beyond the sky, in
former times, she came." She then went on with the
song which she had thus begun, giving a long account
of the deeds and honours of Pélé. This she pronounced
in such a rapid and vociferous manner, accompanied by
such extravagant gestures, that only here and there a
word could be understood. Indeed, towards the close
she appeared to lose all command of herself. When she
had done, I told her she was mistaken in supposing any
supernatural being resided in the volcano; that Pélé
was a creature of their own invention, and existed only
in the imagination of her kahu, or devotees : adding,
that volcanoes and all their accompanying phenomena
were under the powerful control of Jehovah, who,
though uncreated himself, was the Creator and Supporter of heaven and earth, and every thing she beheld.
She replied that it was not so. She did not dispute that
Jehovah was a God, but that he was not the only God.
Pélé was a goddess, and dwelt in her, and through her
would heal the sick chief then present. She wished
him restored, and therefore came to visit him. I said I
also wished Maaro to recover; but if he did recover it
would be by the favour of Jehovah, and that I hoped he
would acknowledge him, and seek to him alone, as he
was the only true Physician, who could save both body
and soul; making the latter happy in another world,
when this world, with all its volcanoes, mountains, and
oceans, should cease to exist.

I then advised her and all present to forsake their
imaginary deity, whose character was distinguished by

all that was.revengeful and destructive, and accept the offers Jehovah had made them by his servants, that they might be happy now, and escape the everlasting death that would overtake all the idolatrous and.wicked.

Assuming a haughty air, she said, "I am Pélé; I shall never die; and those who follow me, when they die, if part of their bones be taken to Kirauea (the name of the volcano), will live with me in the bright fires there." I said, Are you Pélé? She replied, Yes; and was proceeding to state her powers, &c., when Makoa, who had till now stood silent, interrupted her, and said, "It is true you are Pélé, or some of Pélé's party; and it is you that have destroyed the king's land, devoured his people, and spoiled all the fishing-grounds. Ever since you came to the islands, you have been busied in mischief; you spoiled the greater part of the island, shook it to pieces, or cursed it with barrenness, by inundating it with lava. You never did any good; and if I were the king, I would throw you all into the sea, or banish you from the islands. Hawaii would be quiet if you were away."

This was rather unexpected, and seemed to surprise several of the company. However, the pretended Pélé said, "Formerly we did overflow some of the land, but it was only the land of those that were rebels, or were very wicked people.* Now we abide quietly in Kirauea." She then added, "It cannot be said that in these days we destroy the king's people." She mentioned the names of several chiefs, and then asked, "Who destroyed these? Not Pélé, but the rum of the foreigners, whose God you are so fond of. Their diseases and their rum have destroyed more of the king's men than all the vol-canoes on the island:" I told her I regretted that their intercourse with foreigners should have introduced among them diseases to which they were strangers before, and that I hoped they would also receive the advantages of Christian instruction and civilization, which the benevolent in those countries by which they had been injured were now to impart; that intoxication was wholly forbidden by Jehovah the God of Christians, who had declared that no drunkard should enter the kingdom of heaven. I then said I was sorry to see her so deceived, and attempting to deceive others—told her

---

* Broke the restrictions of the tabu, or brought no offerings.

she knew her pretensions were false, and recommended her to consider the consequences of idolatry, and cease to practise her deceptions—to recollect that she would one day die; that God had given her an opportunity of hearing of his love to sinners in the gift of his Son; and that if she applied to him for mercy, although now an idolatrous priestess, she might be saved; but if she did not, a fearful doom awaited her. "I shall not die," she exclaimed, "but *ora no*"-(live spontaneously). After replying to this, I retired; but the spectators, who had manifested by their countenances that they were not uninterested in the discussion, continued in earnest conversation for some time. The name of the priestess, we afterward learned, was Oani. She resided in a neighbouring village, and had that morning arrived at Waiakea on a visit to Maaro.

When the national idolatry was publicly abolished in the year 1819, several priests of Pélé denounced the most awful threatenings of earthquakes, eruptions, &c. from the gods of the volcanoes, in revenge for the insult and neglect then shown by the king and chiefs. But no fires afterward appearing in any of the extinguished volcanoes, no fresh ones having broken out, and those then in action having since that period remained in a state of comparative quiescence, some of the people have been led to conclude that the gods formerly supposed to preside over volcanoes had existed only in their imagination. The fearful apprehensions which they had been accustomed to associate with every idea of Pélé and her companions have in a great measure subsided, and the oppressive power of her priests and priestesses is consequently diminished. There are, however, many who remain in constant dread of her displeasure, and who pay the most submissive and unhesitating obedience to the requisitions of her priests. This is no more than was to be expected, particularly in this part of the island, where the people are far removed from the means of instruction, the example and influence of the principal chiefs and more enlightened part of the population; and it appears matter of surprise that, in the course of three years only, so many should have relinquished their superstitious notions respecting the deities of the volcanoes, when we consider their ignorance and their early impressions, and recollect that while resting at night, perhaps on a bed of lava, they are occasionally

startled from their midnight slumbers by the undulating
earthquake, and are daily reminded of the dreadful
power of this imaginary goddess "by almost every
object that meets their view, from the cliffs which are
washed by the waves of the sea, even to the lofty craters, her ancient seat above the clouds, and amid perpetual snow."

Until this morning, however, none of the servants of
Pélé had ever publicly opposed her pretended right to
that homage and obedience which it was our object to
invite them to render to Jehovah alone; and though it
was encouraging to notice that, by many of the people
present, the pretensions of Oani were disregarded, it
was exceedingly painful to hear an idolatrous priestess
declaring that the conduct of those by whom they had
been sometimes visited from countries called Christian
had been productive of consequences more injurious and
fatal to the unsuspecting and unenlightened Hawaiians
than these dreadful phenomena in nature, which they had
been accustomed to attribute to the most destructive of
their imaginary deities, and to know also that such a
declaration was too true to be contradicted.

A number of people, after they left the place of public
worship, came to our house, and conversed on the blessed-
ness of those who worship and obey Jehovah. They
all said it was good, and that if the king were to come
or send them word, they would build a house for a missionary, a school-house, and chapel, and also observe
the Sabbath-day.

In the afternoon, Mr. Thurston preached at the same
place to an attentive congregation. In company with
Mr. Bishop, I walked over to Ponahawai, where Makoa
collected upwards of one hundred people at the head
man's house, to whom I preached from Rom. x. 13—
"Whosoever shall call upon the name of the Lord shall
be saved." The whole assembly gave good attention,
frequently interrupting me while speaking, by their exclamations. A gray-headed old man, who sat near the
door, listened with apparent interest during the whole
service, and when, towards the close, it was stated that
those who in faith called on the Lord would in another
world obtain everlasting life, he exclaimed, "My days
are almost ended—that cannot be for me; can an old
man live for ever?" He was told that Jesus was willing
to save the souls of all who with humility and sincerity

come to him, both old and young; that he would reanimate their bodies in the resurrection; and that he would give eternal life to as many as believed on his name.

We have more than once had occasion to notice with peculiar interest the impression made on an adult heathen, when some of the sublime and important doctrines of religion are for the first time presented to his mind. Accustomed to contemplate the gods of his ancestors as the patrons of every vice and supernatural monsters of cruelty, deriving satisfaction from the struggles and expiring agonies of the victim offered in sacrifice, he is surprised to hear of the holy nature of God, and the condescending love of Christ; but the idea of the resurrection of the body, the general judgment, and the eternal happiness or misery of all mankind, affects him with a degree of astonishment never witnessed in countries where the Christian religion prevails, and in which, notwithstanding the lamentable ignorance existing in different portions of the community, there are few who have not some indistinct ideas on these subjects. But the heathen, whose mental powers have reached maturity before the truth has been presented, experiences very different sensations; and we have seen the effects produced at these times exhibited in various ways—sometimes by most significant gestures, at other times by involuntary exclamations, or penetrating looks fixed on the speaker; and occasionally, as was the case this afternoon, by their actually interrupting us to inquire, "How can these things be?" or declaring in their own beautiful and figurative language, that the tidings they had heard "broke in upon their minds like the light of the morning."

When the exercises were ended, they congratulated each other on the news they had heard—said it was good, and added, "Let us all attend to it; who is there that does not desire eternal life in the other world?" They afterward made many inquiries about the Sabbath-day, prayer, &c., and asked if they should not be visited again. We told them it was probable that, before long, teachers would come and reside permanently among them.

On our way home we called on Maaro, whom we found very ill. One of his children was also sick, and seemed near dying. We regretted that we had no medicine proper to administer to either.

The wretched picture of uncivilized society which this family exhibited powerfully affected our minds. Maaro's house, like that of the chiefs in general, was large, and accommodated many of his friends and dependants. On one side, near the door, he lay on a mat which was spread on the ground. Two or three domestics sat around—one of them holding a small calabash of water, and another with a kahiri was fanning away the flies. Near the centre of the house, on another mat, spread also on the ground, lay the pale emaciated child, its features distorted with pain, and its feeble voice occasionally uttering the most piteous cries. A native girl sat beside it, driving away the flies and holding a cocoanut-shell in her hand containing a little poè, with which she had been endeavouring to feed it. In the same place, and nearly between the father and the child, two of Maaro's wives and some other chief women were seated on the ground, playing at cards, laughing and jesting over their game. We tried to enter into conversation with them, but they were too intent on the play to pay any attention to what we said. The visitors or attendants of the chief sat in groups in different parts of the house, some carelessly singing, others engaged in earnest conversation.

We could not forbear contrasting the scene here presented with a domestic circle in civilized and Christian society under similar circumstances, where all the alleviations which the tenderest sympathy could impart would be promptly tendered to the suffering individuals. But here, alas! ignorance, cruel idolatry, and familiarity with vice appeared to have destroyed natural affection and all the tender sympathies of humanity in their bosoms. The wife beheld unmoved the sufferings of her husband, and the amusement of the mother was undisturbed by the painful crying of her languishing child.

The state of domestic society in Tahiti and the neighbouring islands, only a few years ago, was even more affecting. Since the introduction of Christianity, so far from being unwilling to take care of their sick relatives and friends, a number of individuals at several of the missionary stations annually devote a part of the produce of their labour to erect houses, purchase medicine, and provide for the comfort of those who are sick and indigent. It is impossible for any people to be more attentive and kind than they now are. Many a time the friend of some one who had been taken ill has called me up at midnight to ask for medicine; and often have I seen a wife or a sister supporting in her lap the head of a sick and perhaps dying husband or brother, night after night, yet refusing to leave them, though almost exhausted with fatigue.

Leaving Maaro, we returned through a highly cultivated part of the district. Every thing in nature was lovely, and the landscape around awakened emotions very different from those excited during our visit to the abode of sickness which we had just left.

In the afternoon of the 11th, we waited on Maaro, the chief, to ask his opinion respecting missionaries settling permanently in his neighbourhood. He said, perhaps it would be well; that if the king and chiefs approved of it, he should desire it. We asked if he would patronise and protect missionaries and their families, provided the king and chiefs approved of their settling at Waiakea. He answered, "Yes, certainly," and at the same time pointed out several places where they might build their houses. We told him that the king, Karaimoku, Kaahumanu, and the governor approved of instructers coming to teach the people of Waiakea; but that we were also desirous to obtain his opinion before any arrangements were made for their removal from Oahu. He again repeated that he thought it would be a good thing, and that if the missionaries came with the approbation of the king and chiefs, he should be glad to witness their arrival. We then took leave of Maaro, and the chiefs that were with him. Messrs. Thurston and Bishop walked to the opposite side of the bay, where we had held a religious exercise yesterday, and here Mr. Thurston preached to an attentive congregation of about sixty people. The head man afterward expressed a strong desire to be instructed, and said all the people would like to learn the palapala and keep the Sabbath-day.

While they were on the western shore, I visited several houses on the eastern side of the settlement, and entered into conversation with the people on the subject of missionaries coming to reside at Waiakea. In general, they approved, saying they had dark minds, and needed instruction. Some, however, seemed to doubt the propriety of foreigners coming to reside permanently among them. They said, they had heard that

in several countries, where foreigners had intermingled
with the original natives, the latter had soon disap-
peared; and, should missionaries come to live at Waiakea, perhaps the land would ultimately become theirs;
and the *kanaka maore* (aborigines) cease to be its occu-
piers. I told them, that had been the case in some
countries; but that the residence of missionaries among
them, so far from producing it, was designed, and eminently calculated, to prevent a consequence so melancholy. At the same time I remarked, that their sanguinary wars, their extensive and cruel practice of
infanticide, their frequent intoxication, and their numerous diseases, partly gendered by vicious habits, had,
according to their own account, diminished the population of the island three-fourths within the last forty
years; and, from the destructive operation of these
causes, there was every reason to fear the Hawaiian
people would soon be annihilated, unless some remedy
was applied. No remedy, I added, was so efficacious
as instruction and civilization; and above all, the principles and doctrines of the Bible, which they could not
become acquainted with, but by the residence of missionaries among them. Such, I informed them, was the
opinion of the friends of missions, who, anxious to
ameliorate their wretched condition, preserve from ob-
livion the remnant of the people, place them among the
nations of the earth, and direct them to the enjoyment
of civilized life, and the participation of immortality and
happiness in another world, had sent them the Word of
God and missionaries, to unfold to them, in their own
language, its divine and invaluable truths. At the close
of this interview, some again repeated that it would be
a good thing for missionaries to come; others expressed
doubt and hesitation.

Many of the people, during their intercourse with
foreigners, have been made acquainted with the leading
facts in the history of South America and the West Indies; and hence the natives of this place, in all probability, derived the ground of their objection.

The inhabitants of Waiakea are peculiarly favoured
in having woods producing timber, such as they use for
building, within three or four miles of their settlement;
while the natives in most parts of the islands have to
fetch it from a much greater distance. In neatness and
elegance of appearance, their houses are not equal to

those of the Society islanders, even before they were instructed by Europeans; but in point of strength and durability they sometimes exceed them. There is also less variety in the form of the Sandwich Island dwellings, which are chiefly of two kinds, viz. the *hale noho* (dwelling-house), or *halau* (a long building), nearly open at one end; and though thatched with different materials, they are all framed in nearly the same way.

The size and quality of a dwelling varies according to the rank and means of its possessor, those of the poor people being mere huts, eight or ten feet square, others twenty feet long, and ten or twelve feet wide, while the houses of the chiefs are from forty to seventy feet long. Their houses are generally separate from each other; even in their most populous villages, however near the houses may be, they are always distinct buildings. Although there are professed house-carpenters who excel in framing, and others who are taught to finish the corners of the house and ridge of the roof, which but few understand, yet, in general, every man erects his own house. If it be of a middling or large size, this, to an individual or a family, is a formidable undertaking, as they have to cut down the trees in the mountains, and bring the wood from six to ten miles on their shoulders with great labour, gather the leaves or grass, braid the cinet, &c., before they can even begin to build.

But when a chief wants a house, he requires the labour of all who hold lands under him; and we have often been surprised at the despatch with which a house is sometimes built. We have known the natives come with their materials in the morning, put up the frame of a middle-sized house in one day, cover it in the next, and on the third day return to their lands. Each division of people has a part of the house allotted by the chief, in proportion to its number; and it is no unusual thing to see upwards of a hundred men at a time working on one house.

A good house, such as they build for the chiefs, will keep out the wind and rain, and last from seven to ten years. But, in general, they do not last more than five years; and those which they are hired to build for foreigners, not much more than half that time. In less than twelve months after my own grass-house was built, the rain came through the roof, from one end to the other, every time there was a heavy shower.

In some of the islands, the natives have recently covered their houses with mud; this, however, does not
appear to render them more durable.

Before they were visited by foreigners, the only tool
employed in building was a stone adze, formed of a
kind of basaltes, or compact lava; and though they now
use an axe in felling the trees, the adze is still their
favourite tool, and many of them use no other. The
stone adze is, however, exchanged for one made with a
plane iron, bent, and tied securely to a handle of light
wood. This they prefer to the European adze, which
they say is too heavy. Sometimes they use a saw,
chisel, and gimlet, in framing their houses, but they are
not yet adepts in the use of these tools; we have often
seen them throw down the saw, and take up their adze,
to finish that which they had commenced cutting with
a saw.

While idolatry existed, a number of superstitious ceremonies were performed, before they could occupy
their houses. Offerings were made to the gods, and
presents to the priest, who entered the house, uttered
prayers, went through other ceremonies, and slept in it
before the owner took possession, in order to prevent
evil spirits from resorting to it, and to secure its inmates
from the effects of incantation.

When the house was finished, it was soon furnished.
A sleeping-mat spread on the ground, and a wooden
pillow, a wicker basket or two to keep their tapa or native cloth in, a few calabashes for water and poë, and
some wooden dishes, of various size and shape, together
with a *haka*, were all they required. This latter article
was sometimes like a stand used by us for hanging hats
and coats on. It was often made with care, and carved,
but more frequently it was a small arm of a tree, with
a number of branches attached to it. These were cut
off within a foot of the main stem, which was planted
in some convenient part of the house, and upon these
natural pegs they used to hang their calabashes, and
other vessels containing victuals. They generally sat
on the ground, and took their food near the door of
their house: sometimes, however, they took their meals
in the more luxurious manner of some of the eastern
nations, lying nearly in a horizontal posture, and resting
on one arm, or reclining on a large cushion or pillow
placed under the breast for that purpose: in this man-

ner, the late king, with the members of his family, and
many of the principal chiefs, were accustomed frequently to take their evening meal. Their intercourse
with foreigners has taught many of the chiefs to prefer
a bedstead to the ground, and a mattress to a mat, to
sit on a chair, eat at a table, use a knife and fork, &c.
This we think advantageous, not only to those who
visit them for purposes of commerce, but to the natives
themselves, as it increases their wants, and consequently stimulates to industry.

CHAPTER XIII.

Former customs on Wairuku river—Affecting instance of infanticide—
Extent of infanticide; motives to its practice; humane efforts of the
chiefs for preventing it—Account of the native methods of curing
diseases—Tradition of the origin of medicine—Waiakea bay—Conversation with natives of the Marquesian islands—Farewell visit to Maaro
—Voyage to Laupahoehoe—Description of a double canoe—Native hospitality.

RETURNING from Pueo, on the 12th I visited Wairuku,
a beautiful stream of water flowing rapidly over a rocky
bed, with frequent falls, and many places eligible for the
erection of water-mills of almost any description. Makoa and the natives pointed out a square rock in the
middle of the stream, on which, during the reign of
Tamehameha, and former kings, a toll used to be paid
by every traveller who passed over the river. Whenever any one approached the stream, he stood on the
brink, and called to the collector of the toll, who resided on the opposite side. He came down with a
broad piece of board, which he placed on the rock
above mentioned. Those who wished to cross met him
there, and deposited on the board whatever articles had
been brought; and if satisfactory, the person was allowed to pass the river. It did not appear that any
uniform toll was required; the amount, or value, being
generally left to the collector. The natives said it was
principally regulated by the rank or number of those
who passed over. In order the better to accommodate
passengers, all kinds of permanently valuable articles
were received. Some paid in native tapa and mats, or

baskets; others paid a hog, a dog, some fowls, a roll of tobacco, or a quantity of dried salt fish.

The river of Wairuku was also distinguished by the markets or fairs held at stated periods on its banks. At those times the people of Puna and the desolate shores of Kaü, even from the south point of the island, brought mats, and mamake tapa, which is a remarkably strong black or brown native cloth, for the manufacture of which the inhabitants of Ora, and some of the inland parts of Puna, are celebrated throughout the whole group of the Sandwich Islands. It is made of a variety of the *morus papyrifera,* which grows spontaneously in those parts. These, together with vast quantities of dried salt fish, were ranged along on the south side of the ravine. The people of Hiro and Hamakua, as far as the north point, brought hogs; tobacco, tapa of various kinds, large mats made of the pandanus leaves, and bundles of *ai pai,*[*] which were collected on the north bank. From bank to bank the traders shouted to each other, and arranged the preliminaries of their bargains. From thence the articles were taken down to the before-mentioned rock in the middle of the stream, which in this place is almost covered with large stones. Here they were examined by the parties immediately concerned, in the presence of the collectors, who stood on each side of the rock, and were the general arbiters, in the event of any disputes arising. To them also was committed the preservation of good order during the fair, and they of course received a suitable remuneration from the different parties. On the above occasions, the banks of the Wairuku must often have presented an interesting scene, in the bustle of which these clerks of the market must have had no inconsiderable share. According to the account of the natives, this institution was in force till the accession of Rihoriho, the late king, since which time it has been abolished.

In the afternoon I called on Maaro, and found him very ill, and averse to conversation. His wives sat in the same room playing at cards, and apparently too intent on their game to be easily diverted.

About twelve years ago, a shocking instance of in-

* Ai pai (hard food). A kind of food made of baked taro, pounded together without water. When properly prepared; it is wrapped in green *ti* leaves, and tied up in bundles containing from twenty to forty pounds each ↑ in this state it will remain several months without injury.

fanticide occurred in this district, exhibiting, in a most affecting manner, the unrestrained violence of malignant passion, and the want of parental affection, which so often characterize savage life.

A man and his wife, tenants of Mr. Young, who has for many years held, under the king, the small district of Kukuwau, situated on the centre of Waiakea bay, resided not far from Maaro's house. They had one child, a fine little boy. A quarrel arose between them on one occasion, respecting this child. The wife refusing to accede to the wishes of the husband, he, in revenge, caught up the child by the head and the feet, broke its back across his knee, and then threw it down in expiring agonies before her. Struck with the atrocity of the act, Mr. Young seized the man, led him before the king, Tamehameha, who was then at Waiakea, and requested that he might be punished. The king inquired, "To whom did the child he has murdered belong?" Mr. Young answered that it was his own son. "Then," said the king, "neither you nor I have any right to interfere; I cannot say any thing to him."

We have long known that the Sandwich islanders practised infanticide, but had no idea of the extent to which it prevailed, until we had made various inquiries during our present tour, and had conversed with Karaimoku, Kapiolani, the governor, and several other chiefs, who, though formerly unwilling to converse on the subject, have, since their reception of Christianity, become more communicative.

It prevails throughout all the islands, and, with the exception of the higher class of chiefs, is, as far as we could learn, practised by all ranks of the people. However numerous the children among the lower orders, parents seldom rear more than two or three, and many spare only one; all the others are destroyed, sometimes shortly after birth, generally during the first year of their age.

The *means* by which it is accomplished, though numerous, it would be improper to describe. Kuakini, the governor of the island, in a conversation I had with him at Kairua, enumerated many different methods, several of which frequently proved fatal to the mother also. Sometimes they strangle their children, but more frequently bury them alive.

Among the Society islanders, who, while they were

idolaters, probably practised infanticide more than any other natives in the Pacific, if the intended victim survived only one day, and frequently not more than a few hours, it was generally saved. Depraved as they were, they could not afterward sacrifice to a barbarous custom an innocent babe, who seemed to look with confidence to its mother' or its nurse, and unconsciously smiled upon those who stood by: hence the parties interested in the child's destruction, which were the parents themselves, or their relations, generally strangled it soon after its birth.   But among the Sandwich islanders, the infant, after living a week, a month, or even a year, was still insecure, as some were destroyed when nearly able to walk.

It is painful to think of the *numbers* thus murdered. All the information we have been able to obtain, and the facts that have come to our knowledge in the neighbourhood where we resided, afford every reason to believe that from the prevalence of infanticide two-thirds of the children perished. We have been told by some of the chiefs, on whose word we can depend, that they have known parents to murder three or four infants, where they have spared one. But even supposing that not more than half the children were thus cut off, what an awful spectacle of depravity is presented! how many infants must have been annually sacrificed to a custom so repugnant to all the tenderest feelings of humanity, that, without the clearest evidence, we should not believe it would be found in the catalogue of human crimes.

The *reasons* they give for this practice manifest a degree of depravity no less affecting. Among the Marquesians, who inhabit a group of islands to the southeast of Hawaii, we are told that children are sometimes, during seasons of extreme scarcity, killed and eaten by their parents, to satisfy hunger. With the Society islanders, the rules of the Areoi institutions and family pride were the principal motives to its practice. Excepting the latter, which operates in a small degree, none of these motives actuate the Sandwich islanders; those, however, by which they are influenced are equally criminal. Some of the natives have told us that children were formerly sacrificed to the sharks infesting their shores, and which through fear they had deified; but as we have never met with persons who have ever offered any, or seen others do it, this possibly may be only report. The principal motive with the greater part of those who practise it is *idleness*; and the reason most frequently assigned, even by the parents themselves, for the murder of their children is, the trouble of bringing them up. In general they are of a changeable disposition, fond of a wandering manner of life, and find their children a restraint, preventing them in some degree from following their roving inclinations. Like other savage nations, they are averse to any more labour than is absolutely necessary. Hence they consider their children a burden, and are unwilling to cultivate a little more ground, or undertake the small additional labour necessary to the support of their offspring during the helpless periods of infancy and childhood. In some cases, when the child has been sickly, and the parents have grown tired of nursing and attending it, they have been known, in order to avoid further attendance and care, to bury it at once; and we have been very credibly informed that children have been buried alive merely because of the irritation they have discovered. On these occasions, when the child has cried more than the parents, particularly the mother, could patiently bear, instead of clasping the little sufferer to her bosom, and soothing by caresses the pains which, though unable to tell them, it has probably felt, she has, to free herself from this annoyance, stopped its cries by thrusting a piece of tapa into its mouth, dug a hole in the floor of the house, and perhaps within a few yards of her bed and the spot where she took her daily meals, has relentlessly buried in the untimely grave her helpless babe!

The Society islanders buried the infants they destroyed among the bushes, at some distance from their houses; but many of the infants in the Sandwich Islands are buried in the houses in which both parents and child had resided together. In the floors, which are frequently of earth or pebbles, a hole is dug two or three feet deep, into which they put the little infant, placed in a broken calabash, and having a piece of native cloth laid upon its mouth to stop its cries. The hole is then filled up with earth, and the inhuman parents themselves have sometimes joined in treading down the earth upon their own innocent but murdered child.

The bare recital of these acts of cruelty has often filled our minds with horror, while those who have been

engaged in the perpetration of them have related all
their tragical circumstances in detail with apparent un-
concern.

How great are the obligations of those whose lot is
cast in countries favoured with the Bible, to whose domestic society Christianity imparts so much happiness.
And how consoling to know that its principles, wherever
imbibed, will produce, even in the most barbarous communities, such a delightful transformation of character,
that the lion and leopard shall become harmless as the
lamb and the kid, "and they shall neither hurt nor
destroy."

In the Sandwich Islands, although not abolished, we
have reason to believe it prevails less extensively
now than it did four or five years ago. The king and
some of the chiefs, especially Karaimoku, since they
have attended to the injunctions of Christianity, and
have been made acquainted with the direct prohibitions
of it in the Bible, have readily expressed in public their
conviction of its criminality, and that committing it is
in fact *pepehi kanaka* (to kill man), under circumstances
which aggravate its guilt. They have also been led to
see its impolicy with respect to their resources, in its
tendency to depopulate the islands, and render them
barren or unprofitable, and, from these views, have
lately exerted themselves to suppress it. Karaimoku,
regent of the islands, has more than once forbidden any
parents to destroy their children, and has threatened to
punish with banishment, if not with death, any who shall
be found guilty of it. After we left Kairua, on our present
tour, Kuakini the governor published among all the people under his jurisdiction a strict prohibition of this barbarous custom. It is, however, only recently that the
chiefs have endeavoured to prevent it, and the people
do not very well brook their interference; so that, notwithstanding their efforts, it is still practised, particularly in remote districts—but in general privately, for
fear of detection and punishment.

The check, however, which infanticide has received
from the humane and enlightened policy of the chiefs
is encouraging. It warrants the most sanguine expectations that as Christianity advances among the Hawaiians, this and other customs equally degrading to their
character and destructive of their race will be entirely
laid aside, as has been the case among the Tahitians;

and there is every reason to presume that the pleasing change which has resulted from the general reception of the gospel among the latter will, under the Divine blessing, be ultimately realized by the Sandwich islanders. May that happy period soon arrive!—for if the total abolition of this cruel practice (though among the least of its benevolent objects) be the only advantage which the establishment of a Christian mission in these distant islands shall confer on their inhabitants, yet, in rescuing every year, through all the succeeding generations of this reviving nation, multitudes from a premature death, the liberal assistance of its friends, and the labours of its several members, will be most amply rewarded.*

On the morning of the 13th, we examined some of the eastern parts of the bay. I also visited Maaro. On arriving at the house in which I had left the sick chief yesterday, the natives told me that he had been removed, that the house where he then was, was tabu, and the tabu would be broken if I should go there. They refused to tell where he was, but did not attempt to prevent my going in search of him. After travelling a mile and a half inland, I reached the house in which he lay, and was immediately invited to enter. The number of small sticks, with the leaves of the ti-plant fastened round them, which I saw fixed in different parts of the house, particularly around the mat on which the chief was reclining, induced me to think they had been performing some incantation for his recovery, as it was by such pieces of leaf as these that they supposed the evil spirit made his escape from the sufferer. I asked one who sat by, and who I supposed was a *kahuna* (doctor), what remedies they were using for his recovery; but they gave me no answer. The chief seemed to have less pain than yesterday, and was much more communicative. He said the native doctors had brought him there in order to try the effect of medicines, which he trusted would give relief. I told him it was right to use every lawful means for the recovery of health; but cautioned

* We have reason to believe this is now in a great measure accomplished. In June, 1824, Kaapumanu publicly enjoined the chiefs of Maui to proclaim by herald that there should be no murder—alluding especially to infanticide: the same regulations have been enforced in other islands; and if the crime is practised now, it is under the same circumstances as secret murder would be perpetrated.

L 2

him particularly against having recourse to the incantations of the priests, or making any offerings to their
former gods, as that was not only foolish and useless,
but offensive to God, the author of all our mercies, with
whom alone were the issues of life and death. He
made no reply, but turned the conversation by saying he
regretted that he was not able to furnish us with a canoe, and that his sickness had not allowed him to be
more with us. I told him we wished to have had more
frequent opportunities of telling him of Jesus Christ;
and endeavouring to impress his mind with the necessity of an early application for the pardon of his sins
and the salvation of his spirit. When I left him, he said
he would think of these things; and, should he get better,
would attend to instruction, and use his influence to induce his people to attend.

Maaro was attended by two or three natives, who
were called *kahuna rapaau mai*, the name given to those
who undertake to cure diseases—from *kahuna*, a priest,
or one expert in his profession—*rapaau*, to heal, or to
apply medicine—and *mai*, disease. Although among
the Sandwich islanders there are none who exclusively
devote themselves to this employment, there are many
who pretend to great skill in the discovery and cure of diseases. They are usually, as their name imports, priests
or sorcerers, and seldom administer medicine unac-
companied by some superstitious ceremony. The knowledge of the art is frequently communicated from father
to son, and thus continued in one family. In their practice they have different departments, and those who are
successful in removing internal complaints are most
esteemed. Febrile disorders are not so prevalent as
in many tropical climates, but asthmatic and pulmonary
affections are frequent, and the latter generally baffle all
their skill. We are not aware that they admit into their
materia medica any but vegetable substances, which are
variously prepared—sometimes baked or heated in a
cocoanut-shell, but often applied after being simply
bruised with a stone. In the selection and employment
of these, they certainly manifest an acquaintance with
the medicinal properties of a number of indigenous herbs
and roots, which is commendable, and may hereafter be
turned to a good account. Several of their applications,
simply as they are prepared, are, however, very powerful, and sometimes fatal, in their effects. They had till

lately no means of employing a warm-bath, but frequently steamed their patients on an oven of heated stones, or placed them over the smoke of a fire covered with green succulent herbs. They have also a singular method of employing friction by rolling a stone or cannon-shot over the part in pain. I went one day into a house belonging to Karaimoku, where a chief was lying on his face, and the kahuna, or his attendant, was rolling a cannon-shot of twelve or fourteen pounds' weight backwards and forwards along his back, in order to alleviate the pain. There were also among them oculists, who were celebrated for curing diseases of the eye, and who were sometimes sent for by persons residing many miles distant. But in surgery they seem to be far behind the Society islanders.

The chiefs and many of the natives, who are accustomed to associate with foreigners, have entirely discarded the native doctors; and in times of sickness apply to the physician connected with the American mission, to the surgeon on shore, or one belonging to any ship in harbour, and show a decided preference to foreign medicine. The great body of the people, however, are generally averse to our remedies, and prefer the attendance of the native doctors. The employment is somewhat profitable; and the fee, which is either a piece of cloth, a mat, a pig, or dog, &c., is usually paid before the kahuna undertakes the case.

In conversation on this subject with the governor at Kairua, I once asked him what first induced them to employ herbs, &c., for the cure of diseases. He said that, many generations back, a man called Koreamoku obtained all their medicinal herbs from the gods, who also taught him the use of them: that after his death he was deified, and a wooden image of him placed in the large temple at Kairua, to which offerings of hogs, fish, and cocoanuts were frequently presented. Oronopuha and Makanuiairomo, two friends and disciples of Koreamoku, continued to practise the art after the death of their master, and were also deified after death, particularly because they were frequently successful in driving away the evil spirits by which the people were afflicted and threatened with death. This is the account they have of the first use of herbs medicinally; and to these deified men the prayers of the kahuna are addressed when medicine is administered to the sick.

During the day we examined various parts of the district on the western side, and sounded in several places along the channel leading into the bay. The district of Waiakea and the bay of the same name, the *Whye-a-te-a* bay of Vancouver,[*] from the southern boundary of the division of Hiro, are situated on the north-east coast of Hawaii, and distant about twenty or twenty-five miles from the eastern point of the island. The highest peak of Mouna Kea bears due west from the sandy beach at the bottom or south end of the bay. In the centre, or rather towards the south-east side, is a small island connected with the shore by a number of rocks, and covered with cocoanut-trees. South-west of this small island the native vessels usually anchor, and are thereby sheltered from all winds to the eastward of north-east. The bottom is good across the whole extent of the bay, but the western side is more exposed to the prevailing trade-winds. There is a shoal extending perhaps two miles from the above-mentioned island. It is therefore necessary, in going into the harbour, to keep near the western shore, which is very bold; the water is deep, and the passage free from rocks. There are three streams of fresh water, which empty themselves into the bay. One on the western angle is called Wairuku. It rises near the summit of Mouna Kea, and after taking a circuitous course for several miles, runs rapidly into the sea. Two others, called Wairama and Waiakea, rise in springs, boiling up through the hollows of the lava, at a short distance from the shore, fill several large fish-ponds, and afterward empty themselves into the sea. Waiakea, on the eastern side of the bay, is tolerably deep, and is navigated by canoes and boats some distance inland.

The face of the country in the vicinity of Waiakea is the most beautiful we have yet seen, which is probably occasioned by the humidity of the atmosphere, the frequent rains that fall here, and the long repose which the district has experienced from volcanic eruptions.

The district of Waiakea, though it does not include more than half the bay, is yet extensive. Kukuwau, in the middle of the bay, is its western boundary, from which, passing along the eastern side, it extends ten or

[*] This bay is now called Byron's Bay, having been visited and explored by Captain Lord Byron, on his late voyage to the Sandwich Islands in his majesty's ship Blonde.

twelve miles towards Kaau, the last district in the division of Puha.

Taking every circumstance into consideration, this appears a most eligible spot for a missionary station. The fertility of the soil, the abundance of fresh water, the convenience of the harbour, the dense population, and the favourable reception we have met with, all combine to give it a stronger claim to immediate attention than any other place we have yet seen, except Kairua. There are 400 houses in the bay, and probably not less than 2000 inhabitants, who would be immediately embraced in the operations of a missionary station here, besides the populous places to the north and south, that might be occasionally visited by itinerant preachers from Waiakea.

In the afternoon I preached in front of the house where we held our worship on the last Sabbath. There were three Marquesians present, who arrived here but a few weeks ago.

It is truly distressing to hear so frequently of the murderous quarrels which take place between the natives of the Marquesas and other islands in the Pacific, and the crews of ships visiting them; which, we think, would be in a great degree prevented were missionaries permanently residing among them. The natives are sometimes exceedingly deceitful and treacherous in their dealings with foreigners, and the conduct of the latter is not always such as to inspire confidence. The missionaries in the Society Islands have often been the means of preventing the consequences to which the misunderstanding of the natives and foreigners would in all probability have led. Once, in particular, about four years ago, a captain who had never visited them before, and has not been there since, touched at a small island to the south-west of Tahiti, bargained with the natives for a number of hogs, agreeing to give in exchange for them tools or clothing. The natives carried to the ship, which was lying off and on, five or six large hogs in a canoe; they were hoisted in, when, instead of returning the stipulated articles, the captain threw down into their canoe a bundle of old iron, principally iron hoops, cast loose the rope by which they held on to the ship, and sailed away. The natives returned to the shore; a council was held, in which it was agreed to take revenge on the first ship that should arrive. In the interim

however, a missionary from one of the Society Islands,
whom they had long known, visited them, and, being
made acquainted with the circumstances, dissuaded
them from their purpose, promised to make up their
loss, and thus, in all probability, the death of several
innocent persons was prevented.

While we were engaged in worship at Waiakea,
Messrs. Bishop and Thurston went over to Pueho, on
the western shore, and Mr. Thurston preached to about
one hundred of the people, at the house of Kapapa, the
head man. When the service was ended, Kapapa accompanied them to the east side of the bay, in the
double canoe which had been hired to convey us to
Laupahoehoe.

At daybreak on the 14th, after morning worship with
the people who crowded our house, we made arrangements for our departure. Mr. Harwood remained, to
return to Oahu in the brig Inore, lying at anchor in the
bay, as he would thereby be enabled to transact some
business for the mission, and also avoid travelling over
the ravines of Hiro and Hamakua.

Soon after six A. M. we embarked on board our
canoe, and passed over the reef to the deep water on the
western side of the bay. The weather was calm, and
the men laboured with their paddles till about eight,
when the *marenai* (east wind) sprang up, and wafted us
pleasantly along the shore. We found our double canoe
very convenient, for it had a *pora*, or stage, raised in the
middle, which provided a comfortable seat, and also kept
our packages above the spray of the sea. The póra is
formed by tying slight poles to the *iäko*, or cross pieces
that connect the two canoes together, from the foremost
iako to the one nearest the stern. The cross pieces
are not straight, but bent like a bow, and form an arch
between the two canoes, which raises the pora, or stage,
at least two feet higher than the sides of the canoe.
When the breeze sprang up, four of the men laid down
their paddles and attended to the sail, while one man sat
in the stern of each canoe with a large paddle to steer.
Our canoe, though made of heavy wood, was thin, and
consequently light, and as the wind increased, seemed
at a rapid rate to skim along the tops of the waves;
dashing through the crested foam with a degree of velocity which, but for the confidence we reposed in the
skill and address of our pilots, would have excited no
small degree of apprehension for our safety.

The canoes of the Sandwich Islands appear eminently calculated for swiftness, being low, narrow, generally light, and drawing but little water. A canoe is always made out of a single tree; some of them are upwards of seventy feet long, one or two feet wide, and sometimes more than three feet deep; though in length they seldom exceed fifty feet. The body of the canoe is generally covered with a black paint, made by the natives of various earthy and vegetable materials, in which the bark, oil, and burnt nuts of the kukui-tree are the principal ingredients. On the upper edge of the canoe is sewed, in a remarkably neat manner, a small strip of hard white wood, from six to eight inches in width, according to the size and length of the canoe. These strips meet and close over the top at both stem and stern, and shoot off much water that would otherwise enter the canoe. All the canoes of these islands are remarkably strong and neatly made, and though not so large as those of New-Zealand, the Society Islands, or some of the other islands to the southward, are certainly better made, and would probably paddle or sail faster than any of them. One man, we have heard, will sometimes paddle a single canoe faster than a good boat's crew could row a whale-boat. Their tackling is simple and convenient; the mast generally has a notch cut at the lower end, and is placed on one of the cross pieces, to which it is tied; the sails they now use are made of mats, and cut in imitation of the sprit-sails of foreign boats, which, they say, they find much better than the kind of sail they had when first visited by foreigners. When sailing with a fresh breeze, the ropes from the lower corners of the sails are always loosened, and held in the hands of persons whose only business it is to keep them properly trimmed. Their paddles, which are large and strong, are generally four or five feet long, have an oval-shaped blade and round handle, and are made of the same hard and heavy wood employed in building their canoes. They are not handsome, and their weight must make paddling very laborious. Neither the canoes nor paddles of the Sandwich islanders are carved like those of many islands in the Pacific. Their canoes are, nevertheless, remarkably neat, and sometimes handsome.

After sailing pleasantly for several hours we approached Laupahoehoe: we had proceeded upwards of

L 3

twenty miles, and had passed not less than fifty ravines
or valleys, but we had not seen a spot where we thought
it would be possible to land without being swamped;
and although we knew we had arrived at the end of our
voyage, we could discover no place by which it seemed
safe to approach the shore, as the surf was beating violently, and the wind blowing directly towards the land.
However, when we came within a few yards of the surf,
we perceived an opening in the rocks, just wide enough
to admit our canoe. Into this our pilots steered with
uncommon address and precision; and before we could
look round we found our canoe on a sandy beach, a few
yards long, entirely defended by rocks of lava from the
rolling surf on the outside.

It was one P. M. when we landed, and walked up to
the house of the head man, where we had a few fish and
some potatoes, that we had brought with us, prepared
for dinner. After the people of the place had been
spoken to on the subject of religion, they said they had
heard there were missionaries living at Oahu, teaching
the king to read, and write, and pray. They had also
heard of Jehovah, but not of Jesus Christ. It was compassionate in the great God, they added, to think of
them, and send his Word among them.

Leaving Laupahoehoe, we ascended the north side of
the deep ravine, at the bottom of which the village is
situated. We reached the top after climbing between
four hundred and five hundred feet, and beheld a beautiful country before us. Over this we travelled about five
miles in a west-north-west direction towards the foot
of Mouna Kea, and after passing three deep ravines
reached Humuula shortly before sunset. This retired
little village is situated on the edge of a wood, extending
along the base of Mouna Kea. We directed our steps
to the principal house in the village, and invited the
people of the neighbourhood to meet us there. They
soon collected, and listened with apparent interest to
a short discourse. Many continued with us till a late
hour in conversation, which to them is usually a source
of no small gratification. We have several times, during our tour, been kept awake by the natives in the
houses where we lodged, who have continued talking
and singing till near daybreak. Circumstances the most
trivial sometimes furnished conversation for hours.
Their songs also afford much amusement, and it is no

unusual thing for the family to entertain their guests with these, or for strangers to gratify their host by reciting those of their own island or neighbourhood. More than once, when we have entered a house, some of the inmates have shortly after commenced a song, accompanied occasionally by a little drum, or the beating of the *raau hura*, musical stick; and the natives who formerly visited Hawaii from the Society Islands excited no small degree of interest by reciting the songs of their country. It is probable that many of the fabulous tales and songs, so popular among them, have originated in the gratification they find in thus spending their time. This kind of amusement is common to most of the South Sea islands. The Sandwich islanders equal the Marquesians, the most lively natives of the Pacific, in the number of their songs, and exceed the Society islanders; but their conversational powers are inferior to those of the latter, who are, perhaps, the most loquacious of them all. An acquaintance with everybody's business used almost to be cultivated as an accomplishment; and inquiries, which to us would appear most officious, were only common civilities. To meet a party, and not ask where they came from, or where they were going, what was their business, and when they intended to return, would be considered indicative of displeasure towards the party thus neglected, or at least of want of interest in their welfare.

Our hostess, who was a widow, treated us kindly, and between seven and eight brought in for supper a small baked pig, and a large dish of taro. This was the more grateful as it had not been required by Makoa in the governor's name, but was furnished by the genuine hospitality which characterizes the South Sea islanders, though not practised so much by the Hawaiians as by some other tribes in the Pacific, and, we believe, much less now than when the Sandwich Islands were first discovered, or during the earlier visits they received.

They are still, however, a hospitable people, and even the poorest would generally share their scanty dish of potatoes with a stranger. Not to entertain a guest with what they have is, among themselves, considered reproachful; and there are many who, if they had but one pig or fowl in the yard, or one root of potatoes in the garden, would cheerfully take them to furnish a repast for a friend. This generous disposition is frequently

abused, and encourages the rambling manner of life of
which many are so fond. It is not unusual for a family,
when they have planted their field with sweet potatoes,
&c., to pay a visit for four or five months to some friend
in a distant part of the island. When the crop is ripe,
they travel home again, and in return are most likely
visited by a friend, who will not think of leaving them
so long as any of their provisions remain unconsumed.
This, however, is only the case where friendship has
previously existed between the parties. A transient
visiter, on arriving among them, will generally have an
entertainment provided, of which the persons who furnish it seldom partake. The family with which we
lodged were, however, induced to join us this evening
at supper, though contrary to their ideas of propriety.
Whenever we have remarked to the natives that their
conduct in this respect is unsocial, they have usually
answered, "Would it be right for us to present food to
our friends, and then sit down and eat of it ourselves!"
Connected with this, another custom, equally at variance
with our views of hospitality, is practised by the guests,
who invariably carry away all that remains of the entertainment, however abundant it may have been. Hence,
whenever a pig, &c. has been dressed for us, and our
party have finished their meal, our boys always put the
remainder into their baskets, and carried it away. To
this we often objected; but they usually replied, "It
is our custom; and if we don't take it, the people will
think you are dissatisfied with what they have provided."

The entertainment given to strangers or visiters is
regulated by the means of the host or the rank of the
guests. In the Society Islands their feasts were formerly characterized by a degree of prodigality extremely
oppressive to the people who had to furnish the provisions. I once saw in the island of Raiatea upwards of
fifty large baked hogs, and a proportionate quantity of
poë, yams, &c. served up at one time for a party of
chiefs on a visit from the Georgian or Windward
Islands. In this respect the Sandwich islanders are not
behind their southern neighbours; but, in their feasts,
the flesh of the dog constitutes the principal meat. I
have seen nearly two hundred dogs cooked at one time:
and during the last visit which Taümuarii, late king of
Tauai, and Kaahumanu, his queen, paid Kuakini, the

governor of this island, a feast was prepared for them by the latter, at which Auna was present, and counted four hundred baked dogs, with fish and hogs, and vegetables in proportion. Sometimes the food is spread out on the ground, which is previously covered with grass or green leaves; the party sit down around it, and the chiefs distribute it among them, after the servants have carved it with a knife, or with a piece of bamboo cane, which, before visited by foreigners, was the only kind of knife they possessed. The serrated edge of the hard bamboo cane, when but recently split, is very sharp; and we have often been surprised at the facility with which they cut up a large hog with no other instrument. The head of a hog, or at least the brains, constituted a dainty for the principal chief of the party; particular portions were given to the priests, if any were present; while the backbone and the tail were the usual perquisites of the person who carved.

In general, however, when such large presents of food are made, each hog or dog when baked is put into a distinct basket, and piled up in heaps in the courtyard in front of the house where the chief is residing; the fish, dogs, and vegetables in separate heaps. When collected, the chief comes out to look at it, and those who have brought it retire. He then calls his stewards, —directs them to select a portion for his own table,— distributes some among the chiefs in the neighbourhood, in which the chief who has provided the feast is frequently included,—and divides the rest among his own followers, who sometimes amount to two or three hundred.

Numbers of dogs, of rather a small size, and something like a terrier, are raised every year as an article of food. They are mostly fed on vegetables; and we have sometimes seen them kept in yards, with small houses to sleep in. A part of the rent of every tenant who occupies land is paid in dogs for his landlord's table. Though often invited by the natives to join them in partaking of the baked dog, we were never induced to taste of one. The natives, however, say it is sweeter than the flesh of the pig, and much more palatable than that of goats or kids, which some refuse to touch, and few care to eat.

These feasts are much less frequent than formerly, particularly among those chiefs who have opportunities for frequent intercourse with foreigners, several of whom now spread their table in the European manner, and invite their friends to dine, or entertain their guests at home, and treat them as members of their family while they remain under their roof.

CHAPTER XIV.

SEVERAL members of the family we had lodged with united with us in our morning worship on the 15th, after which we breakfasted together.

While thus engaged, Makóa, who had remained at the last place where we stopped, arrived with our baggage, and about eight A. M. we were ready to proceed. Unwilling that our hostess should suffer by her kindness, we presented her with as much blue cotton cloth as would amply pay for the supper she had generously furnished last evening, and then set out on our journey.

The wide-extended prospect which our morning walk afforded of the ocean, and the shores of Hamakua, on our right, was agreeably diversified by the occasional appearance of the snow-capped peaks of Mouna Kea, seen through the openings in the trees on our left. The body of the mountain was hid by the wood, and the different peaks only appeared like so many distinct hills at a great distance. The highest peak bore south-west-by-south from Humuula.

The high land over which we passed was generally woody, though the trees were not large. The places that were free from wood were covered with long grass and luxuriant ferns. The houses mostly stood singly, and were scattered over the face of the country. A rich field of potatoes or taro, sometimes five or six

acres in extent, or large plantations of sugar-cane and
bananas, occasionally bordered our path. But though
the soil was excellent, it was only partially cultivated.
The population also appeared less than what we had
seen inhabiting some of the most desolate parts of the
island.

About ten A.M. we reached the pleasant and verdant
valley of Kaura, which separates the divisions of Hiro
and Hamakua.

The geographical divisions of Hawaii and the other
islands of the group are sometimes artificial; and a
stone image, a line of stones somewhat distant from
each other, a path, or a stone wall, serves to separate
the different districts, or larger divisions, from each
other. They are, however, more frequently natural, as
in the present instance, where a watercourse, winding
through the centre of the valley, marked the boundary
of these two divisions. The boundary of the smaller
districts, and even the different farms, as well as the
large divisions, are definitely marked, well understood,
and permanent. Each division, district, village, and
farm, and many of the sites of houses, have a distinct
name, which is often significant of some object or quality distinguishing the place.

On descending to the bottom of the valley, we reached
a heiau dedicated to Pélé, with several rude stone idols,
wrapped up in white and yellow cloth, standing in the
midst of it. A number of wreaths of flowers, pieces
of sugar-cane, and other presents, some of which were
not yet faded, lay strewed around, and we were told
that every passing traveller left a trifling offering before
them. Once in a year, we were also informed, the
inhabitants of Hamakua brought large gifts of hogs,
dogs, and fruit, when the priests and kahu of Pélé assembled to perform certain rites, and partake of the
feast. This annual festival, we were told, was designed
to propitiate the volcanic goddess, and secure their
country from earthquakes, or inundations of lava.
Locks of human hair were among the offerings made to
Pélé. They were frequently presented to this goddess
by those who passed by the crater of Kirauea, on which
occasions they were thrown into the crater, a short
address being made at the same time to the deity supposed to reside there.

We ventured to deviate from the custom of travellers

in general; yet, though we presented no offerings, we
did not proceed to pull down the heiau, and irritate the
people by destroying their idols, but entered into conversation with them on the folly of worshipping such
senseless things, and pointed out the more excellent
way of propitiating the favour of Jehovah, the true
God, with sacrifices of thanksgiving and praise, placing
all their hopes in his mercy, and depending for security
on his providence. They took what we said in good
part, and answered, that though the stones could not
save them, the being whom they represented, or in honour of whom they were erected, was very powerful, and
capable of devouring their land, and destroying the
people. This we denied, and told them that volcanoes
and all their powers were under the control of that God
whom we wished them to choose for their God and
Saviour.—When a drawing had been taken of this beautiful valley, where kukui-trees, plantains, bananas, and
ti-plants were growing spontaneously with unusual richness of foliage and flower, we took leave of the people,
and, continuing our journey, entered Hamakua.

Hiro, which we had now left, though not so extensive
and populous as Kona, is the most fertile and interesting division on the island. The coast from Waiakea to
this place is bold and steep, and intersected by numerous
valleys or ravines; many of these are apparently formed
by the streams from the mountains, which flow through
them into the sea. The rocks along the coast are volcanic, generally a brown vesicular lava. In the sides
and bottoms of some of the ravines, they were occasionally of very hard compact lava, or a kind of basalt.
This part of the island, from the district of Waiakea to
the northern point, appears to have remained many
years undisturbed by volcanic eruptions. The habitations of the natives generally appear in clusters at the
opening of the valleys, or scattered over the face of the
high land. The soil is fertile, and herbage abundant.
The lofty Mouna Kea, rising about the centre of this
division, forms a conspicuous object in every view that
can be taken of it. The base of the mountain on this
side is covered with woods, which occasionally extend
within five or six miles of the shore. While the division
of Kona, on the leeward side of the island, is often
several months without a shower, rain is frequent in this
and the adjoining division of Hamakua, which form the

centre of the windward coast, and is doubtless the
source of their abundant fertility. The climate is warm.
Our thermometer was usually 71° at sunrise, 74° at noon,
and 72° or 73° at sunset. Notwithstanding these natural advantages, the inhabitants, excepting at Waiakea,
did not appear better supplied with the necessaries of
life than those of Kona, or the more barren parts of Hawaii. They had better houses, plenty of vegetables,
some dogs, and a few hogs, but hardly any fish, a principal article of food with the natives in general.

About midday we came to a village called Kearakaha,
where we collected the people, and preached to them.
They listened attentively, and conversed very freely
afterward on what had been said.

Leaving Kearakaha, we continued our walk to Manienie, where we dined, and rested two or three hours.
During our stay, we addressed the people as usual.

Shortly after four in the afternoon, we left Manienie,
and travelled over a well-cultivated tract of country, till
we reached Toumoarii, where we put up for the night,
as we were considerably fatigued with our day's journey, having crossed nearly twenty ravines, some of
which were from three to four hundred feet deep. The
people collected in front of the head man's house, for
religious worship; and the service was concluded with
singing and prayer just as the sun was setting. We
spent the evening in conversation with the people of the
house. Many of them exclaimed, " *Makemake au ia Jesu
Kraist. Aroha nui o Jesu!*"—I desire Jesus Christ,
Great is Jesus's love.

Makoa, as usual, excited much interest among the
natives by the accounts he gave of our journey, &c.
This evening he turned theologian, and while we were
at supper we heard him telling a party around him, in
another part of the house, that heaven was a place where
there was neither salt fish nor calabashes of poë. Indeed, added he, we shall never want any there, for we
shall never be hungry. But in order to get there, much
is to be done. A man that wishes to go there must
live peaceably with his neighbours—must never be idle;
and, moreover, must be a *kanaka opu nui ore*, that is,
must not be a glutton.

We arose at daylight on the 16th, and shortly after
left Taumoarii. We had not travelled more than four
or five miles when we reached Kaahua. After break-

fast we proceeded on our journey over a country equal in fertility to any we had passed since leaving Waiakea. The houses were in general large, containing usually three or four families each. Mr. Goodrich was indisposed through the day, which obliged us to travel but slowly. Near noon we stopped at Koloaha, and, while he reclined beneath the shade of an adjoining grove of trees, I addressed the assembled natives on the subject of religion. After remaining about two hours, we walked to another village, where Mr. Thurston spoke to the people, who gave good attention. We then kept on our way till we reached Maianahae, where a congregation of the people assembled, with whom we conversed some short time, then bade them farewell, and about three P. M. reached Kapulena, where we preached to upwards of one hundred of the people assembled on the occasion.

At this place we thought it best to form ourselves into two parties, in order that we might preach to the natives along the northern parts of the island, and examine the interior between this place and Towaihae. It was therefore arranged that Messrs. Bishop and Goodrich should spend the Sabbath here, and on Monday morning pass over to Waimea, and thence to Towaihae, while Mr. Thurston and myself travelled through the villages on the northern shores.

On Monday morning, Messrs. Bishop and Goodrich commenced their journey to Waimea. Having procured a man to carry their baggage, they left Kapulena, and, taking an inland direction, passed over a pleasant country, gently undulated with hill and dale. The soil was fertile, the vegetation flourishing, and there was considerable cultivation, though but few inhabitants. About noon they reached the valley of Waimea, lying at the foot of Mouna Kea, on the north-west side. Here a number of villages appeared on each side of the path, surrounded with plantations, in which plantains, sugarcane, and taro were seen growing unusually large. At four P. M. they obtained a view of the ocean, and kept on their way towards Towaihae: at night they slept on the ground in the open air.

At break of day on the 19th they began to descend; and after walking about two hours, reached Towaihae, where they were hospitably received by Mr. Young, with whom they spent the day.

Having heard that a schooner from Oahu was at
Keauhou, they left Towaihae in the evening in a canoe
belonging to Mr. Young, and proceeded to Kairua, where
the schooner was lying at anchor.

It was about five o'clock in the afternoon of the 16th
when Mr. Thurston and myself left Kapulena. Wish-
ing to spend the Sabbath in the populous village of Waipio, we travelled fast along the narrow paths bordered
with long grass, or through the well-cultivated plantations of the natives. The Sandwich islanders have no
idea of constructing their roads or foot-paths in a straight
line. In many parts, where the country was level and
open, the paths from one village to another were not
more than a foot wide, and very crooked. We often
had occasion to notice this, but never passed over any
so completely serpentine as those we travelled this
evening.

The sun had set when we reached the high cliff that
formed the southern boundary of Waipio. Steep rocks
not less than five hundred feet high rose immediately
opposite. Viewed from the great elevation at which
we stood, the charming valley, spread out beneath us
like a map, appeared in beautiful miniature. Its numerous inhabitants, cottages, plantations, fish-ponds, and
meandering streams, with the light canoe moving to and
fro on the surface of the latter, gave an air of animation
to the scene, in which the distinct and varied objects
were blended with the most delightful harmony. Makoa
led the way down the steep cliffs. The descent was
difficult, and it was quite dark before we reached the
bottom. A party of natives, returning from a fishing
excursion, ferried us across the stream that ran along
near the place where we descended, and we directed
our steps towards the house of Haa, head-man of the
village. He received us courteously, ordered a clean
mat to be spread for us to recline on, and water for us
to drink; some of his attendants also handed us a large
wooden tobacco-pipe, which is usually passed round
when strangers arrive; this last compliment, however,
we begged leave to decline. Makoa seated himself by
the side of the chief, and gave him a brief outline of our
tour—our object—and the instructions given to the people. In the mean time, fish was prepared for supper
by a fire of sandal-wood, which, instead of filling the
house with disagreeable smoke, perfumed it with a

fragrant odour.   After family worship in the native language, we retired to rest.

The next morning unveiled to view the extent and beauty of the romantic valley. Its entrance from the sea, which was blocked up with sand-hills fifty or sixty feet high, appeared to be a mile or a mile and a half wide. The summits of the hills which bordered the valley seemed six hundred feet above the level of the sea. They were in some parts nearly perpendicular, yet they were clothed with grass, while low straggling shrubs were here and there seen amid the jutting rocks. A number of winding paths led up their steep sides, and in several places rivulets, flowing in beautiful cascades from the top to the bottom, formed a considerable stream, which, meandering along the valley, found a passage through the sand-hills, and emptied itself into the sea. The bottom of the valley was one continued garden, cultivated with taro, bananas, sugar-cane, and other productions of the islands, all growing luxuriantly.   Several large ponds were also seen in different directions, well stocked with excellent fish. A number of small villages, containing from twenty to fifty houses each, stood along the foot of the mountains, at unequal distances on each side, and extended up the valley till projecting cliffs obstructed the view.

Morning worship was attended by our host and his family—and, about half-past ten, the people of the neighbourhood assembled in front of the house. Mr. Thurston preached to them, and was encouraged by the attention given.

In the afternoon he walked up the north side of the valley, and preached to congregations of about one hundred persons, in three different villages. I proceeded about a mile and a half along the south side of the valley to the village of Napope, containing forty-three houses, and preached to the natives. After the service the people complained of their great ignorance, and wished they might be visited again.

At five P. M. I returned, and addressed the people in the place where Mr. Thurston had preached in the morning. About three hundred were present, and listened attentively.

The chief with whom we lodged made many inquiries respecting the way of salvation through Jesus Christ. He also asked about the change, which had taken place in the Society Islands; and afterward observed that Hawaii was a dark land, and would not soon attend to its true interests. He and his family cheerfully united in the devotional exercises of the day, and by his conversation manifested, for an untutored native, an unusual degree of intelligence.

In the evening, as we sat around the door, we heard the voice of wailing and lamentation. On inquiry, it was found to proceed from a neighbouring cottage, where a woman who had been some time ill had just expired. This circumstance led to a conversation on death and a future state, and the necessity of habitual preparedness for the eventful change which awaits all mankind. While we were talking, the moon arose, and shed her mild light upon the valley; her beams were reflected by the rippling stream, and the small lakes beautified the scene. All was serene and still, save the chirping insects in the grass. The echo of the cloth-mallet, which had been heard through the day in different parts of the valley, had now ceased. Though generally a pleasant sound, especially when heard in a solitary valley, indicating the industry of the natives, it had on this day, which was the Sabbath, called forth the most affectionate solicitude for the interesting people of the place; and we could not but desire the speedy arrival of that time when the sacred hours of the Sabbath should be employed in spiritual and devotional exercises. That, however, is not to be expected in the present circumstances of the people; for

> "The sound of the church-going bell
>   These valleys and rocks never heard;
> Never sigh'd at the sound of a knell,
>   Nor smiled when a Sabbath appear'd."

And probably until this day their inhabitants had not been informed that "in six days they should labour and do all their work, and that the seventh is the Sabbath of the Lord their God," which he requires them to sanctify by sacred worship and holy rest.

On the morning of the 18th, we were desirous of witnessing the interment of the person who died last night, but were disappointed; it was, as most of their funerals are, performed in secret. A few particulars relative to their mode of burying we have been able to gather from

the people of this place and other parts of the island.
The bones of the legs and arms, and sometimes the
scull, of their kings and principal chiefs, those who were
supposed to have descended from the gods, or were to
be deified, were usually preserved, as already noticed.
The other parts of the body were burned or buried;
while these bones were either bound up with cinet,
wrapped in cloth, and deposited in temples for adoration, or distributed among the immediate relatives, who,
during their lives, always carried them wherever they
went. This was the case with the bones of Tamehameha; and it is probable that some of his bones were
brought by his son Rihoriho, on his recent visit to England, as they supposed that so long as the bones of the
deceased were revered, his spirit would accompany
them, and exercise a supernatural guardianship over
them.

They did not wash the bodies of the dead, as was the
practice with some of the South Sea islanders. The
bodies of priests, and chiefs of inferior rank, were laid
out straight, wrapped in many folds of native tapa, and
buried in that posture; the priests, generally within the
precincts of the temple in which they had officiated. A
pile of stones, and frequently a circle of high poles, surrounded their grave, and marked the place of their interment, corresponding exactly with the rites of sepulture
practised by some of the tribes on the opposite coast of
North America. It was only the bodies of priests, or
persons of some importance, that were thus buried.
The common people committed their dead to the earth
in a most singular manner. After death, they raised
the upper part of the body, bent the face forward to the
knees; the hands were next put under the hams, and
passed up between the knees, when the head, hands, and
knees were bound together with cinet or cord. The
body was afterward wrapped in a coarse mat, and buried
the first or second day after its decease.

They preferred natural graves whenever available,
and selected for this purpose caves in the sides of their
steep rocks, or large subterranean caverns. Sometimes
the inhabitants of a village, deposited their dead in one
large cavern; but in general each family had a distinct
sepulchral cave. Their artificial graves were either
simple pits dug in the earth or large enclosures. One
of the latter, which we saw at Keahou, was a space

surrounded with high stone walls, appearing much like an ancient heiau or temple. We proposed to several natives of the village to accompany us on a visit to it, and give us an outline of its history; but they appeared startled at the thought—said it was a *wahi ino*, place evil; filled with dead bodies—and objected so strongly to our approaching it, that we deemed it inexpedient to make our intended visit. Occasionally they buried their dead in sequestered places, at a short distance from their habitations, but frequently in their gardens, and sometimes in their houses. Their graves were not deep, and the bodies were usually placed in them in a sitting posture.

No prayer was offered at the grave, except occasionally by the inhabitants of Oahu. All their interments are conducted without any ceremony, and are usually managed with great secrecy. We have often been surprised at this, and believe it arises from the superstitious dread the people entertain respecting the places where dead bodies are deposited, which they believe resorted to by the spirits of those buried there. Like most ignorant and barbarous nations, they imagine that apparitions are frequently seen, and often injure those who come in their way. Their funerals take place in the night, to avoid observation; for, we have been told, that if the people were to see a party carrying a dead body past their houses, they would abuse them, or even throw stones at them, for not taking it some other way, supposing the spirit would return to and fro to the former abode of the deceased, by the path along which the body had been borne to the place of interment.

The worshippers of Pélé threw a part of the bones of their dead into the volcano, under the impression that the spirits of the deceased would then be admitted to the society of the volcanic deities, and that their influence would preserve the survivors from the ravages of volcanic fire.

The fishermen sometimes wrapped their dead in red native cloth, and threw them into the sea, to be devoured by the sharks. Under the influence of a belief in the transmigration of souls, they supposed the spirit of the departed would animate the shark by which the body was devoured, and that the survivors would be spared by those voracious monsters, in the event of their being overtaken by any accident at sea.

The bodies' of criminals who had broken tabu, after having been slain to appease the anger of the god whose tabu, or prohibition, they had broken, were buried within the precincts of the heiau. The bones of human sacrifices, after the flesh had rotted, were piled up in different parts of the heiau in which they had been offered.

Idolatry since 1819 has been abolished, and all ceremonies connected therewith have ceased; the other heathenish modes of burying their dead are only observed by those who are uninstructed, and are not professed worshippers of the true God: those who are inter their dead in a manner more resembling the practice of Christians. The corpse is usually laid in a coffin, which, previous to interment, is borne to the place of worship, attended by the relatives in mourning habiliments, where a short service is performed; it is then carried to the grave: after being deposited there, sometimes the spectators are addressed by the missionary; on other occasions a short prayer only is offered; and as the friends retire, the grave is filled up.

After breakfast, Mr. Thurston walked about five miles up the valley, in order to estimate its population and preach to the people. The whole extent was well cultivated, and presented in every direction the most beautiful prospects. At one of the villages where he stopped about one hundred people collected, to whom he preached the word of salvation. I spent the morning in taking a drawing of the valley from the sand-hills on the beach; and in examining some large heiaus in the neighbourhood, in reference to which the natives taxed our credulity by the legendary tales they related respecting the numbers of victims which had on some occasions been offered. In the days of Umi, they said, that king, after having been victorious in battle over the kings of six of the divisions of Hawaii, was sacrificing captives at Waipio, when the voice of Kuahiro, his god, was heard from the clouds, requiring more men; the king kept sacrificing, and the voice continued calling for more, till he had slain all his men, except one; whom, as he was a great favourite, he refused at first to give up; but the god, being urgent, he sacrificed him also, and the priest and himself were all that remained. Upwards of eighty victims, they added, were offered at that time, in obedience to the audible demands of the insatiate demon. We have heard the same account at other places, of eighty victims being slain at one time; and though, perhaps, the account may exceed the number actually immolated, the tradition serves to show the savage character of the gods, who, in the opinion of the natives, could require such prodigal waste of human life.

In the afternoon we visited *Pakarana*, the puhonua, or place of refuge, for all this part of the island. It was a large enclosure, less extensive, however, than that at Honaunau. The walls, though of great antiquity, were of inferior height and dimensions. In the midst of the enclosure, under a wide-spreading pandanus, was a small house, called *Ke Hale o Riroa* (the house of Riroa), from the circumstance of its containing the bones of a king of that name, who was the grandson of Umi, and, according to their traditions, reigned in Hawaii about fifteen generations back.

We tried, but could not gain admittance to the pahu tabu, or sacred enclosure. We also endeavoured to obtain a sight of the bones of Riroa, but the man who had charge of the house told us we must offer a hog before we could be admitted; that Tamehameha, whenever he entered, had always sent offerings; that Rihoriho, since he had become king, had done the same, and that no one could be admitted on other conditions.

Finding us unwilling to comply, yet anxious to see the bones, they directed us to a rudely carved stone image, about six feet high, standing at one corner of the wall, which they said was *tii*, or image of Riroa. We talked some time with the people around, who were principally priests, on the folly of deifying and worshipping departed men. The only answer, however, which they made was, *Pela no i Hawaii nei:* So it is in Hawaii here.

At five o'clock in the afternoon, about three hundred of the natives of the place assembled for public worship, in front of the head man's house, where they were addressed from Luke xiv. 23. The people were attentive, and frequently interrupted the speaker by their exclamations. Some said, " Jehovah is a good God; the living God is a good God: great is his love."

After the service, they sat talking on what they had heard, and occasionally making inquiries, till the sun had set, and the moon had nearly reached the mid-heaven. The chief, in particular, seemed much interested, and, during the evening, he and several others expressed themselves very desirous that a missionary should come and reside with them, that they might be instructed fully in all these things.

According to the number of houses which we have seen, in all 265, there are at least 1325 inhabitants in this sequestered valley, besides populous villages on each side along the coast, which might be easily visited. This circumstance, together with the fertility of the soil, the abundance of water, the facility with which, at most seasons of the year, supplies can be forwarded by water from Kairua or Towaihae, combine to render this an eligible spot for a missionary station; but, notwithstanding all these favourable circumstances, together with the great desire of the people to be instructed in the important principles of Christianity, it is much to be feared, that unless the funds of the societies are increased, this inviting field, as well as several others, must long remain destitute of moral culture.

The valley of Waipio is a place frequently celebrated in the songs and traditions of Hawaii, as having been the abode of Akea and Miru, the first kings of the island; of Umi and Riroa, kings who make a prominent figure in their history. It is also noted as the residence of Hoakau, king of this part of the island, who appears to have been one of the Neros of the Sandwich Islands, and whose memory is execrable among the people, on account of his cruelties; and of whom it is reported, that if a man was said to have a fine-looking head, he would send his servants to behead the individual, and bring his head before him, when he would wantonly cut, and otherwise disfigure it. . He is said also to have ordered a man's arm to be cut off, and brought to him, only because it was tattooed in a manner more handsome than his own.

An interesting conversation was carried on this evening, with respect to the separate existence of the soul, the resurrection of the body, and the general judgment at the last day. The account of the raising of the widow's son, and the calling of Lazarus from the grave, after he had been dead four days, seemed greatly to interest the natives. We afterward endeavoured to learn from them something respecting their opinions of a state of existence after death. But all they said upon the subject was so contradictory, and mixed with fiction, that it could not be discovered whether they had any definite idea of the nature, or even the existence, of such a state. Some said, that all the souls of the departed went to the *Po*, place of night, and were annihilated, or eaten by the gods there. Others said, that some went to the regions of Akea and Miru. Akea, they said, was the first king of Hawaii. At the expiration of his reign, which terminated with his life at Waipio, where we then were, he descended to a region far below, called Kapapahanaumoku* (the island-bearing rock, or stratum), and founded a kingdom there. Miru, who was his successor, and reigned in Hamakua, descended, when he died, to Akea, and shared the government of the place with him. Their land is a place of darkness; their food lizards and butterflies. There are several streams of water, of which they drink, and some said there were large kahiris,† and wide-spreading koutrees, beneath which they reclined. But, to most of the questions that were asked, they said they could give no answer, as they knew nothing about it; none had ever returned in open daylight, to tell them any thing respecting it; and all they knew was from visions or dreams of the priests. Sometimes, they said, when a recently liberated spirit arrived in the dominions of Miru, the Pluto of Hawaii, he (viz. Miru) would ask it what the kings above were doing, and what were the principal pursuits of the people? and when he had answered, he was sent back to the *ao marama* (state of day or light) with a message from Miru to them, to *iho nui mai ma nei* (to descend altogether to this place). The person so sent would appear to the priests in a dream, deliver his message, and then return to the lower regions.

The account given this evening of the Hawaiian *hades* afforded another proof of the identity between the traditions of the Sandwich and Society islanders: for among the latter, the spirits of the Areois, and

---

* Compounded of *Ka papa*, the rock, or stratum of rock; *hanau*, to bear, or bring forth; and *moku*, an island.

† Though the kahiris were usually small, resembling the one represented in the plate of the native dance at Kairua, they were sometimes upwards of twenty feet high; the hamile twelve or fifteen feet long, beautifully covered with tortoise-shell and the ivory of whales' teeth; and the upper part formed with red, yellow, or black feathers, fastened on a kind of wicker-work, and resembling a cylinder twelve or thirteen inches in diameter. These, however, are only used on state occasions, when they are carried in processions instead of banners, and are fixed in the ground near the tent or house in which the king or principal personages may remain on such occasions.

priests of certain idols, were not eaten by the gods after
the death of their bodies, but went to Miru (pronounced
by both, Meru), where they lived much in the same way
as the departed kings and heroes of Hawaii were supposed to do; or, joining hands, they formed a circle
with those that had gone before, and danced in one
eternal round.

At daylight on the 19th, numbers of the people collected around the house where we had lodged, with
whom we held morning worship. Haa, the chief of
the place, beneath whose friendly roof we had been
most hospitably entertained, then accompanied us to the
beach, where he had prepared a canoe to convey us to
the next district. Shortly after six A. M. we gave him
the parting hand, with sincere thanks for his kindness;
after which we seated ourselves in the canoe, and, in
the midst of many expressions of good-will from those
who had come down to the beach to bid us farewell, we
were safely launched through the surf. We left Waipio,
deeply impressed with a sense of the kind treatment
we had received, and with feelings of sympathy for the
mental darkness and degradation of the interesting people by whom it was inhabited. We could not but hope
that they would soon enjoy the constant light of Christian instruction, and participate in every Christian privilege.   A wide field of usefulness is here presented to a
Christian missionary, and we sincerely hope the direc-
tors of missionary operations will have means sufficient
at their disposal to send a missionary to this, and every
other place where the people are so anxious to be instructed.

After proceeding pleasantly along for five or six miles,
we arrived at *Waimanu*, a little before eight o'clock.

We found Arapai, the chief, and a number of his men,
busy on the beach shipping sandal-wood on board a
sloop belonging to the governor, then lying at anchor
in a small bay off the mouth of the valley. He received us kindly, and directed two of his men to conduct us to his house, which was on the opposite side.
The valley, though not so spacious or cultivated as
Waipio, was equally verdant and picturesque; we could
not but notice the unusual beauty of its natural scenery.
The glittering cascades and waterfalls, that rolled down
the deep sides of the surrounding mountains, seemed
more numerous and beautiful than those at Waipio.

As we crossed the head of the bay, we saw a number of young persons swimming in the surf, which rolled with some violence on the rocky beach. To a spectator nothing can appear more daring, and sometimes alarming, than to see a number of persons splashing about among the waves of the sea as they dash on the shore; yet this is the most popular and delightful of the native sports.

There are perhaps no people more accustomed to the water than the islanders of the Pacific; they seem almost a race of amphibious beings. Familiar with the sea from their birth, they lose all dread of it, and seem nearly as much at home in the water as on dry land. There are few children who are not taken into the sea by their mothers the second or third day after their birth, and many who can swim as soon as they can walk. The heat of the climate is, no doubt, one source of the gratification they find in this amusement, which is so universal that it is scarcely possible to pass along the shore where there are many habitations near, and not see a number of children playing in the sea. Here they remain for hours together, and yet I never knew of but one child being drowned during the number of years I have resided in the islands. They have a variety of games, and gambol as fearlessly in the water as the children of a school do in their play-ground. Sometimes they erect a stage eight or ten feet high on the edge of some deep place, and lay a pole in an oblique direction over the edge of it, perhaps twenty feet above the water; along this they pursue each other to the outermost end, when they jump into the sea. Throwing themselves from the lower yards, or bowsprit, of a ship, is also a favourite sport, but the most general and frequent game is swimming in the surf. The higher the sea and the larger the waves, in their opinion the better the sport. On these occasions they use a board, which they call *papa he naru* (wave-sliding-board), generally five or six feet long, and rather more than a foot wide, sometimes flat, but more frequently slightly convex on both sides. It is usually made of the wood of the *erythrina*, stained quite black, and preserved with great care. After using, it is placed in the sun till perfectly dry, when it is rubbed over with cocoanut oil, frequently wrapped in cloth, and suspended in some part of their dwelling-house. Sometimes they choose a place where the deep water reaches to the beach, but generally prefer a part where the rocks are ten or twenty feet under water, and extend to a distance from the shore, as the surf breaks more violently over these. When playing in these places, each individual takes his board, and, pushing it before him, swims perhaps a quarter of a mile or more out to sea. They do not attempt to go over the billows which roll towards the shore, but watch their approach, and dive under water, allowing the billow to pass over their heads. When they reach the outside of the rocks, where the waves first break, they adjust themselves on one end of the board, lying flat on their faces, and watch the approach of the largest billow; they then poise themselves on its highest edge, and paddling as it were with their hands and feet, ride on the crest of the wave, in the midst of the spray and foam, till within a yard or two of the rocks or the shore; and when the observers would expect to see them dashed to pieces, they steer with great address between the rocks, or slide off their board in a moment, grasp it by the middle, and dive under water, while the wave rolls on, and breaks among the rocks with a roaring noise, the effect of which is greatly heightened by the shouts and laughter of the natives in the water. Those who are expert frequently change their position on the board, sometimes sitting and sometimes standing erect in the midst of the foam. The greatest address is necessary in order to keep on the edge of the wave: for if they get too forward, they are sure to be overturned; and if they fall back, they are buried beneath the succeeding billow.

Occasionally they take a very light canoe; but this, though directed in the same manner as the board, is much more difficult to manage. Sometimes the greater part of the inhabitants of a village go out to this sport when the wind blows fresh towards the shore, and spend the greater part of the day in the water. All ranks and ages appear equally fond of it. We have seen Karaimoku and Kakioeva, two of the highest chiefs in the island, both between fifty and sixty years of age, and large corpulent men, balancing themselves on their narrow board, or splashing about in the foam, with as much satisfaction as youths of sixteen. They frequently play at the mouth of a large river, where the strong current running into the sea and the rolling of the waves towards the shore produce a degree of agitation between the water of the river and the sea that would be fatal to a European, however expert he might be : yet in this they delight : and when the king or queen, or any high chiefs, are playing, none of the common people are allowed to approach these places, lest they should spoil their sport. The chiefs pride themselves much on excelling in some of the games of their country; hence Taumuarii, the late king of Tauai, was celebrated as the most expert swimmer in the surf known in the islands. The only circumstance that ever mars their pleasure in this diversion is the approach of a shark. When this happens, though they sometimes fly in every direction, they frequently unite, set up a loud shout, and make so much splashing in the water as to frighten him away. Their fear of them, however, is very great; and after a party return from this amusement, almost the first question they are asked is, " Were there any sharks ?" The fondness of the natives for the water must strike any person visiting their islands : long before he goes on shore he will see them swimming around his ship : and few ships leave without being accompanied part of the way out of the harbour by the natives, sporting in the water ; but to see fifty or a hundred persons riding on an immense billow, half-immersed in spray and foam, for a distance of several hundred yards together, is one of the most novel and interesting sports a foreigner can witness in the islands.

When we arrived at the house of Arapai, we were welcomed by his wife and several members of his family.

Arapai is evidently a chief of some importance. We saw several large double canoes in his outhouses. The number of his domestics was greater than usual; his house was large, well built, and stocked with a number of useful articles, among which we noticed some large and handsomely stained calabashes, marked with a variety of devices. The calabash is a large kind of gourd, sometimes capable of holding four or five gallons. It is used to contain water and other fluids by the natives of all the islands in the South Sea; but the art of staining it is peculiar to the Sandwich islanders, and is another proof of their superior powers of invention and ingenuity. When the calabash has grown to its full size, they empty it in the usual manner, by placing it in the

sun till the inside is decayed, and may be shaken out.
The shell, which remains entire, except the small perforation made at the stalk for the purpose of discharging
its contents, and serving as a mouth to the vessel, is,
when the calabash is large, sometimes half an inch thick.
In order to stain it, they mix several bruised herbs,
principally the stalks and leaves of the arum, and a
quantity of dark ferruginous earth with water, and fill
the vessel with it. They then draw with a piece of
hard wood or stone on the outside of the calabash whatever figures they wish to ornament it with. These are
various, being either rhomboids, stars, circles, or wave
and straight lines, in separate sections, or crossing each
other at right angles, generally marked with a great degree of accuracy and taste. After the colouring matter
has remained three or four days in the calabashes, they
are put into a native oven and baked. When they are
taken out, all the parts previously marked appear beautifully brown or black, while those places where the
outer skin had not been broken retain their natural
bright-yellow colour. The die is now emptied out, and
the calabash dried in the sun; the whole of the outside
appears perfectly smooth and shining, while the colours
imparted by the above process remain indelible.

Large quantities of kukui, or candle-nuts, hung in long
strings in different parts of Arapai's dwelling. These
are the fruit of the *aleurites triloba*; a tree which is
abundant in the mountains, and highly serviceable to the
natives. It furnishes a gum, which they use in preparing varnish for their tapa, or native cloth. The inner
bark produces a permanent dark-red die, but the nuts
are the most valuable part; they are heart-shaped, about
the size of a walnut, and are produced in abundance.
Sometimes the natives burn them to charcoal, which
they pulverize, and use in tattooing their skin, painting
their canoes, surf-boards, idols, or drums; but they are
generally used as a substitute for candles or lamps.
When designed for this purpose, they are slightly baked
in a native oven, after which the shell, which is exceedingly hard, is taken off, and a hole perforated in the
kernel, through which a rush is passed, and they are
hung up for use, as we saw them at this place. When
employed for fishing by torchlight, four or five strings
are enclosed in the leaves of the pandanus, which not

only keeps them together, but renders the light more brilliant.

When they use them in their houses, ten or twelve are strung on the thin stalk of the cocoanut-leaf, and look like a number of peeled chestnuts on a long skewer. The person who has charge of them lights a nut at one end of the stick, and holds it up till the oil it contains is consumed, when the flame kindles on the one beneath it, and he breaks off the extinct nut with a short piece of wood, which serves as a pair of snuffers. Each nut will burn two or three minutes, and if attended give a tolerable light. We have often had occasion to notice, with admiration, the merciful and abundant provision which the God of nature has made for the comfort of those insulated people, which is strikingly manifested by the spontaneous growth of this valuable tree in all the islands; a great convenience is hereby secured with no other trouble than picking up the nuts from under the trees. The tree is large, the leaves and wood remarkably white; and though the latter is not used by the Sandwich islanders, except occasionally in making fences, small canoes are frequently made of it by the Society islanders. In addition to the above purposes, the nuts are often baked or roasted as an article of food, which the natives eat with salt. The nut contains a large portion of oil, which, possessing the property of drying, is useful in painting; and for this purpose quantities are carried by the Russian vessels to their settlements on the north-west coast of America.

Before we prepared for our departure, we requested that the people of the place might assemble, to hear the word which we had to speak to them. About two hundred collected, and were addressed from John vi. 40. They gave good attention, particularly the wife of Arapai, who was afflicted with an affection of the spine, which prevented her walking without support. She called us to her after the service, and told us she had incurred the displeasure of the gods by eating a fish that was *tabu*, or sacred, and that the disease which rendered her a cripple was her punishment. She said she had felt great pleasure on hearing the invitation of Jesus Christ, desired to go to him and obey his Word; inquiring at the same time very earnestly, if we thought he could and would save her. We told her that eating the tabu fish was not the cause of her suffering, and encouraged

M 3

her to repair, by faith, to Him who was able and willing
to heal her body, if he saw fit, and who would assuredly
save her soul, if she applied in a right manner; repeat-
ing several of the most precious promises of our blessed
Redeemer to those that are weary and heavy-laden with
sin, and desire salvation through his mercy. Numbers
of the people crowded round us when the service was
ended, and with earnestness besought us to sit down,
and repeat several of the truths they had heard respecting the name and attributes of Jehovah, his law, and the
name and offices of Jesus Christ the only Saviour.
They also requested to be more particularly informed in
what manner they should pray to him, and how they
should know when the Sabbath-day came. We told
them to go to Jehovah in prayer, as a child goes to its
parents, assuring them they would find him more ready
to attend to them than the fondest earthly parent was
to listen to his most beloved child. · This did not satisfy
them; we therefore, after observing that God did not
regard so much the *words* as the desires of the heart,
mentioned several expressions of praise, confession, and
petition—which the natives repeated after us till they
could recite them correctly. The chief then sent for a
youth, about sixteen years of age, of whom he seemed
very fond, and after he and his wife had requested him
to attend very particularly to what he should hear, they
requested us to repeat to him what we had told them.
We did so; the youth evidently tried to treasure up the
words in his memory; and when he could repeat correctly what had been told him the parents appeared
highly pleased. Indeed, the greater part of the people
seemed to regard the tidings of *ora roa ia Jesu* (endless
life by Jesus) as the most joyful news they had ever heard;
"breaking upon them," to use the expressions of the
natives on another occasion, "like light in the morning."
The chief's wife, in particular, exclaimed aloud, "Will
my spirit never die? and can this weak body live again?"
When we departed, she rose up, and by the help of two
sticks walked down to the beach with us. Here we
took an affectionate leave, and then stepped into a canoe,
which Arapai had provided to convey us as far as Honokane, the first village in the division of Kohala. As
the canoe pushed off from the shore we again bade them
farewell. When we saw the interesting group standing
on the beach, we could not but feel the most lively

concern for their welfare, and involuntarily besought the great Redeemer that his Holy Spirit might be poured out upon them, that the seed sown among them might take root in their hearts, and produce an abundant harvest to his praise.

After leaving Waimanu, we passed by Laupahoehoe, a second village of that name on this part of the coast, where, according to the accounts of the natives, about eight or nine months before, an immense mass of rocks had suddenly fallen down. The mountain that remained appeared nearly six hundred feet high. The face next the sea was perpendicular, and as smooth as a compact piece of masonry. The rock appeared volcanic, and the different strata of highly vesicular lava were very distinct. In several places we saw the water oozing from the face of the rock 200 or 300 feet from the summit. The mass that had fallen lay in ruins at the base, where it had formed two considerable hills, filled up a large fish-pond and part of the sea, presenting altogether a scene of wide-spread desolation.

The original surface of the ground appeared to have been broken by an earthquake, as some parts were rent by deep chasms, others sunk down six or twelve feet lower than the rest. The shrubs and grass were growing luxuriantly on the upper or original, and lower or fallen surface, while the perpendicular space between them indicated that the latter had recently sunk down from the former. Wrecks of houses were seen in several places, some partly buried by the ruins, others standing just on the edge of the huge rocks that had fallen from above. Several houses were standing in the neighbourhood, but all seemed deserted. The natives said, that in the evening, when the accident took place, a mist or fog was seen to envelop the summits of the precipice, and that, after the sun had set, a luminous appearance like a lambent flame was observed issuing from and playing about the top, which made them think it was a forerunner of Pélé, or volcanic fire. A priest of Pélé and his family, residing in one of the villages below, immediately offered his prayer to the goddess, and told the inhabitants that no harm would befall them.

About ten o'clock at night, however, the whole side of the mountain, for nearly half a mile in extent along the shore, fell down with a horrid crash. Part of two small villages were destroyed, and several of the inhabitants killed, but the natives did not agree as to the numbers; some said twenty were killed, others only eighteen. The people with whom we talked on the spot, and at other places subsequently, could not recollect having heard the natives who escaped say any thing about an earthquake at the time.

We did not land at this place, but passed close to the shore, and continued to sail along at the base of steep mountains, 500 or 600 feet high; and, although nearly perpendicular, they were intersected here and there by winding paths, which we at first thought could be travelled only by goats, but up which we afterward saw one or two groups of travellers pursuing their steep and rugged way. About noon we passed Honokea, a narrow valley which separates the divisions of Hamakua and Kohala, and shortly after reached Honokane, the second village in the latter.

The division of Hamakua, on the north-east side of the island, is, during the greater part of the year, singularly romantic in its appearance, particularly as seen from a vessel four or five miles out at sea. The coast is bold and steep, and the cliffs, from three to five hundred feet high, partially covered with shrubs and herbage, intersected by numerous deep ravines and valleys, frequently in a high state of cultivation, while the whole coast is ornamented with waterfalls and cascades of every description. I once beheld three-and-twenty at one time from a ship's deck—some rolling in one continued stream from the summit of the cliffs to the sea, others foaming and winding among the ledges of rock that arrested their progress, sparkling among the verdant shrubs that fringed their borders, and, altogether, presenting a most delightful spectacle.

We landed at Honokane, and went through the village to the house of Ihikaina, chief woman of the place, and sister to Arapai, the chief of Waimanu, from which this district is distant about twenty miles. Ihikaina received us kindly, and, for our refreshment, provided a duck, some vegetables, and a small quantity of excellent goat's milk, large flocks of which are reared by some of the natives for the supply of ships touching at the islands for refreshments.

The valley contained fifty houses. A number of the people collected round the door of the house, and listened to a short address.

About four P. M. we left Honokane, and passed on
to Pololu. On our way we walked over a long tract
of fragments of rocks, occasioned by the falling down
of a side of the mountain, which took place at the same
time that the mass of rocks fell at Laupahoehoe, which
we had passed in the forenoon.

About seven in the evening we reached Halaua, the
residence of *Miomioi*, a friend and favourite of the late
king Tamehameha. He gave us a hearty welcome, with
the accustomed courtesy of a Hawaiian chief, saying,
" Our house is large, and there are plenty of sleeping-
mats for us." The hospitality of the chiefs, both of the
Society and Sandwich Islands, is always accompanied
with a courtesy of behaviour peculiarly gratifying to
those who are their guests, and indicating a degree of
refinement seldom witnessed among uncivilized nations.
The usual salutation is *Aróhá* (attachment), or *Aróhá nui*
(attachment great); and the customary invitation to
partake of some refreshment is, " The food (*a kakou*)
belonging to you and us is ready ; let us eat together:"
always using the pronoun *kakou*, or *kaua*, which includes
the person addressed, as well as the speaker. On entering a chief's house, should we remark, " Yours is a
strong or convenient house," he would answer, " It is a
good house for (or belonging to) you and me." If, on
entering a house, or examining a fine canoe or piece of
cloth, we should ask who it belongs to, another person
would tell us the possessor's name ; but if we happened
to inquire of the owner himself, he would invariably
answer, " It is *yours* and *mine*." The same desire to
please is manifested in a variety of ways. The manner
in which they frequently ask a favour of each other is
singular, usually prefacing it with, " *I rea oe*"—If pleasing to you. Hence we often have a message or note to
the following effect: " If pleasing to you, I should like
a sheet of writing-paper, or a pen ; but if it would not
give you pleasure to send it, I do not wish it."

Soon after we had entered Miomioi's house, a salt
flying-fish was broiled for supper. A large copper
boiler was also brought out, and tea was made with
some dried mint, which he said he had procured many
months before from ships at Towaihae. He supped at
the same time, but instead of drinking tea, took a large
cocoanut-shell full of *ava*. If an opinion of its taste
might be formed by the distortion of his countenance after

taking it, it must be a most nauseous dose. There
seemed to be about half a pint of it in the cup; its colour was like thick dirty calcareous water. As he took
it, a man stood by his side with a calabash of fresh
water, and the moment he had swallowed the intoxicating dose, he seized the calabash, and drank a hearty
draught of water, to remove the unpleasant taste and
burning effect of the ava.

The *ava* has been used for the purpose of inebriation
by most of the South Sea islanders, and is prepared
from the roots and stalks of a species of pepper plant,
the *piper methysticum* of Forster, which is cultivated for
this purpose in many of the islands, and, being a plant
of slow growth, was frequently tabued from the common
people. The water in which the ava had been mace-
rated was the only intoxicating liquor with which the
natives were acquainted before their intercourse with
foreigners, and was, comparatively speaking, but little
used, and sometimes only medicinally, to cure cutaneous
eruptions and prevent corpulency. But since they have
been so much visited by shipping, the case is very different. They have been taught the art of distillation;
and foreign spirits in some places are so easily obtained,
that inebriety, with all its demoralization and attendant
misery, is ten times more prevalent than formerly. This
is a circumstance deeply to be deplored, especially
when we recollect the immediate cause of its prevalence.

The chief's house was large, and one end of it was
raised by leaves and mats about a foot higher than the
rest of the floor, and partially screened from the other
parts of the house. This was his own sleeping-place,
but he ordered a new mat to be spread, and obligingly
requested us to occupy it. We did so, and enjoyed a
comfortable night's rest.

After an early breakfast with Miomioi and his family,
I embraced the opportunity of addressing his people on
the subject of religion, before they separated to pursue
their various occupations. About fifty were present,
and listened with silent attention.

Miomioi, though not so tall and stout in person as
many of the chiefs, appeared a remarkably active man,
and soon convinced us he had been accustomed to delight in war. His military skill had probably recommended him to the notice and friendship of Tamehameha,

and had secured for him the occupancy of the district of Halaua, the original patrimony of that prince.

Every thing in his house seemed to be preserved with care, but particularly his implements of war. Spears nearly twenty feet long, and highly polished, were suspended in several places, which he was very careful to show us; remarking that Tamehameha always required every man to keep his weapons in order, so as to be ready for war at the shortest notice, and showing at the same time an evident satisfaction at the degree of care with which his own were preserved.

Halaua is a large district on the north-east coast of the island, and, if not the birth-place of Tamehameha, was the land which he inherited from his parents, and, with the exception of a small district in the division of Kona, the only land he possessed in Hawaii prior to the death of Taraiopu, and the celebrated battle of Keei, which took place shortly afterward. Tamehameha seems to have been early distinguished by enterprise, energy, decision of character, and unwearied perseverance in the accomplishment of his objects. Added to these, he possessed a vigorous constitution, and an unrivalled acquaintance with all the warlike games and athletic exercises of his country. To these qualities of mind and body he is probably indebted for the extensive power and protracted dominion which he exercised over the Sandwich Islands. In early life he associated with himself a number of youthful chiefs of his own age and disposition, into whom he had the happy art of instilling, on all occasions, his own spirit, and inspiring them with his own resolution: by these means he most effectually secured their attachment and co-operation. Great undertakings appear to have been his delight, and achievements deemed by others impracticable were those which he regarded as most suitable exercises of his prowess. Miomioi led the way to a spot where, in a small bay, the original coast had been a perpendicular pile of rocks, at least one hundred feet high. Here Tamehameha and his companions, by digging through the rocks, had made a good road, with a regular and gradual descent from the high ground to the sea, up and down which their fishing canoes could be easily drawn.

At another place, he had endeavoured to procure water by digging through the rocks; but after forcing his way through several strata, the lava was found so hard, that he was obliged to give up the undertaking. Probably he had no powder with which to blast the rocks, and not the best tools for working through them. A wide tract of country in the neighbourhood was divided into fields of considerable size, containing several acres each, which he used to keep in good order, and well stocked with potatoes and other vegetables. One of these was called by his name. He was accustomed to cultivate it with his own hands. There were several others called by the names of his principal friends or companions, which, following his example, they used to cultivate themselves; the others were cultivated by their dependants. As the chief walked through the village, he pointed out the houses in which Tamehameha formerly resided, and several groves of *noni*-trees, the *morinda citrifolia*, that he had planted, as Miomioi remarked, before his beard was grown. Tamehameha was undoubtedly a prince possessing shrewdness and great strength of character. During his reign, the knowledge of the people was much enlarged, and their comforts in some respects increased: their acquisition of iron tools facilitated many of their labours; the introduction of firearms changed their mode of.warfare; and in many cases cloth of European manufacture was substituted for that made of native bark. But these improvements appear to be rather the result of their intercourse with foreigners, than of any measures of their sovereign; though the encouragement he gave to all foreigners visiting the islands was, no doubt, advantageous in these respects. He has been called the Alfred of the Hawaiians; but he appears rather to have been their Alexander, ambition and a desire of conquest having been his ruling passions during the greater part of his life—though towards its close avarice superseded them. It has been stated that he projected an invasion of the Society Islands; but the report, from many conversations on the subject with the natives, appears destitute of all foundation. Miomioi also pointed out the family heiau of Tamehameha, of which Tairi was the god, and the heiau was called *Hare o Tairi*, house of Tairi. It was an insignificant pile of stones, on a jutting point of volcanic rocks. Miomioi, however, said that the tabu was very strictly observed, and the punishments incurred by breaking it invariably inflicted on the transgressor; adding, at the same time, that Tame-

hameha always supposed his success, in every enterprise, to be owing to the strict attention he paid to the
service and requirements of his god. Many persons,
he said, had been burned on the adjoining hills, for
having broken the tabu enjoined by the priests of
Tairi.

The TABU formed an important and essential part of
their cruel system of idolatry, and was one of the strongest means of its support.

In most of the Polynesian dialects, the usual meaning
of the word tabu is *sacred*. It does not, however, imply
any moral quality, but expresses a connexion with the
gods, or a separation from ordinary purposes, and ex-
clusive appropriation to persons or things considered
sacred; sometimes it means devoted, as by a vow.
Those chiefs who trace their genealogy to the gods are
called *arii tabu*, chiefs sacred, from their supposed connexion with the gods; and a temple is called a *wahi tabu*,
place sacred, because devoted exclusively to the abode
and worship of the gods. It is a distinct word from
rahui, to prohibit, as the ohelo berries at Kirauea were
said to be prohibited, being *tabu na Pélé*, sacred for Pélé,
and is opposed to the word *noa*, which means general
or common. Hence the system which prohibited females from eating with the men, and from eating, except
on special occasions, any fruits or animals ever offered
in sacrifice to the gods, while it allowed the men to partake of them, was called the *Ai tabu*, eating sacred; but
the present state of things is called the *Ai noa*, eating
generally, or having food in common.

This appears to be the legitimate meaning of the word
tabu, though the natives, when talking with foreigners,
use it more extensively, applying it to every thing prohibited or improper. This, however, is only to accommodate the latter, as they use *kaukau* (a word of Chinese origin) instead of the native word for eat, and *pika-
ninny* for small, supposing they are thereby better
understood.

The tabu, separating whatever it was applied to from
common use, and devoting it to the above purposes, was
one of the most remarkable institutions among the South
Sea islanders; and though it prevailed, with slight variations, in the different groups of the Pacific, it has not
been met with in any other part of the world. Although
employed for civil as well as sacred purposes, the tabu

was entirely a religious ceremony, and could be imposed only by the priests. A religious motive was always assigned for laying it on, though it was often at the instance of the civil authorities; and persons called *kiaimoku*, island keepers, a kind of police officers, were always appointed by the king, to see that the tabu was strictly observed.

The antiquity of the tabū was equal to the other branches of that superstition of which it formed so component a part, and its application was both general and particular, occasional and permanent. The idols, temples, persons, and names of the king and members of the reigning family—the persons of the priests—canoes belonging to the gods—houses, clothes, and mats of the king and priests—and the heads of men who were the devotees of any particular idol,—were always tabu, or sacred. The flesh of hogs, fowls, turtle, and several other kinds of fish, cocoanuts, and almost every thing offered in sacrifice, were tabu to the use of the gods and the men; hence the women were, except in cases of particular indulgence, restricted from using them. Particular places, as those frequented by the king for bathing, were also rendered permanently tabu.

Sometimes an island or a district was tabued, when no canoe or person was allowed to approach it. Particular fruits, animals, and the fish of certain places were occasionally tabu for several months from both men and women.

The seasons generally kept tabu were, on the approach of some great religious ceremony—immediately before going to war—and during the sickness of chiefs. Their duration was various, and much longer in ancient than modern times. Tradition states, that in the days of Umi there was a tabu kept thirty years, during which the men were not allowed to trim their beards, &c. Subsequently, there was one kept five years. Before the reign of Tamehameha, forty days was the usual period; during it, ten or five days, and sometimes only one day. In this respect the tabues, or seasons of restriction, in Hawaii, appear to have exceeded those of the South Sea islands: the longest season of prohibition in Huahine, known to the natives, was the rahui of Mohono which lasted ten or twelve years. It was during this period that the hogs became so numerous and large that they destroyed all the feis, or mountain plantains, excepting those growing on the summits of the highest mountains.

The tabu seasons were either common or strict. During a common tabu, the men were only required to abstain from their usual avocations, and attend at the heiau when the prayers were offered every morning and evening. But, during the season of strict tabu, every fire and light on the island or district must be extinguished; no canoe must be launched on the water, no person must bathe; and, except those whose attendance was required at the temple, no individual must be seen out of doors; no dog must bark, no pig must grunt, no cock must crow,—or the tabu would be broken, and fail to accomplish the object designed. On these occasions, they tied up the mouths of the dogs and pigs, and put the fowls under a calabash, or fastened a piece of cloth over their eyes. All the common people prostrated themselves, with their faces touching the ground, before the sacred chiefs, when they walked out, particularly during tabu; and neither the king nor the priests were allowed to touch any thing,—even their food was put into their mouths by another person.

The tabu was imposed either by proclamation, when the crier or herald of the priests went round, generally in the evening, requiring every light to be extinguished, the path by the sea to be left for the king, the paths inland to be left for the gods, &c. The people, however, were generally prepared, having had previous warning; though this was not always the case. Sometimes it was laid on by fixing certain marks called *unu unu*, the purport of which was well understood, on the places or things tabued. When the fish of a certain part are tabued, a small pole is fixed in the rocks on the coast, in the centre of the place to which is tied a bunch of bamboo leaves, or a piece of white cloth. A cocoanut leaf is tied to the stem of a tree, when the fruit is tabued. The hogs which were tabu, having been devoted to the gods, had a piece of cinet woven through a perforation in one of their ears.

The prohibitions and requisitions of the tabu were strictly enforced, and every breach of them punished with death, unless the delinquents had some very powerful friends who were either priests or chiefs. They were generally offered in sacrifice, strangled, or despatched with a club or a stone within the precincts of the heiau, or they were burnt, as stated by Miomioi.

An institution so universal in its influence, and so inflexible in its demands, contributed very materially to the bondage and oppression of the natives in general. The king, sacred chiefs, and priests appear to have been the only persons to whom its application was easy; the great mass of the people were at no period of their existence exempt from its influence, and no circumstance in life could excuse their obedience to its demands. The females in particular felt all its humiliating and degrading force. From its birth, the child, if a female, was not allowed to be fed with a particle of food that had been kept in the father's dish, or cooked at his fire; and the little boy, after being weaned, was fed with his father's food, and, as soon as he was able, sat down to meals with his father, while his mother was not only obliged to take hers in an outhouse, but was interdicted from tasting the food which he ate. It is not surprising that the abolition of the tabu, effecting for them an emancipation so complete, and an amelioration so important, should be a subject of constant gratulation; and, that every circumstance tending, in the smallest degree, to revive the former tabu, should be viewed with the most distressing apprehensions. The only tabu they now have is the Sabbath, which they call the La tabu (day sacred), and to its extension and perpetuity those who understand it seem to have no objection. Philanthropy will rejoice, that their fears respecting the former are not likely to be realized; for, should Christianity not be embraced by some, and only nominally professed by others, so sensible are the great body of the people of the miseries endured under the tabu system, that it is very improbable it will ever be re-established among them. On the other hand, there is every reason to hope that pure Christianity, which imposes none but moral restrictions, and requires no appropriations but such as it will conduce to their own happiness to make, will eventually pervade every portion of the community; and that, while it teaches them to render a reasonable homage and obedience to the only living and true God, and prepares them for the enjoyment of his presence in a future state, it will elevate the degraded classes, especially the females,* to the rank and influence for which they were designed, and render their domestic society as rational and happy as under the tabu it was abject and wretched.

CHAPTER XV.

Traditions connected with the northern part of Kohala—Methods of procuring sandal-wood—Manufacture of salt at Towaihae—Visit to Waimea—Ascent of Mouna Kea—Arrival of Messrs. Bishop and Goodrich at Kairua—Erection of a place of worship—Observance of the Sabbath—Maritime character of the people—Government of the islands—Hereditary rank—Tenure of lands—Revenue and laws—Embarkation for Oahu.

HAVING seen the most remarkable places in the village, we took leave of Miomioi, and proceeded in a north-north-west direction.

At noon we stopped at Kapaau, an inland village, where, with some difficulty, we collected a congregation of about fifty, principally women, to whom a short discourse was addressed. When we had remained some time for rest and conversation, we resumed our journey, and proceeded towards the north point of the island, near which we passed through the district of *Pauepu*, in which formerly stood a temple called Mokini, celebrated, in the historical accounts of the Hawaiians, as built by Paao, a foreign priest, who resided in Pauepu, and officiated in this temple.

A tradition preserved among them states, that in the reign of *Kahoukapu*, a *kahuna* (priest) arrived at Hawaii, from a foreign country; that he was a white man, and brought with him two idols or gods, one large, and the other small; that they were adopted by the people, and

* Their degraded condition appears to have attracted the notice of the intelligent voyagers by whom the islands were discovered; for, speaking of the Sandwich islanders, Captain King, in his Continuation of Cook's Voyages, remarks, "It must, however, be observed that they fall very short of the other islanders, in that best test of civilization, the respect paid to the women. Here they are not only deprived of the privilege of eating with the men, but the best sorts of food are tabooed, or forbidden them:" and adds, "In their domestic life, they appear to live almost entirely by themselves; and, though we did not observe any instance of personal ill-treatment, yet it is evident they had little regard or attention paid them."—*Cook's Voyages*, vol. iii. p. 130.

placed among the Hawaiian gods; that the above-mentioned temple of Mokini was erected for them, where they were worshipped according to the direction of Paao, who became a powerful man in the nation. The principal event preserved of his life, however, respects a child of Kahoukapu, whose mother was a woman of humble rank, but which was spared at the solicitations of Paao. After his death, his son, Opiri, officiated in his temple; and the only particular worthy of note in their account of his life is his acting as interpreter between the king and a party of white men who arrived at the island. We forbear making any comment on the above, though it naturally originates a variety of interesting inquiries. We heard a similar account of this priest at two other places during our tour, namely, at Kairua, and at the first place we visited after setting out.

During our journey to-day we also passed another place, celebrated as the residence of the brother of *Kana*, a warrior; in comparison with the fabulous account of whose achievements, the descriptions in the Arabian Nights' Entertainments are tame. He is described as having been so tall that he could walk through the sea from one island to another; stand with one foot on the island of Oahu, and the other on Tauai, which is seventy miles distant.

The tale which recounts his adventures states, that the Hawaiians, on one occasion, offended a king of Tahiti; who, in revenge, deprived them of the sun; that after the land had remained some time in darkness, Kana walked through the sea to Tahiti, where Kahoaarii, who, according to their traditions, made the sun, then resided. He obtained the sun, returned, and fixed it in the heavens, where it has remained ever since. Other adventures, equally surprising, are related. The numerous tales of fiction preserved by oral tradition among the people, and from the recital of which they derive so much pleasure, prove that they are not deficient in imagination, and lead us to hope that their mental powers will be hereafter employed on subjects more consistent with truth, and productive of more pure and permanent gratification.

In this part of the island there is another tradition very generally received by the natives, of a somewhat more interesting character; and as it may tend to illustrate the history of the inhabitants, and the means by which the islands were peopled, I shall introduce it in this place.

They have traditions respecting several visits, which in remote times some of the natives made to *Nuuhiva* and *Tahuata*, two islands in the Marquesian group, and to Tahiti, the principal of the Society Islands. One of these accounts the natives call, "The Voyage of Kamapiikai," in which they state that Kamapiikai (child running, or climbing the sea,—from *kama*, a child, *pii*, to run or climb, and *kai*, the sea) was priest of a temple in Kohala, dedicated to Kauenuiakea. The exact period of their history when he lived we have not been able to ascertain; but it is added, that the god appeared to him in a vision, and revealed to him the existence, situation, and distance of *Tahiti*, and directed him to make a voyage thither. In obedience to the communication, he immediately prepared for the voyage, and with about forty of his companions set sail from Hawaii in four double canoes. After an absence of fifteen years, they returned, and gave a most flattering account of Haupokane, the country which they had visited. We know of no island in the neighbourhood called by this name, which appears to be a compound of *Haupo*, sometimes a lap, and *Kane*, one of their gods. Among other things, they described the *one rauena*, a peculiar kind of sandy beach, well stocked with shell-fish, &c. The country, they said, was inhabited by handsome people, whose property was abundant, and the fruits of the earth delicious and plentiful. There was also a stream or fountain, which was called the *wai ora roa* (water of enduring life).

Kamakiipai made three subsequent voyages to the country he had discovered, accompanied by many of the Sandwich islanders. From the fourth voyage they never returned, and were supposed to have perished at sea. or to have taken up their permanent residence at Tahiti. Many were induced to accompany this priest to the country he visited, for the purpose of bathing in the life-giving waters, in consequence of the marvellous change they were reported to produce in those who used them; for it was said, that however infirm, emaciated, or deformed they might be, when they went into the water, they invariably came out young, strong, and handsome.

Without making further remarks, these traditions fur-

nish very strong evidence that the Sandwich islanders
were acquainted with the existence of the Marquesian
and Society Islands long before visited by Captain
Cook; and they also warrant the inference, that in
some remote period the Sandwich islanders have visited or colonized other islands in the Pacific.

About three P. M. we reached Owawarua, and passed
on to Hihiu, where we had an opportunity of speaking
to a small party of natives.

In these villages we saw numbers of canoes and
many large fishing-nets, which are generally made of
a native kind of flax, very strong and durable, but produced by a plant very different from the *phormium tenax*,
which furnishes the flax of New-Zealand, and bearing a
nearer resemblance to the plant used by the natives of
the Society Islands called roa, the *urtica argentea*, or
candicans, of Parkinson. In taking fish out at sea, they
commonly make use of a net, of which they have many
kinds, some very large, others mere hand-nets; they
occasionally employ the hook and line, but never use
the spear or dart, which is a favourite weapon with the
southern islanders.

Quantities of fish were spread out in the sun to dry,
in several places, and the inhabitants of the northern
shores seem better supplied with this article than those
of any other part of the island. The shores of Hawaii
are by no means so well stocked with fish as those of
the Society Islands. The industry of the Hawaiians in
a great degree makes up the deficiency, for they have
numerous small lakes and ponds, frequently artificial,
wherein they breed fish of various kinds, and in tolerable abundance.

It was about seven o'clock in the evening when we
sailed from Hihiu, in a single canoe. The land-breeze
was light, but the canoe went at a tolerably rapid rate,
and about eleven at night we reached Towaihae, where
we were kindly received by Mr. Young. By him we
were informed that Messrs. Bishop and Goodrich had
arrived at Towaihae on the preceding Tuesday, and had
gone to Kairua, expecting to obtain a passage to Oahu,
in a native vessel called the pilot-boat.

Before daylight on the 22d, we were roused by vast
multitudes of people passing through the district from
Waimea with sandal-wood, which had been cut in the
adjacent mountains for Karaimoku, by the people of

Waimea, and which the people of Kohala, as far as the north point, had been ordered to bring down to his store-house on the beach, for the purpose of its being shipped to Oahu. There were between two and three thousand men, carrying each from one to six pieces of sandal-wood, according to their size and weight. It was gene-rally tied on their backs by bands made of ti-leaves, passed over the shoulders and under the arms, and fast-ened across their breast. When they had deposited the wood at the storehouse, they departed to their re-spective homes.

Between seven and eight in the morning, we walked to the warm-springs, a short distance to the southward of the large heiaus, and enjoyed a most refreshing bathe. These springs rise on the beach, a little below high-water mark—of course they are overflowed by every tide; but at low tide the warm water bubbles up through the sand, fills a small kind of cistern made with stones piled close together on the side towards the sea, and affords a very agreeable bathing place. The water is comfortably warm, and is probably impregnated with sulphur: various medicinal qualities are ascribed to it by those who have used it.

The natives of this district manufacture large quan-tities of salt, by evaporating the sea-water. We saw a number of their pans, in the disposition of which they display great ingenuity. They have generally one large pond near the sea, into which the water flows by a chan-nel cut through the rocks, or is carried thither by the natives in large calabashes. After remaining there some time, it is conducted into a number of smaller pans, about six or eight inches in depth, which are made with great care, and frequently lined with large evergreen leaves, in order to prevent absorption. Along the narrow banks or partitions between the different pans we saw a num-ber of large evergreen leaves placed. They were tied up at each end, so as to resemble a shallow dish, and filled with sea-water, in which the crystals of salt were abundant.

The Sandwich islanders eat salt very freely with their food, and use large quantities in preserving their fish. They have, however, besides what they make, salt lakes, which yield them large supplies. The surplus thus furnished they dispose of to vessels touching at the islands, or export to the Russian settlements on the north-west coast of America, where it is in great demand for curing fish, &c.

In the afternoon, Mr. Goodrich returned from Kairua, and informed us that the pilot-boat was at Keauhou, and would sail for Oahu in a fortnight. He also brought the more pleasing intelligence that the governor was engaged in building a chapel for the public worship of God at Kairua, having at the same time enjoined on his people the observance of the Sabbath, as a day of rest from labour and amusement—to be employed, moreover, in religious exercises. This welcome news rendered it desirable that one of us should repair to Kairua, in order to preach there on the coming Sabbath, and encourage them to persevere in the work they had so happily begun.

The 24th was probably the first Christian Sabbath ever enjoyed by the people of Towaihae, which is a village containing one hundred houses. Mr. Thurston preached twice to the people.

About five P. M. on the 25th, Mr. Thurston set out on a visit to the inland district of Waimea, having been furnished with a guide by Mr. Young. It was dark when he reached Ouli, a place belonging to the latter, where he put up for the night.

After worship with the people, on the morning of the 26th, Mr. Thurston walked on to Kalaloa, the residence of the chief of Waimea, *Kumuokapiki*, Stump of Cabbage. Leaving Kalaloa, he walked on to Waiakea, from thence to Waikaloa, Pukalani, and Puukapu, which is sixteen or eighteen miles from the seashore, and is the last village in the district of Waimea. At these places he addressed the people.

The soil over which he had travelled was fertile, well watered, and capable of sustaining many thousand inhabitants. In his walks he had numbered two hundred and twenty houses, and the present population is probably between eleven and twelve hundred.

The surface of the country is gently undulated, tolerably free from rocks, and easy of cultivation. In this district, and throughout the divisions of Hamakua and Kohala, together with the greater part of Hiro, the plough might be introduced with advantage, and the productions of intertropical climates raised in great abundance and excellent quality—as the sugar-cane and other indigenous plants grown at Waimea are unusually large.

From Puukapu he directed his steps towards the sea-shore, and in the twilight of the evening reached Puako, a considerable village, four or five miles to the south-ward of Towaihae, where he took up his lodgings for the night. After addressing the people on the morning of the 27th, Mr. Thurston returned to Towaihae, where he arrived at ten A. M.

About noon the same day, Mr. Goodrich returned from his journey to Mouna Kea. Leaving Towaihae on the 23d, he had walked to Waimea, on the skirts of which he encamped with Mr. Parker, who was employed in shooting wild cattle. With him he spent the Sabbath, which was rainy and unpleasant. Early on Monday the 25th, he commenced his journey up the mountain. The path lay along the side of a deep ravine; the soil was formed of decomposed lava and ashes. At noon he dismissed his native companion, and, taking his great-coat and blanket, began to ascend the more steep and rugged parts. The way was difficult, on account of the rugged volcanic rocks and stunted shrubs that covered the sides of the mountain. In his way, he found num-bers of red and white raspberry bushes, loaded with de-licious fruit. At five P. M., having reached the upper boundary of the trees and bushes that surround the moun-tain, he erected a temporary hut, kindled a small fire, and prepared for his night's repose. The thermometer, shortly after sunset, stood at 43°; and the magnet, though it pointed north when held in the hand, was drawn between two and three degrees to the eastward when placed on the blocks of lava—owing, probably, to the quantity of iron in the mountain.

After a few hours' rest, Mr. Goodrich arose at eleven o'clock at night, and, the moon shining brightly, he re-sumed his journey towards the summit. At midnight he saw the snow about three miles distant, proceeded towards the place, and reached it about one o'clock on the morning of the 26th. The snow was frozen over, and the thermometer stood at 27°. He now directed his steps towards a neighbouring peak, which appeared to be one of the highest; but when he had ascended it he saw several others still higher. He proceeded to-wards one which looked higher than the rest, and bore north-east from the place where he was. On reaching

N 2.

the summit of this second peak, he discovered a heap
of stones, probably erected by some former visiter.
From this peak Mouna Roa bore south-by-west, Mouna
Huararai west-by-south, and the island of Maui north-
west. The several hills or peaks on the summit of
Mouna Kea seemed composed entirely of volcanic matter, principally cinders, pumice, and sand. Mr. Goodrich did not discover apertures or craters on either of
the summits he visited; probably there is a large crater
somewhere adjacent, from which the scoria, sand, and
pumice have been thrown out. The whole of the summit was not covered with snow; there were only frequent patches, apparently several miles in extent, over
which the snow was about eight inches or a foot in
thickness. The ocean to the east and west was visible;
but the high land on the north and south prevented its
being seen in those directions.

Mr. Goodrich commenced his descent about three
o'clock, and after travelling over large beds of sand and
cinders, into which he sank more than ankle deep at
every step, he reached, about sunrise, the place where
he had slept the preceding evening. The descent in
several places, especially over the snow, was steep and
difficult, and rendered the utmost caution necessary.
Continuing his descent, between four and five in the
afternoon he reached the encampment of Mr. Parker.
In his way down, he saw at a distance several herds of
wild cattle, which are very numerous in the mountains
and inland parts of the island, and are the produce of
those taken there and presented to the king by Captain
Vancouver. They were, at his request, tabued for ten
years, during which time they resorted to the mountains, and became so wild and ferocious that the natives
are afraid to go near them. Although there are immense herds of them, they do not attempt to tame any;
and the only advantage they derive is, by employing
persons, principally foreigners, to shoot them, salt the
meat in the mountains, and bring it down to the shore,
for the purpose of provisioning the native vessels. But
this is attended with great labour and expense. They
first carry all the salt to the mountains. When they
have killed the animals, the flesh is cut off their bones,
salted immediately, and afterward put into small barrels, which are brought on men's shoulders ten or fifteen miles to the seashore.

Early on the morning of the 27th, Mr. Goodrich left Mr. Parker, and returned through the fertile district of Waimea to Towaihae.

Nearly six months afterward, Dr. Blatchely and Mr. Ruggles ascended Mouna Keá from Waiakea bay. After travelling six days, they reached the summit of the mountain, where, within the circumference of six miles, they found seven mountains, or peaks, apparently eight hundred or a thousand feet high; their sides were steep, and covered with snow about a foot thick. The summit of the mountain appeared to be formed of decomposed lava, of a reddish brown colour. The peak in the centre, and that on the western side, are the highest.*

In the native language the word *kea*, though seldom used now, formerly meant white. Some white men, who are said to have resided inland, and to have come down to the seashore frequently in the evening, and to have frightened the people, were called *na kea* (the whites).

The snow on the summit of the mountain in all probability induced the natives to call it Mouna Kea (mountain white); or, as we should say, white mountain. They have numerous fabulous tales relative to its being the abode of the gods, and none ever approach its sum-

---

* The following observations respecting a subsequent visit to this mountain from Waiakea, contained in a letter from Mr. Goodrich to Professor Silliman, of New-Haven, are copied from the Philosophical Magazine for September, 1826.

"There appear to be three or four different regions in passing from the seashore to the summit. The first occupies five or six miles, where cultivation is carried on in a degree, and might be to almost any extent; but as yet, not one-twentieth part is cultivated. The next is a sandy region, that is impassable, except in a few foot-paths. Brakes, a species of tall fern, here grow to the size of trees; the bodies of some of them are eighteen inches in diameter. The woody region extends between ten and twenty miles in width. The region higher up produces grass, principally of the bent kind. Strawberries, raspberries, and whortleberries flourish in this region, and herds of wild cattle are seen grazing. It is entirely broken up by hills and valley, composed of lava, with a very shallow soil. The upper region is composed of lava in almost every form, from huge rocks to volcanic sand of the coarser kind. Some of the peaks are composed of coarse sand, and others of loose stones and pebbles. I found a few specimens that I should not hesitate to pronounce fragments of granite. I also found fragments of lava bearing a near resemblance to a geode, filled with green crystals, which I supposed to be augite. Very near to the summit, upon one of the peaks, I found eight or ten dead sheep; they probably fled up there to seek a refuge from the wild dogs; I have heard that there are many wild dogs, sheep, and goats. Dogs and goats I have never seen. I was upon the summit about two o'clock P. M., the wind southwest, much resembling the cold blustering winds of March; the air, being so rare, produced a severe pain in my head, that left me as I descended."

mit—as, they say, some who have gone there have been
turned to stone. We do not know that any have ever
been frozen to death; but neither Mr. Goodrich nor Dr.
Blatchely and his companion could persuade the natives,
whom they engaged as guides up the sides of the mountain, to go near its summit.

We could not but regret that we had no barometer,
or other means of estimating the actual elevation of this
mountain, either here or at Waiakea.

When the missionaries Bishop and Goodrich reached
Kairua, the governor welcomed their return, and they
were agreeably surprised to find him engaged in erecting a building for the worship of the true God. They
learned that he had during the preceding week collected
his people at Kairua, and addressed them on the duty
of observing the Sabbath according to the laws of Jehovah. He also told them it was his desire that they
should cease from work or amusement on that day, and
attend divine service at his house. The people assented
to his proposal, and when the Sabbath arrived, such
numbers assembled, that hundreds were obliged to stand
outside. Numbers also repaired to the house of Thomas
Hopu, to be instructed in what they termed the "new"
religion.

The next day the governor directed the people of Kairua to commence building a house in which they might
all meet to worship God; and in the morning on which
Messrs. Bishop and Goodrich arrived, they had commenced their heart-cheering work.

In the afternoon they walked to the place where the
men were at work. Upwards of fifty persons were employed in carrying stones from an old heiau, which they
were pulling down, to raise the ground and lay the
foundation of the place of worship. It was a pleasing
sight to view the ruins of an idol's temple devoted to
such a purpose; and they could not but hope that the
spirit of Christianity would soon triumph over the superstition, prejudice, and wickedness of idolatry.

The place of worship is sixty feet long and thirty
broad, erected in the native manner, and thatched with
the leaves of the pandanus. The walls are ten feet high,
with doors at each end, and four windows on each side.
It was impossible to behold the work without contemplating it as an intimation of most benevolent designs on
the part of the Lord of missions towards the benighted

tribes around, or without praying that the time might soon arrive when houses for the worship of the living God shall be erected in every district in the islands.[*]

On the 23d Mr. Bishop visited the well, and found that the men had not made much progress. The rocks of lava, though hard, are cellular, so that powder has very little effect, and therefore they proceeded but slowly by blasting it.

The morning of the 24th was the Sabbath, and was unusually still; not a canoe was seen in the bay, and the natives seemed to have left their customary labours and amusements, to spend the day as directed by the governor. Mr. Bishop spent half an hour with him this morning, explaining in English the 21st and 22d chapters of Revelation. I joined them at breakfast, having arrived at Kairua about an hour before daylight. I had left Towaihae on the preceding day at six in the morning, in a canoe kindly furnished by Mr. Young.

About nine A. M. I stopped at Kaparaoa, a small village on the beach, containing twenty-two houses, where I found the people preparing their food for the ensuing day, on which they said the governor had sent word for them to do no work, neither cook any food. When the people were collected I addressed them, and, after answering a number of inquiries, proceeded.

At Kaparaoa I saw a number of curiously carved wooden idols, which formerly belonged to an adjacent temple. I asked the natives if they would part with any? They said, Yes; and I should have purchased one, but had no means of conveying it away, for it was an unwieldy log of heavy wood, twelve or fourteen feet long, curiously carved in rude and frightful imitation of the human figure.

After remaining there till two P. M., I left them making preparation to keep the Sabbath-day, according to the orders they had received from the governor.

About four in the afternoon I landed at Kihoro, a straggling village, inhabited principally by fishermen. A number of people collected, to whom I addressed a short discourse, from 1 John i. 7. This village exhibits another monument of the genius of Tamehameha. A small bay, perhaps half a mile across, runs inland a con-

[*] Recent intelligence conveys the pleasing information, that five or six places of worship and a number of schools have already been erected in Hawaii, and a proportionate number in other islands of the group.

siderable distance. From one side to the other of this
bay Tamehameha built a strong stone wall, six feet high
in some places, and twenty feet wide, by which he had
an excellent fish-pond, not less than two miles in circumference. There were several arches in the wall, which
were guarded by strong stakes driven into the ground
so far apart as to admit the water of the sea, yet sufficiently close to prevent the fish from escaping. It
was well stocked with fish, and water-fowl were seen
swimming on its surface.

The people of this village, as well as the others
through which I had passed, were preparing to keep the
Sabbath, and the conversation naturally turned on the
orders recently issued by the governor. They said it
was a bad thing to commit murder, infanticide, and
theft, which had also been forbidden; that it would be
well to abstain from these crimes; but, they said, they
did not know of what advantage the *palapala*, instruction,
&c., would be.

At breakfast the governor seemed interested in the
narrative of the tour, particularly of the interview we
had with the priestess of Péle at Waiakea.

At half-past ten the bell rang for public worship, and
about eight hundred people, decently dressed, some in
foreign, others in native clothing, assembled under a
large *ranai*, a place sheltered from the sun, formed by
two large canvass awnings and a number of platted
cocoanut-leaves, spread over the place from posts fixed
in the fence which enclosed the court-yard around the
house of the governor's wife. The governor and his
attendants sat on chairs; the rest of the congregation
reclined on their mats, or sat on the ground. After
singing and prayer, I preached from Acts xvi. 30, 31.
The history of the Philippian jailer appeared to interest
them, and after the conclusion of the service the governor, in particular, made many inquiries.

At half-past four in the afternoon the bell rang again,
and the people collected in the place where the services
had been held in the forenoon, and in equal numbers
seated themselves very quietly. The exercises commenced in the usual manner, and I preached on the occasion from Acts v. 14. They were attentive, and appeared much affected with the account of the awful end
of Ananias and Sapphira.

After the public services were finished, Mr. Bishop

visited Thomas Hopu's house, where a small congregation was assembled for conversation and prayer. Mr. Bishop gave them a short exhortation; and many of the people remained afterward to hear more from Thomas about Jesus Christ.

The Sabbath was spent in a manner truly gratifying. No athletic sports were seen on the beach; no noise of playful children, shouting as they gambolled in the surf, nor distant sound of the cloth-beating mallet, was heard through the day; no persons were seen carrying burdens in or out of the village, nor any canoes passing across the bay. It could not but be viewed as the dawn of a bright sabbatic day for the dark shores of Hawaii. Family worship was held at the governor's house, in the native language, in the evening.

Having heard of the arrival of the brig Nio at Towaihae, Mr. Bishop left Kairua in the evening, to return to Oahu.

The natives possess no inconsiderable share of maritime and commercial enterprise. The king and chiefs own fifteen or sixteen vessels, several of which, like the Nio, are brigs of ninety or a hundred tons burden.

The greater part of them, however, are schooners of a smaller size. The larger ones, on a long voyage, are commanded by a foreigner; but among the islands they are manned and navigated by the natives themselves. A native captain and supercargo are appointed to each; the former navigates the vessel, while the latter attends to the cargo. The natives in general make good sailors;

and although their vessels have greatly multiplied within
the last few years, they find constant employ for them,
particularly the small craft, which are continually plying
from one island to another, while their larger ones are
either chartered to foreign merchants, or make distant
voyages on their own account.   They have once sent
a vessel to Canton, loaded with sandal-wood, under the
care of an English captain and mate, but manned by natives.   They have also traded to Kamtschatka and other
parts of the Pacific, and have, within the last few years,
made one or two successful voyages for the purpose of
procuring seal-skins.   The national flag of the islands
(see preceding page), which is an English jack, with
eight or nine horizontal stripes of white, red, and blue,
was given them by the British government many years
ago, accompanied by an assurance that it would be
respected wherever the British flag was acknowledged.
Although they are so expert in the manufacture of their
canoes, they have made but little progress in building
and repairing their ships, or in any of the mechanic arts.
They seem much more fond of the pursuits of commerce, and are tolerable adepts in bartering.   In exchange for foreign articles, they not only give sandal-
wood and salt, but furnish supplies to the numerous
vessels which visit the islands for the purpose of refitting or procuring refreshments.   In the months of March
and April, and of September and October, many vessels,
principally whalers, resort to the Sandwich Islands for
fresh provisions, &c.—we have seen upwards of thirty
lying at anchor off Oahu at one time.   The farmers in
many places dispose of the produce of their land to
these ships; but in Oahu and some other harbours this
trade is almost entirely monopolized by the king and
chiefs.   There is, indeed, a public market, in which the
natives dispose of their stock; but the price is regulated by the chiefs, and two-thirds of the proceeds of
whatever the natives sell is required by them.
 This is not only unpleasant to those who trade with
them, but very oppressive, and retards in no small degree the industry, comfort, and civilization of the people.
In return for most of the supplies which they furnish to
the shipping, they receive Spanish dollars : but the sandal-wood, &c. they usually exchange for articles of
European or Chinese fabrication : the silks, crapes,
umbrellas, furniture, and trunks of the latter are most

in demand; while those of the former are hardware, earthenware, linens, broad-cloth, slops, hats, shoes, canvass, cordage, &c.

The season was approaching when the whalers fishing on the coast of Japan usually put into some of the harbours of these islands. Hence Karaimoku had sent the Nio for a cargo of hogs, to meet the demand for these animals, which he expected would follow their arrival.

About noon on the 28th Mr. Bishop reached Towaihae; and in the evening of the 30th they received the unexpected information that the brig would sail that evening: Messrs. Bishop and Goodrich therefore went on board, leaving Mr. Thurston at Towaihae to preach to the people there on the next day, which was the Sabbath, and afterward join the vessel at the north point of the island, where they were going to take in hogs for Karaimoku, to whom the division of Kohala belonged, though the island in general was under the jurisdiction of Kuakini, the governor. Their system of government is rather complex; and having occasionally mentioned several of its leading members, some further account of it will, perhaps, be acceptable.

The government of the Sandwich Islands is an absolute monarchy. The supreme authority is hereditary. The rank of the principal and inferior chiefs, the offices of the priests, and other situations of honour, influence, and emolument, descend from father to son, and often continue through many generations in the same family, though the power of nomination to every situation of dignity and trust is vested in the king; and persons, by merit or royal favour, frequently rise from comparatively humble rank to the highest station in the islands, as in the instance of Karaimoku, sometimes called by foreigners William Pitt. This individual, from being a chief of the third or fourth rank, has long been prime minister, in dignity next only to the king, and having, in fact, the actual government of the whole of the Sandwich Islands.

Hereditary rank and authority are not confined to the male sex, but are inherited also by the females; and, according to tradition, several of the islands have been once or twice under the government of a queen.

Four distinct classes or ranks in society appear to exist among them. The highest rank includes the king,

queens, and all the branches of the reigning family. It
also includes the chief counsellor or minister of the
king, who, though inferior by birth, is by office and
authority superior to the queens and other members of
the royal family.

The second rank includes the governors of the different islands, and also the chiefs of several large divisions or districts of land. Many of these are the
descendants of the ancient families of Taraiopu, Kehekiri, Teporiorani, and Taeo, who were the kings of
Hawaii, Maui, Oahu, and Tauai, when the islands were
visited by Captain Cook, and retained their power until
subdued by Tamehameha. Several of them were either
the favourite and warlike companions of that prince, or
are descended from those who were; among whom may
be classed Kuakini the governor, Kaahumanu, Piia, Boki,
Wahinepio, Kaikeova, and others.

The third rank is composed of those who hold districts or villages, and pay a regular rent for the land,
cultivating it either by their own dependants and domestics, or letting it out in small allotments to tenants.
This class is by far the most numerous body of chiefs
in the island. Among the principal may be ranked
Kamakau at Kaavaroa, Maaro at Waiakea, Haa at Waipio, Auae at Wairuku, and Kahanaumaitai at Waititi.
They are generally called *haku aina,* proprietors of land.
This rank would also include most of the priests under
the former dispensation.

In the fourth rank may be included the small farmers,
who rent from ten to twenty or thirty acres of land; the
mechanics, namely, canoe and house builders, fishermen,
musicians, and dancers; indeed, all the labouring classes,
those who attach themselves to some chief or farmer,
and labour on his land for their food and clothing, as well
as those who cultivate small portions of land for their
own advantage.

Though the chiefs did not receive that abject and humiliating homage which is frequently paid to superiors
in barbarous nations, where the government is arbitrary,
yet the common people always manifested a degree of
respect to the chiefs according to their rank or office.
This towards the sacred chiefs amounted almost to
adoration, as they were on no occasion allowed to touch
their persons, but prostrated themselves before them,
and could not enter their houses without first receiving

permission. The behaviour among the chiefs was
courteous, and manifested a desire to render themselves
agreeable to each other.; while all observed a degree of
etiquette in their direct intercourse with the king. He
is generally attended by a number of his courtiers or
favourites, called punahele, who join in his amusements
and occupations, except in the affairs of government,
with which they seem to have no concern. When in a
state of inebriation, all marks of distinction were lost;
but at other times even these favourites conducted themselves towards their sovereign with great respect. I
have often seen Kapihe and Kekuanaoa, the two who
accompanied Rihoriho to England, come into his presence, and wait without speaking, whatever their business
might be, till he should address them, and then continue
standing until requested by him to sit down.

In some respects the government resembles the ancient feudal system of the northern nations. During
many periods of their history, not only the separate
islands, but the larger divisions of some of them, have
been under the government of independent kings or
chiefs; and it does not appear that until the reign of
Rihoriho, the late king, they were ever united under one
sovereign. The king is acknowledged in every island
as the lord and proprietor of the soil by hereditary right,
or the laws of conquest. When Tamehameha had subdued the greater part of the islands, he distributed them
among his favourite chiefs and warriors, on condition of
their rendering him, not only military service, but a certain proportion of the produce of their lands. This also
appears to have been their ancient practice on similar
occasions, as the *hoopahora* or *papahora*, division of land
among the *ranakira*, or victors, invariably followed the
conquest of a district or island.

Every island is given by the king to some high chief,
who is supreme governor in it, but is subject to the
king, whose orders he is obliged to see executed, and to
whom he pays a regular rent or tax, according to the
size of the island, or the advantages it may possess.
Each island is separated into a number of permanent
divisions, sometimes fifty or sixty miles in extent. In
Hawaii there are six, Kohala, Kona, &c. Each of the
large divisions is governed by one or two chiefs, appointed by the king or by the governor, and approved
by the former. These large divisions are divided into

districts and villages, which sometimes extend five or
six miles along the coast; at others, not more than half
a mile. A head man, nominated by the governor, usually
presides over these villages, which are again subdivided
into a number of small farms or plantations. The names
of these are generally significant; as. *Towahai*, the
waters broken; from a stream which runs through the
district, and is divided near the sea; *Kairua*, two seas,
from the waters of the bay being separated by a point
of land, &c.

Although this is the usual manner in which the land
is distributed, yet the king holds personally a number
of districts in most of the islands, and several of the
principal chiefs receive districts directly from the king,
and independent of the governor of the island in which
they are situated.

The governor of the island pays over to the king annually, or half-yearly, the rents or taxes required by the
latter. These he receives from the chiefs under him,
who generally pay in the produce of the soil. Sometimes the king requires a certain sum in Spanish dollars,
at other times in sandal-wood.

This, however, is only a modern regulation, introduced since they have become acquainted with the use
of money and the value of sandal-wood. The rent was
originally paid in canoes, native cloth, mats, fishing-nets,
hogs, dogs, and the produce of the soil, for the use of the
king, and the numerous train of favourite chiefs and
dependants by whom he was surrounded, and who were
daily fed from the provisions of his house.

For this tax the governor is responsible, and it is his
business to see it conveyed to the king, or disposed of
according to his order. A second tax is laid on the districts by the governor, for himself. The inhabitants of
those portions of the island, however, which belong to
other chiefs, although they furnish their share towards
the king's revenue, are not called upon to support the
governor of the island, but are expected to send a part
of the produce of the land to their own chiefs. After
this has been paid, additional requisitions are made upon
the poor people cultivating the land, by the petty chiefs
of the districts and villages; these, however, are but
trifling.

There is no standing rule for the amount of rents or
taxes, but they are regulated entirely by the caprice or

necessities of their rulers. Sometimes the poor people take a piece of land, on condition of cultivating a given portion for the chief and the remainder for themselves, making a fresh agreement after every crop.

In addition to the above demands, the common people are in general obliged to labour, if required, part of two days out of seven, in cultivating farms, building houses, &c., for their landlord.

A time is usually appointed for receiving the rent, when the people repair to the governor's with what they have to pay. If the required amount is furnished, they return, and, as they express it *(komo hou)*, enter again on their land. But if unable to pay the required sum, and their landlords are dissatisfied with the presents they have received, or think the tenants have neglected their farm, they are forbidden to return, and the land is offered to another. When, however, the produce brought is nearly equal to the required rent, and the chiefs think the occupants have exerted themselves to procure it, they remit the deficiency, and allow them to return. Besides the stipulated rent, the people are expected to make a number of presents to their chiefs, usually the first fish in season from their artificial ponds, or from the sea if the land they occupy be near the coast, together with the first-fruits of the trees and plantations.

Though these are the usual conditions on which land is held, there are a number of districts called *aina ku pono*, land standing erect, held free from all rent and taxes except a few presents, the value and frequency of which are entirely optional with the occupier. These privileges of exemption from the established usage were probably granted originally in reward for eminent services rendered the king, and they continue permanent; for, should the king, on account of any crime, banish an individual holding one of these districts, the next occupant would enjoy all the privileges of his predecessor.

The common people are generally considered as attached to the soil, and are transferred with the land from one chief to another. In recently conquered districts, they were formerly obliged to abide on the land which they cultivated, as slaves to the victors; at present, though they frequently remain through life the dependants or tenants of the same chief, such continuance appears on their part to be voluntary. No chief

can demand any service or supplies from those who occupy the land of another without his direction.

The king occasionally changes the tenants, of a farm,
without taking the proprietorship from the chief who
may hold it more immediately from himself; and when
the rents are insufficient to meet his wants, if any of the
neighbouring farmers have potatoes and taro in their
fields, he, or any high chief, will send their men, and
hao, seize, the greater part of them, without making
any remuneration to the injured parties.

Besides the sums which the king receives from the
land, and the monopoly of the trade, in live-stock and
other supplies furnished to the shipping at several ports
in the islands, the revenue is augmented by the harbour
dues at Oahu. Every vessel anchoring in the outer
harbour pays sixty dollars, and eighty for entering the
basin, or inner harbour. Till within two or three years,
it was only forty for one, and sixty for the other.* The
pilotage, which is a dollar per foot for every vessel,
both on entering and leaving the harbour, is divided between the government and the pilot.

Another singular method of taxing the people is by
building a new house for the king, or some principal
chief. On the first day the king or chief enters it, the
chiefs and the people of the neighbourhood repair thither
to pay their respects and present their gifts. Custom
obliges every chief to appear on such occasions, or expose himself to the imputation of being disaffected; and
no one is allowed to enter without a present of money.
The amount is proportioned to their rank, or the land
they hold. Some chiefs on such occasions give sixty
dollars; others ten or five, and some only one.

A short time before his embarkation for England, a
large native house was built for Rihoriho, at Honoruru,
in the island of Oahu. During three days after the king
went into it the people came with their gifts. No individual, not even the queens, entered the house without
presenting the king a sum of money; several gave up-

* The demand for these dues originated in their unprofitable voyage to
Canton, in 1816. The cargo of sandal-wood was sold, but instead of a return
in cloths, silks, &c., the vessel came back nearly empty, and in debt. The
king inquired the reason; when the captain, a very incompetent person for
such a business, told him that some of the money had been stolen; that so
much was demanded for pilotage, coming to anchor, &c., as to leave nothing for
the purpose of fitting the vessel for sea, which had occasioned the debt. "If,"
replied the king, "that be the case, we will have a pilot here, and every vessel
that enters the harbour shall pay me for anchorage."

wards of fifty dollars; and we saw more than two thousand dollars received in one day. A similar tax was also levied by Kuakini, the governor at Kairua, when he first entered a handsome framed house, recently erected there.

Until the establishment of a Christian mission among them, the Sandwich islanders had no records, and consequently no written laws. There is, however, a kind of traditionary code, a number of regulations which have been either promulgated by former kings, or followed by general consent, respecting the tenure of lands, right of property, personal security, and exchange or barter, which are well understood, and usually acted upon. The portion of personal labour due from a tenant to his chief is fixed by custom, and a chief would be justified in banishing the person who should refuse it when required: on the other hand, were a chief to banish a man who had rendered it, and paid the stipulated rent, his conduct would be contrary to their opinions of right; and if the man complained to the governor or the king, and no other charge was brought against him, he would most likely be reinstated. The irrigation of their plantations is of great importance in most parts; and there is a law that the water shall be conducted over every plantation twice a week in general, and once a week during the dry season.

On the death of a chief his lands revert to the king or the governor of the island. He may nominate his son, his wife, or any other person, to succeed to his districts, &c., but the appointment must be confirmed by the king or governor before the individual can take possession.

This regulation, next to the tabu, is the most effectual mode of preserving the authority and influence of the king and chiefs.

In cases of assault or murder, except when committed by their own chief, the family and friends of the injured party are, by common consent, justified in retaliating. When they are too weak to attack the offender, they seek the aid of their neighbours, appeal to the chief of the district, or the king, who seldom inflicts a heavier punishment than banishment, even for murder, which, however, is a crime very rarely committed by the natives.

Theft among themselves is severely punished. Formerly, when a garden or house had been robbed, and

and although their vessels have greatly multiplied within
the last few years, they find constant employ for them,
particularly the small craft, which are continually plying
from one island to another, while their larger ones are
either chartered to foreign merchants, or make distant
voyages on their own account. They have once sent
a vessel to Canton, loaded with sandal-wood, under the
care of an English captain and mate, but manned by natives. They have also traded to Kamtschatka and other
parts of the Pacific, and have, within the last few years,
made one or two successful voyages for the purpose of
procuring seal-skins. The national flag of the islands
(see preceding page), which is an English jack, with
eight or nine horizontal stripes of white, red, and blue,
was given them by the British government many years
ago, accompanied by an assurance that it would be
respected wherever the British flag was acknowledged.
Although they are so expert in the manufacture of their
canoes, they have made but little progress in building
and repairing their ships, or in any of the mechanic arts.
They seem much more fond of the pursuits of commerce, and are tolerable adepts in bartering. In exchange for foreign articles, they not only give sandal-
wood and salt, but furnish supplies to the numerous
vessels which visit the islands for the purpose of refitting or procuring refreshments. In the months of March
and April, and of September and October, many vessels,
principally whalers, resort to the Sandwich Islands for
fresh provisions, &c.—we have seen upwards of thirty
lying at anchor off Oahu at one time. The farmers in
many places dispose of the produce of their land to
these ships; but in Oahu and some other harbours this
trade is almost entirely monopolized by the king and
chiefs. There is, indeed, a public market, in which the
natives dispose of their stock; but the price is regulated by the chiefs, and two-thirds of the proceeds of
whatever the natives sell is required by them.

This is not only unpleasant to those who trade with
them, but very oppressive, and retards in no small degree the industry, comfort, and civilization of the people.
In return for most of the supplies which they furnish to
the shipping, they receive Spanish dollars: but the sandal-wood, &c. they usually exchange for articles of
European or Chinese fabrication: the silks, crapes,
umbrellas, furniture, and trunks of the latter are most

in demand; while those of the former are hardware, earthenware, linens, broad-cloth, slops, hats, shoes, canvass, cordage, &c.

The season was approaching when the whalers fishing on the coast of Japan usually put into some of the harbours of these islands. Hence Karaimoku had sent the Nio for a cargo of hogs, to meet the demand for these animals, which he expected would follow their arrival.

About noon on the 28th Mr. Bishop reached Towaihae; and in the evening of the 30th they received the unexpected information that the brig would sail that evening: Messrs. Bishop and Goodrich therefore went on board, leaving Mr. Thurston at Towaihae to preach to the people there on the next day, which was the Sabbath, and afterward join the vessel at the north point of the island, where they were going to take in hogs for Karaimoku, to whom the division of Kohala belonged, though the island in general was under the jurisdiction of Kuakini, the governor. Their system of government is rather complex; and having occasionally mentioned several of its leading members, some further account of it will, perhaps, be acceptable.

The government of the Sandwich Islands is an absolute monarchy. The supreme authority is hereditary. The rank of the principal and inferior chiefs, the offices of the priests, and other situations of honour, influence, and emolument, descend from father to son, and often continue through many generations in the same family, though the power of nomination to every situation of dignity and trust is vested in the king; and persons, by merit or royal favour, frequently rise from comparatively humble rank to the highest station in the islands, as in the instance of Karaimoku, sometimes called by foreigners William Pitt. This individual, from being a chief of the third or fourth rank, has long been prime minister, in dignity next only to the king, and having, in fact, the actual government of the whole of the Sandwich Islands.

Hereditary rank and authority are not confined to the male sex, but are inherited also by the females; and, according to tradition, several of the islands have been once or twice under the government of a queen.

Four distinct classes or ranks in society appear to exist among them. The highest rank includes the king,

queens, and all the branches of the reigning family. It also includes the chief counsellor or minister of the king, who, though inferior by birth, is by office and authority superior to the queens and other members of the royal family.

The second rank includes the governors of the different islands, and also the chiefs of several large divisions or districts of land. Many of these are the descendants of the ancient families of Taraiopu, Kehekiri, Teporiorani, and Taeo, who were the kings of Hawaii, Maui, Oahu, and Tauai, when the islands were visited by Captain Cook, and retained their power until subdued by Tamehameha. Several of them were either the favourite and warlike companions of that prince, or are descended from those who were; among whom may be classed Kuakini the governor, Kaahumanu, Piia, Boki, Wahinepio, Kaikeova, and others.

The third rank is composed of those who hold districts or villages, and pay a regular rent for the land, cultivating it either by their own dependants and domestics, or letting it out in small allotments to tenants. This class is by far the most numerous body of chiefs in the island. Among the principal may be ranked Kamakau at Kaavaroa, Maaro at Waiakea, Haa at Waipio, Auae at Wairuku, and Kahanaumaitai at Waititi. They are generally called *haku aina*, proprietors of land. This rank would also include most of the priests under the former dispensation.

In the fourth rank may be included the small farmers, who rent from ten to twenty or thirty acres of land; the mechanics, namely, canoe and house builders, fishermen, musicians, and dancers; indeed, all the labouring classes, those who attach themselves to some chief or farmer, and labour on his land for their food and clothing, as well as those who cultivate small portions of land for their own advantage.

Though the chiefs did not receive that abject and humiliating homage which is frequently paid to superiors in barbarous nations, where the government is arbitrary, yet the common people always manifested a degree of respect to the chiefs according to their rank or office. This towards the sacred chiefs amounted almost to adoration, as they were on no occasion allowed to touch their persons, but prostrated themselves before them, and could not enter their houses without first receiving

permission. The behaviour among the chiefs was courteous, and manifested a desire to render themselves agreeable to each other; while all observed a degree of etiquette in their direct intercourse with the king. He is generally attended by a number of his courtiers or favourites, called punahele, who join in his amusements and occupations, except in the affairs of government, with which they seem to have no concern. When in a state of inebriation, all marks of distinction were lost; but at other times even these favourites conducted themselves towards their sovereign with great respect. I have often seen Kapihe and Kekuanaoa, the two who accompanied Rihoriho to England, come into his presence, and wait without speaking, whatever their business might be, till he should address them, and then continue standing until requested by him to sit down.

In some respects the government resembles the ancient feudal system of the northern nations. During many periods of their history, not only the separate islands, but the larger divisions of some of them, have been under the government of independent kings or chiefs; and it does not appear that until the reign of Rihoriho, the late king, they were ever united under one sovereign. The king is acknowledged in every island as the lord and proprietor of the soil by hereditary right, or the laws of conquest. When Tamehameha had subdued the greater part of the islands, he distributed them among his favourite chiefs and warriors, on condition of their rendering him, not only military service, but a certain proportion of the produce of their lands. This also appears to have been their ancient practice on similar occasions, as the *hoopahora* or *papahora*, division of land among the *ranakira*, or victors, invariably followed the conquest of a district or island.

Every island is given by the king to some high chief, who is supreme governor in it, but is subject to the king, whose orders he is obliged to see executed, and to whom he pays a regular rent or tax, according to the size of the island, or the advantages it may possess. Each island is separated into a number of permanent divisions, sometimes fifty or sixty miles in extent. In Hawaii there are six, Kohala, Kona, &c. Each of the large divisions is governed by one or two chiefs, appointed by the king or by the governor, and approved by the former. These large divisions are divided into

districts and villages, which sometimes extend five or six miles along the coast; at others, not more than half a mile. A head man, nominated by the governor, usually presides over these villages, which are again subdivided into a number of small farms or plantations. The names of these are generally significant; as *Towahai*, the waters broken, from a stream which runs through the district, and is divided near the sea; *Kairua*, two seas, from the waters of the bay being separated by a point of land, &c.

Although this is the usual manner in which the land is distributed, yet the king holds personally a number of districts in most of the islands, and several of the principal chiefs receive districts directly from the king, and independent of the governor of the island in which they are situated.

The governor of the island pays over to the king annually, or half-yearly, the rents or taxes required by the latter. These he receives from the chiefs under him, who generally pay in the produce of the soil. Sometimes the king requires a certain sum in Spanish dollars, at other times in sandal-wood.

This, however, is only a modern regulation, introduced since they have become acquainted with the use of money and the value of sandal-wood. The rent was originally paid in canoes, native cloth, mats, fishing-nets, hogs, dogs, and the produce of the soil, for the use of the king, and the numerous train of favourite chiefs and dependants by whom he was surrounded, and who were daily fed from the provisions of his house.

For this tax the governor is responsible, and it is his business to see it conveyed to the king, or disposed of according to his order. A second tax is laid on the districts by the governor, for himself. The inhabitants of those portions of the island, however, which belong to other chiefs, although they furnish their share towards the king's revenue, are not called upon to support the governor of the island, but are expected to send a part of the produce of the land to their own chiefs. After this has been paid, additional requisitions are made upon the poor people cultivating the land, by the petty chiefs of the districts and villages; these, however, are but trifling.

There is no standing rule for the amount of rents or taxes, but they are regulated entirely by the caprice or

necessities of their rulers. Sometimes the poor people take a piece of land, on condition of cultivating a given portion for the chief and the remainder for themselves, making a fresh agreement after every crop.

In addition to the above demands, the common people are in general obliged to labour, if required, part of two days out of seven, in cultivating farms, building houses, &c., for their landlord.

A time is usually appointed for receiving the rent, when the people repair to the governor's with what they have to pay. If the required amount is furnished, they return, and, as they express it (*komo hou*), enter again on their land. But if unable to pay the required sum, and their landlords are dissatisfied with the presents they have received, or think the tenants have neglected their farm, they are forbidden to return, and the land is offered to another. When, however, the produce brought is nearly equal to the required rent, and the chiefs think the occupants have exerted themselves to procure it, they remit the deficiency, and allow them to return. Besides the stipulated rent, the people are expected to make a number of presents to their chiefs, usually the first fish in season from their artificial ponds, or from the sea if the land they occupy be near the coast, together with the first-fruits of the trees and plantations.

Though these are the usual conditions on which land is held, there are a number of districts called *aina ku pono*, land standing erect, held free from all rent and taxes except a few presents, the value and frequency of which are entirely optional with the occupier. These privileges of exemption from the established usage were probably granted originally in reward for eminent services rendered the king, and they continue permanent; for should the king, on account of any crime, banish an individual holding one of these districts, the next occupant would enjoy all the privileges of his predecessor.

The common people are generally considered as attached to the soil, and are transferred with the land from one chief to another. In recently conquered districts, they were formerly obliged to abide on the land which they cultivated, as slaves to the victors; at present, though they frequently remain through life the dependants or tenants of the same chief, such continuance appears on their part to be voluntary. No chief

can demand any service or supplies from those who occupy the land of another without his direction.

The king occasionally changes the tenants, of a farm, without taking the proprietorship from the chief who may hold it more immediately from himself; and when the rents are insufficient to meet his wants, if any of the neighbouring farmers have potatoes and taro in their fields, he, or any high chief, will send their men, and *hao*, seize, the greater part of them, without making any remuneration to the injured parties.

Besides the sums which the king receives from the land, and the monopoly of the trade, in live-stock and other supplies furnished to the shipping at several ports in the islands, the revenue is augmented by the harbour dues at Oahu. Every vessel anchoring in the outer harbour pays sixty dollars, and eighty for entering the basin, or inner harbour. Till within two or three years, it was only forty for one, and sixty for the other.* The pilotage, which is a dollar per foot for every vessel, both on entering and leaving the harbour, is divided between the government and the pilot.

Another singular method of taxing the people is by building a new house for the king, or some principal chief. On the first day the king or chief enters it, the chiefs and the people of the neighbourhood repair thither to pay their respects and present their gifts. Custom obliges every chief to appear on such occasions, or expose himself to the imputation of being disaffected; and no one is allowed to enter without a present of money. The amount is proportioned to their rank, or the land they hold. Some chiefs on such occasions give sixty dollars; others ten or five, and some only one.

A short time before his embarkation for England, a large native house was built for Rihoriho, at Honoruru, in the island of Oahu. During three days after the king went into it the people came with their gifts. No individual, not even the queens, entered the house without presenting the king a sum of money; several gave up-

* The demand for these dues originated in their unprofitable voyage to Canton, in 1816. The cargo of sandal-wood was sold, but instead of a return in cloths, silks, &c., the vessel came back nearly empty, and in debt. The king inquired the reason; when the captain, a very incompetent person for such a business, told him that some of the money had been stolen; that so much was demanded for pilotage, coming to anchor, &c., as to leave nothing for the purpose of fitting the vessel for sea, which had occasioned the debt. "If," replied the king, "that be the case, we will have a pilot here, and every vessel that enters the harbour shall pay me for anchorage."

wards of fifty dollars; and we saw more than two thousand dollars received in one day. A similar tax was also levied by Kuakini, the governor at Kairua, when he first entered a handsome framed house, recently erected there.

Until the establishment of a Christian mission among them, the Sandwich islanders had no records, and consequently no written laws. There is, however, a kind of traditionary code, a number of regulations which have been either promulgated by former kings, or followed by general consent, respecting the tenure of lands, right of property, personal security, and exchange or barter, which are well understood, and usually acted upon. The portion of personal labour due from a tenant to his chief is fixed by custom, and a chief would be justified in banishing the person who should refuse it when required: on the other hand, were a chief to banish a man who had rendered it, and paid the stipulated rent, his conduct would be contrary to their opinions of right; and if the man complained to the governor or the king, and no other charge was brought against him, he would most likely be reinstated. The irrigation of their plantations is of great importance in most parts; and there is a law that the water shall be conducted over every plantation twice a week in general, and once a week during the dry season.

On the death of a chief his lands revert to the king or the governor of the island. He may nominate his son, his wife, or any other person, to succeed to his districts, &c., but the appointment must be confirmed by the king or governor before the individual can take possession.

This regulation, next to the tabu, is the most effectual mode of preserving the authority and influence of the king and chiefs.

In cases of assault or murder, except when committed by their own chief, the family and friends of the injured party are, by common consent, justified in retaliating. When they are too weak to attack the offender, they seek the aid of their neighbours, appeal to the chief of the district, or the king, who seldom inflicts a heavier punishment than banishment, even for murder, which, however, is a crime very rarely committed by the natives.

Theft among themselves is severely punished. Formerly, when a garden or house had been robbed, and

and although their vessels have greatly multiplied within
the last few years, they find constant employ for them,
particularly the small craft, which are continually plying
from one island to another, while their larger ones are
either chartered to foreign merchants, or make distant
voyages on their own account. They have once sent
a vessel to Canton, loaded with sandal-wood, under the
care of an English captain and mate, but manned by natives. They have also traded to Kamtschatka and other
parts of the Pacific, and have; within the last few years,
made one or two successful voyages for the purpose of
procuring seal-skins. The national flag of the islands
(see preceding page), which is an English jack, with
eight or nine horizontal stripes of white, red, and blue,
was given them by the British government many years
ago, accompanied by an assurance that it would be
respected wherever the British flag was acknowledged.
Although they are so expert in the manufacture of their
canoes, they have made but little progress in building
and repairing their ships, or in any of the mechanic arts.
They seem much more fond of the pursuits of commerce, and are tolerable adepts in bartering. In exchange for foreign articles, they not only give sandal-
wood and salt, but furnish supplies to the numerous
vessels which visit the islands for the purpose of refitting or procuring refreshments. In the months of March
and April, and of September and October, many vessels,
principally whalers, resort to the Sandwich Islands for
fresh provisions, &c.—we have seen upwards of thirty
lying at anchor off Oahu at one time. The farmers in
many places dispose of the produce of their land to
these ships; but in Oahu and some other harbours this
trade is almost entirely monopolized by the king and
chiefs. There is, indeed, a public market, in which the
natives dispose of their stock; but the price is regulated by the chiefs, and two-thirds of the proceeds of
whatever the natives sell is required by them.

This is not only unpleasant to those who trade with
them, but very oppressive, and retards in no small degree the industry, comfort, and civilization of the people.
In return for most of the supplies which they furnish to
the shipping, they receive Spanish dollars: but the sandal-wood, &c. they usually exchange for articles of
European or Chinese fabrication: the silks, crapes,
umbrellas, furniture, and trunks of the latter are most

in demand; while those of the former are hardware, earthenware, linens, broad-cloth, slops, hats, shoes, canvass, cordage, &c.

The season was approaching when the whalers fishing on the coast of Japan usually put into some of the harbours of these islands. Hence Karaimoku had sent the Nio for a cargo of hogs, to meet the demand for these animals, which he expected would follow their arrival.

About noon on the 28th Mr. Bishop reached Towaihae; and in the evening of the 30th they received the unexpected information that the brig would sail that evening: Messrs. Bishop and Goodrich therefore went on board, leaving Mr. Thurston at Towaihae to preach to the people there on the next day, which was the Sabbath, and afterward join the vessel at the north point of the island, where they were going to take in hogs for Karaimoku, to whom the division of Kohala belonged, though the island in general was under the jurisdiction of Kuakini, the governor. Their system of government is rather complex; and having occasionally mentioned several of its leading members, some further account of it will, perhaps, be acceptable.

The government of the Sandwich Islands is an absolute monarchy. The supreme authority is hereditary. The rank of the principal and inferior chiefs, the offices of the priests, and other situations of honour, influence, and emolument, descend from father to son, and often continue through many generations in the same family, though the power of nomination to every situation of dignity and trust is vested in the king; and persons, by merit or royal favour, frequently rise from comparatively humble rank to the highest station in the islands, as in the instance of Karaimoku, sometimes called by foreigners William Pitt. This individual, from being a chief of the third or fourth rank, has long been prime minister, in dignity next only to the king, and having, in fact, the actual government of the whole of the Sandwich Islands.

Hereditary rank and authority are not confined to the male sex, but are inherited also by the females; and, according to tradition, several of the islands have been once or twice under the government of a queen.

Four distinct classes or ranks in society appear to exist among them. The highest rank includes the king,

queens, and all the branches of the reigning family. It
also includes the chief counsellor or minister of the
king, who, though inferior by birth, is by office and
authority superior to the queens and other members of
the royal family.

The second rank includes the governors of the different islands, and also the chiefs of several large divisions or districts of land. Many of these are the
descendants of the ancient families of Taraiopu, Kehekiri, Teporiorani, and Taeo, who were the kings of
Hawaii, Maui, Oahu, and Tauai, when the islands were
visited by Captain Cook, and retained their power until
subdued by Tamehameha. Several of them were either
the favourite and warlike companions of that prince, or
are descended from those who were; among whom may
be classed Kuakini the governor, Kaahumanu, Piia, Boki,
Wahinepio, Kaikeova, and others.

The third rank is composed of those who hold districts or villages, and pay a regular rent for the land,
cultivating it either by their own dependants and domestics, or letting it out in small allotments to tenants.
This class is by far the most numerous body of chiefs
in the island. Among the principal may be ranked
Kamakau at Kaavaroa, Maaro at Waiakea, Haa at Waipio, Auae at Wairuku, and Kahanaumaitai at Waititi.
They are generally called *haku aina*, proprietors of land.
This rank would also include most of the priests under
the former dispensation.

In the fourth rank may be included the small farmers,
who rent from ten to twenty or thirty acres of land; the
mechanics, namely; canoe and house builders, fishermen,
musicians, and dancers; indeed, all the labouring classes,
those who attach themselves to some chief or farmer,
and labour on his land for their food and clothing, as well
as those who cultivate small portions of land for their
own advantage.

Though the chiefs did not receive that abject and humiliating homage which is frequently paid to superiors
in barbarous nations, where the government is arbitrary,
yet the common people always manifested a degree of
respect to the chiefs according to their rank or office.
This towards the sacred chiefs amounted almost to
adoration, as they were on no occasion allowed to touch
their persons, but prostrated themselves before them,
and could not enter their houses without first receiving

permission. The behaviour among the chiefs was courteous, and manifested a desire to render themselves agreeable to each other; while all observed a degree of etiquette in their direct intercourse with the king. He is generally attended by a number of his courtiers or favourites, called punahele, who join in his amusements and occupations, except in the affairs of government, with which they seem to have no concern. When in a state of inebriation, all marks of distinction were lost; but at other times even these favourites conducted themselves towards their sovereign with great respect. I have often seen Kapihe and Kekuanaoa, the two who accompanied Rihoriho to England, come into his presence, and wait without speaking, whatever their business might be, till he should address them, and then continue standing until requested by him to sit down.

In some respects the government resembles the ancient feudal system of the northern nations. During many periods of their history, not only the separate islands, but the larger divisions of some of them, have been under the government of independent kings or chiefs; and it does not appear that until the reign of Rihoriho, the late king, they were ever united under one sovereign. The king is acknowledged in every island as the lord and proprietor of the soil by hereditary right, or the laws of conquest. When Tamehameha had subdued the greater part of the islands, he distributed them among his favourite chiefs and warriors, on condition of their rendering him, not only military service, but a certain proportion of the produce of their lands. This also appears to have been their ancient practice on similar occasions, as the *hoopahora* or *papahora*, division of land among the *ranakira*, or victors, invariably followed the conquest of a district or island.

Every island is given by the king to some high chief, who is supreme governor in it, but is subject to the king, whose orders he is obliged to see executed, and to whom he pays a regular rent or tax, according to the size of the island, or the advantages it may possess. Each island is separated into a number of permanent divisions, sometimes fifty or sixty miles in extent. In Hawaii there are six, Kohala, Kona, &c. Each of the large divisions is governed by one or two chiefs, appointed by the king or by the governor, and approved by the former. These large divisions are divided into

districts and villages, which sometimes extend five or
six miles along the coast; at others, not more than half
a mile.   A head man, nominated by the governor, usually
presides over these villages, which are again subdivided
into a number of small farms or plantations.   The names
of these are generally significant; as *Towahai*, the
waters broken, from a stream which runs through the
district, and is divided near the sea; *Kairua*, two seas,
from the waters of the bay being separated by a point
of land, &c.

Although this is the usual manner in which the land
is distributed, yet the king holds personally a number
of districts in most of the islands, and several of the
principal chiefs receive districts directly from the king,
and independent of the governor of the island in which
they are situated.

The governor of the island pays over to the king annually, or half-yearly, the rents or taxes required by the
latter.   These he receives from the chiefs under him,
who generally pay in the produce of the soil.   Sometimes the king requires a certain sum in Spanish dollars,
at other times in sandal-wood.

This, however, is only a modern regulation, introduced since they have become acquainted with the use
of money and the value of sandal-wood.   The rent was
originally paid in canoes, native cloth, mats, fishing-nets,
hogs, dogs, and the produce of the soil, for the use of the
king, and the numerous train of favourite chiefs and
dependants by whom he was surrounded, and who were
daily fed from the provisions of his house.

For this tax the governor is responsible, and it is his
business to see it conveyed to the king, or disposed of
according to his order.   A second tax is laid on the districts by the governor, for himself.   The inhabitants of
those portions of the island, however, which belong to
other chiefs, although they furnish their share towards
the king's revenue, are not called upon to support the
governor of the island, but are expected to send a part
of the produce of the land to their own chiefs.   After
this has been paid, additional requisitions are made upon
the poor people cultivating the land, by the petty chiefs
of the districts and villages; these, however, are but
trifling.

There is no standing rule for the amount of rents or
taxes, but they are regulated entirely by the caprice or

necessities of their rulers. Sometimes the poor people take a piece of land, on condition of cultivating a given portion for the chief and the remainder for themselves, making a fresh agreement after every crop.

In addition to the above demands, the common people are in general obliged to labour, if required, part of two days out of seven, in cultivating farms, building houses, &c., for their landlord.

A time is usually appointed for receiving the rent, when the people repair to the governor's with what they have to pay. If the required amount is furnished, they return, and, as they express it (komo hou), enter again on their land. But if unable to pay the required sum, and their landlords are dissatisfied with the presents they have received, or think the tenants have neglected their farm, they are forbidden to return, and the land is offered to another. When, however, the produce brought is nearly equal to the required rent, and the chiefs think the occupants have exerted themselves to procure it, they remit the deficiency, and allow them to return. Besides the stipulated rent, the people are expected to make a number of presents to their chiefs, usually the first fish in season from their artificial ponds, or from the sea if the land they occupy be near the coast, together with the first-fruits of the trees and plantations.

Though these are the usual conditions on which land is held, there are a number of districts called aina ku pono, land standing erect, held free from all rent and taxes except a few presents, the value and frequency of which are entirely optional with the occupier. These privileges of exemption from the established usage were probably granted originally in reward for eminent services rendered the king, and they continue permanent; for, should the king, on account of any crime, banish an individual holding one of these districts, the next occupant would enjoy all the privileges of his predecessor.

The common people are generally considered as attached to the soil, and are transferred with the land from one chief to another. In recently conquered districts, they were formerly obliged to abide on the land which they cultivated, as slaves to the victors; at present, though they frequently remain through life the dependants or tenants of the same chief, such continuance appears on their part to be voluntary. No chief

can demand any service or supplies from those who occupy the land of another without his direction.

The king occasionally changes the tenants, of a farm, without taking the proprietorship from the chief who may hold it more immediately from himself; and when the rents are insufficient to meet his wants, if any of the neighbouring farmers have potatoes and taro in their fields, he, or any high chief, will send their men, and *hao*, seize, the greater part of them, without making any remuneration to the injured parties.

Besides the sums which the king receives from the land, and the monopoly of the trade, in live-stock and other supplies furnished to the shipping at several ports in the islands, the revenue is augmented by the harbour dues at Oahu. Every vessel anchoring in the outer harbour pays sixty dollars, and eighty for entering the basin, or inner harbour. Till within two or three years, it was only forty for one, and sixty for the other.* The pilotage, which is a dollar per foot for every vessel, both on entering and leaving the harbour, is divided between the government and the pilot.

Another singular method of taxing the people is by building a new house for the king, or some principal chief. On the first day the king or chief enters it, the chiefs and the people of the neighbourhood repair thither to pay their respects and present their gifts. Custom obliges every chief to appear on such occasions, or expose himself to the imputation of being disaffected; and no one is allowed to enter without a present of money. The amount is proportioned to their rank, or the land they hold. Some chiefs on such occasions give sixty dollars; others ten or five, and some only one.

A short time before his embarkation for England, a large native house was built for Rihoriho, at Honoruru, in the island of Oahu. During three days after the king went into it the people came with their gifts. No individual, not even the queens, entered the house without presenting the king a sum of money; several gave up-

---

* The demand for these dues originated in their unprofitable voyage to Canton, in 1816. The cargo of sandal-wood was sold, but instead of a return in cloths, silks, &c., the vessel came back nearly empty, and in debt. The king inquired the reason; when the captain, a very incompetent person for such a business, told him that some of the money had been stolen; that so much was demanded for pilotage, coming to anchor, &c., as to leave nothing for the purpose of fitting the vessel for sea, which had occasioned the debt. "If," replied the king, "that be the case, we will have a pilot here, and every vessel that enters the harbour shall pay me for anchorage."

wards of fifty dollars; and we saw more than two thousand dollars received in one day. A similar tax was also levied by Kuakini, the governor at Kairua, when he first entered a handsome framed house, recently erected there.

Until the establishment of a Christian mission among them, the Sandwich islanders had no records, and consequently no written laws. There is, however, a kind of traditionary code, a number of regulations which have been either promulgated by former kings, or followed by general consent, respecting the tenure of lands, right of property, personal security, and exchange or barter, which are well understood, and usually acted upon. The portion of personal labour due from a tenant to his chief is fixed by custom, and a chief would be justified in banishing the person who should refuse it when required: on the other hand, were a chief to banish a man who had rendered it, and paid the stipulated rent, his conduct would be contrary to their opinions of right; and if the man complained to the governor or the king, and no other charge was brought against him, he would most likely be reinstated. The irrigation of their plantations is of great importance in most parts; and there is a law that the water shall be conducted over every plantation twice a week in general, and once a week during the dry season.

On the death of a chief his lands revert to the king or the governor of the island. He may nominate his son, his wife, or any other person, to succeed to his districts, &c., but the appointment must be confirmed by the king or governor before the individual can take possession.

This regulation, next to the tabu, is the most effectual mode of preserving the authority and influence of the king and chiefs.

In cases of assault or murder, except when committed by their own chief, the family and friends of the injured party are, by common consent, justified in retaliating. When they are too weak to attack the offender, they seek the aid of their neighbours, appeal to the chief of the district, or the king, who seldom inflicts a heavier punishment than banishment, even for murder, which, however, is a crime very rarely committed by the natives.

Theft among themselves is severely punished. Formerly, when a garden or house had been robbed, and

and although their vessels have greatly multiplied within
the last few years, they find constant employ for them,
particularly the small craft, which are continually plying
from one island to another, while their larger ones are
either chartered to foreign merchants, or make distant
voyages on their own account. They have once sent
a vessel to Canton, loaded with sandal-wood, under the
care of an English captain and mate, but manned by natives. They have also traded to Kamtschatka and other
parts of the Pacific, and have, within the last few years,
made one or two successful voyages for the purpose of
procuring seal-skins. The national flag of the islands
(see preceding page), which is an English jack, with
eight or nine horizontal stripes of white, red, and blue,
was given them by the British government many years
ago, accompanied by an assurance that it would be
respected wherever the British flag was acknowledged.
Although they are so expert in the manufacture of their
canoes, they have made but little progress in building
and repairing their ships, or in any of the mechanic arts.
They seem much more fond of the pursuits of commerce, and are tolerable adepts in bartering. In exchange for foreign articles, they not only give sandal-
wood and salt, but furnish supplies to the numerous
vessels which visit the islands for the purpose of refitting or procuring refreshments. In the months of March
and April, and of September and October, many vessels,
principally whalers, resort to the Sandwich Islands for
fresh provisions, &c.—we have seen upwards of thirty
lying at anchor off Oahu at one time. The farmers in
many places dispose of the produce of their land to
these ships; but in Oahu and some other harbours this
trade is almost entirely monopolized by the king and
chiefs. There is, indeed, a public market, in which the
natives dispose of their stock; but the price is regulated by the chiefs, and two-thirds of the proceeds of
whatever the natives sell is required by them.

This is not only unpleasant to those who trade with
them, but very oppressive, and retards in no small degree the industry, comfort, and civilization of the people.
In return for most of the supplies which they furnish to
the shipping, they receive Spanish dollars: but the sandal-wood, &c. they usually exchange for articles of
European or Chinese fabrication: the silks, crapes,
umbrellas, furniture, and trunks of the latter are most

in demand; while those of the former are hardware, earthenware, linens, broad-cloth, slops, hats, shoes, canvass, cordage, &c.

The season was approaching when the whalers fishing on the coast of Japan usually put into some of the harbours of these islands. Hence Karaimoku had sent the Nio for a cargo of hogs, to meet the demand for these animals, which he expected would follow their arrival.

About noon on the 28th Mr. Bishop reached Towaihae; and in the evening of the 30th they received the unexpected information that the brig would sail that evening: Messrs. Bishop and Goodrich therefore went on board, leaving Mr. Thurston at Towaihae to preach to the people there on the next day, which was the Sabbath, and afterward join the vessel at the north point of the island, where they were going to take in hogs for Karaimoku, to whom the division of Kohala belonged, though the island in general was under the jurisdiction of Kuakini, the governor. Their system of government is rather complex; and having occasionally mentioned several of its leading members, some further account of it will, perhaps, be acceptable.

The government of the Sandwich Islands is an absolute monarchy. The supreme authority is hereditary. The rank of the principal and inferior chiefs, the offices of the priests, and other situations of honour, influence, and emolument, descend from father to son, and often continue through many generations in the same family, though the power of nomination to every situation of dignity and trust is vested in the king; and persons, by merit or royal favour, frequently rise from comparatively humble rank to the highest station in the islands, as in the instance of Karaimoku, sometimes called by foreigners William Pitt. This individual, from being a chief of the third or fourth rank, has long been prime minister, in dignity next only to the king, and having, in fact, the actual government of the whole of the Sandwich Islands.

Hereditary rank and authority are not confined to the male sex, but are inherited also by the females; and, according to tradition, several of the islands have been once or twice under the government of a queen.

Four distinct classes or ranks in society appear to exist among them. The highest rank includes the king,

queens, and all the branches of the reigning family. It also includes the chief counsellor or minister of the king, who, though inferior by birth, is by office and authority superior to the queens and other members of the royal family.

The second rank includes the governors of the different islands, and also the chiefs of several large divisions or districts of land. Many of these are the descendants of the ancient families of Taraiopu, Kehekiri, Teporiorani, and Taeo, who were the kings of Hawaii, Maui, Oahu, and Tauai, when the islands were visited by Captain Cook, and retained their power until subdued by Tamehameha. Several of them were either the favourite and warlike companions of that prince, or are descended from those who were; among whom may be classed Kuakini the governor, Kaahumanu, Piia, Boki, Wahinepio, Kaikeova, and others.

The third rank is composed of those who hold districts or villages, and pay a regular rent for the land, cultivating it either by their own dependants and domestics, or letting it out in small allotments to tenants. This class is by far the most numerous body of chiefs in the island. Among the principal may be ranked Kamakau at Kaavaroa, Maaro at Waiakea, Haa at Waipio, Auae at Wairuku, and Kahanaumaitai at Waititi. They are generally called *haku aina*, proprietors of land. This rank would also include most of the priests under the former dispensation.

In the fourth rank may be included the small farmers, who rent from ten to twenty or thirty acres of land; the mechanics, namely, canoe and house builders, fishermen, musicians, and dancers; indeed, all the labouring classes, those who attach themselves to some chief or farmer, and labour on his land for their food and clothing, as well as those who cultivate small portions of land for their own advantage.

Though the chiefs did not receive that abject and humiliating homage which is frequently paid to superiors in barbarous nations, where the government is arbitrary, yet the common people always manifested a degree of respect to the chiefs according to their rank or office. This towards the sacred chiefs amounted almost to adoration, as they were on no occasion allowed to touch their persons, but prostrated themselves before them, and could not enter their houses without first receiving

permission. The behaviour among the chiefs was courteous, and manifested a desire to render themselves agreeable to each other; while all observed a degree of etiquette in their direct intercourse with the king. He is generally attended by a number of his courtiers or favourites, called punahele, who join in his amusements and occupations, except in the affairs of government, with which they seem to have no concern. When in a state of inebriation, all marks of distinction were lost; but at other times even these favourites conducted themselves towards their sovereign with great respect. I have often seen Kapihe and Kekuanaoa, the two who accompanied Rihoriho to England, come into his presence, and wait without speaking, whatever their business might be, till he should address them, and then continue standing until requested by him to sit down.

In some respects the government resembles the ancient feudal system of the northern nations. During many periods of their history, not only the separate islands, but the larger divisions of some of them, have been under the government of independent kings or chiefs; and it does not appear that until the reign of Rihoriho, the late king, they were ever united under one sovereign. The king is acknowledged in every island as the lord and proprietor of the soil by hereditary right, or the laws of conquest. When Tamehameha had subdued the greater part of the islands, he distributed them among his favourite chiefs and warriors, on condition of their rendering him, not only military service, but a certain proportion of the produce of their lands. This also appears to have been their ancient practice on similar occasions, as the *hoopahora* or *papahora*, division of land among the *ranakira*, or victors, invariably followed the conquest of a district or island.

Every island is given by the king to some high chief, who is supreme governor in it, but is subject to the king, whose orders he is obliged to see executed, and to whom he pays a regular rent or tax, according to the size of the island, or the advantages it may possess. Each island is separated into a number of permanent divisions, sometimes fifty or sixty miles in extent. In Hawaii there are six, Kohala, Kona, &c. Each of the large divisions is governed by one or two chiefs, appointed by the king or by the governor, and approved by the former. These large divisions are divided into

districts and villages, which sometimes extend five or six miles along the coast; at others, not more than half a mile. A head man, nominated by the governor, usually presides over these villages, which are again subdivided into a number of small farms or plantations. The names of these are generally significant; as, *Towahai*, the waters broken, from a stream which runs through the district, and is divided near the sea; *Kairua*, two seas, from the waters of the bay being separated by a point of land, &c.

Although this is the usual manner in which the land is distributed, yet the king holds personally a number of districts in most of the islands, and several of the principal chiefs receive districts directly from the king, and independent of the governor of the island in which they are situated.

The governor of the island pays over to the king annually, or half-yearly, the rents or taxes required by the latter. These he receives from the chiefs under him, who generally pay in the produce of the soil. Sometimes the king requires a certain sum in Spanish dollars, at other times in sandal-wood.

This, however, is only a modern regulation, introduced since they have become acquainted with the use of money and the value of sandal-wood. The rent was originally paid in canoes, native cloth, mats, fishing-nets, hogs, dogs, and the produce of the soil, for the use of the king, and the numerous train of favourite chiefs and dependants by whom he was surrounded, and who were daily fed from the provisions of his house.

For this tax the governor is responsible, and it is his business to see it conveyed to the king, or disposed of according to his order. A second tax is laid on the districts by the governor, for himself. The inhabitants of those portions of the island, however, which belong to other chiefs, although they furnish their share towards the king's revenue, are not called upon to support the governor of the island, but are expected to send a part of the produce of the land to their own chiefs. After this has been paid, additional requisitions are made upon the poor people cultivating the land, by the petty chiefs of the districts and villages; these, however, are but trifling.

There is no standing rule for the amount of rents or taxes, but they are regulated entirely by the caprice or

necessities of their rulers. Sometimes the poor people take a piece of land, on condition of cultivating a given portion for the chief and the remainder for themselves, making a fresh agreement after every crop.

In addition to the above demands, the common people are in general obliged to labour, if required, part of two days out of seven, in cultivating farms, building houses, &c., for their landlord.

A time is usually appointed for receiving the rent, when the people repair to the governor's with what they have to pay. If the required amount is furnished, they return, and, as they express it *(komo hou)*, enter again on their land. But if unable to pay the required sum, and their landlords are dissatisfied with the presents they have received, or think the tenants have neglected their farm, they are forbidden to return, and the land is offered to another. When, however, the produce brought is nearly equal to the required rent, and the chiefs think the occupants have exerted themselves to procure it, they remit the deficiency, and allow them to return. Besides the stipulated rent, the people are expected to make a number of presents to their chiefs, usually the first fish in season from their artificial ponds, or from the sea if the land they occupy be near the coast, together with the first-fruits of the trees and plantations.

Though these are the usual conditions on which land is held, there are a number of districts called *aina ku pono,* land standing erect, held free from all rent and taxes except a few presents, the value and frequency of which are entirely optional with the occupier. These privileges of exemption from the established usage were probably granted originally in reward for eminent services rendered the king, and they continue permanent; for, should the king, on account of any crime, banish an individual holding one of these districts, the next occupant would enjoy all the privileges of his predecessor.

The common people are generally considered as attached to the soil, and are transferred with the land from one chief to another. In recently conquered districts, they were formerly obliged to abide on the land which they cultivated, as slaves to the victors; at present, though they frequently remain through life the dependants or tenants of the same chief, such continuance appears on their part to be voluntary. No chief

can demand any service or supplies from those who occupy the land of another without his direction.

The king occasionally changes the tenants of a farm,
without taking the proprietorship from the chief who
may hold it more immediately from himself; and when
the rents are insufficient to meet his wants, if any of the
neighbouring farmers have potatoes and taro in their
fields, he, or any high chief, will send their men, and
hao, seize, the greater part of them, without making
any remuneration to the injured parties.

Besides the sums which the king receives from the
land, and the monopoly of the trade, in live-stock and
other supplies furnished to the shipping at several ports
in the islands, the revenue is augmented by the harbour
dues at Oahu. Every vessel anchoring in the outer
harbour pays sixty dollars, and eighty for entering the
basin, or inner harbour. Till within two or three years,
it was only forty for one, and sixty for the other.* The
pilotage, which is a dollar per foot for every vessel,
both on entering and leaving the harbour, is divided between the government and the pilot.

Another singular method of taxing the people is by
building a new house for the king, or some principal
chief. On the first day the king or chief enters it, the
chiefs and the people of the neighbourhood repair thither
to pay their respects and present their gifts. Custom
obliges every chief to appear on such occasions, or expose himself to the imputation of being disaffected; and
no one is allowed to enter without a present of money.
The amount is proportioned to their rank, or the land
they hold. Some chiefs on such occasions give sixty
dollars, others ten or five, and some only one.

A short time before his embarkation for England, a
large native house was built for Rihoriho, at Honoruru,
in the island of Oahu. During three days after the king
went into it the people came with their gifts. No individual, not even the queens, entered the house without
presenting the king a sum of money; several gave up-

* The demand for these dues originated in their unprofitable voyage to
Canton, in 1816. The cargo of sandal-wood was sold, but instead of a return
in cloths, silks, &c., the vessel came back nearly empty, and in debt. The
king inquired the reason; when the captain, a very incompetent person for
such a business, told him that some of the money had been stolen; that so
much was demanded for pilotage, coming to anchor, &c., as to leave nothing for
the purpose of fitting the vessel for sea, which had occasioned the debt. "If,"
replied the king, "that be the case, we will have a pilot here, and every vessel
that enters the harbour shall pay me for anchorage."

wards of fifty dollars; and we saw more than two thousand dollars received in one day. A similar tax was also levied by Kuakini, the governor at Kairua, when he first entered a handsome framed house, recently erected there.

Until the establishment of a Christian mission among them, the Sandwich islanders had no records, and consequently no written laws. There is, however, a kind of traditionary code, a number of regulations which have been either promulgated by former kings, or followed by general consent, respecting the tenure of lands, right of property, personal security, and exchange or barter, which are well understood, and usually acted upon. The portion of personal labour due from a tenant to his chief is fixed by custom, and a chief would be justified in banishing the person who should refuse it when required: on the other hand, were a chief to banish a man who had rendered it, and paid the stipulated rent, his conduct would be contrary to their opinions of right; and if the man complained to the governor or the king, and no other charge was brought against him, he would most likely be reinstated. The irrigation of their plantations is of great importance in most parts; and there is a law that the water shall be conducted over every plantation twice a week in general, and once a week during the dry season.

On the death of a chief his lands revert to the king or the governor of the island. He may nominate his son, his wife, or any other person, to succeed to his districts, &c., but the appointment must be confirmed by the king or governor before the individual can take possession.

This regulation, next to the tabu, is the most effectual mode of preserving the authority and influence of the king and chiefs.

In cases of assault or murder, except when committed by their own chief, the family and friends of the injured party are, by common consent, justified in retaliating. When they are too weak to attack the offender, they seek the aid of their neighbours, appeal to the chief of the district, or the king, who seldom inflicts a heavier punishment than banishment, even for murder, which, however, is a crime very rarely committed by the natives.

Theft among themselves is severely punished. Formerly, when a garden or house had been robbed, and

and although their vessels have greatly multiplied within
the last few years, they find constant employ for them,
particularly the small craft, which are continually plying
from one island to another, while their larger ones are
either chartered to foreign merchants, or make distant
voyages on their own account. They have once sent
a vessel to Canton, loaded with sandal-wood, under the
care of an English captain and mate, but manned by natives. They have also traded to Kamtschatka and other
parts of the Pacific, and have, within the last few years,
made one or two successful voyages for the purpose of
procuring seal-skins. The national flag of the islands
(see preceding page), which is an English jack, with
eight or nine horizontal stripes of white, red, and blue,
was given them by the British government many years
ago, accompanied by an assurance that it would be
respected wherever the British flag was acknowledged.
Although they are so expert in the manufacture of their
canoes, they have made but little progress in building
and repairing their ships, or in any of the mechanic arts.
They seem much more fond of the pursuits of commerce, and are tolerable adepts in bartering. In exchange for foreign articles, they not only give sandal-
wood and salt, but furnish supplies to the numerous
vessels which visit the islands for the purpose of refitting or procuring refreshments. In the months of March
and April, and of September and October, many vessels,
principally whalers, resort to the Sandwich Islands for
fresh provisions, &c.—we have seen upwards of thirty
lying at anchor off Oahu at one time. The farmers in
many places dispose of the produce of their land to
these ships; but in Oahu and some other harbours this
trade is almost entirely monopolized by the king and
chiefs. There is, indeed, a public market, in which the
natives dispose of their stock; but the price is regulated by the chiefs, and two-thirds of the proceeds of
whatever the natives sell is required by them.

This is not only unpleasant to those who trade with
them, but very oppressive, and retards in no small degree the industry, comfort, and civilization of the people.
In return for most of the supplies which they furnish to
the shipping, they receive Spanish dollars: but the sandal-wood, &c. they usually exchange for articles of
European or Chinese fabrication: the silks, crapes,
umbrellas, furniture, and trunks of the latter are most

in demand; while those of the former are hardware, earthenware, linens, broad-cloth, slops, hats, shoes, canvass, cordage, &c.

The season was approaching when the whalers fishing on the coast of Japan usually put into some of the harbours of these islands. Hence Karaimoku had sent the Nio for a cargo of hogs, to meet the demand for these animals, which he expected would follow their arrival.

About noon on the 28th Mr. Bishop reached Towaihae; and in the evening of the 30th they received the unexpected information that the brig would sail that evening: Messrs. Bishop and Goodrich therefore went on board, leaving Mr. Thurston at Towaihae to preach to the people there on the next day, which was the Sabbath, and afterward join the vessel at the north point of the island, where they were going to take in hogs for Karaimoku, to whom the division of Kohala belonged, though the island in general was under the jurisdiction of Kuakini, the governor. Their system of government is rather complex; and having occasionally mentioned several of its leading members, some further account of it will, perhaps, be acceptable.

The government of the Sandwich Islands is an absolute monarchy. The supreme authority is, hereditary. The rank of the principal and inferior chiefs, the offices of the priests, and other situations of honour, influence, and emolument, descend from father to son, and often continue through many generations in the same family, though the power of nomination to every situation of dignity and trust is vested in the king; and persons, by merit or royal favour, frequently rise from comparatively humble rank to the highest station in the islands, as in the instance of Karaimoku, sometimes called by foreigners William Pitt. This individual, from being a chief of the third or fourth rank, has long been prime minister, in dignity next only to the king, and having, in fact, the actual government of the whole of the Sandwich Islands.

Hereditary rank and authority are not confined to the male sex, but are inherited also by the females; and, according to tradition, several of the islands have been once or twice under the government of a queen.

Four distinct classes or ranks in society appear to exist among them. The highest rank includes the king,

queens, and all the branches of the reigning family. It also includes the chief counsellor or minister of the king, who, though inferior by birth, is by office and authority superior to the queens and other members of the royal family.

The second rank includes the governors of the different islands, and also the chiefs of several large divisions or districts of land. Many of these are the descendants of the ancient families of Taraiopu, Kehekiri, Teporiorani, and. Taeo, who were the kings of Hawaii, Maui, Oahu, and Tauai, when the islands were visited by Captain Cook, and retained their power until subdued by Tamehameha. Several of them were either the favourite and warlike companions of that prince, or are descended from those who were; among whom may be classed Kuakini the governor, Kaahumanu, Piia, Boki, Wahinepio, Kaikeova, and others.

The third rank is composed of those who hold districts or villages, and pay a regular rent for the land, cultivating it either by their own dependants and domestics, or letting it out in small allotments to tenants. This class is by far the most numerous body of chiefs in the island. Among the principal may be ranked Kamakau at Kaavaroa, Maaro at Waiakea, Haa at Waipio, Auae at Wairuku, and Kahanaumaitai at Waititi. They are generally called *haku aina*, proprietors of land. This rank would also include most of the priests under the former dispensation.

In the fourth rank may be included the small farmers, who rent from ten to twenty or thirty acres of land; the mechanics, namely, canoe and house builders, fishermen, musicians, and dancers; indeed, all the labouring classes, those who attach themselves to some chief or farmer, and labour on his land for their food and clothing, as well as those who cultivate small portions of land for their own advantage.

Though the chiefs did not receive that abject and humiliating homage which is frequently paid to superiors in barbarous nations, where the government is arbitrary, yet the common people always manifested a degree of respect to the chiefs according to their rank or office. This towards the sacred chiefs amounted almost to adoration, as they were on no occasion allowed to touch their persons, but prostrated themselves before them, and could not enter their houses without first receiving

permission. The behaviour among the chiefs was courteous, and manifested a desire to render themselves agreeable to each other.; while all observed a degree of etiquette in their direct intercourse with the king. He is generally attended by a number of his courtiers or favourites, called punahele, who join in his amusements and occupations, except in the affairs of government, with which they seem to have no concern. When in a state of inebriation, all marks of distinction were lost; but at other times even these favourites conducted themselves towards their sovereign with great respect. I have often seen Kapihe and Kekùanaoa, the two who accompanied Rihoriho to England, come into his presence, and wait without speaking, whatever their business might be, till he should address them, and then continue standing until requested by him to sit down.

In some respects the government resembles the ancient feudal system of the northern nations. During many periods of their history, not only the separate islands, but the larger divisions of some of them, have been under the government of independent kings or chiefs; and it does not appear that until the reign of Rihoriho, the late king, they were ever united under one sovereign. The king is acknowledged in every island as the lord and proprietor of the soil by hereditary right, or the laws of conquest. When Tamehameha had subdued the greater part of the islands, he distributed them among his favourite chiefs and warriors, on condition of their rendering him, not only military service, but a certain proportion of the produce of their lands. This also appears to have been their ancient practice on similar occasions, as the *hoopahora* or *papahora*, division of land among the *ranakira*, or victors, invariably followed the conquest of a district or island.

Every island is given by the king to some high chief, who is supreme governor in it, but is subject to the king, whose orders he is obliged to see executed, and to whom he pays a regular rent or tax, according to the size of the island, or the advantages it may possess. Each island is separated into a number of permanent divisions, sometimes fifty or sixty miles in extent. In Hawaii there are six, Kohala, Kona, &c. Each of the large divisions is governed by one or two chiefs, appointed by the king or by the governor, and approved by the former. These large divisions are divided into

districts and villages, which sometimes extend five or six miles along the coast; at others, not more than half a mile. A head man, nominated by the governor, usually presides over these villages, which are again subdivided into a number of small farms or plantations. The names of these are generally significant; as *Towahai*, the waters broken, from a stream which runs through the district, and is divided near the sea; *Kairua*, two seas, from the waters of the bay being separated by a point of land, &c.

Although this is the usual manner in which the land is distributed, yet the king holds personally a number of districts in most of the islands, and several of the principal chiefs receive districts directly from the king, and independent of the governor of the island in which they are situated.

The governor of the island pays over to the king annually, or half-yearly, the rents or taxes required by the latter. These he receives from the chiefs under him, who generally pay in the produce of the soil. Sometimes the king requires a certain sum in Spanish dollars, at other times in sandal-wood.

This, however, is only a modern regulation, introduced since they have become acquainted with the use of money and the value of sandal-wood. The rent was originally paid in canoes, native cloth, mats, fishing-nets, hogs, dogs, and the produce of the soil, for the use of the king, and the numerous train of favourite chiefs and dependants by whom he was surrounded, and who were daily fed from the provisions of his house.

For this tax the governor is responsible, and it is his business to see it conveyed to the king, or disposed of according to his order. A second tax is laid on the districts by the governor, for himself. The inhabitants of those portions of the island, however, which belong to other chiefs, although they furnish their share towards the king's revenue, are not called upon to support the governor of the island, but are expected to send a part of the produce of the land to their own chiefs. After this has been paid, additional requisitions are made upon the poor people cultivating the land, by the petty chiefs of the districts and villages; these, however, are but trifling.

There is no standing rule for the amount of rents or taxes, but they are regulated entirely by the caprice or

necessities of their rulers. Sometimes the poor people take a piece of land, on condition of cultivating a given portion for the chief and the remainder for themselves, making a fresh agreement after every crop.

In addition to the above demands, the common people are in general obliged to labour, if required, part of two days out of seven, in cultivating farms, building houses, &c., for their landlord.

A time is usually appointed for receiving the rent, when the people repair to the governor's with what they have to pay. If the required amount is furnished, they return, and, as they express it (*komo hou*), enter again on their land. But if unable to pay the required sum, and their landlords are dissatisfied with the presents they have received, or think the tenants have neglected their farm, they are forbidden to return, and the land is offered to another. When, however, the produce brought is nearly equal to the required rent, and the chiefs think the occupants have exerted themselves to procure it, they remit the deficiency, and allow them to return. Besides the stipulated rent, the people are expected to make a number of presents to their chiefs, usually the first fish in season from their artificial ponds, or from the sea if the land they occupy be near the coast, together with the first-fruits of the trees and plantations.

Though these are the usual conditions on which land is held, there are a number of districts called *aina ku pono*, land standing erect, held free from all rent and taxes except a few presents, the value and frequency of which are entirely optional with the occupier. These privileges of exemption from the established usage were probably granted originally in reward for eminent services rendered the king, and they continue permanent; for, should the king, on account of any crime, banish an individual holding one of these districts, the next occupant would enjoy all the privileges of his predecessor.

The common people are generally considered as attached to the soil, and are transferred with the land from one chief to another. In recently conquered districts, they were formerly obliged to abide on the land which they cultivated, as slaves to the victors; at present, though they frequently remain through life the dependants or tenants of the same chief, such continuance appears on their part to be voluntary. No chief

can demand any service or supplies from those who occupy the land of another without his direction.

The king occasionally changes the tenants, of a farm, without taking the proprietorship from the chief who may hold it more immediately from himself; and when the rents are insufficient to meet his wants, if any of the neighbouring farmers have potatoes and taro in their fields, he, or any high chief, will send their men, and *hao*, seize, the greater part of them, without making any remuneration to the injured parties.

Besides the sums which the king receives from the land, and the monopoly of the trade, in live-stock and other supplies furnished to the shipping at several ports in the islands, the revenue is augmented by the harbour dues at Oahu. Every vessel anchoring in the outer harbour pays sixty dollars, and eighty for entering the basin, or inner harbour. Till within two or three years, it was only forty for one, and sixty for the other.* The pilotage, which is a dollar per foot for every vessel, both on entering and leaving the harbour, is divided between the government and the pilot.

Another singular method of taxing the people is by building a new house for the king, or some principal chief. On the first day the king or chief enters it, the chiefs and the people of the neighbourhood repair thither to pay their respects and present their gifts. Custom obliges every chief to appear on such occasions, or expose himself to the imputation of being disaffected; and no one is allowed to enter without a present of money. The amount is proportioned to their rank, or the land they hold. Some chiefs on such occasions give sixty dollars; others ten or five, and some only one.

A short time before his embarkation for England, a large native house was built for Rihoriho, at Hanoruru, in the island of Oahu. During three days after the king went into it the people came with their gifts. No individual, not even the queens, entered the house without presenting the king a sum of money; several gave up-

* The demand for these dues originated in their unprofitable voyage to Canton, in 1816. The cargo of sandal-wood was sold, but instead of a return in cloths, silks, &c., the vessel came back nearly empty, and in debt. The king inquired the reason; when the captain, a very incompetent person for such a business, told him that some of the money had been stolen; that so much was demanded for pilotage, coming to anchor, &c., as to leave nothing for the purpose of fitting the vessel for sea, which had occasioned the debt. "If," replied the king, "that be the case, we will have a pilot here, and every vessel that enters the harbour shall pay me for anchorage."

wards of fifty dollars; and we saw more than two thousand dollars received in one day. A similar tax was also levied by Kuakini, the governor at Kairua, when he first entered a handsome framed house, recently erected there.

Until the establishment of a Christian mission among them, the Sandwich islanders had no records, and consequently no written laws. There is, however, a kind of traditionary code, a number of regulations which have been either promulgated by former kings, or followed by general consent, respecting the tenure of lands, right of property, personal security, and exchange or barter, which are well understood, and usually acted upon. The portion of personal labour due from a tenant to his chief is fixed by custom, and a chief would be justified in banishing the person who should refuse it when required: on the other hand, were a chief to banish a man who had rendered it, and paid the stipulated rent, his conduct would be contrary to their opinions of right; and if the man complained to the governor or the king, and no other charge was brought against him, he would most likely be reinstated. The irrigation of their plantations is of great importance in most parts; and there is a law that the water shall be conducted over every plantation twice a week in general, and once a week during the dry season.

On the death of a chief his lands revert to the king or the governor of the island. He may nominate his son, his wife, or any other person, to succeed to his districts, &c., but the appointment must be confirmed by the king or governor before the individual can take possession.

This regulation, next to the tabu, is the most effectual mode of preserving the authority and influence of the king and chiefs.

In cases of assault or murder, except when committed by their own chief, the family and friends of the injured party are, by common consent, justified in retaliating. When they are too weak to attack the offender, they seek the aid of their neighbours, appeal to the chief of the district, or the king, who seldom inflicts a heavier punishment than banishment, even for murder, which, however, is a crime very rarely committed by the natives.

Theft among themselves is severely punished. Formerly, when a garden or house had been robbed, and

and although their vessels have greatly multiplied within
the last few years, they find constant employ for them,
particularly the small craft, which are continually plying
from one island to another, while their larger ones are
either chartered to foreign merchants, or make distant
voyages on their own account.   They have once sent
a vessel to Canton, loaded with sandal-wood, under the
care of an English captain and mate, but manned by natives.   They have also traded to Kamtschatka and other
parts of the Pacific, and have; within the last few years,
made one or two successful voyages for the purpose of
procuring seal-skins.   The national flag of the islands
(see preceding page), which is an English jack, with
eight or nine horizontal stripes of white, red, and blue,
was given them by the British government many years
ago, accompanied by an assurance that it would be
respected wherever the British flag was acknowledged.
Although they are so expert in the manufacture of their
canoes, they have made but little progress in building
and repairing their ships, or in any of the mechanic arts.
They seem much more fond of the pursuits of commerce, and are tolerable adepts in bartering.   In exchange for foreign articles, they not only give sandal-
wood and salt, but furnish supplies to the numerous
vessels which visit the islands for the purpose of refitting or procuring refreshments.   In the months of March
and April, and of September and October, many vessels,
principally whalers, resort to the Sandwich Islands for
fresh provisions, &c.—we have seen upwards of thirty
lying at anchor off Oahu at one time.   The farmers in
many places dispose of the produce of their land to
these ships; but in Oahu and some other harbours this
trade is almost entirely monopolized by the king and
chiefs.   There is, indeed, a public market, in which the
natives dispose of their stock; but the price is regulated by the chiefs, and two-thirds of the proceeds of
whatever the natives sell is required by them.
   This is not only unpleasant to those who trade with
them, but very oppressive, and retards in no small degree the industry, comfort, and civilization of the people.
In return for most of the supplies which they furnish to
the shipping, they receive Spanish dollars: but the sandal-wood, &c. they usually exchange for articles of
European or Chinese fabrication: the silks, crapes,
umbrellas, furniture, and trunks of the latter are most

in demand; while those of the former are hardware, earthenware, linens, broad-cloth, slops, hats, shoes, canvass, cordage, &c.

The season was approaching when the whalers fishing on the coast of Japan usually put into some of the harbours of these islands. Hence Karaimoku had sent the Nio for a cargo of hogs, to meet the demand for these animals, which he expected would follow their arrival.

About noon on the 28th Mr. Bishop reached Towaihae; and in the evening of the 30th they received the unexpected information that the brig would sail that evening: Messrs. Bishop and Goodrich therefore went on board, leaving Mr. Thurston at Towaihae to preach to the people there on the next day, which was the Sabbath, and afterward join the vessel at the north point of the island, where they were going to take in hogs for Karaimoku, to whom the division of Kohala belonged, though the island in general was under the jurisdiction of Kuakini, the governor. Their system of government is rather complex; and having occasionally mentioned several of its leading members, some further account of it will, perhaps, be acceptable.

The government of the Sandwich Islands is an absolute monarchy. The supreme authority is hereditary. The rank of the principal and inferior chiefs, the offices of the priests, and other situations of honour, influence, and emolument, descend from father to son, and often continue through many generations in the same family, though the power of nomination to every situation of dignity and trust is vested in the king; and persons, by merit or royal favour, frequently rise from comparatively humble rank to the highest station in the islands, as in the instance of Karaimoku, sometimes called by foreigners William Pitt. This individual, from being a chief of the third or fourth rank, has long been prime minister, in dignity next only to the king, and having, in fact, the actual government of the whole of the Sandwich Islands.

Hereditary rank and authority are not confined to the male sex, but are inherited also by the females; and, according to tradition, several of the islands have been once or twice under the government of a queen.

Four distinct classes or ranks in society appear to exist among them. The highest rank includes the king,

queens, and all the branches of the reigning family. It also includes the chief counsellor or minister of the king, who, though inferior by birth, is by office and authority superior to the queens and other members of the royal family.

The second rank includes the governors of the different islands, and also the chiefs of several large divisions or districts of land. Many of these are the descendants of the ancient families of Taraiopu, Kehekiri, Teporiorani, and Taeo, who were the kings of Hawaii, Maui, Oahu, and Tauai, when the islands were visited by Captain Cook, and retained their power until subdued by Tamehameha. Several of them were either the favourite and warlike companions of that prince, or are descended from those who were; among whom may be classed Kuakini the governor, Kaahumanu, Piia, Boki, Wahinepio, Kaikeova, and others.

The third rank is composed of those who hold districts or villages, and pay a regular rent for the land, cultivating it either by their own dependants and domestics, or letting it out in small allotments to tenants. This class is by far the most numerous body of chiefs in the island. Among the principal may be ranked Kamakau at Kaavaroa, Maaro at Waiakea, Haa at Waipio, Auae at Wairuku, and Kahanaumaitai at Waititi. They are generally called *haku aina*, proprietors of land. This rank would also include most of the priests under the former dispensation.

In the fourth rank may be included the small farmers, who rent from ten to twenty or thirty acres of land; the mechanics, namely, canoe and house builders, fishermen, musicians, and dancers; indeed, all the labouring classes, those who attach themselves to some chief or farmer, and labour on his land for their food and clothing, as well as those who cultivate small portions of land for their own advantage.

Though the chiefs did not receive that abject and humiliating homage which is frequently paid to superiors in barbarous nations, where the government is arbitrary, yet the common people always manifested a degree of respect to the chiefs according to their rank or office. This towards the sacred chiefs amounted almost to adoration, as they were on no occasion allowed to touch their persons, but prostrated themselves before them, and could not enter their houses without first receiving

permission. The behaviour among the chiefs was courteous, and manifested a desire to render themselves agreeable to each other; while all observed a degree of etiquette in their direct intercourse with the king. He is generally attended by a number of his courtiers or favourites, called punahele, who join in his amusements and occupations, except in the affairs of government, with which they seem to have no concern. When in a state of inebriation, all marks of distinction were lost; but at other times even these favourites conducted themselves towards their sovereign with great respect. I have often seen Kapihe and Kekuanaoa, the two who accompanied Rihoriho to England, come into his presence, and wait without speaking, whatever their business might be, till he should address them, and then continue standing until requested by him to sit down.

In some respects the government resembles the ancient feudal system of the northern nations. During many periods of their history, not only the separate islands, but the larger divisions of some of them, have been under the government of independent kings or chiefs; and it does not appear that until the reign of Rihoriho, the late king, they were ever united under one sovereign. The king is acknowledged in every island as the lord and proprietor of the soil by hereditary right, or the laws of conquest. When Tamehameha had subdued the greater part of the islands, he distributed them among his favourite chiefs and warriors, on condition of their rendering him, not only military service, but a certain proportion of the produce of their lands. This also appears to have been their ancient practice on similar occasions, as the *hoopahora* or *papahora*, division of land among the *ranakira*, or victors, invariably followed the conquest of a district or island.

Every island is given by the king to some high chief, who is supreme governor in it, but is subject to the king, whose orders he is obliged to see executed, and to whom he pays a regular rent or tax, according to the size of the island, or the advantages it may possess. Each island is separated into a number of permanent divisions, sometimes fifty or sixty miles in extent. In Hawaii there are six, Kohala, Kona, &c. Each of the large divisions is governed by one or two chiefs, appointed by the king or by the governor, and approved by the former. These large divisions are divided into

districts and villages, which sometimes extend five or six miles along the coast; at others, not more than half a mile. A head man, nominated by the governor, usually presides over these villages, which are again subdivided into a number of small farms or plantations. The names of these are generally significant; as *Towahai*, the waters broken, from a stream which runs through the district, and is divided near the sea; *Kairua*, two seas, from the waters of the bay being separated by a point of land, &c.

Although this is the usual manner in which the land is distributed, yet the king holds personally a number of districts in most of the islands, and several of the principal chiefs receive districts directly from the king, and independent of the governor of the island in which they are situated.

The governor of the island pays over to the king annually, or half-yearly, the rents or taxes required by the latter. These he receives from the chiefs under him, who generally pay in the produce of the soil. Sometimes the king requires a certain sum in Spanish dollars, at other times in sandal-wood.

This, however, is only a modern regulation, introduced since they have become acquainted with the use of money and the value of sandal-wood. The rent was originally paid in canoes, native cloth, mats, fishing-nets, hogs, dogs, and the produce of the soil, for the use of the king, and the numerous train of favourite chiefs and dependants by whom he was surrounded, and who were daily fed from the provisions of his house.

For this tax the governor is responsible, and it is his business to see it conveyed to the king, or disposed of according to his order. A second tax is laid on the districts by the governor, for himself. The inhabitants of those portions of the island, however, which belong to other chiefs, although they furnish their share towards the king's revenue, are not called upon to support the governor of the island, but are expected to send a part of the produce of the land to their own chiefs. After this has been paid, additional requisitions are made upon the poor people cultivating the land, by the petty chiefs of the districts and villages; these, however, are but trifling.

There is no standing rule for the amount of rents or taxes, but they are regulated entirely by the caprice or

necessities of their rulers. Sometimes the poor people take a piece of land, on condition of cultivating a given portion for the chief and the remainder for themselves, making a fresh agreement after every crop.

In addition to the above demands, the common people are in general obliged to labour, if required, part of two days out of seven, in cultivating farms, building houses, &c., for their landlord.

A time is usually appointed for receiving the rent, when the people repair to the governor's with what they have to pay. If the required amount is furnished, they return, and, as they express it (*komo hou*), enter again on their land. But if unable to pay the required sum, and their landlords are dissatisfied with the presents they have received, or think the tenants have neglected their farm, they are forbidden to return, and the land is offered to another. When, however, the produce brought is nearly equal to the required rent, and the chiefs think the occupants have exerted themselves to procure it, they remit the deficiency, and allow them to return. Besides the stipulated rent, the people are expected to make a number of presents to their chiefs, usually the first fish in season from their artificial ponds, or from the sea if the land they occupy be near the coast, together with the first-fruits of the trees and plantations.

Though these are the usual conditions on which land is held, there are a number of districts called *aina ku pono*, land standing erect, held free from all rent and taxes except a few presents, the value and frequency of which are entirely optional with the occupier. These privileges of exemption from the established usage were probably granted originally in reward for eminent services rendered the king, and they continue permanent; for, should the king, on account of any crime, banish an individual holding one of these districts, the next occupant would enjoy all the privileges of his predecessor.

The common people are generally considered as attached to the soil, and are transferred with the land from one chief to another. In recently conquered districts, they were formerly obliged to abide on the land which they cultivated, as slaves to the victors; at present, though they frequently remain through life the dependants or tenants of the same chief, such continuance appears on their part to be voluntary. No chief

can demand any service or supplies from those who occupy the land of another without his direction.

The king occasionally changes the tenants, of a farm,
without taking the proprietorship from the chief who
may hold it more immediately from himself; and when
the rents are insufficient to meet his wants, if any of the
neighbouring farmers have potatoes and taro in their
fields, he, or any high chief, will send their men, and
hao, seize, the greater part of them, without making
any remuneration to the injured parties.

Besides the sums which the king receives from the
land, and the monopoly of the trade, in live-stock and
other supplies furnished to the shipping at several ports
in the islands, the revenue is augmented by the harbour
dues at Oahu. Every vessel anchoring in the outer
harbour pays sixty dollars, and eighty for entering the
basin, or inner harbour. Till within two or three years,
it was only forty for one, and sixty for the other.* The
pilotage, which is a dollar per foot for every vessel,
both on entering and leaving the harbour, is divided between the government and the pilot.

Another singular method of taxing the people is by
building a new house for the king, or some principal
chief. On the first day the king or chief enters it, the
chiefs and the people of the neighbourhood repair thither
to pay their respects and present their gifts. Custom
obliges every chief to appear on such occasions, or expose himself to the imputation of being disaffected; and
no one is allowed to enter without a present of money.
The amount is proportioned to their rank, or the land
they hold. Some chiefs on such occasions give sixty
dollars; others ten or five, and some only one.

A short time before his embarkation for England, a
large native house was built for Rihoriho, at Honoruru,
in the island of Oahu. During three days after the king
went into it the people came with their gifts. No individual, not even the queens, entered the house without
presenting the king a sum of money; several gave up-

<hr>

* The demand for these dues originated in their unprofitable voyage to
Canton, in 1816. The cargo of sandal-wood was sold, but instead of a return
in cloths, silks, &c., the vessel came back nearly empty, and in debt. The
king inquired the reason; when the captain, a very incompetent person for
such a business, told him that some of the money had been stolen; that so
much was demanded for pilotage, coming to anchor, &c., as to leave nothing for
the purpose of fitting the vessel for sea, which had occasioned the debt. "If,"
replied the king, "that be the case, we will have a pilot here, and every vessel
that enters the harbour shall pay me for anchorage."

wards of fifty dollars; and we saw more than two thousand dollars received in one day. A similar tax was also levied by Kuakini, the governor at Kairua, when he first entered a handsome framed house, recently erected there.

Until the establishment of a Christian mission among them, the Sandwich islanders had no records, and consequently no written laws. There is, however, a kind of traditionary code, a number of regulations which have been either promulgated by former kings, or followed by general consent, respecting the tenure of lands, right of property, personal security, and exchange or barter, which are well understood, and usually acted upon. The portion of personal labour due from a tenant to his chief is fixed by custom, and a chief would be justified in banishing the person who should refuse it when required: on the other hand, were a chief to banish a man who had rendered it, and paid the stipulated rent, his conduct would be contrary to their opinions of right; and if the man complained to the governor or the king, and no other charge was brought against him, he would most likely be reinstated. The irrigation of their plantations is of great importance in most parts; and there is a law that the water shall be conducted over every plantation twice a week in general, and once a week during the dry season.

On the death of a chief his lands revert to the king or the governor of the island. He may nominate his son, his wife, or any other person, to succeed to his districts, &c., but the appointment must be confirmed by the king or governor before the individual can take possession. This regulation, next to the tabu, is the most effectual mode of preserving the authority and influence of the king and chiefs.

In cases of assault or murder, except when committed by their own chief, the family and friends of the injured party are, by common consent, justified in retaliating. When they are too weak to attack the offender, they seek the aid of their neighbours, appeal to the chief of the district, or the king, who seldom inflicts a heavier punishment than banishment, even for murder, which, however, is a crime very rarely committed by the natives.

Theft among themselves is severely punished. Formerly, when a garden or house had been robbed, and

siderable distance. From one side to the other of this
bay Tamehameha built a strong stone wall, six feet high
in some places, and twenty feet wide, by which he had
an excellent fish-pond, not less than two miles in circumference, There were several arches in the wall, which
were guarded by strong stakes driven into the ground
so far apart as to admit the water of the sea, yet sufficiently close to prevent the fish from escaping.   It
was well stocked with fish, and water-fowl were seen
swimming on its surface.

The people of this village, as well as the others
through which I had passed, were preparing to keep the
Sabbath, and the conversation naturally turned on the
orders recently issued by the governor.   They said it
was a bad thing to commit murder, infanticide, and
theft, which had also been forbidden ; that it would be
well to abstain from these crimes ; but, they said, they
did not know of what advantage the *palapala*, instruction,
&c., would be.

At breakfast the governor seemed interested in the
narrative of the tour, particularly of the interview we
had with the priestess of Pélé at Waiakea.

At half-past ten the bell rang for public worship, and
about eight hundred people, decently dressed, some in
foreign, others in native clothing, assembled under a
large *ranai*, a place sheltered from the sun, formed by
two large canvass awnings and a number of platted
cocoanut-leaves, spread over the place from posts fixed
in the fence which enclosed the court-yard around the
house of the governor's wife.   The governor and his
attendants sat on chairs ; the rest of the congregation
reclined on their mats, or sat on the ground.   After
singing and prayer, I preached from Acts xvi. 30, 31.
The history of the Philippian jailer appeared to interest
them, and after the conclusion of the service the governor, in particular, made many inquiries.

At half-past four in the afternoon the bell rang again,
and the people collected in the place where the services
had been held in the forenoon, and in equal numbers
seated themselves very quietly.   The exercises commenced in the usual manner, and I preached on the occasion from Acts v. 14.   They were attentive, and appeared much affected with the account of the awful end
of Ananias and Sapphira.

After the public services were finished, Mr. Bishop

visited Thomas Hopu's house, where a small congregation was assembled for conversation and prayer. Mr. Bishop gave them a short exhortation; and many of the people remained afterward to hear more from Thomas about Jesus Christ.

The Sabbath was spent in a manner truly gratifying. No athletic sports were seen on the beach; no noise of playful children, shouting as they gambolled in the surf, nor distant sound of the cloth-beating mallet, was heard through the day; no persons were seen carrying burdens in or out of the village, nor any canoes passing across the bay. It could not but be viewed as the dawn of a bright sabbatic day for the dark shores of Hawaii. Family worship was held at the governor's house, in the native language, in the evening.

Having heard of the arrival of the brig Nio at Towaihae, Mr. Bishop left Kairua in the evening, to return to Oahu.

The natives possess no inconsiderable share of maritime and commercial enterprise. The king and chiefs own fifteen or sixteen vessels, several of which, like the Nio, are brigs of ninety or a hundred tons burden.

The greater part of them, however, are schooners of a smaller size. The larger ones, on a long voyage, are commanded by a foreigner; but among the islands they are manned and navigated by the natives themselves. A native captain and supercargo are appointed to each; the former navigates the vessel, while the latter attends to the cargo. The natives in general make good sailors;

and although their vessels have greatly multiplied within the last few years, they find constant employ for them, particularly the small craft, which are continually plying from one island to another, while their larger ones are either chartered to foreign merchants, or make distant voyages on their own account. They have once sent a vessel to Canton, loaded with sandal-wood, under the care of an English captain and mate, but manned by natives. They have also traded to Kamtschatka and other parts of the Pacific, and have, within the last few years, made one or two successful voyages for the purpose of procuring seal-skins. The national flag of the islands (see preceding page), which is an English jack, with eight or nine horizontal stripes of white, red, and blue, was given them by the British government many years ago, accompanied by an assurance that it would be respected wherever the British flag was acknowledged. Although they are so expert in the manufacture of their canoes, they have made but little progress in building and repairing their ships, or in any of the mechanic arts. They seem much more fond of the pursuits of commerce, and are tolerable adepts in bartering. In exchange for foreign articles, they not only give sandal-wood and salt, but furnish supplies to the numerous vessels which visit the islands for the purpose of refitting or procuring refreshments. In the months of March and April, and of September and October, many vessels, principally whalers, resort to the Sandwich Islands for fresh provisions, &c.—we have seen upwards of thirty lying at anchor off Oahu at one time. The farmers in many places dispose of the produce of their land to these ships; but in Oahu and some other harbours this trade is almost entirely monopolized by the king and chiefs. There is, indeed, a public market, in which the natives dispose of their stock; but the price is regulated by the chiefs, and two-thirds of the proceeds of whatever the natives sell is required by them.

This is not only unpleasant to those who trade with them, but very oppressive, and retards in no small degree the industry, comfort, and civilization of the people. In return for most of the supplies which they furnish to the shipping, they receive Spanish dollars: but the sandal-wood, &c. they usually exchange for articles of European or Chinese fabrication: the silks, crapes, umbrellas, furniture, and trunks of the latter are most

in demand; while those of the former are hardware, earthenware, linens, broad-cloth, slops, hats, shoes, canvass, cordage, &c.

The season was approaching when the whalers fishing on the coast of Japan usually put into some of the harbours of these islands. Hence Karaimoku had sent the Nio for a cargo of hogs, to meet the demand for these animals, which he expected would follow their arrival.

About noon on the 28th Mr. Bishop reached Towai-hae; and in the evening of the 30th they received the unexpected information that the brig would sail that evening: Messrs. Bishop and Goodrich therefore went on board, leaving Mr. Thurston at Towaihae to preach to the people there on the next day, which was the Sabbath, and afterward join the vessel at the north point of the island, where they were going to take in hogs for Karaimoku, to whom the division of Kohala belonged, though the island in general was under the jurisdiction of Kuakini, the governor. Their system of government is rather complex; and having occasionally mentioned several of its leading members, some further account of it will, perhaps, be acceptable.

The government of the Sandwich Islands is an absolute monarchy. The supreme authority is hereditary. The rank of the principal and inferior chiefs, the offices of the priests, and other situations of honour, influence, and emolument, descend from father to son, and often continue through many generations in the same family, though the power of nomination to every situation of dignity and trust is vested in the king; and persons, by merit or royal favour, frequently rise from comparatively humble rank to the highest station in the islands, as in the instance of Karaimoku, sometimes called by foreigners William Pitt. This individual, from being a chief of the third or fourth rank, has long been prime minister, in dignity next only to the king, and having, in fact, the actual government of the whole of the Sandwich Islands.

Hereditary rank and authority are not confined to the male sex, but are inherited also by the females; and, according to tradition, several of the islands have been once or twice under the government of a queen.

Four distinct classes or ranks in society appear to exist among them. The highest rank includes the king,

queens, and all the branches of the reigning family. It also includes the chief counsellor or minister of the king, who, though inferior by birth, is by office and authority superior to the queens and other members of the royal family.

The second rank includes the governors of the different islands, and also the chiefs of several large divisions or districts of land. Many of these are the descendants of the ancient families of Taraiopu, Kehekiri, Teporiorani, and Taeo, who were the kings of Hawaii, Maui, Oahu, and Tauai, when the islands were visited by Captain Cook, and retained their power until subdued by Tamehameha. Several of them were either the favourite and warlike companions of that prince, or are descended from those who were; among whom may be classed Kuakini the governor, Kaahumanu, Piia, Boki, Wahinepio, Kaikeova, and others.

The third rank is composed of those who hold districts or villages, and pay a regular rent for the land, cultivating it either by their own dependants and domestics, or letting it out in small allotments to tenants. This class is by far the most numerous body of chiefs in the island. Among the principal may be ranked Kamakau at Kaavaroa, Maaro at Waiakea, Haa at Waipio, Auàe at Wairuku, and Kahanaumaitai at Waititi. They are generally called *haku aina*, proprietors of land. This rank would also include most of the priests under the former dispensation.

In the fourth rank may be included the small farmers, who rent from ten to twenty or thirty acres of land; the mechanics, namely, canoe and house builders, fishermen, musicians, and dancers; indeed, all the labouring classes, those who attach themselves to some chief or farmer, and labour on his land for their food and clothing, as well as those who cultivate small portions of land for their own advantage.

Though the chiefs did not receive that abject and humiliating homage which is frequently paid to superiors in barbarous nations, where the government is arbitrary, yet the common people always manifested a degree of respect to the chiefs according to their rank or office. This towards the sacred chiefs amounted almost to adoration, as they were on no occasion allowed to touch their persons, but prostrated themselves before them, and could not enter their houses without first receiving

permission. The behaviour among the chiefs was courteous, and manifested a desire to render themselves agreeable to each other; while all observed a degree of etiquette in their direct intercourse with the king. He is generally attended by a number of his courtiers or favourites, called punahele, who join in his amusements and occupations, except in the affairs of government, with which they seem to have no concern. When in a state of inebriation, all marks of distinction were lost; but at other times even these favourites conducted themselves towards their sovereign with great respect. I have often seen Kapihe and Kekuanaoa, the two who accompanied Rihoriho to England, come into his presence, and wait without speaking, whatever their business might be, till he should address them, and then continue standing until requested by him to sit down.

In some respects the government resembles the ancient feudal system of the northern nations. During many periods of their history, not only the separate islands, but the larger divisions of some of them, have been under the government of independent kings or chiefs; and it does not appear that until the reign of Rihoriho, the late king, they were ever united under one sovereign. The king is acknowledged in every island as the lord and proprietor of the soil by hereditary right, or the laws of conquest. When Tamehameha had subdued the greater part of the islands, he distributed them among his favourite chiefs and warriors, on condition of their rendering him, not only military service, but a certain proportion of the produce of their lands. This also appears to have been their ancient practice on similar occasions, as the *hoopahora* or *papahora*, division of land among the *ranakira*, or victors, invariably followed the conquest of a district or island.

Every island is given by the king to some high chief, who is supreme governor in it, but is subject to the king, whose orders he is obliged to see executed, and to whom he pays a regular rent or tax, according to the size of the island, or the advantages it may possess. Each island is separated into a number of permanent divisions, sometimes fifty or sixty miles in extent. In Hawaii there are six, Kohala, Kona, &c. Each of the large divisions is governed by one or two chiefs, appointed by the king or by the governor, and approved by the former. These large divisions are divided into

districts and villages, which sometimes extend five or six miles along the coast; at others, not more than half a mile. A head man, nominated by the governor, usually presides over these villages, which are again subdivided into a number of small farms or plantations. The names of these are generally significant; as *Towahai*, the waters broken, from a stream which runs through the district, and is divided near the sea; *Kairua*, two seas, from the waters of the bay being separated by a point of land, &c.

Although this is the usual manner in which the land is distributed, yet the king holds personally a number of districts in most of the islands, and several of the principal chiefs receive districts directly from the king and independent of the governor of the island in which they are situated.

The governor of the island pays over to the king annually, or half-yearly, the rents or taxes required by the latter. These he receives from the chiefs under him, who generally pay in the produce of the soil. Sometimes the king requires a certain sum in Spanish dollars, at other times in sandal-wood.

This, however, is only a modern regulation, introduced since they have become acquainted with the use of money and the value of sandal-wood. The rent was originally paid in canoes, native cloth, mats, fishing-nets, hogs, dogs, and the produce of the soil, for the use of the king, and the numerous train of favourite chiefs and dependants by whom he was surrounded, and who were daily fed from the provisions of his house.

For this tax the governor is responsible, and it is his business to see it conveyed to the king, or disposed of according to his order. A second tax is laid on the districts by the governor, for himself. The inhabitants of those portions of the island, however, which belong to other chiefs, although they furnish their share towards the king's revenue, are not called upon to support the governor of the island, but are expected to send a part of the produce of the land to their own chiefs. After this has been paid, additional requisitions are made upon the poor people cultivating the land, by the petty chiefs of the districts and villages; these, however, are but trifling.

There is no standing rule for the amount of rents or taxes, but they are regulated entirely by the caprice or

necessities of their rulers. Sometimes the poor people take a piece of land, on condition of cultivating a given portion for the chief and the remainder for themselves, making a fresh agreement after every crop.

In addition to the above demands, the common people are in general obliged to labour, if required, part of two days out of seven, in cultivating farms, building houses, &c., for their landlord.

A time is usually appointed for receiving the rent, when the people repair to the governor's with what they have to pay. If the required amount is furnished, they return, and, as they express it *(komo hou)*, enter again on their land. But if unable to pay the required sum, and their landlords are dissatisfied with the presents they have received, or think the tenants have neglected their farm, they are forbidden to return, and the land is offered to another. When, however, the produce brought is nearly equal to the required rent, and the chiefs think the occupants have exerted themselves to procure it, they remit the deficiency, and allow them to return. Besides the stipulated rent, the people are expected to make a number of presents to their chiefs, usually the first fish in season from their artificial ponds, or from the sea if the land they occupy be near the coast, together with the first-fruits of the trees and plantations.

Though these are the usual conditions on which land is held, there are a number of districts called *aina ku pono,* land standing erect, held free from all rent and taxes except a few presents, the value and frequency of which are entirely optional with the occupier. These privileges of exemption from the established usage were probably granted originally in reward for eminent services rendered the king, and they continue permanent; for, should the king, on account of any crime, banish an individual holding one of these districts, the next occupant would enjoy all the privileges of his predecessor.

The common people are generally considered as attached to the soil, and are transferred with the land from one chief to another. In recently conquered districts, they were formerly obliged to abide on the land which they cultivated, as slaves to the victors; at present, though they frequently remain through life the dependants or tenants of the same chief, such continuance appears on their part to be voluntary. No chief

can demand any service or supplies from those who occupy the land of another without his direction.

The king occasionally changes the tenants of a farm, without taking the proprietorship from the chief who may hold it more immediately from himself; and when the rents are insufficient to meet his wants, if any of the neighbouring farmers have potatoes and taro in their fields, he, or any high chief, will send their men, and *hao*, seize, the greater part of them, without making any remuneration to the injured parties.

Besides the sums which the king receives from the land, and the monopoly of the trade, in live-stock and other supplies furnished to the shipping at several ports in the islands, the revenue is augmented by the harbour dues at Oahu. Every vessel anchoring in the outer harbour pays sixty dollars, and eighty for entering the basin, or inner harbour. Till within two or three years, it was only forty for one, and sixty for the other.* The pilotage, which is a dollar per foot for every vessel, both on entering and leaving the harbour, is divided between the government and the pilot.

Another singular method of taxing the people is by building a new house for the king, or some principal chief. On the first day the king or chief enters it, the chiefs and the people of the neighbourhood repair thither to pay their respects and present their gifts. Custom obliges every chief to appear on such occasions, or expose himself to the imputation of being disaffected; and no one is allowed to enter without a present of money. The amount is proportioned to their rank, or the land they hold. Some chiefs on such occasions give sixty dollars; others ten or five, and some only one.

A short time before his embarkation for England, a large native house was built for Rihoriho, at Honoruru, in the island of Oahu. During three days after the king went into it the people came with their gifts. No individual, not even the queens, entered the house without presenting the king a sum of money; several gave up-

* The demand for these dues originated in their unprofitable voyage to Canton, in 1816. The cargo of sandal-wood was sold, but instead of a return in cloths, silks, &c., the vessel came back nearly empty, and in debt. The king inquired the reason; when the captain, a very incompetent person for such a business, told him that some of the money had been stolen; that so much was demanded for pilotage, coming to anchor, &c., as to leave nothing for the purpose of fitting the vessel for sea, which had occasioned the debt. "If," replied the king, "that be the case, we will have a pilot here, and every vessel that enters the harbour shall pay me for anchorage "

wards of fifty dollars; and we saw more than two thousand dollars received in one day. A similar tax was also levied by Kuakini, the governor at Kairua, when he first entered a handsome framed house, recently erected there.

Until the establishment of a Christian mission among them, the Sandwich islanders had no records, and consequently no written laws. There is, however, a kind of traditionary code, a number of regulations which have been either promulgated by former kings, or followed by general consent, respecting the tenure of lands, right of property, personal security, and exchange or barter, which are well understood, and usually acted upon. The portion of personal labour due from a tenant to his chief is fixed by custom, and a chief would be justified in banishing the person who should refuse it when required: on the other-hand, were a chief to banish a man who had rendered it, and paid the stipulated rent, his conduct would be contrary to their opinions of right; and if the man complained to the governor or the king, and no other charge was brought against him, he would most likely be reinstated. The irrigation of their plantations is of great importance in most parts; and there is a law that the water shall be conducted over every plantation twice a week in general, and once a week during the dry season.

On the death of a chief his lands revert to the king or the governor of the island. He may nominate his son, his wife, or any other person, to succeed to his districts, &c., but the appointment must be confirmed by the king or governor before the individual can take possession.

This regulation, next to the tabu, is the most effectual mode of preserving the authority and influence of the king and chiefs.

In cases of assault or murder, except when committed by their own chief, the family and friends of the injured party are, by common consent, justified in retaliating. When they are too weak to attack the offender, they seek the aid of their neighbours, appeal to the chief of the district, or the king, who seldom inflicts a heavier punishment than banishment, even for murder, which, however, is a crime very rarely committed by the natives.

Theft among themselves is severely punished. Formerly, when a garden or house had been robbed, and

the robbers were discovered, those whose goods had
been stolen repaired to the house or plantation of the
offenders, and *hao*, seized, whatever they could find.
This regulation was so well established, that though
the guilty party should be the strongest, they would not
dare to resist the retaliation; for, in the event of their
making any opposition, the people of a whole district
would support those who were thus punishing the individuals by whom theft had been perpetrated.

When robbery had been committed on the property
of a high chief, or to any great amount, the thief, in
some of the islands, was frequently bound hand and foot,
placed in an old decayed canoe, towed out to sea, and
turned adrift. The canoe speedily filled, and the culprit, being bound, soon sank beneath the waves.

Adultery among the highest ranks has been punished
with death by decapitation.

In the transactions of barter among themselves, there
are several regulations which they punctually observe.
No bargain was considered binding till the articles
were actually exchanged, and the respective owners expressed themselves satisfied. Afterward there was no
withdrawing, however injurious the bargain might be to
either party.

There is in the Sandwich Islands no class of men,
either peasants or mechanics, who are regularly employed as day-labourers, or who receive for their work
a stipulated payment, except those employed by foreigners. In hiring workmen to dig stone, burn lime,
build a house or canoe, &c., it is a common practice
among the natives themselves to make the bargain with
a petty chief, who requires the labour of all his dependants in its fulfilment. They usually pay beforehand;
and those who have received such remuneration are
bound, when called upon, to perform their work, or
have their property seized and their plantations plundered.

These and several similar regulations are generally
received, and govern the conduct of the people. The
king can dispense with any of them; but such conduct
would be contrary to the established usage, and is seldom done. The will of the king, however, being the
supreme law, the government is more or less arbitrary,
as his disposition is humane, or vindictive and cruel.
His power extends, not only over the property, but over

the liberty and lives, of the people. This power is delegated by him to the governors of the different islands, and by them again to the chiefs of the districts. A chief takes the life of one of his own people for any offence he may commit, and no one thinks he has a right to interfere. But though the power of the chiefs is so absolute over their own people, it extends no further. A chief dare not for any offence punish a man belonging to another, but must complain to the chief on whose land the offender resides.

The king is chief magistrate over the whole islands. The governors sustain the same office in the islands under their jurisdiction, and the chiefs of the districts are the arbitrators in all quarrels among their own people. A man dissatisfied with the decisions of his chief may appeal to the governor, and finally to the king. They have no regular police, but the king has generally a number of chiefs in attendance, who, with the assistance of their own dependants, execute his orders. The governors and high chiefs have the same, and employ them in a similar manner when occasion requires.

The house or front yard of the king or governor is the usual court of justice, and it is sometimes quite a court of equity. Judgment is seldom given till both parties are heard face to face. They have several ordeals for trying those accused of different crimes. One of the most singular is the *wai haruru*, shaking water. A large calabash or wooden dish of water is placed in the midst of a circle, on one side of which the accused party is seated. A prayer is offered by the priest; and the suspected individuals are required, one by one, to hold both hands, with the fingers spread out, over the dish, while the priest or the chief looks steadfastly at the face of the water; and it is said that when the person who has committed the crime spreads his hands over the vessel, the water trembles. Probably conscious guilt and superstitious dread may make the hands of the culprit shake, and occasion the tremulous appearance of the water in which they are reflected. No unnecessary delays take place in the redress of grievances or the administration of justice. I was once sitting with Karaimoku, when a poor woman came to complain of the chief of her district, who, she said, had kept the water running through his own plantation for several days, while the potatoes and taro in her garden were parched up with drought. After making a few inquiries, he called Kaiakoiri, one of his favourite chiefs, and said, " Go with this woman; and if the chief has kept back the water, open the channels, and let it flow over her field immediately." The chief girded up his *maro*, and, followed by the woman, set off for the district in which she resided.—No lawyers are employed to conduct their public trials; every man advocates his own cause, usually sitting cross-legged before the judge; and I have often been pleased with the address the different parties have displayed in exhibiting or enforcing their respective claims.

There is no national council, neither have the people any voice in the proceedings of government. But the king, though accountable to no one for the measures he adopts, seldom acts, in any affair of importance, without the advice of his confidential chiefs. These counsellors are in no degree responsible for the advice they give, nor liable to suffer from any conduct the king may pursue. He, however, always pays a deference to their opinion, and seldom acts in opposition to their wishes. In all matters of importance, it is customary to summon the governors and principal chiefs of the several islands to a national council, when the subject is freely discussed. Their deliberations are generally conducted with great privacy, and seldom known among the people till finally arranged, when they are promulgated throughout the island by the king's heralds or messengers. The king sends his orders directly to the governor of the island, or principal chief of the district. Formerly a courier bore a verbal message—now he carries a written despatch. The office of messenger, as well as that of herald, is hereditary, and considered honourable, as those who sustain it must necessarily have possessed the confidence of the king and chiefs.

The Hawaiian system of government—whether derived from the country whence the first settlers emigrated, or established by warlike chieftains in a subsequent period of their history, as an expedient to secure conquests, to command the services of their tenants on occasions of war, and to perpetuate the influence which military prowess or success in the first instance had given them—exhibits, in its decided monarchical character, the hereditary descent of rank and office, and other distinguishing features, considerable advancement from a state of barbarism, and warrants the conclusion that they have been an organized community for many generations.   But whatever antiquity their system may possess, they have made but little progress in the art of good government.   The well-being of the subject seems to have been but rarely regarded by the rulers, who appear to have considered the lower orders in general as a kind of property, to be employed only in promoting the interests of their superiors; and the ardent love of wealth which an acquaintance with the productions of foreign countries has excited in most of the chiefs has not improved the condition of the people.   Industry receives no encouragement; and even those whom natural energy of character would induce to cultivate a larger portion of land than was absolutely necessary for their bare subsistence, are deterred from the attempt by the apprehension of thereby exposing themselves to the rapacity of avaricious or necessitous chiefs.   Nothing can be more detrimental to the true interest of the chiefs and the civilization and happiness of the people than the abject dependence of the latter, the uncertain tenure of lands, the insecurity of personal property, the exactions of the chiefs, and the restrictions on trade with the shipping, which they impose.   As the nation in general becomes enlightened, it is to be presumed that the policy of the rulers will be more liberal, and the general prosperity of the islands proportionably advanced.

On the 31st, Mr. Thurston preached twice at Towaihae to attentive congregations—and with the labours of the day closed a month of toil and interest greater than any he had before spent in the Sandwich Islands.   In the retrospect, he could not but hope some good would result to the people.

Early on the 1st of September, Mr. Thurston left Towaihae in a canoe furnished by Mr. Young, and at eight in the forenoon reached the place where the Nio was lying at anchor, on board of which he joined Messrs. Goodrich and Bishop.   Soon after four in the afternoon, they weighed anchor and made sail.   When they left Hawaii, the master intended touching at Maui; but contrary winds obliged them to shape their course towards Oahu, where they safely arrived late in the evening of the 3d, and had the satisfaction of finding the mission family in the enjoyment of comfortable health

CHAPTER XVI.

Traditions respecting the origin of the islands—Marriage among the natives
—Account of foreigners who visited the Sandwich Islands before they were
discovered by Captain Cook—Preaching at Kairua—Traditions of a deluge
—Visit to Maui—Memoir of the late king and queen of the islands—Notice
of Boki, their principal attendant—Return to Oahu.

THE time which I spent at Kairua was, chiefly occupied in conversation with the governor on the history
and traditions of the island, the advantages of instruction, and the blessings which the general adoption of
Christianity would confer on the people. On this latter
subject the governor uniformly expressed his conviction
of its utility, and said he had therefore sent a messenger
round among the people, requesting them to renounce
their former evil practices, and keep the Sabbath according to the direction of the Word of God.

Adjacent to the governor's house stand the ruins of
Ahuena, an ancient heiau, where the war-god was often
kept, and human sacrifices offered. Since the abolition
of idolatry, the governor has converted it into a fort—
has widened the stone wall next the sea, and placed upon
it a number of cannon. The idols are all destroyed, excepting three, which are planted on the wall, one at
each end, and the other in the centre, where they stand
like sentinels amid the guns, as if designed, by their
frightful appearance, to terrify an enemy. On the 29th
I visited the ruins, and took a sketch of one of the idols,
which stood sixteen feet above the wall, was upwards
of three feet in breadth, and had been carved out of a
single tree.

The annexed figure may be considered as a fair specimen of the greater part of Hawaiian idols. The head
has generally a most horrid appearance, the mouth being
large, and usually extended wide, exhibiting a row of
large teeth, resembling in no small degree the cogs in
the wheel of an engine, and adapted to excite terror
rather than inspire confidence in the beholder. Some
of their idols were of stone, and many were constructed with a kind of wicker-work covered with red
feathers.

Hawaiian Idol.

In the evening our conversation at the governor's turnéd on the origin of the people of Hawaii and the other islands of the Pacific—a topic which often engaged our attention, and respecting which, in the various inquiries we made, we often had occasion to regret that the traditions of the natives furnished such scanty information on a subject so interesting and important.

This portion, however, though small, and surrounded
by an incredible mass of fiction, is still worth preserving.

The general opinions entertained by the natives themselves relative to their origin are, either that the first inhabitants were created on the islands, descended from the
gods by whom they were first inhabited, or that they came
from a country which they called Tahiti. Many, as was
the case with the chiefs at Maui, and also the governor
at this place, suppose that, according to the accounts
of the priests of Tane, Tanaroa, and other gods, the first
man was made by *Haumea*, a female deity. We have
not, however, met with any who pretend to know of
what material he was formed. Others, again, suppose
the chiefs to have descended from Akea, who appears
to have been the connecting link between the gods and
the men; but this supposes the chiefs and the common
people to have been derived from different sources. The
accounts they have of their ancestors having arrived in
a canoe from Tahiti are far more general and popular
among the people.

When some of our party were at Towaihae, the subject was discussed. Mr. Young said, among the many
traditionary accounts of the origin of the island and its
inhabitants, one was, that in former times, when there
was nothing but sea, an immense bird settled on the
water, and laid an egg, which, soon bursting, produced
the island of Hawaii. Shortly after this, a man and
woman, with a hog, a dog, and a pair of fowls, arrived
in a canoe from the Society Islands, took-up their abode
on the eastern shores, and were the progenitors of the
present inhabitants.

Another account prevalent among the natives of Oahu
states, that a number of persons arrived in a canoe from
Tahiti, and perceiving the Sandwich Islands were fertile, and inhabited only by gods or spirits, took up their
abode on one of them, having asked permission of the
gods, and presented an offering, which rendered them
propitious to their settlement.

Though these accounts do not prove that the Sandwich islanders came originally from the Georgian
Islands, they afford a strong presumption in favour of
such an opinion.

Tahiti is the name of the principal island in the group,
called by Captain Cook the Georgian Islands. It is the

Otaheite of Cook; the *Taïti* of Bougainville; and the *Taheitee*, or *Tahitee*, of Forster. In the language of the Georgian and Society Islands, the word *tahiti* also signifies to pull up or take out of the ground, as herbs or trees are taken up with a view to transplantation, and to select or extract passages from a book or language, to be translated into another. Hence a book of scripture extracts is called, words, *tahitihea*.

In the language of the Sandwich Islands, we do not know that the word is ever used in the latter sense, and very rarely in the former. It is generally employed to denote any foreign country, and seems equivalent to the English word *abroad*, as applied to parts beyond the sea. But though this is the signification of the word among the Sandwich islanders at the present time, it is probable that it was primarily used to designate the whole of the southern group, or the principal island among them; and it may lead us to infer, either that Tahiti and the Georgian and Society Islands were all the foreign countries the Hawaiians were acquainted with, or that they considered the Marquesian Islands contiguous, and politically connected with them, and that these being the only foreign countries originally known to them, they have applied the term to every other part with which they have subsequently become acquainted. In some of the ancient traditions of the Society islanders, Opoa in Raiatea, the most celebrated place in the islands, the birth-place of Oro, and the spot where the human species were created, &c., is called *Hawaii*.

It is an opinion generally received, that the various tribes inhabiting the islands of the Pacific have an Asiatic, and probably a Malayan, origin. Applied to a great part of them, this opinion is supported by a variety of facts; but with respect to those groups with which we are acquainted, additional evidence appears necessary to confirm such a conclusion.

The natives of the eastern part of New-Holland, and the intertropical islands within thirty degrees east, including New-Caledonia, the New-Hebrides, and the Figiis, appear to be one nation, and in all probability came originally from the Asiatic islands to the northward, as their skin is black, and their hair woolly or crisped, like the inhabitants of the mountainous parts of several of the Asiatic islands. But the inhabitants

of all the islands to the east of the Figiis, including the
Friendly Islands and New-Zealand, though they have
many characteristics in common with these, have a
number essentially distinct.

The natives of Chatham Island and New-Zealand, in
the south; the Sandwich Islands, in the north; the
Friendly Islands, in the west; and all the intermediate
islands, as far as Easter Island, in the east, are one
people. Their mythology, traditions, manners and customs, language, and physical appearance, in their main
features, are, so far as we have had an opportunity of
becoming acquainted with them, identically the same,
yet differing in many respects from those of the islands
to the westward of Tongatabu.

The dress of the Figiians, &c. is not the same as that
of the natives of New-Zealand, Tahiti, and the other
islands; they do not appear to wear the cloak, or the
tiputa. In war, they throw long spears to a considerable distance, and use the bow and arrow, which the
others only employ in their amusements.

The difference in their physical character is greater;
the dark complexion, woolly hair, and slender make,
indicate them to be a different people.

Various points of resemblance have been shown between the aborigines of America and the natives of the
eastern islands of the Pacific, in their modes of war,
instruments, gymnastic games, rafts or canoes, treatment of their children, dressing their hair, feather head-
dresses of the chiefs, girdles, and particularly the *tiputa*
of the latter, which, in shape and use, exactly resembles
the *poncho* of the Peruvians.

These circumstances seem to favour the conjecture
that the inhabitants of the islands west of Tongatabu
have an Asiatic origin entirely; but that the natives of
the eastern islands may be a mixed race, who have
emigrated from the American continent, and from the
Asiatic islands; that the proximity of the Friendly and
Figii Islands may have given both a variety of words
and usages in common, while the people to which the
former belong have remained in many respects distinct.

The nation inhabiting the eastern parts of the Pacific
has spread itself over an immense tract of ocean, extending upwards of seventy degrees north and south
from New-Zealand and Chatham Island to the Sandwich
group, and between sixty and seventy degrees east and

west from Tongatabu to Easter Island. This last is not farther from the islands adjacent to the continent than some of these groups are from any other inhabited island. The Sandwich Islands are above twenty degrees from the Marquesas, and thirty-six from Tahiti, yet inhabited by the same race of people.

The day after the conversation took place which led to the above remarks, the pilot-boat arrived at Kairua, on her way to Maui. On first coming to anchor, *Kahiori*, the master, said he should sail in the evening; but when I told him I would go with him, if he would wait till the Sabbath was over, he cheerfully agreed to do so. By him the governor received a note on business, written by Kamakau, the interesting chief of Kaavaroa, which, after he had read it, he showed me, saying he admired the diligence and perseverance of Kamakau, who, with but little instruction, had learned to write very well. "This letter-writing," added the governor, "is a very good thing." It also appears to them a most surprising art, which, till they saw what had been acquired by the natives of the southern islands, they imagined could never be attained by persons in their circumstances. Supposing it beyond the powers of man to invent the plan of communicating words by marks on paper, they have sometimes asked us, if, in the first instance, the knowledge of it were not communicated to mankind by God himself.

In the governor's family is an interesting girl, who is called his daughter, and has been spoken of as the future consort of the young prince Kauikeoule, instead of Nahienaena, his sister.

Marriage contracts in the Sandwich Islands are usually concluded by the parents or relations of both parties, or by the man and the parents or friends of the woman.

We are not aware that the parents of the woman receive any thing from the husband, or give any dowry with the wife. Their ceremonies on the occasion are very few, and chiefly consist in the bridegroom's casting a piece of tapa or native cloth over the bride, in the presence of her parents or relations. Feasting is general, and the friends of both parties contribute towards furnishing the entertainment.

The marriage tie is loose, and the husband can dismiss his wife on any occasion.

O 2

' The number of males is much greater than that of females in all the islands, in consequence of the girls being more frequently destroyed in infancy, as less useful than the males for purposes of war, fishing, &c. We do not know the exact proportion here; but in the Society Islands, in all our early schools, the proportion of girls to boys was as three to four, or four to five, though, since the abolition of infanticide, the numbers are equal.

Polygamy is allowed among all ranks, but practised only by the chiefs, whose means enable them to maintain a plurality of wives.

Among the higher ranks, marriage seems to be conducted on principles of political expediency, with a view to strengthen alliances and family influence; and among the reigning family, brothers and sisters marry. This custom, so revolting to every idea of moral propriety that the mind is shocked at the thought of its existence, appears to have been long in use; and very recently a marriage was proposed at Maui, between the young prince and princess, both children of the same parents: a council of chiefs was held on the subject, and all were favourable. The opinion of the missionaries was asked. The chiefs assigned as a reason, that, being the highest chiefs in the islands, they could not marry any others who were their equals, and ought not to form any alliances with inferiors, as it was desirable that the supreme rank they held should descend to their posterity. They were told that such marriages were forbidden in the Word of God, were held in abhorrence by all civilized and Christian nations, and had seldom been known to leave any descendants to wear the honour or sustain the rank the contracting parties desired thus to perpetuate.

Several of the chiefs present made no profession of Christianity, and consequently were uninfluenced by some of the remarks; but the concluding observation appeared of importance to them all. They said they thought there was some truth in it; that the late king Tamehameha, father of Rihoriho, had several wives who were his near relations, and even his daughter-in-law, yet left no children, except those of whom Keopuolani was the mother, and who, though a sacred chief of higher rank than her husband, was the granddaughter of a princess of another island, and distantly connected with his family, and that the same was the case with Rihoriho.

The marriage was postponed; and it appears to be the opinion of the chiefs in general that it ought not to take place. The individuals themselves are entirely passive in the affair; and we view it as a happy circumstance, subversive of an evil custom, and tending to produce moral feelings highly advantageous, and illustrative of the collateral advantages arising from the influence of Christian missionaries.

An interesting conversation took place this evening, relative to the first visits the islanders received from foreigners. The possession of pieces of iron, particularly one supposed to be the point of a broadsword, by the natives of Tauai (Atooi), when discovered by Captain Cook, induced some of his companions to think they were not the first European visiters to the islands. We have endeavoured to ascertain, by inquiring of the most intelligent of the natives, whether or not this was the fact.

They have three accounts of foreigners arriving at Hawaii prior to Capt. Cook. The first was the priest Paao, who landed at Kohala, and to whom the priests of that neighbourhood traced their genealogy until very recently. Of this priest some account is given in a preceding chapter.

The second account states, that during the lifetime of Opiri, the son of Paao, a number of foreigners (white men), arrived at Hawaii, landed somewhere in the southwest part of the island, and repaired to the mountains, where they took up their abode. The natives regarded them with a superstitious curiosity and dread, and knew not whether to consider them as gods or men. Opiri was sent for by the king of that part of the island where they were residing, and consulted as to the conduct to be observed towards them. According to his advice, a large present of provisions was cooked and carried to them. Opiri led the procession, accompanied by several men, each carrying a bamboo cane, with a piece of white native cloth tied to the end of it. When the strangers saw them approaching their retreat, they came out to meet them. The natives placed the baked pigs and potatoes, &c. on the grass, fixed their white banners in the ground, and then retreated a few paces. The foreigners approached. Opiri addressed them. They answered, received the presents, and afterward conversed with the people through the medium of Opiri. The facility with which they could communicate their thoughts by means of Opiri, the governor said, was attributed to the supposed influence of Opiri with his gods. The foreigners, they imagined, were supernatural beings, and, as such, were treated with every possible mark of respect. After remaining some time on the island, they returned to their own country. No account is preserved of the kind of vessel in which they arrived or departed. The name of the principal person among them was Manahini; and it is a singular fact, that in the Marquesian, Society, and Sandwich Islands the term manahini is still employed to designate a stranger, visiter, or guest.

The third account is much more recent and precise, though the period at which it took place is uncertain.

It states, that a number of years after the departure of *Manahini-ma* (Manahini and his party), in the reign of Kahoukapu, king at Kaavaroa, seven foreigners arrived at Kearake'kua bay, the spot where Captain Cook landed. They came in a painted boat, with an awning or canopy over the stern, but without mast or sails. They were all dressed; the colour of their clothes was white or yellow, and one of them wore a *pahi*, long knife, the name by which they still call a sword, at his side, and had a feather in his hat. The natives received them kindly. They married native women, were made chiefs, proved themselves warriors, and ultimately became very powerful in the island of Hawaii, which, it is said, was for some time governed by them.

There are in the Sandwich Islands a number of persons distinguished by a lighter colour in their skin, and corresponding brown curly hair, called *ehu*, who are, by all the natives of the islands, considered as the descendants of these foreigners, who acknowledge themselves to be such, and esteem their origin by no means dishonourable.

Another party is said to have afterward arrived at the same place, but the accounts the natives give of their landing are not very distinct; and we feel undecided whether there were two distinct parties, or only two different accounts of the same event.

We have heard from one of the chiefs of Hawaii that there is a tradition of a ship having touched at the island

of Maui prior to the arrival of Captain Cook ; but, with the exception of this chief, all the natives we have conversed with on the subject, and we have conversed with many, declare that they had no idea of a ship before Capt. Cook was seen off Tauai. The ship they called *motu*, an island, probably supposing it was an island with all its inhabitants.

Marvellous reports respecting the ships and people were circulated through the islands, between the first discovery off Tauai and the return of the vessels from the north-west coast of America. *Aa mo*, skin of lizard's egg, a native of Tauai, who was on board one of the ships, procured a piece of canvass about a yard and a half long, which Tiha, king of Tauai, sent as a present to Poriorani, king of Oahu. He gave it to his queen Opuhani, by whom it was worn on the most conspicuous part of her dress in a public procession, and attracted more attention than any thing else. The piece of cloth was called Aa mo, after the man who had the honour of bringing it from the ships.

The most unaccountable circumstance connected with the priest Paao is his arriving alone, though he might be the only survivor of his party. If such a person ever did arrive, we should think he was a Roman Catholic priest, and the reported gods an image and a crucifix.

The different parties that subsequently arrived were probably, if any inference may be drawn from the accounts of the natives, survivors of the crew of some Spanish ship wrecked in the neighbourhood, perhaps on the numerous reefs to the north-west ; or they might have been culprits committed by their countrymen to the mercy of the waves. The circumstance of the first party leaving the island in the same boat in which they arrived would lead us to suppose they had been wrecked, and had escaped in their boat, or had constructed a bark out of the wreck of their ship, as has subsequently been the case with two vessels wrecked in the vicinity of these islands.

It is possible that one or other of the islands might have been seen by some Spanish ship passing between Acapulco and Manilla ; but it is not probable that they were ever visited by any of these ships. An event so interesting to the people would not have been left out of their traditions, which contain many things much less important; and had the Spaniards discovered them, however jealous they might be of such a discovery becoming known to other nations, that jealousy would not have prevented their availing themselves of the facilities which the islands afforded for refitting or recruiting their vessels, which must frequently have been most desirable during the period their ships were accustomed to traverse these seas.

These accounts, but particularly the latter, are generally known, and have been related by different persons at distant places. All agree respecting the boat, clothing, sword, &c. of the party who arrived at Kearake'kua. Among others, the late king Rihoriho gave us a detailed account of their landing, &c. only a short time before he embarked for England. We feel but little doubt of the fact; but the country whence they came, the place whither they were bound, the occasion of their visit, and a variety of interesting particulars connected therewith, will probably remain undiscovered.

The 31st was the Sabbath. The stillness of every thing around, the decent apparel of those who were seen passing and repassing, together with the numbers of canoes all drawn up on the beach, under the shade of the cocoanut or kou-trees, combined to mark the return of the *la tabu*, or sacred day. An unusual number attended family prayers at the governor's house in the morning; and at half-past ten the bell was rung for public worship. About eight hundred people assembled under the ranai, and I preached to them from Heb. xi. 7. And after a succinct account of the deluge, I endeavoured to exhibit the advantages of faith, and the consequences of wickedness and unbelief, as illustrated in the salvation of Noah and the destruction of the rest of mankind.

After the conclusion of the service, several persons present requested me to remain till they had made some inquiries respecting the deluge, Noah, &c.

They said they were informed by their fathers that all the land had once been overflowed by the sea, except a small peak on the top of Mouna Kea, where two human beings were preserved from the destruction that overtook the rest; but they said they had never before heard of a ship, or of Noah, having always been accustomed

to call it the *kai a Kahinárii* (sea of Kahinárii). After conversing with them some time, I returned to the governor's.

The afternoon was principally employed in conversation with him on the flood, and the repeopling of the earth by the descendants of Noah. The governor seemed to doubt whether it were possible that the Hawaiians could be the descendants of Noah; but said he thought their progenitors must have been created on the islands. I told him the account in the Bible had every evidence that could be wished to support it; referred him to his own traditions, not only of Hawaii having been peopled by persons who came in canoes from a foreign country, but of their having in their turn visited other islands and planted colonies, as in the days of Kamapiikai—the superiority of their war-canoes in former days—the resemblance in manners, customs, traditions, and language between themselves and other islanders in the Pacific, many thousand miles distant.

The longevity of mankind in the days of Noah also surprised him. Comparing it with the period of human life at the present time, he said, "By-and-by men will not live more than forty years."

At half-past four in the afternoon the bell rang again, and the people collected in numbers about equal to those who attended in the morning. I preached to them from the words, "Be not weary in well-doing, for in due season ye shall reap, if ye faint not"

Numbers thronged the governor's house at evening worship. The conversation afterward turned upon the identity of the body at the resurrection, and the reward of the righteous in heaven. The governor asked if people would know each other in heaven; and when answered in the affirmative, said he thought Christian relations would be very happy when they met there. Some who were present asked, "If there is no eating and drinking or wearing of clothes in heaven, wherein does its goodness consist?" This was a natural question for a Hawaiian to ask; who never had an idea of happiness, except in the gratification of his natural appetites and feelings. In answer to the question, they were, however, informed that the joys of heaven were intellectual and spiritual, and would infinitely exceed, both in their nature and duration, every earthly enjoyment. At a late hour I took leave of the governor and

his family, thanking him at the same time for the hospitable entertainment we had received, and the great
facilities he had afforded for accomplishing the objects
of our visit.

About three o'clock in the morning, being awoke by
the shouts of the men who were heaving up the anchor
of the pilot-boat, I repaired on board, and immediately
afterward we sailed with a gentle breeze blowing from
the land. The wind was light and baffling, and it was
noon before we reached Towaihae, where I learned with
disappointment that the Nio had sailed to Oahu. On
landing I was welcomed by Mr. Young, with whom I
remained till the pilot-boat was ready to sail for Lahaina.

Late in the evening of the 2d of September, after
preaching to the people of the place at Mr. Young's
house, I went again on board the pilot-boat, but found
her so full of sandal-wood that there was not room for
any person below, while the decks were crowded with
natives. The weather was unfavourable for getting
under way till nearly daylight; and every person on
board was completely drenched by the heavy rain that
fell during the night.

During the forenoon of the 3d, we drifted slowly to
the northward, and about noon took in eight hundred
dried fish, after which we made sail for Maui. The
weather was warm, the wind light; and all on board
being obliged to keep on deck, without any screen or
shade from the scorching rays of a vertical sun, the
situation was very uncomfortable. At three P. M. we
took the channel-breeze, which soon wafted us across to
the south-east part of Maui.

As the shores of Hawaii receded from my view, a
variety of reflections insensibly arose in my mind. The
tour which, in the society of my companions, I had made
had been replete with interest. The varied and sublime
phenomena of nature had elevated our conceptions of
"nature's God;" the manners and customs of the inhabitants had increased our interest in their welfare;
while their superstition, moral degradation, ignorance,
and vice had called forth our sincerest commiseration.
We had made known the nature and consequences of
sin, spoken of the love of God, and had exhibited the
Lord Jesus Christ as the only Saviour to multitudes
who had never before heard his name, or been directed

to worship the holy and living God, and who would probably never hear these truths again. We cherish the hope that, under the Divine blessing, lasting good will result, even from this transient visit.

Many of the individuals we have met on these occasions, we shall in all probability meet no more till the morning of the resurrection. May we meet them then on the right-hand of the Son of God?

At sunset we arrived off Morokini, but were shortly after becalmed. The current, however, was in our favour through the night, and at daylight on the 4th we found ourselves off the east end of the district of Lahaina, and about a mile distant from the shore. Many of the natives jumped into the sea, and swam to the beach, holding their clothes above their heads with one hand, and swimming with the other.

On landing I waited on Keopuolani, the king's mother, whom I found ill; Karaimoku, Kaahumanu, Kalakua, and several other chiefs were reclining around her, weeping. After some time, Karaimoku proposed that they should unitedly pray for her recovery, and his proposal was acceded to.

Towards evening I visited the governor of the island, and also the king, who was then at Maui. The subsequent voyage of the latter to Great Britain, accompanied by his queen, and the melancholy event which terminated their lives while in London, excited considerable interest, and will probably be considered sufficient apology for a short account of them, although the event took place after my visit to Maui at this time.

The late king of the Sandwich Islands was the son of Tamehameha, former king, and Keopuolani, daughter of Kauikeouli, and Kakuiapoiwa. He was born in the eastern part of Hawaii, in the year 1795 or 1796. The name by which he was generally known was *Rihoriho*, which was only a contraction of *Kalaninui-rihoriho*, literally, the heaven's great black—from *Ka lani*, the heavens, *nui*, great, and *rihoriho*, applied to any thing burned to blackness. On public occasions he was sometimes called Tamehameha, after his father, though names are not always hereditary. Besides these, he had a variety of other names, the most common of which was *Iolani*. The word *lani*, heaven or sky, formed a component part

in the name of most chiefs of distinction. The following is a fac-simile of the official signature of the late
king.

The early habits of Rihoriho did not warrant any
great expectations. His natural disposition was frank,
and humane. The natives always spoke of him as
good-natured, except when he was under the influence
of ardent spirits; his manners were perfectly free, at
the same time dignified, and always agreeable to those
who were about him. His mind was naturally inquisitive. The questions he usually presented to foreigners
were by no means trifling; and his memory was retentive. His general knowledge of the world was much
greater than could have been expected. I have heard
him entertain a party of chiefs for hours together with
accounts of different parts of the earth, describing the
extensive lakes, the mountains, and mines of North and
South America—the elephants and inhabitants of India
—the houses, manufactures, &c. of England—with no
small accuracy, considering he had never seen them.
He had a great thirst for knowledge, and was diligent in
his studies. I recollect his remarking one day, when
he opened his writing-desk, that he expected more advantage from that desk than from a fine brig belonging
to him, lying at anchor opposite the house in which we
were sitting. Mr. Bingham and myself were his daily
teachers, and have often been surprised at his unwearied
perseverance. I have sat beside him at his desk sometimes from nine or ten o'clock in the morning till nearly
sunset, during which period his pen or his book has not
been out of his hand more than three-quarters of an
hour, while he was at dinner.

We do not know that Christianity exerted any decisive influence on his heart. He was willing to receive
the missionaries on their first arrival—availed himself
of their knowledge, to increase his own—and, during

the latter years of his life, was decidedly favourable to
their object; declared his conviction of the truth of
Christianity; attended public worship himself on the
Sabbath, and recommended the same to his people.

His moral character was not marked by that cruelty,
rapacity, and insensibility to the sufferings of the people,
which frequently distinguish the abitrary chiefs of uncivilized nations. He appears in general to have been
kind; and, in several places on our tour, the mothers
showed us their children, and told us that when Rihoriho passed that way, he had kissed them—a condescension they seemed to think much of, and which they
will probably remember to the end of their days. But,
though generous in his disposition, and humane in his
conduct towards his subjects, he was addicted to intoxication—whether from natural inclination or the influence
and example of others is not now to be determined;
frequently, to my own knowledge, it has been entirely
from the latter. Had he in early life been privileged to
associate with individuals whose conduct and principles
were favourable to virtue and religion, there is every
reason to suppose his moral character, with respect at
least to this vice, would have been as irreproachable as
his mental habits were commendable. But, alas for
him! it was quite the reverse.

Though not distinguished by the ardour and strength
of character so conspicuous in his father, he possessed
both decision and enterprise: the abolition of the national idolatry was a striking instance of the former;
and his voyage to England, of the latter.

The motives by which he was induced to undertake
a voyage so long and hazardous were highly commendable. They were—a desire to see for himself countries
of which he had heard such various and interesting
accounts; a wish to have a personal interview with his
majesty the king of Great Britain, or the chief members of the British government—for the purpose of
confirming the cession of the Sandwich Islands, and
placing himself and his dominions under British protection.

It was also his intention to make himself acquainted
with the tenor and forms of administering justice in the
courts of law, the principles of commerce, and other
subjects important to the welfare of the islands.

The melancholy death of the late king and queen,

which took place shortly after their arrival in England,
not only prevented the full accomplishment of these
desirable objects, but awakened very generally a degree
of apprehension that the people of the islands, unacquainted with the true circumstances of their death,
would be led to suppose they had been neglected, unkindly treated, or even poisoned in revenge of the death
of Captain Cook, and that the feelings of friendship
with which they had been accustomed to regard the
people of England might be followed by enmity or distrust. The fears of those who felt interested in the
welfare of the Hawaiians, though natural, were groundless. The British government had entertained the
young ruler of the Sandwich Islands, his consort, and
attendants with its accustomed hospitality; and when
they were attacked by diseases incident to a northern
climate, but unknown in their native islands, every attention that humanity could suggest, and every alleviation
that the first medical skill in London could afford, was
most promptly rendered. After their decease, the highest respect was paid to their remains, and in honourable
regard to the feelings of the nation who had suffered this
painful bereavement, a British frigate, under the command of Captain Lord Byron, was appointed to convey to
the Sandwich Islands the bodies of the king and queen,
that their sorrowing people might have the mournful
satisfaction of depositing their ashes among the tombs
of their ancestors.

By the return of a highly esteemed missionary friend,
Rev. C. S. Stewart, I have learned that the Blonde
reached the islands in the month of May, 1825: the
natives were in some degree prepared for the arrival, by
the intelligence of the death of their king and queen,
which they had received about two months before from
Valparaiso. Shortly after, the vessel having the remains
of the king and queen on board had anchored off Oahu,
Boki, the principal chief, who had accompanied the
king to England, attended by those of his countrymen
who had also returned, proceeded on shore: on landing,
he was met by his elder brother Karaimoku, and other
distinguished chiefs, and after the first emotions of joy
at meeting again, and sorrow on account of the loss all
had sustained, were somewhat abated, the survivors
and their friends walked in solemn and mournful procession to the place of worship, where thanksgivings
were presented to God, for the merciful preservation

of those who were thus privileged to meet again, and supplications were made that the afflicting dispensation, which all so deeply felt, might exert a salutary influence in the minds of the surviving chiefs, and the sorrowing nation at large.

Karaimoku, the late prime minister, and present regent of the islands, then arose and said, "We have lost our king and queen, they have died in a foreign land; we shall see them no more; it is right that we should weep, but let us not entertain hard thoughts of God. *God has not done wrong.* The evil is with us: let us bow under his hand; let all amusement cease; let our daily avocations be suspended; and let the nation, by prayer and a cessation from ordinary pursuits, humble itself before God fourteen days." Before the assembly separated, Boki stood up, and, in a brief outline of the voyage, narrated the most prominent events that had transpired since his departure from the islands —calling their attention in particular to the suitable and important advice he had received from his majesty the king of Great Britain, in an audience with which he was graciously favoured, viz. To return to his native country, attend to general and religious instruction himself, and endeavour to enlighten and reform the people. The peculiar circumstances of the people at this time, the increased satisfaction they had for some time felt in attending every means of instruction within their reach, and the pleasing change in favour of religion which many had experienced, rendered this recommendation, so congenial to their feelings, from a source so distinguished, unusually acceptable. A deep and favourable impression was produced on all present, a new impulse was given to the means already employed for the instruction and improvement of the people, from which most advantageous results have already appeared. They were also made acquainted, by Boki and his companions, with the kind reception, generous treatment, and marked attentions which the late king and queen and their suite had received while in England. This intelligence, communicated by those whose testimony would be received with the most entire credence, would at once confirm the attachment and confidence they have so long felt towards England.

No disturbance of the general tranquillity, nor change in the government, of the islands has resulted from this

event. Rihoriho' left a younger brother, *Kauikeouli,*
about ten years of age, who is acknowledged by the
chiefs as his successor. A regency will govern during
his minority, and the executive authority will probably
continue to be exercised by *Karaimoku,* and the other
chiefs with whom Rihoriho left it when he embarked
for England.

The queen, who accompanied him, and who died at the
same time, has left a fond mother and an affectionate
people to lament her loss: she was the daughter of
Tamehameha and Talakua, and was born about the
year 1797 or 1798, being two years younger than Rihoriho, and about twenty-six years of age when she
left the islands. Like all the persons of distinction she
had many names, but that by which she was generally
known was *Kamehamaru* (shade of Kameha), from *kameha,* a contraction of her father's name, and *maru,* shade.
She was distinguished for good nature, and was much
beloved by all her subjects. The poor people, when
unable to pay their rent, or under the displeasure of the
king and chiefs, or embarrassed on any other account,
frequently repaired to her, and found a friend whose aid
was never refused. She was also kind to those foreigners who might be distressed in the islands, and though
she never harboured any or countenanced their absconding from their ships, she has often fed them when
hungry, and given them native tapa for clothing.

Kamehamaru was at all times lively and agreeable in
company; and though her application to her book and
her pen was equal to that of the king, her improvement
in learning was more gradual, and her general knowledge less extensive.

She excelled, however, in the management of his
domestic affairs, which were conducted by her with
great judgment and address, and, though formerly accustomed to use ardent spirits, from the time she put herself under Christian instruction, she entirely discontinued that and every other practice inconsistent with
her profession of Christianity. Her attendance on the
duties of religion was maintained with commendable
regularity.

Her influence contributed very materially to the pleasing change that has recently taken place, in connexion
with the labours of the missionaries in the islands. For
the instruction and moral improvement of the people,

she manifested no ordinary concern. Long before many of the leading chiefs were favourable to the instruction of the people or their reception of Christianity, Kamehamaru on every suitable occasion recommended to her own servants to serve Jehovah the living God, and attend to every means of improvement within their reach. It was truly pleasing to observe, so soon after she had embraced Christianity herself, an anxiety to induce her people to follow her example. At Honoruru she erected a school, in which upwards of forty children and young persons, principally connected with her establishment, were daily taught to read and write, and instructed in the first principles of religion, by a native teacher, whom she almost entirely supported. In this school she took a lively interest, and marked the progress of the scholars with evident satisfaction; in order to encourage the pupils, she frequently visited the school during the hours of instruction, accompanied by a number of chief women. She also attended the public examinations, and noticed those who on these occasions excelled, frequently presenting a favourite scholar with a slate, a copy-book, pencil, pen, or some other token of her approbation.

In her death the missionaries have lost a sincere friend, and her subjects a queen who always delighted to alleviate their distresses and promote their interests.

Her disposition was affectionate. I have seen her and the king sitting beside the couch of Keopuolani, her mother-in-law, day after day, when the latter has been ill; and on these occasions, though there might be several servants in constant attendance, she would allow no individual but her husband or herself to hand to the patient any thing she might want, or even fan the flies from her person.

The circumstances attending her departure from the islands were peculiarly affecting. The king had gone on board L'Aigle; but the boat was waiting to convey her to the ship. She arose from the mat on which she had been reclining; embraced her mother and other relations most affectionately, and passed through the crowd towards the boat. The people fell down on their knees as she walked along, pressing and saluting her feet—frequently bathing them with tears of unfeigned sorrow—and making loud wailings, in which

their traditions, which contain many things much less important ; and had the Spaniards discovered them, however jealous they might be of such a discovery becoming known to other nations, that jealousy would not have prevented their availing themselves of the facilities which the islands afforded for refitting or recruiting their vessels, which must frequently have been most desirable during the period their ships were accustomed to traverse these seas.

These accounts, but particularly the latter, are generally known, and have been related by different persons at distant places. All agree respecting the boat, clothing, sword, &c. of the party who arrived at Kearake'kua. Among others, the late king Rihoriho gave us a detailed account of their landing, &c. only a short time before he embarked for England. We feel but little doubt of the fact.; but the country whence they came, the place whither they were bound, the occasion of their visit, and a variety of interesting particulars connected therewith, will probably remain undiscovered.

The 31st was the Sabbath. The stillness of every thing around, the decent apparel of those who were seen passing and repassing, together with the numbers of canoes all drawn up on the beach, under the shade of the cocoanut or kou-trees, combined to mark the return of the *la tabu*, or sacred day. An unusual number attended family prayers at the governor's house in the morning; and at half-past ten the bell was rung for public worship. About eight hundred people assembled under the ranai, and I preached to them from Heb. xi. 7. And after a succinct account of the deluge, I endeavoured to exhibit the advantages of faith, and the consequences of wickedness and unbelief, as illustrated in the salvation of Noah and the destruction of the rest of mankind.

After the conclusion of the service, several persons present requested me to remain till they had made some inquiries respecting the deluge, Noah, &c.

They said they were informed by their fathers that all the land had once been overflowed by the sea, except a small peak on the top of Mouna Kea, where two human beings were preserved from the destruction that overtook the rest ; but they said they had never before heard of a ship, or of Noah, having always been accustomed

to call it the *kai a Kahinárii* (sea of Kahinárii). After conversing with them some time, I returned to the governor's.

The afternoon was principally employed in conversation with him on the flood, and the repeopling of the earth by the descendants of Noah. The governor seemed to doubt whether it were possible that the Hawaiians could be the descendants of Noah; but said he thought their progenitors must have been created on the islands. I told him the account in the Bible had every evidence that could be wished to support it; referred him to his own traditions, not only of Hawaii having been peopled by persons who came in canoes from a foreign country, but of their having in their turn visited other islands and planted colonies, as in the days of Kamapiikai—the superiority of their war-canoes in former days—the resemblance in manners, customs, traditions, and language between themselves and other islanders in the Pacific, many thousand miles distant.

The longevity of mankind in the days of Noah also surprised him. Comparing it with the period of human life at the present time, he said, "By-and-by men will not live more than forty years."

At half-past four in the afternoon the bell rang again, and the people collected in numbers about equal to those who attended in the morning. I preached to them from the words, " Be not weary in well-doing, for in due season ye shall reap, if ye faint not "

Numbers thronged the governor's house at evening worship. The conversation afterward turned upon the identity of the body at the resurrection, and the reward of the righteous in heaven. The governor asked if people would know each other in heaven; and when answered in the affirmative, said he thought Christian relations would be very happy when they met there. Some who were present asked, " If there is no eating and drinking or wearing of clothes in heaven, wherein does its goodness consist ?" This was a natural question for a Hawaiian to ask; who never had an idea of happiness, except in the gratification of his natural appetites and feelings. In answer to the question, they were, however, informed that the joys of heaven were intellectual and spiritual, and would infinitely exceed, both in their nature and duration, every earthly enjoyment. At a late hour I took leave of the governor and

his family, thanking him at the same time for the hospitable entertainment we had received; and the great facilities he had afforded for accomplishing the objects of our visit.

About three o'clock in the morning, being awoke by the shouts of the men who were heaving up the anchor of the pilot-boat, I repaired on board, and immediately afterward we sailed with a gentle breeze blowing from the land. The wind was light and baffling, and it was noon before we reached Towaihae, where I learned with disappointment that the Nio had sailed to Oahu. On landing I was welcomed by Mr. Young, with whom I remained till the pilot-boat was ready to sail for Lahaina.

Late in the evening of the 2d of September, after preaching to the people of the place at Mr. Young's house, I went again on board the pilot-boat, but found her so full of sandal-wood that there was not room for any person below, while the decks were crowded with natives. The weather was unfavourable for getting under way till nearly daylight; and every person on board was completely drenched by the heavy rain that fell during the night.

During the forenoon of the 3d, we drifted slowly to the northward, and about noon took in eight hundred dried fish, after which we made sail for Maui. The weather was warm, the wind light; and all on board being obliged to keep on deck, without any screen or shade from the scorching rays of a vertical sun, the situation was very uncomfortable. At three P. M. we took the channel-breeze, which soon wafted us across to the south-east part of Maui.

As the shores of Hawaii receded from my view, a variety of reflections insensibly arose in my mind. The tour which, in the society of my companions, I had made had been replete with interest. The varied and sublime phenomena of nature had elevated our conceptions of "nature's God;" the manners and customs of the inhabitants had increased our interest in their welfare; while their superstition, moral degradation, ignorance, and vice had called forth our sincerest commiseration. We had made known the nature and consequences of sin, spoken of the love of God, and had exhibited the Lord Jesus Christ as the only Saviour to multitudes who had never before heard his name, or been directed

to worship the holy and living God, and who would probably never hear these truths again. We cherish the hope that, under the Divine blessing, lasting good will result, even from this transient visit.

Many of the individuals we have met on these occasions, we shall in all probability meet no more till the morning of the resurrection. May we meet them then on the right-hand of the Son of God!

At sunset we arrived off Morokini, but were shortly after becalmed. The current, however, was in our favour through the night, and at daylight on the 4th we found ourselves off the east end of the district of Lahaina, and about a mile distant from the shore. Many of the natives jumped into the sea, and swam to the beach, holding their clothes above their heads with one hand, and swimming with the other.

On landing I waited on Keopuolani, the king's mother, whom I found ill; Karaimoku, Kaahumanu, Kalakua, and several other chiefs were reclining around her, weeping. After some time, Karaimoku proposed that they should unitedly pray for her recovery, and his proposal was acceded to.

Towards evening I visited the governor of the island, and also the king, who was then at Maui. The subsequent voyage of the latter to Great Britain, accompanied by his queen, and the melancholy event which terminated their lives while in London, excited considerable interest, and will probably be considered sufficient apology for a short account of them, although the event took place after my visit to Maui at this time.

The late king of the Sandwich Islands was the son of Tamehameha, former king, and Keopuolani, daughter of Kauikeouli, and Kakuiapoiwa. He was born in the eastern part of Hawaii, in the year 1795 or 1796. The name by which he was generally known was *Rihoriho*, which was only a contraction of *Kalaninui-rihoriho*, literally, the heaven's great black—from *Ka lani*, the heavens, *nui*, great, and *rihoriho*, applied to any thing burned to blackness. On public occasions he was sometimes called Tamehameha, after his father, though names are not always hereditary. Besides these, he had a variety of other names, the most common of which was *Iolani*. The word *lani*, heaven or sky, formed a component part

in the name of most chiefs of distinction. The following is a fac-simile of the official signature of the late
king.

Tamehameha

The early habits of Rihoriho did not warrant any
great expectations. His natural disposition was frank,
and humane. The natives always spoke of him as
good-natured, except when he was under the influence
of ardent spirits; his manners were perfectly free, at
the same time dignified, and always agreeable to those
who were about him. His mind was naturally inquisitive. The questions he usually presented to foreigners
were by no means trifling; and his memory was retentive. His general knowledge of the world was much
greater than could have been expected. I have heard
him entertain a party of chiefs for hours together with
accounts of different parts of the earth, describing the
extensive lakes, the mountains, and mines of North and
South America—the elephants and inhabitants of India
—the houses, manufactures, &c. of England—with no
small accuracy, considering he had never seen them.
He had a great thirst for knowledge, and was diligent in
his studies. I recollect his remarking one day, when
he opened his writing-desk, that he expected more advantage from that desk than from a fine brig belonging
to him, lying at anchor opposite the house in which we
were sitting. Mr. Bingham and myself were his daily
teachers, and have often been surprised at his unwearied
perseverance. I have sat beside him at his desk sometimes from nine or ten o'clock in the morning till nearly
sunset, during which period his pen or his book has not
been out of his hand more than three-quarters of an
hour, while he was at dinner.
  We do not know that Christianity exerted any decisive influence on his heart. He was willing to receive
the missionaries on their first arrival—availed himself
of their knowledge, to increase his own—and, during

the latter years of his life, was decidedly favourable to their object; declared his conviction of the truth of Christianity; attended public worship himself on the Sabbath, and recommended the same to his people.

His moral character was not marked by that cruelty, rapacity, and insensibility to the sufferings of the people, which frequently distinguish the abitrary chiefs of uncivilized nations. He appears in general to have been kind; and, in several places on our tour, the mothers showed us their children, and told us that when Rihoriho passed that way, he had kissed them—a condescension they seemed to think much of, and which they will probably remember to the end of their days. But, though generous in his disposition, and humane in his conduct towards his subjects, he was addicted to intoxication—whether from natural inclination or the influence and example of others is not now to be determined; frequently, to my own knowledge, it has been entirely from the latter. Had he in early life been privileged to associate with individuals whose conduct and principles were favourable to virtue and religion, there is every reason to suppose his moral character, with respect at least to this vice, would have been as irreproachable as his mental habits were commendable. But, alas for him! it was quite the reverse.

Though not distinguished by the ardour and strength of character so conspicuous in his father, he possessed both decision and enterprise: the abolition of the national idolatry was a striking instance of the former; and his voyage to England, of the latter.

The motives by which he was induced to undertake a voyage so long and hazardous were highly commendable. They were—a desire to see for himself countries of which he had heard such various and interesting accounts; a wish to have a personal interview with his majesty the king of Great Britain, or the chief members of the British government—for the purpose of confirming the cession of the Sandwich Islands, and placing himself and his dominions under British protection.

It was also his intention to make himself acquainted with the tenor and forms of administering justice in the courts of law, the principles of commerce, and other subjects important to the welfare of the islands.

The melancholy death of the late king and queen,

which took place shortly after their arrival in England,
not only prevented the full accomplishment of these
desirable objects, but awakened very generally a degree
of apprehension that the people of the islands, unacquainted with the true circumstances of their death,
would be led to suppose they had been neglected, unkindly treated, or even poisoned in revenge of the death
of Captain Cook, and that the feelings of friendship
with which they had been accustomed to regard the
people of England might be followed by enmity or distrust. The fears of those who felt interested in the
welfare of the Hawaiians, though natural, were groundless. The British government had entertained the
young ruler of the Sandwich Islands, his consort, and
attendants with its accustomed hospitality; and when
they were attacked by diseases incident to a northern
climate, but unknown in their native islands, every attention that humanity could suggest, and every alleviation
that the first medical skill in London could afford, was
most promptly rendered. After their decease, the highest respect was paid to their remains, and in honourable
regard to the feelings of the nation who had suffered this
painful bereavement, a British frigate, under the command of Captain Lord Byron, was appointed to convey to
the Sandwich Islands the bodies of the king and queen,
that their sorrowing people might have the mournful
satisfaction of depositing their ashes among the tombs
of their ancestors.

By the return of a highly esteemed missionary friend,
Rev. C. S. Stewart, I have learned that the Blonde
reached the islands in the month of May, 1825: the
natives were in some degree prepared for the arrival, by
the intelligence of the death of their king and queen,
which they had received about two months before from
Valparaiso. Shortly after, the vessel having the remains
of the king and queen on board had anchored off Oahu,
Boki, the principal chief, who had accompanied the
king to England, attended by those of his countrymen
who had also returned, proceeded on shore: on landing,
he was met by his elder brother Karaimoku, and other
distinguished chiefs, and after the first emotions of joy
at meeting again, and sorrow on account of the loss all
had sustained, were somewhat abated, the survivors
and their friends walked in solemn and mournful procession to the place of worship, where thanksgivings
were presented to God, for the merciful preservation

of those who were thus privileged to meet again, and
supplications were made that the afflicting dispensation,
which all so deeply felt, might exert a salutary influence
in the minds of the surviving chiefs, and the sorrowing
nation at large.

Karaimoku, the late prime minister, and present
regent of the islands, then arose and said, " We have
lost our king and queen, they have died in a foreign
land; we shall see them no more; it is right that we
should weep, but let us not entertain hard thoughts of
God. *God has not done wrong.* The evil is with us:
let us bow under his hand; let all amusement cease;
let our daily avocations be suspended; and let the nation, by prayer and a cessation from ordinary pursuits,
humble itself before God fourteen days." Before the
assembly separated, Boki stood up, and, in a brief outline of the voyage, narrated the most prominent events
that had transpired since his departure from the islands
—calling their attention in particular to the suitable
and important advice he had received from his majesty
the king of Great Britain, in an audience with which he
was graciously favoured, viz. To return to his native
country, attend to general and religious instruction himself, and endeavour to enlighten and reform the people.
The peculiar circumstances of the people at this time,
the increased satisfaction they had for some time felt
in attending every means of instruction within their
reach, and the pleasing change in favour of religion which
many had experienced, rendered this recommendation, so congenial to their feelings, from a source so
distinguished, unusually acceptable. A deep and favourable impression was produced on all present, a new
impulse was given to the means already employed for
the instruction and improvement of the people, from
which most advantageous results have already appeared.
They were also made acquainted, by Boki and his companions, with the kind reception, generous treatment,
and marked attentions which the late king and queen
and their suite had received while in England. This
intelligence, communicated by those whose testimony
would be received with the most entire credence, would
at once confirm the attachment and confidence they
have so long felt towards England.

No disturbance of the general tranquillity, nor change
in the government, of the islands has resulted from this

event. Rihoriho' left a younger brother, *Kauikeouli*, about ten years of age, who is acknowledged by the chiefs as his successor. A regency will govern during his minority, and the executive authority will probably continue to be exercised by *Karaimoku*, and the other chiefs with whom Rihoriho left it when he embarked for England.

The queen, who accompanied him, and who died at the same time, has left a fond mother and an affectionate people to lament her loss: she was the daughter of Tamehameha and Talakua, and was born about the year 1797 or 1798, being two years younger than Rihoriho, and about twenty-six years of age when she left the islands. Like all the persons of distinction she had many names, but that by which she was generally known was *Kamehamaru* (shade of Kameha), from *kameha*, a contraction of her father's name, and *maru*, shade. She was distinguished for good nature, and was much beloved by all her subjects. The poor people, when unable to pay their rent, or under the displeasure of the king and chiefs, or embarrassed on any other account, frequently repaired to her, and found a friend whose aid was never refused. She was also kind to those foreigners who might be distressed in the islands, and though she never harboured any or countenanced their absconding from their ships, she has often fed them when hungry, and given them native tapa for clothing.

Kamehamaru was at all times lively and agreeable in company; and though her application to her book and her pen was equal to that of the king, her improvement in learning was more gradual, and her general knowledge less extensive.

She excelled, however, in the management of his domestic affairs, which were conducted by her with great judgment and address, and, though formerly accustomed to use ardent spirits, from the time she put herself under Christian instruction, she entirely discontinued that and every other practice inconsistent with her profession of Christianity. Her attendance on the duties of religion was maintained with commendable regularity.

Her influence contributed very materially to the pleasing change that has recently taken place, in connexion with the labours of the missionaries in the islands. For the instruction and moral improvement of the people,

she manifested no ordinary concern. Long before
many of the leading chiefs were favourable to the instruction of the people or their reception of Christianity, Kamehamaru on every suitable occasion recommended to her own servants to serve Jehovah the living
God, and attend to every means of improvement within
their reach. It was truly pleasing to observe, so soon
after she had embraced Christianity herself, an anxiety
to induce her people to follow her example. At Honoruru she erected a school, in which upwards of forty
children and young persons, principally connected with
her establishment, were daily taught to read and write,
and instructed in the first principles of religion, by a
native teacher, whom she almost entirely supported. In
this school she took a lively interest, and marked the
progress of the scholars with evident satisfaction; in
order to encourage the pupils, she frequently visited
the school during the hours of instruction, accompanied
by a number of chief women. She also attended the
public examinations, and noticed those who on these
occasions excelled, frequently presenting a favourite
scholar with a slate, a copy-book, pencil, pen, or some
other token of her approbation.

In her death the missionaries have lost a sincere
friend, and her subjects a queen who always delighted
to alleviate their distresses and promote their interests.

Her disposition was affectionate. I have seen her
and the king sitting beside the couch of Keopuolani, her
mother-in-law, day after day, when the latter has been
ill; and on these occasions, though there might be several servants in constant attendance, she would allow
no individual but her husband or herself to hand to the
patient any thing she might want, or even fan the flies
from her person.

The circumstances attending her departure from the
islands were peculiarly affecting. The king had gone
on board L'Aigle; but the boat was waiting to convey
her to the ship. She arose from the mat on which she
had been reclining, embraced her mother and other
relations most affectionately, and passed through the
crowd towards the boat. The people fell down on
their knees as she walked along, pressing and saluting
her feet—frequently bathing them with tears of unfeigned sorrow—and making loud wailings, in which

his family, thanking him at the same time for the hospitable entertainment we had received, and the great
facilities he had afforded for accomplishing the objects
of our visit.

About three o'clock in the morning, being awoke by
the shouts of the men who were heaving up the anchor
of the pilot-boat, I repaired on board, and immediately
afterward we sailed with a gentle breeze blowing from
the land. The wind was light and baffling, and it was
noon before we reached Towaihae, where I learned with
disappointment that the Nio had sailed to Oahu. On
landing I was welcomed by Mr. Young, with whom I
remained till the pilot-boat was ready to sail for Lahaina.

Late in the evening of the 2d of September, after
preaching to the people of the place at Mr. Young's
house, I went again on board the pilot-boat, but found
her so full of sandal-wood that there was not room for
any person below, while the decks were crowded with
natives. The weather was unfavourable for getting
under way till nearly daylight; and every person on
board was completely drenched by the heavy rain that
fell during the night.

During the forenoon of the 3d, we drifted slowly to
the northward, and about noon took in eight hundred
dried fish, after which we made sail for Maui. The
weather was warm, the wind light: and all on board
being obliged to keep on deck, without any screen or
shade from the scorching rays of a vertical sun, the
situation was very uncomfortable. At three P. M. we
took the channel-breeze, which soon wafted us across to
the south-east part of Maui.

As the shores of Hawaii receded from my view, a
variety of reflections insensibly arose in my mind. The
tour which, in the society of my companions, I had made
had been replete with interest. The varied and sublime
phenomena of nature had elevated our conceptions of
"nature's God;" the manners and customs of the inhabitants had increased our interest in their welfare;
while their superstition, moral degradation, ignorance,
and vice had called forth our sincerest commiseration.
We had made known the nature and consequences of
sin, spoken of the love of God, and had exhibited the
Lord Jesus Christ as the only Saviour to multitudes
who had never before heard his name, or been directed

'to worship the holy and living God, and who would probably never hear these truths again. We cherish the hope that, under the Divine blessing, lasting good will result, even from this transient visit.

Many. of the individuals we have met on these occa-sions, we shall in all probability meet no. more till the morning of the resurrection. May we meet them then on the right-hand of the Son of God?

At sunset we arrived off Morokini, but were shortly after becalmed. The current, however, was in our favour through the night, and at daylight on the 4th we found ourselves off the east end of the district of Laha-aina, and about a mile distant from the shore. Many of the natives jumped into the sea, and swam to the beach, holding their clothes above their heads with one hand, and swimming with the other.

On landing I waited on Keopuolani, the king's mother, whom I found ill; Karaimoku, Kaahumanu, Kalakua, and several other chiefs were reclining around her, weeping. After some time, Karaimoku proposed that they should unitedly pray for her recovery, and his pro-posal was acceded to.

Towards evening I visited the governor of the island, and also the king, who was then at Maui. The subse-quent voyage of the latter to Great Britain, accom-panied by his queen, and the melancholy event which terminated their lives while in London, excited con-siderable interest, and will probably be considered suffi-cient apology for a short account of them, although the event took place after my visit to Maui at this time.

The late king of the Sandwich Islands was the son of Tamehameha, former king, and Keopuolani, daughter of Kauikeouli, and Kakuiapoiwa. He was born in the eastern part of Hawaii, in the year 1795 or 1796. The name by which he was generally known was *Rihoriho*, which was only a contraction of *Kalaninui-rihoriho*, lite-rally, the heaven's great black—from *Ka lani*, the heav-ens, *nui*, great, and *rihoriho*, applied to any thing burned to blackness. On public occasions he was sometimes called Tamehameha, after his father, though names are not always hereditary. Besides these, he had a variety of other names, the most common of which was *Iolani*. The word *lani*, heaven or sky, formed a component part

in the name of most chiefs of distinction. The following is a fac-simile of the official signature of the late
king.

Tamehameha

The early habits of Rihoriho did not warrant any
great expectations. His natural disposition was frank,
and humane. The natives always spoke of him as
good-natured, except when he was under the influence
of ardent spirits; his manners were perfectly free, at
the same time dignified, and always agreeable to those
who were about him.' His mind was naturally inquisitive. The questions he usually presented to foreigners
were by no means trifling; and his memory was retentive.
His general knowledge of the world was much
greater than could have been expected. I have heard
him entertain a party of chiefs for hours together with
accounts of different parts of the earth, describing the
extensive lakes, the mountains, and mines of North and
South America—the elephants and inhabitants of India
—the houses, manufactures, &c. of England—with no
small accuracy, considering he had never seen them.
He had a great thirst for knowledge, and was diligent in
his studies. I recollect his remarking one day, when
he opened his writing-desk, that he expected more advantage from that desk than from a fine brig belonging
to him, lying at anchor opposite the house in which we
were sitting. Mr. Bingham and myself were his daily
teachers, and have often been surprised at his unwearied
perseverance. I have sat beside him at his desk sometimes from nine or ten o'clock in the morning till nearly
sunset, during which period his pen or his book has not
been out of his hand more than three-quarters of an
hour, while he was at dinner.
We do not know that Christianity exerted any decisive influence on his heart. He was willing to receive
the missionaries on their first arrival—availed himself
of their knowledge, to increase his own—and, during

the latter years of his life, was decidedly favourable to their object; declared his conviction of the truth of Christianity; attended public worship himself on the Sabbath, and recommended the same to his people.

His moral character was not marked by that cruelty, rapacity, and insensibility to the sufferings of the people, which frequently distinguish the abitrary chiefs of uncivilized nations. He appears in general to have been kind; and, in several places on our tour, the mothers showed us their children, and told us that when Rihoriho passed that way, he had kissed them—a condescension they seemed to think much of, and which they will probably remember to the end of their days. But, though generous in his disposition, and humane in his conduct towards his subjects, he was addicted to intoxication—whether from natural inclination or the influence and example of others is not now to be determined; frequently, to my own knowledge, it has been entirely from the latter. Had he in early life been privileged to associate with individuals whose conduct and principles were favourable to virtue and religion, there is every reason to suppose his moral character, with respect at least to this vice, would have been as irreproachable as his mental habits were commendable. But, alas for him! it was quite the reverse.

Though not distinguished by the ardour and strength of character so conspicuous in his father, he possessed both decision and enterprise: the abolition of the national idolatry was a striking instance of the former; and his voyage to England, of the latter.

The motives by which he was induced to undertake a voyage so long and hazardous were highly commendable. They were—a desire to see for himself countries of which he had heard such various and interesting accounts; a wish to have a personal interview with his majesty the king of Great Britain, or the chief members of the British government—for the purpose of confirming the cession of the Sandwich Islands, and placing himself and his dominions under British protection.

It was also his intention to make himself acquainted with the tenor and forms of administering justice in the courts of law, the principles of commerce, and other subjects important to the welfare of the islands.

The melancholy death of the late king and queen,

which took place shortly after their arrival in England,
not only prevented the full accomplishment of these
desirable objects, but awakened very generally a degree
of apprehension that the people of the islands, unacquainted with the true circumstances of their death,
would be led to suppose they had been neglected, unkindly treated, or even poisoned in revenge of the death
of Captain Cook, and that the feelings of friendship
with which they had been accustomed to regard the
people of England might be followed by enmity or distrust. The fears of those who felt interested in the
welfare of the Hawaiians, though natural, were groundless. The British government had entertained the
young ruler of the Sandwich Islands, his consort, and
attendants with its accustomed hospitality; and when
they were attacked by diseases incident to a northern
climate, but unknown in their native islands, every attention that humanity could suggest, and every alleviation
that the first medical skill in London could afford, was
most promptly rendered. After their decease, the highest respect was paid to their remains, and in honourable
regard to the feelings of the nation who had suffered this
painful bereavement, a British frigate, under the command of Captain Lord Byron, was appointed to convey to
the Sandwich Islands the bodies of the king and queen,
that their sorrowing people might have the mournful
satisfaction of depositing their ashes among the tombs
of their ancestors.

By the return of a highly esteemed missionary friend,
Rev. C. S. Stewart, I have learned that the Blonde
reached the islands in the month of May, 1825: the
natives were in some degree prepared for the arrival, by
the intelligence of the death of their king and queen,
which they had received about two months before from
Valparaiso. Shortly after, the vessel having the remains
of the king and queen on board had anchored off Oahu,
Boki, the principal chief, who had accompanied the
king to England, attended by those of his countrymen
who had also returned, proceeded on shore: on landing,
he was met by his elder brother Karaimoku, and other
distinguished chiefs, and after the first emotions of joy
at meeting again, and sorrow on account of the loss all
had sustained, were somewhat abated, the survivors
and their friends walked in solemn and mournful procession to the place of worship, where thanksgivings
were presented to God, for the merciful preservation

of those who were thus privileged to meet again, and
supplications were made that the afflicting dispensation,
which all so deeply felt, might exert a salutary influence
in the minds of the surviving chiefs, and the sorrowing
nation at large.

Karaimoku, the late prime minister, and present
regent of the islands, then arose and said, " We have
lost our king and queen, they have died in a foreign
land; we shall see them no more ; it is right that we
should weep, but let us not entertain hard thoughts of
God. ' *God has not done wrong*. The evil is with us :
let us bow under his hand ; let all amusement cease;
let our daily avocations be suspended ; and let the nation, by prayer and a cessation from ordinary pursuits,
humble itself before God fourteen days." Before the
assembly separated, Boki stood up, and, in a brief outline of the voyage, narrated the most prominent events
that had transpired since his departure from the islands
—calling their attention in particular to the suitable
and important advice he had received from his majesty
the king of Great Britain, in an audience with which he
was graciously favoured, viz. To return to his native
country, attend to general and religious instruction himself, and endeavour to enlighten and reform the people.
The peculiar circumstances of the people at this time,
the increased satisfaction they had for some time felt
in attending every means of instruction within their
reach, and the pleasing change in favour of religion which
many had experienced, rendered this recommendation, so congenial to their feelings, from a source so
distinguished, unusually acceptable. A deep and favourable impression was produced on all present, a new
impulse was given to the means already employed for
the instruction and improvement of the people, from
which most advantageous results have already appeared.
They were also made acquainted, by Boki and his companions, with the kind reception, generous treatment,
and marked attentions which the late king and queen
and their suite had received while in England. This
intelligence, communicated by those whose testimony
would be received with the most entire credence, would
at once confirm the attachment and confidence they
have so long felt towards England.

No disturbance of the general tranquillity, nor change
in the government, of the islands has resulted from this

event.   Rihoriho' left a younger brother, *Kauikeouli*,
about ten years of age, who is acknowledged by the
chiefs as his successor.   A regency will govern during
his minority, and the executive authority will probably
continue to be exercised by *Karaimoku*, and the other
chiefs with whom Rihoriho left it when he embarked
for England.

The queen, who accompanied him, and who died at the
same time, has left a fond mother and an affectionate
people to lament her loss: she was the daughter of
Tamehameha and Talakua, and was born about the
year 1797 or 1798, being two years younger than Rihoriho, and about twenty-six years of age when she
left the islands.   Like all the persons of distinction she
had many names, but that by which she was generally
known was *Kamehamaru* (shade of Kameha), from *kameha*, a contraction of her father's name, and *maru*, shade.
She was distinguished for good nature, and was much
beloved by all her subjects.   The poor people, when
unable to pay their rent, or under the displeasure of the
king and chiefs, or embarrassed on any other account,
frequently repaired to her, and found a friend whose aid
was never refused.   She was also kind to those foreigners who might be distressed in the islands, and though
she never harboured any or countenanced their absconding from their ships, she has often fed them when
hungry, and given them native tapa for clothing.

Kamehamaru was at all times lively and agreeable in
company ; and though her application to her book and
her pen was equal to that of the king, her improvement
in learning was more gradual, and her general knowledge less extensive.

She excelled, however, in the management of his
domestic affairs, which were conducted by her with
great judgment and address, and, though formerly accustomed to use ardent spirits, from the time she put herself under Christian instruction, she entirely discontinued that and every other practice inconsistent with
her profession of Christianity.   Her attendance on the
duties of religion was maintained with commendable
regularity.

Her influence contributed very materially to the pleasing change that has recently taken place, in connexion
with the labours of the missionaries in the islands.   For
the instruction and moral improvement of the people,

she manifested no ordinary concern. Long before many of the leading chiefs were favourable to the instruction of the people or their reception of Christianity, Kamehamaru on every suitable occasion recommended to her own servants to serve Jehovah the living God, and attend to every means of improvement within their reach. It was truly pleasing to observe, so soon after she had embraced Christianity herself, an anxiety to induce her people to follow her example. At Honoruru she erected a school, in which upwards of forty children and young persons, principally connected with her establishment, were daily taught to read and write, and instructed in the first principles of religion, by a native teacher, whom she almost entirely supported. In this school she took a lively interest, and marked the progress of the scholars with evident satisfaction; in order to encourage the pupils, she frequently visited the school during the hours of instruction, accompanied by a number of chief women. She also attended the public examinations, and noticed those who on these occasions excelled, frequently presenting a favourite scholar with a slate, a copy-book, pencil, pen, or some other token of her approbation.

In her death the missionaries have lost a sincere friend, and her subjects a queen who always delighted to alleviate their distresses and promote their interests.

Her disposition was affectionate. I have seen her and the king sitting beside the couch of Keopuolani, her mother-in-law, day after day, when the latter has been ill; and on these occasions, though there might be several servants in constant attendance, she would allow no individual but her husband or herself to hand to the patient any thing she might want, or even fan the flies from her person.

The circumstances attending her departure from the islands were peculiarly affecting. The king had gone on board L'Aigle; but the boat was waiting to convey her to the ship. She arose from the mat on which she had been reclining; embraced her mother and other relations most affectionately, and passed through the crowd towards the boat. The people fell down on their knees as she walked along, pressing and saluting her feet—frequently bathing them with tears of unfeigned sorrow—and making loud wailings, in which

his family, thanking him at the same time for the hospitable entertainment we had received, and the great facilities he had afforded for accomplishing the objects of our visit.

About three o'clock in the morning, being awoke by the shouts of the men who were heaving up the anchor of the pilot-boat, I repaired on board, and immediately afterward we sailed with a gentle breeze blowing from the land. The wind was light and baffling, and it was noon before we reached Towaihae, where I learned with disappointment that the Nio had sailed to Oahu. On landing I was welcomed by Mr. Young, with whom I remained till the pilot-boat was ready to sail for Lahaina.

Late in the evening of the 2d of September, after preaching to the people of the place at Mr. Young's house, I went again on board the pilot-boat, but found her so full of sandal-wood that there was not room for any person below, while the decks were crowded with natives. The weather was unfavourable for getting under way till nearly daylight; and every person on board was completely drenched by the heavy rain that fell during the night.

During the forenoon of the 3d, we drifted slowly to the northward, and about noon took in eight hundred dried fish, after which we made sail for Maui. The weather was warm, the wind light: and all on board being obliged to keep on deck, without any screen or shade from the scorching rays of a vertical sun, the situation was very uncomfortable. At three P. M. we took the channel-breeze, which soon wafted us across to the south-east part of Maui.

As the shores of Hawaii receded from my view, a variety of reflections insensibly arose in my mind. The tour which, in the society of my companions, I had made had been replete with interest. The varied and sublime phenomena of nature had elevated our conceptions of "nature's God;" the manners and customs of the inhabitants had increased our interest in their welfare; while their superstition, moral degradation, ignorance, and vice had called forth our sincerest commiseration. We had made known the nature and consequences of sin, spoken of the love of God, and had exhibited the Lord Jesus Christ as the only Saviour to multitudes who had never before heard his name, or been directed

to worship the holy and living God, and who would probably never hear these truths again. We cherish the hope that, under the Divine blessing, lasting good will result, even from this transient visit.

Many of the individuals we have met on these occasions, we shall in all probability meet no more till the morning of the resurrection. May we meet them then on the right-hand of the Son of God!

At sunset we arrived off Morokini, but were shortly after becalmed. The current, however, was in our favour through the night, and at daylight on the 4th we found ourselves off the east end of the district of Laha-ina, and about a mile distant from the shore. Many of the natives jumped into the sea, and swam to the beach, holding their clothes above their heads with one hand, and swimming with the other.

On landing I waited on Keopuolani, the king's mother, whom I found ill; Karaimoku, Kaahumanu, Kalakua, and several other chiefs were reclining around her, weeping. After some time, Karaimoku proposed that they should unitedly pray for her recovery, and his proposal was acceded to.

Towards evening I visited the governor of the island, and also the king, who was then at Maui. The subsequent voyage of the latter to Great Britain, accompanied by his queen, and the melancholy event which terminated their lives while in London, excited considerable interest, and will probably be considered sufficient apology for a short account of them, although the event took place after my visit to Maui at this time.

The late king of the Sandwich Islands was the son of Tamehameha, former king, and Keopuolani, daughter of Kauikeouli, and Kakuiapoiwa. He was born in the eastern part of Hawaii, in the year 1795 or 1796. The name by which he was generally known was *Rihoriho*, which was only a contraction of *Kalaninui-rihoriho*, literally, the heaven's great black—from *Ka lani*, the heavens, *nui*, great, and *rihoriho*, applied to any thing burned to blackness. On public occasions he was sometimes called Tamehameha, after his father, though names are not always hereditary. Besides these, he had a variety of other names, the most common of which was *Iolani*. The word *lani*, heaven or sky, formed a component part

in the name of most chiefs of distinction. The following is a fac-simile of the official signature of the late
king.

The early habits of Rihoriho did not warrant any
great expectations. His natural disposition was frank,
and humane. The natives always spoke of him as
good-natured, except when he was under the influence
of ardent spirits; his manners were perfectly free, at
the same time dignified, and always agreeable to those
who were about him. His mind was naturally inquisitive. The questions he usually presented to foreigners
were by no means trifling; and his memory was retentive.
tive. His general knowledge of the world was much
greater than could have been expected. I have heard
him entertain a party of chiefs for hours together with
accounts of different parts of the earth, describing the
extensive lakes, the mountains, and mines of North and
South America—the elephants and inhabitants of India
—the houses, manufactures, &c. of England—with no
small accuracy, considering he had never seen them.
He had a great thirst for knowledge, and was diligent in
his studies. I recollect his remarking one day, when
he opened his writing-desk, that he expected more advantage from that desk than from a fine brig belonging
to him, lying at anchor opposite the house in which we
were sitting. Mr. Bingham and myself were his daily
teachers, and have often been surprised at his unwearied
perseverance. I have sat beside him at his desk sometimes from nine or ten o'clock in the morning till nearly
sunset, during which period his pen or his book has not
been out of his hand more than three-quarters of an
hour, while he was at dinner.

We do not know that Christianity exerted any decisive influence on his heart. He was willing to receive
the missionaries on their first arrival—availed himself
of their knowledge, to increase his own—and, during

the latter years of his life, was decidedly favourable to their object; declared his conviction of the truth of Christianity; attended public worship himself on the Sabbath, and recommended the same to his people.

His moral character was not marked by that cruelty, rapacity, and insensibility to the sufferings of the people, which frequently distinguish the abitrary chiefs of uncivilized nations. He appears in general to have been kind; and, in several places on our tour, the mothers showed us their children, and told us that when Rihoriho passed that way, he had kissed them—a condescension they seemed to think much of, and which they will probably remember to the end of their days. But, though generous in his disposition, and humane in his conduct towards his subjects, he was addicted to intoxication—whether from natural inclination or the influence and example of others is not now to be determined; frequently, to my own knowledge, it has been entirely from the latter. Had he in early life been privileged to associate with individuals whose conduct and principles were favourable to virtue and religion, there is every reason to suppose his moral character, with respect at least to this vice, would have been as irreproachable as his mental habits were commendable. But, alas for him! it was quite the reverse.

Though not distinguished by the ardour and strength of character so conspicuous in his father, he possessed both decision and enterprise: the abolition of the national idolatry was a striking instance of the former; and his voyage to England, of the latter.

The motives by which he was induced to undertake a voyage so long and hazardous were highly commendable. They were—a desire to see for himself countries of which he had heard such various and interesting accounts; a wish to have a personal interview with his majesty the king of Great Britain, or the chief members of the British government—for the purpose of confirming the cession of the Sandwich Islands, and placing himself and his dominions under British protection.

It was also his intention to make himself acquainted with the tenor and forms of administering justice in the courts of law, the principles of commerce, and other subjects important to the welfare of the islands.

The melancholy death of the late king and queen,

which took place shortly after their arrival in England,
not only prevented the full accomplishment of these
desirable objects, but awakened very generally a degree
of apprehension that the people of the islands, unacquainted with the true circumstances of their death,
would be led to suppose they had been neglected, unkindly treated, or even poisoned in revenge of the death
of. Captain Cook, and that the feelings of friendship
with which they had been accustomed to regard the
people of England might be followed by enmity or distrust.   The fears of those who felt. interested in the
welfare of the Hawaiians, though natural, were groundless.   The British government had entertained the
young ruler of the Sandwich Islands, his consort, and
attendants with its accustomed hospitality; and when
they were attacked by diseases incident to a northern
climate, but unknown in their native islands, every attention that humanity could suggest, and every alleviation
that the first medical skill in London could afford, was
most promptly rendered.   After their decease, the highest respect was paid to their remains, and in honourable
regard to the feelings of the nation who had suffered this
painful bereavement, a British frigate, under the command of Captain Lord Byron, was appointed to convey to
the Sandwich Islands the bodies of the king and queen,
that their sorrowing people might have the mournful
satisfaction of depositing their ashes among the tombs
of their ancestors.

By the return of a highly esteemed missionary friend,
Rev. C. S. Stewart, I have learned that the Blonde
reached the islands in the month of May, 1825: the
natives were in some degree prepared for the arrival, by
the intelligence of the death of their king and queen,
which they had received about two months before from
Valparaiso.   Shortly after, the vessel having the remains
of the king and queen on board had anchored off Oahu,
Boki, the principal chief, who had accompanied the
king to England, attended by those of his countrymen
who had also returned, proceeded on shore : on landing,
he was met by his elder brother Karaimoku, and other
distinguished chiefs, and after the first emotions of joy
at meeting again, and sorrow on account of the loss all
had sustained, were somewhat abated, the survivors
and their friends walked in solemn and mournful procession to the place of worship, where thanksgivings
were presented to God, for the merciful preservation

of. those who were thus privileged to meet again, and supplications were made that the afflicting dispensation, which all so deeply felt, might exert a salutary influence in the minds of the surviving chiefs, and the sorrowing nation at large.

Karaimoku, the late prime minister, and present regent of the islands, then arose and said, "We have lost our king and queen, they have died in a foreign land; we shall see them no more; it is right that we should weep, but let us not entertain hard thoughts of God. *God has not done wrong.* The evil is with us: let us bow under his hand; let all amusement cease; let our daily avocations be suspended; and let the nation, by prayer and a cessation from ordinary pursuits, humble itself before God fourteen days." Before the assembly separated, Boki stood up, and, in a brief outline of the voyage, narrated the most prominent events that had transpired since his departure from the islands —calling their attention in particular to the suitable and important advice he had received from his majesty the king of Great Britain, in an audience with which he was graciously favoured, viz. To return to his native country, attend to general and religious instruction himself, and endeavour to enlighten and reform the people. The peculiar circumstances of the people at this time, the increased satisfaction they had for some time felt in attending every means of instruction within their reach, and the pleasing change in favour of religion which many had experienced, rendered this recommendation, so congenial to their feelings, from a source so distinguished, unusually acceptable. A deep and favourable impression was produced on all present, a new impulse was given to the means already employed for the instruction and improvement of the people, from which most advantageous results have already appeared. They were also made acquainted, by Boki and his companions, with the kind reception, generous treatment, and marked attentions which the late king and queen and their suite had received while in England. This intelligence, communicated by those whose testimony would be received with the most entire credence, would at once confirm the attachment and confidence they have so long felt towards England.

No disturbance of the general tranquillity, nor change in the government, of the islands has resulted from this

event.   Rihoriho' left a younger brother, *Kauikeouli*, about ten years of age, who is acknowledged by the chiefs as his successor.   A regency will govern during his minority, and the executive authority will probably continue to be exercised by *Karaimoku*, and the other chiefs with whom Rihoriho left it when he embarked for England.

The queen, who accompanied him, and who died at the same time, has left a fond mother and an affectionate people to lament her loss: she was the daughter of Tamehameha and Talakua, and was born about the year 1797 or 1798, being two years younger than Rihoriho, and about twenty-six years of age when she left the islands.   Like all the persons of distinction she had many names, but that by which she was generally known was *Kamehamaru* (shade of Kameha), from *kameha*, a contraction of her father's name, and *maru*, shade. She was distinguished for good nature, and was much beloved by all her subjects.   The poor people, when unable to pay their rent, or under the displeasure of the king and chiefs, or embarrassed on any other account, frequently repaired to her, and found a friend whose aid was never refused.   She was also kind to those foreigners who might be distressed in the islands, and though she never harboured any or countenanced their absconding from their ships, she has often fed them when hungry, and given them native *tapa* for clothing.

Kamehamaru was at all times lively and agreeable in company ; and though her application to her book and her pen was equal to that of the king, her improvement in learning was more gradual, and her general knowledge less extensive.

She excelled, however, in the management of his domestic affairs, which were conducted by her with great judgment and address, and, though formerly accustomed to use ardent spirits, from the time she put herself under Christian instruction, she entirely discontinued that and every other practice inconsistent with her profession of Christianity.   Her attendance on the duties of religion was maintained with commendable regularity.

Her influence contributed very materially to the pleasing change that has recently taken place, in connexion with the labours of the missionaries in the islands.   For the instruction and moral improvement of the people,

she manifested no ordinary concern. Long before
many of the leading chiefs were favourable to the instruction of the people or their reception of Christianity, Kamehamaru on every suitable occasion recommended to her own servants to serve Jehovah the living
God, and attend to every means of improvement within
their reach. It was truly pleasing to observe, so soon
after she had embraced Christianity herself, an anxiety
to induce her people to follow her example. At Honoruru she erected a school, in which upwards of forty
children and young persons, principally connected with
her establishment, were daily taught to read and write,
and instructed in the first principles of religion, by a
native teacher, whom she almost entirely supported. In
this school she took a lively interest, and marked the
progress of the scholars with evident satisfaction; in
order to encourage the pupils, she frequently visited
the school during the hours of instruction, accompanied
by a number of chief women. She also attended the
public examinations, and noticed those who on these
occasions excelled, frequently presenting a favourite
scholar with a slate, a copy-book, pencil, pen, or some
other token of her approbation.

In her death the missionaries have lost a sincere
friend, and her subjects a queen who always delighted
to alleviate their distresses and promote their interests.

Her disposition was affectionate. I have seen her
and the king sitting beside the couch of Keopuolani, her
mother-in-law, day after day, when the latter has been
ill; and on these occasions, though there might be several servants in constant attendance, she would allow
no individual but her husband or herself to hand to the
patient any thing she might want, or even fan the flies
from her person.

The circumstances attending her departure from the
islands were peculiarly affecting. The king had gone
on board L'Aigle; but the boat was waiting to convey
her to the ship. She arose from the mat on which she
had been reclining; embraced her mother and other
relations most affectionately, and passed through the
crowd towards the boat. The people fell down on
their knees as she walked along, pressing and saluting
her feet—frequently bathing them with tears of unfeigned sorrow—and making loud wailings, in which

his family, thanking him at the same time for the hospitable entertainment we had received; and the great
facilities he had afforded for accomplishing the objects
of our visit.

About three o'clock in the morning, being awoke by
the shouts of the men who were heaving up the anchor
of the pilot-boat, I repaired on board, and immediately
afterward we sailed with a gentle breeze blowing from
the land. The wind was light and baffling, and it was
noon before we reached Towaihae, where I learned with
disappointment that the Nio had sailed to Oahu. On
landing I was welcomed by Mr. Young, with whom I
remained till the pilot-boat was ready to sail for Lahaina.

Late in the evening of the 2d of September, after
preaching to the people of the place at Mr. Young's
house, I went again on board the pilot-boat, but found
her so full of sandal-wood that there was not room for
any person below, while the decks were crowded with
natives. The weather was unfavourable for getting
under way till nearly daylight; and every person on
board was completely drenched by the heavy rain that
fell during the night.

During the forenoon of the 3d, we drifted slowly to
the northward, and about noon took in eight hundred
dried fish, after which we made sail for Maui. The
weather was warm, the wind light: and all on board
being obliged to keep on deck, without any screen or
shade from the scorching rays of a vertical sun, the
situation was very uncomfortable. At three P. M. we
took the channel-breeze, which soon wafted us across to
the south-east part of Maui.

As the shores of Hawaii receded from my view, a
variety of reflections insensibly arose in my mind. The
tour which, in the society of my companions, I had made
had been replete with interest. The varied and sublime
phenomena of nature had elevated our conceptions of
"nature's God;" the manners and customs of the inhabitants had increased our interest in their welfare;
while their superstition, moral degradation, ignorance,
and vice had called forth our sincerest commiseration.
We had made known the nature and consequences of
sin, spoken of the love of God, and had exhibited the
Lord Jesus Christ as the only Saviour to multitudes
who had never before heard his name, or been directed

to worship the holy and living God, and who would probably never hear these truths again. We cherish the hope that, under the Divine blessing, lasting good will result, even from this transient visit.

Many of the individuals we have met on these occasions, we shall in all probability meet no more till the morning of the resurrection. May we meet them then on the right-hand of the Son of God?

At sunset we arrived off Morokini, but were shortly after becalmed. The current, however, was in our favour through the night, and at daylight on the 4th we found ourselves off the east end of the district of Lahaaina, and about a mile distant from the shore. Many of the natives jumped into the sea, and swam to the beach, holding their clothes above their heads with one hand, and swimming with the other.

On landing I waited on Keopuolani, the king's mother, whom I found ill; Karaimoku, Kaahumanu, Kalakua, and several other chiefs were reclining around her, weeping. After some time, Karaimoku proposed that they should unitedly pray for her recovery, and his proposal was acceded to.

Towards evening I visited the governor of the island, and also the king, who was then at Maui. The subsequent voyage of the latter to Great Britain, accompanied by his queen, and the melancholy event which terminated their lives while in London, excited considerable interest, and will probably be considered sufficient apology for a short account of them, although the event took place after my visit to Maui at this time.

The late king of the Sandwich Islands was the son of Tamehameha, former king, and Keopuolani, daughter of Kauikeouli, and Kakuiapoiwa. He was born in the eastern part of Hawaii, in the year 1795 or 1796. The name by which he was generally known was *Rihoriho*, which was only a contraction of *Kalaninui-rihoriho*, literally, the heaven's great black—from *Ka lani*, the heavens, *nui*, great, and *rihoriho*, applied to any thing burned to blackness. On public occasions he was sometimes called Tamehameha, after his father, though names are not always hereditary. Besides these, he had a variety of other names, the most common of which was *Iolani*. The word *lani*, heaven or sky, formed a component part

in the name of most chiefs of distinction. The following is a fac-simile of the official signature of the late
king.

Tamehameha

The early habits of Rihoriho did not warrant any
great expectations. His natural disposition was frank,
and humane. The natives always spoke of him as
good-natured, except when he was under the influence
of ardent spirits; his manners were perfectly free, at
the same time dignified, and always agreeable to those
who were about him. His mind was naturally inquisitive. The questions he usually presented to foreigners
were by no means trifling; and his memory was retentive. His general knowledge of the world was much
greater than could have been expected. I have heard
him entertain a party of chiefs for hours together with
accounts of different parts of the earth, describing the
extensive lakes, the mountains, and mines of North and
South America—the elephants and inhabitants of India
—the houses, manufactures, &c. of England—with no
small accuracy, considering he had never seen them.
He had a great thirst for knowledge, and was diligent in
his studies. I recollect his remarking one day, when
he opened his writing-desk, that he expected more advantage from that desk than from a fine brig belonging
to him, lying at anchor opposite the house in which we
were sitting. Mr. Bingham and myself were his daily
teachers, and have often been surprised at his unwearied
perseverance. I have sat beside him at his desk sometimes from nine or ten o'clock in the morning till nearly
sunset, during which period his pen or his book has not
been out of his hand more than three-quarters of an
hour, while he was at dinner.

We do not know that Christianity exerted any decisive influence on his heart. He was willing to receive
the missionaries on their first arrival—availed himself
of their knowledge, to increase his own—and, during

the latter years of his life, was decidedly favourable to their object; declared his conviction of the truth of Christianity; attended public worship himself on the Sabbath, and recommended the same to his people.

His moral character was not marked by that cruelty, rapacity, and insensibility to the sufferings of the people, which frequently distinguish the arbitrary chiefs of uncivilized nations. He appears in general to have been kind; and, in several places on our tour, the mothers showed us their children, and told us that when Rihoriho passed that way, he had kissed them—a condescension they seemed to think much of, and which they will probably remember to the end of their days. But, though generous in his disposition, and humane in his conduct towards his subjects, he was addicted to intoxication—whether from natural inclination or the influence and example of others is not now to be determined; frequently, to my own knowledge, it has been entirely from the latter. Had he in early life been privileged to associate with individuals whose conduct and principles were favourable to virtue and religion, there is every reason to suppose his moral character, with respect at least to this vice, would have been as irreproachable as his mental habits were commendable. But, alas for him! it was quite the reverse.

Though not distinguished by the ardour and strength of character so conspicuous in his father, he possessed both decision and enterprise: the abolition of the national idolatry was a striking instance of the former; and his voyage to England, of the latter.

The motives by which he was induced to undertake a voyage so long and hazardous were highly commendable. They were—a desire to see for himself countries of which he had heard such various and interesting accounts; a wish to have a personal interview with his majesty the king of Great Britain, or the chief members of the British government—for the purpose of confirming the cession of the Sandwich Islands, and placing himself and his dominions under British protection.

It was also his intention to make himself acquainted with the tenor and forms of administering justice in the courts of law, the principles of commerce, and other subjects important to the welfare of the islands.

The melancholy death of the late king and queen,

which took place shortly after their arrival in England,
not only prevented the full accomplishment of these
desirable objects, but awakened very generally a degree
of apprehension that the people of the islands, unacquainted with the true circumstances of their death,
would be led to suppose they had been neglected, unkindly treated, or even poisoned in revenge of the death
of Captain Cook, and that the feelings of friendship
with which they had been accustomed to regard the
people of England might be followed by enmity or distrust. The fears of those who felt interested in the
welfare of the Hawaiians, though natural, were groundless. The British government had entertained the
young ruler of the Sandwich Islands, his consort, and
attendants with its accustomed hospitality; and when
they were attacked by diseases incident to a northern
climate, but unknown in their native islands, every attention that humanity could suggest, and every alleviation
that the first medical skill in London could afford, was
most promptly rendered. After their decease, the highest respect was paid to their remains, and in honourable
regard to the feelings of the nation who had suffered this
painful bereavement, a British frigate, under the command of Captain Lord Byron, was appointed to convey to
the Sandwich Islands the bodies of the king and queen,
that their sorrowing people might have the mournful
satisfaction of depositing their ashes among the tombs
of their ancestors.

By the return of a highly esteemed missionary friend,
Rev. C. S. Stewart, I have learned that the Blonde
reached the islands in the month of May, 1825: the
natives were in some degree prepared for the arrival, by
the intelligence of the death of their king and queen,
which they had received about two months before from
Valparaiso. Shortly after, the vessel having the remains
of the king and queen on board had anchored off Oahu,
Boki, the principal chief, who had accompanied the
king to England, attended by those of his countrymen
who had also returned, proceeded on shore: on landing,
he was met by his elder brother Karaimoku, and other
distinguished chiefs, and after the first emotions of joy
at meeting again, and sorrow on account of the loss all
had sustained, were somewhat abated, the survivors
and their friends walked in solemn and mournful pro.
cession to the place of worship, where thanksgivings
were presented to God, for the merciful preservation

of those who were thus privileged to meet again, and supplications were made that the afflicting dispensation, which all so deeply felt, might exert a salutary influence in the minds of the surviving chiefs, and the sorrowing nation at large.

Karaimoku, the late prime minister, and present regent of the islands, then arose and said, " We have lost our king and queen, they have died in a foreign land; we shall see them no more ; it is right that we should weep, but let us not entertain hard thoughts of God. *God has not done wrong.* The evil is with us : let us bow under his hand ; let all amusement cease ; let our daily avocations be suspended ; and let the nation, by prayer and a cessation from ordinary pursuits, humble itself before God fourteen days." Before the assembly separated, Boki stood up, and, in a brief outline of the voyage, narrated the most prominent events that had transpired since his departure from the islands —calling their attention in particular to the suitable and important advice he had received from his majesty the king of Great Britain, in an audience with which he was graciously favoured, viz.   To return to his native country, attend to general and religious instruction himself, and endeavour to enlighten and reform the people. The peculiar circumstances of the people at this time, the increased satisfaction they had for some time felt in attending every means of instruction within their reach, and the pleasing change in favour of religion which many had experienced, rendered this recommendation, so congenial to their feelings, from a source so distinguished, unusually acceptable.   A deep and favourable impression was produced on all present, a new impulse was given to the means already employed for the instruction and improvement of the people, from which most advantageous results have already appeared. They were also made acquainted, by Boki and his companions, with the kind reception, generous treatment, and marked attentions which the late king and queen and their suite had received while in England.   This intelligence, communicated by those whose testimony would be received with the most entire credence, would at once confirm the attachment and confidence they have so long felt towards England.

No disturbance of the general tranquillity, nor change in the government, of the islands has resulted from this

event. Rihoriho' left a younger brother, *Kauikeouli*,
about ten years of age, who is acknowledged by the
chiefs as his successor. A regency will govern during
his minority, and the executive authority will probably
continue to be exercised by *Karaimoku*, and the other
chiefs with whom Rihoriho left it when he embarked
for England.

The queen, who accompanied him, and who died at the
same time, has left a fond mother and an affectionate
people to lament her loss: she was the daughter of
Tamehameha and Talakua, and was born about the
year 1797 or 1798, being two years younger than Rihoriho, and about twenty-six years of age when she
left the islands. Like all the persons of distinction she
had many names, but that by which she was generally
known was *Kamehamaru* (shade of Kameha), from *kameha*, a contraction of herfather's name, and *maru*, shade.
She was distinguished for good nature, and was much
beloved by all her subjects. The poor people, when
unable to pay their rent, or under the displeasure of the
king and chiefs, or embarrassed on any other account,
frequently repaired to her, and found a friend whose aid
was never refused. She was also kind to those foreigners who might be distressed in the islands, and though
she never harboured any or countenanced their absconding from their ships, she has often fed them when
hungry, and given them native tapa for clothing.

Kamehamaru was at all times lively and agreeable in
company; and though her application to her book and
her pen was equal to that of the king, her improvement
in learning was more gradual, and her general knowledge less extensive.

She excelled, however, in the management of his
domestic affairs, which were conducted by her with
great judgment and address, and, though formerly accustomed to use ardent spirits, from the time she put herself under Christian instruction, she entirely discontinued that and every other practice inconsistent with
her profession of Christianity. Her attendance on the
duties of religion was maintained with commendable
regularity.

Her influence contributed very materially to the pleasing change that has recently taken place, in connexion
with the labours of the missionaries in the islands. For
the instruction and moral improvement of the people,

she manifested no ordinary concern. Long before
many of the leading chiefs were favourable to the instruction of the people or their reception of Christianity, Kamehamaru on every suitable occasion recommended to her own servants to serve Jehovah the living
God, and attend to every means of improvement within
their reach. It was truly pleasing to observe, so soon
after she had embraced Christianity herself, an anxiety
to induce her people to follow her example. At Honoruru she erected a school, in which upwards of forty
children and young persons, principally connected with
her establishment, were daily taught to read and write,
and instructed in the first principles of religion, by a
native teacher, whom she almost entirely supported. In
this school she took a lively interest, and marked the
progress of the scholars with evident satisfaction; in
order to encourage the pupils, she frequently visited
the school during the hours of instruction, accompanied
by a number of chief women. She also attended the
public examinations, and noticed those who on these
occasions excelled, frequently presenting a favourite
scholar with a slate, a copy-book, pencil, pen, or some
other token of her approbation.

In her death the missionaries have lost a sincere
friend, and her subjects a queen who always delighted
to alleviate their distresses and promote their interests.

Her disposition was affectionate. I have seen her
and the king sitting beside the couch of Keopuolani, her
mother-in-law, day after day, when the latter has been
ill; and on these occasions, though there might be several servants in constant attendance, she would allow
no individual but her husband or herself to hand to the
patient any thing she might want, or even fan the flies
from her person.

The circumstances attending her departure from the
islands were peculiarly affecting. The king had gone
on board L'Aigle; but the boat was waiting to convey
her to the ship. She arose from the mat on which she
had been reclining, embraced her mother and other
relations most affectionately, and passed through the
crowd towards the boat. The people fell down on
their knees as she walked along, pressing and saluting
her feet—frequently bathing them with tears of unfeigned sorrow—and making loud wailings, in which

his family, thanking him at the same time for the hospitable entertainment we had received, and the great facilities he had afforded for accomplishing the objects of our visit.

About three o'clock in the morning, being awoke by the shouts of the men who were heaving up the anchor of the pilot-boat, I repaired on board, and immediately afterward we sailed with a gentle breeze blowing from the land. The wind was light and baffling, and it was noon before we reached Towaihae, where I learned with disappointment that the Nio had sailed to Oahu. On landing I was welcomed by Mr. Young, with whom I remained till the pilot-boat was ready to sail for Lahaina.

Late in the evening of the 2d of September, after preaching to the people of the place at Mr. Young's house, I went again on board the pilot-boat, but found her so full of sandal-wood that there was not room for any person below, while the decks were crowded with natives. The weather was unfavourable for getting under way till nearly daylight; and every person on board was completely drenched by the heavy rain that fell during the night.

During the forenoon of the 3d, we drifted slowly to the northward, and about noon took in eight hundred dried fish, after which we made sail for Maui. The weather was warm, the wind light: and all on board being obliged to keep on deck, without any screen or shade from the scorching rays of a vertical sun, the situation was very uncomfortable. At three P.M. we took the channel-breeze, which soon wafted us across to the south-east part of Maui.

As the shores of Hawaii receded from my view, a variety of reflections insensibly arose in my mind. The tour which, in the society of my companions, I had made had been replete with interest. The varied and sublime phenomena of nature had elevated our conceptions of "nature's God;" the manners and customs of the inhabitants had increased our interest in their welfare; while their superstition, moral degradation, ignorance, and vice had called forth our sincerest commiseration. We had made known the nature and consequences of sin, spoken of the love of God, and had exhibited the Lord Jesus Christ as the only Saviour to multitudes who had never before heard his name, or been directed

to worship the holy and living God, and who would probably never hear these truths again. We cherish the hope that, under the Divine blessing, lasting good will result, even from this transient visit.

Many of the individuals we have met on these occasions, we shall in all probability meet no more till the morning of the resurrection. May we meet them then on the right-hand of the Son of God?

At sunset we arrived off Morokini, but were shortly after becalmed. The current, however, was in our favour through the night, and at daylight on the 4th we found ourselves off the east end of the district of Lahaaina, and about a mile distant from the shore. Many of the natives jumped into the sea, and swam to the beach, holding their clothes above their heads with one hand, and swimming with the other.

On landing I waited on Keopuolani, the king's mother, whom I found ill; Karaimoku, Kaahumanu, Kalakua, and several other chiefs were reclining around her, weeping. After some time, Karaimoku proposed that they should unitedly pray for her recovery, and his proposal was acceded to.

Towards evening I visited the governor of the island, and also the king, who was then at Maui. The subsequent voyage of the latter to Great Britain, accompanied by his queen, and the melancholy event which terminated their lives while in London, excited considerable interest, and will probably be considered sufficient apology for a short account of them, although the event took place after my visit to Maui at this time.

The late king of the Sandwich Islands was the son of Tamehameha, former king, and Keopuolani, daughter of Kauikeouli, and Kakuiapoiwa. He was born in the eastern part of Hawaii, in the year 1795 or 1796. The name by which he was generally known was *Rihoriho*, which was only a contraction of *Kalaninui-rihoriho*, literally, the heaven's great black—from *Ka lani*, the heavens, *nui*, great, and *rihoriho*, applied to any thing burned to blackness. On public occasions he was sometimes called Tamehameha, after his father, though names are not always hereditary. Besides these, he had a variety of other names, the most common of which was *Iolani*. The word *lani*, heaven or sky, formed a component part

in the name of most chiefs of distinction. The following is a fac-simile of the official signature of the late king.

Tamehameha

The early habits of Rihoriho did not warrant any great expectations. His natural disposition was frank, and humane. The natives always spoke of him as good-natured, except when he was under the influence of ardent spirits; his manners were perfectly free, at the same time dignified, and always agreeable to those who were about him. His mind was naturally inquisitive. The questions he usually presented to foreigners were by no means trifling; and his memory was retentive. His general knowledge of the world was much greater than could have been expected. I have heard him entertain a party of chiefs for hours together with accounts of different parts of the earth, describing the extensive lakes, the mountains, and mines of North and South America—the elephants and inhabitants of India —the houses, manufactures, &c. of England—with no small accuracy, considering he had never seen them. He had a great thirst for knowledge, and was diligent in his studies. I recollect his remarking one day, when he opened his writing-desk, that he expected more advantage from that desk than from a fine brig belonging to him, lying at anchor opposite the house in which we were sitting. Mr. Bingham and myself were his daily teachers, and have often been surprised at his unwearied perseverance. I have sat beside him at his desk sometimes from nine or ten o'clock in the morning till nearly sunset, during which period his pen or his book has not been out of his hand more than three-quarters of an hour, while he was at dinner.

We do not know that Christianity exerted any decisive influence on his heart. He was willing to receive the missionaries on their first arrival—availed himself of their knowledge, to increase his own—and, during

the latter years of his life, was decidedly favourable to their object; declared his conviction of the truth of Christianity; attended public worship himself on the Sabbath, and recommended the same to his people.

His moral character was not marked by that cruelty, rapacity, and insensibility to the sufferings of the people, which frequently distinguish the abitrary chiefs of uncivilized nations. He appears in general to have been kind; and, in several places on our tour, the mothers showed us their children, and told us that when Rihoriho passed that way, he had kissed them—a condescension they seemed to think much of, and which they will probably remember to the end of their days. But, though generous in his disposition, and humane in his conduct towards his subjects, he was addicted to intoxication—whether from natural inclination or the influence and example of others is not now to be determined; frequently, to my own knowledge, it has been entirely from the latter. Had he in early life been privileged to associate with individuals whose conduct and principles were favourable to virtue and religion, there is every reason to suppose his moral character, with respect at least to this vice, would have been as irreproachable as his mental habits were commendable. But, alas for him! it was quite the reverse.

Though not distinguished by the ardour and strength of character so conspicuous in his father, he possessed both decision and enterprise: the abolition of the national idolatry was a striking instance of the former; and his voyage to England, of the latter.

The motives by which he was induced to undertake a voyage so long and hazardous were highly commendable. They were—a desire to see for himself countries of which he had heard such various and interesting accounts; a wish to have a personal interview with his majesty the king of Great Britain, or the chief members of the British government—for the purpose of confirming the cession of the Sandwich Islands, and placing himself and his dominions under British protection.

It was also his intention to make himself acquainted with the tenor and forms of administering justice in the courts of law, the principles of commerce, and other subjects important to the welfare of the islands.

The melancholy death of the late king and queen,

answered, received the presents, and afterward conversed with the people through the medium of Opiri. The facility with which they could communicate their thoughts by means of Opiri, the governor said, was attributed to the supposed influence of Opiri with his gods. The foreigners, they imagined, were supernatural beings, and, as such, were treated with every possible mark of respect. After remaining some time on the island, they returned to their own country. No account is preserved of the kind of vessel in which they arrived or departed. The name of the principal person among them was Manahini ; and it is a singular fact, that in the Marquesian, Society, and Sandwich Islands the term manahini is still employed to designate a stranger, visiter, or guest.

The third account is much more recent and precise, though the period at which it took place is uncertain.

It states, that a number of years after the departure of *Manahini-ma* (Manahini and his party), in the reign of Kahoukapu, king at Kaavaroa, seven foreigners arrived at Kearake'kua bay, the spot where Captain Cook landed. They came in a painted boat, with an awning or canopy over the stern, but without mast or sails. They were all dressed ; the colour of their clothes was white or yellow, and one of them wore a *pahi*, long knife, the name by which they still call a sword, at his side, and had a feather in his hat. The natives received them kindly. They married native women, were made chiefs, proved themselves warriors, and ultimately became very powerful in the island of Hawaii, which, it is said, was for some time governed by them.

There are in the Sandwich Islands a number of persons distinguished by a lighter colour in their skin, and corresponding brown curly hair, called *ehu*, who are, by all the natives of the islands, considered as the descendants of these foreigners, who acknowledge themselves to be such, and esteem their origin by no means dishonourable.

Another party is said to have afterward arrived at the same place, but the accounts the natives give of their landing are not very distinct ; and we feel undecided whether there were two distinct parties, or only two different accounts of the same event.

We have heard from one of the chiefs of Hawaii that there is a tradition of a ship having touched at the island

of Maui prior to the arrival of Captain Cook; but, with
the exception of this chief, all the natives we have conversed with on the subject, and we have conversed with
many, declare that they had no idea of a ship before
Capt. Cook was seen off Tauai. The ship they called
motu, an island, probably supposing it was an island with
all its inhabitants.

Marvellous reports respecting the ships and people
were circulated through the islands, between the first
discovery off Tauai and the return of the vessels from
the north-west coast of America. *Aa mo*, skin of lizard's
egg, a native of Tauai, who was on board one of the
ships, procured a piece of canvass about a yard and a
half long, which Tiha, king of Tauai, sent as a present
to Poriorani, king of Oahu. He gave it to his queen
Opuhani, by whom it was worn on the most conspicuous part of her dress in a public procession, and attracted
more attention than any thing else. The piece of cloth
was called Aa mo, after the man who had the honour
of bringing it from the ships.

The most unaccountable circumstance connected with
the priest Paao is his arriving alone, though he might
be the only survivor of his party. If such a person
ever did arrive, we should think he was a Roman Catholic priest, and the reported gods an image and a
crucifix.

The different parties that subsequently arrived were
probably, if any inference may be drawn from the accounts of the natives, survivors of the crew of some
Spanish ship wrecked in the neighbourhood, perhaps on
the numerous reefs to the north-west; or they might
have been culprits committed by their countrymen to
the mercy of the waves. The circumstance of the first
party leaving the island in the same boat in which they
arrived would lead us to suppose they had been wrecked,
and had escaped in their boat, or had constructed a bark
out of the wreck of their ship, as has subsequently been
the case with two vessels wrecked in the vicinity of
these islands.

It is possible that one or other of the islands might have
been seen by some Spanish ship passing between Acapulco and Manilla; but it is not probable that they were
ever visited by any of these ships. An event so interesting to the people would not have been left out of

their traditions, which contain many things much less
important; and had the Spaniards discovered them,
however jealous they might be of such a discovery
becoming known to other nations, that jealousy would
not have prevented their availing themselves of the
facilities which the islands afforded for refitting or recruiting their vessels, which must frequently have been
most desirable during the period their ships were accustomed to traverse these seas.

These accounts, but particularly the latter, are generally known, and have been related by different persons
at distant places. All agree respecting the boat, clothing, sword, &c. of the party who arrived at Kearake'kua.
Among others, the late king Rihoriho gave us a detailed
account of their landing, &c. only a short time before
he embarked for England. We feel but little doubt of
the fact; but the country whence they came, the place
whither they were bound, the occasion of their visit,
and a variety of interesting particulars connected therewith, will probably remain undiscovered.

The 31st was the Sabbath. The stillness of every
thing around, the decent apparel of those who were seen
passing and repassing, together with the numbers of
canoes all drawn up on the beach, under the shade of
the cocoanut or kou-trees, combined to mark the return
of the *la tabu*, or sacred day. An unusual number attended family prayers at the governor's house in the
morning; and at half-past ten the bell was rung for
public worship. About eight hundred people assembled
under the ranai, and I preached to them from Heb. xi. 7.
And after a succinct account of the deluge, I endeavoured to exhibit the advantages of faith, and the consequences of wickedness and unbelief, as illustrated in
the salvation of Noah and the destruction of the rest
of mankind.

After the conclusion of the service, several persons
present requested me to remain till they had made some
inquiries respecting the deluge, Noah, &c.

They said they were informed by their fathers that
all the land had once been overflowed by the sea, except
a small peak on the top of Mouna Kea, where two human
beings were preserved from the destruction that overtook the rest; but they said they had never before heard
of a ship, or of Noah, having always been accustomed

to call it the *kai a Kahinárii* (sea of Kahinárii). After conversing with them some time, I returned to the governor's.

The afternoon was principally employed in conversation with him on the flood, and the repeopling of the earth by the descendants of Noah. The governor seemed to doubt whether it were possible that the Hawaiians could be the descendants of Noah; but said he thought their progenitors must have been created on the islands. I told him the account in the Bible had every evidence that could be wished to support it; referred him to his own traditions, not only of Hawaii having been peopled by persons who came in canoes from a foreign country, but of their having in their turn visited other islands and planted colonies, as in the days of Kamapiikai—the superiority of their war-canoes in former days—the resemblance in manners, customs, traditions, and language between themselves and other islanders in the Pacific, many thousand miles distant.

The longevity of mankind in the days of Noah also surprised him. Comparing it with the period of human life at the present time, he said, "By-and-by men will not live more than forty years."

At half-past four in the afternoon the bell rang again, and the people collected in numbers about equal to those who attended in the morning. I preached to them from the words, "Be not weary in well-doing, for in due season ye shall reap, if ye faint not."

Numbers thronged the governor's house at evening worship. The conversation afterward turned upon the identity of the body at the resurrection, and the reward of the righteous in heaven. The governor asked if people would know each other in heaven; and when answered in the affirmative, said he thought Christian relations would be very happy when they met there. Some who were present asked, "If there is no eating and drinking or wearing of clothes in heaven, wherein does its goodness consist?" This was a natural question for a Hawaiian to ask; who never had an idea of happiness, except in the gratification of his natural appetites and feelings. In answer to the question, they were, however, informed that the joys of heaven were intellectual and spiritual, and would infinitely exceed, both in their nature and duration, every earthly enjoyment. At a late hour I took leave of the governor and

his family, thanking him at the same time for the hospitable entertainment we had received, and the great facilities he had afforded for accomplishing the objects of our visit.

About three o'clock in the morning, being awoke by the shouts of the men who were heaving up the anchor of the pilot-boat, I repaired on board, and immediately afterward we sailed with a gentle breeze blowing from the land. The wind was light and baffling, and it was noon before we reached Towaihae, where I learned with disappointment that the Nio had sailed to Oahu. On landing I was welcomed by Mr. Young, with whom I remained till the pilot-boat was ready to sail for Lahaina.

Late in the evening of the 2d of September, after preaching to the people of the place at Mr. Young's house, I went again on board the pilot-boat, but found her so full of sandal-wood that there was not room for any person below, while the decks were crowded with natives. The weather was unfavourable for getting under way till nearly daylight; and every person on board was completely drenched by the heavy rain that fell during the night.

During the forenoon of the 3d, we drifted slowly to the northward, and about noon took in eight hundred dried fish, after which we made sail for Maui. The weather was warm, the wind light: and all on board being obliged to keep on deck, without any screen or shade from the scorching rays of a vertical sun, the situation was very uncomfortable. At three P. M. we took the channel-breeze, which soon wafted us across to the south-east part of Maui.

As the shores of Hawaii receded from my view, a variety of reflections insensibly arose in my mind. The tour which, in the society of my companions, I had made had been replete with interest. The varied and sublime phenomena of nature had elevated our conceptions of "nature's God;" the manners and customs of the inhabitants had increased our interest in their welfare; while their superstition, moral degradation, ignorance, and vice had called forth our sincerest commiseration. We had made known the nature and consequences of sin, spoken of the love of God, and had exhibited the Lord Jesus Christ as the only Saviour to multitudes who had never before heard his name, or been directed

to worship the holy and living God, and who would probably never hear these truths again. We cherish the hope that, under the Divine blessing, lasting good will result, even from this transient visit.

Many of the individuals we have met on these occasions, we shall in all probability meet no more till the morning of the resurrection. May we meet them then on the right-hand of the Son of God!

At sunset we arrived off Morokini, but were shortly after becalmed. The current, however, was in our favour through the night, and at daylight on the 4th we found ourselves off the east end of the district of Lahaina, and about a mile distant from the shore. Many of the natives jumped into the sea, and swam to the beach, holding their clothes above their heads with one hand, and swimming with the other.

On landing I waited on Keopuolani, the king's mother, whom I found ill; Karaimoku, Kaahumanu, Kalakua, and several other chiefs were reclining around her, weeping. After some time, Karaimoku proposed that they should unitedly pray for her recovery, and his proposal was acceded to.

Towards evening I visited the governor of the island, and also the king, who was then at Maui. The subsequent voyage of the latter to Great Britain, accompanied by his queen, and the melancholy event which terminated their lives while in London, excited considerable interest, and will probably be considered sufficient apology for a short account of them, although the event took place after my visit to Maui at this time.

The late king of the Sandwich Islands was the son of Tamehameha, former king, and Keopuolani, daughter of Kauikeouli, and Kakuiapoiwa. He was born in the eastern part of Hawaii, in the year 1795 or 1796. The name by which he was generally known was *Rihoriho*, which was only a contraction of *Kalaninui-rihoriho*, literally, the heaven's great black—from *Ka lani*, the heavens, *nui*, great, and *rihoriho*, applied to any thing burned to blackness. On public occasions he was sometimes called Tamehameha, after his father, though names are not always hereditary. Besides these, he had a variety of other names, the most common of which was *Iolani*. The word *lani*, heaven or sky, formed a component part

in the name of most chiefs of distinction. The following is a fac-simile of the official signature of the late king.

The early habits of Rihoriho did not warrant any great expectations. His natural disposition was frank, and humane. The natives always spoke of him as good-natured, except when he was under the influence of ardent spirits; his manners were perfectly free, at the same time dignified, and always agreeable to those who were about him.' His mind was naturally inquisitive. The questions he usually presented to foreigners were by no means trifling; and his memory was retentive. His general knowledge of the world was much greater than could have been expected. I have heard him entertain a party of chiefs for hours together with accounts of different parts of the earth, describing the extensive lakes, the mountains, and mines of North and South America—the elephants and inhabitants of India—the houses, manufactures, &c. of England—with no small accuracy, considering he had never seen them. He had a great thirst for knowledge, and was diligent in his studies. I recollect his remarking one day, when he opened his writing-desk, that he expected more advantage from that desk than from a fine brig belonging to him, lying at anchor opposite the house in which we were sitting. Mr. Bingham and myself were his daily teachers, and have often been surprised at his unwearied perseverance. I have sat beside him at his desk sometimes from nine or ten o'clock in the morning till nearly sunset, during which period his pen or his book has not been out of his hand more than three-quarters of an hour, while he was at dinner. ·

. We do not know that Christianity exerted any decisive influence on his heart. He was willing to receive the missionaries on their first arrival—availed himself of their knowledge, to increase his own—and, during

the latter years of his life, was decidedly favourable to
their object; declared his conviction of the truth of
Christianity; attended public worship himself on the
Sabbath, and recommended the same to his people.

His moral character was not marked by that cruelty,
rapacity, and insensibility to the sufferings of the people,
which frequently distinguish the abitrary chiefs of uncivilized nations. He appears in general to have been
kind; and, in several places on our tour, the mothers
showed us their children, and told us that when Rihoriho passed that way, he had kissed them—a condescension they seemed to think much of, and which they
will probably remember to the end of their days. But,
though generous in his disposition, and humane in his
conduct towards his subjects, he was addicted to intoxication—whether from natural inclination or the influence
and example of others is not now to be determined;
frequently, to my own knowledge, it has been entirely
from the latter. Had he in early life been privileged to
associate with individuals whose conduct and principles
were favourable to virtue and religion, there is every
reason to suppose his moral character, with respect at
least to this vice, would have been as irreproachable as
his mental habits were commendable. But, alas for
him! it was quite the reverse.

Though not distinguished by the ardour and strength
of character so conspicuous in his father, he possessed
both decision and enterprise: the abolition of the national idolatry was a striking instance of the former;
and his voyage to England, of the latter.

The motives by which he was induced to undertake
a voyage so long and hazardous were highly commendable. They were—a desire to see for himself countries
of which he had heard such various and interesting
accounts; a wish to have a personal interview with his
majesty the king of Great Britain, or the chief members of the British government—for the purpose of
confirming the cession of the Sandwich Islands, and
placing himself and his dominions under British protection.

It was also his intention to make himself acquainted
with the tenor and forms of administering justice in the
courts of law, the principles of commerce, and other
subjects important to the welfare of the islands.

The melancholy death of the late king and queen,

which took place shortly after their arrival in England,
not only prevented the full accomplishment of these
desirable objects, but awakened very generally a degree
of apprehension that the people of the islands, unacquainted with the true circumstances of their death,
would be led to suppose they had been neglected, unkindly treated, or even poisoned in revenge of the death
of Captain Cook, and that the feelings of friendship
with which they had been accustomed to regard the
people of England might be followed by enmity or distrust. The fears of those who felt interested in the
welfare of the Hawaiians, though natural, were groundless. The British government had entertained the
young ruler of the Sandwich Islands, his consort, and
attendants with its accustomed hospitality; and when
they were attacked by diseases incident to a northern
climate, but unknown in their native islands, every attention that humanity could suggest, and every alleviation
that the first medical skill in London could afford, was
most promptly rendered. After their decease, the highest respect was paid to their remains, and in honourable
regard to the feelings of the nation who had suffered this
painful bereavement, a British frigate, under the command of Captain Lord Byron, was appointed to convey to
the Sandwich Islands the bodies of the king and queen,
that their sorrowing people might have the mournful
satisfaction of depositing their ashes among the tombs
of their ancestors.

By the return of a highly esteemed missionary friend,
Rev. C. S. Stewart, I have learned that the Blonde
reached the islands in the month of May, 1825: the
natives were in some degree prepared for the arrival, by
the intelligence of the death of their king and queen,
which they had received about two months before from
Valparaiso. Shortly after, the vessel having the remains
of the king and queen on board had anchored off Oahu,
Boki, the principal chief, who had accompanied the
king to England, attended by those of his countrymen
who had also returned, proceeded on shore: on landing,
he was met by his elder brother Karaimoku, and other
distinguished chiefs, and after the first emotions of joy
at meeting again, and sorrow on account of the loss all
had sustained, were somewhat abated, the survivors
and their friends walked in solemn and mournful procession to the place of worship, where thanksgivings
were presented to God, for the merciful preservation

of those who were thus privileged to meet again, and supplications were made that the afflicting dispensation, which all so deeply felt, might exert a salutary influence in the minds of the surviving chiefs, and the sorrowing nation at large.

Karaimoku, the late prime minister, and present regent of the islands, then arose and said, " We have lost our king and queen, they have died in a foreign land; we shall see them no more ; it is right that we should weep, but let us not entertain hard thoughts of God. *God has not done wrong.* The evil is with us: let us bow under his hand; let all amusement cease; let our daily avocations be suspended ; and let the nation, by prayer and a cessation from ordinary pursuits, humble itself before God fourteen days." Before the assembly separated, Boki stood up, and, in a brief outline of the voyage, narrated the most prominent events that had transpired since his departure from the islands —calling their attention in particular to the suitable and important advice he had received from his majesty the king of Great Britain, in an audience with which he was graciously favoured, viz. To return to his native country, attend to general and religious instruction himself, and endeavour to enlighten and reform the people. The peculiar circumstances of the people at this time, the increased satisfaction they had for some time felt in attending every means of instruction within their reach, and the pleasing change in favour of religion which many had experienced, rendered this recommendation, so congenial to their feelings, from a source so distinguished, unusually acceptable. A deep and favourable impression was produced on all present, a new impulse was given to the means already employed for the instruction and improvement of the people, from which most advantageous results have already appeared. They were also made acquainted, by Boki and his companions, with the kind reception, generous treatment, and marked attentions which the late king and queen and their suite had received while in England. This intelligence, communicated by those whose testimony would be received with the most entire credence, would at once confirm the attachment and confidence they have so long felt towards England.

No disturbance of the general tranquillity, nor change in the government, of the islands has resulted from this

event. Rihoriho' left a younger brother, *Kauikeouli*, about ten years of age, who is acknowledged by the chiefs as his successor. A regency will govern during his minority, and the executive authority will probably continue to be exercised by *Karaimoku*, and the other chiefs with whom Rihoriho left it when he embarked for England.

The queen, who accompanied him, and who died at the same time, has left a fond mother and an affectionate people to lament her loss: she was the daughter of Tamehameha and Talakua, and was born about the year 1797 or 1798, being two years younger than Rihoriho, and about twenty-six years of age when she left the islands. Like all the persons of distinction she had many names, but that by which she was generally known was *Kamehamaru* (shade of Kameha), from *kameha*, a contraction of her father's name, and *maru*, shade. She was distinguished for good nature, and was much beloved by all her subjects. The poor people, when unable to pay their rent, or under the displeasure of the king and chiefs, or embarrassed on any other account, frequently repaired to her, and found a friend whose aid was never refused. She was also kind to those foreigners who might be distressed in the islands, and though she never harboured any or countenanced their absconding from their ships, she has often fed them when hungry, and given them native tapa for clothing.

Kamehamaru was at all times lively and agreeable in company; and though her application to her book and her pen was equal to that of the king, her improvement in learning was more gradual, and her general knowledge less extensive.

She excelled, however, in the management of his domestic affairs, which were conducted by her with great judgment and address, and, though formerly accustomed to use ardent spirits, from the time she put herself under Christian instruction, she entirely discontinued that and every other practice inconsistent with her profession of Christianity. Her attendance on the duties of religion was maintained with commendable regularity.

Her influence contributed very materially to the pleasing change that has recently taken place, in connexion with the labours of the missionaries in the islands. For the instruction and moral improvement of the people,

she manifested no ordinary concern. Long before
many of the leading chiefs were favourable to the instruction of the people or their reception of Christianity, Kamehamaru on every suitable occasion recommended to her own servants to serve Jehovah the living
God, and attend to every means of improvement within
their reach. It was truly pleasing to observe, so soon
after she had embraced Christianity herself, an anxiety
to induce her people to follow her example. At Honoruru she erected a school, in which upwards of forty
children and young persons, principally connected with
her establishment, were daily taught to read and write,
and instructed in the first principles of religion, by a
native teacher, whom she almost entirely supported. In
this school she took a lively interest, and marked the
progress of the scholars with evident satisfaction; in
order to encourage the pupils, she frequently visited
the school during the hours of instruction, accompanied
by a number of chief women. She also attended the
public examinations, and noticed those who on these
occasions excelled, frequently presenting a favourite
scholar with a slate, a copy-book, pencil, pen, or some
other token of her approbation.

In her death the missionaries have lost a sincere
friend, and her subjects a queen who always delighted
to alleviate their distresses and promote their interests.

Her disposition was affectionate. I have seen her
and the king sitting beside the couch of Keopuolani, her
mother-in-law, day after day, when the latter has been
ill; and on these occasions, though there might be several servants in constant attendance, she would allow
no individual but her husband or herself to hand to the
patient any thing she might want, or even fan the flies
from her person.

The circumstances attending her departure from the
islands were peculiarly affecting. The king had gone
on board L'Aigle; but the boat was waiting to convey
her to the ship. She arose from the mat on which she
had been reclining; embraced her mother and other
relations most affectionately, and passed through the
crowd towards the boat. The people fell down on
their knees as she walked along, pressing and saluting
her feet—frequently bathing them with tears of unfeigned sorrow—and making loud wailings, in which

his family, thanking him at the same time for the hospitable entertainment we had received, and the great facilities he had afforded for accomplishing the objects of our visit.

About three o'clock in the morning, being awoke by the shouts of the men who were heaving up the anchor of the pilot-boat, I repaired on board, and immediately afterward we sailed with a gentle breeze blowing from the land. The wind was light and baffling, and it was noon before we reached Towaihae, where I learned with disappointment that the Nio had sailed to Oahu. On landing I was welcomed by Mr. Young, with whom I remained till the pilot-boat was ready to sail for Lahaina.

Late in the evening of the 2d of September, after preaching to the people of the place at Mr. Young's house, I went again on board the pilot-boat, but found her so full of sandal-wood that there was not room for any person below, while the decks were crowded with natives. The weather was unfavourable for getting under way till nearly daylight; and every person on board was completely drenched by the heavy rain that fell during the night.

During the forenoon of the 3d, we drifted slowly to the northward, and about noon took in eight hundred dried fish, after which we made sail for Maui. The weather was warm, the wind light: and all on board being obliged to keep on deck, without any screen or shade from the scorching rays of a vertical sun, the situation was very uncomfortable. At three P. M. we took the channel-breeze, which soon wafted us across to the south-east part of Maui.

As the shores of Hawaii receded from my view, a variety of reflections insensibly arose in my mind. The tour which, in the society of my companions, I had made had been replete with interest. The varied and sublime phenomena of nature had elevated our conceptions of "nature's God;" the manners and customs of the inhabitants had increased our interest in their welfare; while their superstition, moral degradation, ignorance, and vice had called forth our sincerest commiseration. We had made known the nature and consequences of sin, spoken of the love of God, and had exhibited the Lord Jesus Christ as the only Saviour to multitudes who had never before heard his name, or been directed

to worship the holy and living God, and who would probably never hear these truths again. We cherish the hope that, under the Divine blessing, lasting good will result, even from this transient visit.

Many of the individuals we have met on these occasions, we shall in all probability meet no more till the morning of the resurrection. May we meet them then on the right-hand of the Son of God?

At sunset we arrived off Morokini, but were shortly after becalmed. The current, however, was in our favour through the night, and at daylight on the 4th we found ourselves off the east end of the district of Lahaina, and about a mile distant from the shore. Many of the natives jumped into the sea, and swam to the beach, holding their clothes above their heads with one hand, and swimming with the other.

On landing I waited on Keopuolani, the king's mother, whom I found ill; Karaimoku, Kaahumanu, Kalakua, and several other chiefs were reclining around her, weeping. After some time, Karaimoku proposed that they should unitedly pray for her recovery, and his proposal was acceded to.

Towards evening I visited the governor of the island, and also the king, who was then at Maui. The subsequent voyage of the latter to Great Britain, accompanied by his queen, and the melancholy event which terminated their lives while in London, excited considerable interest, and will probably be considered sufficient apology for a short account of them, although the event took place after my visit to Maui at this time.

The late king of the Sandwich Islands was the son of Tamehameha, former king, and Keopuolani, daughter of Kauikeouli, and Kakuiapoiwa. He was born in the eastern part of Hawaii, in the year 1795 or 1796. The name by which he was generally known was *Rihoriho*, which was only a contraction of *Kalaninui-rihoriho*, literally, the heaven's great black—from *Ka lani*, the heavens, *nui*, great, and *rihoriho*, applied to any thing burned to blackness. On public occasions he was sometimes called Tamehameha, after his father, though names are not always hereditary. Besides these, he had a variety of other names, the most common of which was *Iolani*. The word *lani*, heaven or sky, formed a component part

in the name of most chiefs of distinction. The following is a fac-simile of the official signature of the late
king.

Tamehameha

The early habits of Rihoriho did not warrant any
great expectations. His natural disposition was frank,
and humane. The natives always spoke of him as
good-natured, except when he was under the influence
of ardent spirits; his manners were perfectly free, at
the same time dignified, and always agreeable to those
who were about him. His mind was naturally inquisitive. The questions he usually presented to foreigners
were by no means trifling; and his memory was retentive. His general knowledge of the world was much
greater than could have been expected. I have heard
him entertain a party of chiefs for hours together with
accounts of different parts of the earth, describing the
extensive lakes, the mountains, and mines of North and
South America—the elephants and inhabitants of India
—the houses, manufactures, &c. of England—with no
small accuracy, considering he had never seen them.
He had a great thirst for knowledge, and was diligent in
his studies. I recollect his remarking one day, when
he opened his writing-desk, that he expected more advantage from that desk than from a fine brig belonging
to him, lying at anchor opposite the house in which we
were sitting. Mr. Bingham and myself were his daily
teachers, and have often been surprised at his unwearied
perseverance. I have sat beside him at his desk sometimes from nine or ten o'clock in the morning till nearly
sunset, during which period his pen or his book has not
been out of his hand more than three-quarters of an
hour, while he was at dinner.
We do not know that Christianity exerted any decisive influence on his heart. He was willing to receive
the missionaries on their first arrival—availed himself
of their knowledge, to increase his own—and, during

the latter years of his life, was decidedly favourable to
their object; declared his conviction of the truth of
Christianity; attended public worship himself on the
Sabbath, and recommended the same to his people.

His moral character was not marked by that cruelty,
rapacity, and insensibility to the sufferings of the people,
which frequently distinguish the abitrary chiefs of uncivilized nations. He appears in general to have been
kind; and, in several places on our tour, the mothers
showed us their children, and told us that when Rihoriho passed that way, he had kissed them—a condescension they seemed to think much of, and which they
will probably remember to the end of their days. But,
though generous in his disposition, and humane in his
conduct towards his subjects, he was addicted to intoxication—whether from natural inclination or the influence
and example of others is not now to be determined;
frequently, to my own knowledge, it has been entirely
from the latter. Had he in early life been privileged to
associate with individuals whose conduct and principles
were favourable to virtue and religion, there is every
reason to suppose his moral character, with respect at
least to this vice, would have been as irreproachable as
his mental habits were commendable. But, alas for
him! it was quite the reverse.

Though not distinguished by the ardour and strength
of character so conspicuous in his father, he possessed
both decision and enterprise: the abolition of the national idolatry was a striking instance of the former;
and his voyage to England, of the latter.

The motives by which he was induced to undertake
a voyage so long and hazardous were highly commendable. They were—a desire to see for himself countries
of which he had heard such various and interesting
accounts; a wish to have a personal interview with his
majesty the king of Great Britain, or the chief members of the British government—for the purpose of
confirming the cession of the Sandwich Islands, and
placing himself and his dominions under British protection.

It was also his intention to make himself acquainted
with the tenor and forms of administering justice in the
courts of law, the principles of commerce, and other
subjects important to the welfare of the islands.

The melancholy death of the late king and queen,

which took place shortly after their arrival in England, not only prevented the full accomplishment of these desirable objects, but awakened very generally a degree of apprehension that the people of the islands, unacquainted with the true circumstances of their death, would be led to suppose they had been neglected, unkindly treated, or even poisoned in revenge of the death of Captain Cook, and that the feelings of friendship with which they had been accustomed to regard the people of England might be followed by enmity or distrust. The fears of those who felt interested in the welfare of the Hawaiians, though natural, were groundless. The British government had entertained the young ruler of the Sandwich Islands, his consort, and attendants with its accustomed hospitality; and when they were attacked by diseases incident to a northern climate, but unknown in their native islands, every attention that humanity could suggest, and every alleviation that the first medical skill in London could afford, was most promptly rendered. After their decease, the highest respect was paid to their remains, and in honourable regard to the feelings of the nation who had suffered this painful bereavement, a British frigate, under the command of Captain Lord Byron, was appointed to convey to the Sandwich Islands the bodies of the king and queen, that their sorrowing people might have the mournful satisfaction of depositing their ashes among the tombs of their ancestors.

By the return of a highly esteemed missionary friend, Rev. C. S. Stewart, I have learned that the Blonde reached the islands in the month of May, 1825: the natives were in some degree prepared for the arrival, by the intelligence of the death of their king and queen, which they had received about two months before from Valparaiso. Shortly after, the vessel having the remains of the king and queen on board had anchored off Oahu, Boki, the principal chief, who had accompanied the king to England, attended by those of his countrymen who had also returned, proceeded on shore: on landing, he was met by his elder brother Karaimoku, and other distinguished chiefs, and after the first emotions of joy at meeting again, and sorrow on account of the loss all had sustained, were somewhat abated, the survivors and their friends walked in solemn and mournful procession to the place of worship, where thanksgivings were presented to God, for the merciful preservation

of those who were thus privileged to meet again, and supplications were made that the afflicting dispensation, which all so deeply felt, might exert a salutary influence in the minds of the surviving chiefs, and the sorrowing nation at large.

Karaimoku, the late prime minister, and present regent of the islands, then arose and said, "We have lost our king and queen, they have died in a foreign land; we shall see them no more; it is right that we should weep, but let us not entertain hard thoughts of God. *God has not done wrong.* The evil is with us: let us bow under his hand; let all amusement cease; let our daily avocations be suspended; and let the nation, by prayer and a cessation from ordinary pursuits, humble itself before God fourteen days." Before the assembly separated, Boki stood up, and, in a brief outline of the voyage, narrated the most prominent events that had transpired since his departure from the islands —calling their attention in particular to the suitable and important advice he had received from his majesty the king of Great Britain, in an audience with which he was graciously favoured, viz. To return to his native country, attend to general and religious instruction himself, and endeavour to enlighten and reform the people. The peculiar circumstances of the people at this time, the increased satisfaction they had for some time felt in attending every means of instruction within their reach, and the pleasing change in favour of religion which many had experienced, rendered this recommendation, so congenial to their feelings, from a source so distinguished, unusually acceptable. A deep and favourable impression was produced on all present, a new impulse was given to the means already employed for the instruction and improvement of the people, from which most advantageous results have already appeared. They were also made acquainted, by Boki and his companions, with the kind reception, generous treatment, and marked attentions which the late king and queen and their suite had received while in England. This intelligence, communicated by those whose testimony would be received with the most entire credence, would at once confirm the attachment and confidence they have so long felt towards England.

No disturbance of the general tranquillity, nor change in the government, of the islands has resulted from this

event. Rihoriho' left a younger brother, *Kauikeouli*, about ten years of age, who is acknowledged by the chiefs as his successor. A regency will.govern during his minority, and the executive authority will probably continue to be exercised by *Karaimoku*, and the other chiefs with whom Rihoriho left it when he embarked for England.

The queen, who accompanied him, and who died at the same time, has left a fond mother and an affectionate people to lament her loss: she was the daughter of Tamehameha and Talakua, and was born about the year 1797 or 1798, being two years younger than Rihoriho, and about twenty-six years of age when she left the islands. Like all the persons of distinction she had many names, but that by which she was generally known was *Kamehamaru* (shade of Kameha), from *kameha*, a contraction of herfather's name, and *maru*, shade. She was distinguished for good nature, and was much beloved by all her subjects. The poor people, when unable to pay their rent, or under the displeasure of the king and chiefs, or embarrassed on any other account, frequently repaired to her, and found a friend whose aid was never refused. She was also kind to those foreigners who might be distressed in the islands, and though she never harboured any or countenanced their absconding from their ships, she has often fed them when hungry, and given them native tapa for clothing.

Kamehamaru was at all times lively and agreeable in company; and though her application to her book and her pen was equal to that of the king, her improvement in learning was more gradual, and her general knowledge less extensive.

She excelled, however, in the management of his domestic affairs, which were conducted by her with great judgment and address, and, though formerly accustomed to use ardent spirits, from the time she put herself under Christian instruction, she entirely discontinued that and every other practice inconsistent with her profession of Christianity. Her attendance on the duties of religion was maintained with commendable regularity.

Her influence contributed very materially to the pleasing change that has recently taken place, in connexion with the labours of the missionaries in the islands. For the instruction and moral improvement of the people,

she manifested no ordinary concern. Long before many of the leading chiefs were favourable to the instruction of the people or their reception of Christianity, Kamehamaru on every suitable occasion recommended to her own servants to serve Jehovah the living God, and attend to every means of improvement within their reach. It was truly pleasing to observe, so soon after she had embraced Christianity herself, an anxiety to induce her people to follow her example. At Honoruru she erected a school, in which upwards of forty children and young persons, principally connected with her establishment, were daily taught to read and write, and instructed in the first principles of religion, by a native teacher, whom she almost entirely supported. In this school she took a lively interest, and marked the progress of the scholars with evident satisfaction; in order to encourage the pupils, she frequently visited the school during the hours of instruction, accompanied by a number of chief women. She also attended the public examinations, and noticed those who on these occasions excelled, frequently presenting a favourite scholar with a slate, a copy-book, pencil, pen, or some other token of her approbation.

In her death the missionaries have lost a sincere friend, and her subjects a queen who always delighted to alleviate their distresses and promote their interests.

Her disposition was affectionate. I have seen her and the king sitting beside the couch of Keopuolani, her mother-in-law, day after day, when the latter has been ill; and on these occasions, though there might be several servants in constant attendance, she would allow no individual but her husband or herself to hand to the patient any thing she might want, or even fan the flies from her person.

The circumstances attending her departure from the islands were peculiarly affecting. The king had gone on board L'Aigle; but the boat was waiting to convey her to the ship. She arose from the mat on which she had been reclining; embraced her mother and other relations most affectionately, and passed through the crowd towards the boat. The people fell down on their knees as she walked along, pressing and saluting her feet—frequently bathing them with tears of unfeigned sorrow—and making loud wailings, in which

his family, thanking him at the same time for the hospitable entertainment we had received; and the great
facilities he had afforded for accomplishing the objects
of our visit.

About three o'clock in the morning, being awoke by
the shouts of the men who were heaving up the anchor
of the pilot-boat, I repaired on board, and immediately
afterward we sailed with a gentle breeze blowing from
the land. The wind was light and baffling, and it was
noon before we reached Towaihae, where I learned with
disappointment that the Nio had sailed to Oahu. On
landing I was welcomed by Mr. Young, with whom I
remained till the pilot-boat was ready to sail for Lahaina.

Late in the evening of the 2d of September, after
preaching to the people of the place at Mr. Young's
house, I went again on board the pilot-boat, but found
her so full of sandal-wood that there was not room for
any person below, while the decks were crowded with
natives. The weather was unfavourable for getting
under way till nearly daylight; and every person on
board was completely drenched by the heavy rain that
fell during the night.

During the forenoon of the 3d, we drifted slowly to
the northward, and about noon took in eight hundred
dried fish, after which we made sail for Maui. The
weather was warm, the wind light: and all on board
being obliged to keep on deck, without any screen or
shade from the scorching rays of a vertical sun, the
situation was very uncomfortable. At three P. M. we
took the channel-breeze, which soon wafted us across to
the south-east part of Maui.

As the shores of Hawaii receded from my view, a
variety of reflections insensibly arose in my mind. The
tour which, in the society of my companions, I had made
had been replete with interest. The varied and sublime
phenomena of nature had elevated our conceptions of
" nature's God;" the manners and customs of the inhabitants had increased our interest in their welfare;
while their superstition, moral degradation, ignorance,
and vice had called forth our sincerest commiseration.
We had made known the nature and consequences of
sin, spoken of the love of God, and had exhibited the
Lord Jesus Christ as the only Saviour to multitudes
who had never before heard his name, or been directed

to worship the holy and living God, and who would probably never hear these truths again. We cherish the hope that, under the Divine blessing, lasting good will result, even from this transient visit.

Many of the individuals we have met on these occasions, we shall in all probability meet no more till the morning of the resurrection. May we meet them then on the right-hand of the Son of God?

At sunset we arrived off Morokini, but were shortly after becalmed. The current, however, was in our favour through the night, and at daylight on the 4th we found ourselves off the east end of the district of Lahaina, and about a mile distant from the shore. Many of the natives jumped into the sea, and swam to the beach, holding their clothes above their heads with one hand, and swimming with the other.

On landing I waited on Keopuolani, the king's mother, whom I found ill; Karaimoku, Kaahumanu, Kalakua, and several other chiefs were reclining around her, weeping. After some time, Karaimoku proposed that they should unitedly pray for her recovery, and his proposal was acceded to.

Towards evening I visited the governor of the island, and also the king, who was then at Maui. The subsequent voyage of the latter to Great Britain, accompanied by his queen, and the melancholy event which terminated their lives while in London, excited considerable interest, and will probably be considered sufficient apology for a short account of them, although the event took place after my visit to Maui at this time.

The late king of the Sandwich Islands was the son of Tamehameha, former king, and Keopuolani, daughter of Kauikeouli, and Kakuiapoiwa. He was born in the eastern part of Hawaii, in the year 1795 or 1796. The name by which he was generally known was *Rihoriho*, which was only a contraction of *Kalaninui-rihoriho*, literally, the heaven's great black—from *Ka lani*, the heavens, *nui*, great, and *rihoriho*, applied to any thing burned to blackness. On public occasions he was sometimes called Tamehameha, after his father, though names are not always hereditary. Besides these, he had a variety of other names, the most common of which was *Iolani*. The word *lani*, heaven or sky, formed a component part

in the name of most chiefs of distinction. The following is a fac-simile of the official signature of the late
king.

Tamehameha

The early habits of Rihoriho did not warrant any
great expectations. His natural disposition was frank,
and humane. The natives always spoke of him as
good-natured, except when he was under the influence
of ardent spirits; his manners were perfectly free, at
the same time dignified, and always agreeable to those
who were about him. His mind was naturally inquisitive. The questions he usually presented to foreigners
were by no means trifling; and his memory was retentive. His general knowledge of the world was much
greater than could have been expected. I have heard
him entertain a party of chiefs for hours together with
accounts of different parts of the earth, describing the
extensive lakes, the mountains, and mines of North and
South America—the elephants and inhabitants of India
—the houses, manufactures, &c. of England—with no
small accuracy, considering he had never seen them.
He had a great thirst for knowledge, and was diligent in
his studies. I recollect his remarking one day, when
he opened his writing-desk, that he expected more advantage from that desk than from a fine brig belonging
to him, lying at anchor opposite the house in which we
were sitting. Mr. Bingham and myself were his daily
teachers, and have often been surprised at his unwearied
perseverance. I have sat beside him at his desk sometimes from nine or ten o'clock in the morning till nearly
sunset, during which period his pen or his book has not
been out of his hand more than three-quarters of an
hour, while he was at dinner.

We do not know that Christianity exerted any decisive influence on his heart. He was willing to receive
the missionaries on their first arrival—availed himself
of their knowledge, to increase his own—and, during

the latter years of his life, was decidedly favourable to
their object; declared his conviction of the truth of
Christianity; attended public worship himself on the
Sabbath, and recommended the same to his people.

His moral character was not marked by that cruelty,
rapacity, and insensibility to the sufferings of the people,
which frequently distinguish the abitrary chiefs of uncivilized nations. He appears in general to have been
kind; and, in several places on our tour, the mothers
showed us their children, and told us that when Rihoriho passed that way, he had kissed them—a condescension they seemed to think much of, and which they
will probably remember to the end of their days. But,
though generous in his disposition, and humane in his
conduct towards his subjects, he was addicted to intoxication—whether from natural inclination or the influence
and example of others is not now to be determined;
frequently, to my own knowledge, it has been entirely
from the latter. Had he in early life been privileged to
associate with individuals whose conduct and principles
were favourable to virtue and religion, there is every
reason to suppose his moral character, with respect at
least to this vice, would have been as irreproachable as
his mental habits were commendable. But, alas for
him! it was quite the reverse.

Though not distinguished by the ardour and strength
of character so conspicuous in his father, he possessed
both decision and enterprise: the abolition of the national idolatry was a striking instance of the former;
and his voyage to England, of the latter.

The motives by which he was induced to undertake
a voyage so long and hazardous were highly commendable. They were—a desire to see for himself countries
of which he had heard such various and interesting
accounts; a wish to have a personal interview with his
majesty the king of Great Britain, or the chief members of the British government—for the purpose of
confirming the cession of the Sandwich Islands, and
placing himself and his dominions under British protection.

It was also his intention to make himself acquainted
with the tenor and forms of administering justice in the
courts of law, the principles of commerce, and other
subjects important to the welfare of the islands.

The melancholy death of the late king and queen,

which took place shortly after their arrival in England, not only prevented the full accomplishment of these desirable objects, but awakened very generally a degree of apprehension that the people of the islands, unacquainted with the true circumstances of their death, would be led to suppose they had been neglected, unkindly treated, or even poisoned in revenge of the death of Captain Cook, and that the feelings of friendship with which they had been accustomed to regard the people of England might be followed by enmity or distrust. The fears of those who felt interested in the welfare of the Hawaiians, though natural, were groundless. The British government had entertained the young ruler of the Sandwich Islands, his consort, and attendants with its accustomed hospitality; and when they were attacked by diseases incident to a northern climate, but unknown in their native islands, every attention that humanity could suggest, and every alleviation that the first medical skill in London could afford, was most promptly rendered. After their decease, the highest respect was paid to their remains, and in honourable regard to the feelings of the nation who had suffered this painful bereavement, a British frigate, under the command of Captain Lord Byron, was appointed to convey to the Sandwich Islands the bodies of the king and queen, that their sorrowing people might have the mournful satisfaction of depositing their ashes among the tombs of their ancestors.

By the return of a highly esteemed missionary friend, Rev. C. S. Stewart, I have learned that the Blonde reached the islands in the month of May, 1825: the natives were in some degree prepared for the arrival, by the intelligence of the death of their king and queen, which they had received about two months before from Valparaiso. Shortly after, the vessel having the remains of the king and queen on board had anchored off Oahu, Boki, the principal chief, who had accompanied the king to England, attended by those of his countrymen who had also returned, proceeded on shore: on landing, he was met by his elder brother Karaimoku, and other distinguished chiefs, and after the first emotions of joy at meeting again, and sorrow on account of the loss all had sustained, were somewhat abated, the survivors and their friends walked in solemn and mournful procession to the place of worship, where thanksgivings were presented to God, for the merciful preservation

of those who were thus privileged to meet again, and supplications were made that the afflicting dispensation, which all so deeply felt, might exert a salutary influence in the minds of the surviving chiefs, and the sorrowing nation at large.

Karaimoku, the late prime minister, and present regent of the islands, then arose and said, "We have lost our king and queen, they have died in a foreign land; we shall see them no more; it is right that we should weep, but let us not entertain hard thoughts of God. *God has not done wrong.* The evil is with us: let us bow under his hand; let all amusement cease; let our daily avocations be suspended; and let the nation, by prayer and a cessation from ordinary pursuits, humble itself before God fourteen days." Before the assembly separated, Boki stood up, and, in a brief outline of the voyage, narrated the most prominent events that had transpired since his departure from the islands —calling their attention in particular to the suitable and important advice he had received from his majesty the king of Great Britain, in an audience with which he was graciously favoured, viz. To return to his native country, attend to general and religious instruction himself, and endeavour to enlighten and reform the people. The peculiar circumstances of the people at this time, the increased satisfaction they had for some time felt in attending every means of instruction within their reach, and the pleasing change in favour of religion which many had experienced, rendered this recommendation, so congenial to their feelings, from a source so distinguished, unusually acceptable. A deep and favourable impression was produced on all present, a new impulse was given to the means already employed for the instruction and improvement of the people, from which most advantageous results have already appeared. They were also made acquainted, by Boki and his companions, with the kind reception, generous treatment, and marked attentions which the late king and queen and their suite had received while in England. This intelligence, communicated by those whose testimony would be received with the most entire credence, would at once confirm the attachment and confidence they have so long felt towards England.

No disturbance of the general tranquillity, nor change in the government, of the islands has resulted from this

event.   Rihoriho' left a younger brother, *Kauikeouli,*
about ten years of age, who is acknowledged by the
chiefs as his successor.   A regency will govern during
his minority, and the executive authority will probably
continue to be exercised by *Karaimoku,* and the other
chiefs with whom Rihoriho left it when he embarked
for England.

The queen, who accompanied him, and who died at the
same time, has left a fond mother and an affectionate
people to lament her loss: she was the daughter of
Tamehameha and Talakua, and was born about the
year 1797 or 1798, being two years younger than Rihoriho, and about twenty-six years of age when she
left the islands.   Like all the persons of distinction she
had many names, but that by which she was generally
known was *Kamehamaru* (shade of Kameha), from *kameha,* a contraction of her father's name, and *maru,* shade.
She was distinguished for good nature, and was much
beloved by all her subjects.   The poor people, when
unable to pay their rent, or under the displeasure of the
king and chiefs, or embarrassed on any other account,
frequently repaired to her, and found a friend whose aid
was never refused.   She was also kind to those foreigners who might be distressed in the islands, and though
she never harboured any or countenanced their absconding from their ships, she has often fed them when
hungry, and given them native tapa for clothing.

Kamehamaru was at all times lively and agreeable in
company ; and though her application to her book and
her pen was equal to that of the king, her improvement
in learning was more gradual, and her general knowledge less extensive.

She excelled, however, in the management of his
domestic affairs, which were conducted by her with
great judgment and address, and, though formerly accustomed to use ardent spirits, from the time she put herself under Christian instruction, she entirely discontinued that and every other practice inconsistent with
her profession of Christianity.   Her attendance on the
duties of religion was maintained with commendable
regularity.

Her influence contributed very materially to the pleasing change that has recently taken place, in connexion
with the labours of the missionaries in the islands. For
the instruction and moral improvement of the people,

she manifested no ordinary concern. Long before many of the leading chiefs were favourable to the instruction of the people, or their reception of Christianity, Kamehamaru on every suitable occasion recommended to her own servants to serve Jehovah the living God, and attend to every means of improvement within their reach. It was truly pleasing to observe, so soon after she had embraced Christianity herself, an anxiety to induce her people to follow her example. At Honoruru she erected a school, in which upwards of forty children and young persons, principally connected with her establishment, were daily taught to read and write, and instructed in the first principles of religion, by a native teacher, whom she almost entirely supported. In this school she took a lively interest, and marked the progress of the scholars with evident satisfaction; in order to encourage the pupils, she frequently visited the school during the hours of instruction, accompanied by a number of chief women. She also attended the public examinations, and noticed those who on these occasions excelled, frequently presenting a favourite scholar with a slate, a copy-book, pencil, pen, or some other token of her approbation.

In her death the missionaries have lost a sincere friend, and her subjects a queen who always delighted to alleviate their distresses and promote their interests.

Her disposition was affectionate. I have seen her and the king sitting beside the couch of Keopuolani, her mother-in-law, day after day, when the latter has been ill; and on these occasions, though there might be several servants in constant attendance, she would allow no individual but her husband or herself to hand to the patient any thing she might want, or even fan the flies from her person.

The circumstances attending her departure from the islands were peculiarly affecting. The king had gone on board L'Aigle; but the boat was waiting to convey her to the ship. She arose from the mat on which she had been reclining, embraced her mother and other relations most affectionately, and passed through the crowd towards the boat. The people fell down on their knees as she walked along, pressing and saluting her feet—frequently bathing them with tears of unfeigned sorrow—and making loud wailings, in which

his family, thanking him at the same time for the hospitable entertainment we had received; and the great facilities he had afforded for accomplishing the objects of our visit.

About three o'clock in the morning, being awoke by the shouts of the men who were heaving up the anchor of the pilot-boat, I repaired on board, and immediately afterward we sailed with a gentle breeze blowing from the land. The wind was light and baffling, and it was noon before we reached Towaihae, where I learned with disappointment that the Nio had sailed to Oahu. On landing I was welcomed by Mr. Young, with whom I remained till the pilot-boat was ready to sail for Lahaina.

Late in the evening of the 2d of September, after preaching to the people of the place at Mr. Young's house, I went again on board the pilot-boat, but found her so full of sandal-wood that there was not room for any person below, while the decks were crowded with natives. The weather was unfavourable for getting under way till nearly daylight; and every person on board was completely drenched by the heavy rain that fell during the night.

During the forenoon of the 3d, we drifted slowly to the northward, and about noon took in eight hundred dried fish, after which we made sail for Maui. The weather was warm, the wind light: and all on board being obliged to keep on deck, without any screen or shade from the scorching rays of a vertical sun, the situation was very uncomfortable. At three P.M. we took the channel-breeze, which soon wafted us across to the south-east part of Maui.

As the shores of Hawaii receded from my view, a variety of reflections insensibly arose in my mind. The tour which, in the society of my companions, I had made had been replete with interest. The varied and sublime phenomena of nature had elevated our conceptions of "nature's God;" the manners and customs of the inhabitants had increased our interest in their welfare; while their superstition, moral degradation, ignorance, and vice had called forth our sincerest commiseration. We had made known the nature and consequences of sin, spoken of the love of God, and had exhibited the Lord Jesus Christ as the only Saviour to multitudes who had never before heard his name, or been directed

to worship the holy and living God, and who would probably never hear these truths again. We cherish the hope that, under the Divine blessing, lasting good will result, even from this transient visit.

Many of the individuals we have met on these occasions, we shall in all probability meet no more till the morning of the resurrection. May we meet them then on the right-hand of the Son of God!

At sunset we arrived off Morokini, but were shortly after becalmed. The current, however, was in our favour through the night, and at daylight on the 4th we found ourselves off the east end of the district of Lahaina, and about a mile distant from the shore. Many of the natives jumped into the sea, and swam to the beach, holding their clothes above their heads with one hand, and swimming with the other.

On landing I waited on Keopuolani, the king's mother, whom I found ill; Karaimoku, Kaahumanu, Kalakua, and several other chiefs were reclining around her, weeping. After some time, Karaimoku proposed that they should unitedly pray for her recovery, and his proposal was acceded to.

Towards evening I visited the governor of the island, and also the king, who was then at Maui. The subsequent voyage of the latter to Great Britain, accompanied by his queen, and the melancholy event which terminated their lives while in London, excited considerable interest, and will probably be considered sufficient apology for a short account of them, although the event took place after my visit to Maui at this time.

The late king of the Sandwich Islands was the son of Tamehameha, former king, and Keopuolani, daughter of Kauikeouli, and Kakuiapoiwa. He was born in the eastern part of Hawaii, in the year 1795 or 1796. The name by which he was generally known was *Rihoriho*, which was only a contraction of *Kalaninui-rihoriho*, literally, the heaven's great black—from *Ka lani*, the heavens, *nui*, great, and *rihoriho*, applied to any thing burned to blackness. On public occasions he was sometimes called Tamehameha, after his father, though names are not always hereditary. Besides these, he had a variety of other names, the most common of which was *Iolani*. The word *lani*, heaven or sky, formed a component part

in the name of most chiefs of distinction. The following is a fac-simile of the official signature of the late king.

Tamehameha

The early habits of Rihoriho did not warrant any great expectations. His natural disposition was frank, and humane. The natives always spoke of him as good-natured, except when he was under the influence of ardent spirits; his manners were perfectly free, at the same time dignified, and always agreeable to those who were about him. His mind was naturally inquisitive. The questions he usually presented to foreigners were by no means trifling; and his memory was retentive. His general knowledge of the world was much greater than could have been expected. I have heard him entertain a party of chiefs for hours together with accounts of different parts of the earth, describing the extensive lakes, the mountains, and mines of North and South America—the elephants and inhabitants of India —the houses, manufactures, &c. of England—with no small accuracy, considering he had never seen them. He had a great thirst for knowledge, and was diligent in his studies. I recollect his remarking one day, when he opened his writing-desk, that he expected more advantage from that desk than from a fine brig belonging to him, lying at anchor opposite the house in which we were sitting. Mr. Bingham and myself were his daily teachers, and have often been surprised at his unwearied perseverance. I have sat beside him at his desk sometimes from nine or ten o'clock in the morning till nearly sunset, during which period his pen or his book has not been out of his hand more than three-quarters of an hour, while he was at dinner.

We do not know that Christianity exerted any decisive influence on his heart. He was willing to receive the missionaries on their first arrival—availed himself of their knowledge, to increase his own—and, during

the latter years of his life, was decidedly favourable to their object; declared his conviction of the truth of Christianity; attended public worship himself on the Sabbath, and recommended the same to his people.

His moral character was not marked by that cruelty, rapacity, and insensibility to the sufferings of the people, which frequently distinguish the abitrary chiefs of uncivilized nations. He appears in general to have been kind; and, in several places on our tour, the mothers showed us their children, and told us that when Rihoriho passed that way, he had kissed them—a condescension they seemed to think much of, and which they will probably remember to the end of their days. But, though generous in his disposition, and humane in his conduct towards his subjects, he was addicted to intoxication—whether from natural inclination or the influence and example of others is not now to be determined; frequently, to my own knowledge, it has been entirely from the latter. Had he in early life been privileged to associate with individuals whose conduct and principles were favourable to virtue and religion, there is every reason to suppose his moral character, with respect at least to this vice, would have been as irreproachable as his mental habits were commendable. But, alas for him! it was quite the reverse.

Though not distinguished by the ardour and strength of character so conspicuous in his father, he possessed both decision and enterprise: the abolition of the national idolatry was a striking instance of the former; and his voyage to England, of the latter.

The motives by which he was induced to undertake a voyage so long and hazardous were highly commendable. They were—a desire to see for himself countries of which he had heard such various and interesting accounts; a wish to have a personal interview with his majesty the king of Great Britain, or the chief members of the British government—for the purpose of confirming the cession of the Sandwich Islands, and placing himself and his dominions under British protection.

It was also his intention to make himself acquainted with the tenor and forms of administering justice in the courts of law, the principles of commerce, and other subjects important to the welfare of the islands.

The melancholy death of the late king and queen,

which took place shortly after their arrival in England,
not only prevented the full accomplishment of these
desirable objects, but awakened very generally a degree
of apprehension that the people of the islands, unacquainted with the true circumstances of their death,
would be led to suppose they had been neglected, unkindly treated, or even poisoned in revenge of the death
of Captain Cook, and that the feelings of friendship
with which they had been accustomed to regard the
people of England might be followed by enmity or distrust. The fears of those who felt interested in the
welfare of the Hawaiians, though natural, were groundless. The British government had entertained the
young ruler of the Sandwich Islands, his consort, and
attendants with its accustomed hospitality; and when
they were attacked by diseases incident to a northern
climate, but unknown in their native islands, every attention that humanity could suggest, and every alleviation
that the first medical skill in London could afford, was
most promptly rendered. After their decease, the highest respect was paid to their remains, and in honourable
regard to the feelings of the nation who had suffered this
painful bereavement, a British frigate, under the command of Captain Lord Byron, was appointed to convey to
the Sandwich Islands the bodies of the king and queen,
that their sorrowing people might have the mournful
satisfaction of depositing their ashes among the tombs
of their ancestors.

By the return of a highly esteemed missionary friend,
Rev. C. S. Stewart, I have learned that the Blonde
reached the islands in the month of May, 1825: the
natives were in some degree prepared for the arrival, by
the intelligence of the death of their king and queen,
which they had received about two months before from
Valparaiso. Shortly after, the vessel having the remains
of the king and queen on board had anchored off Oahu,
Boki, the principal chief, who had accompanied the
king to England, attended by those of his countrymen
who had also returned, proceeded on shore: on landing,
he was met by his elder brother Karaimoku, and other
distinguished chiefs, and after the first emotions of joy
at meeting again, and sorrow on account of the loss all
had sustained, were somewhat abated, the survivors
and their friends walked in solemn and mournful procession to the place of worship, where thanksgivings
were presented to God, for the merciful preservation

of those who were thus privileged to meet again, and supplications were made that the afflicting dispensation, which all so deeply felt, might exert a salutary influence in the minds of the surviving chiefs, and the sorrowing nation at large.

Karaimoku, the late prime minister, and present regent of the islands, then arose and said, "We have lost our king and queen, they have died in a foreign land; we shall see them no more; it is right that we should weep, but let us not entertain hard thoughts of God. *God has not done wrong.* The evil is with us: let us bow under his hand; let all amusement cease; let our daily avocations be suspended; and let the nation, by prayer and a cessation from ordinary pursuits, humble itself before God fourteen days." Before the assembly separated, Boki stood up, and, in a brief outline of the voyage, narrated the most prominent events that had transpired since his departure from the islands —calling their attention in particular to the suitable and important advice he had received from his majesty the king of Great Britain, in an audience with which he was graciously favoured, viz. To return to his native country, attend to general and religious instruction himself, and endeavour to enlighten and reform the people. The peculiar circumstances of the people at this time, the increased satisfaction they had for some time felt in attending every means of instruction within their reach, and the pleasing change in favour of religion which many had experienced, rendered this recommendation, so congenial to their feelings, from a source so distinguished, unusually acceptable. A deep and favourable impression was produced on all present, a new impulse was given to the means already employed for the instruction and improvement of the people, from which most advantageous results have already appeared. They were also made acquainted, by Boki and his companions, with the kind reception, generous treatment, and marked attentions which the late king and queen and their suite had received while in England. This intelligence, communicated by those whose testimony would be received with the most entire credence, would at once confirm the attachment and confidence they have so long felt towards England.

No disturbance of the general tranquillity, nor change in the government, of the islands has resulted from this

their traditions, which contain many things much less
important; and had the Spaniards discovered them,
however jealous they might be of such a discovery
becoming known to other nations, that jealousy would
not have prevented their availing themselves of the
facilities which the islands afforded for refitting or recruiting their vessels, which must frequently have been
most desirable during the period their ships were accustomed to traverse these seas.

These accounts, but particularly the latter, are generally known, and have been related by different persons
at distant places. All agree respecting the boat, clothing, sword, &c. of the party who arrived at Kearake'kua.
Among others, the late king Rihoriho gave us a detailed
account of their landing, &c. only a short time before
he embarked for England. We feel but little doubt of
the fact; but the country whence they came, the place
whither they were bound, the occasion of their visit,
and a variety of interesting particulars connected therewith, will probably remain undiscovered.

The 31st was the Sabbath. The stillness of every
thing around, the decent apparel of those who were seen
passing and repassing, together with the numbers of
canoes all drawn up on the beach, under the shade of
the cocoanut or kou-trees, combined to mark the return
of the *la tabu,* or sacred day. An unusual number attended family prayers at the governor's house in the
morning; and at half-past ten the bell was rung for
public worship. About eight hundred people assembled
under the ranai, and I preached to them from Heb. xi. 7.
And after a succinct account of the deluge, I endeavoured to exhibit the advantages of faith, and the consequences of wickedness and unbelief, as illustrated in
the salvation of Noah and the destruction of the rest
of mankind.

After the conclusion of the service, several persons
present requested me to remain till they had made some
inquiries respecting the deluge, Noah, &c.

They said they were informed by their fathers that
all the land had once been overflowed by the sea, except
a small peak on the top of Mouna Kea, where two human
beings were preserved from the destruction that overtook the rest; but they said they had never before heard
of a ship, or of Noah, having always been accustomed

to call it the *kai a Kahinárii* (sea of Kahinárii). After conversing with them some time, I returned to the governor's.

The afternoon was principally employed in conversation with him on the flood, and the repeopling of the earth by the descendants of Noah. The governor seemed to doubt whether it were possible that the Hawaiians could be the descendants of Noah; but said he thought their progenitors must have been created on the islands. I told him the account in the Bible had every evidence that could be wished to support it; referred him to his own traditions, not only of Hawaii having been peopled by persons who came in canoes from a foreign country, but of their having in their turn visited other islands and planted colonies, as in the days of Kamapiikai—the superiority of their war-canoes in former days—the resemblance in manners, customs, traditions, and language between themselves and other islanders in the Pacific, many thousand miles distant.

The longevity of mankind in the days of Noah also surprised him. Comparing it with the period of human life at the present time, he said, "By-and-by men will not live more than forty years."

At half-past four in the afternoon the bell rang again, and the people collected in numbers about equal to those who attended in the morning. I preached to them from the words, " Be not weary in well-doing, for in due season ye shall reap, if ye faint not "

Numbers thronged the governor's house at evening worship. The conversation afterward turned upon the identity of the body at the resurrection, and the reward of the righteous in heaven. The governor asked if people would know each other in heaven; and when answered in the affirmative, said he thought Christian relations would be very happy when they met there. Some who were present asked, " If there is no eating and drinking or wearing of clothes in heaven, wherein does its goodness consist ?" This was a natural question for a Hawaiian to ask; who never had an idea of happiness, except in the gratification of his natural appetites and feelings. In answer to the question, they were, however, informed that the joys of heaven were intellectual and spiritual, and would infinitely exceed, both in their nature and duration, every earthly enjoyment. At a late hour I took leave of the governor and

his family, thanking him at the same time for the hospitable entertainment we had received; and the great facilities he had afforded for accomplishing the objects of our visit.

About three o'clock in the morning, being awoke by the shouts of the men who were heaving up the anchor of the pilot-boat, I repaired on board, and immediately afterward we sailed with a gentle breeze blowing from the land. The wind was light and baffling, and it was noon before we reached Towaihae, where I learned with disappointment that the Nio had sailed to Oahu. On landing I was welcomed by Mr. Young, with whom I remained till the pilot-boat was ready to sail for Lahaina.

Late in the evening of the 2d of September, after preaching to the people of the place at Mr. Young's house, I went again on board the pilot-boat, but found her so full of sandal-wood that there was not room for any person below, while the decks were crowded with natives. The weather was unfavourable for getting under way till nearly daylight; and every person on board was completely drenched by the heavy rain that fell during the night.

During the forenoon of the 3d, we drifted slowly to the northward, and about noon took in eight hundred dried fish, after which we made sail for Maui. The weather was warm, the wind light: and all on board being obliged to keep on deck, without any screen or shade from the scorching rays of a vertical sun, the situation was very uncomfortable. At three P. M. we took the channel-breeze, which soon wafted us across to the south-east part of Maui.

As the shores of Hawaii receded from my view, a variety of reflections insensibly arose in my mind. The tour which, in the society of my companions, I had made had been replete with interest. The varied and sublime phenomena of nature had elevated our conceptions of "nature's God;" the manners and customs of the inhabitants had increased our interest in their welfare; while their superstition, moral degradation, ignorance, and vice had called forth our sincerest commiseration. We had made known the nature and consequences of sin, spoken of the love of God, and had exhibited the Lord Jesus Christ as the only Saviour to multitudes who had never before heard his name, or been directed

to worship the holy and living God, and who would probably never hear these truths again. We cherish the hope that, under the Divine blessing, lasting good will result, even from this transient visit.

Many of the individuals we have met on these occasions, we shall in all probability meet no more till the morning of the resurrection. May we meet them then on the right-hand of the Son of God?

At sunset we arrived off Morokini, but were shortly after becalmed. The current, however, was in our favour through the night, and at daylight on the 4th we found ourselves off the east end of the district of Lahaina, and about a mile distant from the shore. Many of the natives jumped into the sea, and swam to the beach, holding their clothes above their heads with one hand, and swimming with the other.

On landing I waited on Keopuolani, the king's mother, whom I found ill; Karaimoku, Kaahumanu, Kalakua, and several other chiefs were reclining around her, weeping. After some time, Karaimoku proposed that they should unitedly pray for her recovery, and his proposal was acceded to.

Towards evening I visited the governor of the island, and also the king, who was then at Maui. The subsequent voyage of the latter to Great Britain, accompanied by his queen, and the melancholy event which terminated their lives while in London, excited considerable interest, and will probably be considered sufficient apology for a short account of them, although the event took place after my visit to Maui at this time.

The late king of the Sandwich Islands was the son of Tamehameha, former king, and Keopuolani, daughter of Kauikeouli, and Kakuiapoiwa. He was born in the eastern part of Hawaii, in the year 1795 or 1796. The name by which he was generally known was *Rihoriho*, which was only a contraction of *Kalaninui-rihoriho*, literally, the heaven's great black—from *Ka lani*, the heavens, *nui*, great, and *rihoriho*, applied to any thing burned to blackness. On public occasions he was sometimes called Tamehameha, after his father, though names are not always hereditary. Besides these, he had a variety of other names, the most common of which was *Iolani*. The word *lani*, heaven or sky, formed a component part

in the name of most chiefs of distinction. The following is a fac-simile of the official signature of the late
king.

Tamehameha

The early habits of Rihoriho did not warrant any
great expectations. His natural disposition was frank,
and humane. The natives always spoke of him as
good-natured, except when he was under the influence
of ardent spirits; his manners were perfectly free, at
the same time dignified, and always agreeable to those
who were about him. His mind was naturally inquisitive. The questions he usually presented to foreigners
were by no means trifling; and his memory was retentive. His general knowledge of the world was much
greater than could have been expected. I have heard
him entertain a party of chiefs for hours together with
accounts of different parts of the earth, describing the
extensive lakes, the mountains, and mines of North and
South America—the elephants and inhabitants of India
—the houses, manufactures, &c. of England—with no
small accuracy, considering he had never seen them.
He had a great thirst for knowledge, and was diligent in
his studies. I recollect his remarking one day, when
he opened his writing-desk, that he expected more advantage from that desk than from a fine brig belonging
to him, lying at anchor opposite the house in which we
were sitting. Mr. Bingham and myself were his daily
teachers, and have often been surprised at his unwearied
perseverance. I have sat beside him at his desk sometimes from nine or ten o'clock in the morning till nearly
sunset, during which period his pen or his book has not
been out of his hand more than three-quarters of an
hour, while he was at dinner.

We do not know that Christianity exerted any decisive influence on his heart. He was willing to receive
the missionaries on their first arrival—availed himself
of their knowledge, to increase his own—and, during

the latter years of his life, was decidedly favourable to their object; declared his conviction of the truth of Christianity; attended public worship himself on the Sabbath, and recommended the same to his people.

His moral character was not marked by that cruelty, rapacity, and insensibility to the sufferings of the people, which frequently distinguish the arbitrary chiefs of uncivilized nations. He appears in general to have been kind ; and, in several places on our tour, the mothers showed us their children, and told us that when Rihoriho passed that way, he had kissed them—a condescension they seemed to think much of, and which they will probably remember to the end of their days. But, though generous in his disposition, and humane in his conduct towards his subjects, he was addicted to intoxication—whether from natural inclination or the influence and-example of others is not now to be determined; frequently, to my own knowledge, it has been entirely from the latter. Had he in early life been privileged to associate with individuals whose conduct and principles were favourable to virtue and religion, there is every reason to suppose his moral character, with respect at least to this vice, would have been as irreproachable as his mental habits were commendable. But, alas for him! it was quite the reverse.

Though not distinguished by the ardour and strength of character so conspicuous in his father, he possessed both decision and enterprise: the abolition of the national idolatry was a striking instance of the former; and his voyage to England, of the latter.

The motives by which he was induced to undertake a voyage so long and hazardous were highly commendable. They were—a desire to see for himself countries of which he had heard such various and interesting accounts; a wish to have a personal interview with his majesty the king of Great Britain, or the chief members of the British government—for the purpose of confirming the cession of the Sandwich Islands, and placing himself and his dominions under British protection.

It was also his intention to make himself acquainted with the tenor and forms of administering justice in the courts of law, the principles of commerce, and other subjects important to the welfare of the islands.

The melancholy death of the late king and queen,

which took place shortly after their arrival in England, not only prevented the full accomplishment of these desirable objects, but awakened very generally a degree of apprehension that the people of the islands, unacquainted with the true circumstances of their death, would be led to suppose they had been neglected, unkindly treated, or even poisoned in revenge of the death of Captain Cook, and that the feelings of friendship with which they had been accustomed to regard the people of England might be followed by enmity or distrust. The fears of those who felt interested in the welfare of the Hawaiians, though natural, were groundless. The British government had entertained the young ruler of the Sandwich Islands, his consort, and attendants with its accustomed hospitality; and when they were attacked by diseases incident to a northern climate, but unknown in their native islands, every attention that humanity could suggest, and every alleviation that the first medical skill in London could afford, was most promptly rendered. After their decease, the highest respect was paid to their remains, and in honourable regard to the feelings of the nation who had suffered this painful bereavement, a British frigate, under the command of Captain Lord Byron, was appointed to convey to the Sandwich Islands the bodies of the king and queen, that their sorrowing people might have the mournful satisfaction of depositing their ashes among the tombs of their ancestors.

By the return of a highly esteemed missionary friend, Rev. C. S. Stewart, I have learned that the Blonde reached the islands in the month of May, 1825: the natives were in some degree prepared for the arrival, by the intelligence of the death of their king and queen, which they had received about two months before from Valparaiso. Shortly after, the vessel having the remains of the king and queen on board had anchored off Oahu, Boki, the principal chief, who had accompanied the king to England, attended by those of his countrymen who had also returned, proceeded on shore: on landing, he was met by his elder brother Karaimoku, and other distinguished chiefs, and after the first emotions of joy at meeting again, and sorrow on account of the loss all had sustained, were somewhat abated, the survivors and their friends walked in solemn and mournful procession to the place of worship, where thanksgivings were presented to God, for the merciful preservation

of those who were thus privileged to meet again, and supplications were made that the afflicting dispensation, which all so deeply felt, might exert a salutary influence in the minds of the surviving chiefs, and the sorrowing nation at large.

Karaimoku, the late prime minister, and present regent of the islands, then arose and said, " We have lost our king and queen, they have died in a foreign land; we shall see them no more; it is right that we should weep, but let us not entertain hard thoughts of God. *God has not done wrong.* The evil is with us: let us bow under his hand; let all amusement cease; let our daily avocations be suspended; and let the nation, by prayer and a cessation from ordinary pursuits, humble itself before God fourteen days." Before the assembly separated, Boki stood up, and, in a brief outline of the voyage, narrated the most prominent events that had transpired since his departure from the islands —calling their attention in particular to the suitable and important advice he had received from his majesty the king of Great Britain, in an audience with which he was graciously favoured, viz. To return to his native country, attend to general and religious instruction himself, and endeavour to enlighten and reform the people. The peculiar circumstances of the people at this time, the increased satisfaction they had for some time felt in attending every means of instruction within their reach, and the pleasing change in favour of religion which many had experienced, rendered this recommendation, so congenial to their feelings, from a source so distinguished, unusually acceptable. A deep and favourable impression was produced on all present, a new impulse was given to the means already employed for the instruction and improvement of the people, from which most advantageous results have already appeared. They were also made acquainted, by Boki and his companions, with the kind reception, generous treatment, and marked attentions which the late king and queen and their suite had received while in England. This intelligence, communicated by those whose testimony would be received with the most entire credence, would at once confirm the attachment and confidence they have so long felt towards England.

No disturbance of the general tranquillity, nor change in the government, of the islands has resulted from this

event. Rihoriho' left a younger brother, *Kauikeouli,*
about ten years of age, who is acknowledged by the
chiefs as his successor. A regency will govern during
his minority, and the executive authority will probably
continue to be exercised by *Karaimoku,* and the other
chiefs with whom Rihoriho left it when he embarked
for England.

The queen, who accompanied him, and who died at the
same time, has left a fond mother and an affectionate
people to lament her loss; she was the daughter of
Tamehameha and Talakua, and was born about the
year 1797 or 1798, being two years younger than Rihoriho, and about twenty-six years of age when she
left the islands. Like all the persons of distinction she
had many names, but that by which she was generally
known was *Kamehamaru* (shade of Kameha), from *kameha,* a contraction of her father's name, and *maru,* shade.
She was distinguished for good nature, and was much
beloved by all her subjects. The poor people, when
unable to pay their rent, or under the displeasure of the
king and chiefs, or embarrassed on any other account,
frequently repaired to her, and found a friend whose aid
was never refused. She was also kind to those foreigners who might be distressed in the islands, and though
she never harboured any or countenanced their absconding from their ships, she has often fed them when
hungry, and given them native tapa for clothing.

Kamehamaru was at all times lively and agreeable in
company; and though her application to her book and
her pen was equal to that of the king, her improvement
in learning was more gradual, and her general knowledge less extensive.

She excelled, however, in the management of his
domestic affairs, which were conducted by her with
great judgment and address, and, though formerly accustomed to use ardent spirits, from the time she put herself under Christian instruction, she entirely discontinued that and every other practice inconsistent with
her profession of Christianity. Her attendance on the
duties of religion was maintained with commendable
regularity.

Her influence contributed very materially to the pleasing change that has recently taken place, in connexion
with the labours of the missionaries in the islands. For
the instruction and moral improvement of the people,

she manifested no ordinary concern. Long before
many of the leading chiefs were favourable to the instruction of the people or their reception of Christianity, Kamehamaru on every suitable occasion recommended to her own servants to serve Jehovah the living
God, and attend to every means of improvement within
their reach. It was truly pleasing to observe, so soon
after she had embraced Christianity herself, an anxiety
to induce her people to follow her example. At Honoruru she erected a school, in which upwards of forty
children and young persons, principally connected with
her establishment, were daily taught to read and write,
and instructed in the first principles of religion, by a
native teacher, whom she almost entirely supported. In
this school she took a lively interest, and marked the
progress of the scholars with evident satisfaction; in
order to encourage the pupils, she frequently visited
the school during the hours of instruction, accompanied
by a number of chief women. She also attended the
public examinations, and noticed those who on these
occasions excelled, frequently presenting a favourite
scholar with a slate, a copy-book, pencil, pen, or some
other token of her approbation.

In her death the missionaries have lost a sincere
friend, and her subjects a queen who always delighted
to alleviate their distresses and promote their interests.

Her disposition was affectionate. I have seen her
and the king sitting beside the couch of Keopuolani, her
mother-in-law, day after day, when the latter has been
ill; and on these occasions, though there might be several servants in constant attendance, she would allow
no individual but her husband or herself to hand to the
patient any thing she might want, or even fan the flies
from her person.

The circumstances attending her departure from the
islands were peculiarly affecting. The king had gone
on board L'Aigle; but the boat was waiting to convey
her to the ship. She arose from the mat on which she
had been reclining; embraced her mother and other
relations most affectionately, and passed through the
crowd towards the boat. The people fell down on
their knees as she walked along, pressing and saluting
her feet—frequently bathing them with tears of unfeigned sorrow—and making loud wailings, in which

they were joined by the thousands who thronged the shore.

On reaching the water-side, she turned and beckoned to the people to cease their cries. As soon as they were silent, she said, "I am going to a distant land, and perhaps we shall not meet again. Let us pray to Jehovah, that he may preserve us on the water and you on the shore." She then called *Auna*, a native teacher from the Society Islands, and requested him to pray. He did so; at the conclusion she waved her hand to the people, and said, "*Arohá muiroukou*" (attachment great to you): she then stepped into the boat, evidently much affected. The multitude followed her, not only to the beach, but into the sea, where many, wading into the water, stood waving their hands, exhibiting every attitude of sorrow, and uttering their loud *u-e! u-e!* (alas! alas!) till the boat had pulled far out to sea.

The death of the king and queen, so soon after their arrival in England, was an event in many respects deeply to be deplored. The officers of the London Missionary Society were unable to gain access to them until they should have been introduced to his majesty; and one of them, I believe the king, died on the very day on which that introduction was to have taken place. The same circumstance also prevented many Christian friends, who felt interested in their welfare, from that intercourse with them which, under the blessing of God, might have been expected to have strengthened the religious impressions they had received from the instructions of the missionaries. In their visit to England they were accompanied by a suite, which, though much less numerous than that which invariably attended their movements in their native islands, included nevertheless, several individuals of rank and influence. Among the principal of these was Boki, the governor of the island of Oahu, and Liliha, his wife; Kauruheimarama, a distant relation of the king; Kakuanaoa and Kapihe, two of his favourite companions; the latter of whom was a man of an amiable disposition, and, considering the circumstances under which he had been brought up, possessed general intelligence. He had made a voyage to Canton in China, for the purpose of acquiring mercantile information; and, from the circumstance of his commanding the finest vessel belonging to the king, a brig of about ninety tons burden, called the *Haaheo Hawaii* (pride of Hawaii), he was sometimes called the admiral, although that is an office to which there is nothing analogous in the present maritime system of the Hawaiians. With this individual, who died at Valparaiso, on his return to the islands, and the others who survived the death of the king, particularly with Boki, the officers of the London Missionary Society had several interviews, and received the strongest assurances of their continued patronage and support of the Christian mission established in the Sandwich Islands. Many benevolent individuals had also an opportunity of testifying the deep interest they felt in the civil, moral, and religious improvement of their countrymen.

It is a pleasing fact, in connexion with the present circumstances of the nation, that almost every chief of rank and influence in the Sandwich Islands is favourably disposed towards the instruction of the natives and the promulgation of the gospel. A deep sense of the kindness of the friends by whom the chiefs who survived the king and queen were visited at Portsmouth, appears to have remained on the minds of the Hawaiian chiefs long after their return to their native land; for when the Rev. C. S. Stewart, an American missionary, was about to leave the Sandwich Islands for Great Britain, Boki gave him a special charge to present his grateful regards to the *Bishop of Portsmouth.* Mr. S. told him he was not aware that there was such a dignitary; but Boki said, Yes, there was, for he visited him, with some of his friends, when they were on the point of sailing from England. I at first heard that the late Dr. Bogue was the individual to whom Boki referred; but I have since learned, that in consequence of severe domestic affliction at that time it is uncertain whether he did or did not; and that the Sandwich Island chief referred either to the Rev. C. Simeon of Cambridge, or the Rev. J. Griffin, by both of whom he was visited.

Among the letters I was favoured to receive from the islands by the return of his majesty's ship Blonde, those from Boki and Liliha, or, as she was frequently called while in England, Madam Boki, were of a character so interesting, that I think I shall be pardoned for inserting one of them. It is from Boki, the chief who was with the king in London. I shall translate it very literally

his family, thanking him at the same time for the hospitable entertainment we had received; and the great facilities he had afforded for accomplishing the objects of our visit.

About three o'clock in the morning, being awoke by the shouts of the men who were heaving up the anchor of the pilot-boat, I repaired on board, and immediately afterward we sailed with a gentle breeze blowing from the land. The wind was light and baffling, and it was noon before we reached Towaihae, where I learned with disappointment that the Nio had sailed to Oahu. On landing I was welcomed by Mr. Young, with whom I remained till the pilot-boat was ready to sail for Lahaina.

Late in the evening of the 2d of September, after preaching to the people of the place at Mr. Young's house, I went again on board the pilot-boat, but found her so full of sandal-wood that there was not room for any person below, while the decks were crowded with natives. The weather was unfavourable for getting under way till nearly daylight; and every person on board was completely drenched by the heavy rain that fell during the night.

During the forenoon of the 3d, we drifted slowly to the northward, and about noon took in eight hundred dried fish, after which we made sail for Maui. The weather was warm, the wind light: and all on board being obliged to keep on deck, without any screen or shade from the scorching rays of a vertical sun, the situation was very uncomfortable. At three P. M. we took the channel-breeze, which soon wafted us across to the south-east part of Maui.

As the shores of Hawaii receded from my view, a variety of reflections insensibly arose in my mind. The tour which, in the society of my companions, I had made had been replete with interest. The varied and sublime phenomena of nature had elevated our conceptions of "nature's God;" the manners and customs of the inhabitants had increased our interest in their welfare; while their superstition, moral degradation, ignorance, and vice had called forth our sincerest commiseration. We had made known the nature and consequences of sin, spoken of the love of God, and had exhibited the Lord Jesus Christ as the only Saviour to multitudes who had never before heard his name, or been directed

to worship the holy and living God, and who would probably never hear these truths again. We cherish the hope that, under the Divine blessing, lasting good will result, even from this transient visit.

Many of the individuals we have met on these occasions, we shall in all probability meet no more till the morning of the resurrection. May we meet them then on the right-hand of the Son of God!

At sunset we arrived off Morokini, but were shortly after becalmed. The current, however, was in our favour through the night, and at daylight on the 4th we found ourselves off the east end of the district of Lahaoina, and about a mile distant from the shore. Many of the natives jumped into the sea, and swam to the beach, holding their clothes above their heads with one hand, and swimming with the other.

On landing I waited on Keopuolani, the king's mother, whom I found ill; Karaimoku, Kaahumanu, Kalakua, and several other chiefs were reclining around her, weeping. After some time, Karaimoku proposed that they should unitedly pray for her recovery, and his proposal was acceded to.

Towards evening I visited the governor of the island, and also the king, who was then at Maui. The subsequent voyage of the latter to Great Britain, accompanied by his queen, and the melancholy event which terminated their lives while in London, excited considerable interest, and will probably be considered sufficient apology for a short account of them, although the event took place after my visit to Maui at this time.

The late king of the Sandwich Islands was the son of Tamehameha, former king, and Keopuolani, daughter of Kauikeouli, and Kakuiapoiwa. He was born in the eastern part of Hawaii, in the year 1795 or 1796. The name by which he was generally known was *Rihoriho*, which was only a contraction of *Kalaninui-rihoriho*, literally, the heaven's great black—from *Ka lani*, the heavens, *nui*, great, and *rihoriho*, applied to any thing burned to blackness. On public occasions he was sometimes called Tamehameha, after his father, though names are not always hereditary. Besides these, he had a variety of other names, the most common of which was *Iolani*. The word *lani*, heaven or sky, formed a component part

in the name of most chiefs of distinction. The following is a fac-simile of the official signature of the late
king.

The early habits of Rihoriho did not warrant any
great expectations. His natural disposition was frank,
and humane. The natives always spoke of him as
good-natured, except when he was under the influence
of ardent spirits; his manners were perfectly free, at
the same time dignified, and always agreeable to those
who were about him. His mind was naturally inquisitive. The questions he usually presented to foreigners
were by no means trifling; and his memory was retentive. His general knowledge of the world was much
greater than could have been expected. I have heard
him entertain a party of chiefs for hours together with
accounts of different parts of the earth, describing the
extensive lakes, the mountains, and mines of North and
South America—the elephants and inhabitants of India
—the houses, manufactures, &c. of England—with no
small accuracy, considering he had never seen them.
He had a great thirst for knowledge, and was diligent in
his studies. I recollect his remarking one day, when
he opened his writing-desk, that he expected more advantage from that desk than from a fine brig belonging
to him, lying at anchor opposite the house in which we
were sitting. Mr. Bingham and myself were his daily
teachers, and have often been surprised at his unwearied
perseverance. I have sat beside him at his desk sometimes from nine or ten o'clock in the morning till nearly
sunset, during which period his pen or his book has not
been out of his hand more than three-quarters of an
hour, while he was at dinner.

We do not know that Christianity exerted any decisive influence on his heart. He was willing to receive
the missionaries on their first arrival—availed himself
of their knowledge, to increase his own—and, during

the latter years of his life, was decidedly favourable to
their object; declared his conviction of the truth of
Christianity; attended public worship himself on the
Sabbath, and recommended the same to his people.

His moral character was not marked by that cruelty,
rapacity, and insensibility to the sufferings of the people,
which frequently distinguish the abitrary chiefs of. uncivilized nations. He appears in general to have been
kind; and, in several places on our tour, the mothers
showed us their children, and told us that when Rihoriho passed that way, he had kissed them—a condescension they seemed to think much of, and which they
will probably remember to the end of their days. But,
though generous in his disposition, and humane in his
conduct towards his subjects, he was addicted to intoxication—whether from natural inclination or the influence
and example of others is not now to be determined;
frequently, to my own knowledge, it has been entirely
from the latter. Had he in early life been privileged to
associate with individuals whose conduct and principles
were favourable to virtue and religion, there is every
reason to suppose his moral character, with respect at
least to this vice, would have been as irreproachable as
his mental habits were commendable. But, alas for
him! it was quite the reverse.

Though not distinguished by the ardour and strength
of character so conspicuous in his father, he possessed
both decision and enterprise: the abolition of the national idolatry was a striking instance of the former;
and his voyage to England, of the latter.

The motives by which he was induced to undertake
a voyage so long and hazardous were highly commendable. They were—a desire to see for himself countries
of which he had heard such various and interesting
accounts; a wish to have a personal interview with his
majesty the king of Great Britain, or the chief members of the British government—for the purpose of
confirming the cession of the Sandwich Islands, and
placing himself and his dominions under British protection.

It was also his intention to make himself acquainted
with the tenor and forms of administering justice in the
courts of law, the principles of commerce, and other
subjects important to the welfare of the islands.

The melancholy death of the late king and queen,

which took place shortly after their arrival in England, not only prevented the full accomplishment of these desirable objects, but awakened very generally a degree of apprehension that the people of the islands, unacquainted with the true circumstances of their death, would be led to suppose they had been neglected, unkindly treated, or even poisoned in revenge of the death of Captain Cook, and that the feelings of friendship with which they had been accustomed to regard the people of England might be followed by enmity or distrust. The fears of those who felt interested in the welfare of the Hawaiians, though natural, were groundless. The British government had entertained the young ruler of the Sandwich Islands, his consort, and attendants with its accustomed hospitality; and when they were attacked by diseases incident to a northern climate, but unknown in their native islands, every attention that humanity could suggest, and every alleviation that the first medical skill in London could afford, was most promptly rendered. After their decease, the highest respect was paid to their remains, and in honourable regard to the feelings of the nation who had suffered this painful bereavement, a British frigate, under the command of Captain Lord Byron, was appointed to convey to the Sandwich Islands the bodies of the king and queen, that their sorrowing people might have the mournful satisfaction of depositing their ashes among the tombs of their ancestors.

By the return of a highly esteemed missionary friend, Rev. C. S. Stewart, I have learned that the Blonde reached the islands in the month of May, 1825: the natives were in some degree prepared for the arrival, by the intelligence of the death of their king and queen, which they had received about two months before from Valparaiso. Shortly after, the vessel having the remains of the king and queen on board had anchored off Oahu, Boki, the principal chief, who had accompanied the king to England, attended by those of his countrymen who had also returned, proceeded on shore: on landing, he was met by his elder brother Karaimoku, and other distinguished chiefs, and after the first emotions of joy at meeting again, and sorrow on account of the loss all had sustained, were somewhat abated, the survivors and their friends walked in solemn and mournful procession to the place of worship, where thanksgivings were presented to God, for the merciful preservation

of those who were thus privileged to meet again, and supplications were made that the afflicting dispensation, which all so deeply felt, might exert a salutary influence in the minds of the surviving chiefs, and the sorrowing nation at large.

Karaimoku, the late prime minister, and present regent of the islands, then arose and said, "We have lost our king and queen, they have died in a foreign land; we shall see them no more; it is right that we should weep, but let us not entertain hard thoughts of God. *God has not done wrong.* The evil is with us: let us bow under his hand; let all amusement cease; let our daily avocations be suspended; and let the nation, by prayer and a cessation from ordinary pursuits, humble itself before God fourteen days." Before the assembly separated, Boki stood up, and, in a brief outline of the voyage, narrated the most prominent events that had transpired since his departure from the islands —calling their attention in particular to the suitable and important advice he had received from his majesty the king of Great Britain, in an audience with which he was graciously favoured, viz. To return to his native country, attend to general and religious instruction himself, and endeavour to enlighten and reform the people. The peculiar circumstances of the people at this time, the increased satisfaction they had for some time felt in attending every means of instruction within their reach, and the pleasing change in favour of religion which many had experienced, rendered this recommendation, so congenial to their feelings, from a source so distinguished, unusually acceptable. A deep and favourable impression was produced on all present, a new impulse was given to the means already employed for the instruction and improvement of the people, from which most advantageous results have already appeared. They were also made acquainted, by Boki and his companions, with the kind reception, generous treatment, and marked attentions which the late king and queen and their suite had received while in England. This intelligence, communicated by those whose testimony would be received with the most entire credence, would at once confirm the attachment and confidence they have so long felt towards England.

No disturbance of the general tranquillity, nor change in the government, of the islands has resulted from this

answered, received the presents, and afterward conversed with the people through the medium of Opiri. The facility with which they could communicate their thoughts by means of Opiri, the governor said, was attributed to the supposed influence of Opiri with his gods. The foreigners, they imagined, were supernatural beings, and, as such, were treated with every possible mark of respect. After remaining some time on the island, they returned to their own country. No account is preserved of the kind of vessel in which they arrived or departed. The name of the principal person among them was Manahini; and it is a singular fact, that in the Marquesian, Society, and Sandwich Islands the term manahini is still employed to designate a stranger, visiter, or guest.

The third account is much more recent and precise; though the period at which it took place is uncertain.

It states, that a number of years after the departure of *Manahini-ma* (Manahini and his party), in the reign of Kahoukapu, king at Kaavaroa, seven foreigners arrived at Kearake'kua bay, the spot where Captain Cook landed. They came in a painted boat, with an awning or canopy over the stern, but without mast or sails. They were all dressed; the colour of their clothes was white or yellow, and one of them wore a *pahi*, long knife, the name by which they still call a sword, at his side, and had a feather in his hat. The natives received them kindly. They married native women, were made chiefs, proved themselves warriors, and ultimately became very powerful in the island of Hawaii, which, it is said, was for some time governed by them.

There are in the Sandwich Islands a number of persons distinguished by a lighter colour in their skin, and corresponding brown curly hair, called *ehu*, who are, by all the natives of the islands, considered as the descendants of these foreigners, who acknowledge themselves to be such, and esteem their origin by no means dishonourable.

Another party is said to have afterward arrived at the same place, but the accounts the natives give of their landing are not very distinct; and we feel undecided whether there were two distinct parties, or only two different accounts of the same event.

We have heard from one of the chiefs of Hawaii that there is a tradition of a ship having touched at the island

of Maui prior to the arrival of Captain Cook; but, with
the exception of this chief, all the natives we have conversed with on the subject, and we have conversed with
many, declare that they had no idea of a ship before
Capt. Cook was seen off Tauai. The ship they called
motu, an island, probably supposing it was an island with
all its inhabitants.

Marvellous reports respecting the ships and people
were circulated through the islands, between the first
discovery off Tauai and the return of the vessels from
the north-west coast of America. *Aa mo*, skin of lizard's
egg, a native of Tauai, who was on board one of the
ships, procured a piece of canvass about a yard and a
half long, which Tiha, king of Tauai, sent as a present
to Poriorani, king of Oahu. He gave it to his queen
Opuhani, by whom it was worn on the most conspicuous part of her dress in a public procession, and attracted
more attention than any thing else. The piece of cloth
was called Aa mo, after the man who had the honour
of bringing it from the ships.

The most unaccountable circumstance connected with
the priest Paao is his arriving alone, though he might
be the only survivor of his party. If such a person
ever did arrive, we should think he was a Roman Catholic priest, and the reported gods an image and a
crucifix.

The different parties that subsequently arrived were
probably, if any inference may be drawn from the accounts of the natives, survivors of the crew of some
Spanish ship wrecked in the neighbourhood, perhaps on
the numerous reefs to the north-west; or they might
have been culprits committed by their countrymen to
the mercy of the waves. The circumstance of the first
party leaving the island in the same boat in which they
arrived would lead us to suppose they had been wrecked,
and had escaped in their boat, or had constructed a bark
out of the wreck of their ship, as has subsequently been
the case with two vessels wrecked in the vicinity of
these islands.

It is possible that one or other of the islands might have
been seen by some Spanish ship passing between Acapulco and Manilla; but it is not probable that they were
ever visited by any of these ships. An event so interesting to the people would not have been left out of

their traditions, which contain many things much less
important; and had the Spaniards discovered them,
however jealous 'they might be of such a discovery
becoming known to other nations, that jealousy would
not have prevented their availing themselves of the
facilities which the islands afforded for refitting or recruiting their vessels, which must frequently have been
most desirable during the period their ships were accustomed to traverse these seas.

These accounts, but particularly the latter, are generally known, and have been related by different persons
at distant places. All agree respecting the boat, clothing, sword, &c. of the party who arrived at Kearake'kua.
Among others, the late king Rihoriho gave us a detailed
account of their landing, &c. only a short time before
he embarked for England. We feel but 'little doubt of
the fact; but the country whence they came, the place
whither they were bound, the occasion of their visit,
and a variety of interesting particulars connected therewith, will probably remain undiscovered.

The 31st was the Sabbath. The stillness of every
thing around, the decent apparel of those who were seen
passing and repassing, together with the numbers of
canoes all drawn up on the beach, under the shade of
the cocoanut or kou-trees, combined to mark the return
of the *la tabu*, or sacred day. An unusual number attended family prayers at the governor's house in the
morning; and at half-past ten the bell was rung for
public worship. About eight hundred people assembled
under the ranai, and I preached to them from Heb. xi. 7.
And after a succinct account of the deluge, I endeavoured to exhibit the advantages of faith, and the consequences of wickedness and unbelief, as illustrated in
the salvation of Noah and the destruction of the rest
of mankind.

After the conclusion of the service, several persons
present requested me to remain till they had made some
inquiries respecting the deluge, Noah, &c.

They said they were informed by their fathers that
all the land had once been overflowed by the sea, except
a small peak on the top of Mouna Kea, where two human
beings were preserved from the destruction that overtook the rest; but they said they had never before heard
of a ship, or of Noah, having always been accustomed

to call it the *kai a Kahinárii* (sea of Kahinárii). After conversing with them some time, I returned to the governor's.

The afternoon was principally employed in conversation with him on the flood, and the repeopling of the earth by the descendants of Noah. The governor seemed to doubt whether it were possible that the Hawaiians could be the descendants of Noah; but said he thought their progenitors must have been created on the islands. I told him the account in the Bible had every evidence that could be wished to support it; referred him to his own traditions, not only of Hawaii having been peopled by persons who came in canoes from a foreign country, but of their having in their turn visited other islands and planted colonies, as in the days of Kamapiikai—the superiority of their war-canoes in former days—the resemblance in manners, customs, traditions, and language between themselves and other islanders in the Pacific, many thousand miles distant.

The longevity of mankind in the days of Noah also surprised him. Comparing it with the period of human life at the present time, he said, "By-and-by men will not live more than forty years."

At half-past four in the afternoon the bell rang again, and the people collected in numbers about equal to those who attended in the morning. I preached to them from the words, "Be not weary in well-doing, for in due season ye shall reap, if ye faint not"

Numbers thronged the governor's house at evening worship. The conversation afterward turned upon the identity of the body at the resurrection, and the reward of the righteous in heaven. The governor asked if people would know each other in heaven; and when answered in the affirmative, said he thought Christian relations would be very happy when they met there. Some who were present asked, "If there is no eating and drinking or wearing of clothes in heaven, wherein does its goodness consist?" This was a natural question for a Hawaiian to ask; who never had an idea of happiness, except in the gratification of his natural appetites and feelings. In answer to the question, they were, however, informed that the joys of heaven were intellectual and spiritual, and would infinitely exceed, both in their nature and duration, every earthly enjoyment. At a late hour I took leave of the governor and

his family, thanking him at the same time for the hospitable entertainment we had received; and the great
facilities he had afforded for accomplishing the objects
of our visit.

About three o'clock in the morning, being awoke by
the shouts of the men who were heaving up the anchor
of the pilot-boat, I repaired on board, and immediately
afterward we sailed with a gentle breeze blowing from
the land. The wind was light and baffling, and it was
noon before we reached Towaihae, where I learned with
disappointment that the Nio had sailed to Oahu. On
landing I was welcomed by Mr. Young, with whom I
remained till the pilot-boat was ready to sail for Lahaina.

Late in the evening of the 2d of September, after
preaching to the people of the place at Mr. Young's
house, I went again on board the pilot-boat, but found
her so full of sandal-wood that there was not room for
any person below, while the decks were crowded with
natives. The weather was unfavourable for getting
under way till nearly daylight; and every person on
board was completely drenched by the heavy rain that
fell during the night.

During the forenoon of the 3d, we drifted slowly to
the northward, and about noon took in eight hundred
dried fish, after which we made sail for Maui. The
weather was warm, the wind light; and all on board
being obliged to keep on deck, without any screen or
shade from the scorching rays of a vertical sun, the
situation was very uncomfortable. At three P. M. we
took the channel-breeze, which soon wafted us across to
the south-east part of Maui.

As the shores of Hawaii receded from my view, a
variety of reflections insensibly arose in my mind. The
tour which, in the society of my companions, I had made
had been replete with interest. The varied and sublime
phenomena of nature had elevated our conceptions of
" nature's God;" the manners and customs of the inhabitants had increased our interest in their welfare;
while their superstition, moral degradation, ignorance,
and vice had called forth our sincerest commiseration.
We had made known the nature and consequences of
sin, spoken of the love of God, and had exhibited the
Lord Jesus Christ as the only Saviour to multitudes
who had never before heard his name, or been directed

to worship the holy and living God, and who would
probably never hear these truths again. We cherish the
hope that, under the Divine blessing, lasting good will
result, even from this transient visit.

Many of the individuals we have met on these occasions, we shall in all probability meet no more till the
morning of the resurrection. May we meet them then
on the right-hand of the Son of God?

At sunset we arrived off Morokini, but were shortly
after becalmed. The current, however, was in our
favour through the night, and at daylight on the 4th we
found ourselves off the east end of the district of Lahaoina, and about a mile distant from the shore. Many of
the natives jumped into the sea, and swam to the beach,
holding their clothes above their heads with one hand,
and swimming with the other.

On landing I waited on Keopuolani, the king's mother,
whom I found ill; Karaimoku, Kaahumanu, Kalakua,
and several other chiefs were reclining around her,
weeping. After some time, Karaimoku proposed that
they should unitedly pray for her recovery, and his proposal was acceded to.

Towards evening I visited the governor of the island,
and also the king, who was then at Maui. The subsequent voyage of the latter to Great Britain, accompanied by his queen, and the melancholy event which
terminated their lives while in London, excited considerable interest, and will probably be considered sufficient apology for a short account of them, although
the event took place after my visit to Maui at this
time.

The late king of the Sandwich Islands was the son
of Tamehameha, former king, and Keopuolani, daughter
of Kauikeouli, and Kakuiapoiwa. He was born in the
eastern part of Hawaii, in the year 1795 or 1796. The
name by which he was generally known was *Rihoriho*,
which was only a contraction of *Kalaninui-rihoriho*, literally, the heaven's great black—from *Ka lani*, the heavens, *nui*, great, and *rihoriho*, applied to any thing burned
to blackness. On public occasions he was sometimes
called Tamehameha, after his father, though names are
not always hereditary. Besides these, he had a variety
of other names, the most common of which was *Iolani*.
The word *lani*, heaven or sky, formed a component part

in the name of most chiefs of distinction. The following is a fac-simile of the official signature of the late king.

Tamehameha

The early habits of Rihoriho did not warrant any great expectations. His natural disposition was frank, and humane. The natives always spoke of him as good-natured, except when he was under the influence of ardent spirits; his manners were perfectly free, at the same time dignified, and always agreeable to those who were about him. His mind was naturally inquisitive. The questions he usually presented to foreigners were by no means trifling; and his memory was retentive. His general knowledge of the world was much greater than could have been expected. I have heard him entertain a party of chiefs for hours together with accounts of different parts of the earth, describing the extensive lakes, the mountains, and mines of North and South America—the elephants and inhabitants of India —the houses, manufactures, &c. of England—with no small accuracy, considering he had never seen them. He had a great thirst for knowledge, and was diligent in his studies. I recollect his remarking one day, when he opened his writing-desk, that he expected more advantage from that desk than from a fine brig belonging to him, lying at anchor opposite the house in which we were sitting. Mr. Bingham and myself were his daily teachers, and have often been surprised at his unwearied perseverance. I have sat beside him at his desk sometimes from nine or ten o'clock in the morning till nearly sunset, during which period his pen or his book has not been out of his hand more than three-quarters of an hour, while he was at dinner.

We do not know that Christianity exerted any decisive influence on his heart. He was willing to receive the missionaries on their first arrival—availed himself of their knowledge, to increase his own—and, during

the latter years of his life, was decidedly favourable to their object; declared his conviction of the truth of Christianity; attended public worship himself on the Sabbath, and recommended the same to his people.

His moral character was not marked by that cruelty, rapacity, and insensibility to the sufferings of the people, which frequently distinguish the abitrary chiefs of uncivilized nations. He appears in general to have been kind; and, in several places on our tour, the mothers showed us their children, and told us that when Rihoriho passed that way, he had kissed them—a condescension they seemed to think much of, and which they will probably remember to the end of their days. But, though generous in his disposition, and humane in his conduct towards his subjects, he was addicted to intoxication—whether from natural inclination or the influence and example of others is not now to be determined; frequently, to my own knowledge, it has been entirely from the latter. Had he in early life been privileged to associate with individuals whose conduct and principles were favourable to virtue and religion, there is every reason to suppose his moral character, with respect at least to this vice, would have been as irreproachable as his mental habits were commendable. But, alas for him! it was quite the reverse.

Though not distinguished by the ardour and strength of character so conspicuous in his father, he possessed both decision and enterprise: the abolition of the national idolatry was a striking instance of the former; and his voyage to England, of the latter.

The motives by which he was induced to undertake a voyage so long and hazardous were highly commendable. They were—a desire to see for himself countries of which he had heard such various and interesting accounts; a wish to have a personal interview with his majesty the king of Great Britain, or the chief members of the British government—for the purpose of confirming the cession of the Sandwich Islands, and placing himself and his dominions under British protection.

It was also his intention to make himself acquainted with the tenor and forms of administering justice in the courts of law, the principles of commerce, and other subjects important to the welfare of the islands.

The melancholy death of the late king and queen,

which took place shortly after their arrival in England,
not only prevented the full accomplishment of these
desirable objects, but awakened very generally a degree
of apprehension that the people of the islands, unacquainted with the true circumstances of their death,
would be led to suppose they had been neglected, unkindly treated, or even poisoned in revenge of the death
of Captain Cook, and that the feelings of friendship
with which they had been accustomed to regard the
people of England might be followed by enmity or distrust.   The fears of those who felt interested in the
welfare of the Hawaiians, though natural, were groundless.   The British government had entertained the
young ruler of the Sandwich Islands, his consort, and
attendants with its accustomed hospitality; and when
they were attacked by diseases incident to a northern
climate, but unknown in their native islands, every attention that humanity could suggest, and every alleviation
that the first medical skill in London could afford, was
most promptly rendered.   After their decease, the highest respect was paid to their remains, and in honourable
regard to the feelings of the nation who had suffered this
painful bereavement, a British frigate, under the command of Captain Lord Byron, was appointed to convey to
the Sandwich Islands the bodies of the king and queen,·
that their sorrowing people might have the mournful
satisfaction of depositing their ashes among the tombs
of their ancestors.

By the return of a highly esteemed missionary friend,
Rev. C. S. Stewart, I have learned that the Blonde
reached the islands in the month of May, 1825: the
natives were in some degree prepared for the arrival, by
the intelligence of the death of their king and queen,
which they had received about two months before from
Valparaiso.   Shortly after, the vessel having the remains
of the king and queen on board had anchored off Oahu,
Boki, the principal chief, who had accompanied the
king to England, attended by those of his countrymen
who had also returned, proceeded on shore: on landing,
he was met by his elder brother Karaimoku, and other
distinguished chiefs, and after the first emotions of joy
at meeting again, and sorrow on account of the loss all
had sustained, were somewhat abated, the survivors
and their friends walked in solemn and mournful procession to the place of worship, where thanksgivings
were presented to God, for the merciful preservation

of those who were thus privileged to meet again, and supplications were made that the afflicting dispensation, which all so deeply felt, might exert a salutary influence in the minds of the surviving chiefs, and the sorrowing nation at large.

Karaimoku, the late prime minister, and present regent of the islands, then arose and said, " We have lost our king and queen, they have died in a foreign land; we shall see them no more ; it is right that we should weep, but let us not entertain hard thoughts of God. *God has not done wrong.* The evil is with us: let us bow under his hand; let all amusement cease ; let our daily avocations be suspended ; and let the nation, by prayer and a cessation from ordinary pursuits, humble itself before God fourteen days." Before the assembly separated, Boki stood up, and, in a brief outline of the voyage, narrated the most prominent events that had transpired since his departure from the islands —calling their attention in particular to the suitable and important advice he had received from his majesty the king of Great Britain, in an audience with which he was graciously favoured, viz. To return to his native country, attend to general and religious instruction himself, and endeavour to enlighten and reform the people. The peculiar circumstances of the people at this time, the increased satisfaction they had for some time felt in attending every means of instruction within their reach, and the pleasing change in favour of religion which many had experienced, rendered this recommendation, so congenial to their feelings, from a source so distinguished, unusually acceptable. A deep and favourable impression was produced on all present, a new impulse was given to the means already employed for the instruction and improvement of the people, from which most advantageous results have already appeared. They were also made acquainted, by Boki and his companions, with the kind reception, generous treatment, and marked attentions which the late king and queen and their suite had received while in England. This intelligence, communicated by those whose testimony would be received with the most entire credence, would at once confirm the attachment and confidence they have so long felt towards England.

No disturbance of the general tranquillity, nor change in the government, of the islands has resulted from this

event.   Rihoriho' left a younger brother, *Kauikeouli*,
about ten years of age, who is acknowledged by the
chiefs as his successor.   A regency will govern during
his minority, and the executive authority will probably
continue to be exercised by *Karaimoku*, and the other
chiefs with whom Rihoriho left it when he embarked
for England.

The queen, who accompanied him, and who died at the
same time, has left a fond mother and an affectionate
people to lament her loss; she was the daughter of
Tamehameha and Talakua, and was born about the
year 1797 or 1798, being two years younger than Rihoriho, and about twenty-six years of age when she
left the islands.   Like all the persons of distinction she
had many names, but that by which she was generally
known was *Kamehamaru* (shade of Kameha), from *kameha*, a contraction of herfather's name, and *maru*, shade.
She was distinguished for good nature, and was much
beloved by all her subjects.   The poor people, when
unable to pay their rent, or under the displeasure of the
king and chiefs, or embarrassed on any other account,
frequently repaired to her, and found a friend whose aid
was never refused.   She was also kind to those foreigners who might be distressed in the islands, and though
she never harboured any or countenanced their absconding from their ships, she has often fed them when
hungry, and given them native tapa for clothing.

Kamehamaru was at all times lively and agreeable in
company ; and though her application to her book and
her pen was equal to that of the king, her improvement
in learning was more gradual, and her general knowledge less extensive.

She excelled, however, in the management of his
domestic affairs, which were conducted by her with
great judgment and address, and, though formerly accustomed to use ardent spirits, from the time she put herself under Christian instruction, she entirely discontinued that and every other practice inconsistent with
her profession of Christianity.   Her attendance on the
duties of religion was maintained with commendable
regularity.

Her influence contributed very materially to the pleasing change that has recently taken place, in connexion
with the labours of the missionaries in the islands. For
the instruction and moral improvement of the people,

she manifested no ordinary concern. Long before
many of the leading chiefs were favourable to the instruction of the people or their reception of Christianity, Kamehamaru on every suitable occasion recommended to her own servants to serve Jehovah the living
God, and attend to every means of improvement within
their reach. It was truly pleasing to observe, so soon
after she had embraced Christianity herself, an anxiety
to induce her people to follow her example. At Honoruru she erected a school, in which upwards of forty
children and young persons, principally connected with
her establishment, were daily taught to read and write,
and instructed in the first principles of religion, by a
native teacher, whom she almost entirely supported. In
this school she took a lively interest, and marked the
progress of the scholars with evident satisfaction; in
order to encourage the pupils, she frequently visited
the school during the hours of instruction, accompanied
by a number of chief women. She also attended the
public examinations, and noticed those who on these
occasions excelled, frequently presenting a favourite
scholar with a slate, a copy-book, pencil, pen, or some
other token of her approbation.

In her death the missionaries have lost a sincere
friend, and her subjects a queen who always delighted
to alleviate their distresses and promote their interests.

Her disposition was affectionate. I have seen her
and the king sitting beside the couch of Keopuolani, her
mother-in-law, day after day, when the latter has been
ill; and on these occasions, though there might be several servants in constant attendance, she would allow
no individual but her husband or herself to hand to the
patient any thing she might want, or even fan the flies
from her person.

The circumstances attending her departure from the
islands were peculiarly affecting. The king had gone
on board L'Aigle; but the boat was waiting to convey
her to the ship. She arose from the mat on which she
had been reclining; embraced her mother and other
relations most affectionately, and passed through the
crowd towards the boat. The people fell down on
their knees as she walked along, pressing and saluting
her feet—frequently bathing them with tears of unfeigned sorrow—and making loud wailings, in which

his family, thanking him at the same time for the hospitable entertainment we had received; and the great facilities he had afforded for accomplishing the objects of our visit.

About three o'clock in the morning, being awoke by the shouts of the men who were heaving up the anchor of the pilot-boat, I repaired on board, and immediately afterward we sailed with a gentle breeze blowing from the land. The wind was light and baffling, and it was noon before we reached Towaihae, where I learned with disappointment that the Nio had sailed to Oahu. On landing I was welcomed by Mr. Young, with whom I remained till the pilot-boat was ready to sail for Lahaina.

Late in the evening of the 2d of September, after preaching to the people of the place at Mr. Young's house, I went again on board the pilot-boat, but found her so full of sandal-wood that there was not room for any person below, while the decks were crowded with natives. The weather was unfavourable for getting under way till nearly daylight; and every person on board was completely drenched by the heavy rain that fell during the night.

During the forenoon of the 3d, we drifted slowly to the northward, and about noon took in eight hundred dried fish, after which we made sail for Maui. The weather was warm, the wind light: and all on board being obliged to keep on deck, without any screen or shade from the scorching rays of a vertical sun, the situation was very uncomfortable. At three P. M. we took the channel-breeze, which soon wafted us across to the south-east part of Maui.

As the shores of Hawaii receded from my view, a variety of reflections insensibly arose in my mind. The tour which, in the society of my companions, I had made had been replete with interest. The varied and sublime phenomena of nature had elevated our conceptions of "nature's God;" the manners and customs of the inhabitants had increased our interest in their welfare; while their superstition, moral degradation, ignorance, and vice had called forth our sincerest commiseration. We had made known the nature and consequences of sin, spoken of the love of God, and had exhibited the Lord Jesus Christ as the only Saviour to multitudes who had never before heard his name, or been directed

to worship the holy and living God, and who would probably never hear these truths again. We cherish the hope that, under the Divine blessing, lasting good will result, even from this transient visit.

Many of the individuals we have met on these occasions, we shall in all probability meet no more till the morning of the resurrection. May we meet them then on the right-hand of the Son of God?

At sunset we arrived off Morokini, but were shortly after becalmed. The current, however, was in our favour through the night, and at daylight on the 4th we found ourselves off the east end of the district of Laha-ʌina, and about a mile distant from the shore. Many of the natives jumped into the sea, and swam to the beach, holding their clothes above their heads with one hand, and swimming with the other.

On landing I waited on Keopuolani, the king's mother, whom I found ill; Karaimoku, Kaahumanu, Kalakua, and several other chiefs were reclining around her, weeping. After some time, Karaimoku proposed that they should unitedly pray for her recovery, and his proposal was acceded to.

Towards evening I visited the governor of the island, and also the king, who was then at Maui. The subsequent voyage of the latter to Great Britain, accompanied by his queen, and the melancholy event which terminated their lives while in London, excited considerable interest, and will probably be considered sufficient apology for a short account of them, although the event took place after my visit to Maui at this time.

The late king of the Sandwich Islands was the son of Tamehameha, former king, and Keopuolani, daughter of Kauikeouli, and Kakuiapoiwa. He was born in the eastern part of Hawaii, in the year 1795 or 1796. The name by which he was generally known was *Rihoriho*, which was only a contraction of *Kalaninui-rihoriho*, literally, the heaven's great black—from *Ka lani*, the heavens, *nui*, great, and *rihoriho*, applied to any thing burned to blackness. On public occasions he was sometimes called Tamehameha, after his father, though names are not always hereditary. Besides these, he had a variety of other names, the most common of which was *Iolani*. The word *lani*, heaven or sky, formed a component part

in the name of most chiefs of distinction. The following is a fac-simile of the official signature of the late
king.

Tamehameha

The early habits of Rihoriho did not warrant any
great expectations. His natural disposition was frank,
and humane. The natives always spoke of him as
good-natured, except when he was under the influence
of ardent spirits; his manners were perfectly free, at
the same time dignified, and always agreeable to those
who were about him. His mind was naturally inquisitive. The questions he usually presented to foreigners
were by no means trifling; and his memory was retentive. His general knowledge of the world was much
greater than could have been expected. I have heard
him entertain a party of chiefs for hours together with
accounts of different parts of the earth, describing the
extensive lakes, the mountains, and mines of North and
South America—the elephants and inhabitants of India
—the houses, manufactures, &c. of England—with no
small accuracy, considering he had never seen them.
He had a great thirst for knowledge, and was diligent in
his studies. I recollect his remarking one day, when
he opened his writing-desk, that he expected more advantage from that desk than from a fine brig belonging
to him, lying at anchor opposite the house in which we
were sitting. Mr. Bingham and myself were his daily
teachers, and have often been surprised at his unwearied
perseverance. I have sat beside him at his desk sometimes from nine or ten o'clock in the morning till nearly
sunset, during which period his pen or his book has not
been out of his hand more than three-quarters of an
hour, while he was at dinner.

We do not know that Christianity exerted any decisive influence on his heart. He was willing to receive
the missionaries on their first arrival—availed himself
of their knowledge, to increase his own—and, during

the latter years of his life, was decidedly favourable to their object; declared his conviction of the truth of Christianity; attended public worship himself on the Sabbath, and recommended the same to his people.

His moral character was not marked by that cruelty, rapacity, and insensibility to the sufferings of the people, which frequently distinguish the arbitrary chiefs of uncivilized nations. He appears in general to have been kind; and, in several places on our tour, the mothers showed us their children, and told us that when Rihoriho passed that way, he had kissed them—a condescension they seemed to think much of, and which they will probably remember to the end of their days. But, though generous in his disposition, and humane in his conduct towards his subjects, he was addicted to intoxication—whether from natural inclination or the influence and-example of others is not now to be determined; frequently, to my own knowledge, it has been entirely from the latter. Had he in early life been privileged to associate with individuals whose conduct and principles were favourable to virtue and religion, there is every reason to suppose his moral character, with respect at least to this vice, would have been as irreproachable as his mental habits were commendable. But, alas for him! it was quite the reverse.

Though not distinguished by the ardour and strength of character so conspicuous in his father, he possessed both decision and enterprise: the abolition of the national idolatry was a striking instance of the former; and his voyage to England, of the latter.

The motives by which he was induced to undertake a voyage so long and hazardous were highly commendable. They were—a desire to see for himself countries of which he had heard such various and interesting accounts; a wish to have a personal interview with his majesty the king of Great Britain, or the chief members of the British government—for the purpose of confirming the cession of the Sandwich Islands, and placing himself and his dominions under British protection.

It was also his intention to make himself acquainted with the tenor and forms of administering justice in the courts of law, the principles of commerce, and other subjects important to the welfare of the islands.

The melancholy death of the late king and queen,

which took place shortly after their arrival in England, not only prevented the full accomplishment of these desirable objects, but awakened very generally a degree of apprehension that the people of the islands, unacquainted with the true circumstances of their death, would be led to suppose they had been neglected, unkindly treated, or even poisoned in revenge of the death of Captain Cook, and that the feelings of friendship with which they had been accustomed to regard the people of England might be followed by enmity or distrust. The fears of those who felt interested in the welfare of the Hawaiians, though natural, were groundless. The British government had entertained the young ruler of the Sandwich Islands, his consort, and attendants with its accustomed hospitality; and when they were attacked by diseases incident to a northern climate, but unknown in their native islands, every attention that humanity could suggest, and every alleviation that the first medical skill in London could afford, was most promptly rendered. After their decease, the highest respect was paid to their remains, and in honourable regard to the feelings of the nation who had suffered this painful bereavement, a British frigate, under the command of Captain Lord Byron, was appointed to convey to the Sandwich Islands the bodies of the king and queen, that their sorrowing people might have the mournful satisfaction of depositing their ashes among the tombs of their ancestors.

By the return of a highly esteemed missionary friend, Rev. C. S. Stewart, I have learned that the Blonde reached the islands in the month of May, 1825: the natives were in some degree prepared for the arrival, by the intelligence of the death of their king and queen, which they had received about two months before from Valparaiso. Shortly after, the vessel having the remains of the king and queen on board had anchored off Oahu, Boki, the principal chief, who had accompanied the king to England, attended by those of his countrymen who had also returned, proceeded on shore: on landing, he was met by his elder brother Karaimoku, and other distinguished chiefs, and after the first emotions of joy at meeting again, and sorrow on account of the loss all had sustained, were somewhat abated, the survivors and their friends walked in solemn and mournful procession to the place of worship, where thanksgivings were presented to God, for the merciful preservation

of those who were thus privileged to meet again, and supplications were made that the afflicting dispensation, which all so deeply felt, might exert a salutary influence in the minds of the surviving chiefs, and the sorrowing nation at large.

Karaimoku, the late prime minister, and present regent of the islands, then arose and said, " We have lost our king and queen, they have died in a foreign land; we shall see them no more ; it is right that we should weep, but let us not entertain hard thoughts of God. ' *God has not done wrong.* The evil is with us : let us bow under his hand ; let all amusement cease ; let our daily avocations be suspended ; and let the nation, by prayer and a cessation from ordinary pursuits, humble itself before God fourteen days." Before the assembly separated, Boki stood up, and, in a brief outline of the voyage, narrated the most prominent events that had transpired since his departure from the islands —calling their attention in particular to the suitable and important advice he had received from his majesty the king of Great Britain, in an audience with which he was graciously favoured, viz.   To return to his native country, attend to general and religious instruction himself, and endeavour to enlighten and reform the people. The peculiar circumstances of the people at this time, the increased satisfaction they had for some time felt in attending every means of instruction within their reach, and the pleasing change in favour of religion which many had experienced, rendered this recommendation, so congenial to their feelings, from a source so distinguished, unusually acceptable.   A deep and favourable impression was produced on all present, a new impulse was given to the means already employed for the instruction and improvement of the people, from which most advantageous results have already appeared. They were also made acquainted, by Boki and his companions, with the kind reception, generous treatment, and marked attentions which the late king and queen and their suite had received while in England.   This intelligence, communicated by those whose testimony would be received with the most entire credence, would at once confirm the attachment and confidence they have so long felt towards England.

No disturbance of the general tranquillity, nor change in the government, of the islands has resulted from this

event. Rihoriho' left a younger brother, *Kauikeouli*, about ten years of age, who is acknowledged by the chiefs as his successor. A regency will govern during his minority, and the executive authority will probably continue to be exercised by *Karaimoku*, and the other chiefs with whom Rihoriho left it when he embarked for England.

The queen, who accompanied him, and who died at the same time, has left a fond mother and an affectionate people to lament her loss: she was the daughter of Tamehameha and Talakua, and was born about the year 1797 or 1798, being two years younger than Rihoriho, and about twenty-six years of age when she left the islands. Like all the persons of distinction she had many names, but that by which she was generally known was *Kamehamaru* (shade of Kameha), from *kameha*, a contraction of herfather's name, and *maru*, shade. She was distinguished for good nature, and was much beloved by all her subjects. The poor people, when unable to pay their rent, or under the displeasure of the king and chiefs, or embarrassed on any other account, frequently repaired to her, and found a friend whose aid was never refused. She was also kind to those foreigners who might be distressed in the islands, and though she never harboured any or countenanced their absconding from their ships, she has often fed them when hungry, and given them native tapa for clothing.

Kamehamaru was at all times lively and agreeable in company; and though her application to her book and her pen was equal to that of the king, her improvement in learning was more gradual, and her general knowledge less extensive.

She excelled, however, in the management of his domestic affairs, which were conducted by her with great judgment and address, and, though formerly accustomed to use ardent spirits, from the time she put herself under Christian instruction, she entirely discontinued that and every other practice inconsistent with her profession of Christianity. Her attendance on the duties of religion was maintained with commendable regularity.

Her influence contributed very materially to the pleasing change that has recently taken place, in connexion with the labours of the missionaries in the islands. For the instruction and moral improvement of the people,

she manifested no ordinary concern. Long before
many of the leading chiefs were favourable to the instruction of the people or their reception of Christianity, Kamehamaru on every suitable occasion recommended to her own servants to serve Jehovah the living
God, and attend to every means of improvement within
their reach. It was truly pleasing to observe, so soon
after she had embraced Christianity herself, an anxiety
to induce her people to follow her example. At Honoruru she erected a school, in which upwards of forty
children and young persons, principally connected with
her establishment, were daily taught to read and write,
and instructed in the first principles of religion, by a
native teacher, whom she almost entirely supported. In
this school she took a lively interest, and marked the
progress of the scholars with evident satisfaction; in
order to encourage the pupils, she frequently visited
the school during the hours of instruction, accompanied
by a number of chief women. She also attended the
public examinations, and noticed those who on these
occasions excelled, frequently presenting a favourite
scholar with a slate, a copy-book, pencil, pen, or some
other token of her approbation.

In her death the missionaries have lost a sincere
friend, and her subjects a queen who always delighted
to alleviate their distresses and promote their interests.

Her disposition was affectionate. I have seen her
and the king sitting beside the couch of Keopuolani, her
mother-in-law, day after day, when the latter has been
ill; and on these occasions, though there might be several servants in constant attendance, she would allow
no individual but her husband or herself to hand to the
patient any thing she might want, or even fan the flies
from her person.

The circumstances attending her departure from the
islands were peculiarly affecting. The king had gone
on board L'Aigle; but the boat was waiting to convey
her to the ship. She arose from the mat on which she
had been reclining, embraced her mother and other
relations most affectionately, and passed through the
crowd towards the boat. The people fell down on
their knees as she walked along, pressing and saluting
her feet—frequently bathing them with tears of unfeigned sorrow—and making loud wailings, in which

they were joined by the thousands who thronged the shore.

On reaching the water-side, she turned and beckoned to the people to cease their cries. As soon as they were silent, she said, "I am going to a distant land, and perhaps we shall not meet again. Let us pray to Jehovah, that he may preserve us on the water and you on the shore." She then called *Auna*, a native teacher from the Society Islands, and requested him to pray. He did so; at the conclusion she waved her hand to the people, and said, "*Arohá nui oukou*" (attachment great to you): she then stepped into the boat, evidently much affected. The multitude followed her, not only to the beach, but into the sea, where many, wading into the water, stood waving their hands, exhibiting every attitude of sorrow, and uttering their loud *u-e! u-e!* (alas! alas!) till the boat had pulled far out to sea.

The death of the king and queen, so soon after their arrival in England, was an event in many respects deeply to be deplored. The officers of the London Missionary Society were unable to gain access to them until they should have been introduced to his majesty; and one of them, I believe the king, died on the very day on which that introduction was to have taken place. The same circumstance also prevented many Christian friends, who felt interested in their welfare, from that intercourse with them which, under the blessing of God, might have been expected to have strengthened the religious impressions they had received from the instructions of the missionaries. In their visit to England they were accompanied by a suite, which, though much less numerous than that which invariably attended their movements in their native islands, included nevertheless, several individuals of rank and influence. Among the principal of these was Boki, the governor of the island of Oahu, and Liliha, his wife; Kauruheimarama, a distant relation of the king; Kakuanaoa and Kapihe, two of his favourite companions; the latter of whom was a man of an amiable disposition, and, considering the circumstances under which he had been brought up, possessed general intelligence. He had made a voyage to Canton in China, for the purpose of acquiring mercantile information; and, from the circumstance of his commanding the finest vessel belonging to the king, a brig of about ninety tons burden, called the *Haaheo Hawaii* (pride of Hawaii), he was sometimes called the admiral, although that is an office to which there is nothing analogous in the present maritime system of the Hawaiians. With this individual, who died at Valparaiso, on his return to the islands, and the others who survived the death of the king, particularly with Boki, the officers of the London Missionary Society had several interviews, and received the strongest assurances of their continued patronage and support of the Christian mission established in the Sandwich Islands. Many benevolent individuals had also an opportunity of testifying the deep interest they felt in the civil, moral, and religious improvement of their countrymen.

It is a pleasing fact, in connexion with the present circumstances of the nation, that almost every chief of rank and influence in the Sandwich Islands is favourably disposed towards the instruction of the natives and the promulgation of the gospel. A deep sense of the kindness of the friends by whom the chiefs who survived the king and queen were visited at Portsmouth, appears to have remained on the minds of the Hawaiian chiefs long after their return to their native land; for when the Rev. C. S. Stewart, an American missionary, was about to leave the Sandwich Islands for Great Britain, Boki gave him a special charge to present his grateful regards to the *Bishop of Portsmouth.* Mr. S. told him he was not aware that there was such a dignitary; but Boki said, Yes, there was, for he visited him, with some of his friends, when they were on the point of sailing from England. I at first heard that the late Dr. Bogue was the individual to whom Boki referred; but I have since learned, that in consequence of severe domestic affliction at that time it is uncertain whether he did or did not; and that the Sandwich Island chief referred either to the Rev. C. Simeon of Cambridge, or the Rev. J. Griffin, by both of whom he was visited.

Among the letters I was favoured to receive from the islands by the return of his majesty's ship Blonde, those from Boki and Liliha, or, as she was frequently called while in England, Madam Boki, were of a character so interesting, that I think I shall be pardoned for inserting one of them. It is from Boki, the chief who was with the king in London. I shall translate it very literally

" Oahu. *The first of the Twins is the month*
(answering to our *October*), 1825.

" Affection for you, Mr. Ellis, and sympathy with you, Mrs.
Ellis, in your illness. This is my entreaty: return you hither,
and we shall be right. Grief was ours on your returning.
Heard before this have you of the death of the king: but all things
here are correct. We are serving God: we are making ourselves strong in His Word. Turned have the chiefs to instruction: their desire is towards God. I speak unto them, and encourage them concerning the Word of God, that it may be well
with our land.

" Attachment to you two, attachment to the
ministers, and the missionaries all.

" CAPTAIN BOKI."

At ten o'clock in the forenoon of the 9th I took leave
of my kind friends at Lahaina, and in company with
Messrs. Bingham and Richards went on board the Ta-
mahorolani, bound to Oahu. It was, however, four
o'clock in the afternoon before the vessel hove-up her
anchor. We were becalmed till nine in the evening,
when a fresh breeze sprang up; we passed down the
channel between Morokai and Ranai; and between nine
and ten in the forenoon of the 10th arrived off the harbour of Honoruru.

On landing I was grateful to meet my family in health
and comfort, except Mrs. Ellis, who was confined by
severe indisposition. I united with Messrs. Thurston,
Bishop, and Goodrich, who had previously arrived, in
grateful acknowledgments to God for the unremitted
care and distinguishing goodness which we had enjoyed
in accomplishing the interesting tour, from which, under
circumstances of no small mercy, we had now returned.

APPENDIX.

In the course of our tour around Hawaii, we met with a few specimens of what may perhaps be termed the first efforts of an uncivilized people towards the construction of a language of symbols. Along the southern coast, both on the east and west sides, we frequently saw a number of straight lines, semicircles, or concentric rings, with some rude imitations of the human figure, cut or carved in the compact rocks of lava. They did not appear to have been cut with an iron instrument, but with a stone hatchet, or a stone less frangible than the rock on which they were portrayed. On inquiry, we found that they had been made by former travellers, from a motive similar to that which induces a person to carve his initials on a stone or tree, or a traveller to record his name in an album, to inform his successors that he has been there. When there were a number of concentric circles with a dot or mark in the centre, the dot signified a man, and the number of rings denoted the number in the party who had circumambulated the island. When there was a ring and a number of marks, it denoted the same; the number of marks showing of how many the party consisted; and the ring, that they had travelled completely round the island; but when there was only a semicircle, it denoted that they had returned after reaching the place where it was made. In some of the islands we have seen the outline of a fish portrayed in the same manner, to denote that one of that species or size had been taken near the spot; sometimes the dimensions of an exceedingly large fruit, &c. are marked in the same way.

With this slight exception, if such it can be called, the natives of the Sandwich and other islands had no signs for sounds or ideas, nor any pictorial representation of events. Theirs was entirely an oral language; and, whatever view we take of it, presents the most interesting phenomenon connected with the inhabitants of the Pacific. A grammatical analysis would exceed my present limits ; a few brief remarks, however, will convey some idea of its peculiarities ; and a copious grammar, prepared by my respected colleagues, the American missionaries in those islands, and myself, may perhaps be published at no distant period.

The language of the Hawaiians is a dialect of what the missionaries in the South Seas have called the Polynesian language, spoken in all the islands which lie to the east of the Friendly Islands, including New-Zealand and Chatham Island. The extent to which it prevails, the degree of perfection it has attained, the slight analogy between it and any one known language, the insulated situation, and the uncivilized character of the people by whom it is spoken, prove that, notwithstanding the rude state of their society, they have bestowed no small attention to its cultivation, and lead to the inference that it has been for many ages a distinct language ; while the obscurity that veils its origin, as well as that of the people by whom it is used, prevents our forming any satisfactory conclusion as to the source whence it was derived.

The numerals are similar to those of the Malays ? and it has many words in common with that language, yet the construction of the words and the rules of syntax appear different. In the specimen of languages spoken in Sumatra, given by Mr. Marsden in his history of that island, some words appear in each, common in the South Seas ; and it is difficult to determine in which they preponderate. In looking over the Malayan grammar and dictionary by the same gentleman, many words appear similar in sound and signification ; but there are a number of radical words common to all the Polynesian languages, as *kanaka*, man, *ao*, light, *pouri*, darkness, *po*, night, *ra* or *la*, sun, *marama*, moon, *maitai*, good, *ino*, bad, *ai*, to eat, and *moe*, to sleep, which, though very nearly the same in all the South Sea languages, appear to have no affinity with *orang*, *trang*, *klam*, *malam*, *mataari*, and *shems*, *bulan*, *baik*, *baruk*, *makan*, and *tidor*, words of the same meaning in Malayan : notwithstanding this, there is a striking resemblance in others, and a great part of the language was doubtless derived from the same source.

Since my return to England, I have had an opportunity of conversing with the Madagasse youth now in this country for the purposes of education, and from them, as well as a vocabulary which I have seen, I was surprised to learn, that in several points the aboriginal languages of Madagascar and the South Sea islands are strikingly analogous, if not identical, though the islands are about 10,000 geographical miles distant from each other.

With the aboriginal languages of South America we have had no opportunity of comparing it; some of the words of that

country, in their simplicity of construction and vowel terminations, as Peru, Quito (pronounced *kito*), Parana, Oronoko, &c.,
appear like Polynesian words.

In the Sandwich Islands, as well as the Tahitian language,
there are a number of words that appear true Hebrew roots, and
in the conjugation of the verbs there is a striking similarity; the
causative active and the causative passive being formed by a
prefix and suffix to the verb.

In many respects it is unique, and in some defective, but not
in that degree which might be expected from the limited knowledge of the people. The simple construction of the words, the
predominancy of vowels, and the uniform terminations, are its
great peculiarities. The syllables are in general composed of
two letters, and never more than three. There are no sibilants
in the language, nor any double consonants. Every word and
syllable terminates with a vowel; and the natives cannot pronounce two consonants without an intervening vowel; nor a
word terminating with a consonant, without either dropping the
final letter, or adding a vowel; hence they pronounce Britain,
Beritani, boat, *boti*; while there are many words, and even sentences, without a consonant, as *e i ai oe ia ïa ae e ao ïa*, literally,
" speak now to him by the side that he learn." The frequent use
of the *k* renders their speech more masculine than that of the
Tahitians, in which the *t* predominates.

The sound of their language is peculiarly soft and harmonious; great attention is also paid to euphony, on account of
which the article is often varied; the same is the case in the
Tahitian, in which the word *tavovóvovó* signifies the rolling of
thunder.

Each of the dialects appears adapted for poetry, and none
more so than the Hawaiian, in which the *l* frequently occurs.
Whether the smoothness of their language induced the natives
to cultivate metrical composition, or their fondness for the latter
has occasioned the multiplicity of vowels and soft flowing
arrangement of the sentences, which distinguish their language,
it is difficult to conjecture. In native poetry, rhyming terminations are neglected, and the chief art appears to consist in the
compilation of short metrical sentences, agreeing in accent and
cadence at the conclusion of each, or at the end of a certain
number of sentences. Rude as their native poetry is, they are
passionately fond of it. When they first began to learn to read and
spell, it was impossible for them to repeat a column of spelling,
or recite a lesson, without chanting or singing it. They had one
tune for the monosyllables, another for the dissyllables, &c., and
we have heard three or four members of a family sitting for an
hour together in an evening, and reciting their school lessons in
perfect concord. Most of the traditions of remarkable events in
their history are preserved in songs committed to memory, by

persons attached to the king or chiefs; or strolling musicians, who travel through the islands, and recite them on occasions of public festivity. The late king had one of these *bards* attached from infancy to his household, who, like some of the ancient bards, was blind, and who, when required, would recite a *hura* (song) on any particular event relating to the family of his sovereign. The office was hereditary; the songs are transmitted from father to son; and whatever defects might attach to their performances, considered as works of art, they were not wanting in effect; being highly figurative and delivered in strains of plaintive sadness, or wild enthusiasm, they produced great excitement of feeling. Sometimes their interest was local, and respected some particular family, but the most popular were the national songs. When I first visited the Sandwich Islands, one on the defeat of Kekuaokalani, the rival of Rihoriho, who was slain in the battle of Tuamoo, was in the mouth of almost every native we met; another, nearly as popular, was a panegyric on the late king, composed on his accession to the government; and soon after his departure for England, several bards were employed in celebrating that event. In my voyage from Hawaii, three or four females, fellow-passengers, were thus employed during the greater part of the passage, which afforded me an opportunity of observing the process. They first agreed on two or three ideas, arranged them in a kind of metrical sentence, with great attention to the accent of the concluding word, and then repeated it in concert. If it sounded discordantly, they altered it; if not, they repeated it several times, and then proceeded to form a new sentence. The *k* in most of the islands is generally used in common intercourse, but it is never admitted into their poetical compositions, in which the *t* is universally and invariably employed.

The following verses, extracted from a collection of hymns in the native language, comprising sixty pages, are a translation of lines on the " Sandwich Mission," by W. B. Tappan, on the embarkation of the missionaries from New-Haven (America), in 1822. The *k* is employed, though contrary to the practice of the natives. The original commences with—

" Wake, isles of the south, your redemption is near,
No longer repose in the borders of gloom.''

HAWAIIAN.

I na moku i paa i ka pouri mau,
Uhia 'ka naau po wale rakou,
Ano hei e puka no maila ke ao,
Hoku Bet'lehema, ka Hoku ao mau.

Huïa ka rere a pau me ka kii,
E hooreïa kɐ taumaha a pau ;
I k'alana maitai rakou e ora'i,
Tabu ka heiau na ke Akua mau.

E ake rakou i nana wave ae,
Ka wehea mai'ka araura maitai,
A o ka kúkuna 'ka Mesia mau,
" A kali na moku kona kanawai."

ORIGINAL.

On the islands that sit in the regions of night,
    The lands of despair, to oblivion a prey,
The morning will open with healing and light,
    And the young star of Bethlehem will ripen to day.

The altar and idol, in dust overthrown,
    The incense forbade that was hallow'd with blood ;
The priest of Melchisedec there shall atone,
    And the shrines of Hawaii be sacred to God.

The heathen will hasten to welcome the time,
    The day-spring the prophet in vision foresaw,
When the beams of Messiah will 'lumine each clime,
    And the isles of the ocean shall wait for his law.

Notwithstanding its defects, the Hawaiian has its excellences.
Ideas are frequently conveyed with great force and precision ;
verbs not only express the action, but the manner of it distinctly ; hence, to send a message would be *orero*, to send a
messenger, *kono*, to send a parcel, *houna*, to break a stick, *haki*,
to break a string, *moku*, to break a cup, *naha*, to break a law, *koo-
maloka*, &c. Considering it is a language that has received no
additions from the intercourse of the natives with other countries,
and is devoid of all technical terms of art and science, it is, as
well as the other dialects, exceedingly copious. Some idea of
this may be formed from the circumstance of there being in the
Tahitian upwards of 1400 words commencing with the letter *a*.
The greatest imperfections we have discovered occur in the
degrees of the adjectives, and the deficiency of the auxiliary verb
to be, which is implied, but not expressed. The natives cannot
say, *I am*, or *it is* ; yet they can say a thing remains, as, *ke
waiho maira ka waa i raira*, the canoe remains there ; and their
verbs are used in the participial form, by simply adding the termination *ana*, equivalent to *ing* in English. Hence in asking a
native, what he is doing ; the question would be, *He aha-ana
oe?* Whating you? The answer would be, *He ai ana wau*,
Eating (am) I. The *He* denoting the present tense preceding
the question, the answer corresponds ; but if he wished to say,
what he was eating, the noun would be placed between the verb

VOL. IV.—P

and its participial termination, as *He ai* poe *ana* wau, literally, *Eat* poe-*ing* I. In every other respect their language appears to possess all the parts of speech, and some in greater variety and perfection than any language we are acquainted with.

In reducing the language to a written form, the American missionaries adopted the Roman character, as the English missionaries had done before in the southern dialects. The English alphabet possesses a redundancy of consonants, and, though rather deficient in vowels, answers tolerably well to express all the native sounds. The Hawaiian alphabet consists of seventeen letters: five vowels, *a, e, i, o, u,* and twelve consonants, *b, d, h, k, l, m, n, p, r, t, v, w,* to which *f, g, s,* and *z,* have been added, for the purpose of preserving the identity of foreign words. The consonants are founded as in English, though we have been obliged to give them different names, for the natives could not say *el* or *em,* but invariably pronounced *ela* and *ema;* it being therefore necessary to retain the final vowel, that was thought sufficient, and the other was rejected. The vowels are sounded more after the manner of the Continental languages than the English; *A,* as in ah, and sometimes as *a* in far, but never as *a* in fate; *E,* as *a* in gale, ape, and mate; *I,* as *ee* in green, *e* in me, or *i* in machine. The short sound of *i* in bit seldom occurs, and the long sound of *i* in wine is expressed by the diphthong *ai;* *O,* as *o* in no and mote; *U,* as *u* in rude, or *oo* in moon. Several of the consonants are interchangeable, particularly the *l* and *r,* the *b* and *p, t* and *k.* There are no silent letters. I have known a native, acquainted with the power of the letters, spell a word when it has been correctly pronounced, though he had never seen it written; for, in pronouncing a word, it is necessary to pronounce every letter of which it is composed.

Articles.—They have two articles, definite (*he*) and indefinite (*ke* or *ka*), answering to the English *the* and *a* or *an.* The articles precede the nouns to which they belong.

Nouns.—The nouns undergo no inflection, or change of termination, the number, case, and gender being denoted by distinct words or particles prefixed or added. Hence *o,* which is only the sign of the nominative, has been usually placed before Tahiti and Hawaii, making Otaheiti and Owyhee; though the *o* is no part of the word, any more than *no* the sign of the possessive, as *no Hawaii,* of Hawaii, and *i* the sign of the objective, as *i Hawaii,* to Hawaii.

Pronouns.—The scheme of pronouns is copious and precise, having not only a singular, dual, and plural number, but a double dual and plural; the first including the speaker and spoken-*to,* as *thou* and I, and *ye* and *I;* the second, the speaker and party spoken *of,* as *he* and *I,* and *they* and *I.* Each of these combinations is clearly expressed by a distinct pronoun. The following specimen will convey some idea of their extent and peculiarity:—

DECLENSION OF HAWAIIAN PRONOUNS EXEMPLIFIED.

First Person Singular.

Nom.

Owau		*Owau* ke kumu	*I* (am) the teacher
Wau		I aku la *wau*	*I* said
Au	I	E hele *au*	*I* (will) go
Na'u		*Na'u* e hanu	*I* (will) work
O'u		*Na'u* la e hana	*I* will do it, or make it
———		Aore *o'u* ike	*I* (do) not know.

Poss.

Na'u		*Na'u* ka ia	*Mine* the fish
No'u		*No'u* ka rore	*Mine* the cloth
Ka'u	Mine,	*No'u* oukou i ike ai	*Of me* ye know
Ko'u	my,	*Ka'u* palapala	*My* paper
A'u	or	*Ko'u* hale	*My* house
O'u	of me	Ka pene *a'u*	The pen *of me*
———		Ka kamaa *o'u*	The shoes *of me*

Obj.

Wau	Me	Nana *wau* i hana	He *me* made or did make
Ia'u	Me	Mai pepehi mai *ia'u*	(Do) not kill *me*
Ia'u	To me	I mia *ia'u*	Speak *to me*
Ia'u	By me	Roaa *iu a*	Obtained *by me*
E au	By me	Aoia e au	Instructed *by me*
Me au	With me	Noho me au	Dwell *with me*.

Second Person Singular.

Nom.

O oe		*O oe* ke kahuna	*You* (are) the preacher
Oe	Thou	E pule *oe*	Pray *thou*
Nau	or	*Nau* no makou i hana	*Thou* alone us (didst) make
Ou	You	Aohe *ou* rohe ?	(Did) not *you* hear ?
Kau		He aha *kau* noho wale nei?	Why (do) *you* remain idle ?

Poss.

Nau		*Nau* ka ai	*Thine* the food
Nou		*Nou* ka kanaka	*Thine* the man
Nou	Thine,	*Nou* rakou i hele a.	*Of thee* they went
Kau	Thy, or	*Kau* keiki	*Thy* son
Kou	of thee	*Kou* wahi	*Thy* place
Au		Ka orero *au*	The speech *of you*
Ou		Ke aroha *ou*	The love *of you*.

A peculiar break in the first person singular possessive (which makes the pronouns resemble two syllables, while in the second person they are sounded as one long syllable) is the only distinction between them.

Obj.

Oe	Thee	Nana *oe* i hoora	He *thee* saved
Ia oe	You	E hoouna wau *ia oe*	I send *you*
Ia oe	To you	Orero aku *ia oe*	Speak *to you*
Ia oe	By you	Roaa *ia oe*	Obtained *by you*
E oe	By you	Palapalaia *e oe*	Written *by you*
Me oe	With you	Hele pu *me oe*	Go *with you*.

Third Person Singular.

Nom.

Oia, or		*Oia* ka haku	He (is) the lord, or pro-
Oiala	He,		prietor
Ia	She,	E cra *ia*	Live (will) *it*
Kela	or	I aroha *kela*	Loved *he*
Nana	It	*Nana* i orero	He spake
Naia		*Naia* i hai mai	He declared
Na kela		*Na kela* i makana	He gave,

Poss.

Naia	⎫	Naia ka taro	His the taro
Noia	⎬	Noia ka rore	His the cloth
Noia		Noia } wau e eha'i	Of him I was hurt
		Nona	
Kaia		Ka a ia palapala	His book or letter
Koia		Koia ia kapa	His native cloth
Na kela		Na kela ka puaa	His the hog
No kela		No kela ka raau	His the wood
Ka kela		Ka kela ka wai	His the water
Ko kela		Ko kela ia waiwai	His that property
Nana		Nana ia buka	His that book
Nona		Nona ka aina	His the land
Kana		Kana kamarii	His children
Kona		Kona pono	His duty
Ana		Kawahine ana	The wife of him
Ona		Ka kanawai ona	The law of him.

(vertical label: His, her, or its, and of him, her, or it.)

Obj.

Him, her, or it.

Ia	It	Na ke Akua ia i makana	God it gave
Ia ia	Him	Aroha ia ia	Love him
Ia ia	To him	Kahea aku ia ia	Call to him
Ia ia	By him	Roaa ia ia	Obtained by him
E ia	By him	Hoorahaia e ia	Proclaimed by him
Ke ia	Him	Nana kela i hoouna	He him sent
I kela	To him	Hoavi i kela	Give to him
I kela	Him	Malama i kela	Keep him
E kela	By him	Kuaiia e kela	Bought by him
Ona	Him	Haihai ma hope ona	Follow after him
I ona	To him	Hele ana i ona	Going to him.

DUAL.

First Person.

O kaua	⎫	O kaua ke hele	You and I go
Kaua	Thou and I	E noho kaua	Sit you and I
Na kaua, or taua		Na kaua ia e rave	You and I it will take
O maua	⎫	O maua ke ike	He and I know
Maua	He, she, or it, and I	I rohe maua	She and I heard
Na maua		Na maua e nana	He and I will look.

The possessive and objective cases of the first person dual, and second person, *orua*, ye twe, and the third person, *raua*, they two, have their several forms of *nominative, possessive,* and *objective* cases constructed in a manner similar to those of the singular.

Nom.　　　　*First Person Plural.*

O kakou	⎫ We, including the party speaking, and the party addressed ⎬	O *kakou* ke rohe	We hear
Kakou		E himeni *kakou*	Let sing us
Na kakou		Na *kakou* e malana	Ye and I (will) take heed
O makou	⎫ We, excluding the party addressed ⎬	O *makou* wale no	They and I only
Makou		Ke horoi nei *makou*	Washing (are) we
Na makou		Na *makou* e ave aku	We, i. e. our party, will take away

The other cases and persons of the plural are as numerous and precise as in the singular and dual. The adjective pronouns are possessive, demonstrative, interrogative, and relative.

Adjectives.—The adjective follows the noun to which it belongs. There are several degrees of comparison, though the form of the adjective undergoes no change: the degrees are expressed by distinct words. There is, properly speaking, no superlative; it is, however, expressed by prefixing the definite article, as *ke kiekie, ke nui,* the high, the great.

Verbs,—The verbs are active, passive, and neuter. The regular active verb, in the Hawaiian dialect, admits of four conjugations, as *rohe,* to hear, *hoo-rohe,* to cause to hear, *rohe-iä,* heard, and *hoo-rohe-iä,* to cause to be heard. Some of the verbs admit the second and fourth, but reject the third, as *noho,* to sit, *hoo-noho,* to cause to sit, and *hoo-noho-ia,* to cause to be seated. Others again allow the third and fourth, but not the second, as *pepehi,* to beat, *pepehi-ia,* beaten, and *hoo-pepehi-ia,* to cause to be beaten. The verbs usually precede the nouns and pronouns, as *here au,* go I, and *e noho marie oe,* sit still you, instead of, I go, and you sit still.

The adverbs, prepositions, conjunctions, and interjections are numerous; but a description of them, and their relative situation in the construction of their sentences, would take up too much room.

Their numerals resemble the Malayan more than any other part of their language.

NUMERALS.

A kahi one	arima five	avaru eight
arua two	uono six	aiva nine
atoru three	ahitu seven	umi ten.
ahaa four		

Eleven would be either *umi-kumu-ma-kahi,* ten the root and one, or *umi-akahi-keu,* ten one over; this would be continued by adding the units to the ten till twenty, which they call *iva-kurua,* forty they call *kanahaa,* for seventy-six they would say forty twenty ten and six, and continue counting by forties till 400, which they call a *rau,* then they add till 4000, which they call *máno,* 40,000 they call *lehu,* and 400,000 a *kini;* beyond this we do not know that they carry their calculations; the above words are sometimes doubled, as *manomano kinikini;* they are, however, only used thus to express a large but indefinite number. Their selection of the number four in calculations is singular; thus, 864,895 would be, according to their method of reckoning, two kini, or 400,000s, one lehu, 40,000, six mano, or 4000s, two rau, or 400s, two kanaha, or 40s, one umi, or ten and five. They calculate time by the moon; allow twelve to a year; have a distinct name for every moon, and every night of the moon, and reckon the parts of a month by the number of nights, as *po akoru ainei*, nights three ago, instead of three days ago. The following are some of the most common words in their language:

Akua	God.	buaa	hog.
kanaka	man.	ilio	dog.
wahine	woman.	moa	fowl.
kama	child.	manu	bird.
ra, or la	sun.	ia	fish.
mahina	moon.	wai	water.
hokú	star.	ahi	fire.
lani	heaven, or sky.	uru	bread-fruit.
ao	light.	maia	plantain
pouri	darkness.	ai	food.
makani	wind.	inu	to drink.
uä	rain.	here	to walk.
vera	hot.	noho	to sit.
anu	cold.	moe	to sleep.
hare	house.	orero	to speak.
waa	canoe.	ereere	black.
mata	face and eye.	keokeo	white.
rauoho	hair.	ura	red.
ihu	nose.	lenalena	yellow.
waha	mouth.	kapa	native cloth.
kino	body.	rore	foreign do.
poo	head.	ora	to live.
naau	stomach.	make	to die.
rima	hands and arms.	ai	to eat.
wawae	legs and feet.	polulu	spear.
uhane	spirit.	mouna	mountain.
eha	pain.	ihe	javelin.
rea	pleasure.	bu	a hill.
maitai	good.	papale	a hat.
ino	bad	hao	iron.
pono	correct.	pohaku	stone
heva	wrong, guilt.	repo	dirt.
raau	tree, wood.	area	hard.
rau	leaf.	nolunolu	soft.
kai	sea.	ma	a sling.
aina	land.	rua	a pit.
heiau	a temple.	kamaa	shoes.

The following specimen of native composition will convey some idea of their idiom. The translation is servile; and with this I shall close these remarks on their language. It is a letter written by the late king in answer to one I sent, acquainting him with my second arrival in the islands, on the 4th of Feb., 1823.

" *Mr. Ellis, eo.*
Mr. Ellis, attend

" *Aroha ino oe, me ko wahine, me na keiki a*
Attachment great (to) you; and your wife, with children all

pau a orua. I ola oukou ia Jehova ia laua o
of ye two. Preserved (have) you (been) by Jehovah they two

Iesu Kraist. Eia kau wahi olero ia oe, Mr. Ellis, apopo a
Jesus Christ. This (is) my word to you, Mr. Ellis, to-morrow

kela la ku a ahiahi, a ku hoi mai. I ka tabu a
or the day after when evening, then I return. On the Sabbath

leila ua ite kaua. A i makemake oe e here mai ianei maitai
then (shall) meet we. But if desire you to come here, well

no hoi. Ike ware oe i na'rii o Tahiti. Aroha ware
also. Seen indeed (have) you the chiefs of Tahiti. Attachment

na'rii o Bolabola.
only to the chiefs of Borabora.*

" *I ola oe ia Jehova ia Jesu Kraist.*
Saved (may) you (be) by Jehovah by Jesus Christ.

" Iolani."

* The term for the Society Islands.

THE END.

THE FAMILY LIBRARY.

In presenting to the American public a list of the Works composing the Family Library, the publishers avail themselves of the opportunity afforded them to offer their thanks for the very liberal encouragement they have enjoyed, and still continue to receive, and for the numerous expressions of approbation that have been bestowed upon their undertaking.

The general estimation in which the work is held is proved by the great number of copies that have been sold, and by the constantly increasing demand, which in the case of many of the volumes has been so great as to call for several successive editions.

No pains and no expense have been spared in procuring and selecting works of the highest character, both of foreign and native writers,—and the list of contributors includes, among other distinguished names, those of

Professors H. H. Milman,
" Leslie,
" Jameson,
" Wilson,
" G. Bush,
" Euler, and
" Griscom,
Lord Dover,
Sir Walter Scott,
Sir David Brewster,
John Galt, Esq.,
J. G. Lockhart, LL.D.,
Robert Southey, LL.D.,
J. S Memes, LL.D.,
Hugh Murray, Esq.,
Allan Cunningham, Esq.,

H. G. Bell, Esq.,
G. P. R. James, Esq.,
Horace Smith, Esq.,
B. B. Thatcher, Esq.,
Sharon Turner, F.S.A.,
Mrs. Jameson,
J. A. St. John, Esq.,
John Abercrombie, M.D.,
P. F. Tytler, Esq.,
Robert Mudie, Esq.,
John Barrow, Esq.,
Rev. J. Williams, A.M.,
" G. R. Gleig,
" George Croly,
" M. Russell, LL.D.,
" E. Smedley,

With the assistance and co-operation of persons of such eminent talents and high reputation, a series of works has been commenced and is still in progress, embracing almost every department of science and literature, and combining with great excellence of execution the advantages of exceedingly low price, convenience of form, and beauty of illustration. While the trifling cost has placed the several works within the reach of all classes of readers, the interesting nature of the subjects, and the pleasing manner in which they are treated, render them well suited for the perusal of young persons, and valuable auxiliaries to parents and teachers in the important offices of guiding and cultivating the youthful mind ; and the care that has been taken to exclude every thing that could in the slightest degree have a prejudicial influence in a moral or religious point of view, entitles the series to the entire confidence of the most scrupulous.

With these recommendations, the publication will be found deserving of a place in every well-selected Library, and as *each work is complete in itself,* and may be purchased separately from the others, it will furnish a valuable variety of literary presents, of school-books, and of volumes for family reading, adapted to the means and tastes of all classes of readers.

The publication of the Family Library is still in progress, and will be continued by the addition of every appropriate work that is produced either in England or America, so long as the publishers continue to receive the same encouragement which has hitherto attended their enterprise. At present the series embraces the following:—

Nos. 1, 2, 3. Milman's *History of the Jews.* With Plates.

4, 5. Lockhart's *Life of Napoleon Bonaparte.* With Plates.

6. Southey's *Life of Nelson.*

7. Williams's *Life of Alexander the Great.* With Plates.

8. *Natural History of Insects.*

9. Galt's *Life of Lord Byron.*

10. Bush's *Life of Mohammed.*

11. Scott's *Letters on Demonology and Witchcraft.* Plate.

12, 13. Gleig's *History of the Bible.* With Maps.

14. *Discovery and Adventure in the Polar Seas, &c.* By Professor Leslie, Professor Jameson, and Hugh Murray, Esq.

15. Croly's *Life of George the Fourth.* With a Portrait.

16. *Discovery and Adventure in Africa.* By Prof. Jameson, James Wilson, Esq., and Hugh Murray, Esq. With a Map and Engravings.

17, 18, 19. Cunningham's *Lives of Eminent Painters and Sculptors.* With Portraits.

20. James's *History of Chivalry and the Crusades.* Plate.

21, 22. Bell's *Life of Mary Queen of Scots.* Portrait.

23. Russell's *Ancient and Modern Egypt.* With Plates.

24. Fletcher's *History of Poland.* With a Plate.

25. Smith's *Festivals, Games, and Amusements.* With Plates.

26. Brewster's *Life of Sir Isaac Newton.* With Plates.

27. Russell's *History of Palestine, or the Holy Land.* Plates.

28. Memes' *Memoirs of the Empress Josephine.* Plates.

29. *The Court and Camp of Bonaparte.* With Plates.

30. *Lives of Early Navigators.* With Portraits.

31. *A Description of Pitcairn's Island,* &c. Engravings.

32. Turner's *Sacred History of the World.*

33, 34. Mrs. Jameson's *Memoirs of Celebrated Female Sovereigns.*

35, 36. Landers' *Africa.* With Engravings and Maps.

37. Abercrombie *on the Intellectual Powers, &c.*

38, 39, 40. St. John's *Lives of Celebrated Travellers.*

41, 42. Lord Dover's *Life of Frederic II. King of Prussia.* With a Portrait.

43, 44. *Sketches from Venetian History.* With Plates.

45, 46. Thatcher's *Indian Biography.* With Plates.

47, 48, 49. *History of India.*

50. Brewster's *Letters on Natural Magic.* Engravings.

51, 52. Taylor's *History of Ireland.* With Engravings.

53. *Discoveries on the Northern Coasts of America.*

54. Humboldt's *Travels.* Plates.

55, 56. Euler's *Letters on Natural Philosophy.* Engravings.

57. Mudie's *Guide to the Observation of Nature.* Engravings.

58. Abercrombie, on the *Philosophy of the Moral Feelings.*

59. James's *History of Charlemagne.* With a Portrait.

60. Russell's *History of Nubia and Abyssinia.*

61, 62. Russell's *Life of Oliver Cromwell.* With a Portrait

OPINIONS OF THE FAMILY LIBRARY.

"The publishers have hitherto fully deserved their daily increasing reputation by the good taste and judgment which have influenced the selections of works for the Family Library."—*Albany Daily Advertiser.*

"The Family Library—A title which, from the valuable and entertaining matter the collection contains, as well as from the careful style of its execution, it well deserves. No family, indeed, in which there are children to be brought up, ought to be without this Library, as it furnishes the readiest resources for that education which ought to accompany or succeed that of the boarding-school or the academy, and is infinitely more conducive than either to the cultivation of the intellect."—*Monthly Review.*

"It is the duty of every person having a family to put this excellent Library into the hands of his children."—*N. Y. Mercantile Advertiser.*

"It is one of the recommendations of the Family Library, that it embraces a large circle of interesting matter, of important information and agreeable entertainment, in a concise manner and a cheap form. It is eminently calculated for a popular series—published at a price so low, that persons of the most moderate income may purchase it—combining a matter and a style that the most ordinary mind may comprehend it, at the same time that it is calculated to raise the moral and intellectual character of the people."—*Constellation.*

"We have repeatedly borne testimony to the utility of this work. It is one of the best that has ever been issued from the American press, and should be in the library of *every* family desirous of treasuring up useful knowledge."—*Boston Statesman.*

"We venture the assertion that there is no publication in the country more suitably adapted to the taste and requirements of the great mass of community, or better calculated to raise the intellectual character of the middling classes of society, than the Family Library."—*Boston Masonic Mirror.*

"We have so often recommended this enterprising and useful publication (the Family Library), that we can here only add, that each successive number appears to confirm its merited popularity."—*N. Y. American.*

"The little volumes of this series truly comport with their title, and are in themselves a Family Library."—*N. Y. Commercial Advertiser.*

"We recommend the whole set of the Family Library as one of the cheapest means of affording pleasing instruction, and imparting a proper pride in books, with which we are acquainted."—*U. S. Gazette.*

"It will prove instructing and amusing to all classes. We are pleased to learn that the works comprising this Library have become, as they ought to be, quite popular among the heads of families."—*N. Y. Gazette.*

"The Family Library is, what its name implies, a collection of various original works of the best kind, containing reading useful and interesting to the family circle. It is neatly printed, and should be in every family that can afford it—the price being moderate."—*New-England Palladium.*

"We are pleased to see that the publishers have obtained sufficient encouragement to continue their valuable Family Library."—*Baltimore Republican.*

"The Family Library presents, in a compendious and convenient form, well-written histories of popular men, kingdoms, sciences, &c. arranged and edited by able writers, and drawn entirely from the most correct and accredited authorities. It is, as it professes to be, a Family Library, from which, at little expense, a household may prepare themselves for a consideration of those elementary subjects of education and society, without a due acquaintance with which neither man nor woman has claim to be well bred, or to take their proper place among those with whom they ehide."—*Charleston Gazette.*

Lightning Source UK Ltd.
Milton Keynes UK
UKHW022232141118
332357UK00012B/399/P